REUTERS

OUR WORLD NOW

3

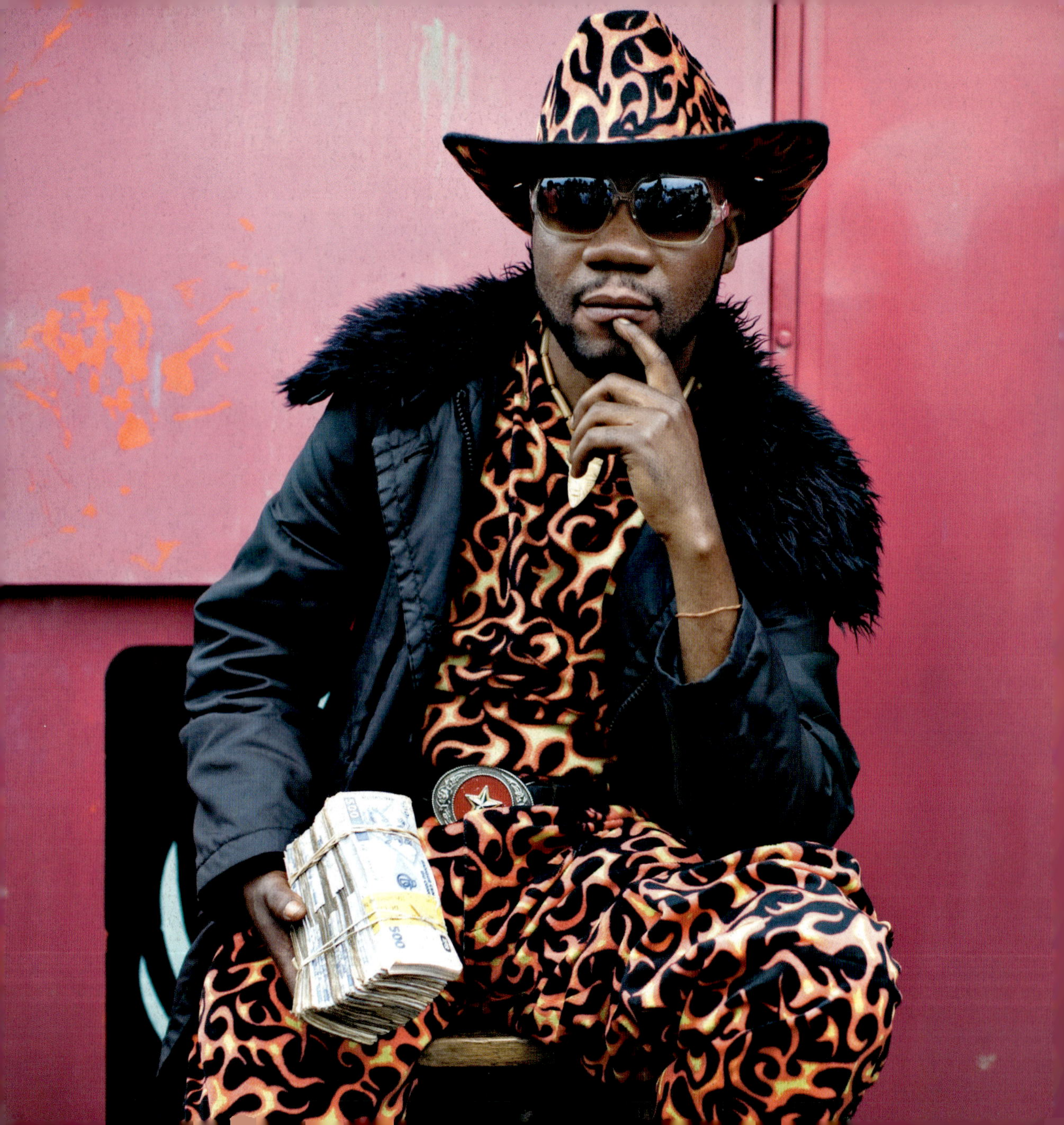

REUTERS

OUR WORLD NOW 3

With 348 colour illustrations

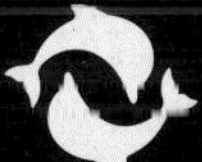

Thames & Hudson

PAGE 2 Money changer Kwami Longange
poses for a portrait on a street corner
in Goma in eastern Congo. Longange,
nicknamed 'le Bon' – the Good – is a *sapeur*,
the local name for a dandy dresser. He has
some 200 different coordinated outfits that
he wears to work as a money changer and
musician. 9 February 2009. Goma, Democratic
Republic of Congo. Finbarr O'Reilly.

Reuters Vice-President, Pictures Ayperi Karabuda Ecer
Reuters Head of Visual Projects Jassim Ahmad
Reuters Pictures Projects Manager Shannon Ghannam

Introduction by Jeremy Gaunt

First published in the United Kingdom in 2010 by
Thames & Hudson Ltd, 181A High Holborn, London WC1V 7QX

thamesandhudson.com

Copyright © Thomson Reuters 2010

License pictures from Reuters for professional use at reuters.com/pictures

British Library Cataloguing-in-Publication Data
A catalogue record for this book is available from the British Library

ISBN 978-0-500-28869-6

Printed and bound in Spain by Graficas Estella

Contents

01

02

03

04

2009

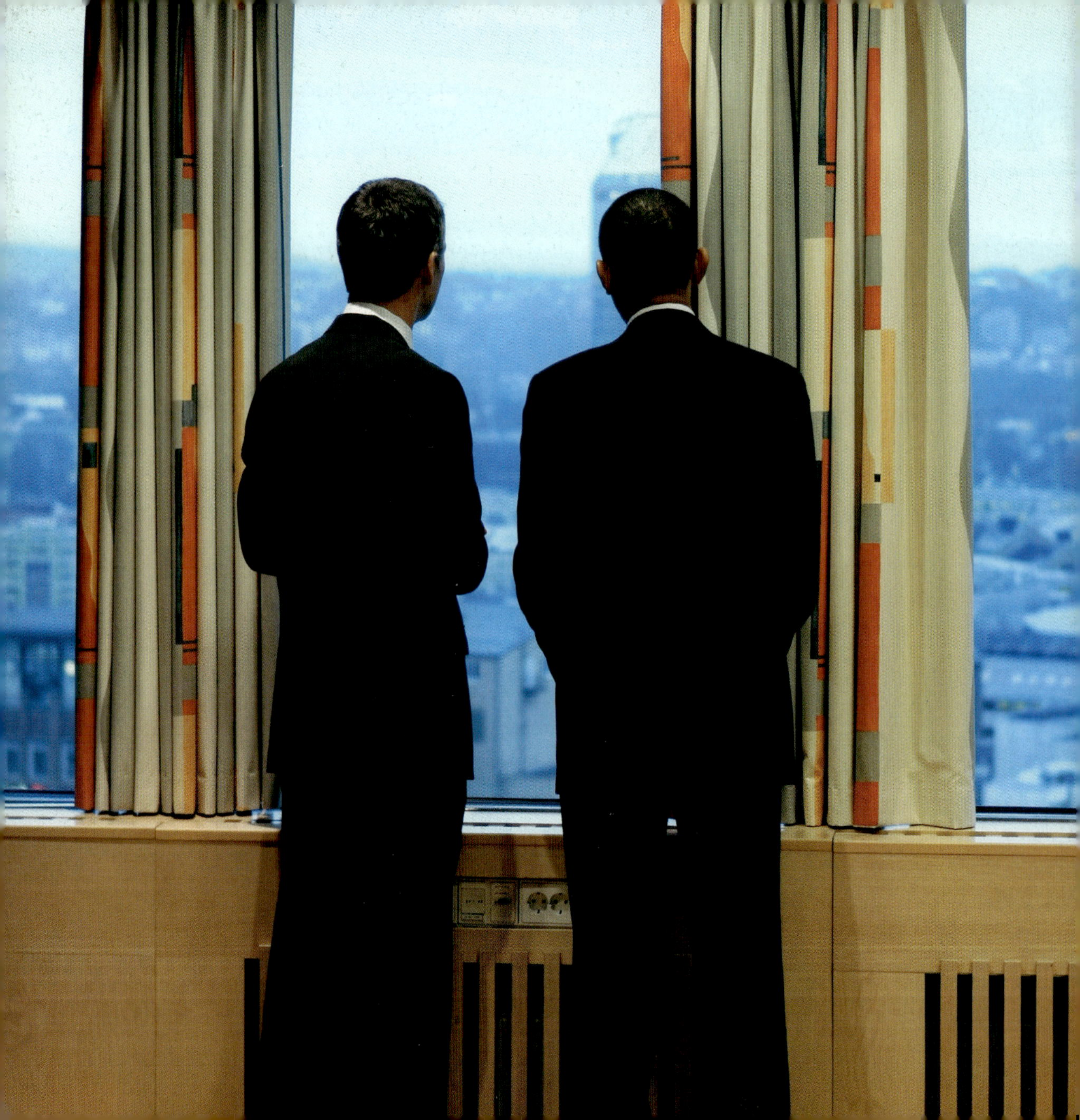

Introduction

Backed-up plumbing, mould, marijuana plants, abandoned grandparents, even a suicide...

Orange County Sheriff's Deputy Ramona Figueroa says nothing she finds surprises her any more as she enforces eviction orders on foreclosed properties in the U.S. state of California. Thousands of people have been thrown out of their homes on her beat, either because they have been unable to maintain mortgage repayments or because they rent from a landlord who has failed to pay. From one foreclosure every four or five years, the veteran deputy of 25 years found herself overseeing as many as one a day in 2009 amidst the worst recession in decades.

A world away in Tajikistan, Rakhima Vosirova, a mother of four, has faced parallel struggles. Lack of opportunity at home had already sent her husband thousands of miles away to Moscow to find work before the crisis hit. When it did, it destroyed his full-time job and left him scrambling to earn enough to send back to feed his family. A $1,400–1,700 monthly remittance to Rakhima and the kids dwindled to less than $100.

It is hard to believe that it is a decade since we were transfixed by the dawn of what many avowed would be a bright new future. Fireworks and celebrations rolled across the globe, lighting up, in turn, Beijing's Forbidden City, the Parthenon in Athens, the Eiffel Tower in Paris and the Statue of Liberty in New York Harbor. A new era as well as a new millennium were proclaimed.

There were fears back then, chiefly of the so-called Y2K virus, a supposed glitch in computer programming that would bring technology to its knees. That never happened, but plenty of other disasters have. The rise of terrorism and of global religious conflict, the 2004 Indian Ocean tsunami, violence in Darfur, wars in Afghanistan and Iraq, the credit crunch, a deteriorating environment, even piracy on the high seas have all grabbed the headlines.

This book is a collection of images taken by Reuters photographers throughout 2009, documenting our world 10 years on from those millennium celebrations. An exhausted U.S. soldier hauntingly catches some rest on the Afghanistan front. A Tamil woman fixes her hair in a refugee camp. Devotees wear surgical masks to ward off H1N1 swine flu during a pilgrimage in Mexico. Financiers face the wrath of protesters.

 U.S. President Barack Obama (right), in Oslo to receive the Nobel Peace Prize, looks over the city with Norwegian Prime Minister Jens Stoltenberg. 10 December 2009. Oslo, Norway. Kevin Lamarque.

In-depth Witness features present
powerful photo essays from around the
world, from Pakistan to Rio, Mumbai to
Siberia. 'I am hunting for an image that will
show the world what is happening here,'
Reuters photographer Adrees Latif recalls
telling refugees from Pakistan's Swat Valley,
angry that he is invading their privacy. His
words encapsulate what he and his fellow
Reuters photographers do across the globe
on a daily basis.

As the new decade begins, hundreds
of millions of people have been lifted
out of poverty as new economic powers
including China, India and Brazil rise to
challenge the stalwarts of the 20th century.
A trip to London in autumn 2009 tells the
tale: gloom-defying shoppers from China
are to be seen flocking to luxury stores,
outspending Arab royalty and replacing
Russia's departing super-rich.

These new economies have been at the
forefront of fighting the global downturn
and financial meltdown. Not for nothing

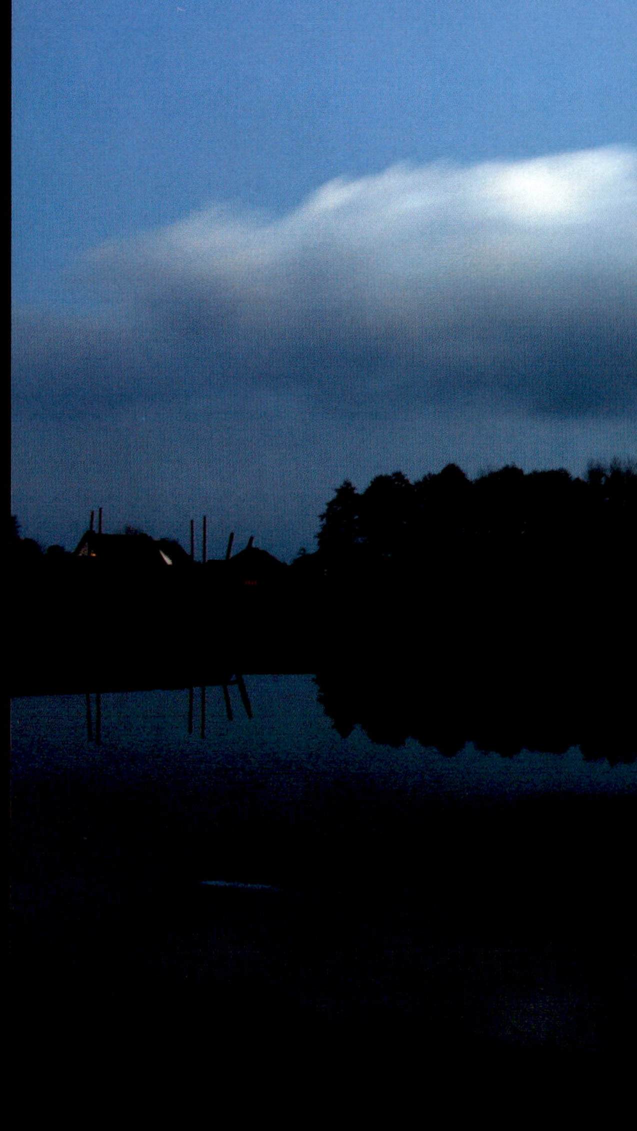

RIGHT Steam billows from the cooling towers
of Jänschwalde brown coal power station
on the German–Polish border. One of the
most polluting plants in Europe, Jänschwalde
has been awarded EU funding to develop
pioneering technology to trap and bury its
carbon dioxide emissions. 2 December 2009.
Jänschwalde, Germany. Pawel Kopczynski

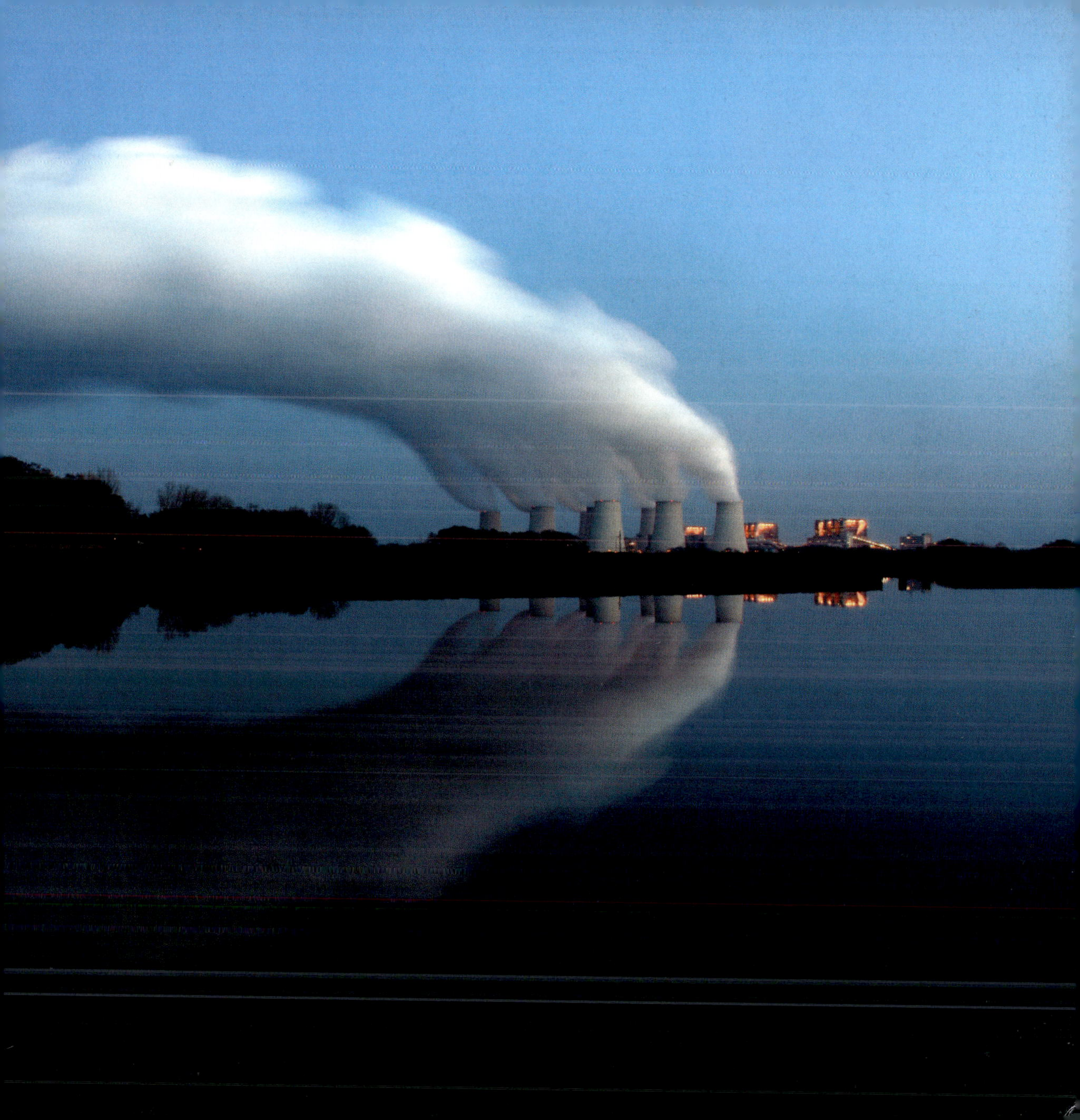

and more relevant G20 of wealthy nations, charged with steering the global economy towards stable and sustainable growth.

The benefits of past growth have not been even. Twenty years after the fall of communism, nostalgia for the Soviet era is keenly felt in many areas of the former Soviet sphere where capitalism has failed to lift living standards and corruption has flourished.

In the United States, meanwhile, a new president, Barack Obama, has broken many moulds, from being the first African-American commander-in-chief to seeking greater engagement with the Muslim world and openly declaring a campaign to rid the world of nuclear weapons. It earned him a Nobel Peace Prize.

But the glow of approval that bathed Obama at the start of 2009 – captured in these pages at his glittering inauguration – has since dimmed as his country's economic troubles have contined and his bill to introduce universal health care has been mired in fractious political debate.

The world of technology, meanwhile, has exploded, bringing improvements in health and education. The cost of computing has tumbled. Smart phones have made always-on, mobile internet access a reality. High definition digital images and sound are becoming the norm. Movies are

Beijing to Brooklyn. Home-based remote working is ever more commonplace across many sectors. Even fishermen in India use mobile phones to check prices for their catch. Traditional media business models are being hastily reinvented.

This proliferation has created a wireless generation of bloggers, Tweeters and Facebookers, zapping personal and professional information around the world at a speed previous generations could only dream of. Reuters itself sources breaking images from the public via the YourView feature on its websites.

In the realm of politics, the potential of such media to reach a previously disengaged part of the electorate was dramatically demonstrated in Barack Obama's election campaign. The power of new technology was also glimpsed in Iran in 2009, when demonstrators – many of them headscarf-clad women in the green that came to symbolize their protest – erupted with rage after disputed elections. Tweets, the 140-character microblog messages distributed via Twitter.com, relayed news of protest and the ensuing government crackdown at the push of a button. Video footage was zapped around the world on YouTube.

There is a broader freedom of expression now for billions of people as a result of such technology combined with ever cheaper computing. But as our interconnected world grapples with the consequences of the technology we have created, we all also share a sobering struggle with the ancient forces of our planet.

The sand dunes had been advancing for decades in Ilha Grande, Brazil, before, two years ago, they finally swallowed the houses of Raimundo do Nascimento and 12 other families. Standing on the 14 metre (46 foot) dune that now completely covers his old home, the 53-year-old Brazilian remembers a childhood landscape of cashew trees as far as he could see. Not a dune was in sight. 'It is beautiful now, but beauty brings misery,' he said. 'The cause of this is natural, but it is man-made as well.'

In southern China, the impact of unfettered industrial development is all too evident in the river that runs through Shangba. The river's flow ranges from murky white to a bright orange and the waters are so viscous that they barely ripple in the breeze. The river brings death, not sustenance, according to experts who say the local hamlets have become cancer villages.

'All the fish died, even chickens and ducks that drank from the river died. If you put your leg in the water, you'll get rashes and a terrible itch,' said rice farmer He Shuncai.

Pollution, climate change, deforestation and huge population increases brought the leaders of the world together in Copenhagen at the end of 2009 in a political fight to find ways to halt environmental degradation without killing off the economic growth that billions still desperately need to rescue them from hunger and poverty.

The United States, Russia, China and the European Union will likely play the lead roles in averting climate change in the years ahead, but it is little countries on the front line that have thus far taken the prize for drawing attention to what is at stake.

For the Maldives, it is the threat of rising sea levels on their tropical archipelago, set to be submerged by 2100 if U.N. predictions are correct. Clad in black diving suits and masks, the country's president and ministers gathered for a cabinet meeting in October nearly 4 metres (13 feet) under the crystalline waters. A black-and-white striped Humbug Damselfish darted around a backdrop of white coral, as President Mohamed Nasheed and the ministers used a white plastic slate and waterproof pencils to sign an 'SOS' message from their country during the 30-minute meeting.

Nepal's government delivered a similar 'SOS' a month or so later, this time 5,242 metres (17,200 feet) above sea level. Wearing oxygen masks and padded jackets, Nepal's prime minister and more than 20 ministers met at the base camp of Mount Everest to raise awareness of the threat to millions of people from disappearing glaciers.

Elsewhere, floods and drought have struck regions as far apart as the Philippines and Greece, dust storms have blanketed Sydney, the snows of Kilimanjaro are melting and people worldwide have been shaken by a new globalized flu pandemic.

But there are also frequent flashes of humour and humanity within these pages – a Chinese child apes grown-ups at a dance, an Argentine footballer cradles his baby, an Indian boy plays in a salt pan, an Afghan man embraces his mother. Reuters award-winning photographers bear daily witness to life across the globe, from headline stories to the small, telling details of ordinary experience.

This is the third volume of the annual *Our World Now* collectors' series, a vivid window on our world as we begin the second decade of the new millennium.

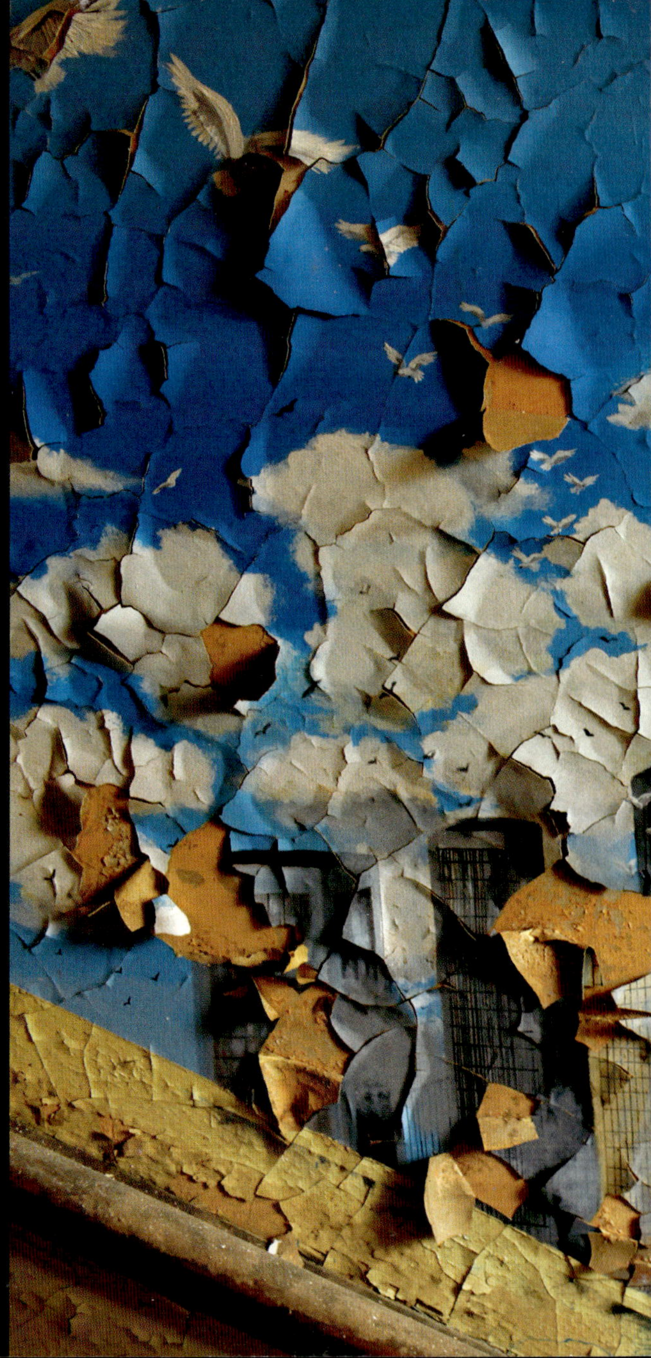

RIGHT Paint peels off a mural depicting Manhattan's Twin Towers in flames in the former Madison School in Youngstown, Ohio. School closures are a common fate in the former steel town, whose population has fallen by more than half since the 1930s, leaving 4,500 vacant structures in a town of about 75,000 people. 21 November 2009. Youngstown, United States. Brian Snyder.

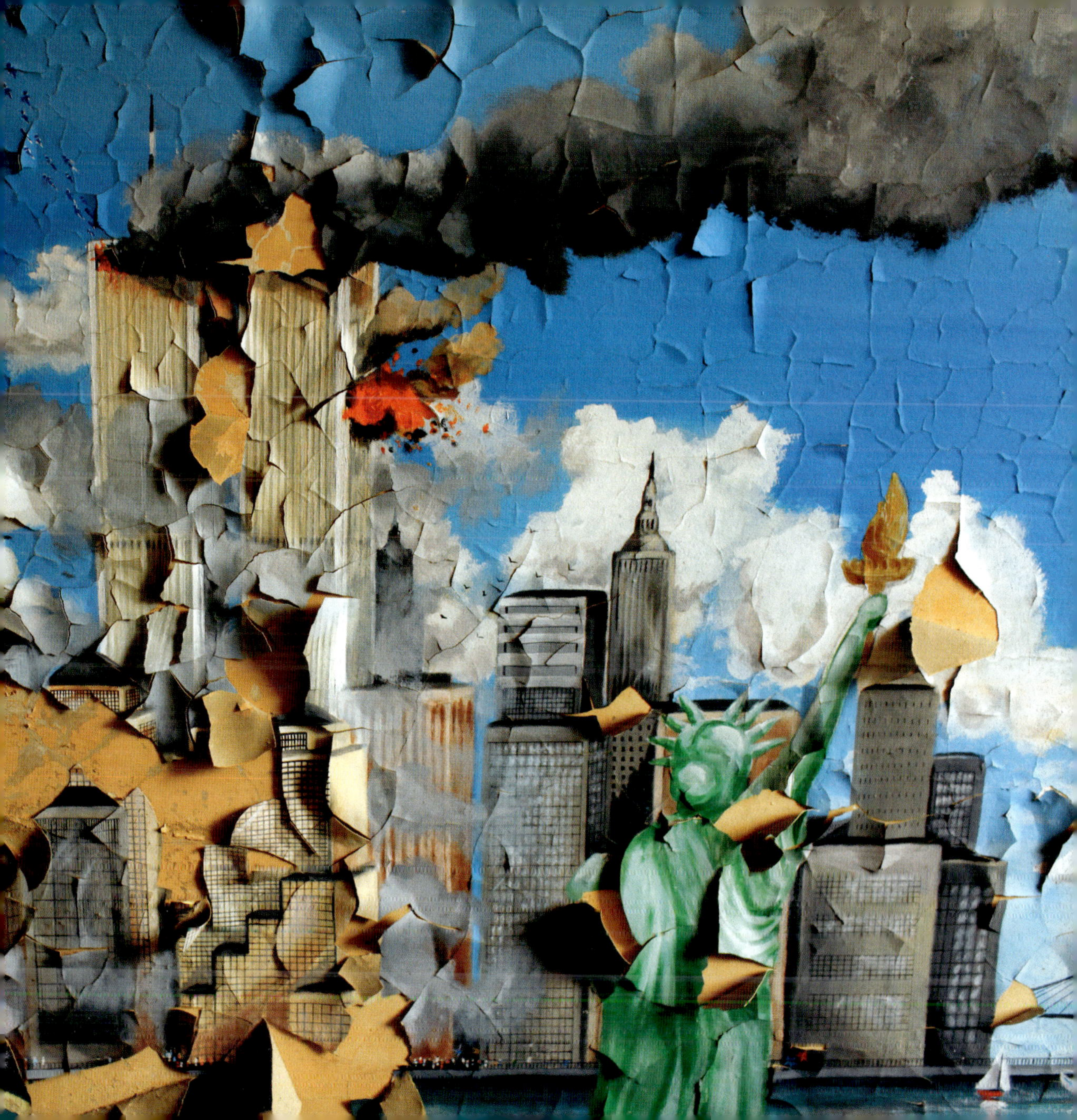

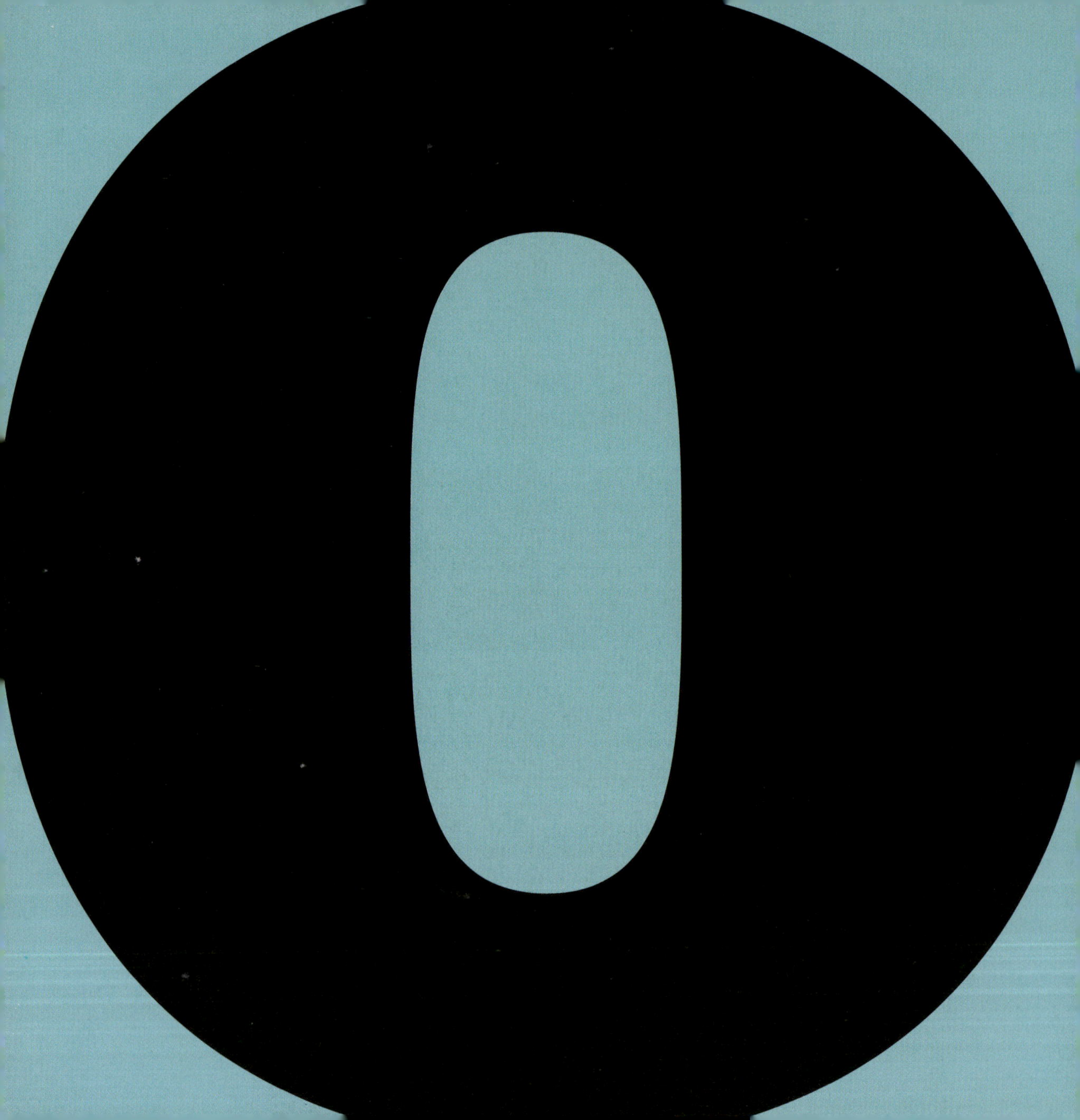

1

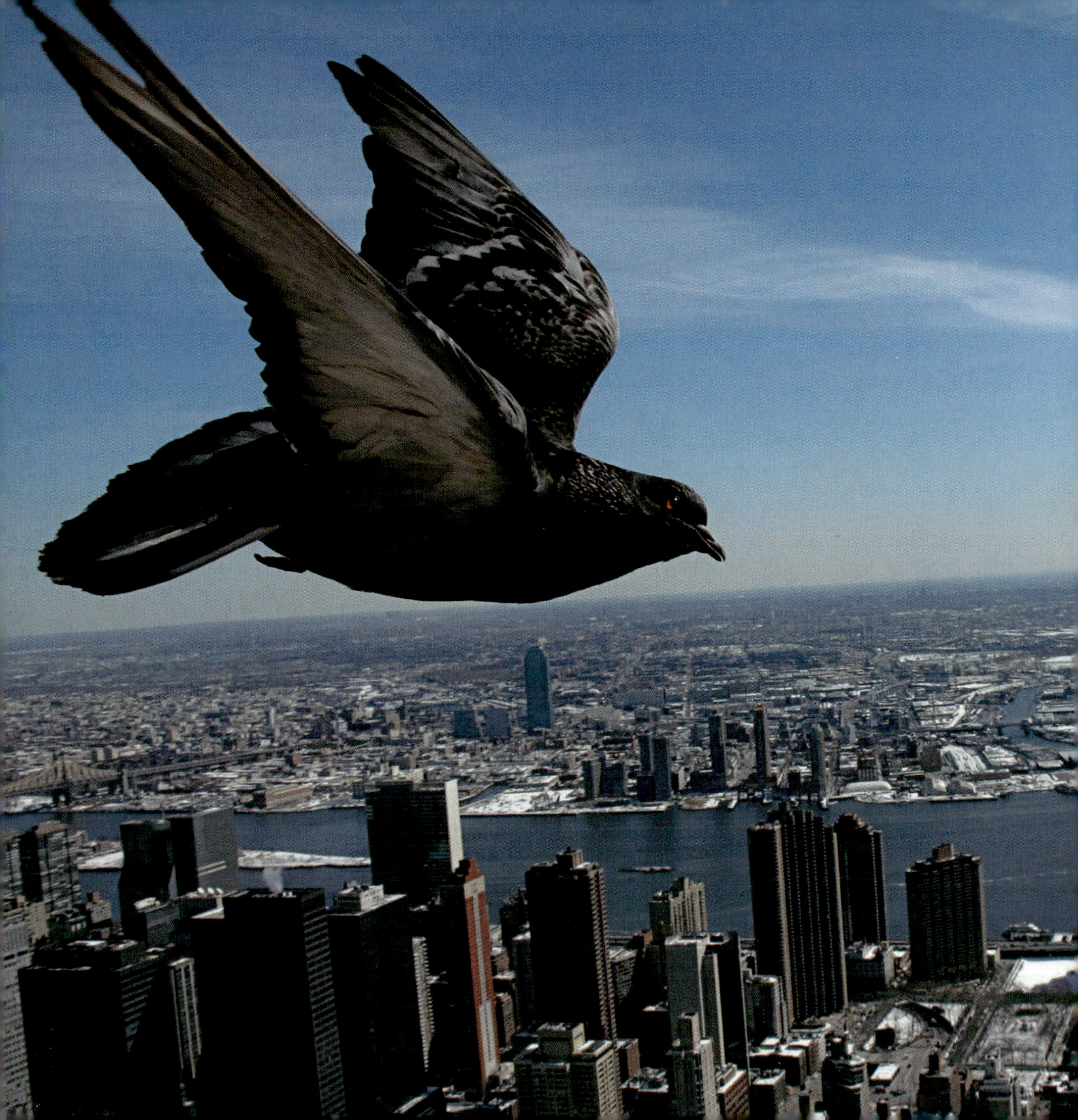

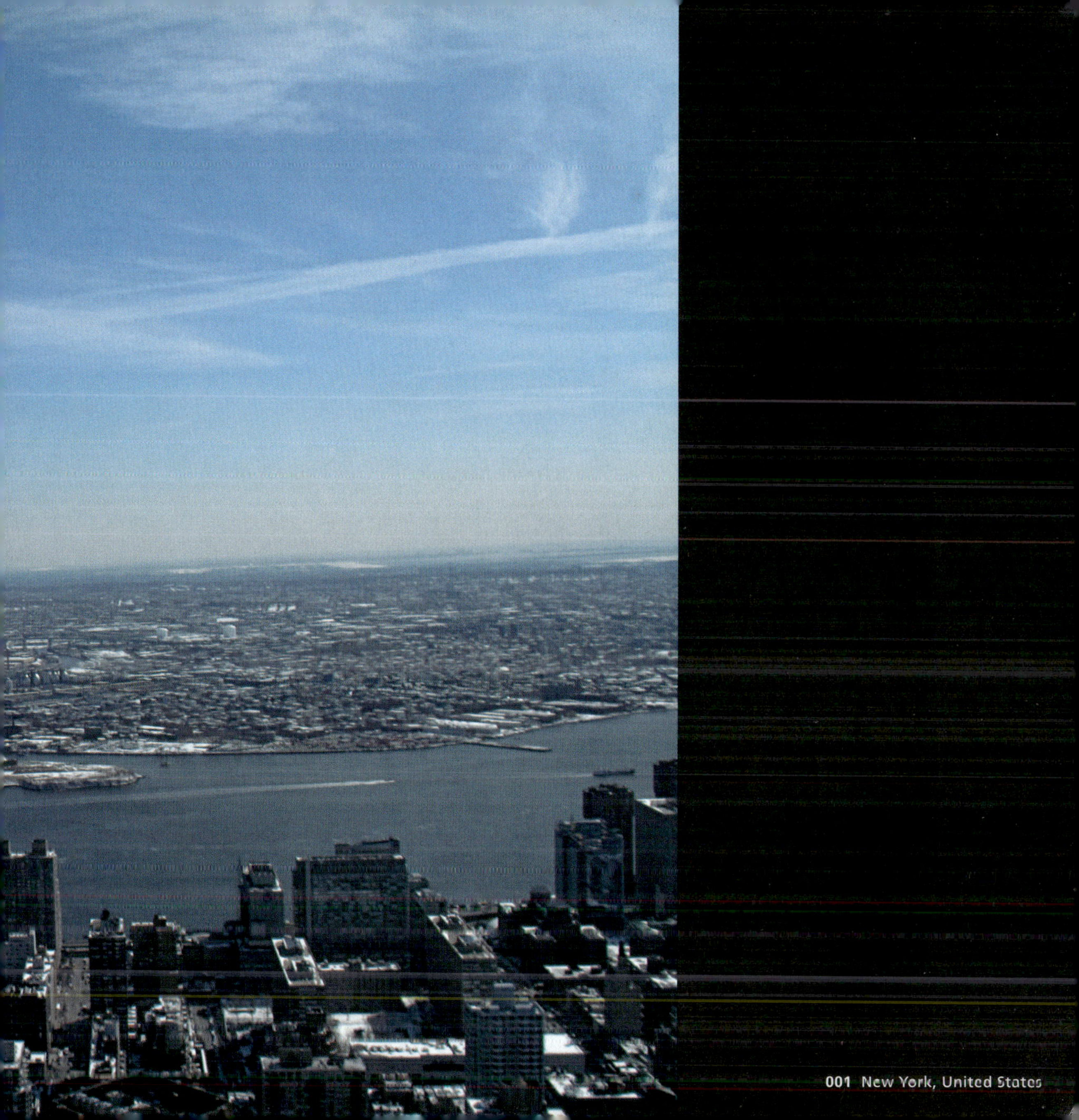
001 New York, United States

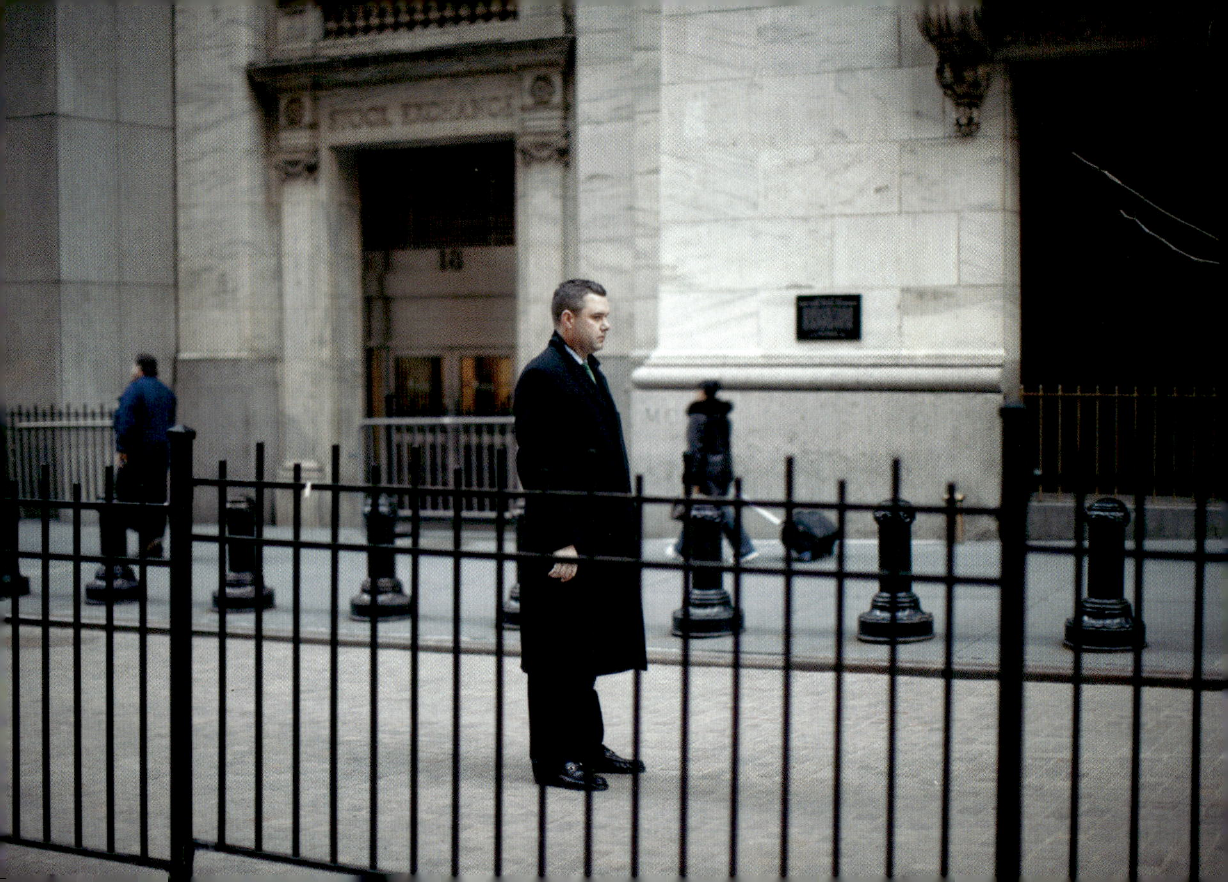

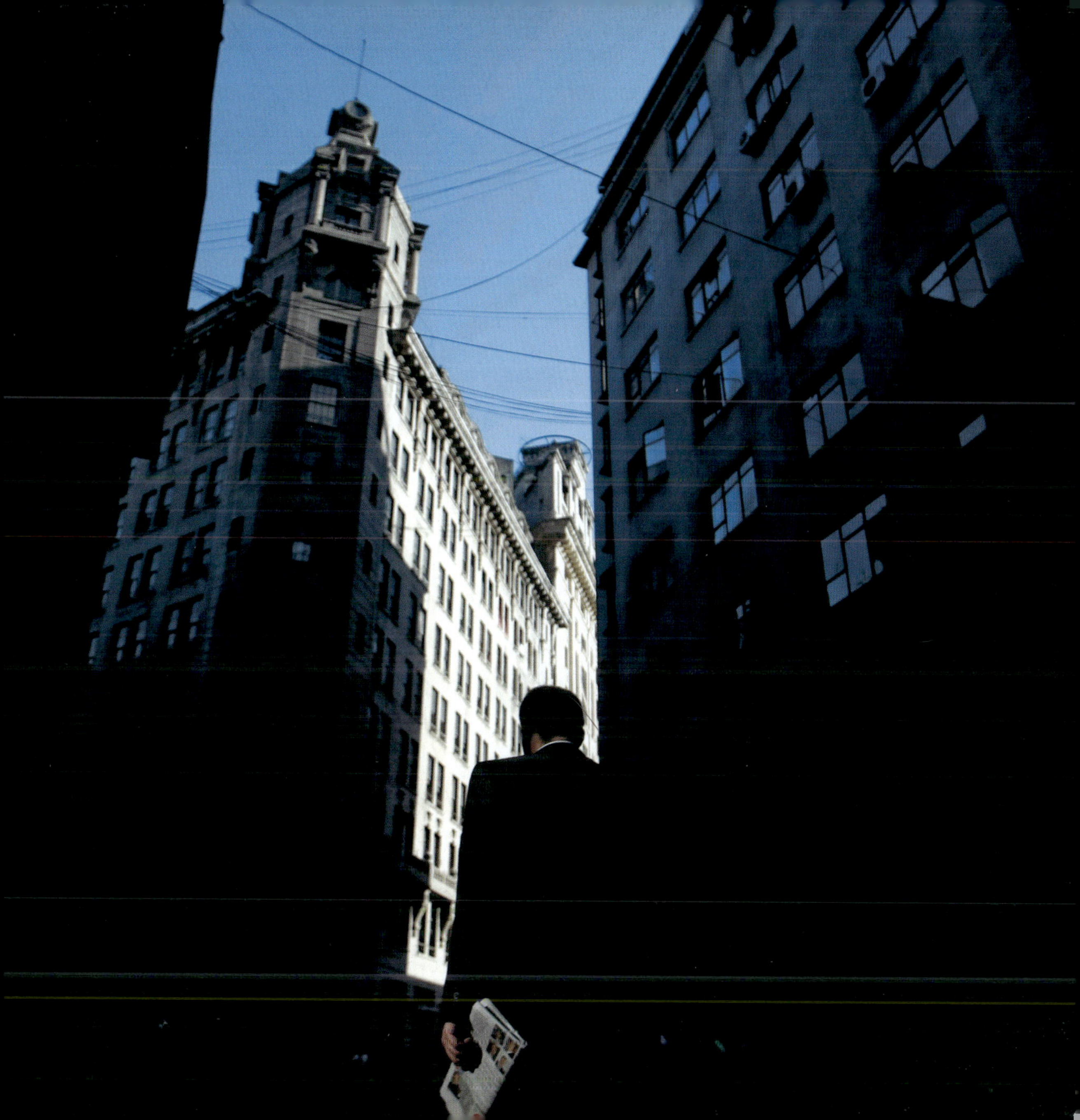

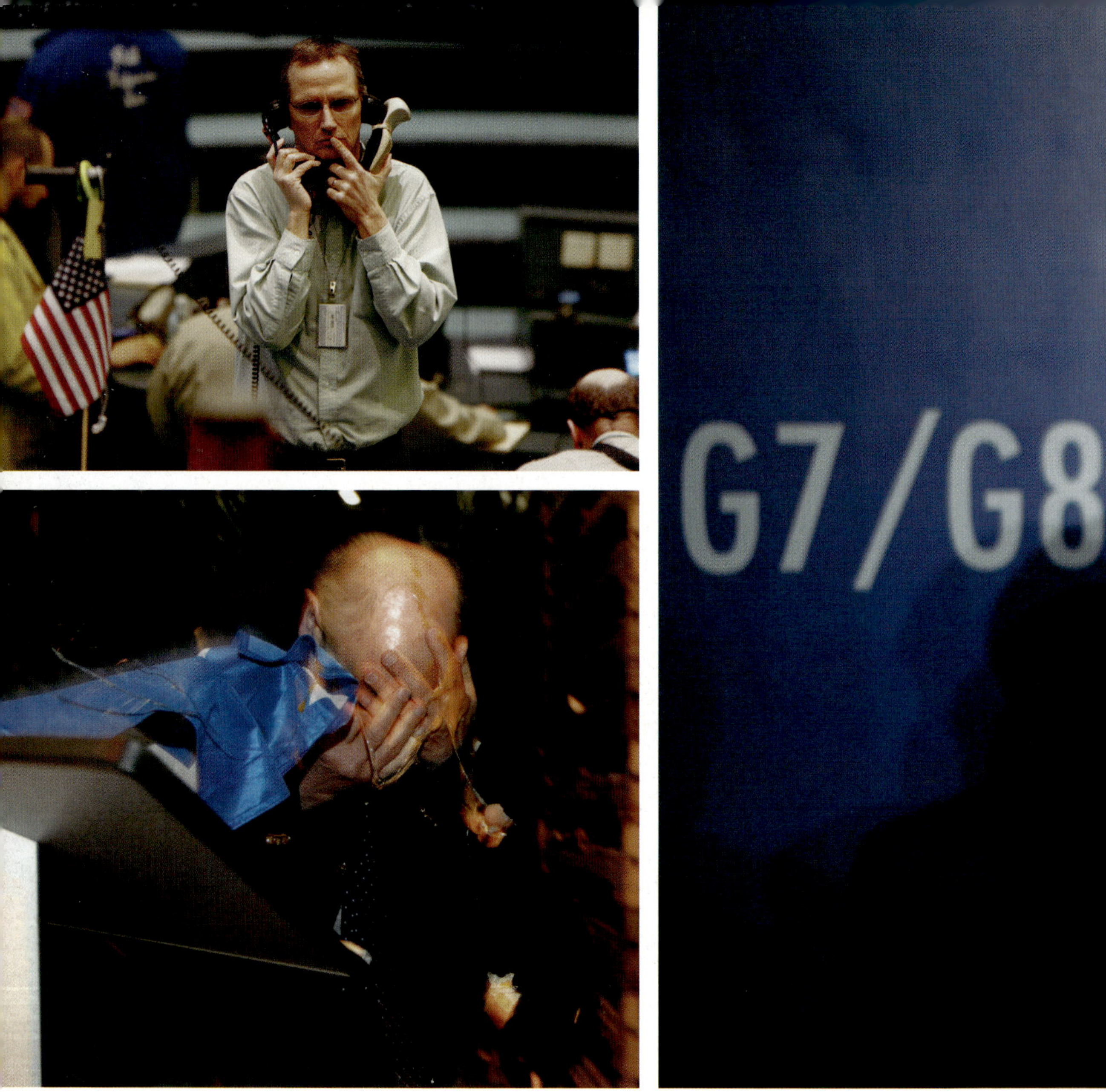

004 [TOP] New York, United States   **005** [ABOVE] Clairoix, France

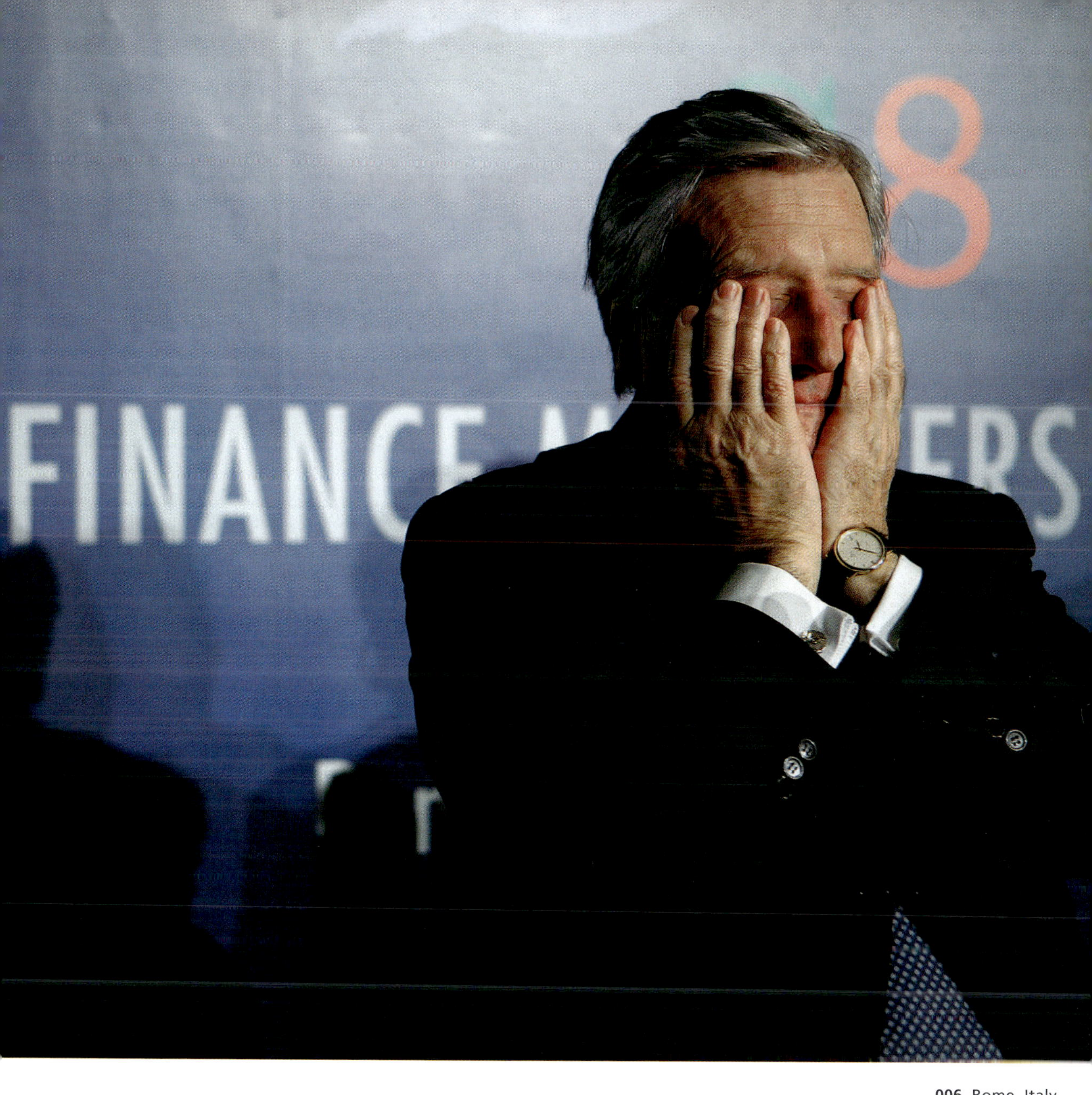
FINANCE M   ERS
8

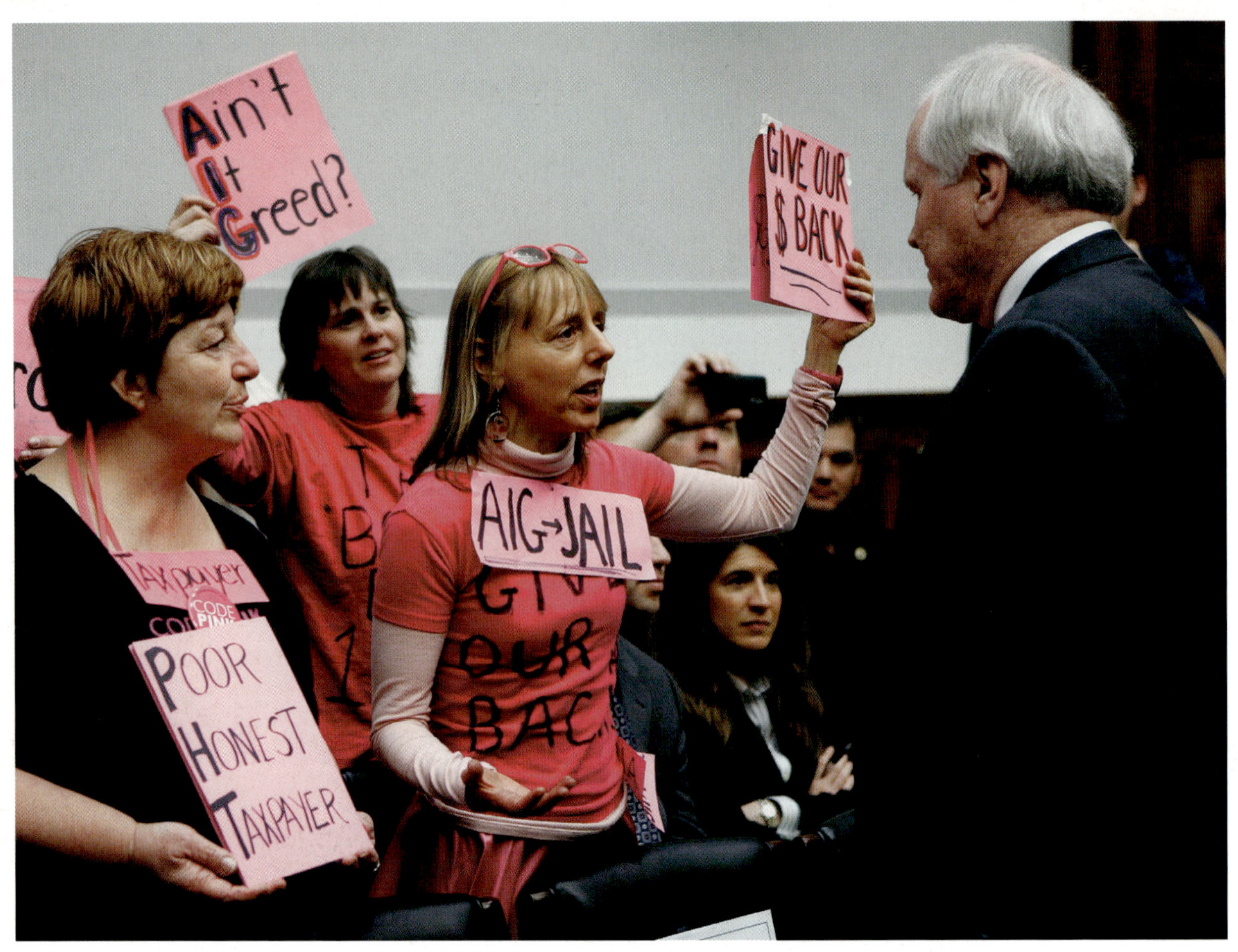

Ain't it Greed?
GIVE OUR $ BACK
POOR HONEST TAXPAYER
AIG→JAIL
CODE PINK
Taxpayer

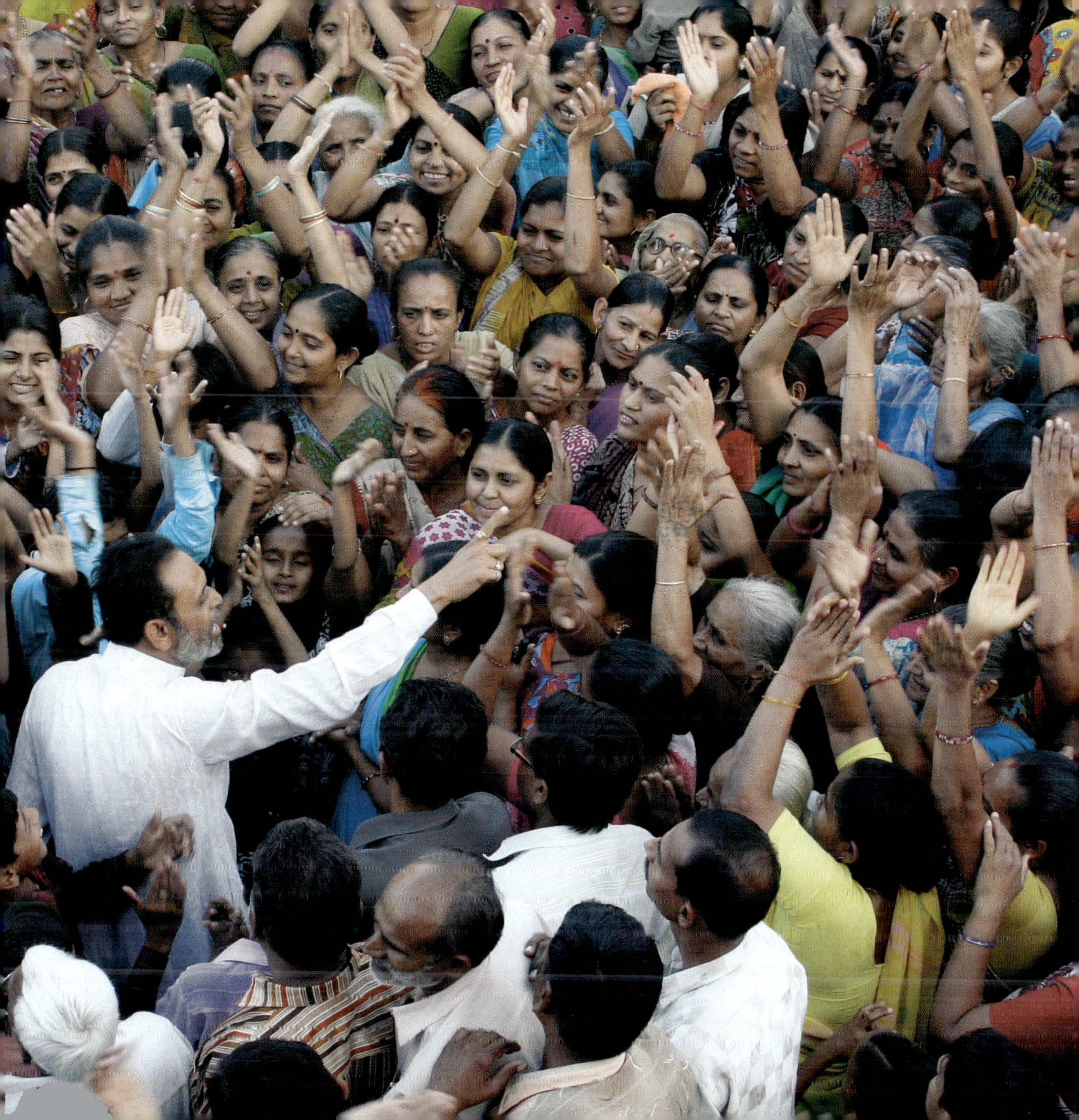

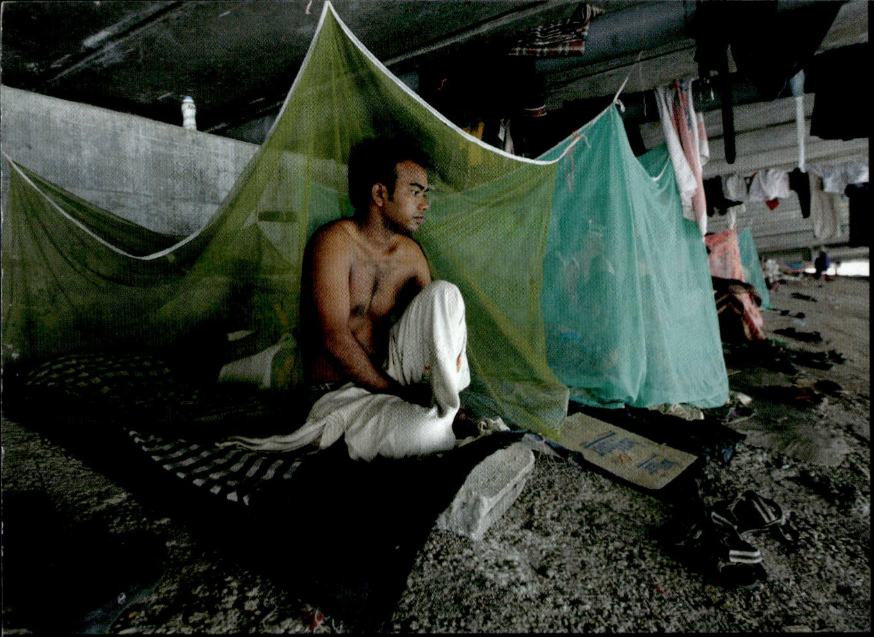

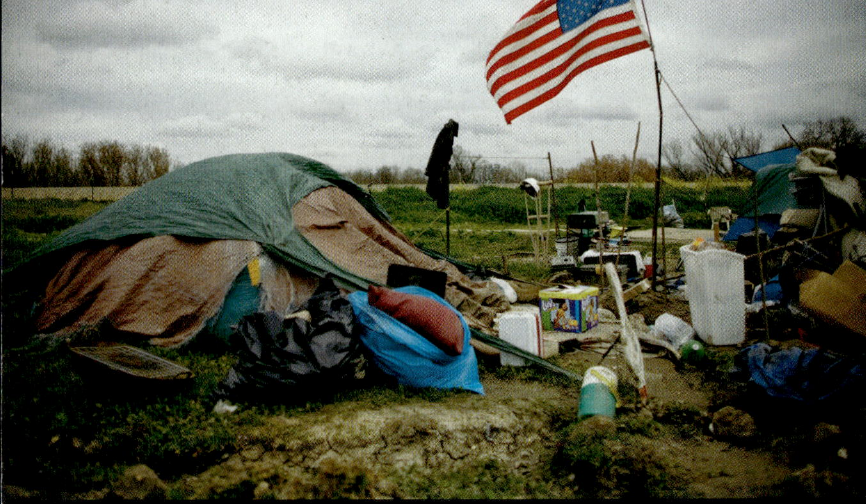

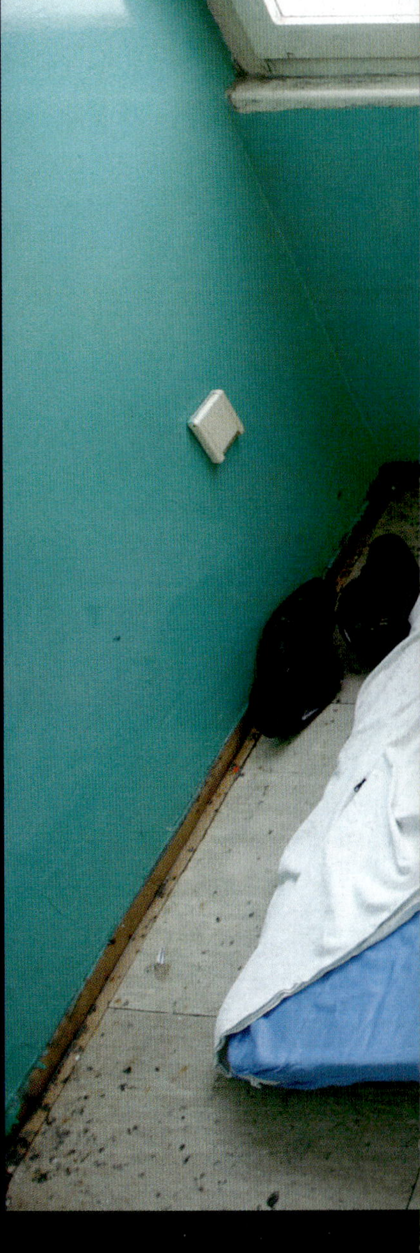

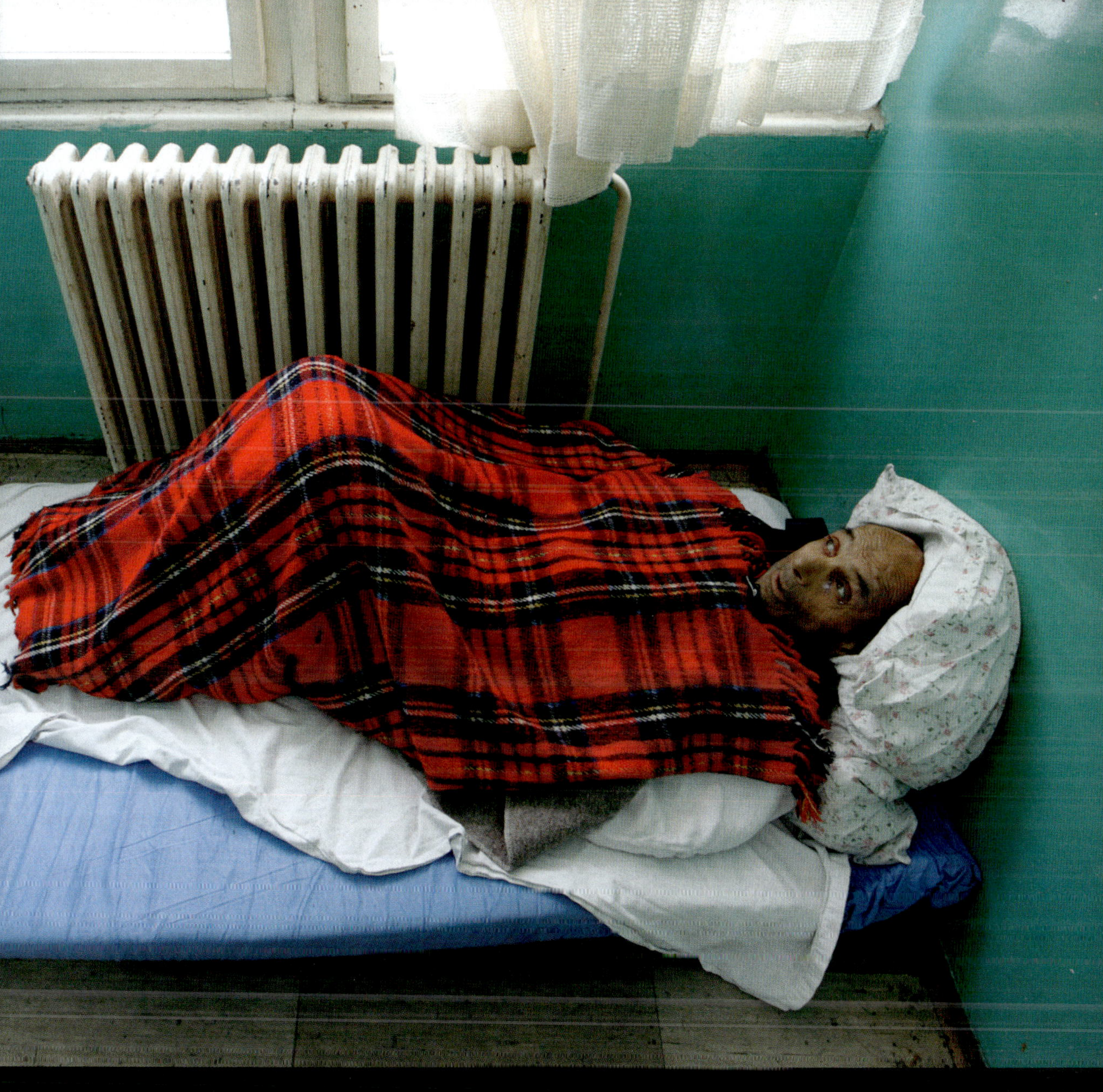

011 Belgrade, Serbia

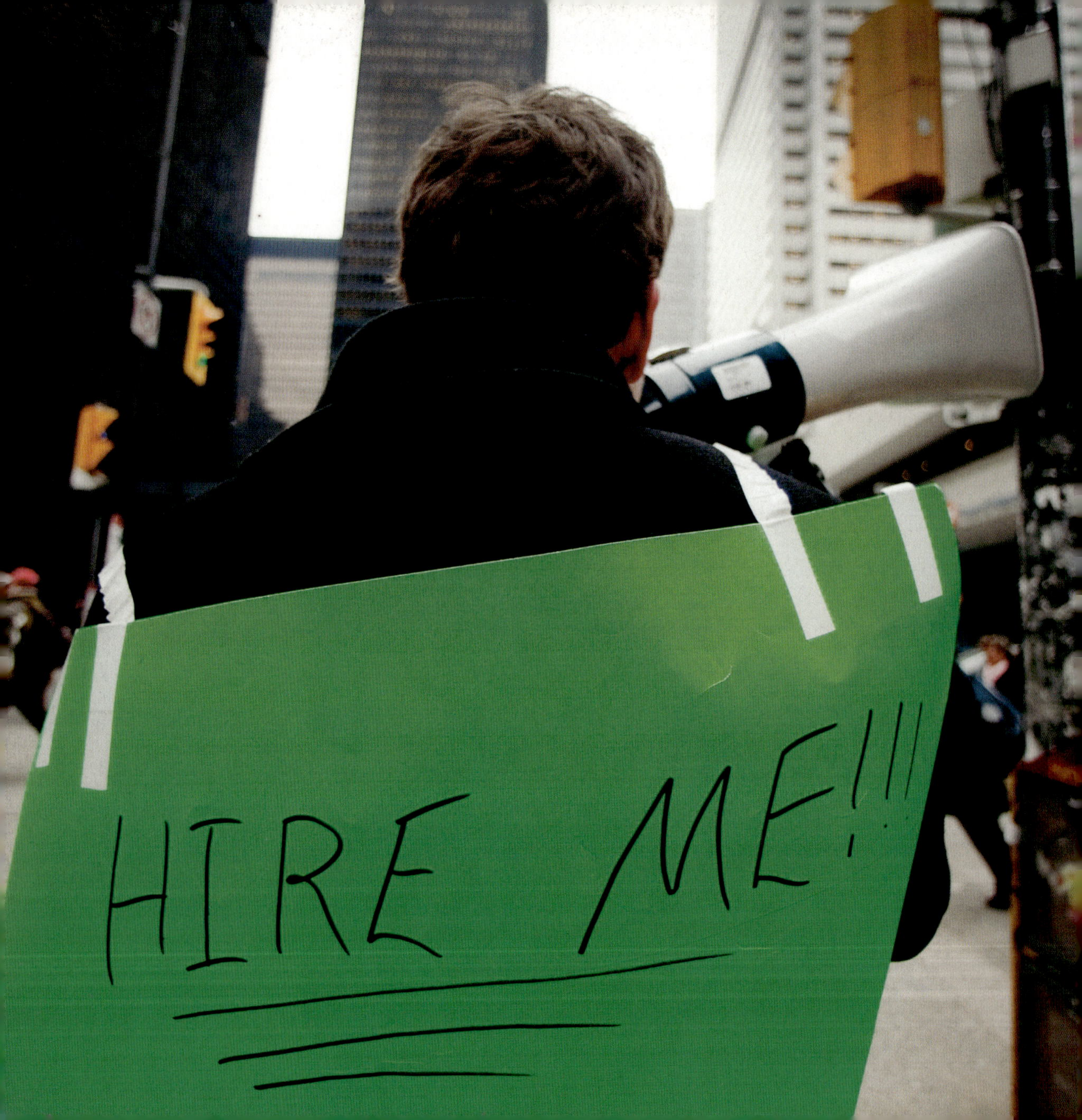

HIRE ME!!!

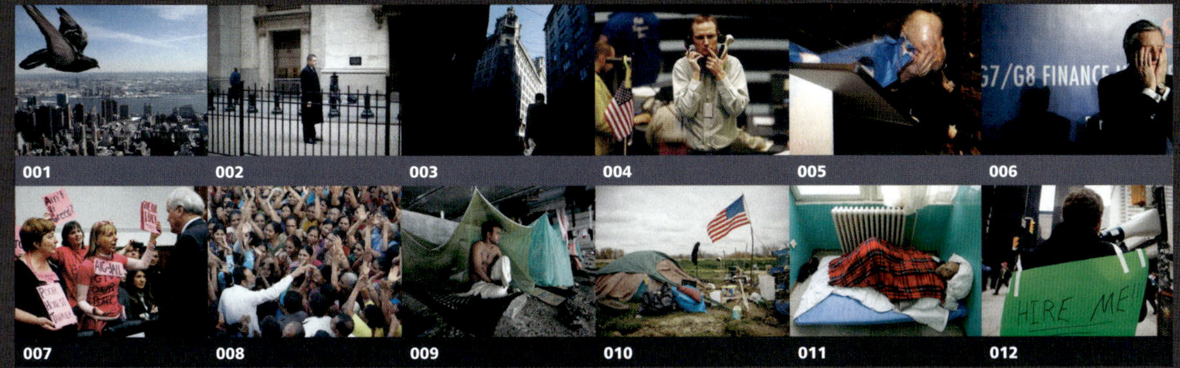

001 A pigeon flies over New York. 3 March 2009. New York, United States. Gleb Garanich.

002 A man stands outside the New York Stock Exchange. 25 March 2009. New York, United States. Eric Thayer.

003 Men walk through the financial district next to Santiago's stock exchange. 11 February 2009. Santiago, Chile. Ivan Alvarado.

004 A man works at the gold futures trading pit at the New York Mercantile Exchange. 12 February 2009. New York, United States. Mike Segar.

005 Louis Forzy, Clairoix Continental factory director, is hit by eggs and a trade union flag thrown by protesting employees. Continental announced that it would close its site in Clairoix, northern France, as well as its plant in Hanover, Germany, in response to a global collapse in orders. 12 March 2009. Clairoix, France. Benoit Tessier.

006 European Central Bank President Jean-Claude Trichet gestures as he attends a news conference during a meeting of G7 finance ministers and central bank governors. 14 February 2009. Rome, Italy. Alessia Pierdomenico.

007 Edward Liddy, CEO of American International Group Inc., is greeted by protesters as he arrives on Capitol Hill to testify before the House Financial Services Subcommittee on Capital Markets, Insurance, and Government Sponsored Enterprises. Hefty bonuses paid to AIG executives following a $180 billion government bailout sparked outrage in the United States, with some employees receiving death threats. 18 March 2009. Washington, DC, United States. Jason Reed.

008 Family members of unemployed diamond workers take part in street protests in the western Indian city of Ahmedabad. The diamond industry in Gujarat was badly hit by the recession. 22 January 2009. Ahmedabad, India. Amit Dave.

009 A Bangladeshi worker sits near mosquito nets under a bridge behind the Bangladesh High Commission in Kuala Lumpur. Hundreds of Bangladeshi workers took up residence along the cemented banks of Gombak river after fleeing employers who failed to pay their wages as the recession bit into Malaysia's construction, manufacturing and services industries. 25 February 2009. Kuala Lumpur, Malaysia. Zainal Abd Halim.

010 A U.S. flag flies over a campsite in a tent city for the homeless in Sacramento, California. 15 March 2009. Sacramento, United States. Max Whittaker.

011 A man lies on a mattress in Belgrade's only state-run homeless shelter, where resources were stretched to the limit in winter 2008–9. 8 January 2009. Belgrade, Serbia. Marko Djurica.

012 Lukas Stewart, bearing a sign strapped to his back, uses a megaphone to attract the attention of potential employers as he hands out résumés in Toronto's financial district. 5 March 2009. Toronto, Canada. Mark Blinch.

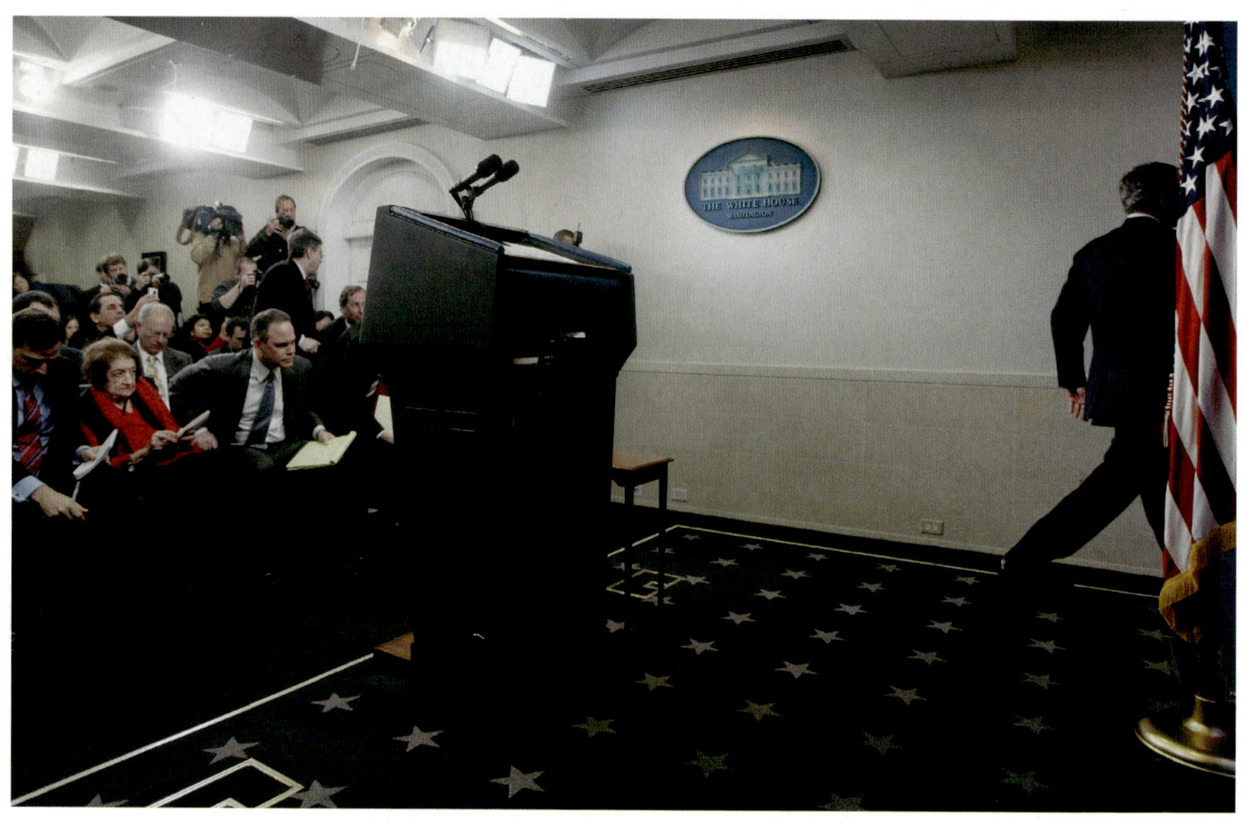

013 [ABOVE]   **014** [OPPOSITE] Washington, DC, United States

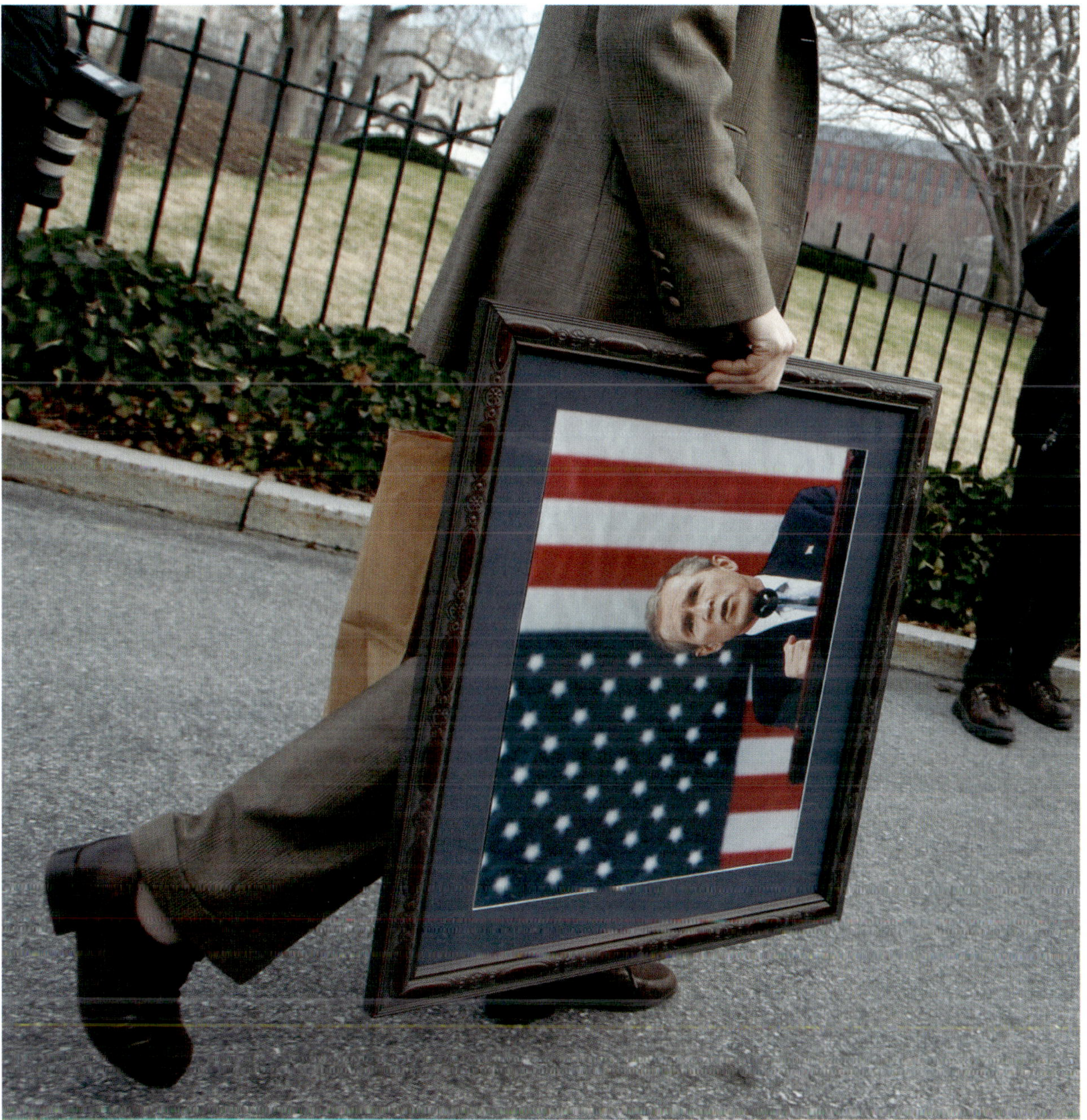

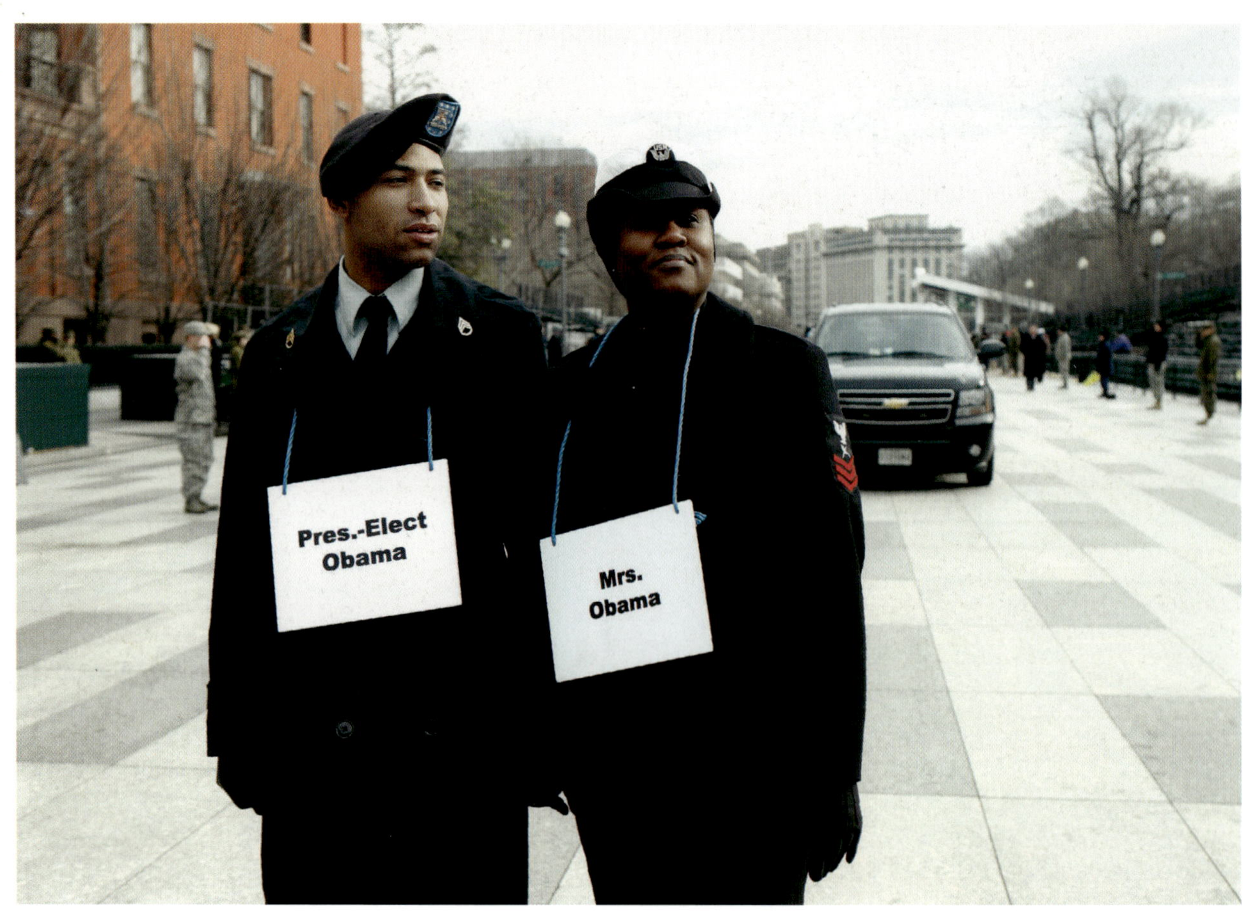

015 Washington, DC, United States

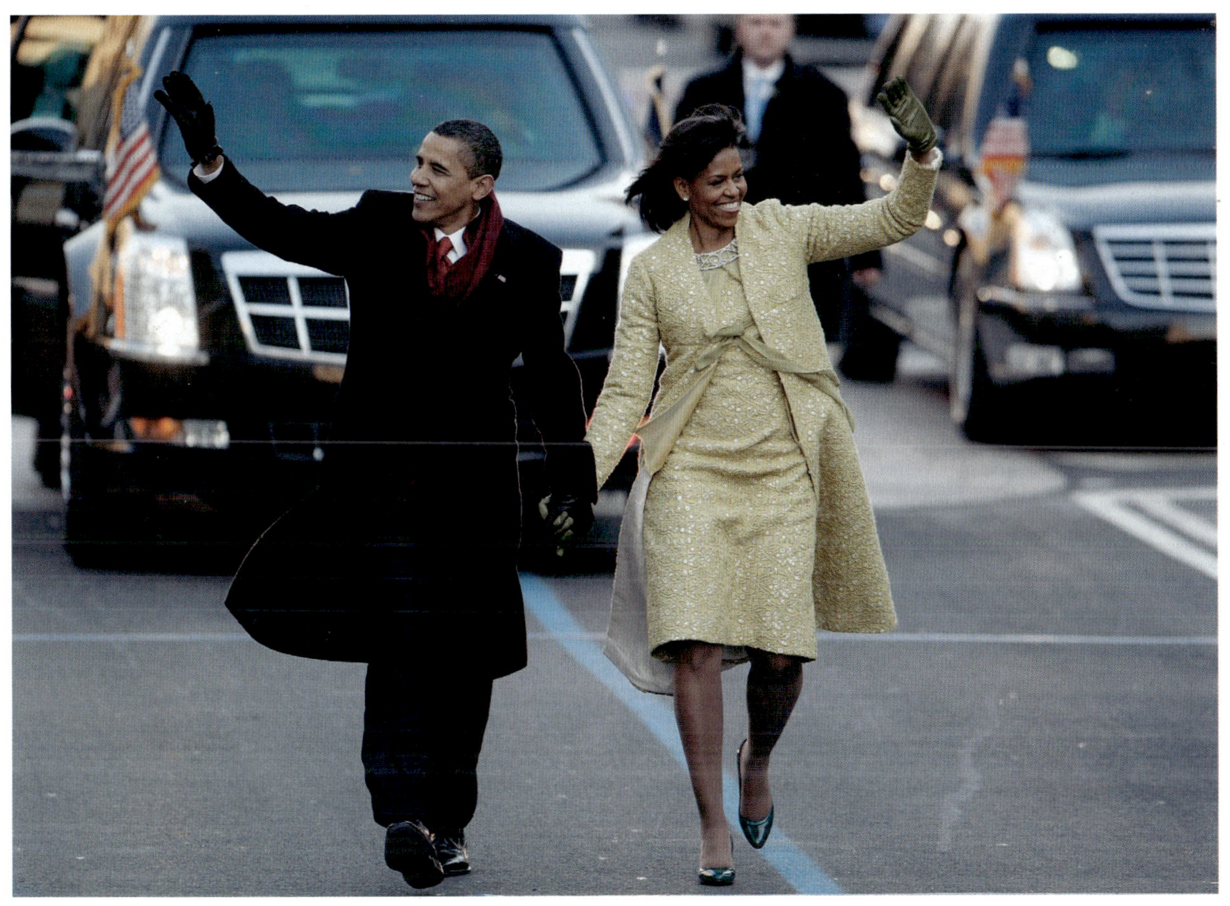

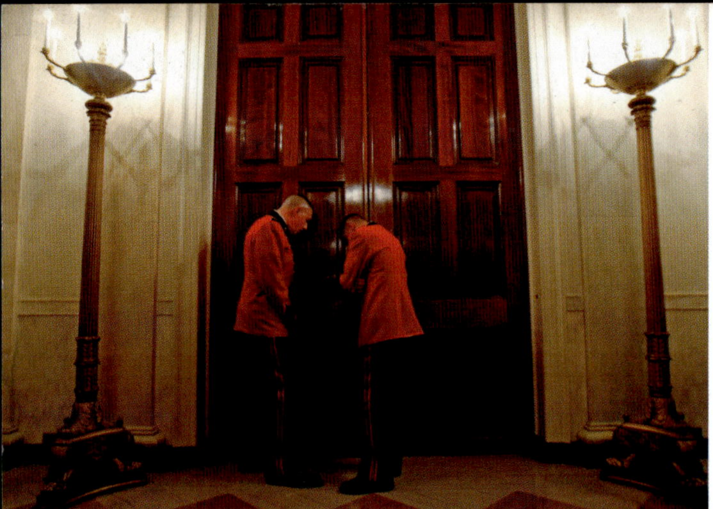

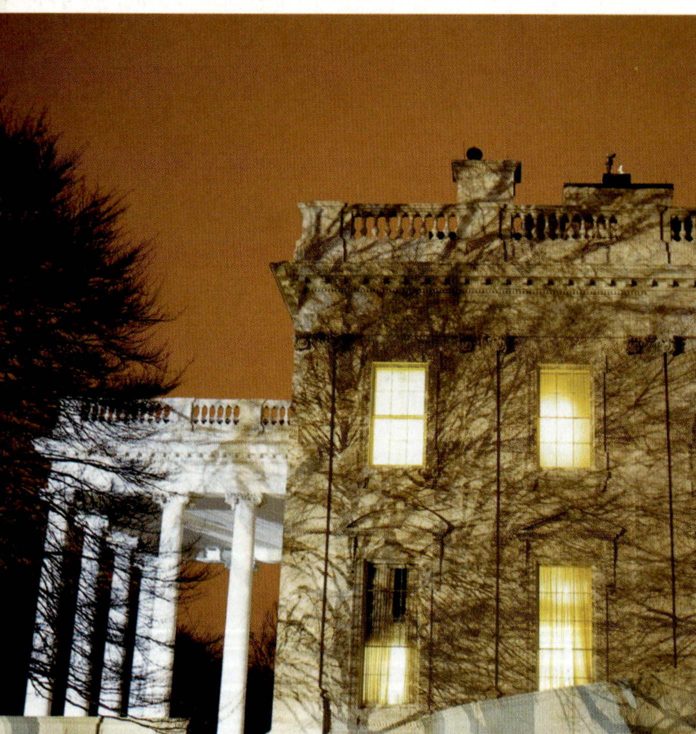

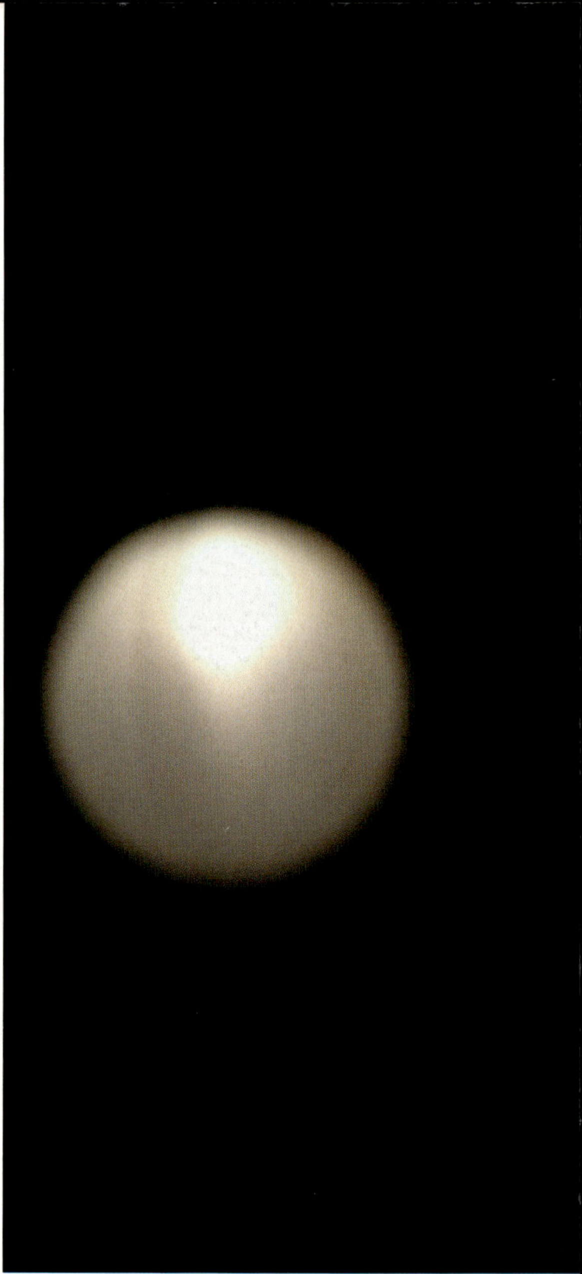

017 [TOP]   018 [ABOVE] Washington, DC, United States

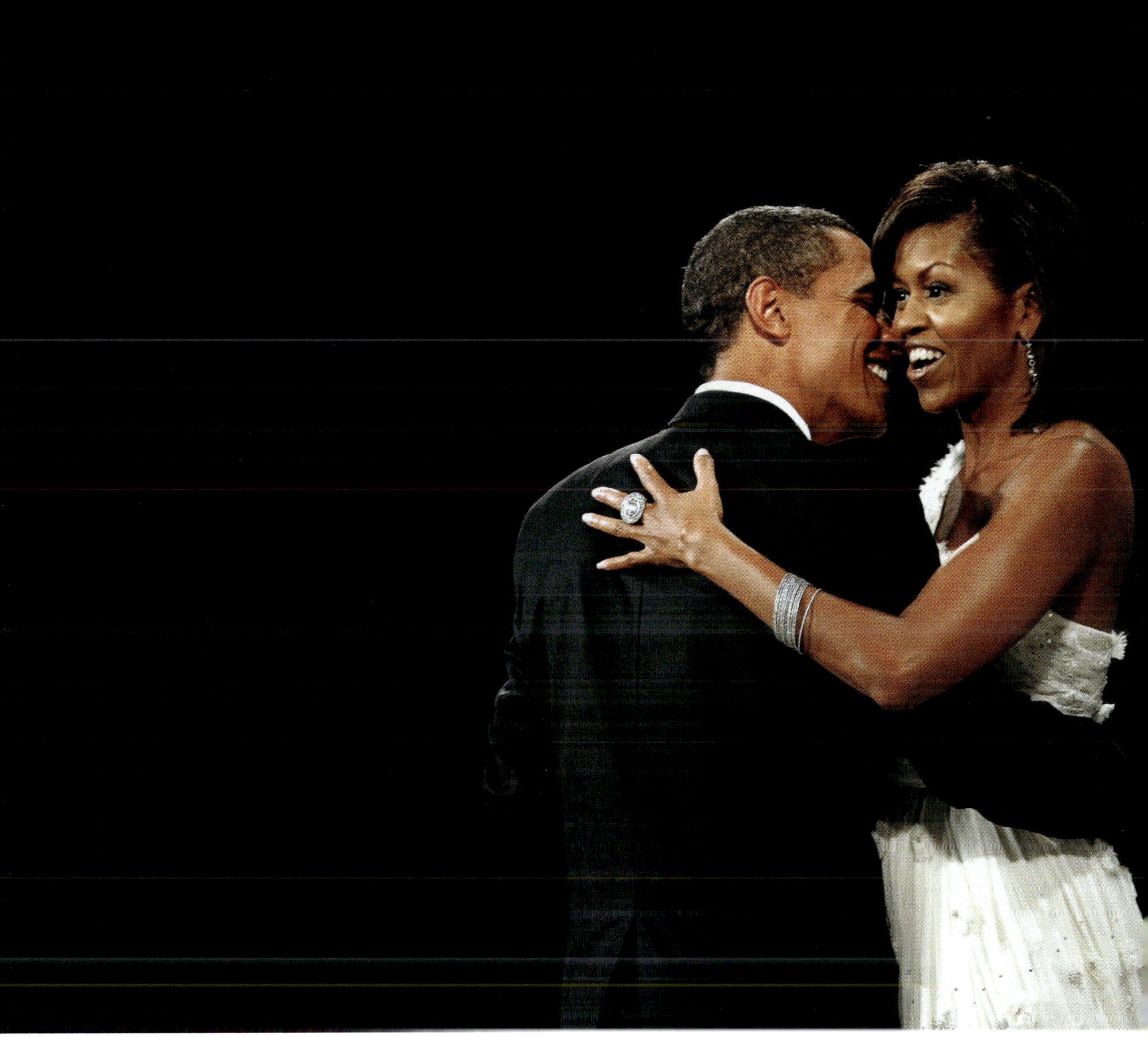

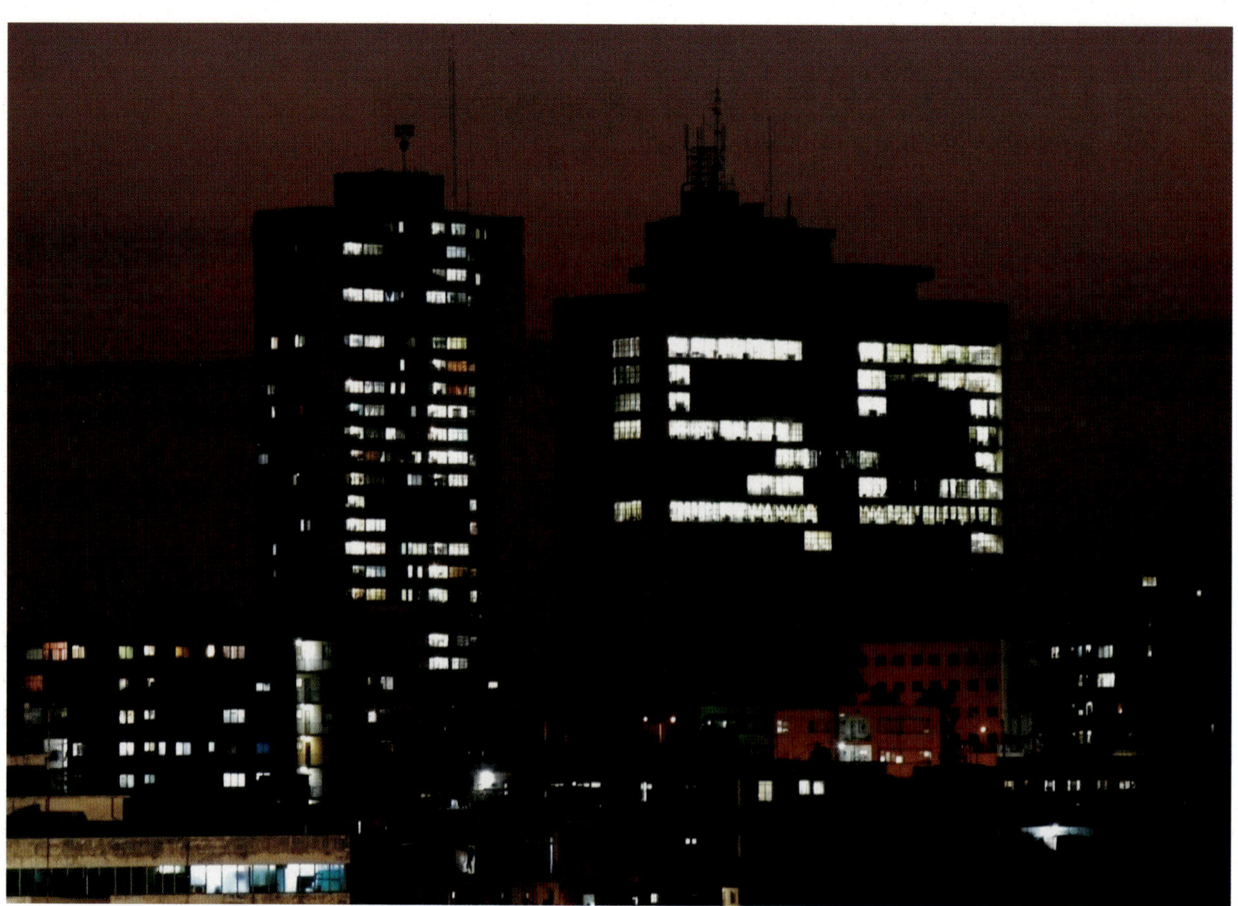

020 Havana, Cuba

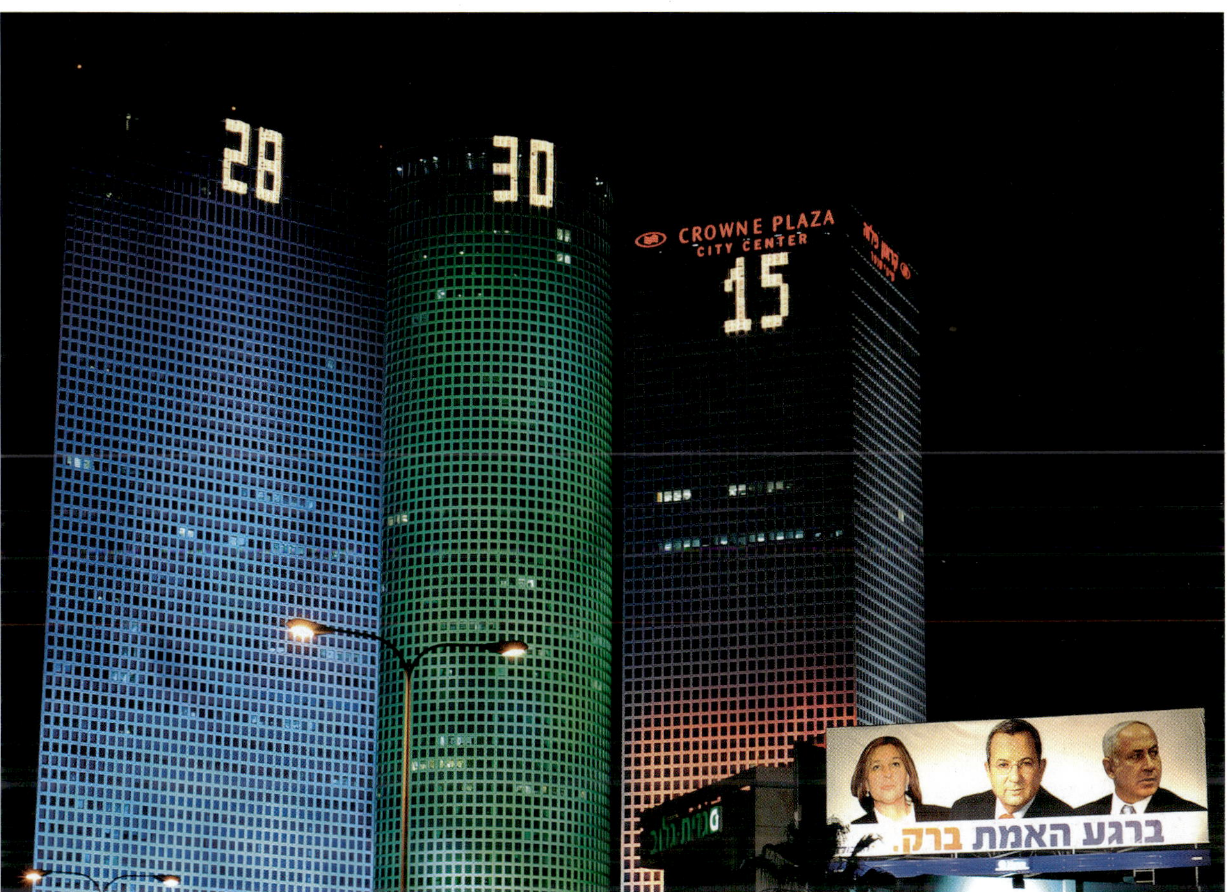

28
30
CROWNE PLAZA
CITY CENTER
15
ברגע האמת ברק.

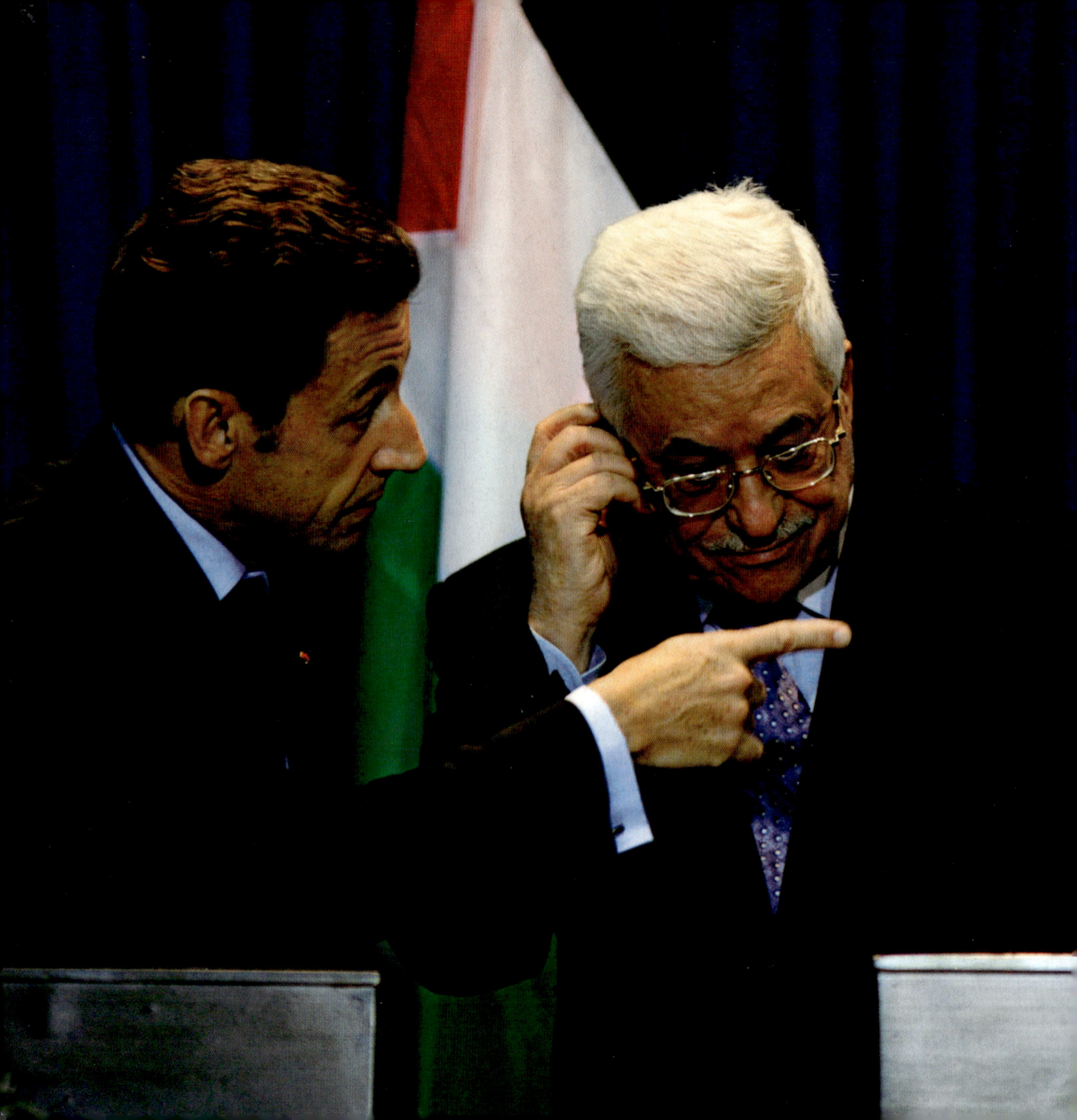

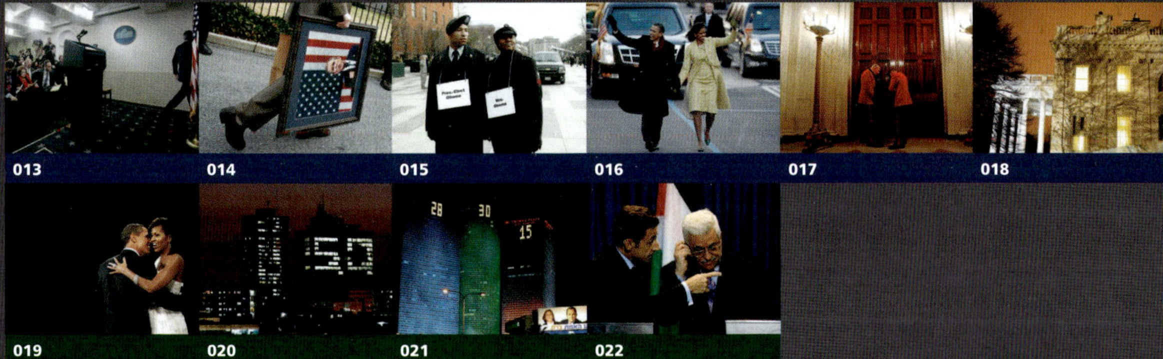

013 Outgoing U.S. President George W. Bush departs the stage after his final news conference in the Brady Press Briefing room at the White House. 12 January 2009. Washington, DC, United States. Jason Reed.

014 A member of the White House staff walks off with a portrait of President George W. Bush ahead of Barack Obama's inauguration as the 44th president of the United States. 13 January 2009. Washington, DC, United States. Jason Reed.

015 U.S. Army Staff Sergeant Derrick Brooks and U.S. Navy Yeoman First Class LaSean McCray stand in as President-elect Barack Obama and his wife Michelle during a rehearsal for Obama's inaugural parade. 11 January 2009. Washington, DC, United States. Kevin Lamarque.

016 President Barack Obama, the newly sworn-in 44th president of the United States, waves as he and his wife Michelle walk down Pennsylvania Avenue during his inaugural parade. 20 January 2009. Washington, DC, United States. Jim Young.

017 Members of the President's Own United States Marine Band listen through a door as musician Stevie Wonder performs during a ceremony at the White House. Wonder was awarded the Library of Congress Gershwin Prize in recognition of a lifetime of contributions to popular music. 25 February 2009. Washington, DC, United States. Jim Young.

018 Shadows are cast on the White House in the early morning. 4 February 2009. Washington, DC, United States. Larry Downing.

019 U.S. President Barack Obama and first lady Michelle Obama dance at the Home States Ball following his inauguration. 20 January 2009. Washington, DC, United States. Carlos Barria.

020 Lights form the number 50 on the Cuban Transport Ministry building in Havana, part of celebrations to mark the 50th anniversary of the 1959 revolution that brought Fidel Castro to power and transformed the island into a communist state. 2 January 2009. Havana, Cuba. Enrique De La Osa.

021 Azrieli Towers in Tel Aviv display general election exit poll results for three of Israel's political parties: (from left) Likud, Kadima and Yisrael Beiteinu. 10 February 2009. Tel Aviv, Israel. Amir Cohen.

022 Palestinian President Mahmoud Abbas (right) and France's President Nicolas Sarkozy hold a joint news conference in the West Bank city of Ramallah. 5 January 2009. Ramallah, West Bank. Fadi Arouri.

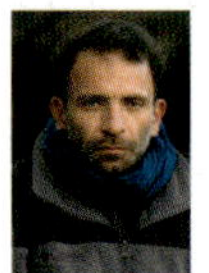

YANNIS BEHRAKIS
Chief photographer, Israel and Palestinian territories
Born: Greece, Athens, 1960
Based: Jerusalem
Nationality: Greek

West of Route 232

A call from Gaza on a Saturday morning usually means bad news. I was getting ready to take my two-year-old daughter Rebecca to the Jerusalem zoo when the phone rang. 'Yannis, Israeli jets bombed Gaza, there are hundreds dead and wounded.' It was Suhaib Salem, Reuters senior photographer in Gaza. 'I'm on my way to the hospital,' he said. 'I'll call you again when I have the first pictures.' I grabbed my cameras and rushed out of the house. I think I shouted 'Daddy has to work…'.

Over the next three weeks I was privileged to lead a team of more than 20 photographers and photo editors from Israel, the Palestinian territories, Greece, France, Croatia, the United States and the Netherlands, working together, most of the time under great pressure and danger, to photograph events for a world audience. The toughest job was that of our photographers in Gaza, who worked round the clock in extreme danger. Worse, their families were also in the front line. Some days at the hospital, waiting to shoot pictures of victims of the bombing, Suhaib told me he would find himself checking for familiar faces among the bloodied bodies.

The Israeli army sealed off Gaza, so all of our international photographers had to remain on the Israeli side of the border. Even so, I needed to call for reinforcements to cover events in the West Bank and also Israeli towns within 50–60 km (30–40 miles) of Gaza, in reach of Hamas Grad missiles. A team of photographers remained constantly near the border. Every day they would wake at around 5 a.m. and sneak into the Israeli closed military zone west of Route 232, which runs north-to-south parallel to the border. Photographers operating here were regularly detained by the Israeli military police and in some cases their equipment was confiscated. Most of the time we filed pictures from petrol stations or from our cars along Route 232.

Powerful emotions still run deep, east and west of Route 232. The team produced many unforgettable images. Ismail Zaydah, working in Gaza, captured exclusive pictures of the bombing of a U.N. school in the northern Gaza Strip, which left scores dead and wounded. The next day, Jerusalem-based Baz Ratner photographed an Israeli mother protecting her two children as they waited to see their reservist father. But the best day for us was when the fighting ceased and we counted all our staff safe and sound.

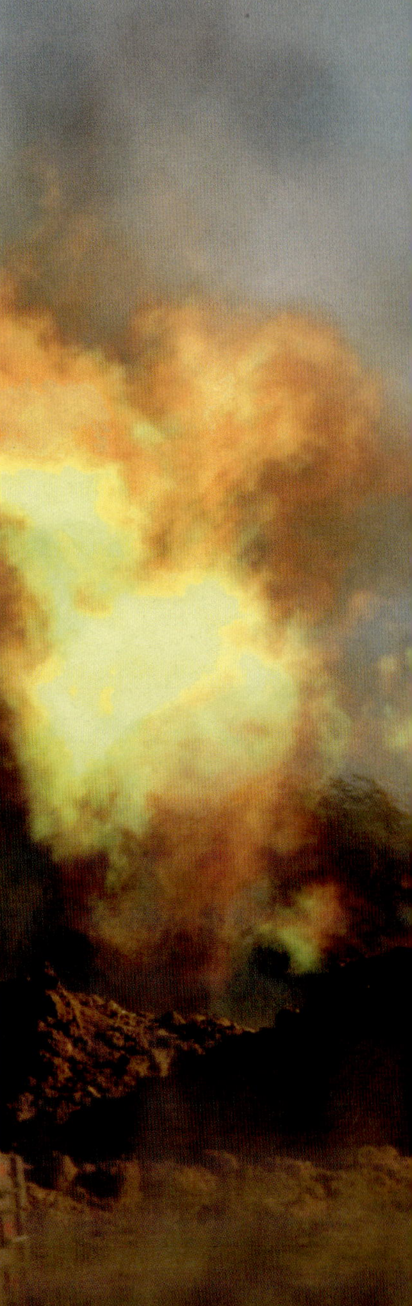

023 An Israeli soldier covers his ears as a mobile artillery unit fires a shell towards Gaza. 6 January 2009. Israel–Gaza border. Baz Ratner.

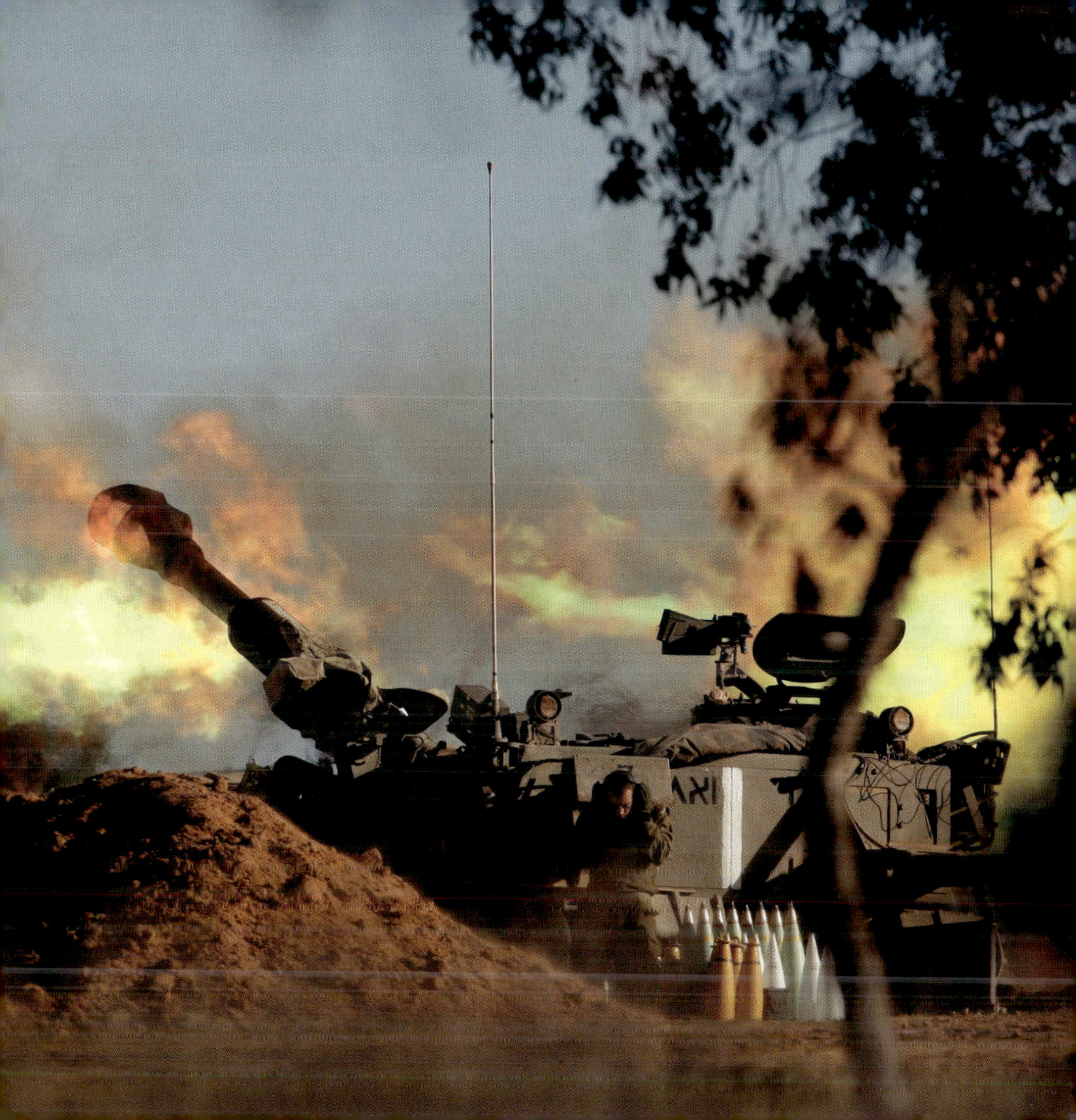

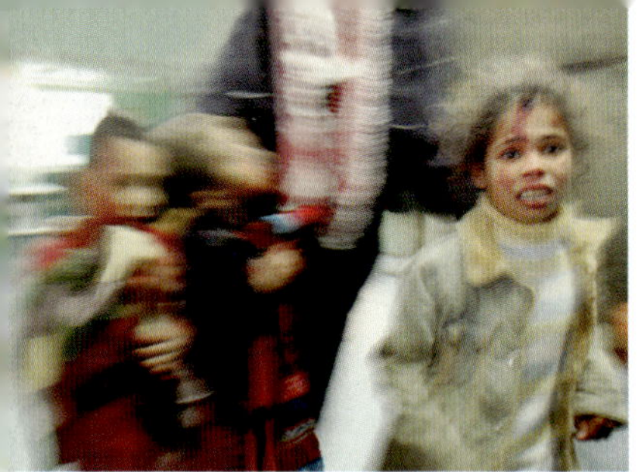
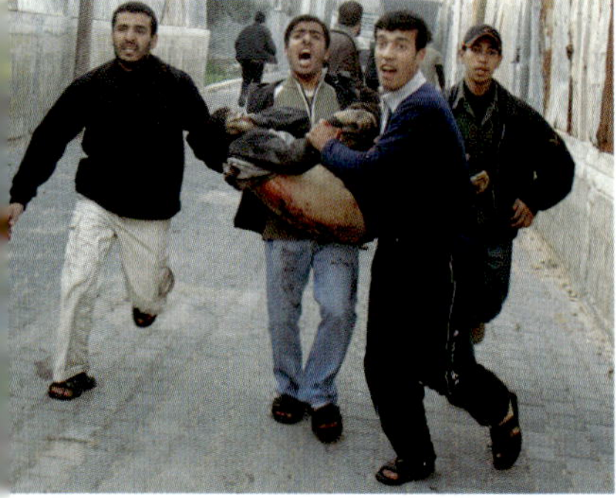
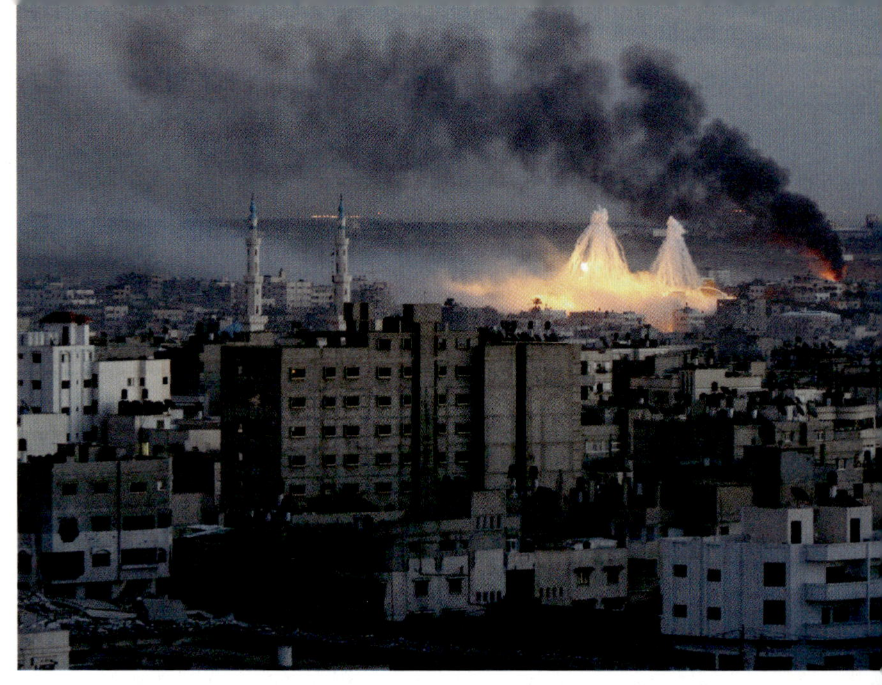

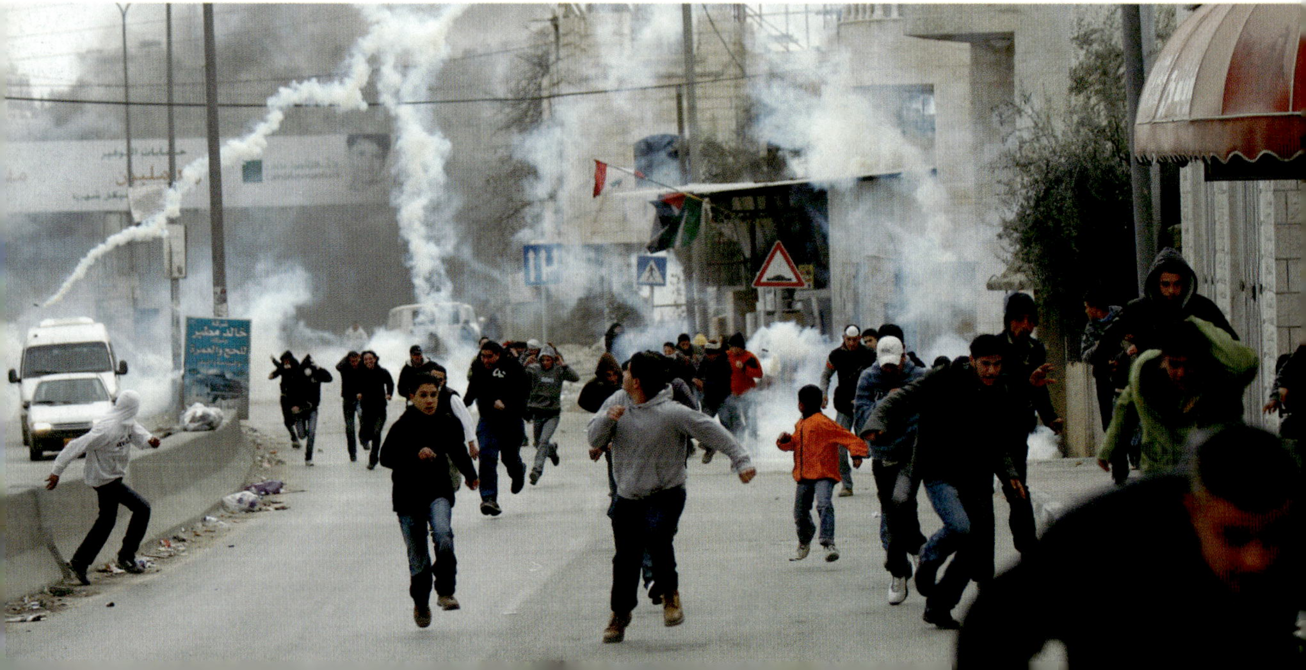

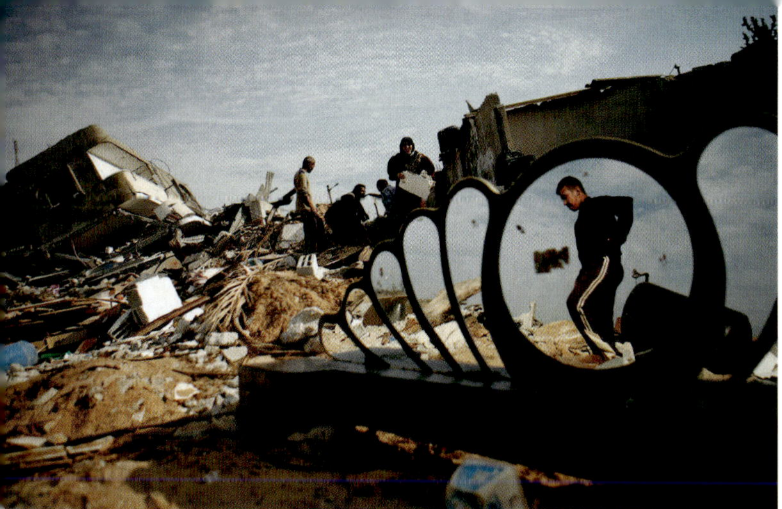

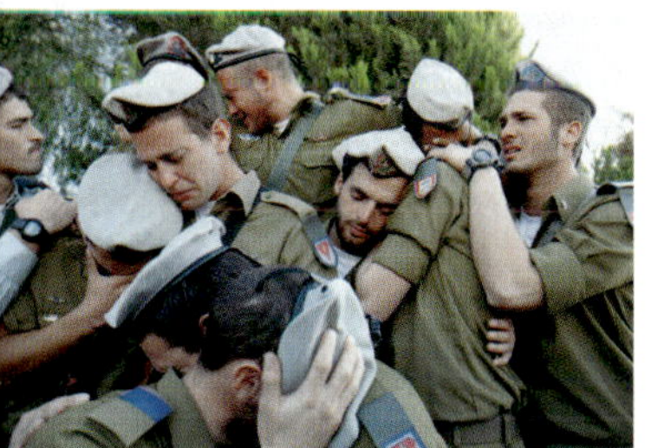

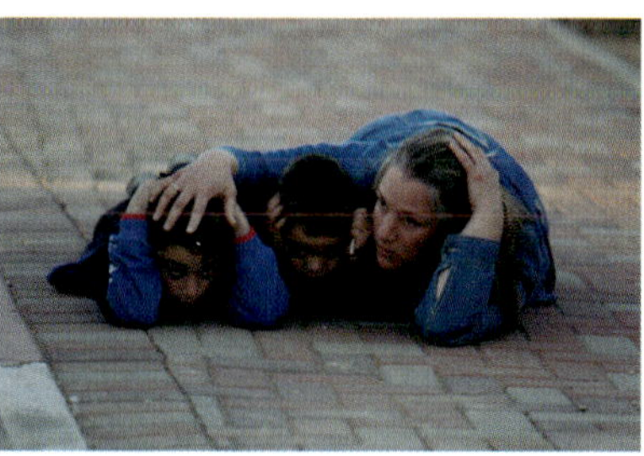

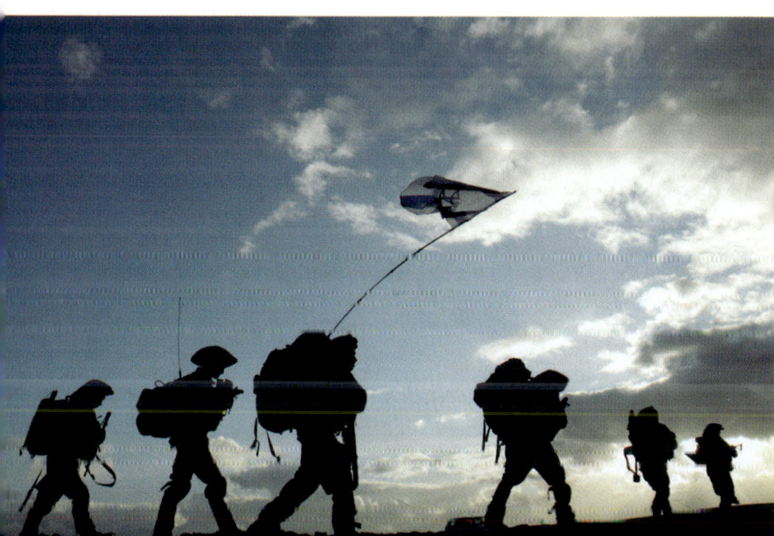

024 Wounded Palestinian children rush into Shifa Hospital in Gaza. 5 January 2009. Gaza. Suhaib Salem. **025** A wounded Palestinian is carried near a U.N. school in the northern Gaza Strip. 6 January 2009. Jabalya, Gaza. Ismail Zaydah. **026** Smoke rises and missiles explode during Israel's offensive in Gaza. 8 January 2009. Gaza. Mohammed Salem. **027** Palestinian stone-throwers in the West Bank run for cover from teargas fired by Israeli border police during scuffles at Qalandiya checkpoint near Ramallah. 16 January 2009. Qalandiya, West Bank. Fadi Arouri. **028** A Palestinian woman salvages belongings from the rubble of her destroyed house in the village of Johr el-Deek. 21 January 2009. Johr el-Deek, Gaza. Jerry Lampen. **029** Israeli soldiers mourn their comrade Alex Mashavisky at a cemetery in Beersheba. 7 January 2009. Beersheba, Israel. Eric Gaillard. **030** An Israeli woman shelters her children during a Palestinian rocket attack near Kfar Aza, just outside the northern Gaza Strip. 7 January 2009. Kfar Aza, Israel. Baz Ratner. **031** Israeli soldiers cross the border back to Israel after an early morning combat mission on the day that a unilateral Israeli ceasefire signalled the end of the war. 18 January 2009. Israel–Gaza border. Yannis Behrakis.

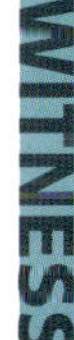

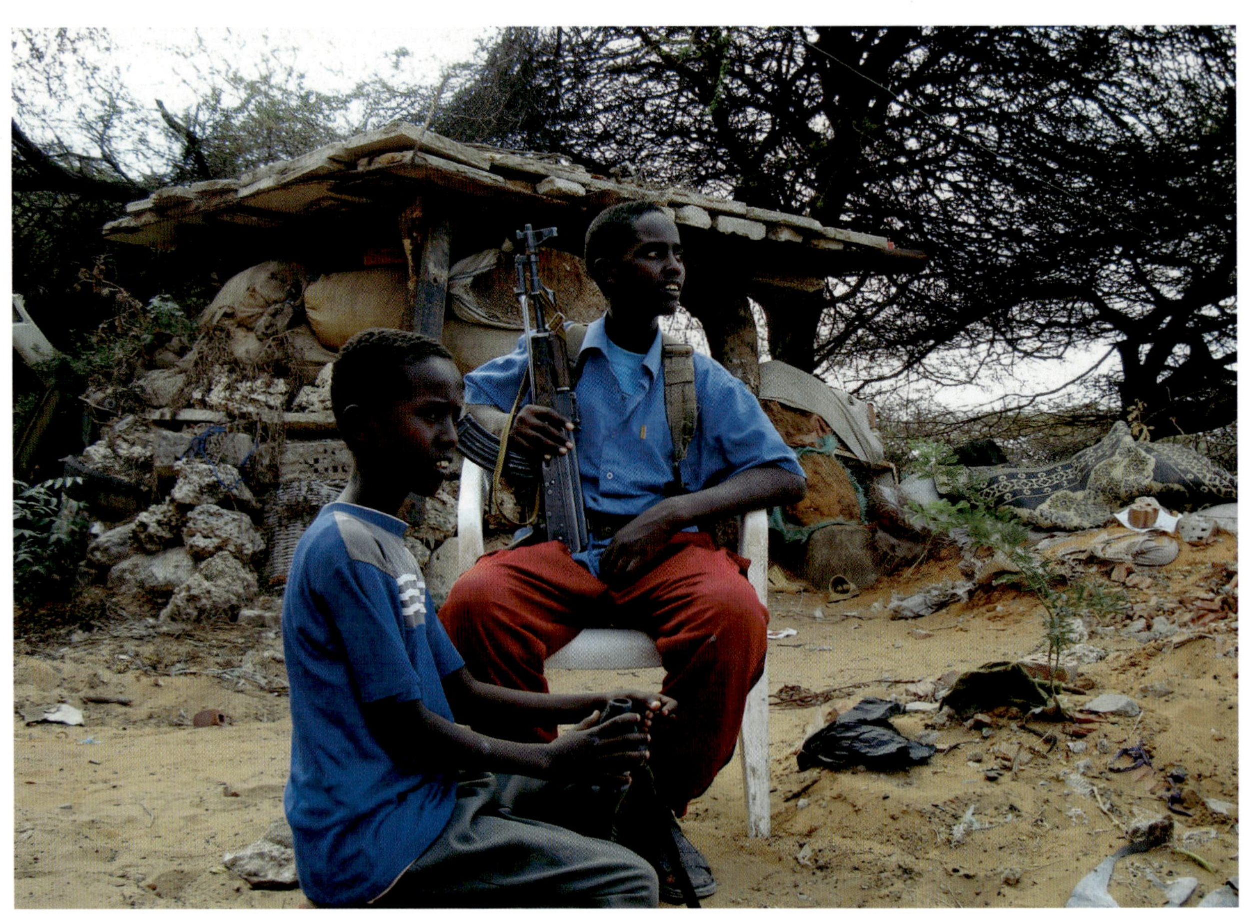

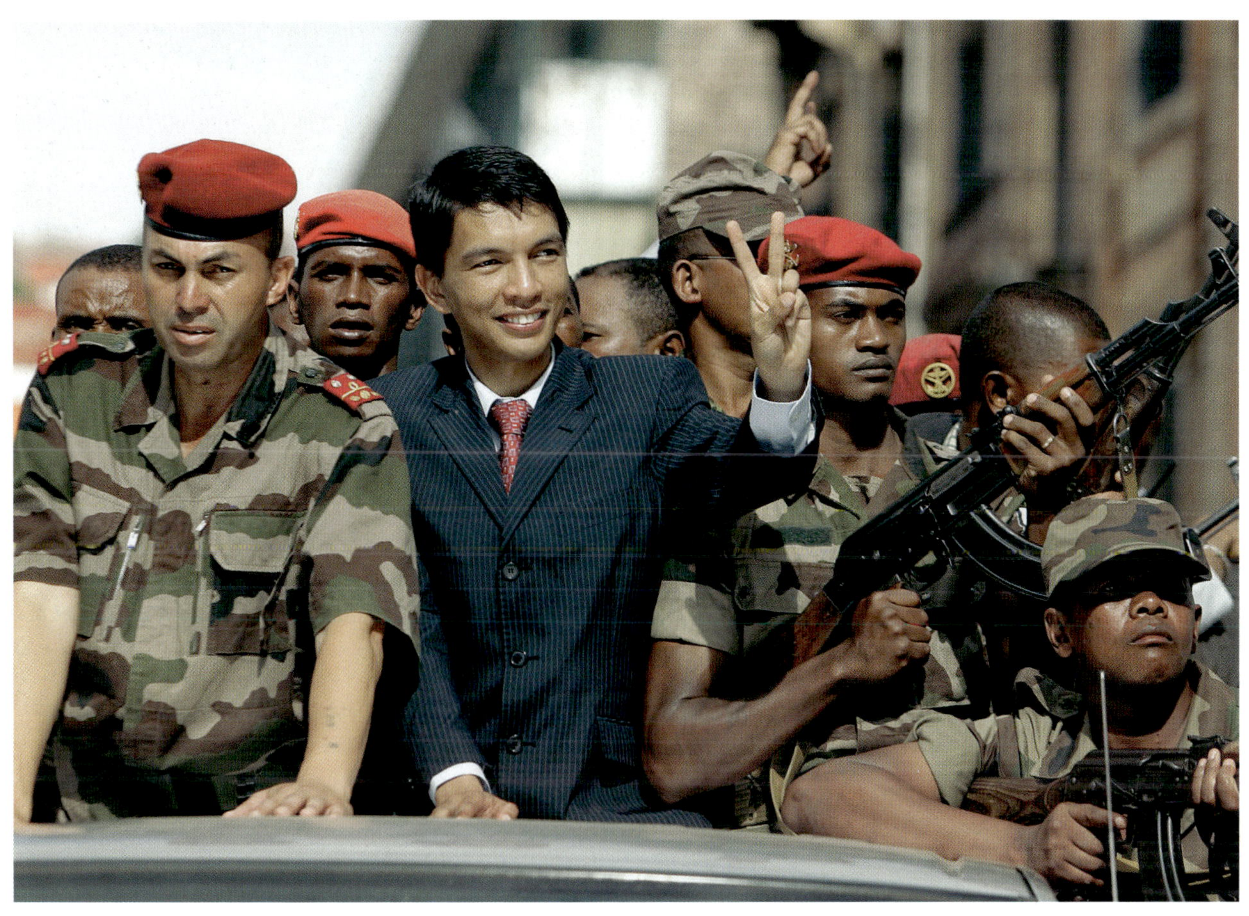

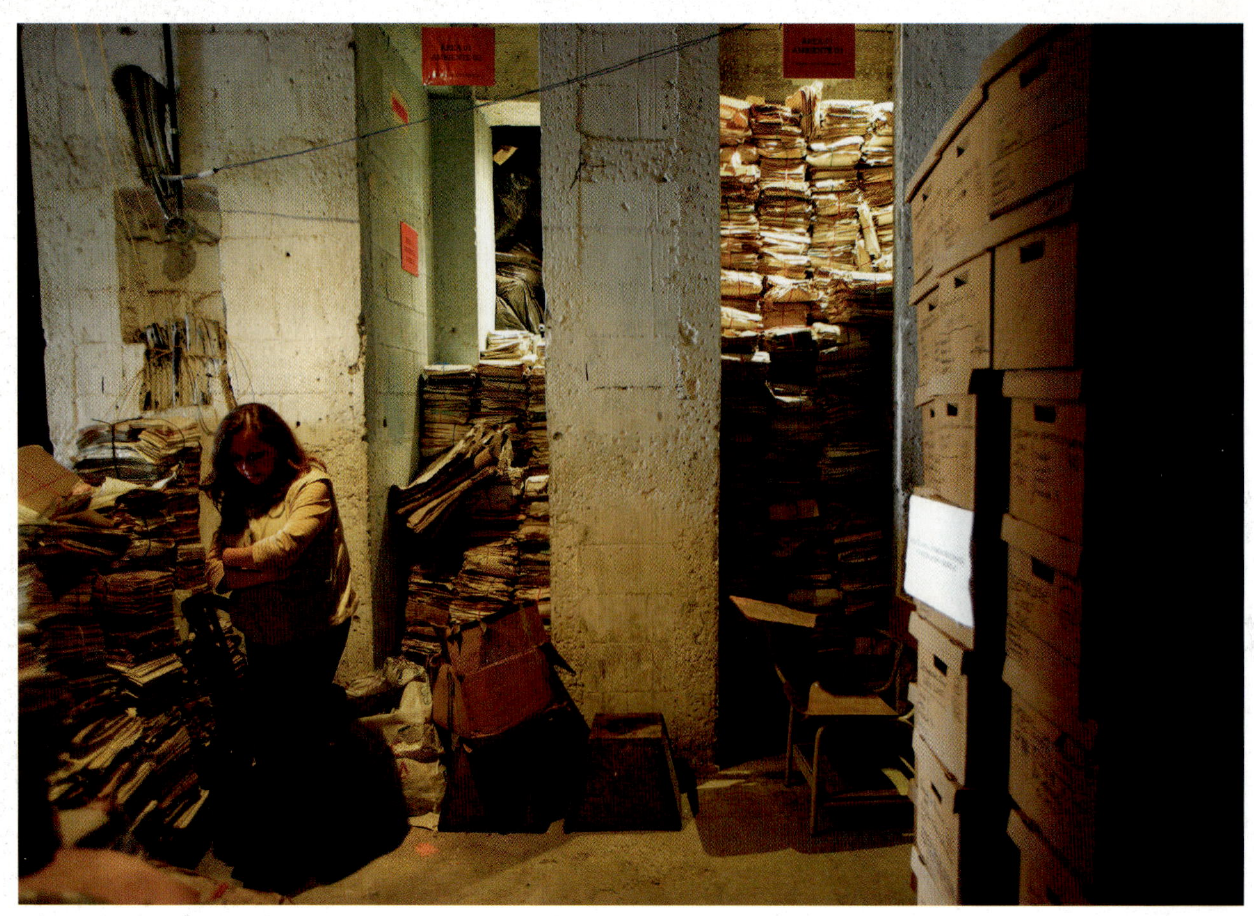

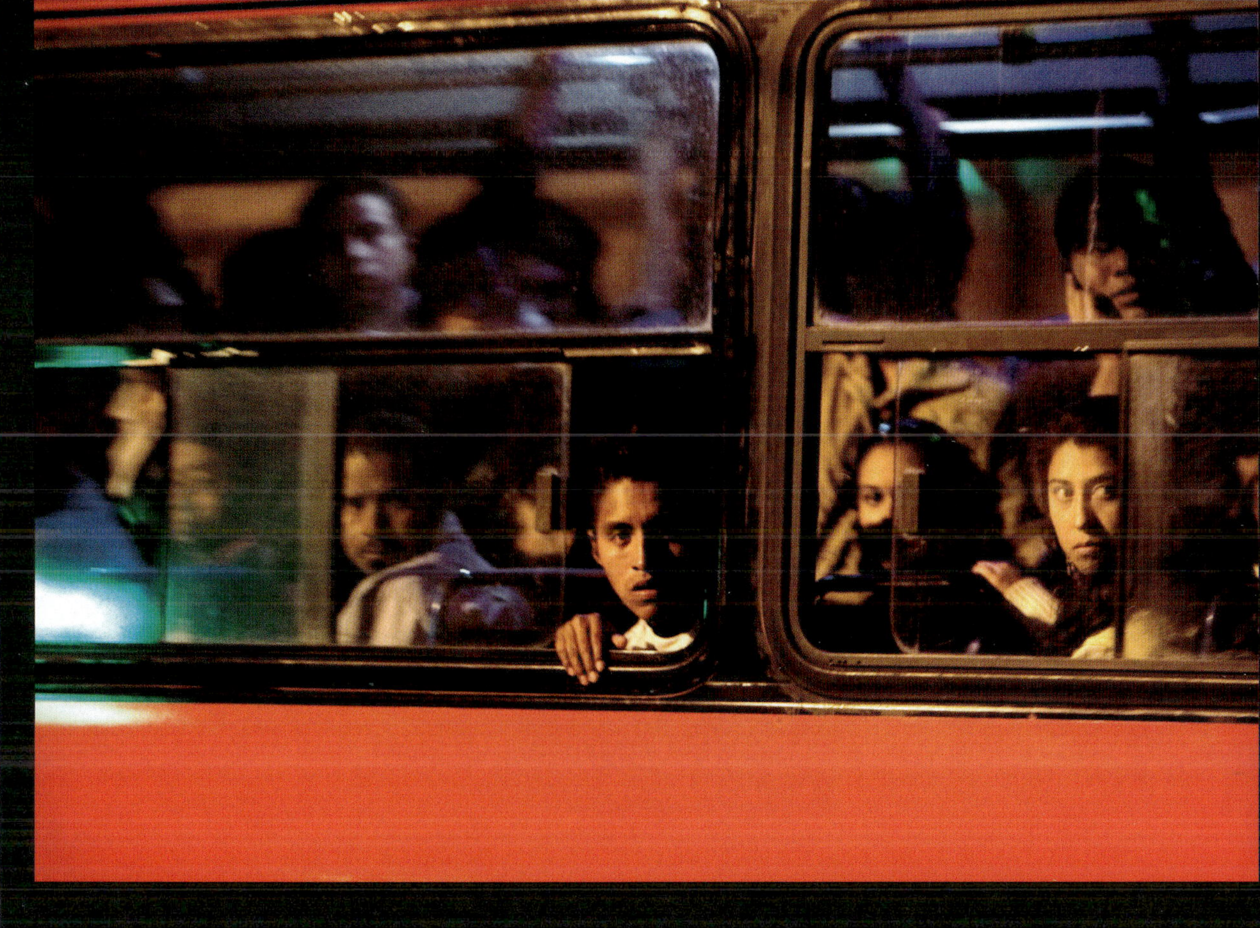

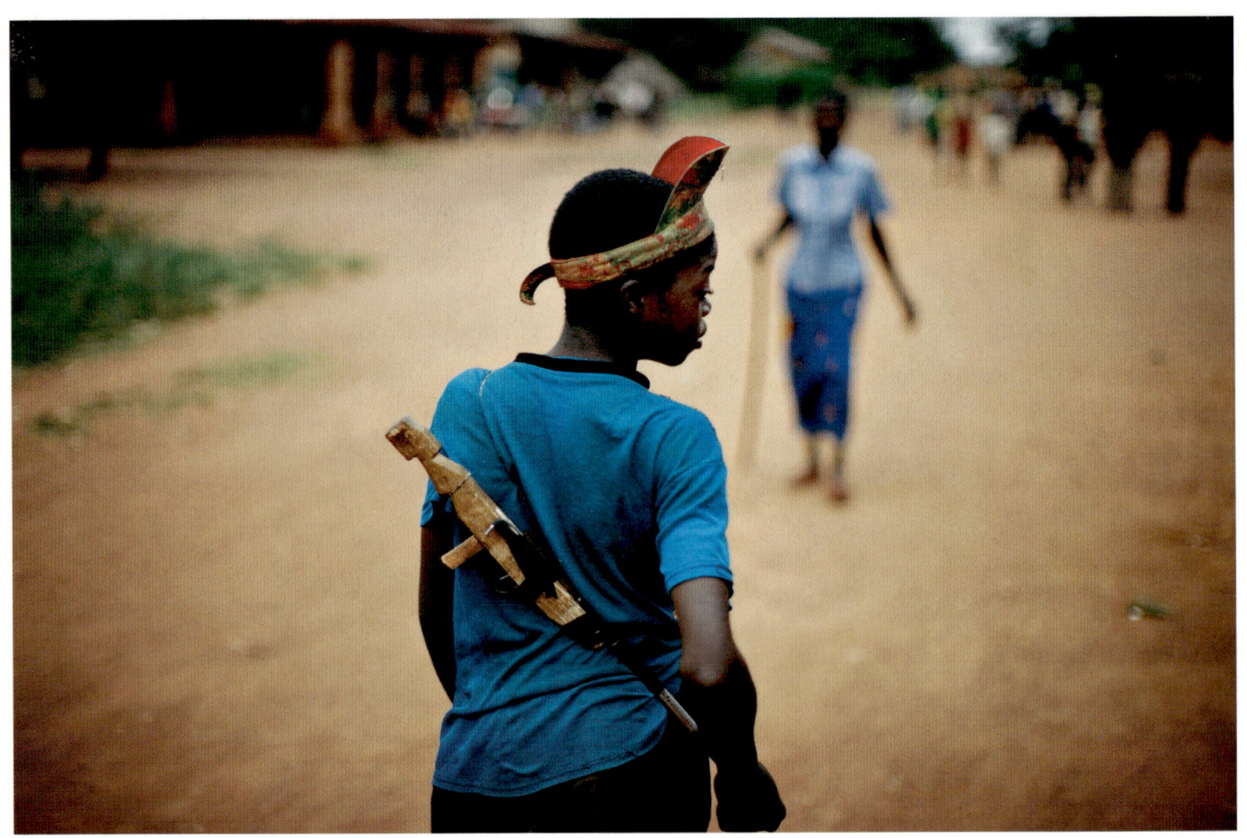

036 Bangadi, Congo

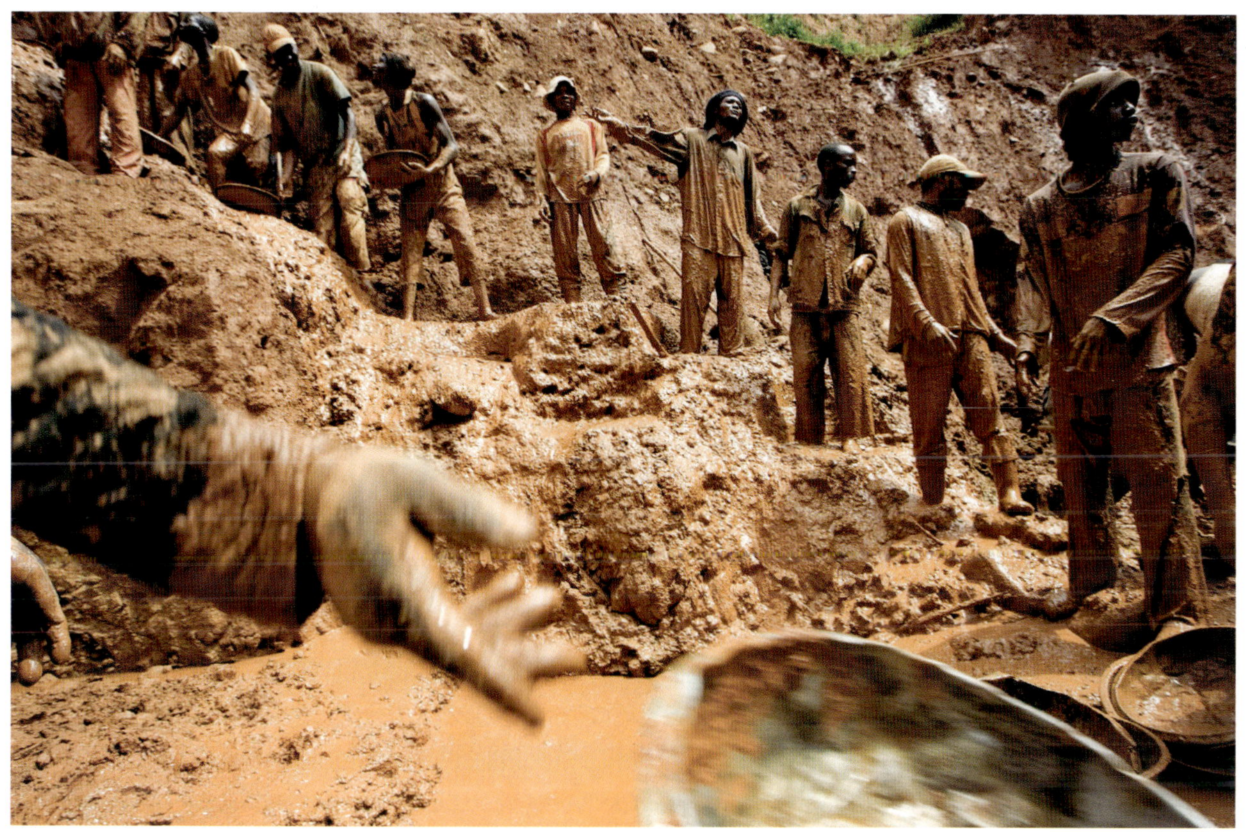

037 Kobu. Congo

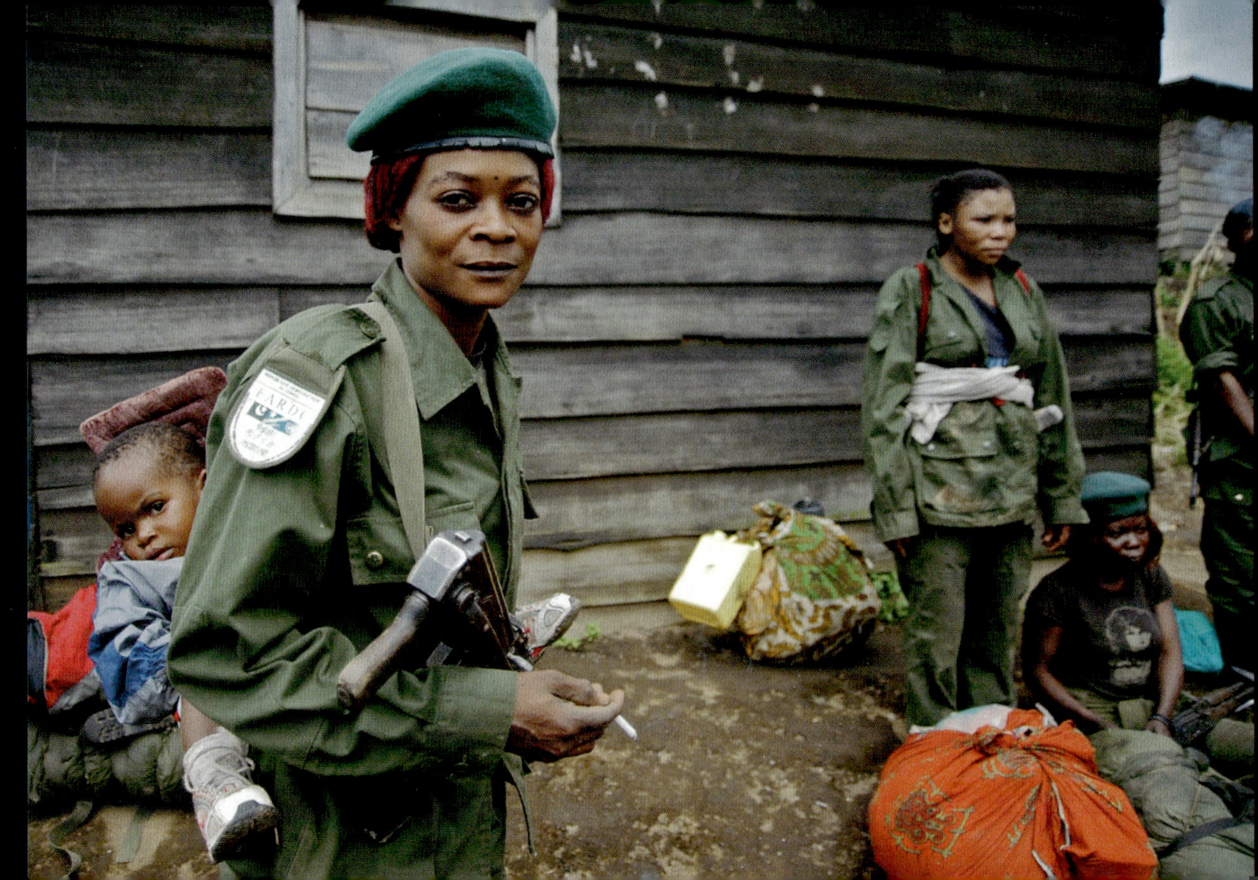

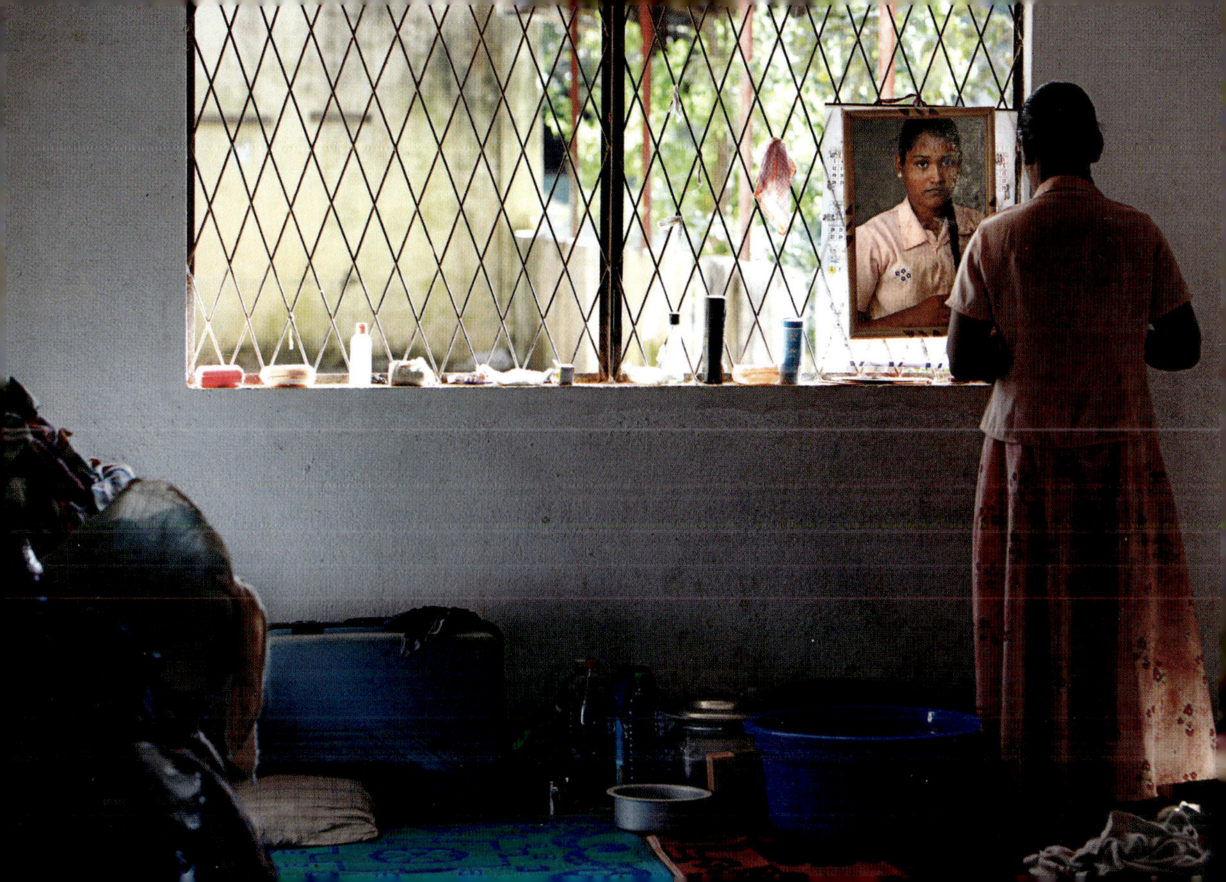

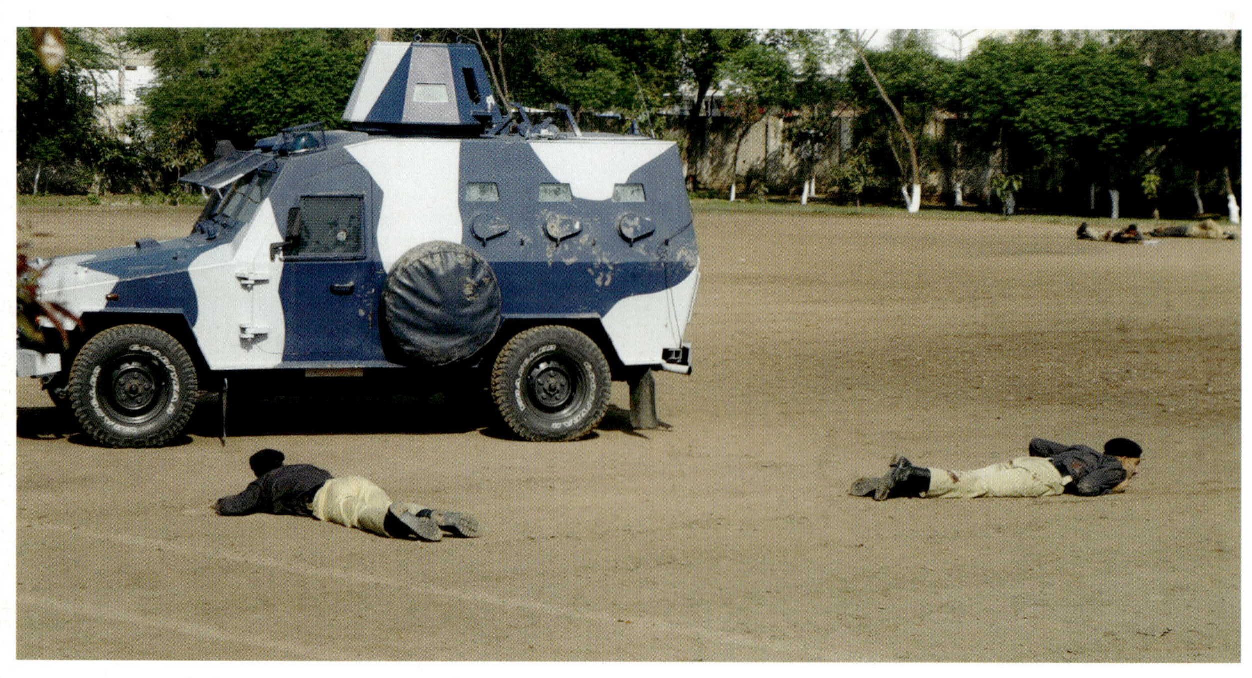

040 [ABOVE] **041** [OPPOSITE] Lahore, Pakistan

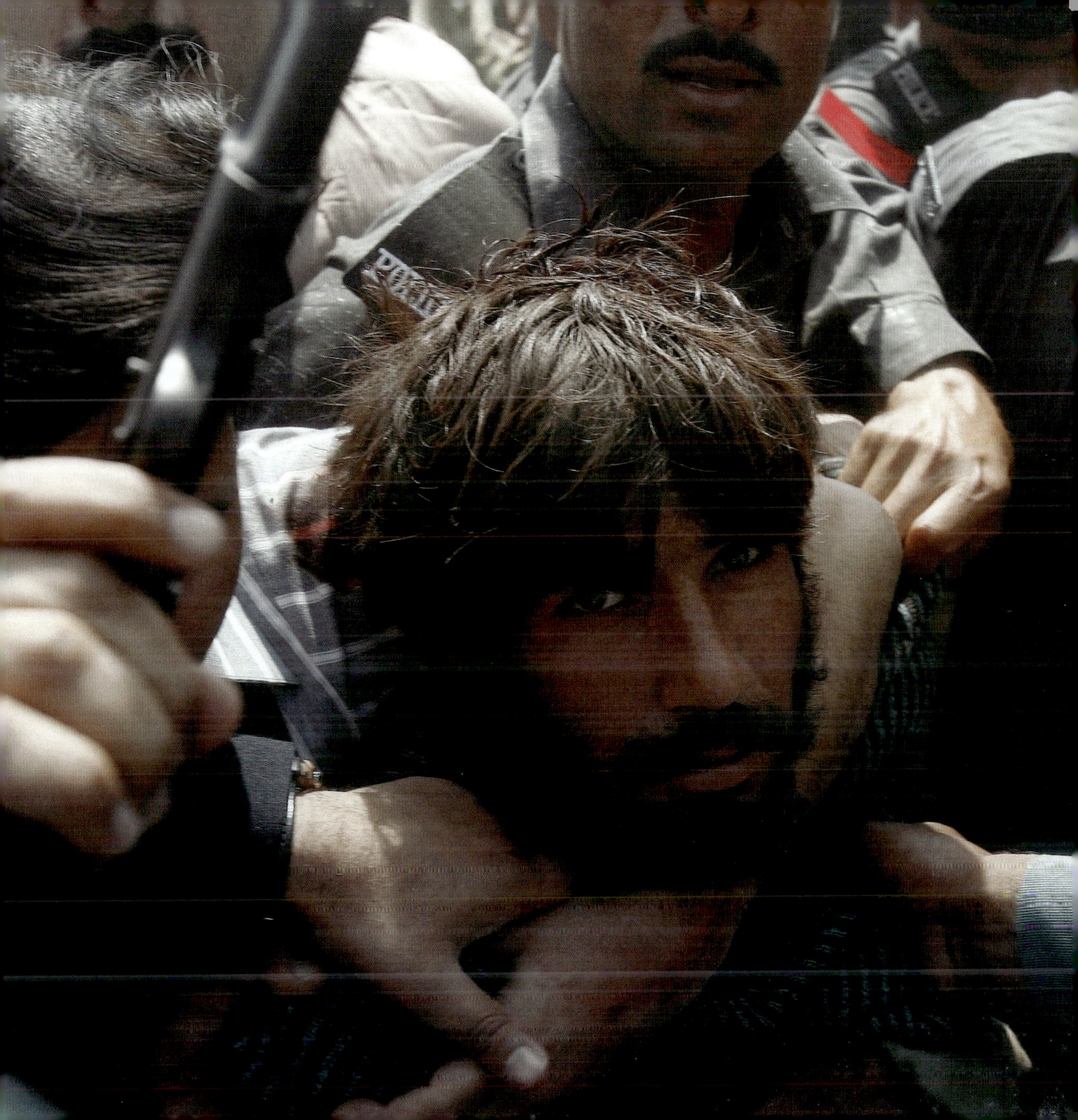

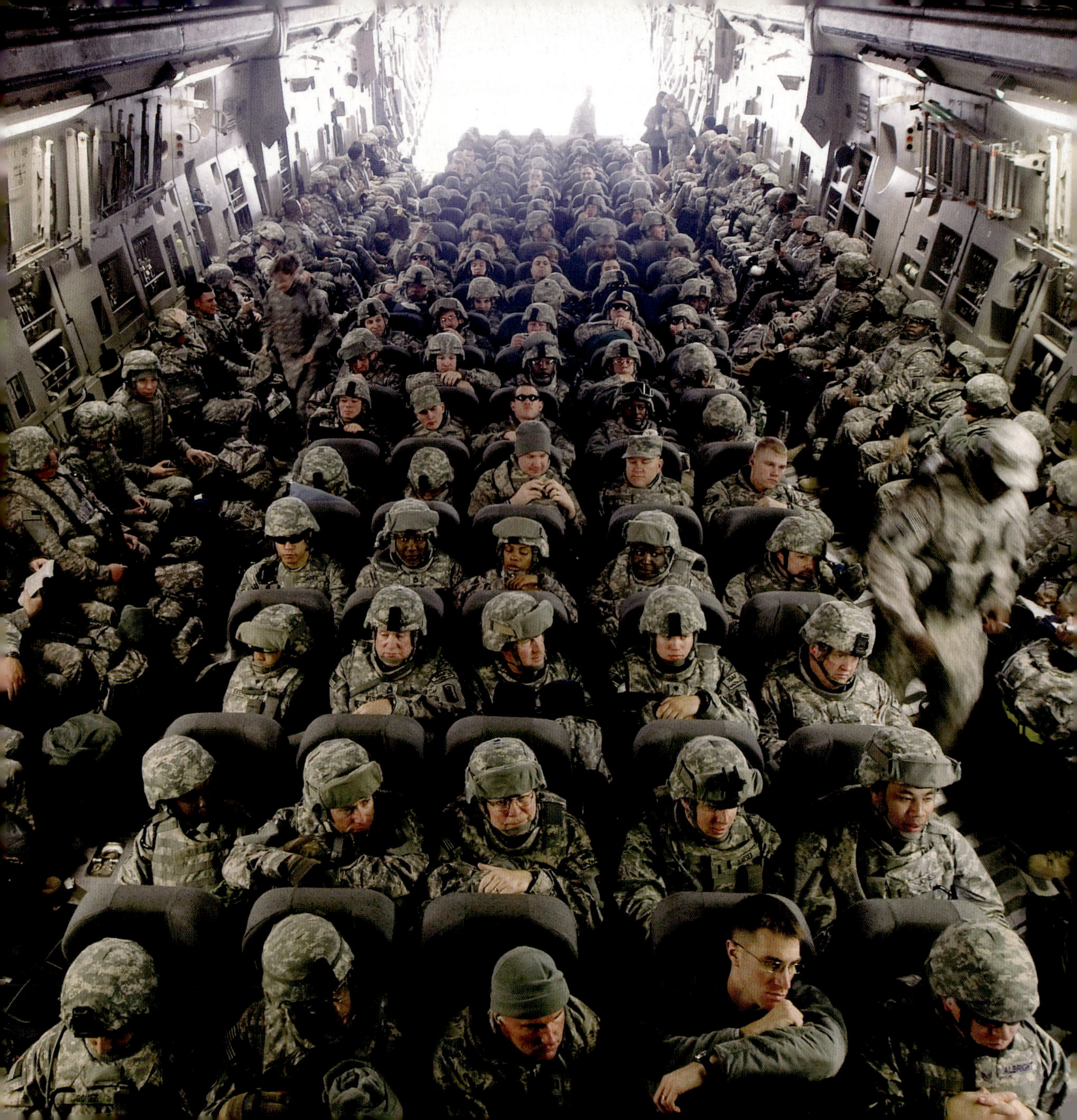

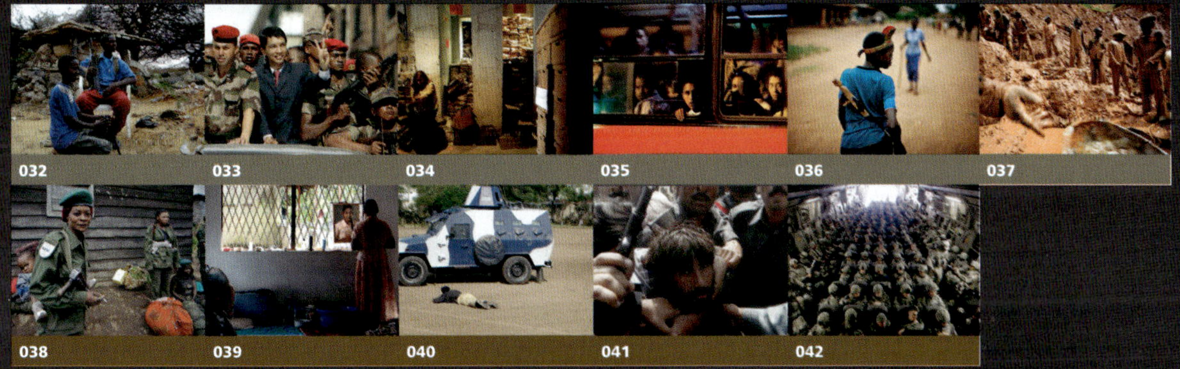

032 Somali Islamist insurgents are seen at one of the bases vacated by Ethiopian troops in the capital Mogadishu. Ethiopia pulled out of Somalia in January 2009, having entered in late 2006 to topple an Islamist movement in Mogadishu. 13 January 2009. Mogadishu, Somalia. Feisal Omar.

033 Madagascar's opposition leader Andry Rajoelina greets his supporters after making his way into the presidential palace in the capital Antananarivo. Rajoelina, 35, seized power after leading a campaign of violent street protests that led to the military-backed ousting of former leader Marc Ravalomanana. 17 March 2009. Antananarivo, Madagascar. Siphiwe Sibeko.

034 A human rights worker stands among documents at a police station archive in Guatemala City. Information long hidden in dusty archives could implicate hundreds of former officers accused of killing students and leftists during Guatemala's 36-year civil war, according to human rights activists. 24 March 2009. Guatemala City, Guatemala. Daniel LeClair.

035 Bus passengers look at a crime scene after an attack on a public bus in Guatemala City. Police reported one passenger killed and the driver seriously injured. The Association of Urban Bus Companies said nearly 200 drivers, assistants and bus owners had been killed over the previous year in a battle between bus companies and organized gangs of extortionists. 16 February 2009. Guatemala City, Guatemala. Daniel LeClair.

036 A member of a local self-defence force walks in the village of Bangadi in northeastern Congo. Some 900 Congolese civilians were killed in the previous three months in attacks and massacres by Ugandan Lord's Resistance Army rebels. 19 February 2009. Bangadi, Congo. Finbarr O'Reilly.

037 Gold miners form a human chain while digging an open pit in the Kilomoto concession near the village of Kobu in northeastern Congo. Civil conflict in the Democratic Republic of Congo has been driven for more than a decade by the violent struggle for control over the country's vast natural resources. 23 February 2009. Kobu, Congo. Finbarr O'Reilly.

038 A government soldier carries her baby on her back at Mushake in eastern Congo. 26 January 2009. Mushake, Congo. Alissa Everett.

039 A Tamil woman who escaped fighting between the Sri Lankan army and Tamil Tiger rebels fixes her hair in a classroom at a refugee camp in Vavuniya, northern Sri Lanka. 23 February 2009. Vavuniya, Sri Lanka. Nir Elias.

040 Policemen lie injured near a police training centre in Lahore after an attack by militants who rampaged through the complex, killing eight recruits and wounding scores. 30 March 2009. Lahore, Pakistan. Mohsin Raza.

041 Police officials detain a suspected militant following a shooting at a police training centre. Four militants were killed and three arrested after an eight-hour stand-off. 30 March 2009. Lahore, Pakistan. Mohsin Raza.

042 U.S. servicemen in a C-17 Globemaster await take-off from Manas Air Base near Kyrgyzstan's capital Bishkek. The base supports U.S. operations in nearby Afghanistan. 13 February 2009. Bishkek, Kyrgyzstan. Shamil Zhumatov.

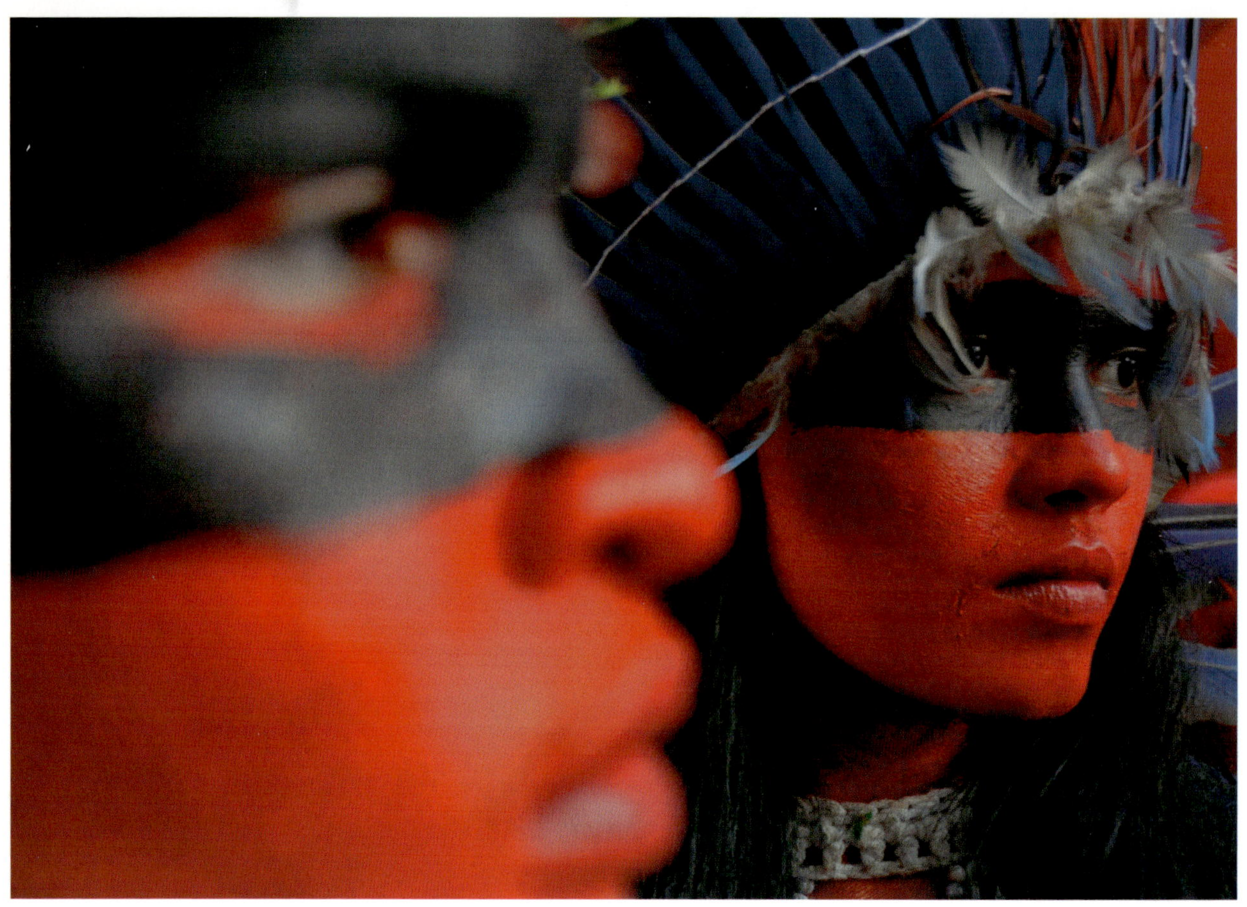

043 Belém, Brazil

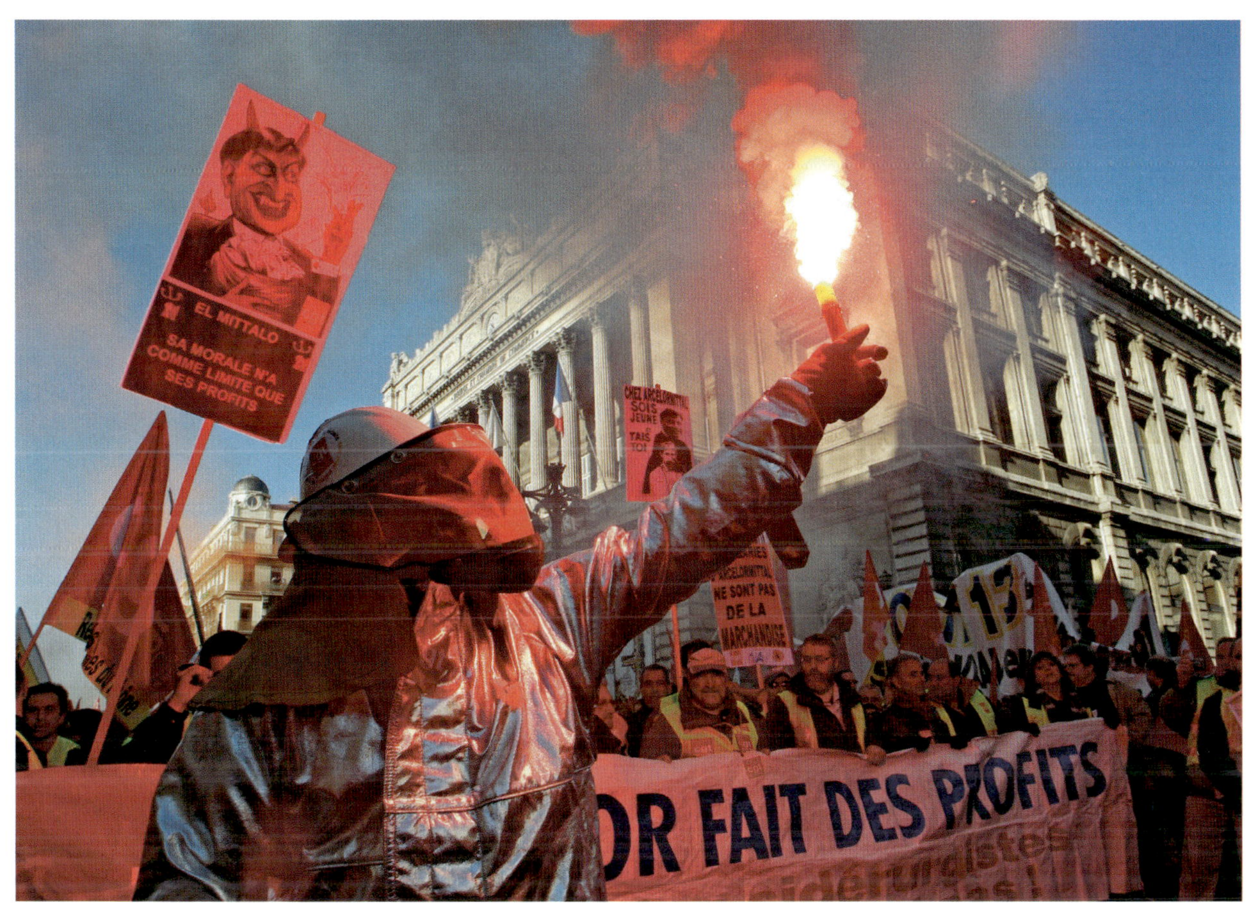EL MITTALO
SA MORALE N'A
COMME LIMITE QUE
SES PROFITS
CHEZ ARCELORMITTAL
SOIS JEUNE
&
TAIS
TOI
ARCELORMITTAL
NE SONT PAS
DE LA
MARCHANDISE
OR FAIT DES PROFITS

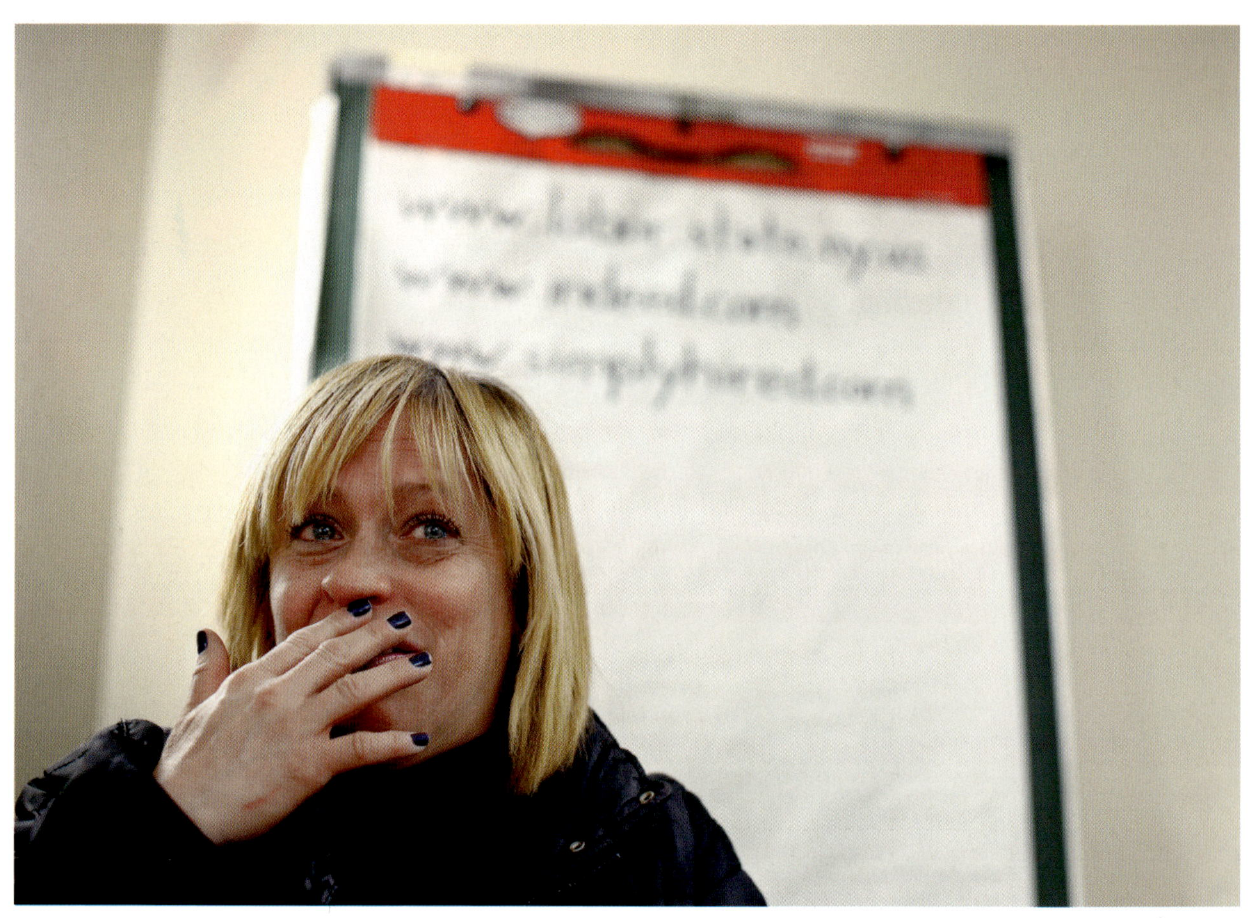

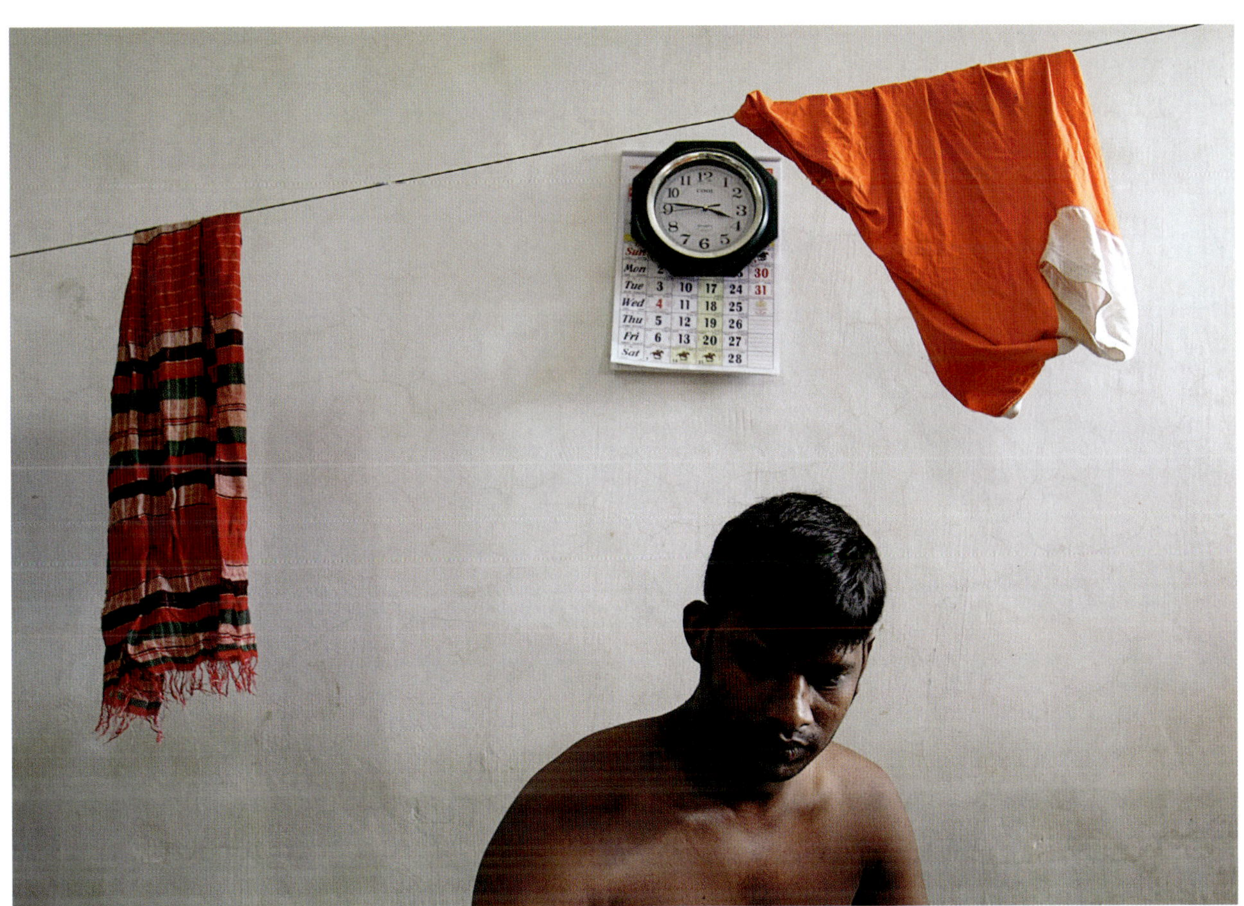

Sun
Mon
Tue   3   10   17   24   31
Wed   4   11   18   25
Thu   5   12   19   26
Fri   6   13   20   27
Sat   28
30

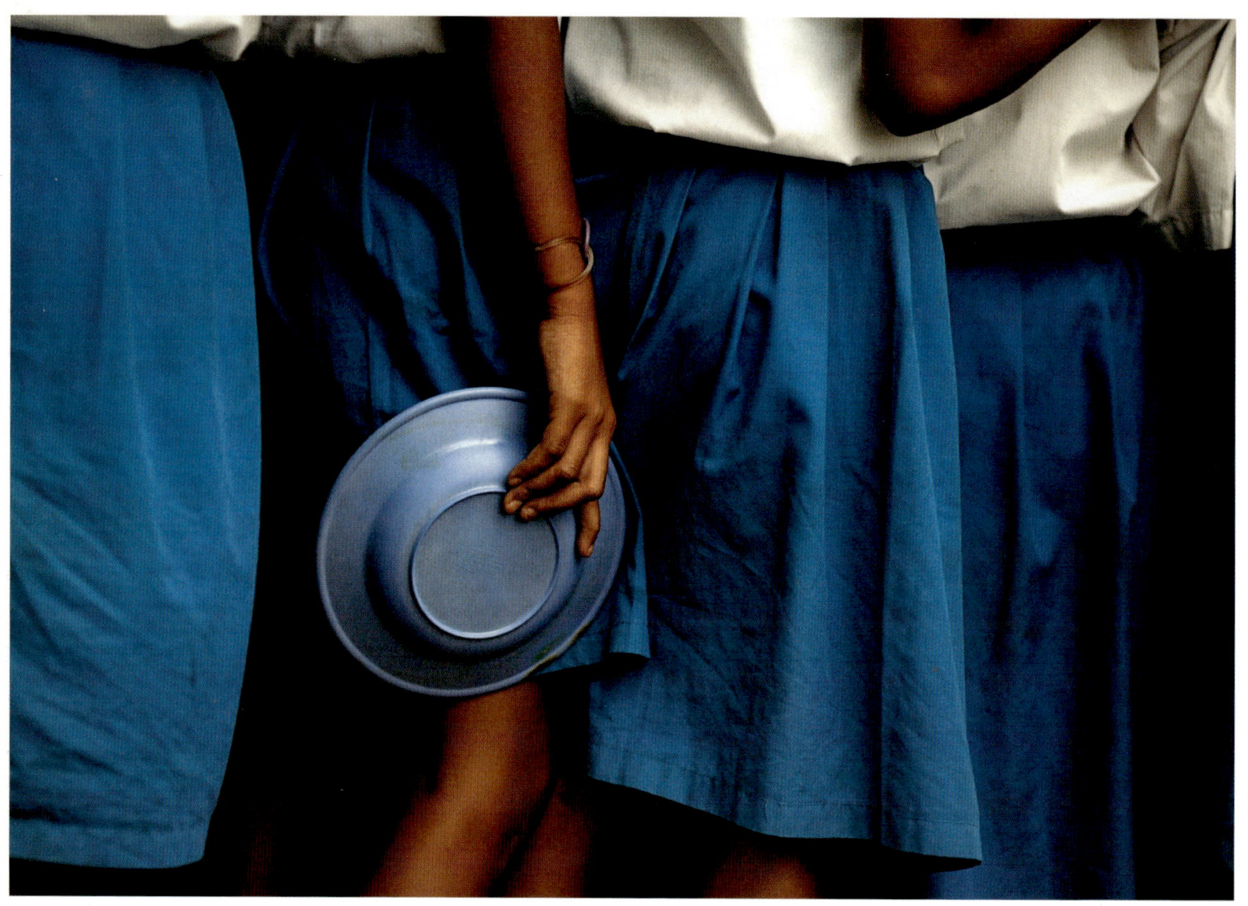

047 Jakarta, Indonesia

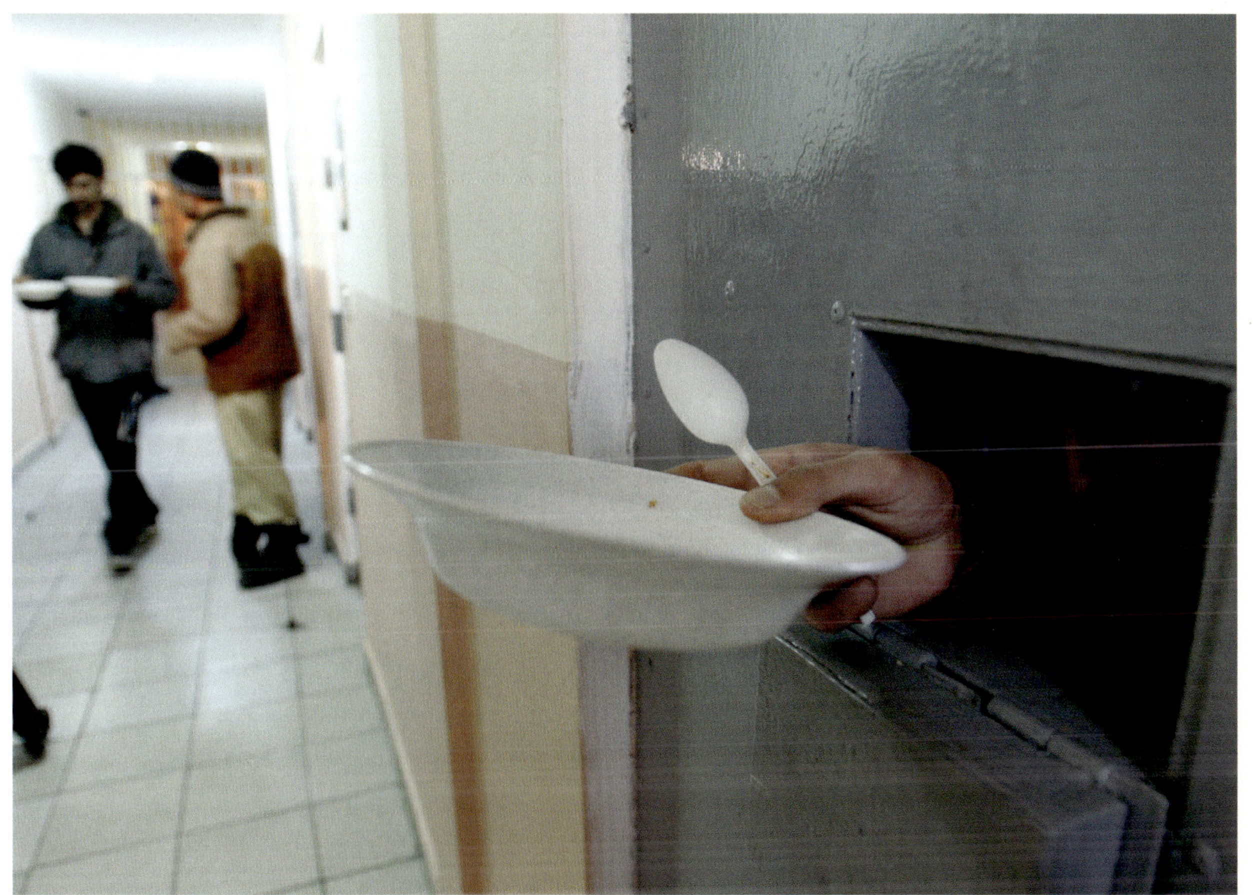

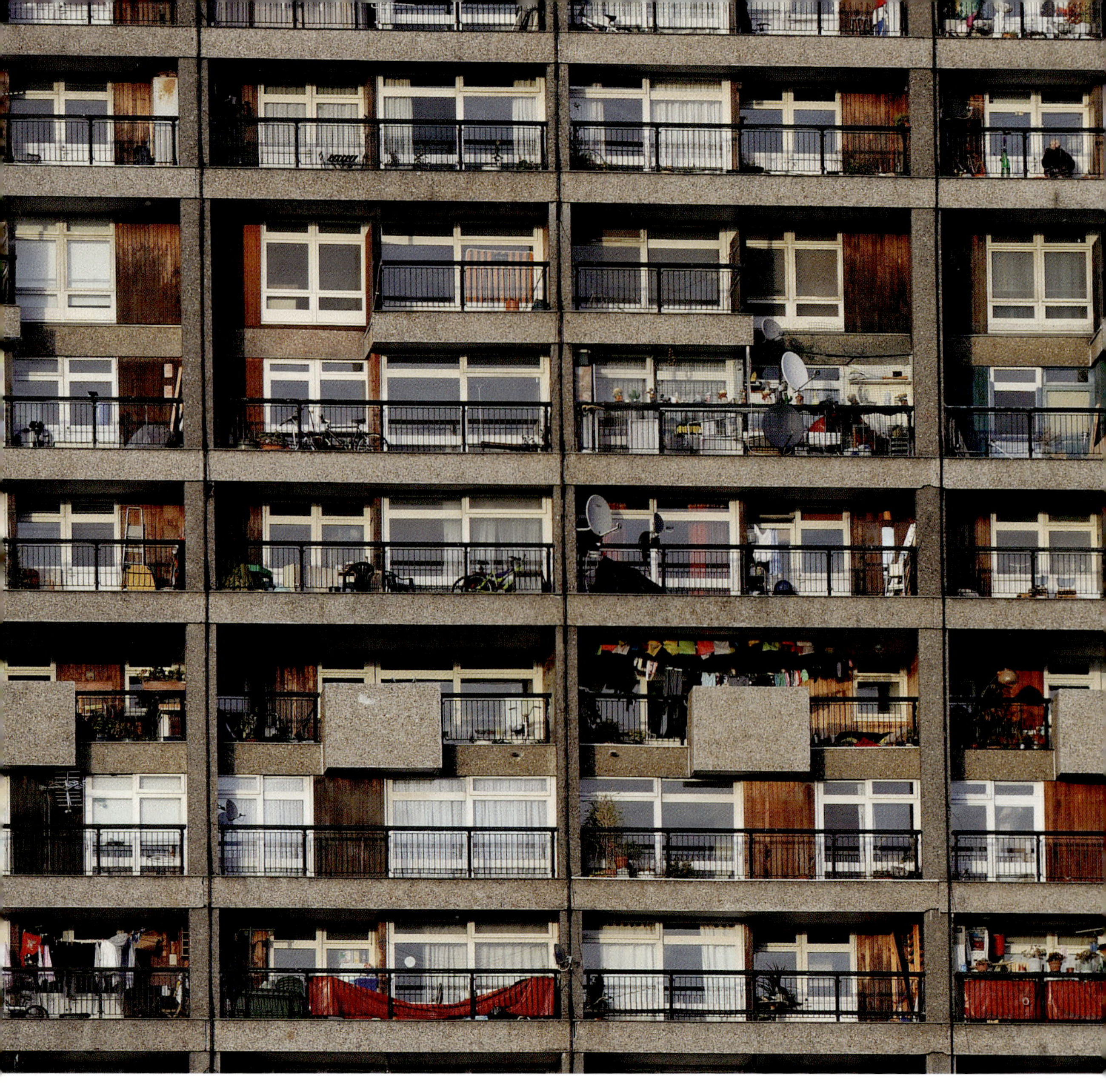

049 London, Britain

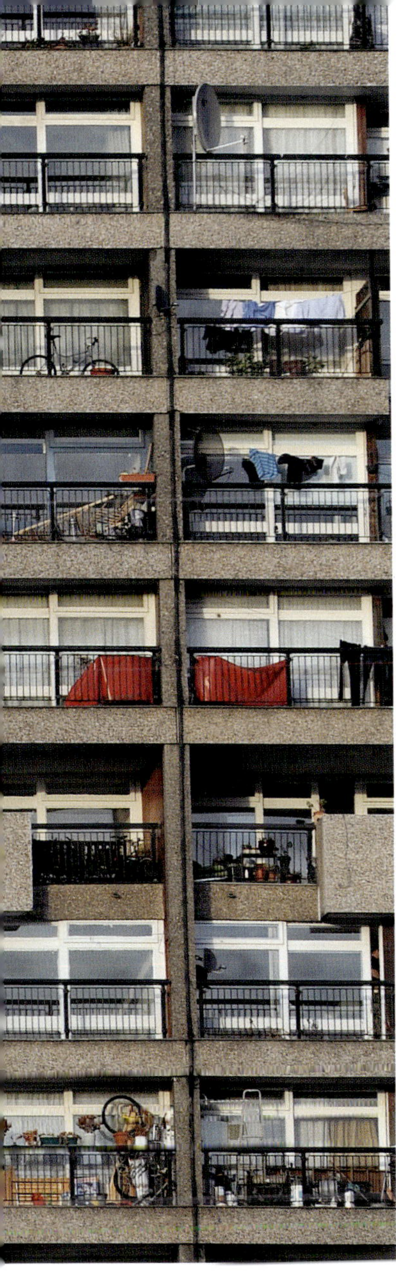

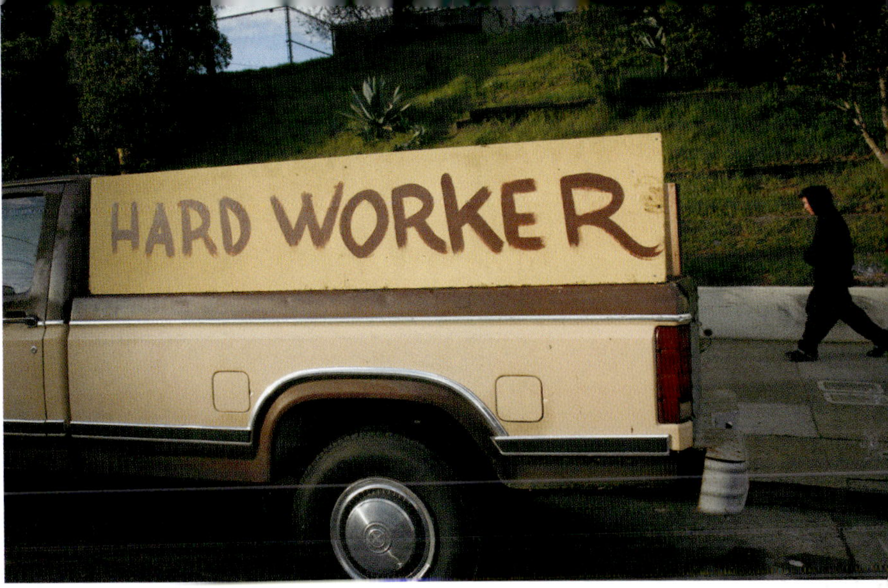
HARD WORKER

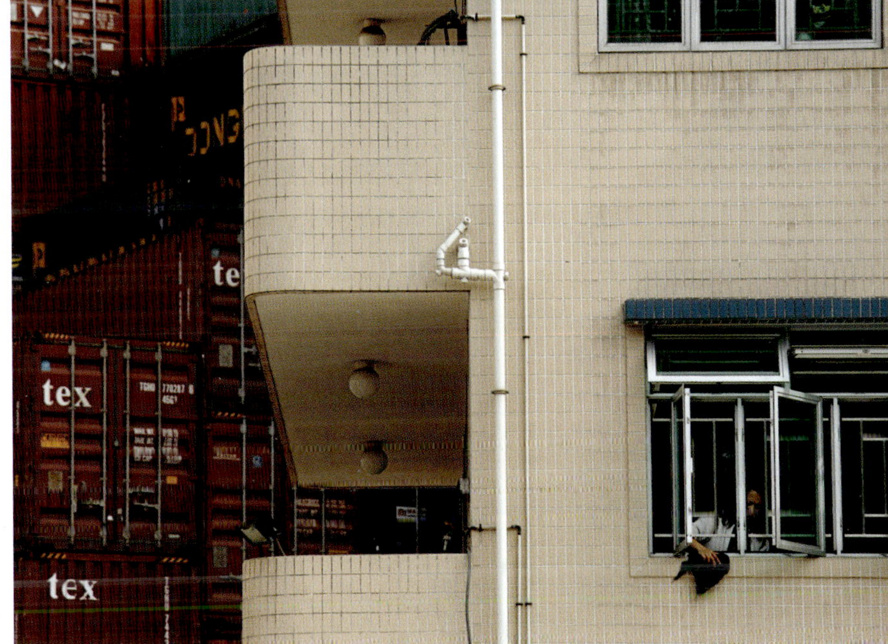
tex
tex
te

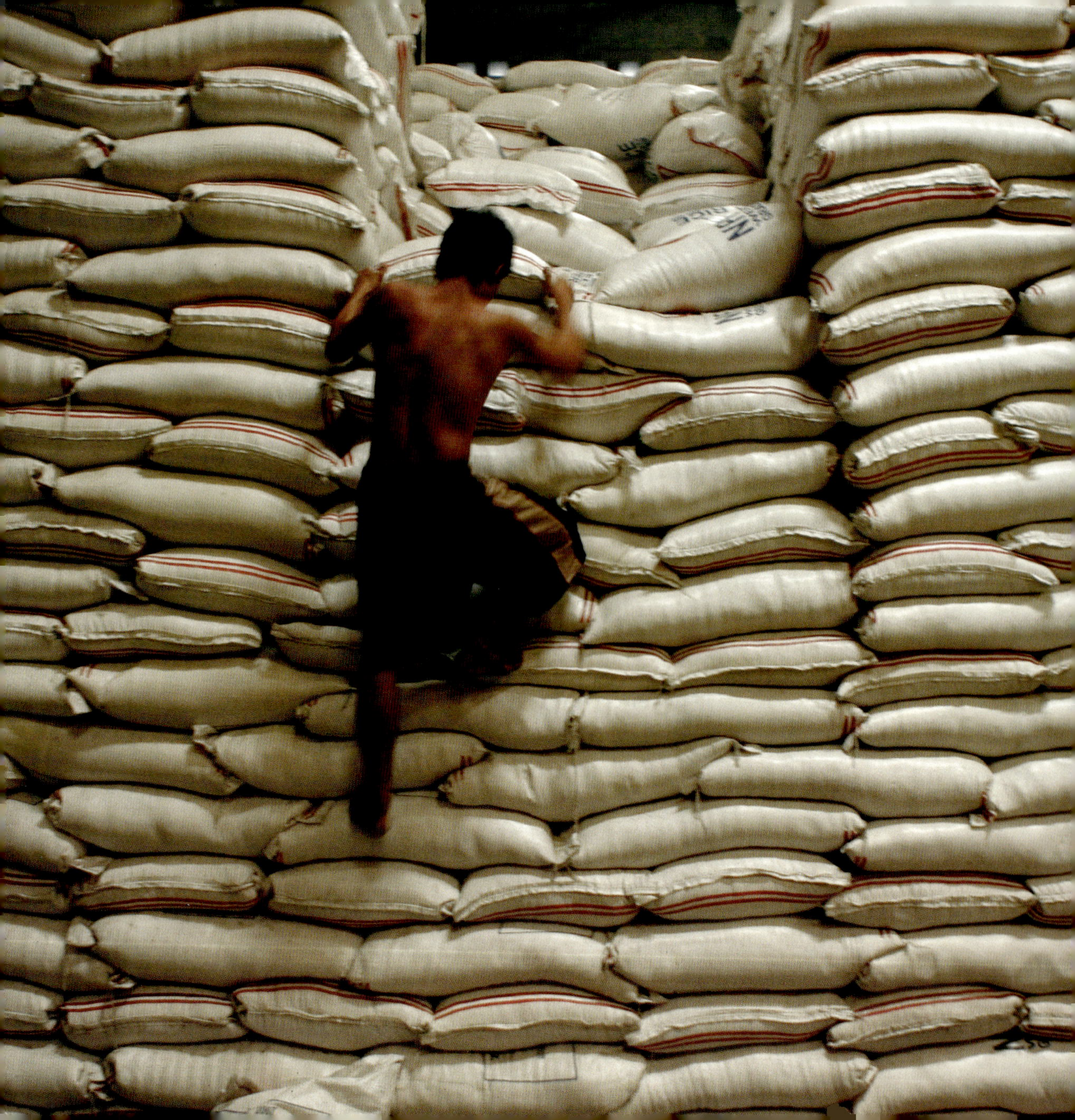

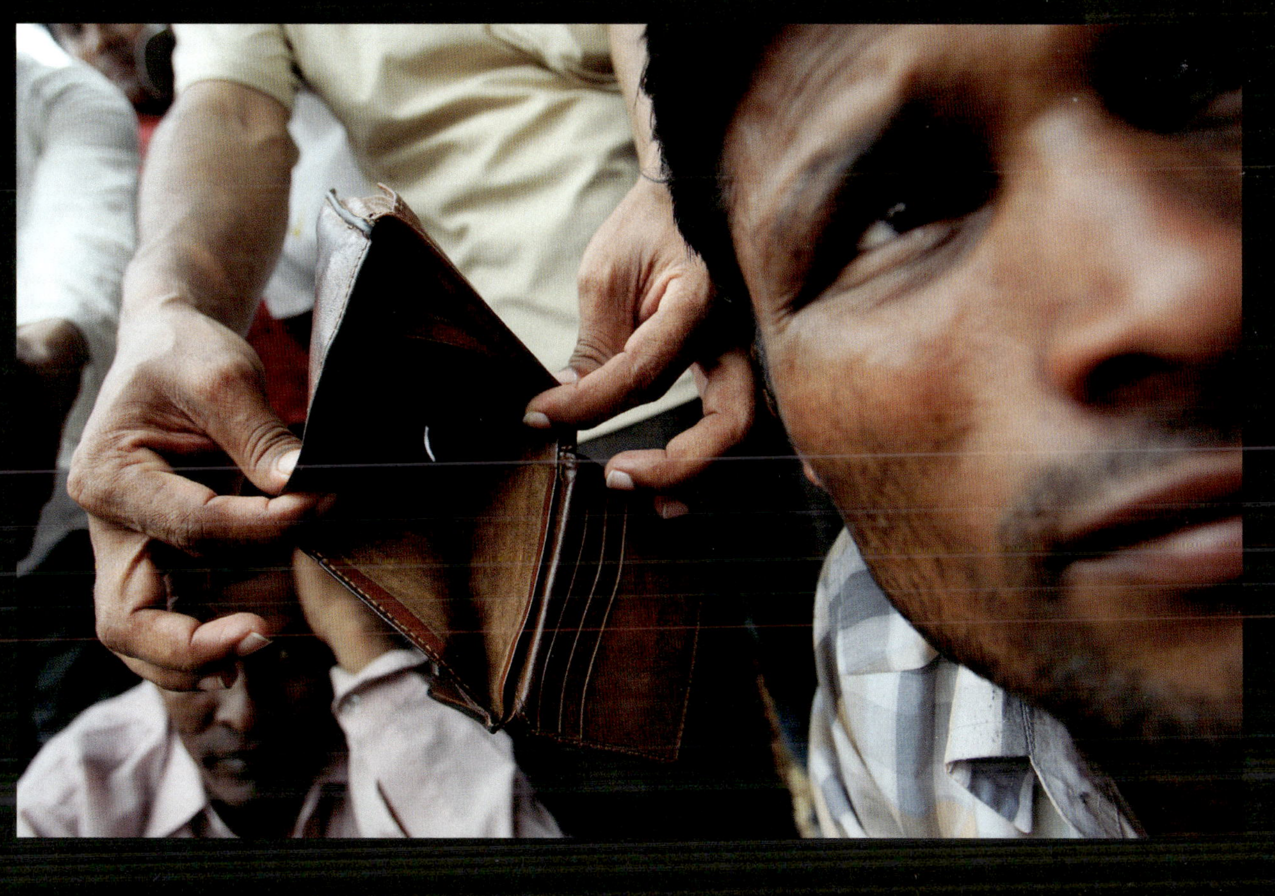

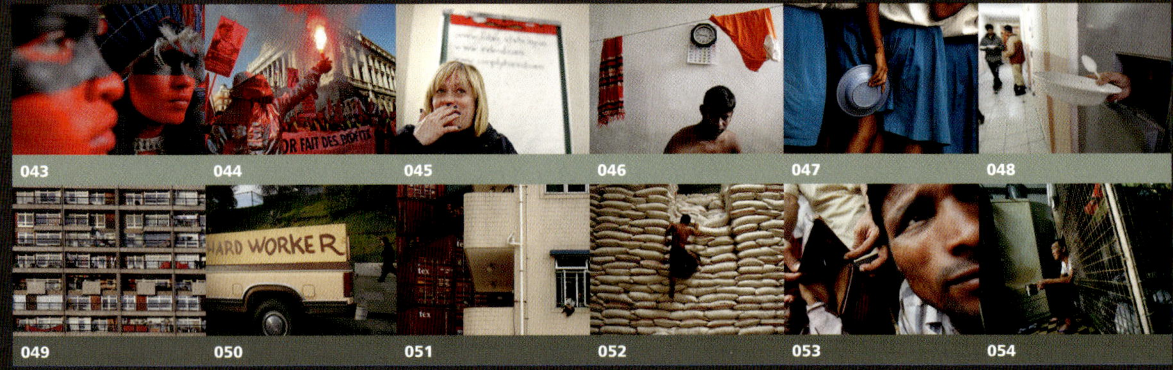

043 Indigenous people march during the 2009 World Social Forum in Belém, Brazil. Timed to coincide with the meeting of world business leaders in Davos, Switzerland, the event attracted about 100,000 leftist activists and environmentalists. 27 January 2009. Belém, Brazil. Paulo Santos.

044 Arcelor Mittal steel workers take part in a protest march in Marseille. Up to 2.5 million people demonstrated around France on 29 January to demand more action from government and companies to protect jobs and salaries. 29 January 2009. Marseille, France. Jean-Paul Pelissier.

045 Lillian Nazario, recently unemployed, wipes away a tear at the Manhattan branch of the New York State Department of Labor. 4 March 2009. New York, United States. Shannon Stapleton.

046 A migrant labourer from Bangladesh sits in a temporary dormitory near Johor Bahru. The Malaysian government cancelled some 55,000 visas for migrant labourers in the face of the global economic downturn, Malaysian media reported. 20 March 2009. Johor Bahru, Malaysia. Vivek Prakash.

047 Kartini Emergency School students queue for food in a slum area of north Jakarta. The school, which provides free education to more than 2,000 poor children, is run and funded by philanthropist twins Sri Irianingsih and Sri Rossyati. 26 February 2009. Jakarta, Indonesia. Beawiharta.

048 A would-be immigrant awaits lunch in a detention camp for illegal migrants in Chop, western Ukraine. Thousands of migrants from India, Afghanistan, China, Iraq, Somalia, Chechnya and Georgia have begun to attempt to reach the European Union through Ukraine's Carpathian mountains. 6 February 2009. Chop, Ukraine. Gleb Garanich.

049 A woman sits on her balcony (top right) in a tower block in west London. 22 January 2009. London, Britain. Toby Melville.

050 A pick-up truck bears a hand-painted sign reading 'hard worker' in San Francisco. California's unemployment rate was at a 14-year high at the beginning of 2009. 25 January 2009. San Francisco, United States. Robert Galbraith.

051 Unused shipping containers are seen piled up at a storage depot behind an apartment block in northwest Hong Kong. Hundreds of thousands more empty containers were expected to flood the territory as a result of China's slowing exports. 18 February 2009. Hong Kong, China. Bobby Yip.

052 A worker climbs on sacks of government-subsidized rice at a warehouse in Manila. 14 January 2009. Manila, Philippines. Romeo Ranoco.

053 A migrant worker from Bangladesh shows his empty wallet to the camera as a group of over 50 Bangladeshi workers gather near Singapore's Ministry of Manpower, urging the government to help them retrieve overdue pay from former employers. 16 February 2009. Singapore. Vivek Prakash.

054 Kong Siu-kau, 63, sits on his bed in the cage home where he has lived for several years. Cages are stacked on top of each other, several blocks to a room, and are barely big enough for a bed. 20 March 2009. Hong Kong, China. Bobby Yip.

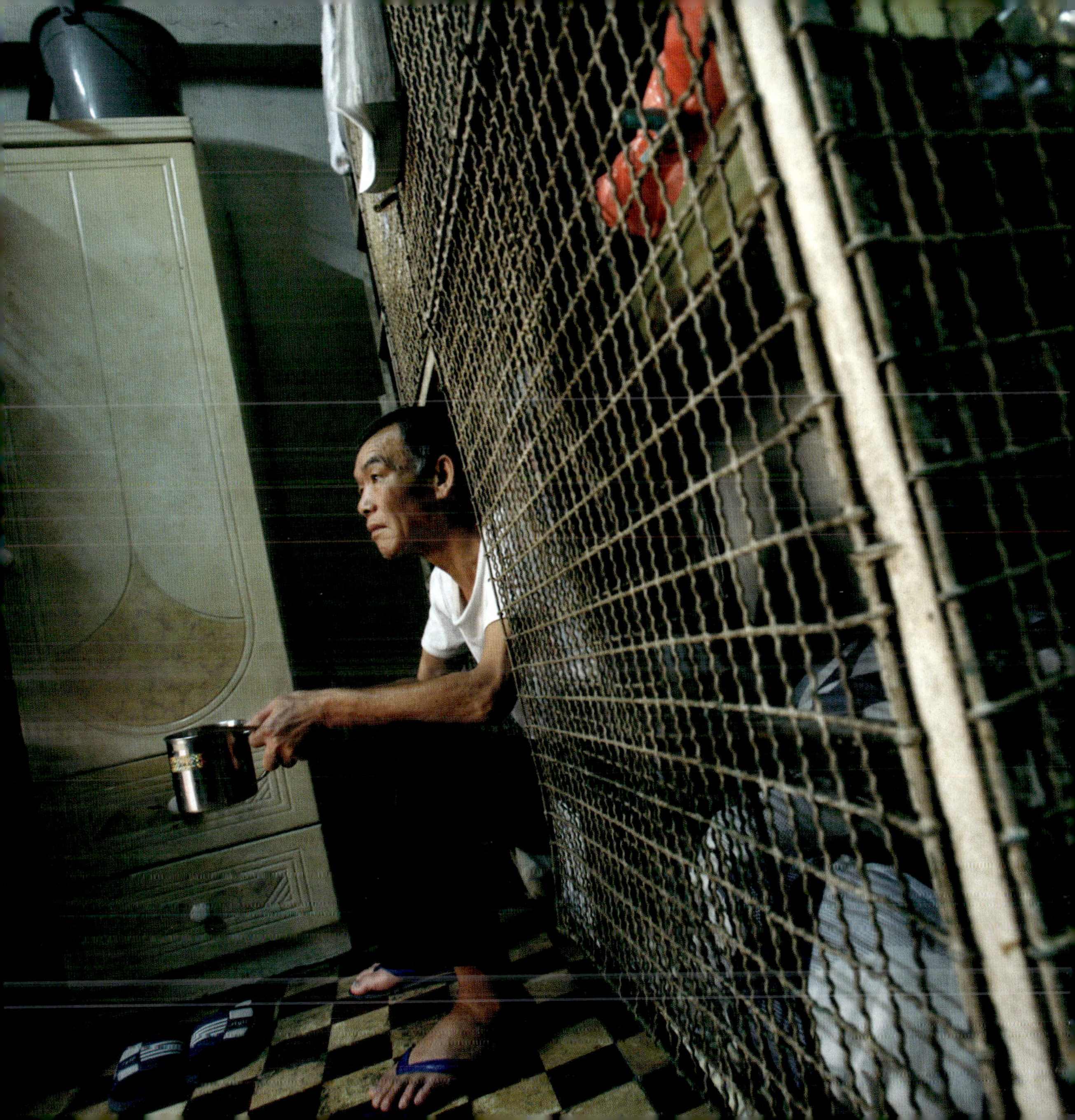

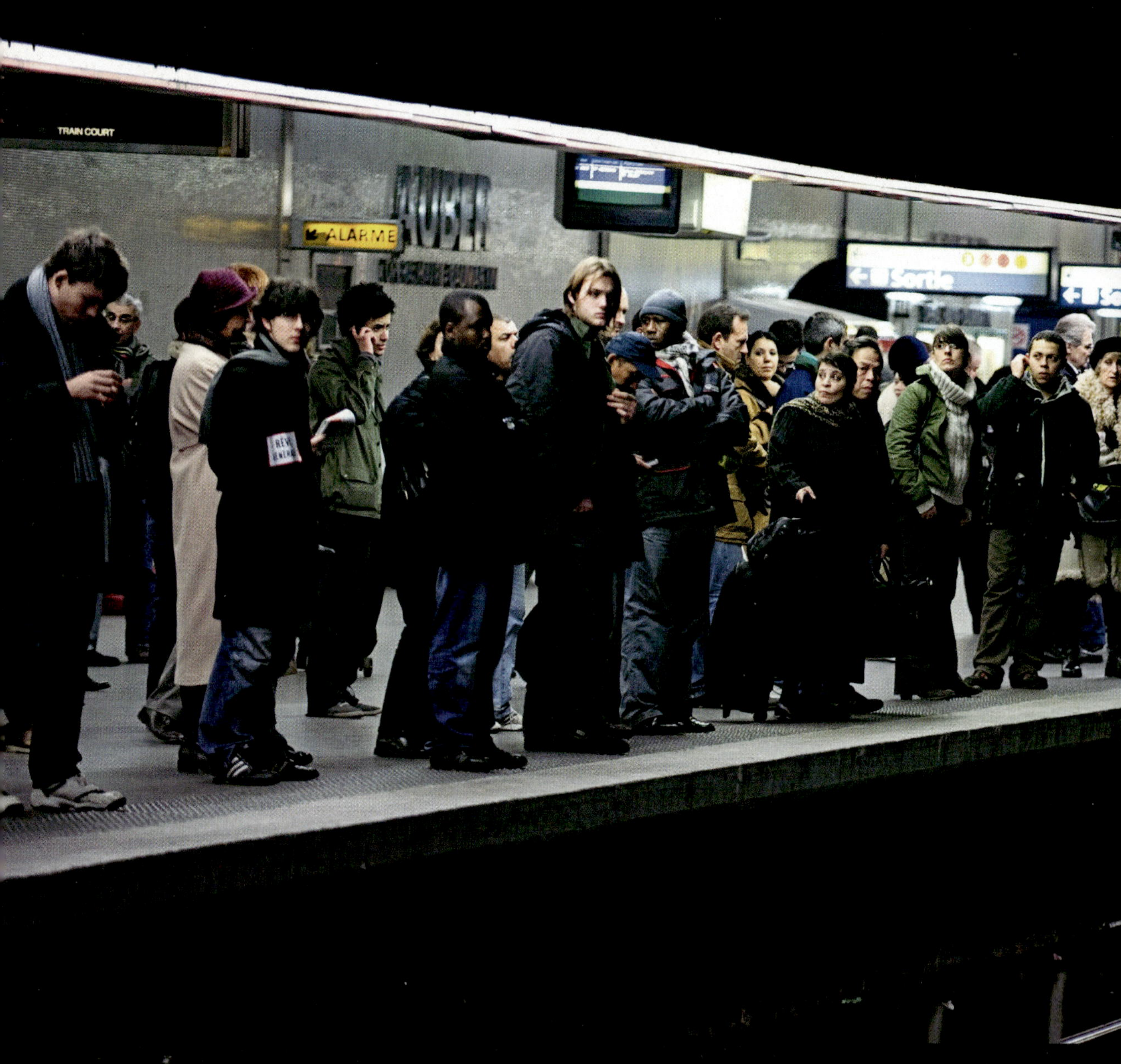

TRAIN COURT
ALARME
AUBER
Sortie

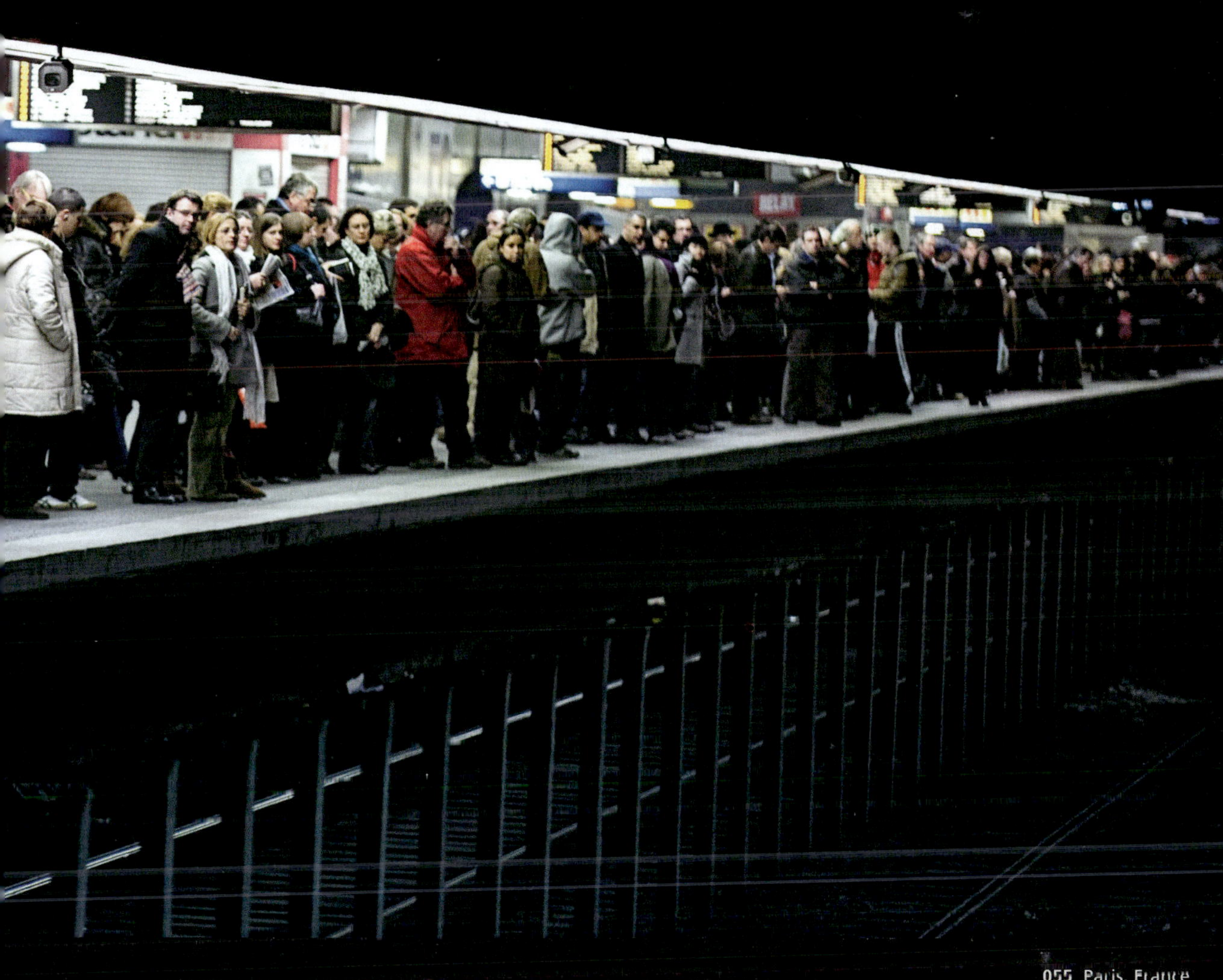

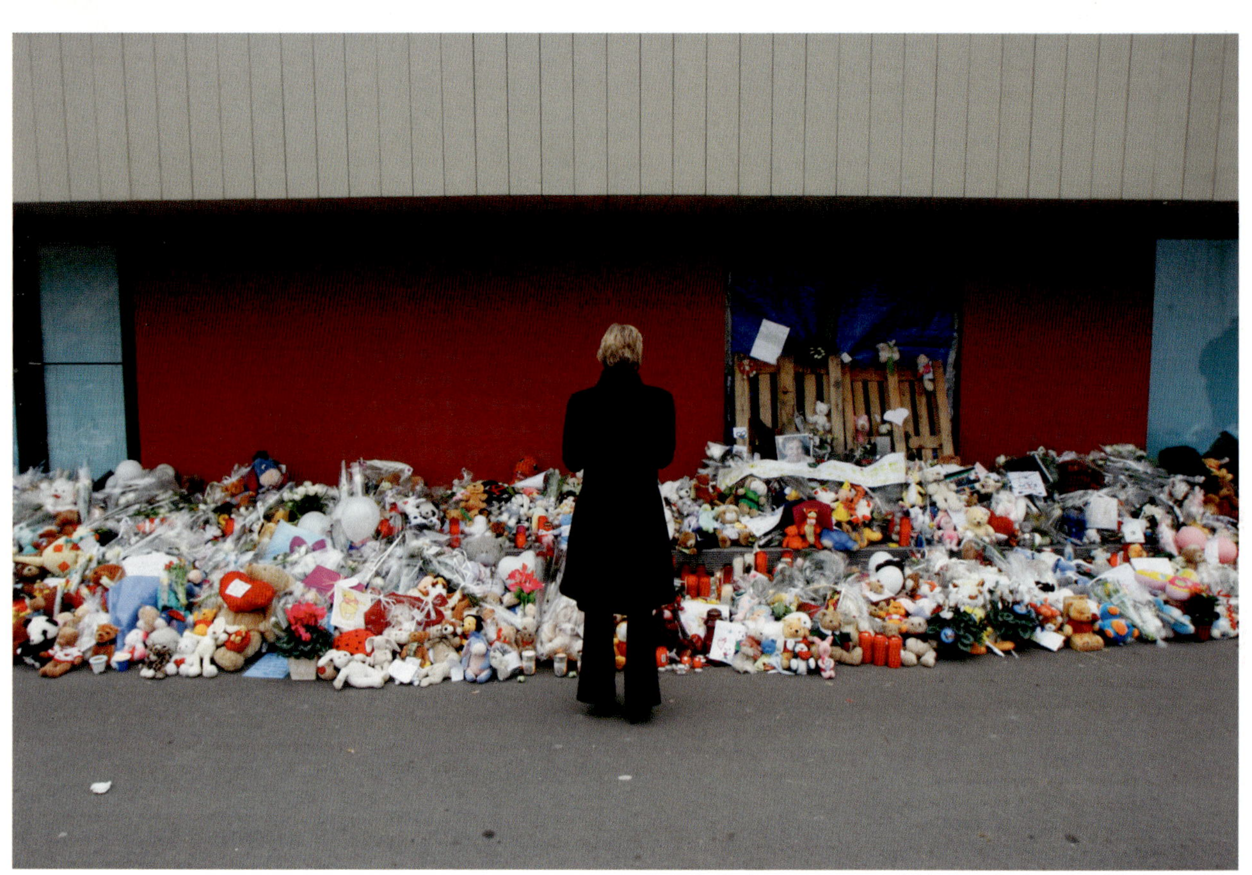

056 Dendermonde, Belgium

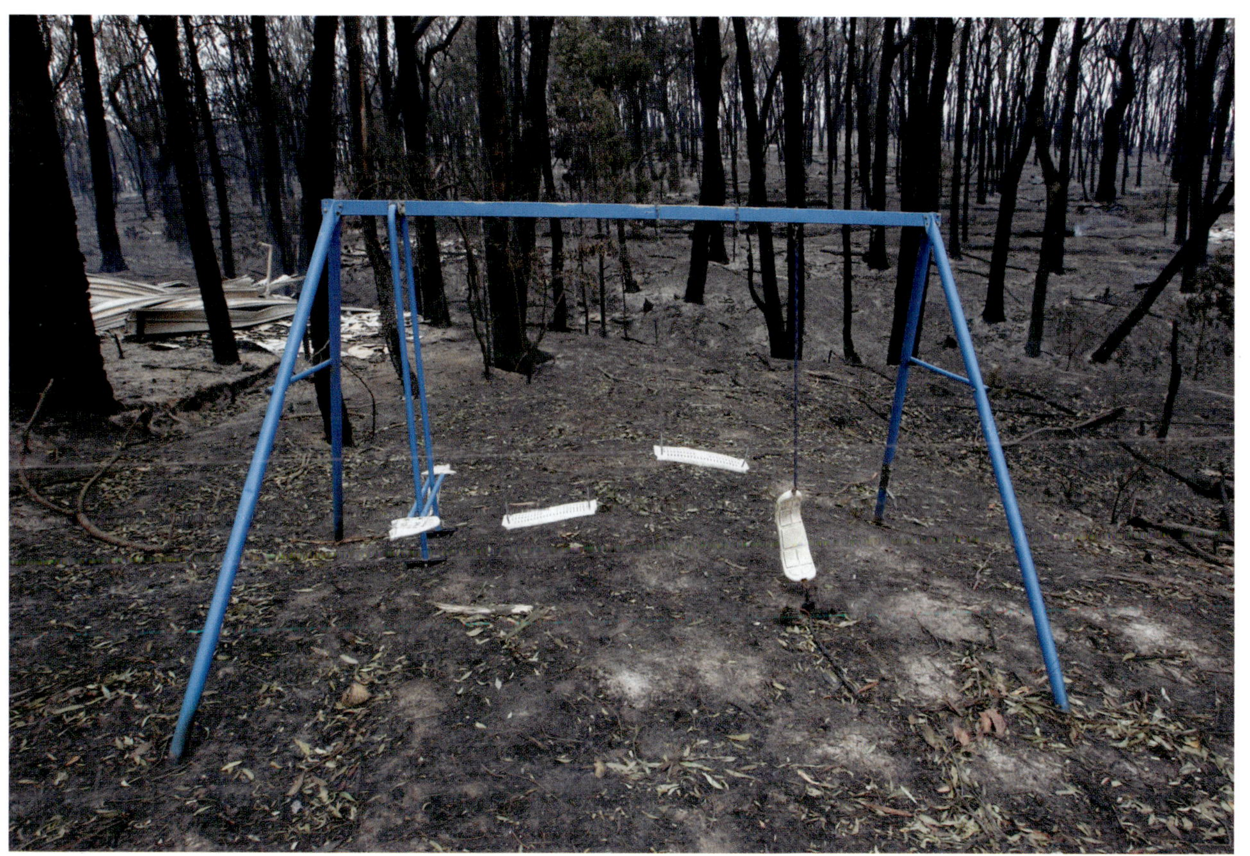

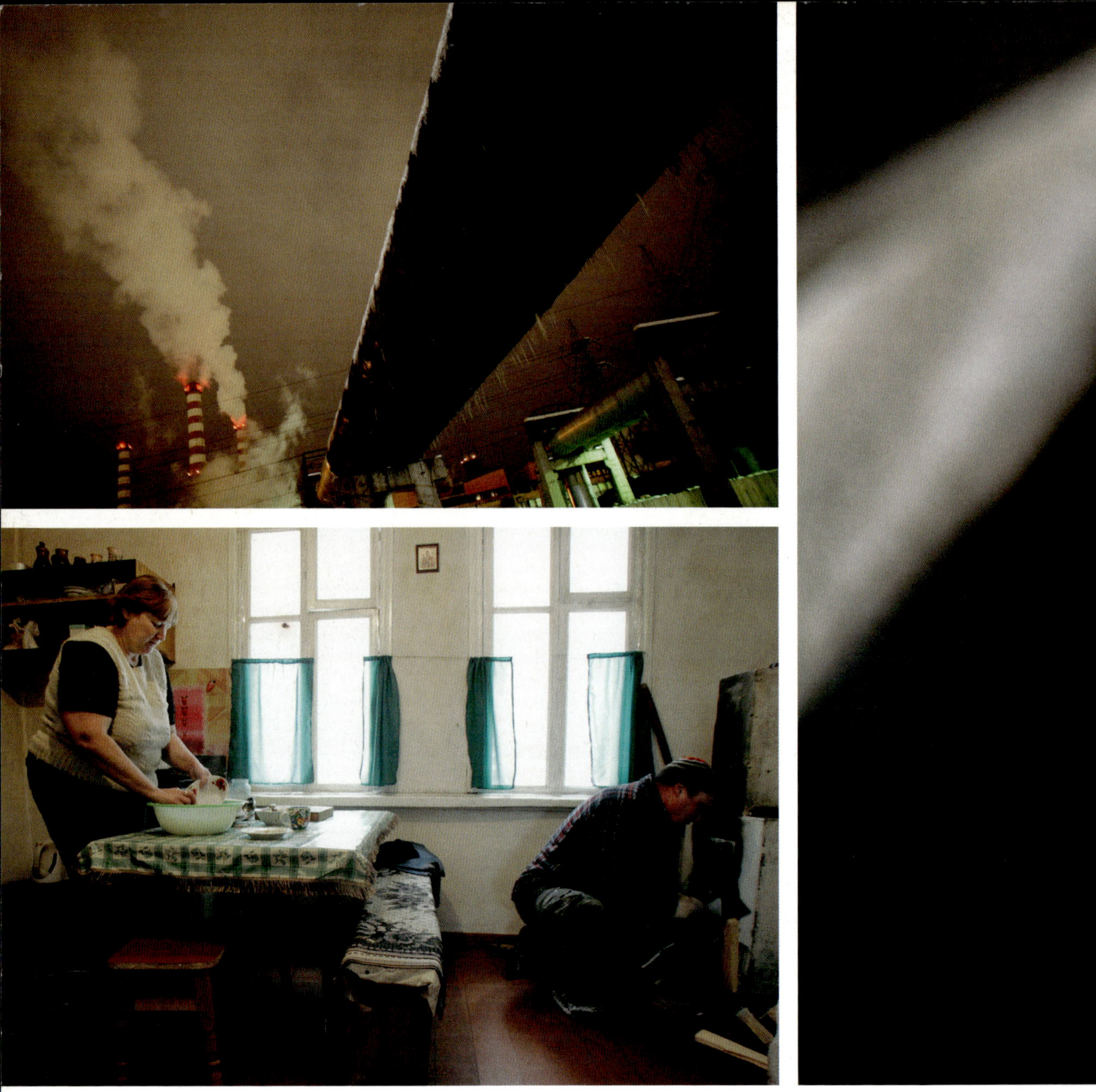

058 [TOP] Sofia, Bulgaria   **059** [ABOVE] Bilogorodka, Ukraine

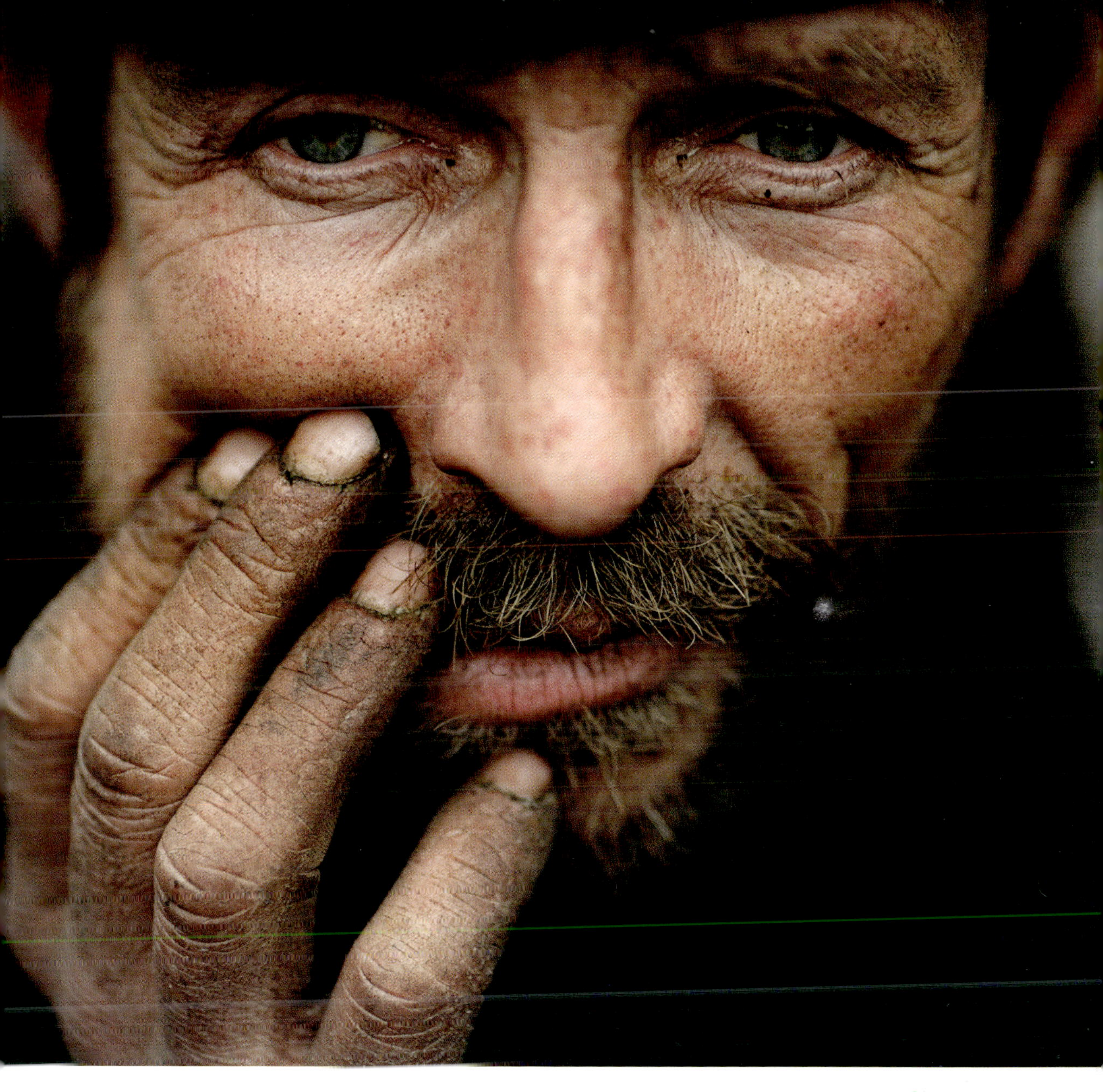

060 Kakanj, Bosnia

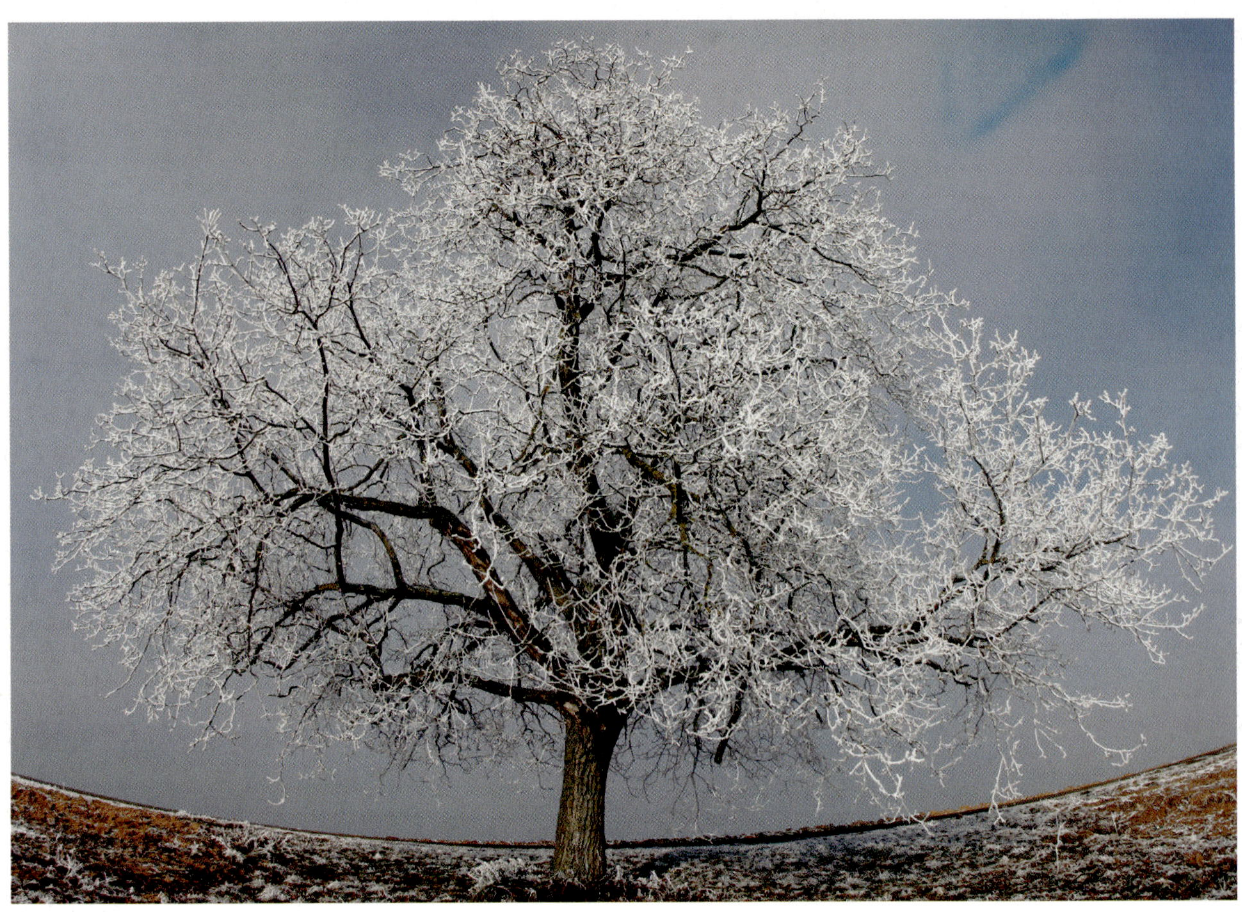

061 Strasbourg, France

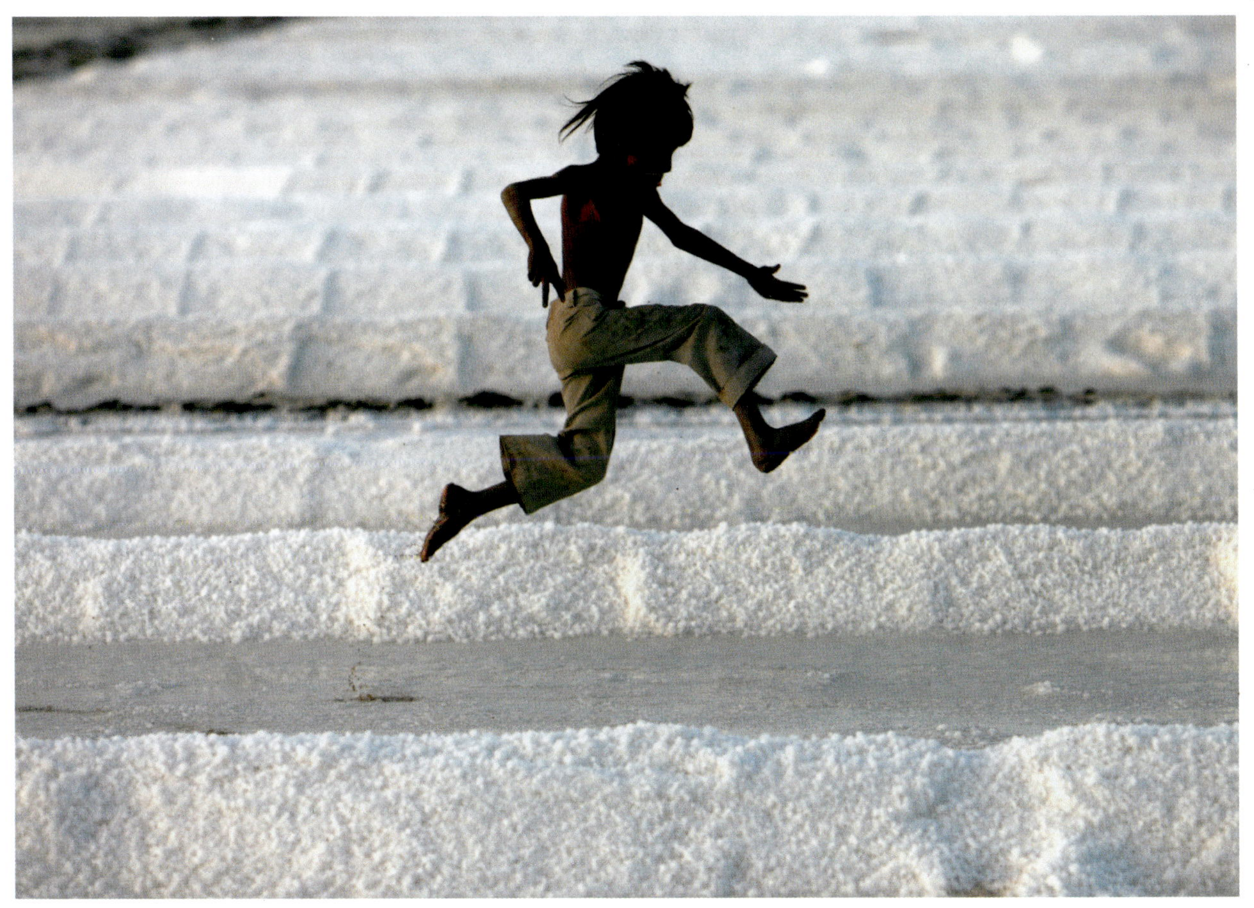

082 Bhavnagar, India

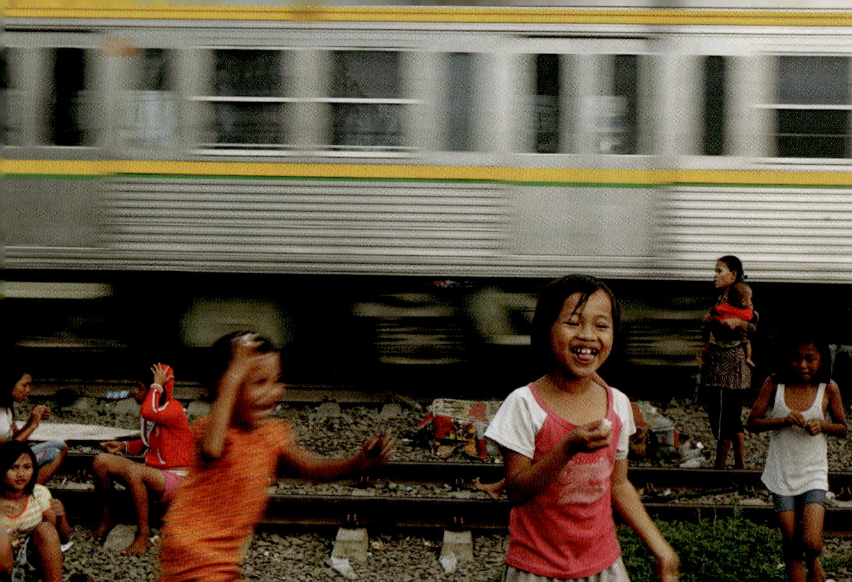

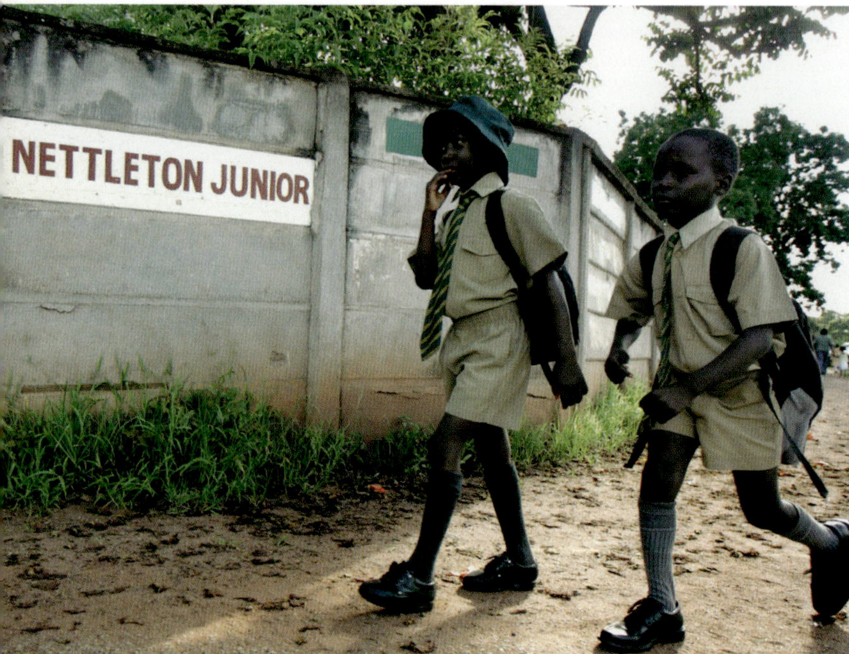

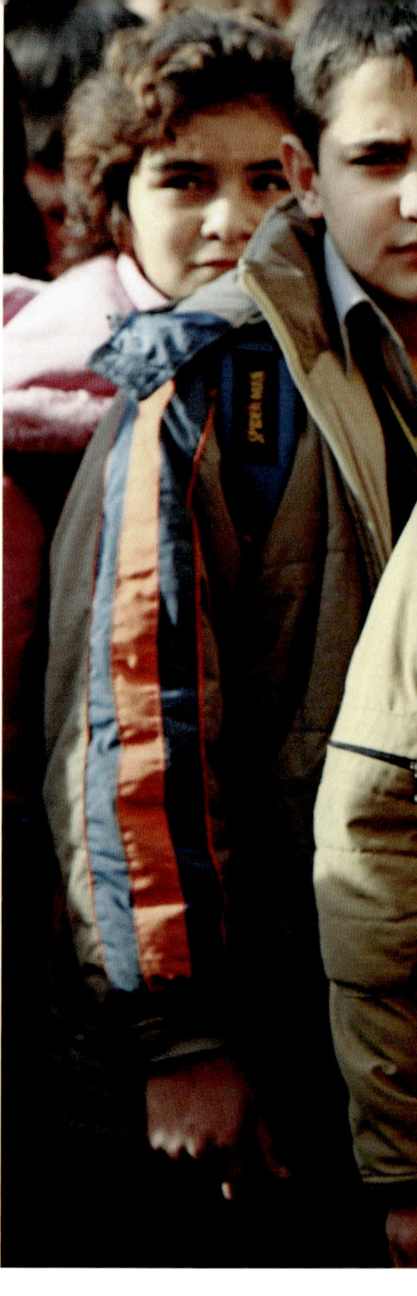

063 [TOP] Jakarta, Indonesia   **064** [ABOVE] Harare, Zimbabwe

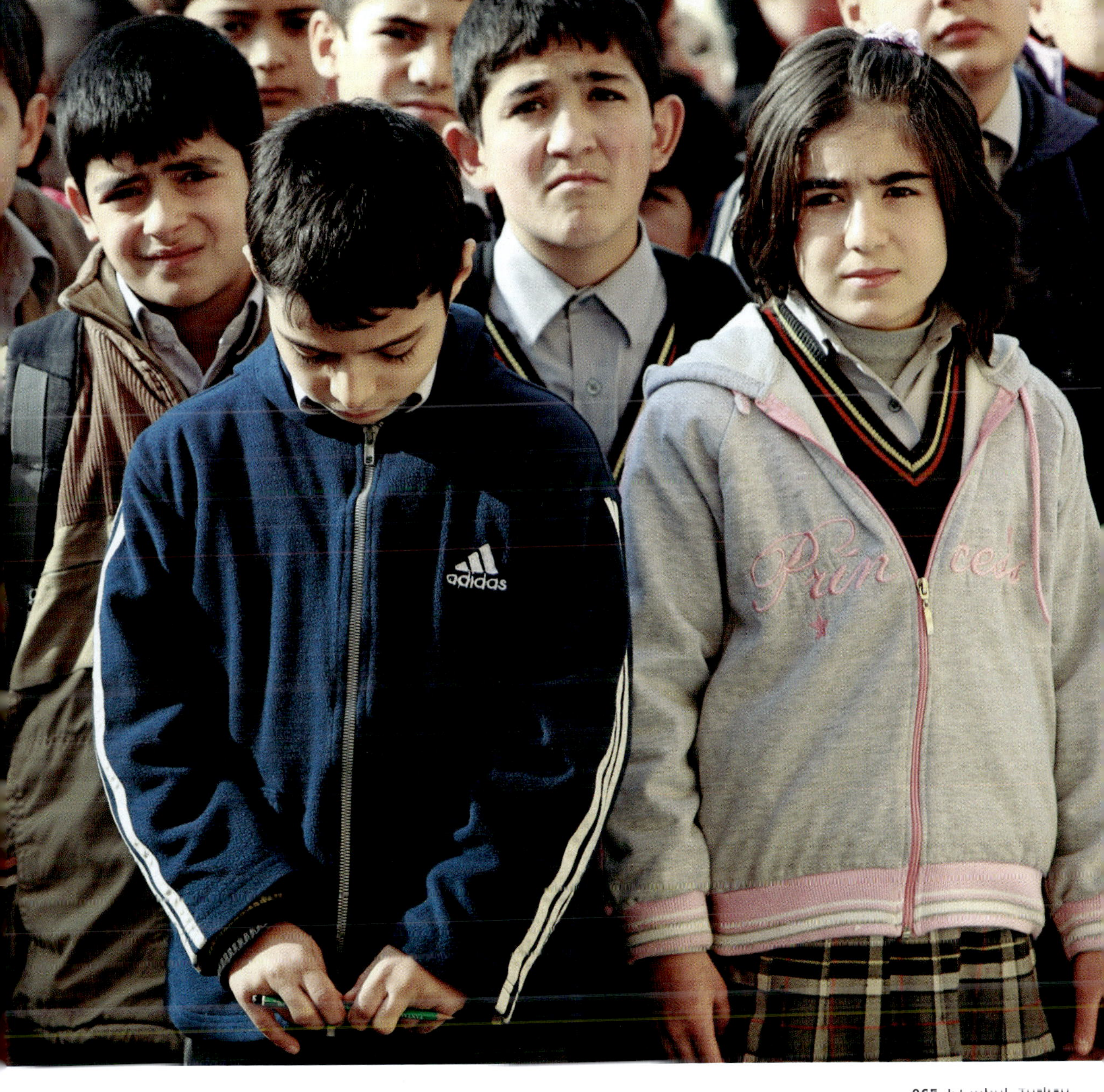

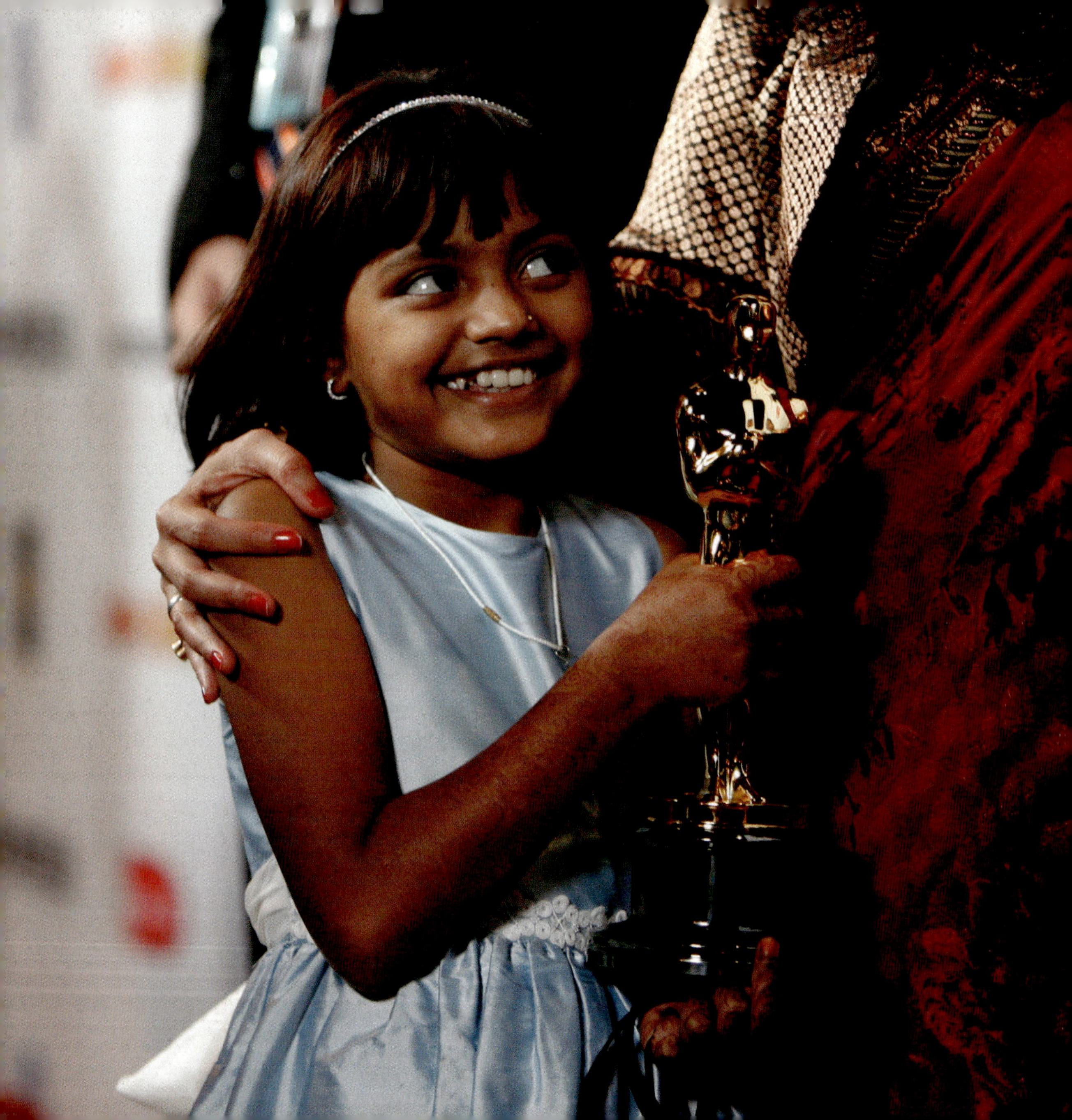

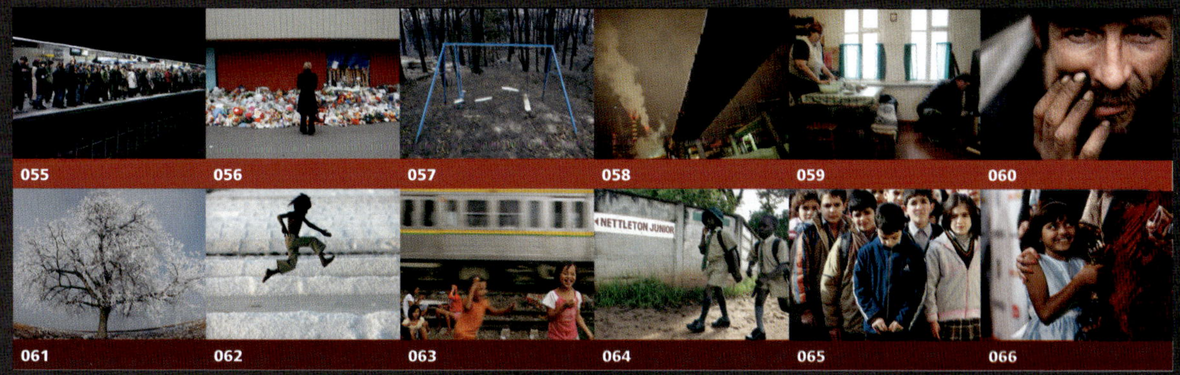

055 Commuters wait on a platform in central Paris as a one-day nationwide strike hit transport services. Hundreds of thousands of workers across France took part in the strike to pressure the government to take greater measures to tackle the economic crisis. 29 January 2009. Paris, France. Gonzalo Fuentes.

056 A woman stands in front of a Belgian childcare centre where two infants and a woman were murdered and 12 others injured in a frenzied knife attack on 23 January. 26 January 2009. Dendermonde, Belgium. Francois Lenoir.

057 A children's swing destroyed by bushfires is seen in the town of Heathcote Junction, 55 km (35 miles) north of Melbourne. The bushfires in Victoria state left 210 people dead and 10,000 homeless. 8 February 2009. Heathcote Junction, Australia. Mick Tsikas.

058 Druzhba thermal power station is seen in the Bulgarian capital Sofia. A row over gas payments between Moscow and Kiev led to a two-week cut in Russian gas supplies via Ukraine in the dead of winter, creating what Bulgaria called a 'crisis situation'. 6 January 2009. Sofia, Bulgaria. Stoyan Nenov.

059 With gas supplies from Russia cut off due to a row over payments, a Ukrainian man puts firewood into the stove as his wife cooks in the village of Bilogorodka, 30 km (20 miles) from the capital Kiev. 8 January 2009. Bilogorodka, Ukraine. Konstantin Chernichkin.

060 Former Bosnian soldier Ferid Sinan pauses while working in his coalmine, where he also lives, near the central Bosnian town of Kakanj. Sinan dug the dangerous and illegal mine himself, and collects poor quality coal with primitive tools and his bare hands to make a living. 3 March 2009. Kakanj, Bosnia. Damir Sagolj.

061 A tree covered in frost is pictured in the countryside near Strasbourg as sub-freezing winter temperatures hit the region. 12 January 2009. Strasbourg, France. Vincent Kessler.

062 A worker's son plays in a salt pan near Bhavnagar, in the western Indian state of Gujarat. 5 March 2009. Bhavnagar, India. Arko Datta.

063 Children play alongside the Bekasi commuter rail line in the Tanah Abang area of Jakarta. Hundreds of poor families have set up makeshift homes along this stretch of railway tracks. 6 January 2009. Jakarta, Indonesia. Beawiharta.

064 Students walk to school in Zimbabwe's capital Harare. Schools failed to open for the start of the new school year as teachers went on strike demanding the government pay their salary in foreign currency. 27 January 2009. Harare, Zimbabwe. Philimon Bulawayo.

065 Primary school students in Istanbul observe a minute of silence in memory of Palestinian children killed in Israeli attacks on the Gaza Strip. Commemorations were held in primary schools across the country. 13 January 2009. Istanbul, Turkey. Osman Orsal.

066 Cast member Rubina Ali from the movie *Slumdog Millionaire* holds the Oscar awarded to director Danny Boyle in Los Angeles. 22 February 2009. Los Angeles, United States. Mario Anzuoni.

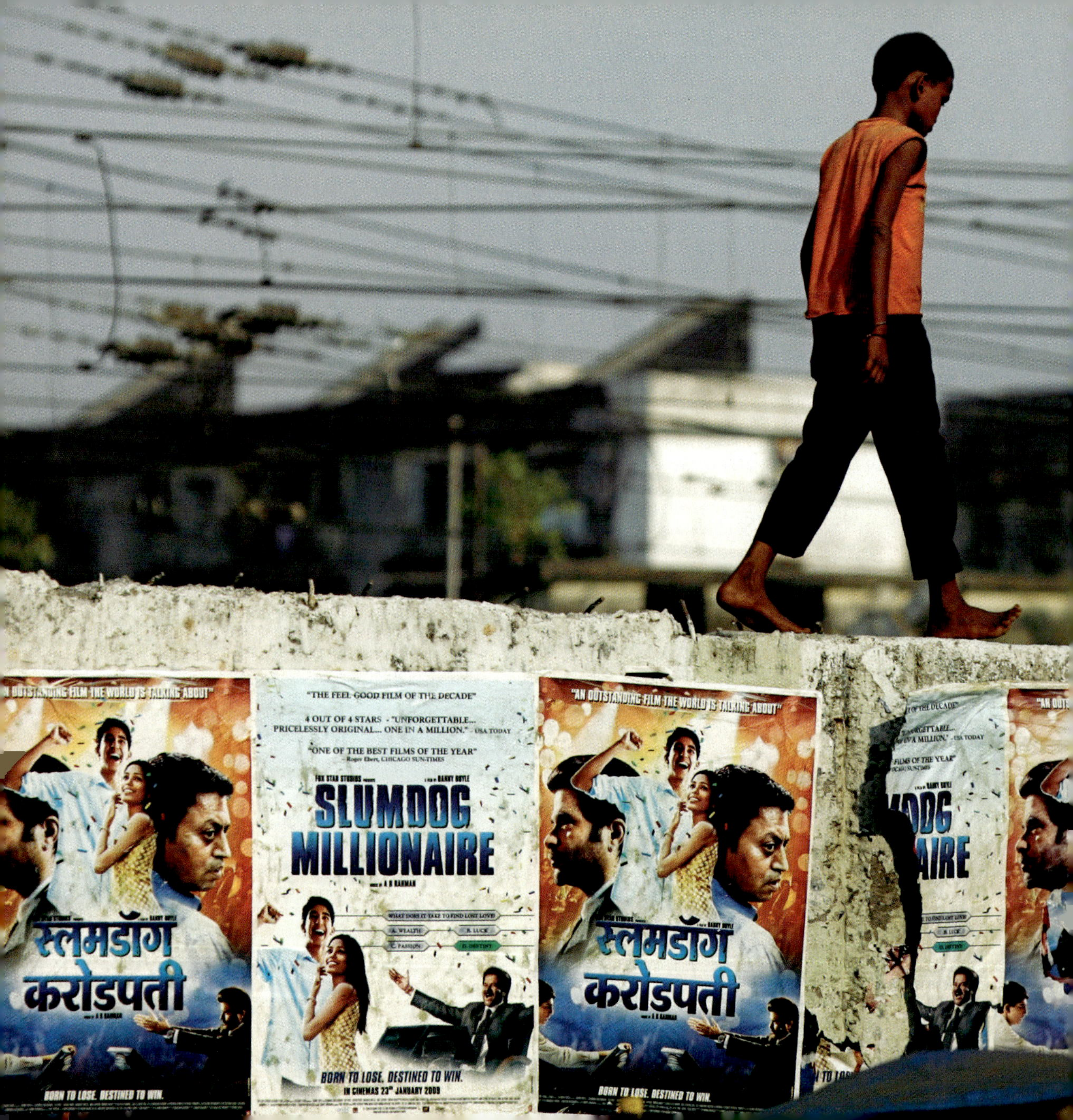

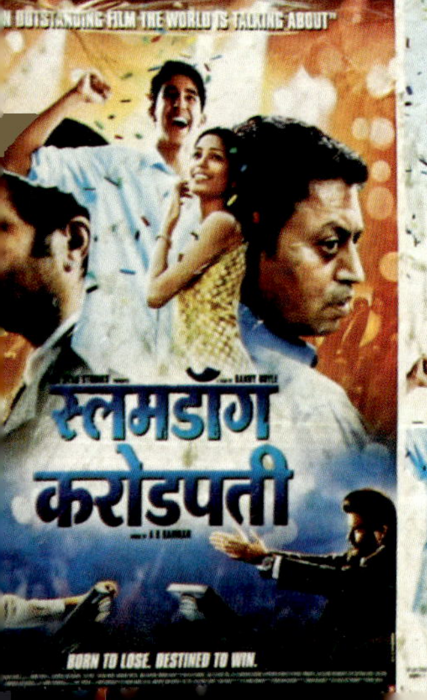
"AN OUTSTANDING FILM THE WORLD IS TALKING ABOUT"
स्लमडॉग
करोड़पती
BORN TO LOSE. DESTINED TO WIN.
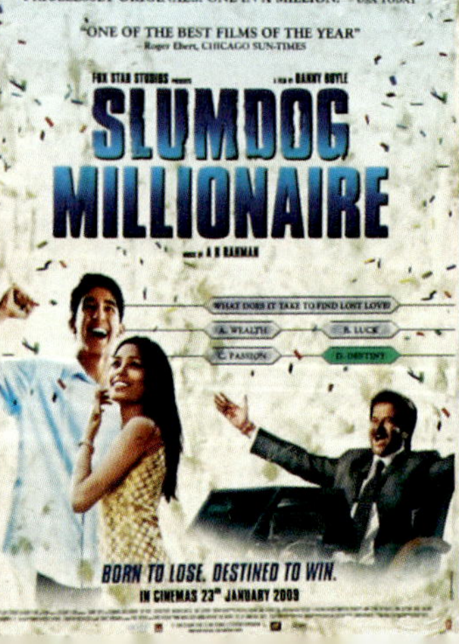
"THE FEEL-GOOD FILM OF THE DECADE"
4 OUT OF 4 STARS - "UNFORGETTABLE...
PRICELESSLY ORIGINAL... ONE IN A MILLION." - USA TODAY
"ONE OF THE BEST FILMS OF THE YEAR"
- Roger Ebert, CHICAGO SUN-TIMES
FOX STAR STUDIOS presents
A FILM BY DANNY BOYLE
SLUMDOG
MILLIONAIRE
MUSIC BY A R RAHMAN
WHAT DOES IT TAKE TO FIND LOST LOVE?
A. WEALTH
B. LUCK
C. PASSION
D. DESTINY
BORN TO LOSE. DESTINED TO WIN.
IN CINEMAS 23rd JANUARY 2009
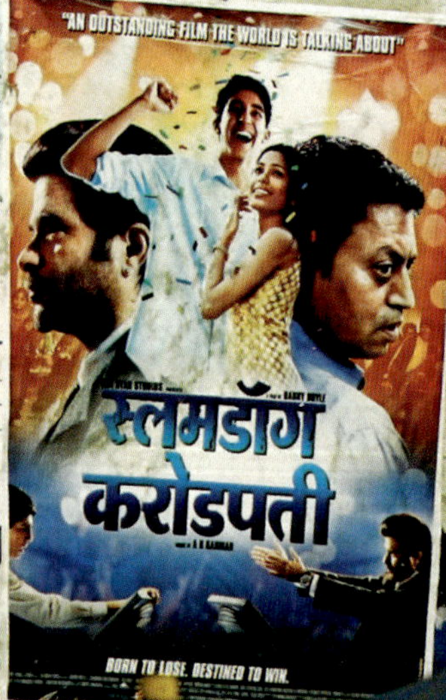
"AN OUTSTANDING FILM THE WORLD IS TALKING ABOUT"
स्लमडॉग
करोड़पती
BORN TO LOSE. DESTINED TO WIN.
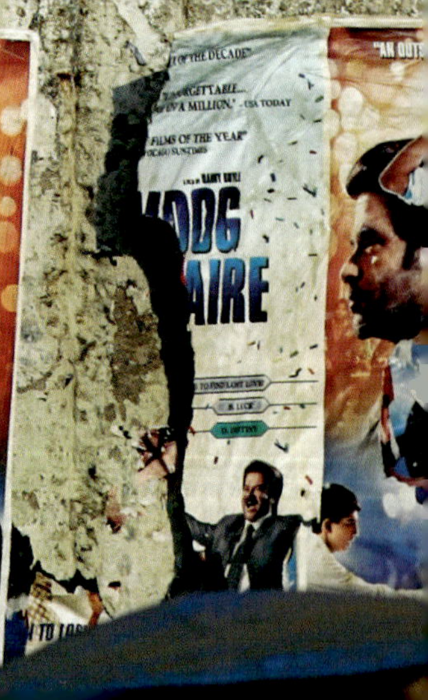
OF THE DECADE"
FORGETTABLE...
IN A MILLION." - USA TODAY
FILMS OF THE YEAR"
CHICAGO SUN-TIMES
MDOG
AIRE
"AN OUT

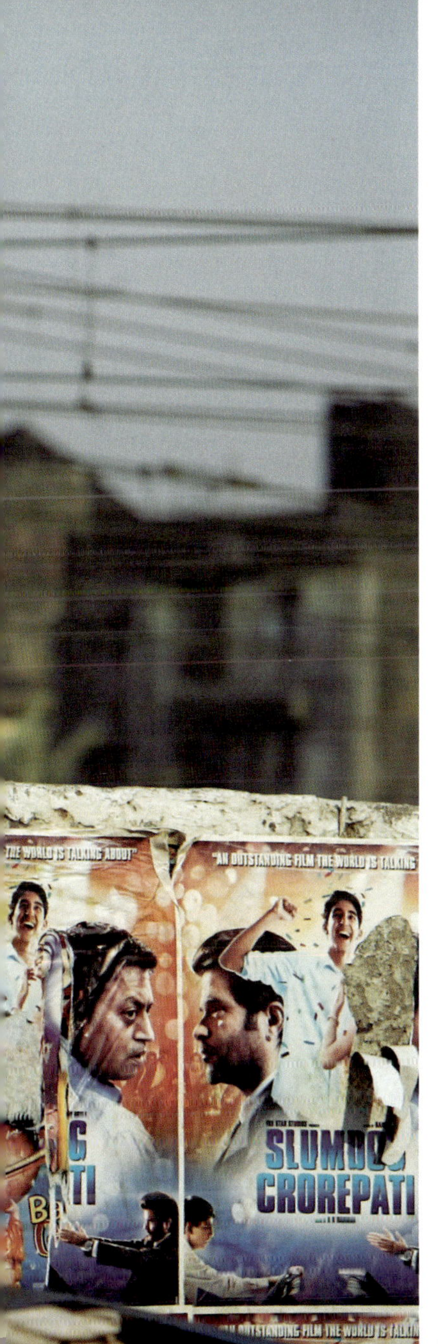

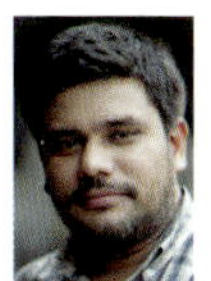

ARKO DATTA
Photographer
Born: Delhi, India, 1969
Based: Mumbai
Nationality: Indian

From Mumbai to L.A.

'R-u-b-i-n-a'. Each letter was formed slowly and carefully as the girl playing young Latika in *Slumdog Millionaire* gave me one of her first autographs. It was certainly a first for me: collecting the autograph of a child barely 10 years old, who was to walk the red carpet at the Oscars and then return home to a Mumbai slum.

Mumbai is no stranger to contrasts. Skyscrapers and some of the world's richest men share the cityscape with sprawling slums and struggling labourers. Backdrop to it all is the Indian film industry, Bollywood, sowing its glittering dreams of a better life.

Rubina Ali and Azharuddin Ismail, who played little Salim, seemed to leapfrog over all this overnight. I first met them before the film had become such a phenomenal success. Rubina's neighbours already called her a 'little queen': in her school uniform, hair in bunches, there was a twinkle in her eye that poverty had failed to dim. Azhar was fascinated to hold my camera and look through its viewfinder. And yet their homes were no more than a room in a slum in Rubina's case; a cloth roof held up by a stick for Azhar.

On the day of the Oscars ceremony, I walked down the gutter-fringed lanes of their slum. People had put out a television and cheered every time they saw Rubina and Azhar, staying up late into the night to watch as *Slumdog* bagged award after award.

On their return, the entire neighbourhood came out to greet them. But the lows were quick to come. Rubina's biological mother and stepmother fought a battle over her custody that was closely followed by local media. Azhar gave the waiting press their sound-bites, only to be unceremoniously slapped by his father in front of the cameras. His father, ill with tuberculosis, died on 4 September 2009 in the new flat bought for Azhar and his family by the trust set up by director Danny Boyle and producer Christian Colson.

Rubina and Azhar do finally have a proper roof over their heads. The 'Jai Ho' trust, named after the movie's award-winning track, is intended to pay for their education and living costs until they turn 18. But I wonder what goes on in their young minds. Is theirs a fairy tale that came true? Or is there bewilderment at being launched from abject poverty to dizzying celebrity – a transformation that would disorient most adults?

067 A boy living on the street walks along a wall displaying publicity posters for the movie *Slumdog Millionaire*. 22 January 2009. Mumbai, India.

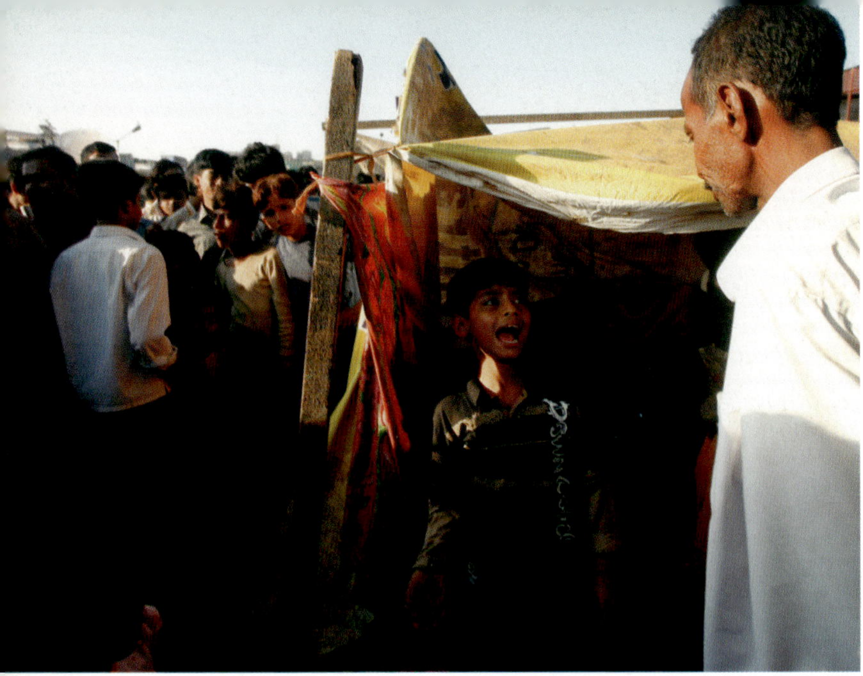

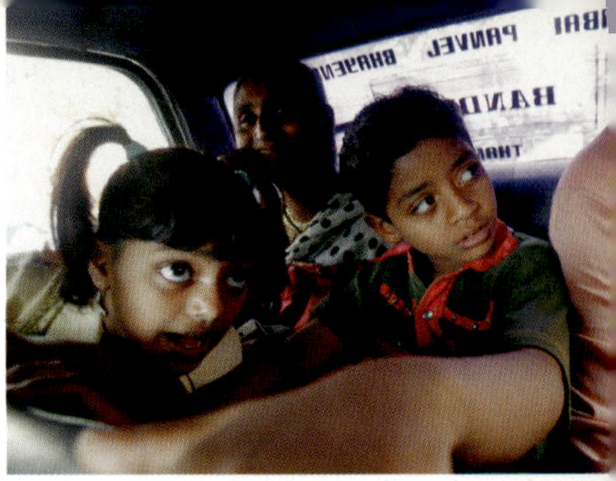

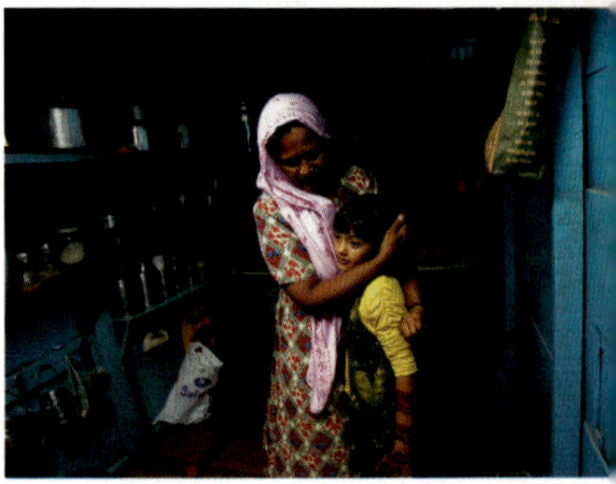

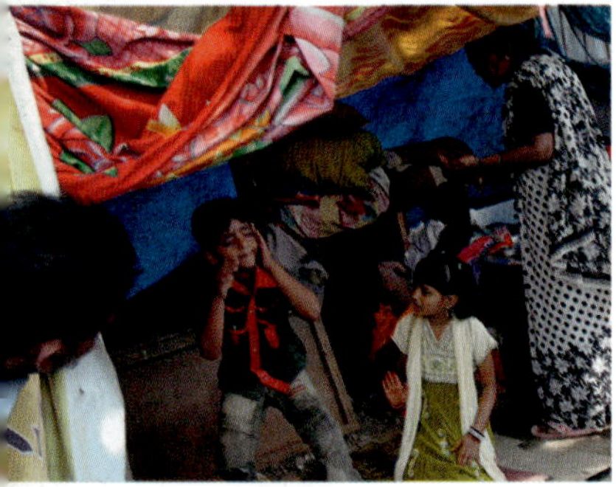

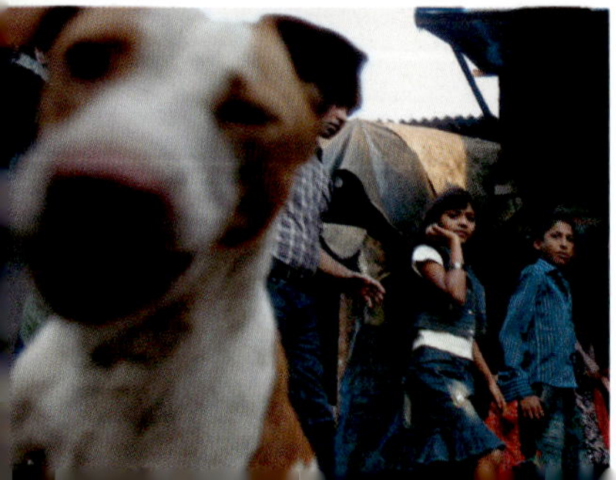

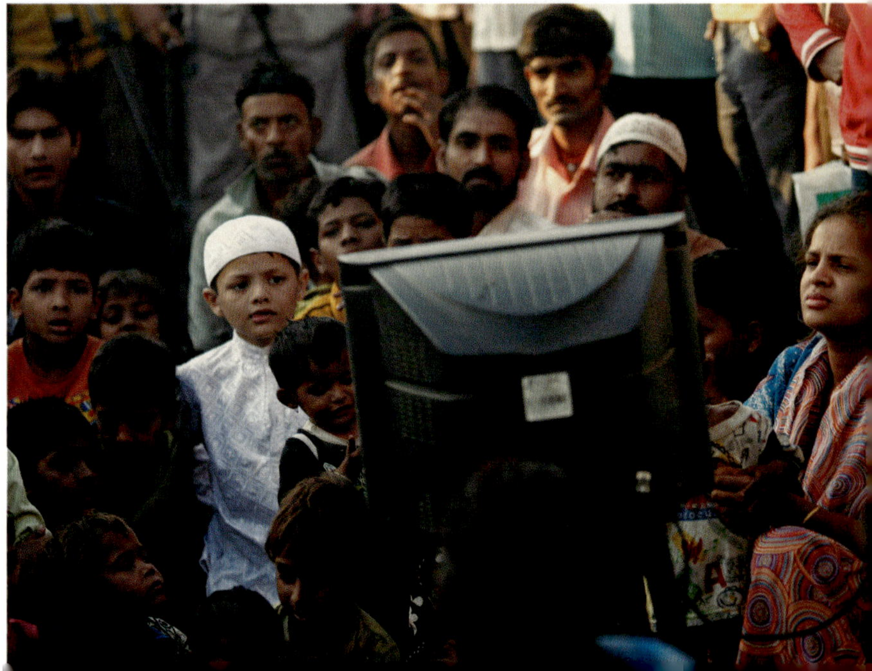

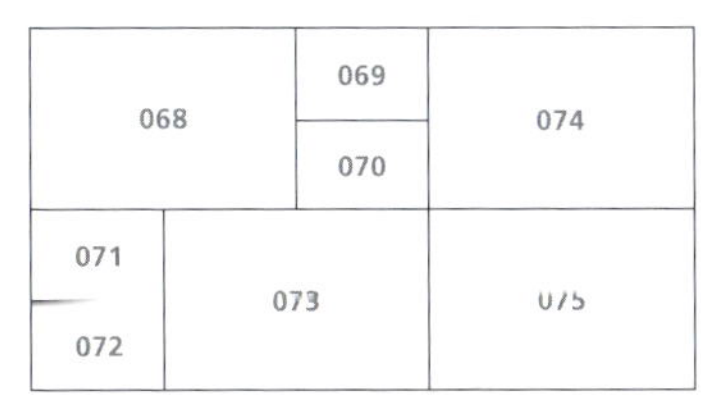

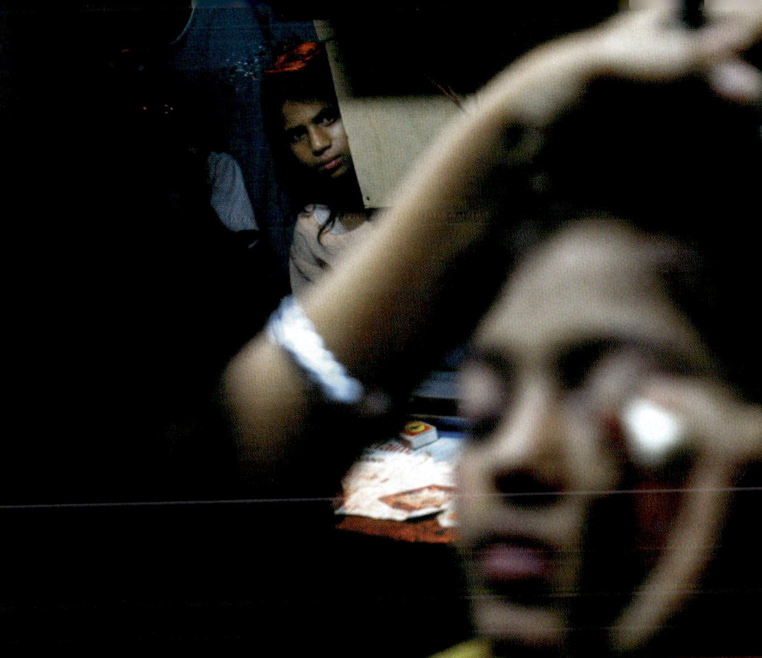

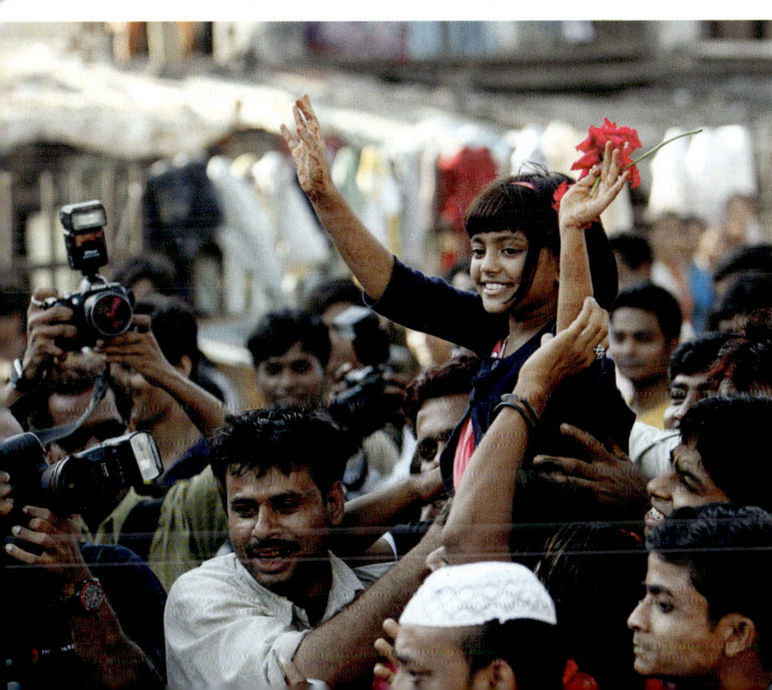

068 Azharuddin Ismail, who played the part of young Salim in *Slumdog Millionaire*, reacts to his father in their shack in a Mumbai slum after returning from Los Angeles, where he attended the 81st Academy Awards. 26 February 2009. **069** Rubina Ali (left), who played the part of young Latika, and Azharuddin Ismail look towards a billboard image of Bollywood star Salman Khan as they travel in a taxi to collect their passports and U.S. visas. 19 February 2009. **070** Rubina Ali is hugged by her grandmother, Jamila, prior to leaving for the airport. 20 February 2009. **071** Azharuddin Ismail gets ready as his mother Shameem (right) and Rubina Ali look on, before leaving to collect their passports. 19 February 2009. **072** Rubina Ali walks in her Mumbai slum neighbourhood to meet friends. 20 February 2009. **073** Neighbours of Azharuddin Ismail gather to watch the Oscars ceremony on television outside their homes. 23 February 2009. **074** A relative applies make-up to Rubina Ali. 20 February 2009. **075** Neighbours carry Rubina Ali back to her home in celebration on her return to Mumbai from the United States. 26 February 2009. Arko Datta.

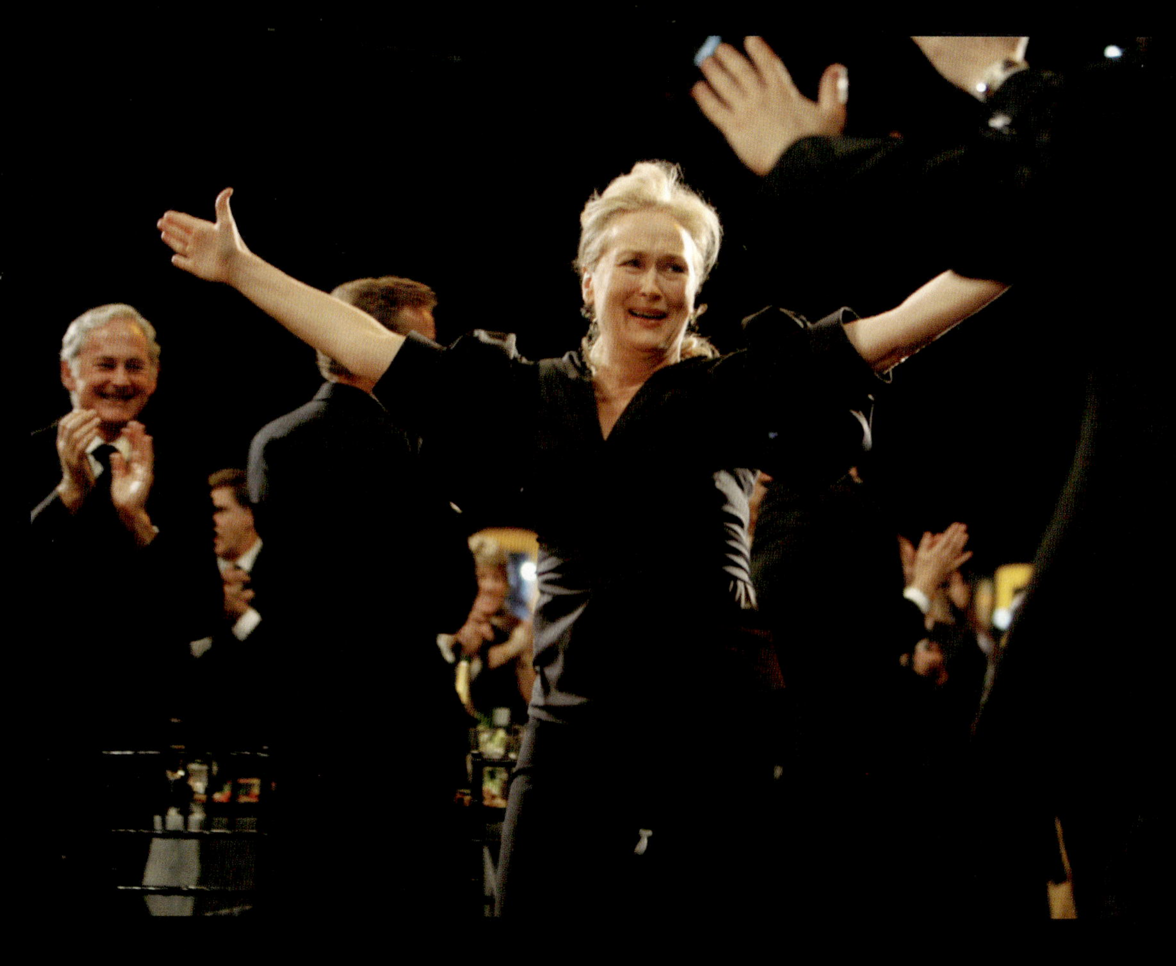

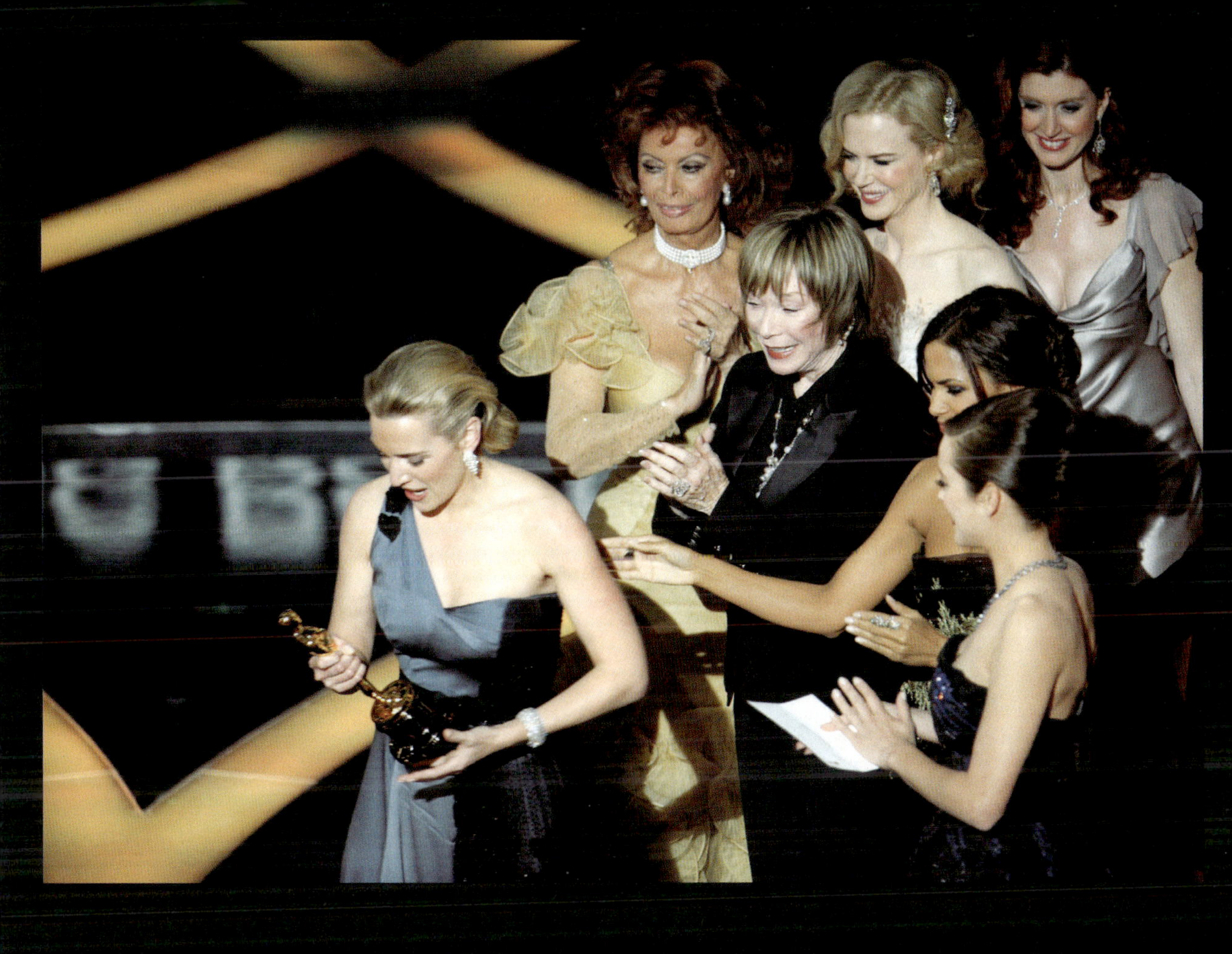

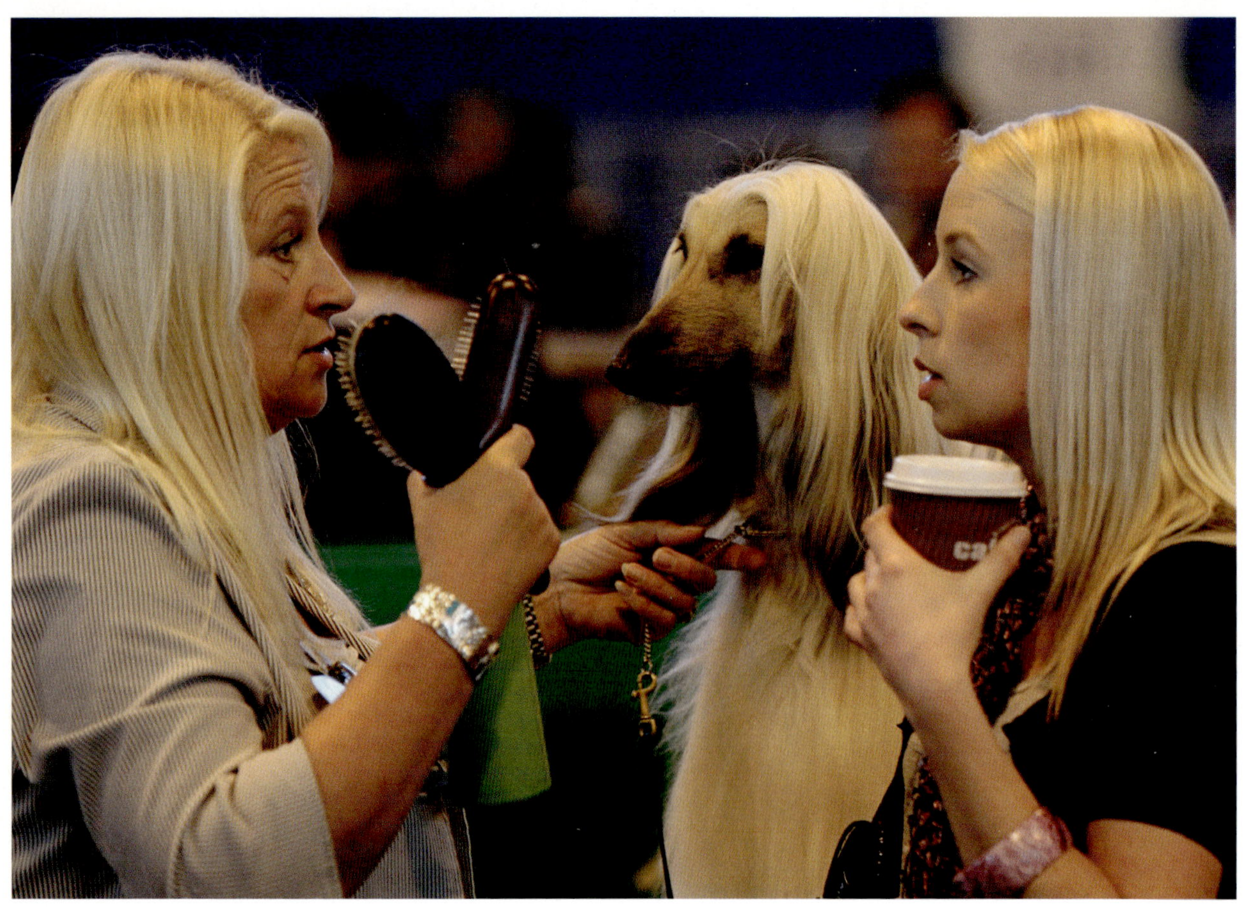

078 Birmingham, Britain

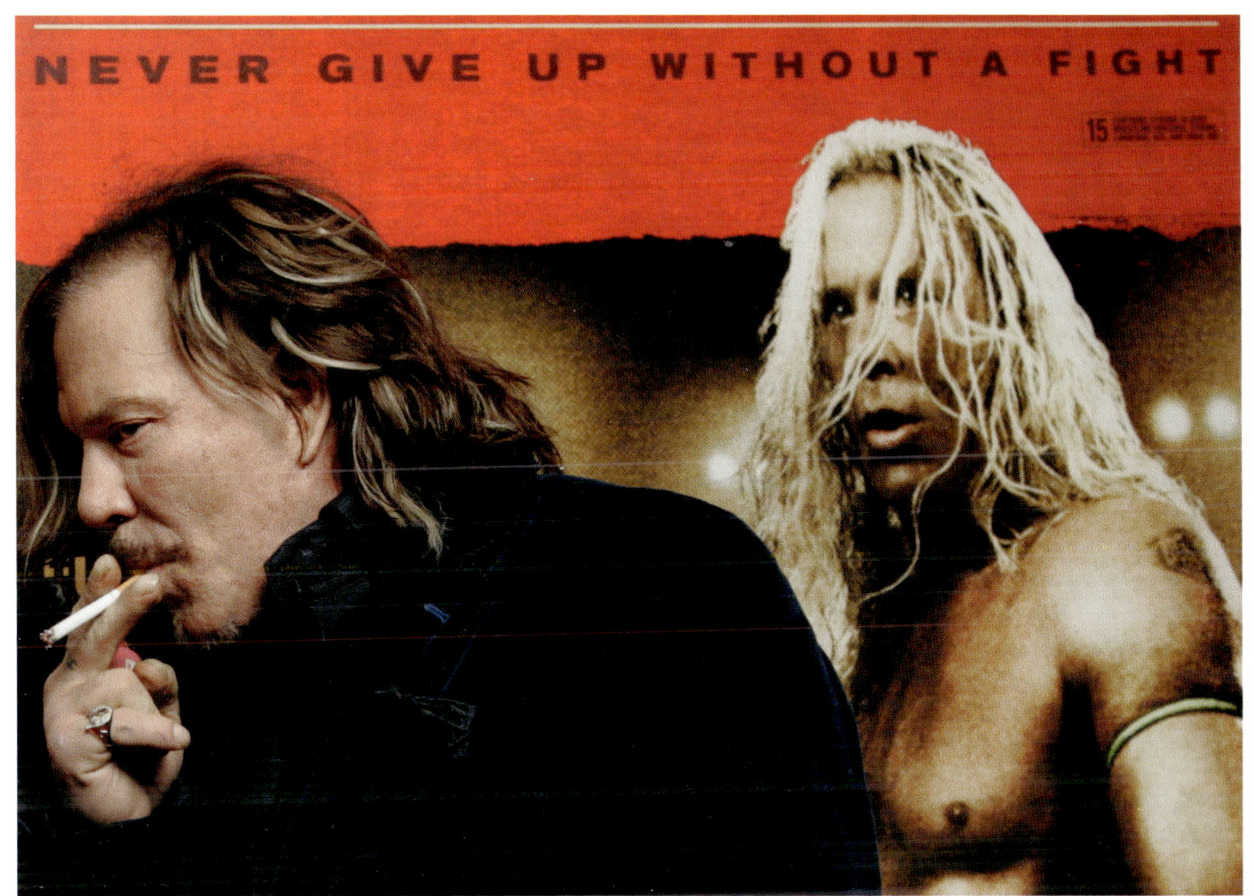

NEVER GIVE UP WITHOUT A FIGHT
15

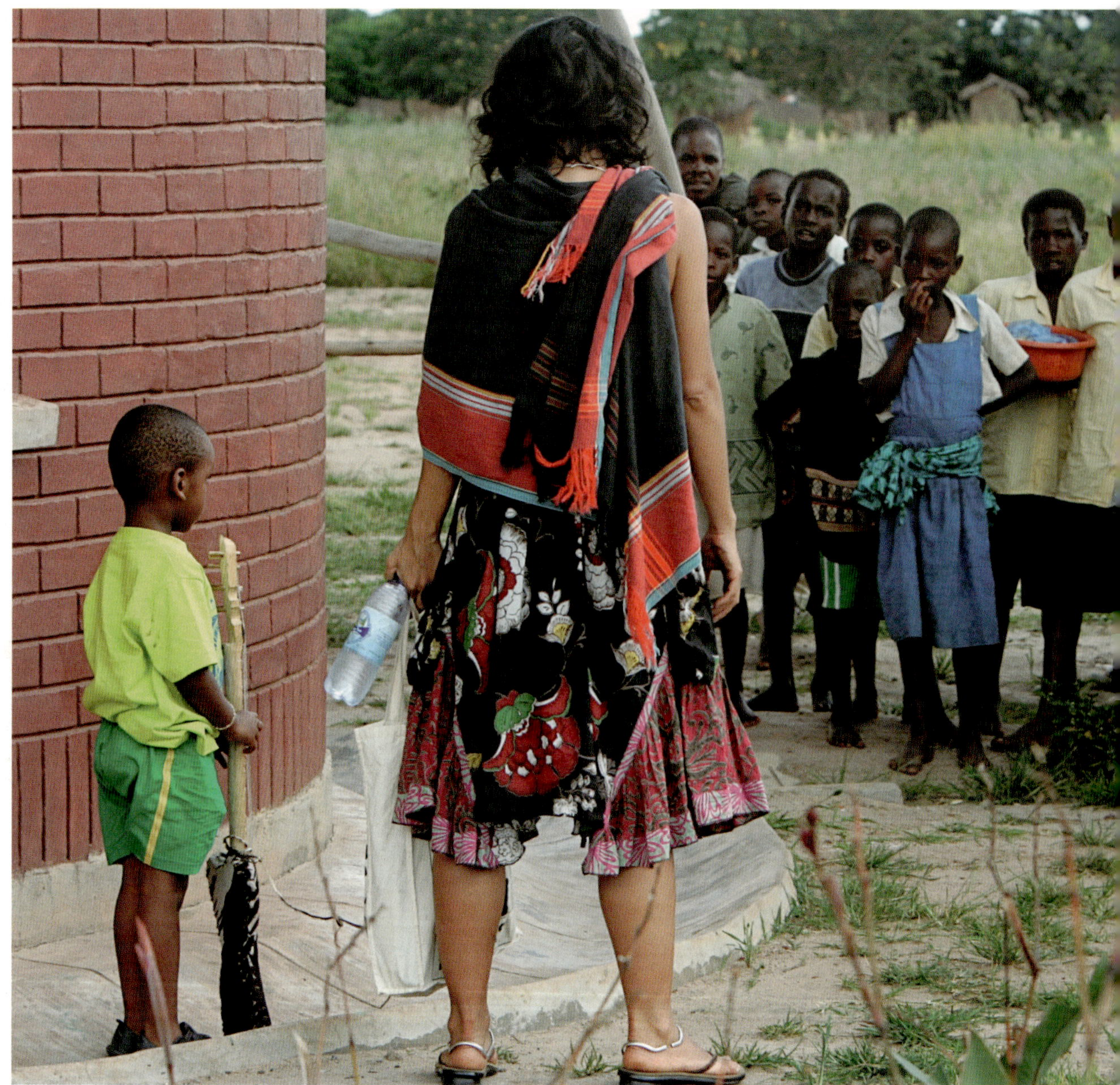

080 Namitete, Malawi

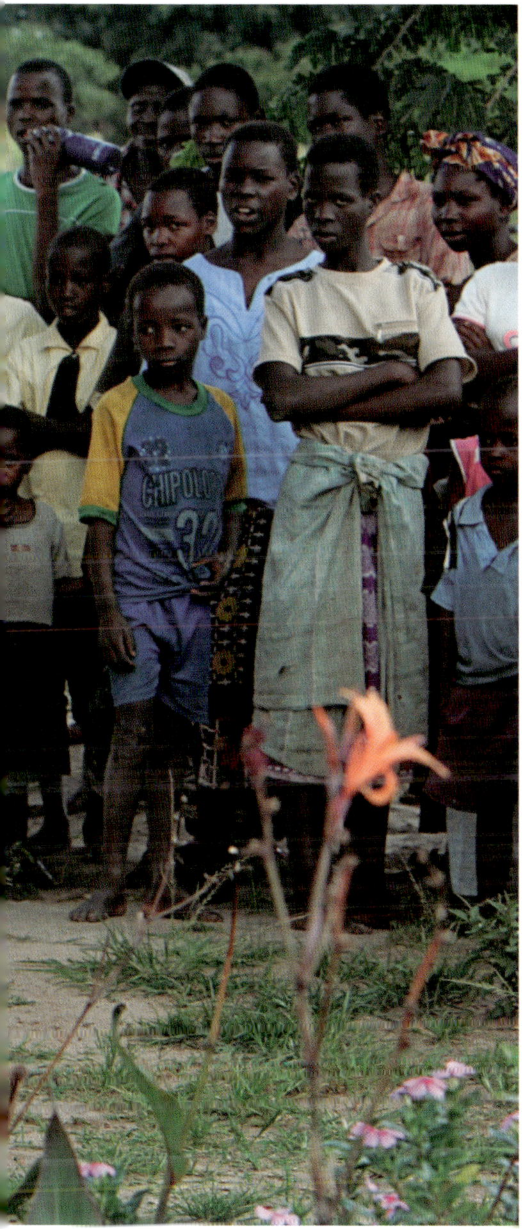

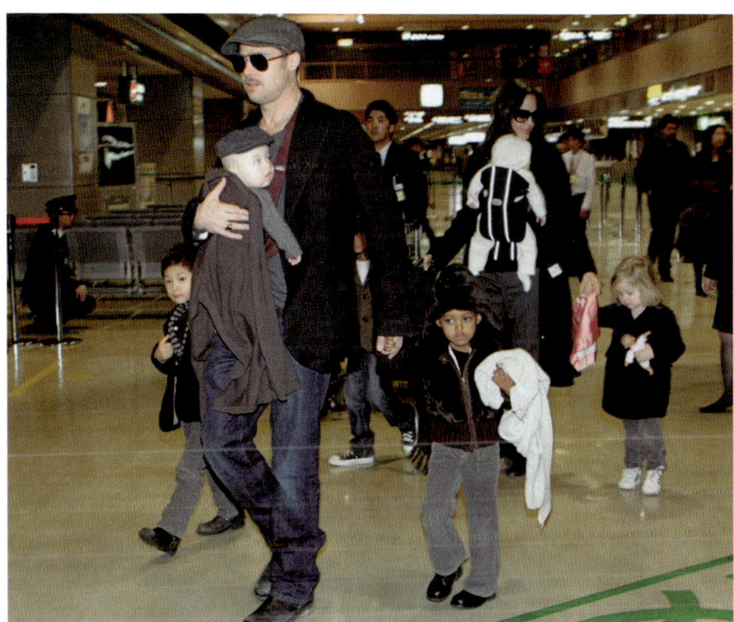

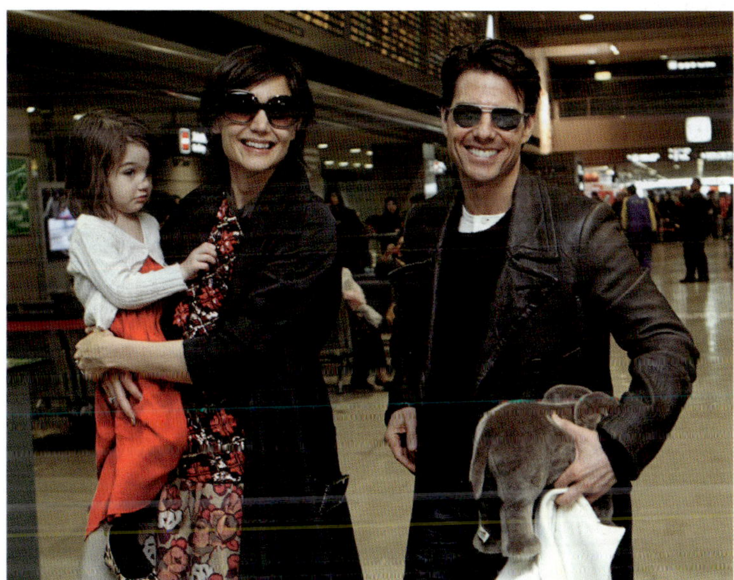

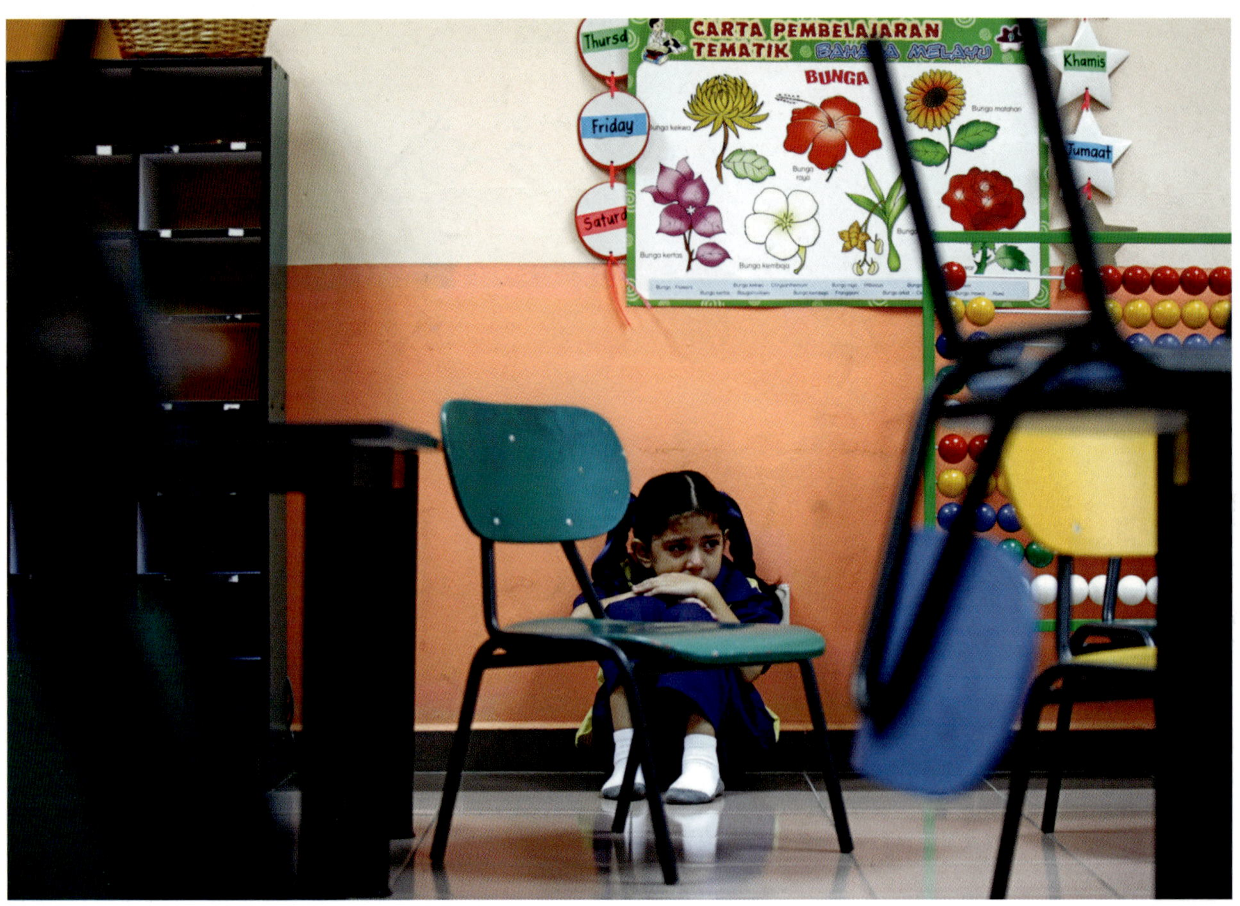

Thursd
Friday
Saturd
CARTA PEMBELAJARAN
TEMATIK
BAHASA MELAYU
BUNGA
Bunga kekwa
Bunga raya
Bunga matahari
Bunga kertas
Bunga kembaja
Khamis
Jumaat

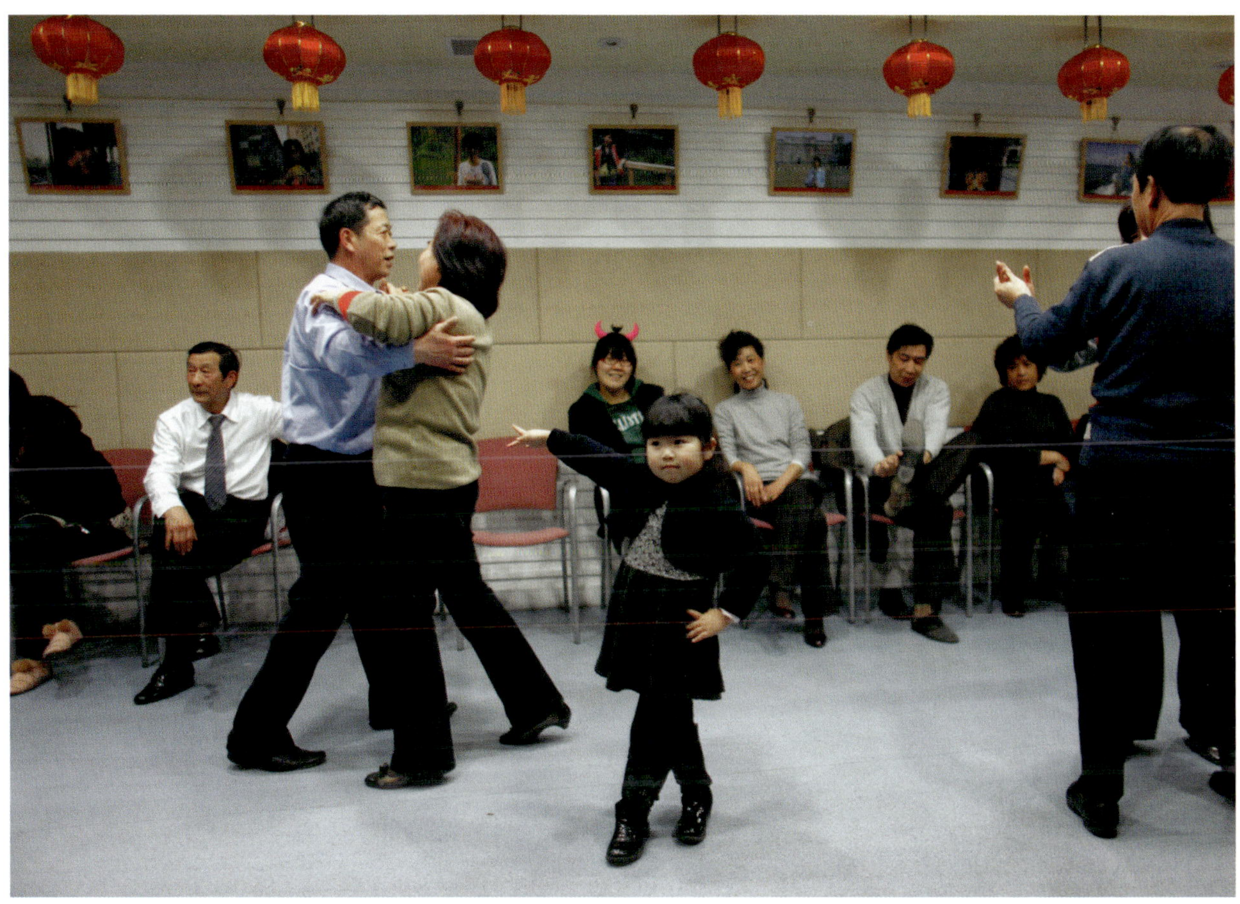

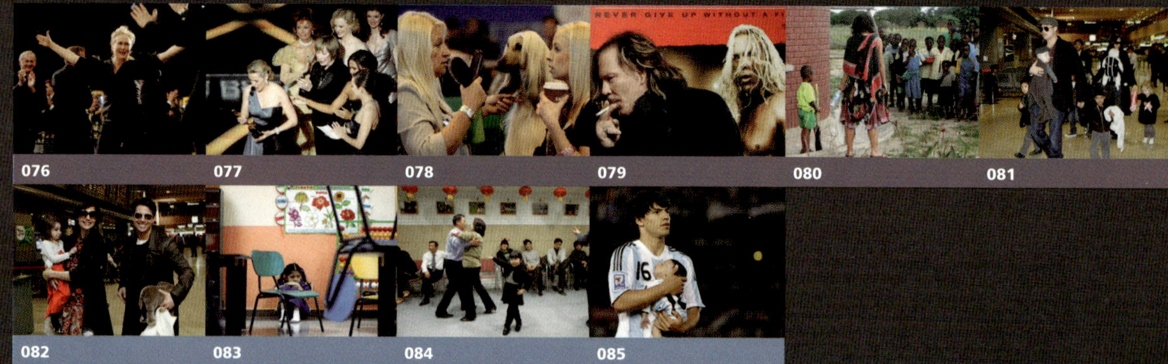

076 U.S. actress Meryl Streep reacts to winning the award for Outstanding Performance by a Female Actor in a Leading Role for *Doubt* at the 15th annual Screen Actors Guild Awards in Los Angeles. 25 January 2009. Los Angeles, United States. Mario Anzuoni.

077 British actress Kate Winslet accepts the Oscar for best actress for her role in *The Reader* in front of former best actress winners (left to right) Sophia Loren, Shirley MacLaine, Nicole Kidman, Halle Berry and Marion Cotillard during the 81st Academy Awards in Hollywood. 22 February 2009. Los Angeles, United States. Gary Hershorn.

078 Women stand with their Afghan Hound before entering the parade ring during the Crufts dog show. 5 March 2009. Birmingham, Britain. Darren Staples.

079 U.S. actor Mickey Rourke arrives for the British premiere of his film *The Wrestler*. 5 January 2009. London, Britain. Luke MacGregor.

080 Madonna's adopted son David Banda (left) looks at pupils at a school financed by the U.S. pop star in Namitete, some 50 km (30 miles) south of Malawi's capital Lilongwe. A Malawian court ruled in April that Madonna could not adopt a second Malawian child, Mercy James, because the singer was not a resident of the country. The Supreme Court later overturned that decision. 30 March 2009. Namitete, Malawi. Antony Njuguna.

081 U.S. actors Brad Pitt and Angelina Jolie arrive with their children at Narita International Airport, near Tokyo. From left to right: Pax, Knox Leon (carried by Pitt), Maddox (obscured), Zahara, Vivienne Marcheline (carried by Jolie) and Shiloh. 27 January 2009. Tokyo, Japan. Toru Hanai.

082 U.S. actors Tom Cruise and his wife Katie Holmes, holding their daughter Suri, arrive at Narita International Airport. 8 March 2009. Tokyo, Japan. Toru Hanai.

083 Aleeya Amran, 6, refuses to attend class during her first day at Putrajaya Presint 9 (1) Primary School in Putrajaya outside Kuala Lumpur. 5 January 2009. Kuala Lumpur, Malaysia. Bazuki Muhammad.

084 A child dances during a community function celebrating the upcoming Lantern Festival in Shanghai. The festival marks the last day of the Chinese New Year celebrations. 6 February 2009. Shanghai, China. Aly Song.

085 Argentina's Sergio Aguero, son-in-law of coach Diego Maradona, carries his son onto the field for the pre-game ceremony before their World Cup 2010 qualifying soccer match against Venezuela. 28 March 2009. Buenos Aires, Argentina. Santiago Pandolfi.

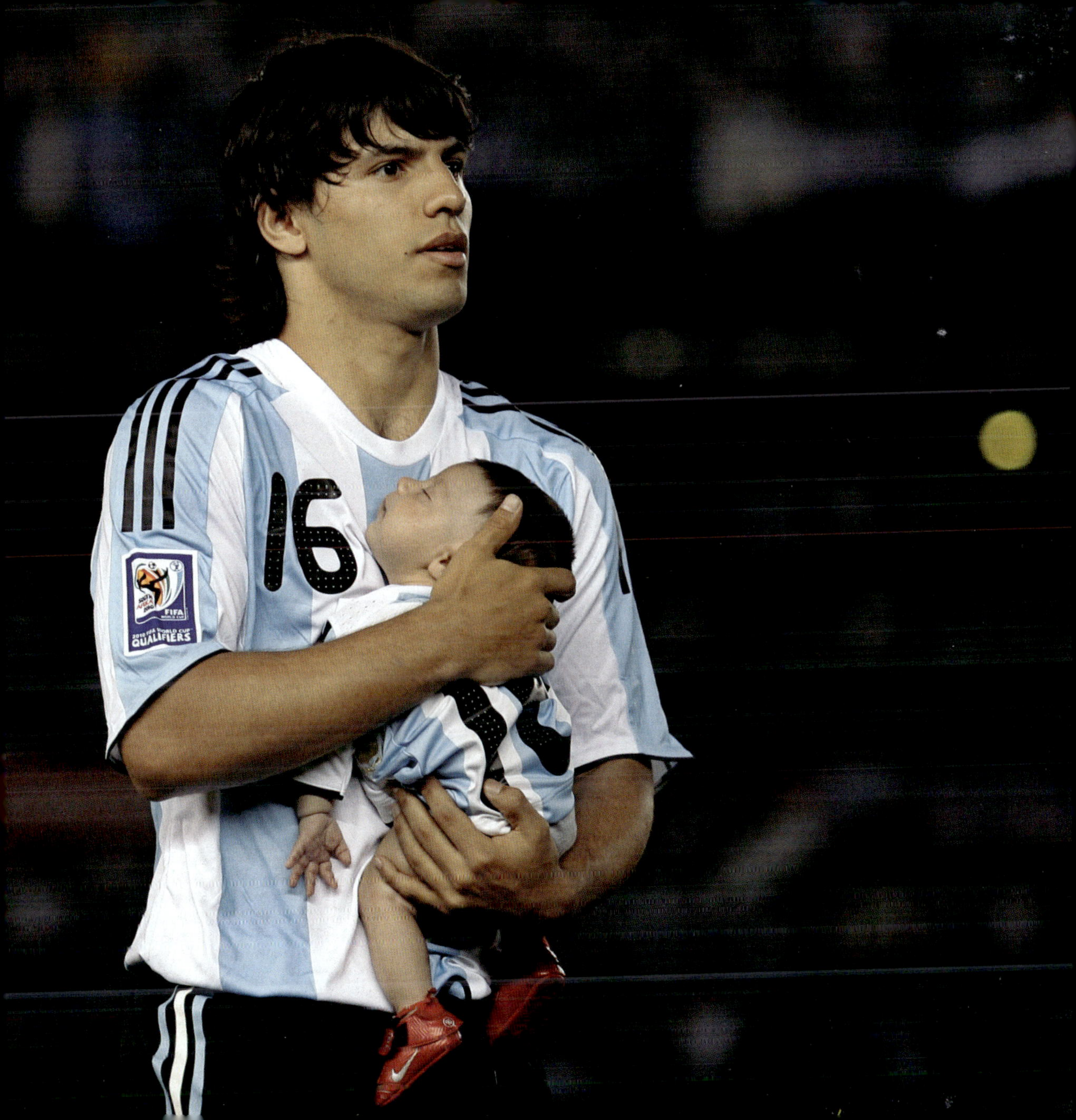

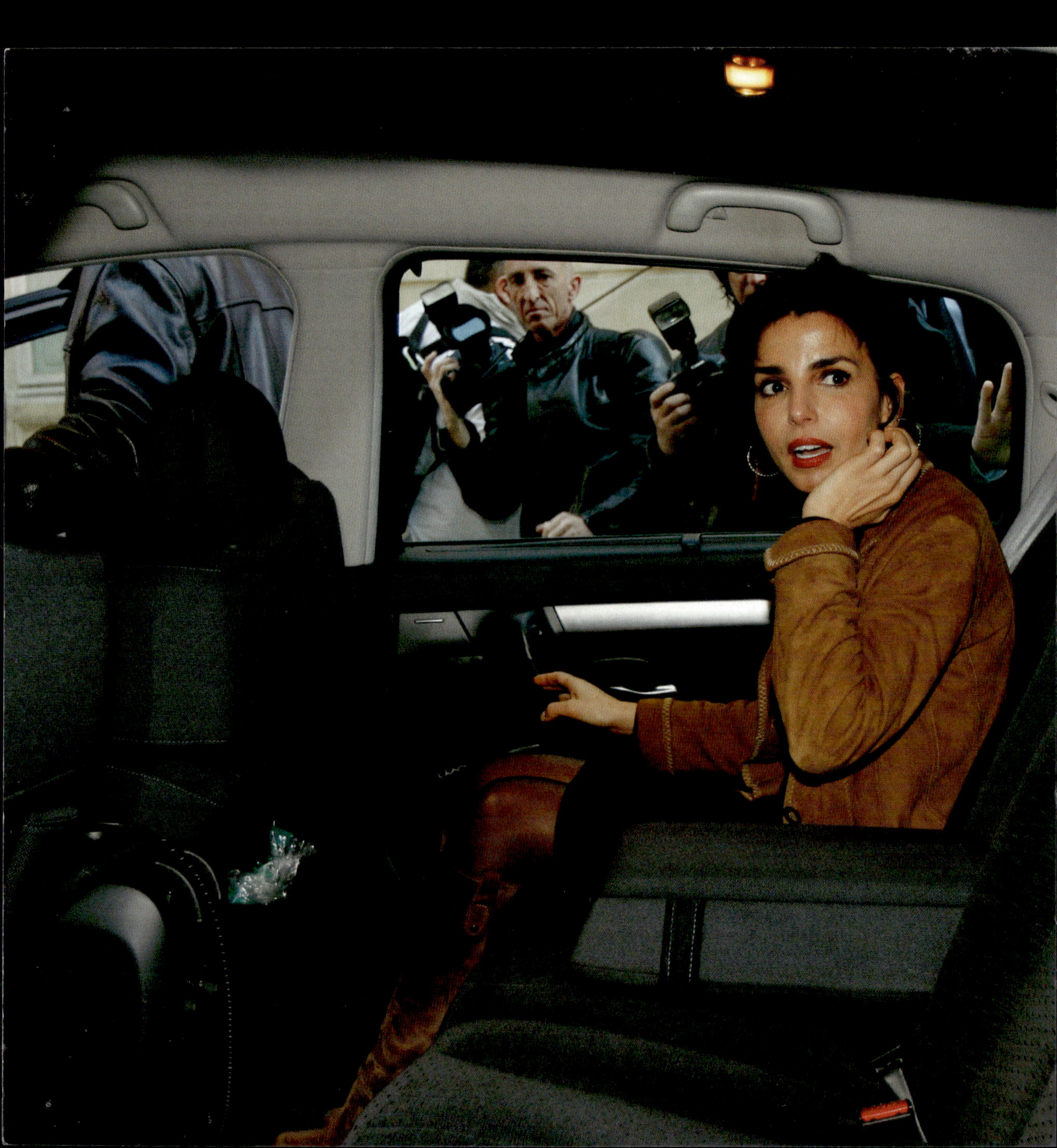

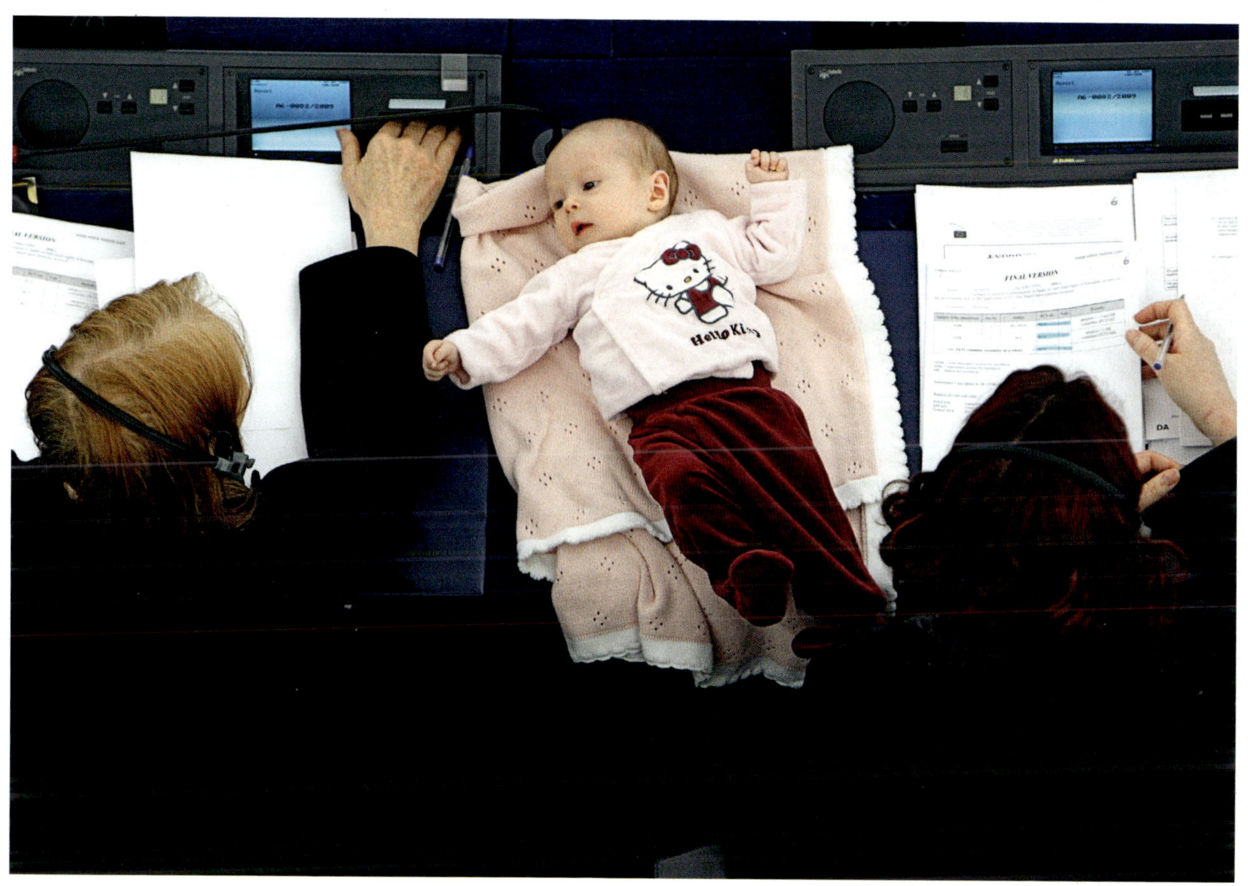

086 [OPPOSITE] Toulon, France

087 Strasbourg, France

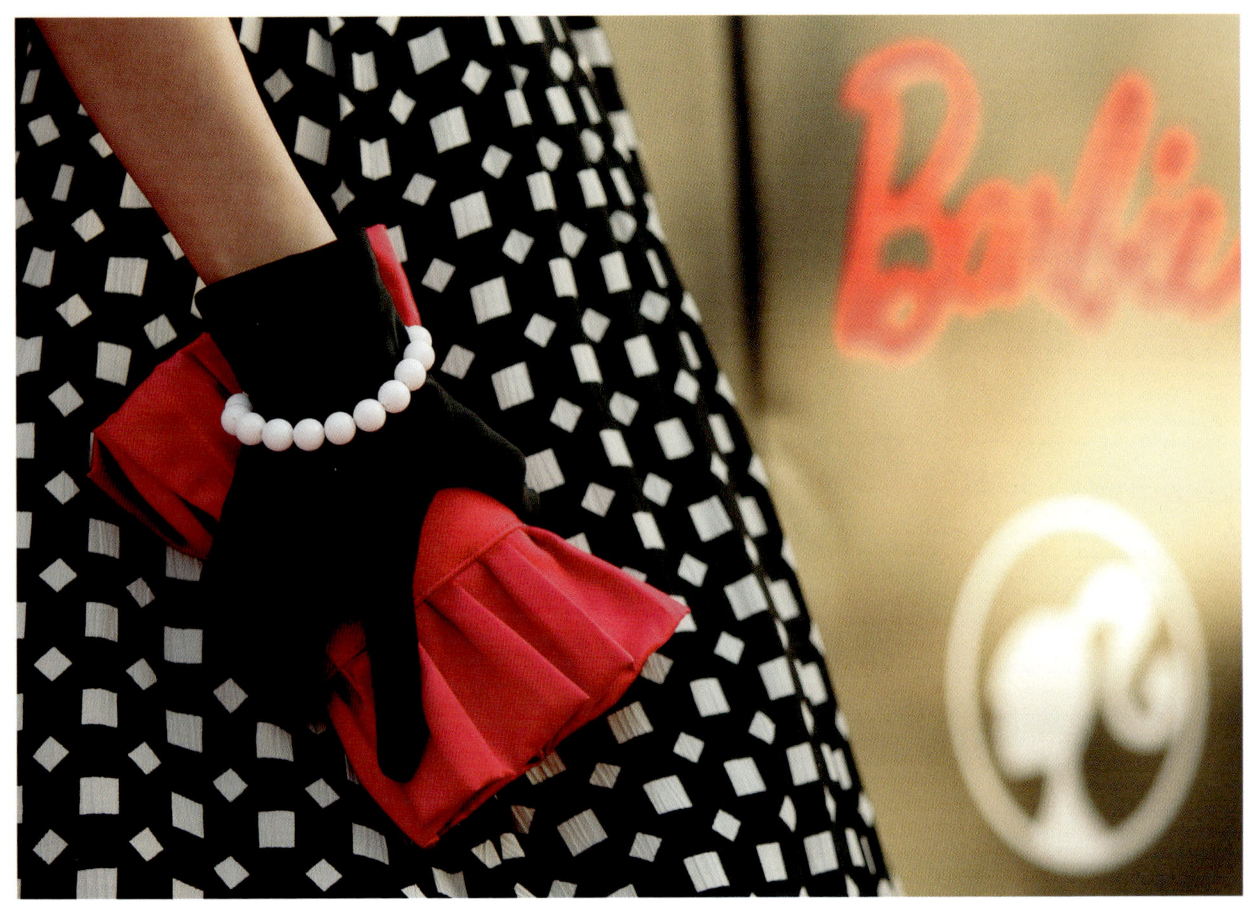

088 Malibu, United States

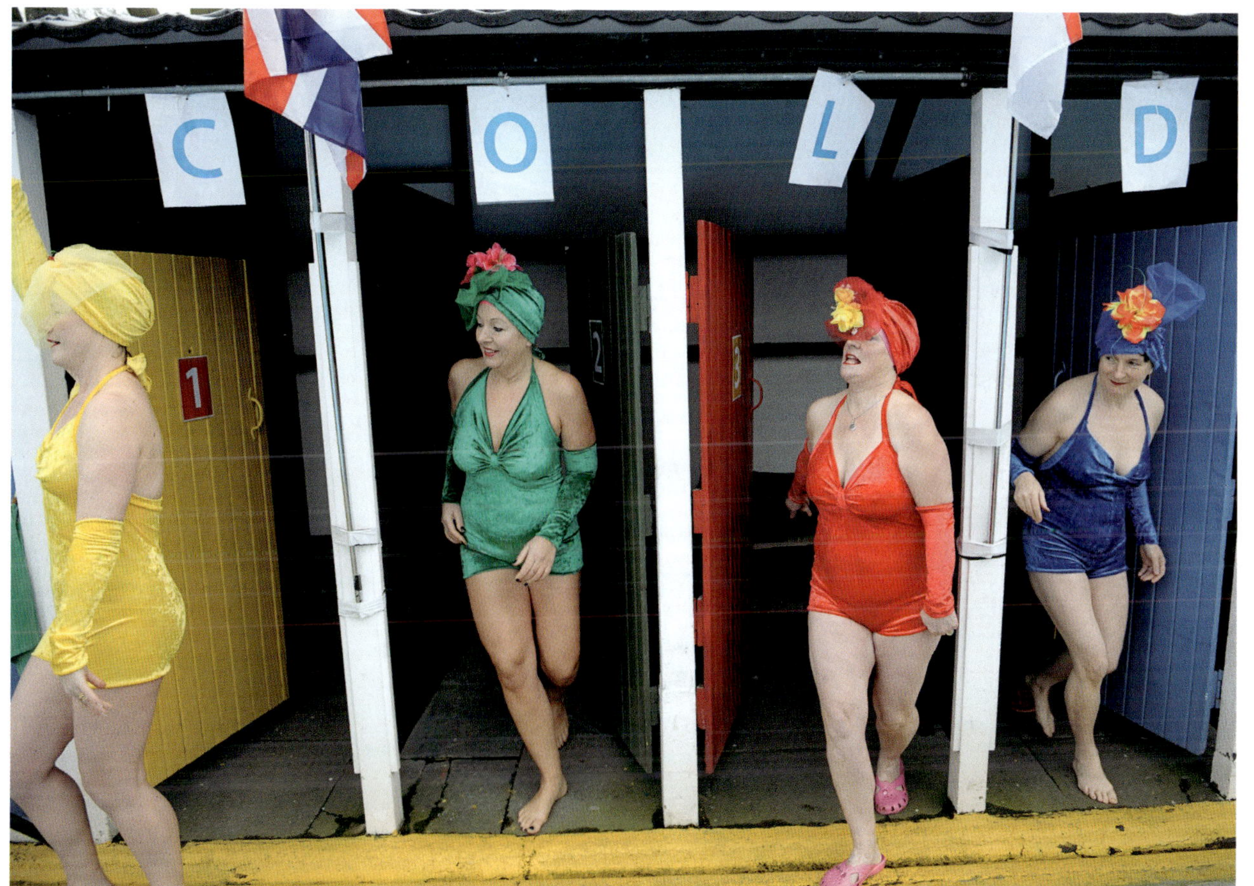
C
O
L
D
1
2
3

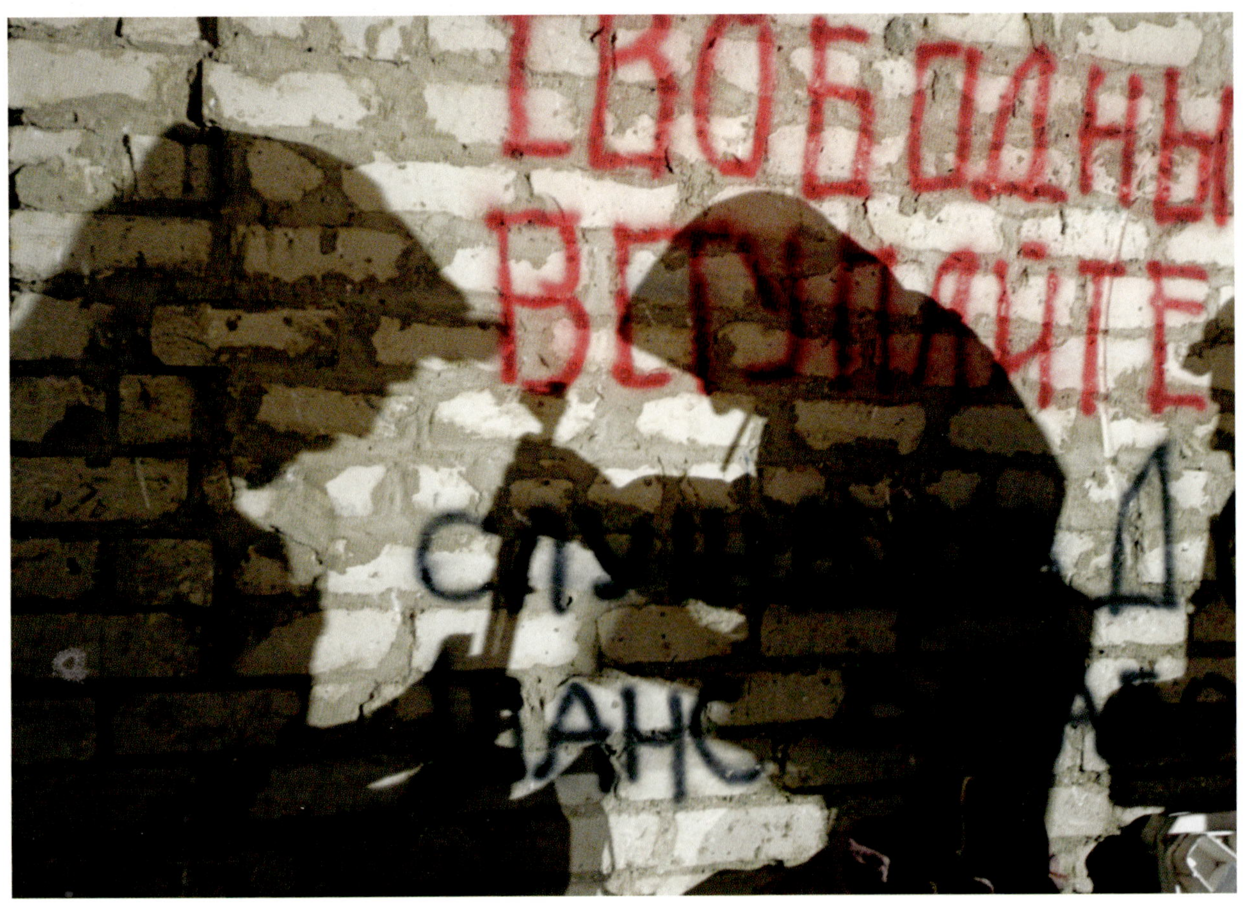
СВОБОДНЫ
ВЕРНИТЕ

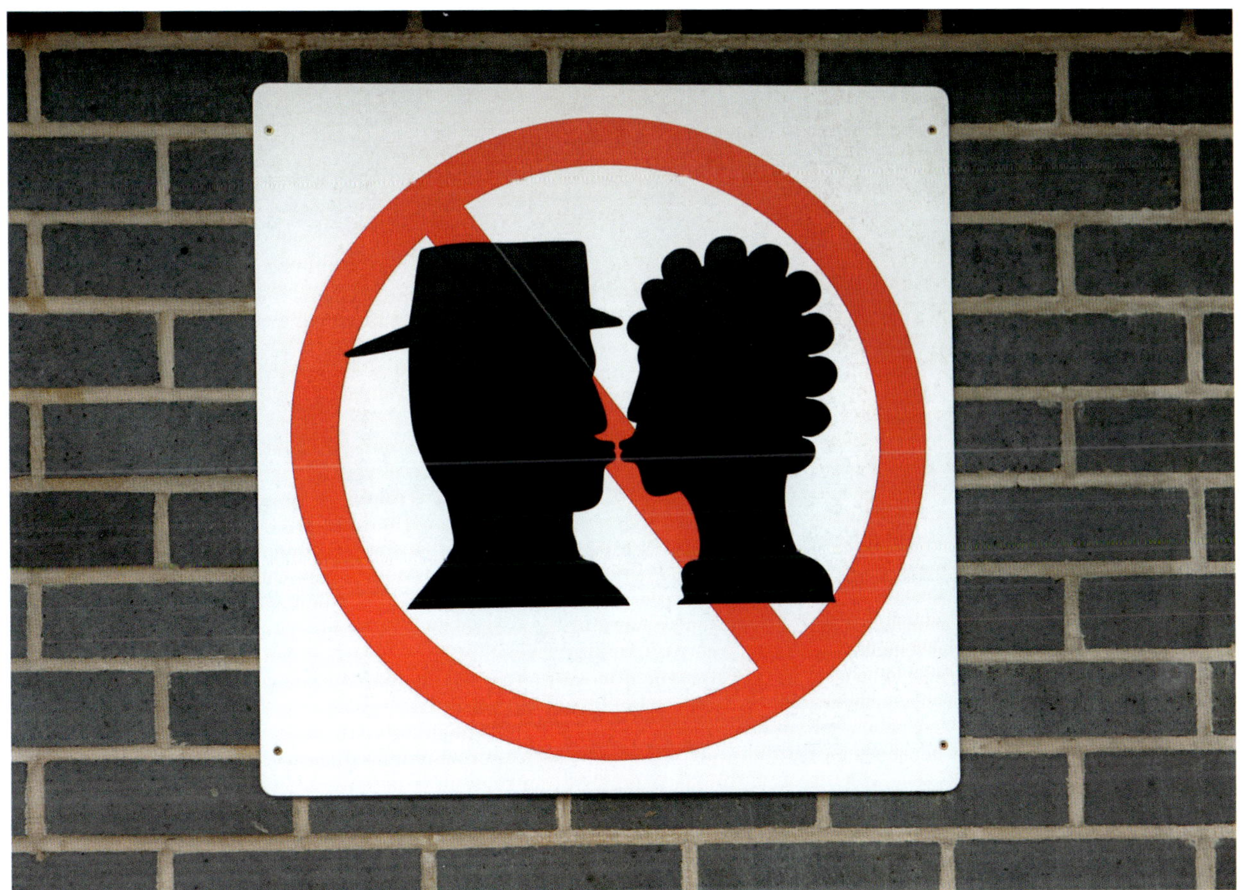

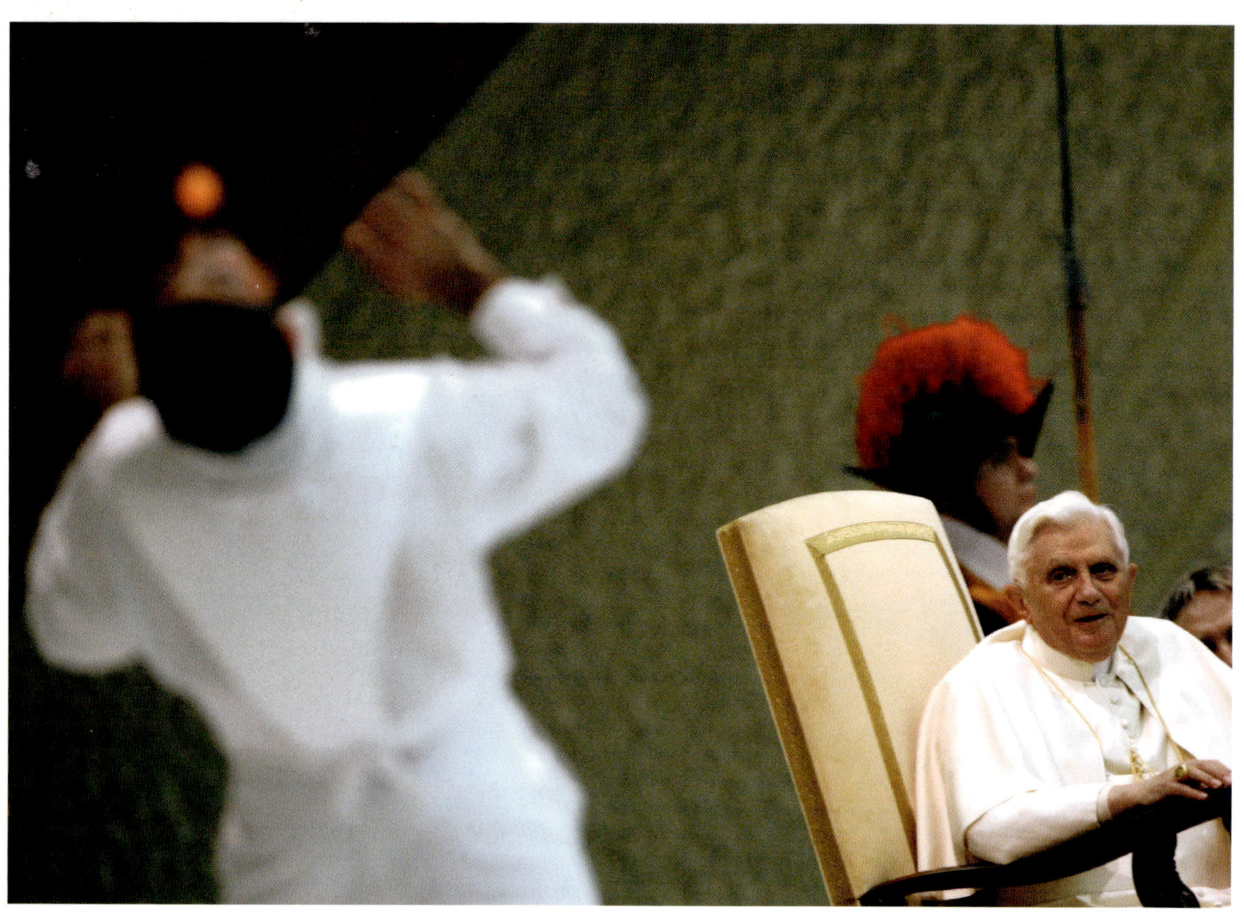

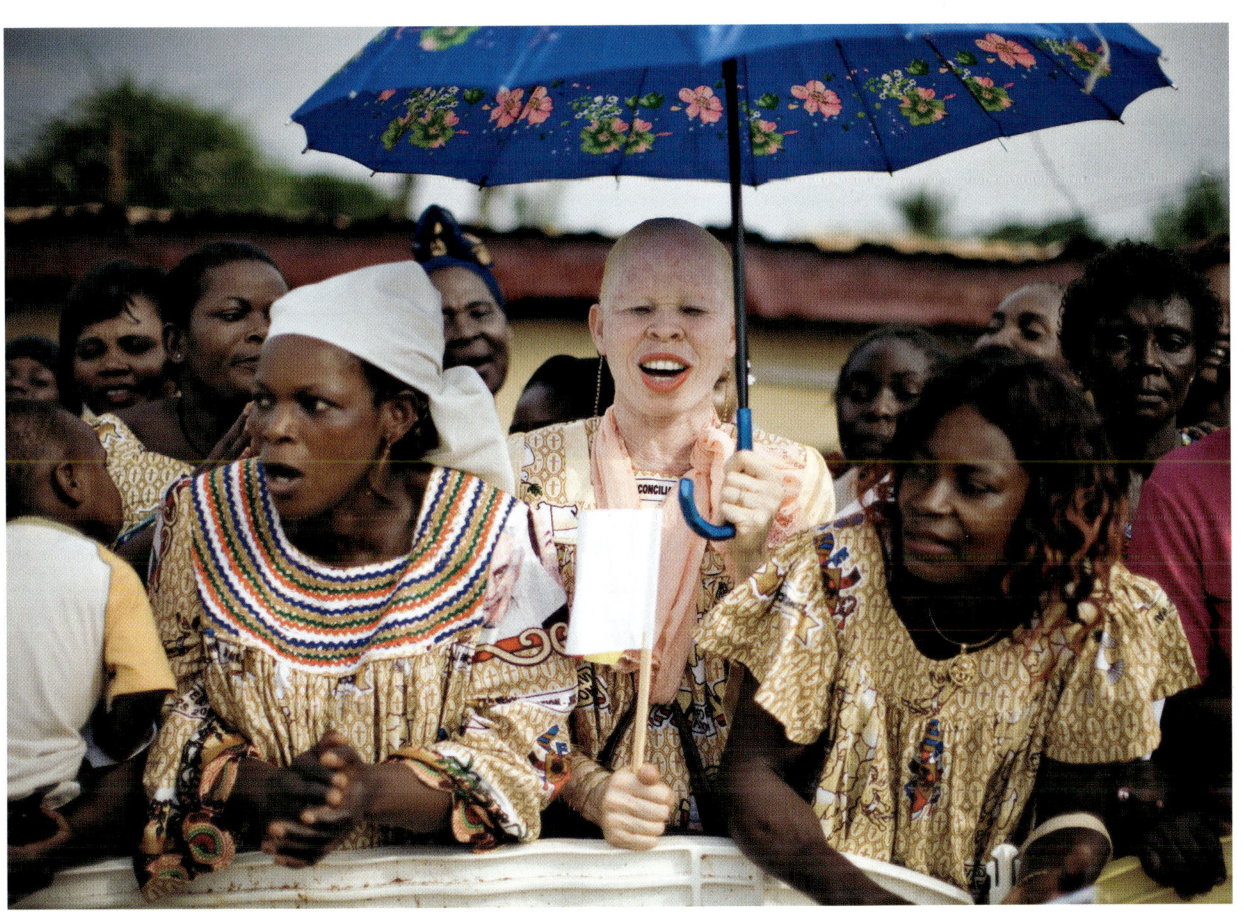

093 Yaounde, Cameroon

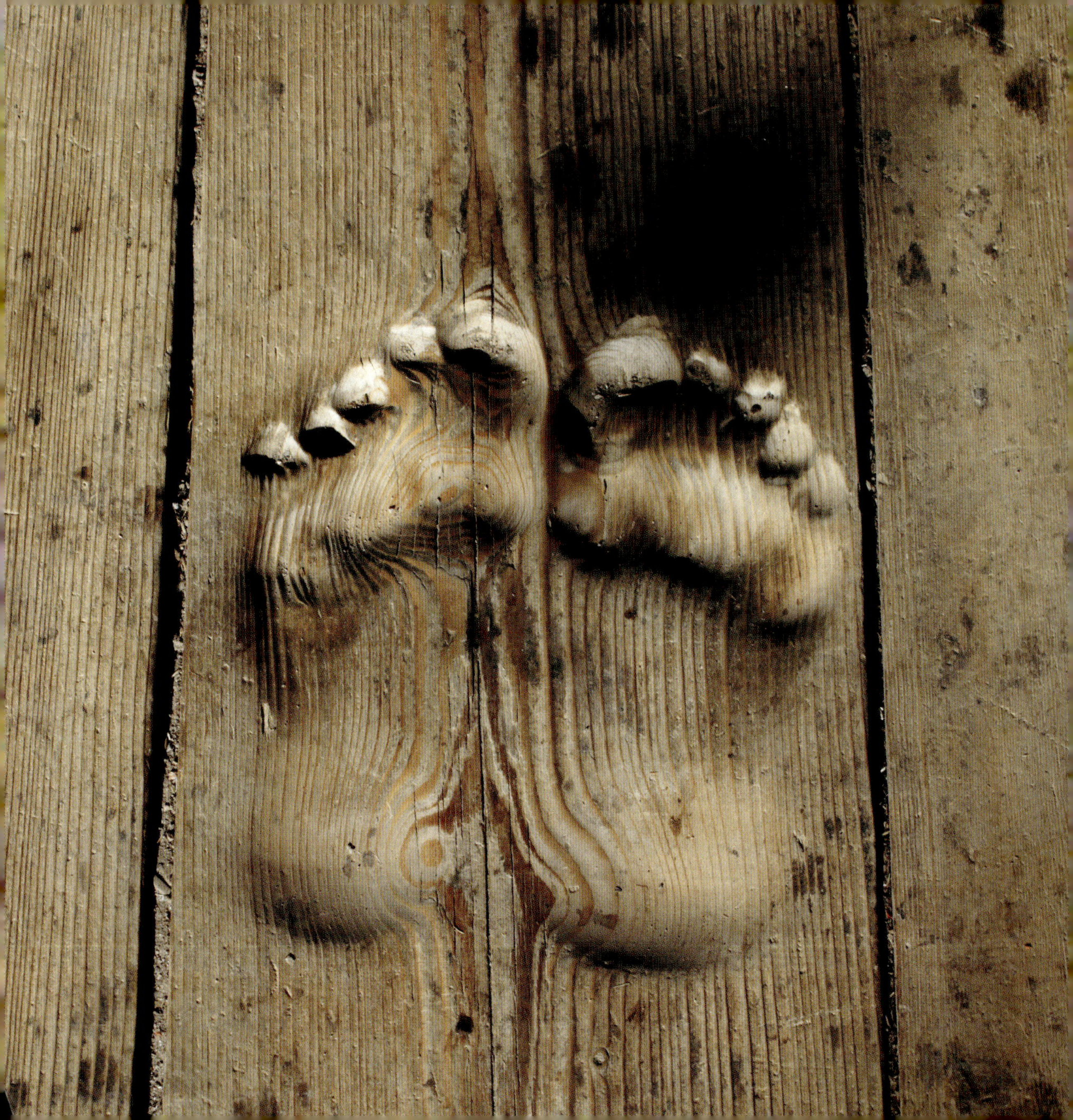

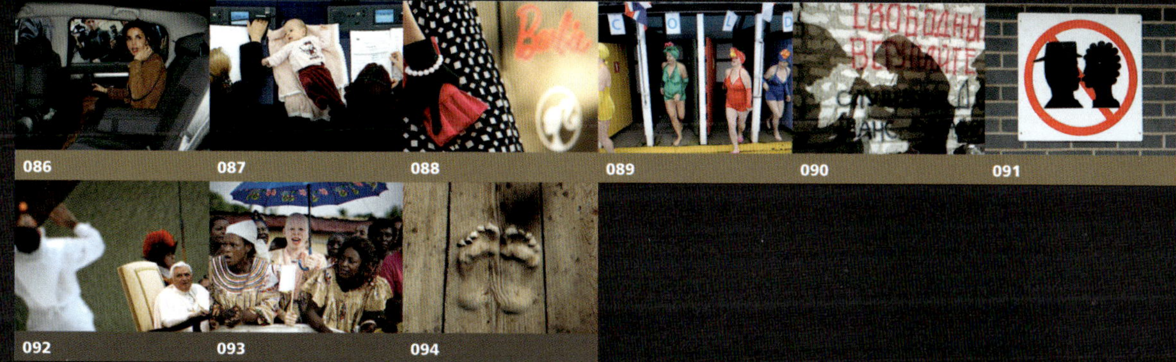

086 087 088 089 090 091
092 093 094

086 France's then Justice Minister Rachida Dati gets into a car after the inauguration of the administrative court of Toulon in southeastern France. Photos of Dati returning to work only five days after giving birth to a baby girl in January sparked speculation that she feared being politically sidelined. 23 February 2009. Toulon, France. Jean-Paul Pelissier.

087 Denmark's member of the European Parliament Hanne Dahl (right) takes part in a voting session with her baby alongside. 26 March 2009. Strasbourg, France. Vincent Kessler.

088 A guest arrives at Barbie's 50th birthday party at the Barbie real-life Malibu Dream House in California. 9 March 2009. Malibu, United States. Mario Anzuoni.

089 Swimmers prepare to participate in the opening ceremony of the UK Cold Water Swimming Championships at Tooting Bec Lido in London. 24 January 2009. London, Britain. Kieran Doherty.

090 Shadows are cast on a wall during a live action role-playing game based on the computer game S.T.A.L.K.E.R., near the village of Sengileyevskoe in Russia's southern Stavropol region. The game is set in the radioactive exclusion zone around the Chernobyl nuclear reactor after a second, fictional disaster. Players must fight for survival against mutant creatures. 21 March 2009. Sengileyevskoe, Russia. Eduard Korniyenko.

091 A 'No Kissing' sign is displayed outside Warrington Bank Quay railway station in northern England. The controversial sign was erected at the drop-off point after departing passengers and drivers blocked access to the station with their vehicles while saying goodbye, local media reported. 16 February 2009. Warrington, Britain. Gordon Jack.

092 A juggler of Circus Medrano performs in front of Pope Benedict during his Wednesday general audience in Paul VI hall at the Vatican. 28 January 2009. Vatican. Tony Gentile.

093 A woman with albinism stands in a crowd waiting to catch a glimpse of Pope Benedict in Cameroon's capital Yaounde. The pope began his third day in the country by meeting leaders of Cameroon's Muslim community before saying mass to a crowd of tens of thousands at Yaounde's open-air stadium. 19 March 2009. Yaounde, Cameroon. Finbarr O'Reilly.

094 Footprints carved in wood are seen at a monastery near Tongren, Qinghai province, as Tibetan monks and pilgrims gathered to celebrate Monlam, one of the most important festivals in Tibetan Buddhism. Locals believe the footprints were made by a worshipper who prayed at the same spot for decades. 5 February 2009. Tongren, China. Reinhard Krause.

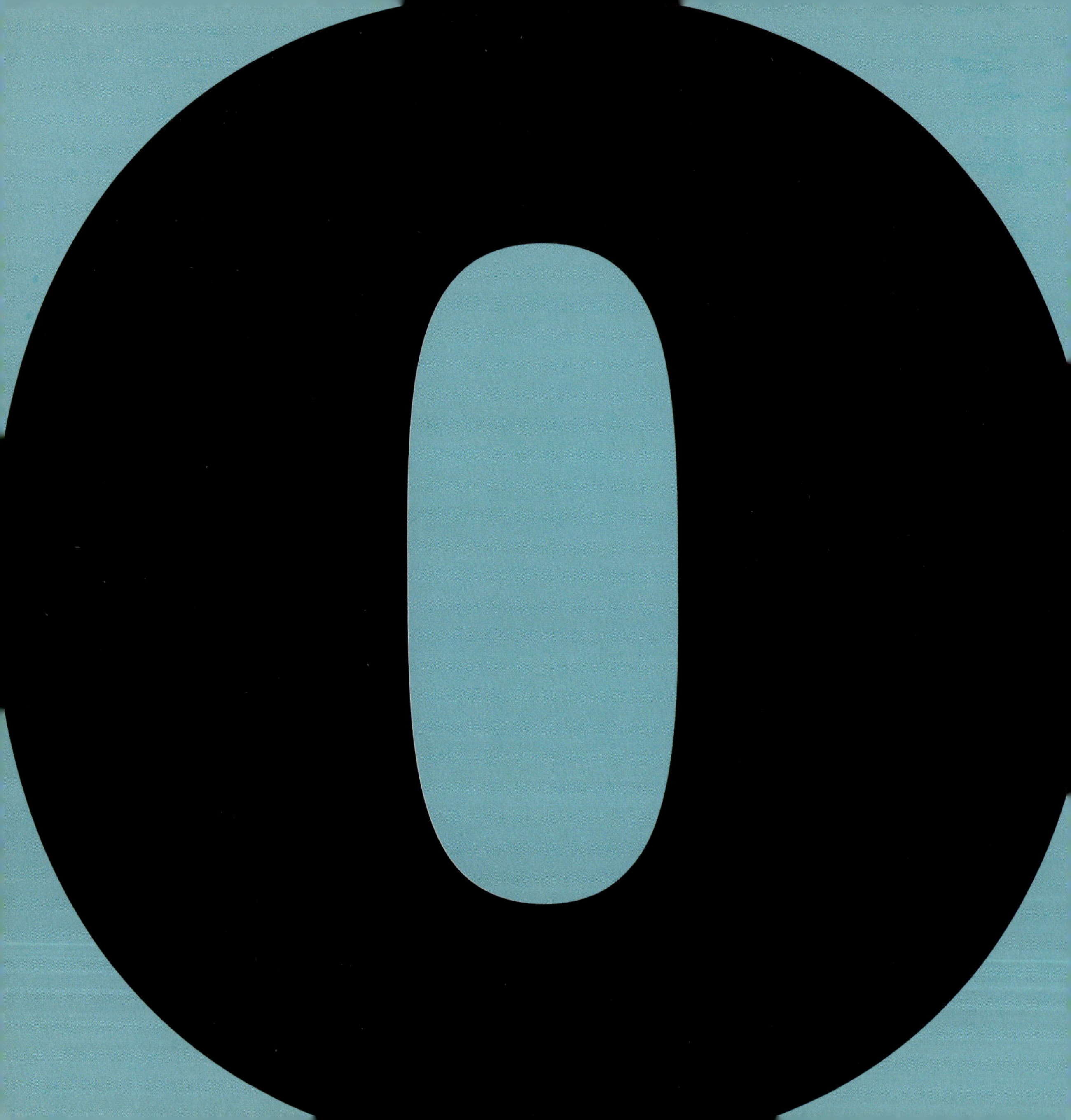

2

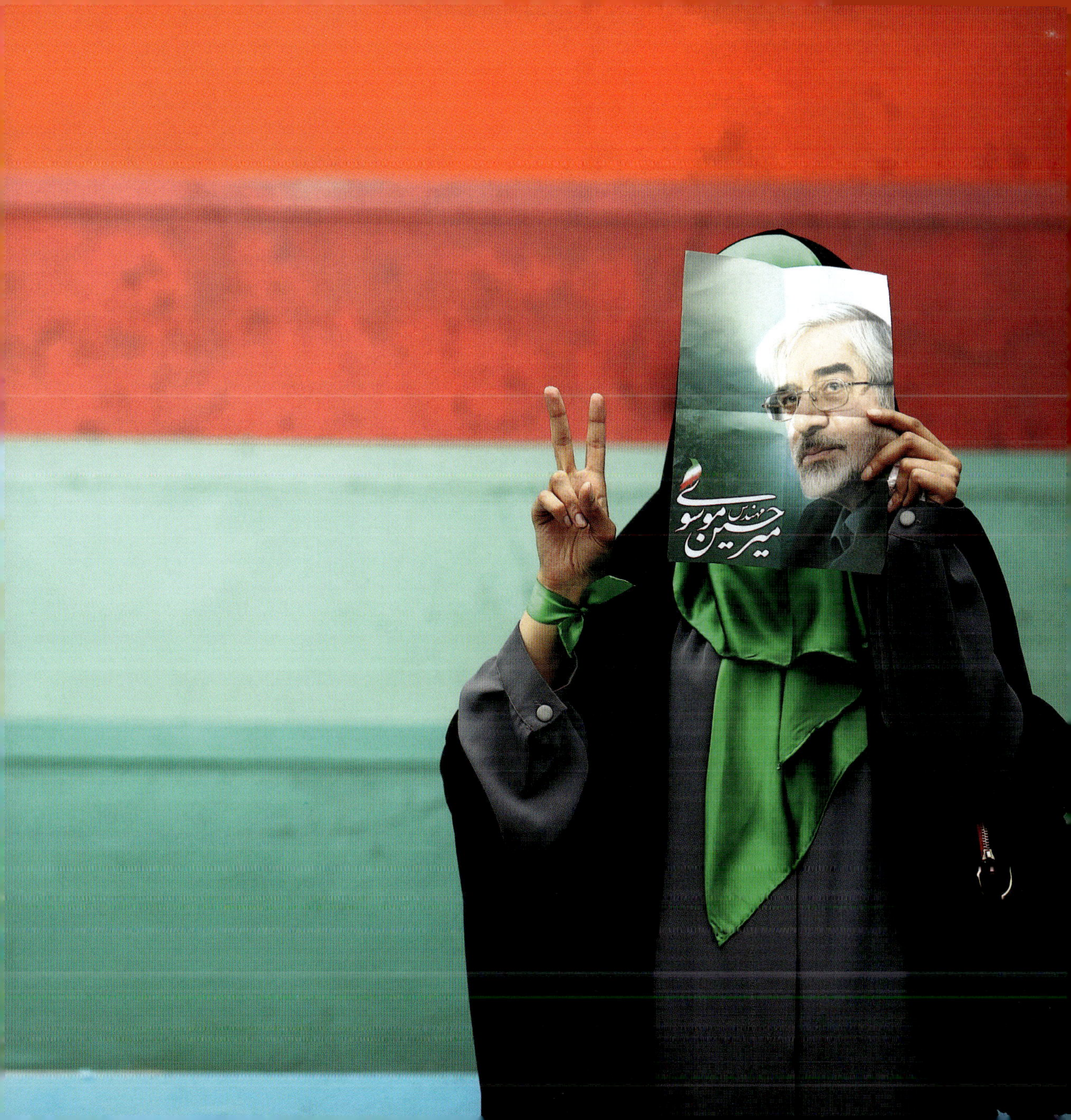

مهندس میرحسین موسوی

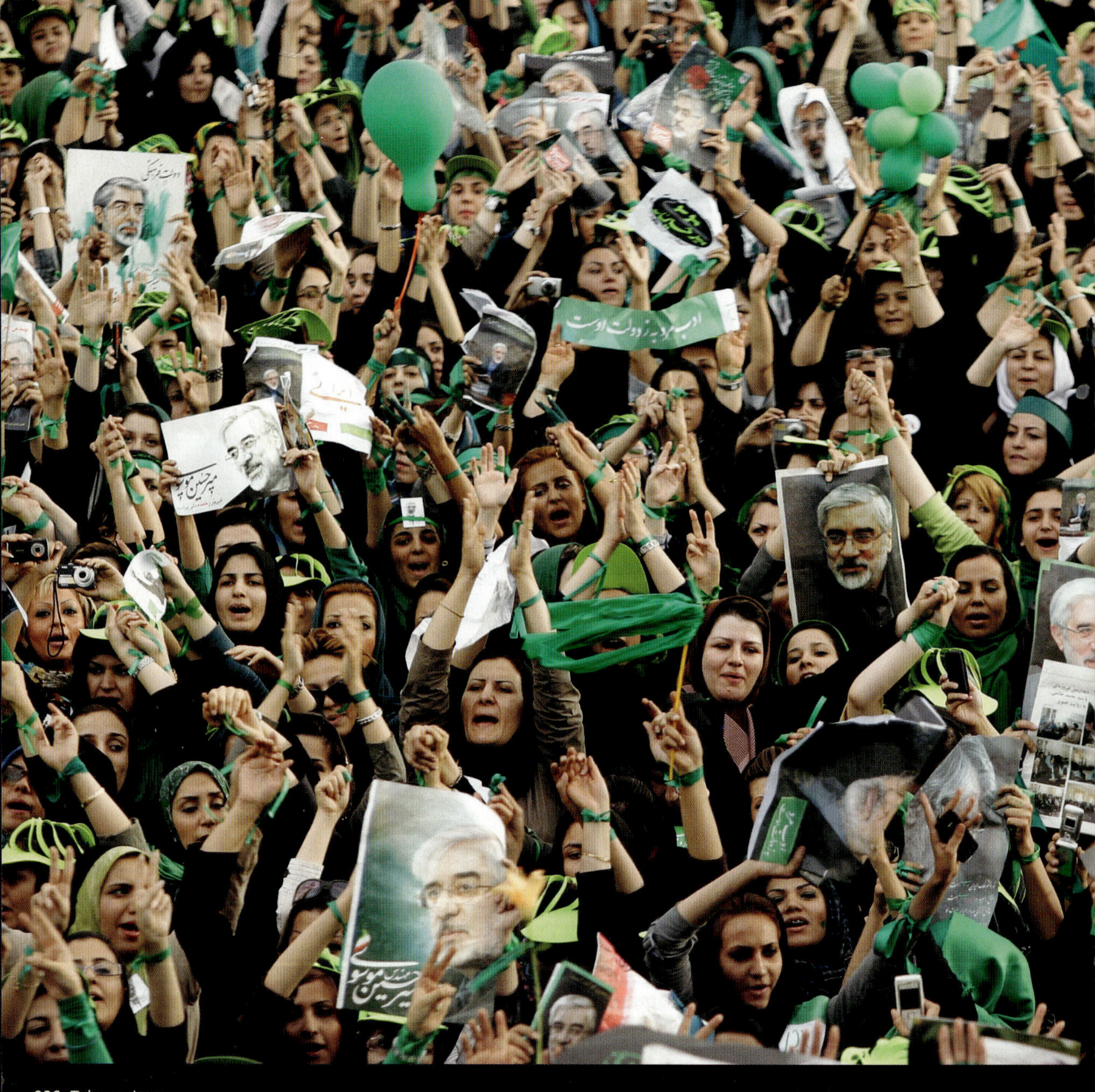

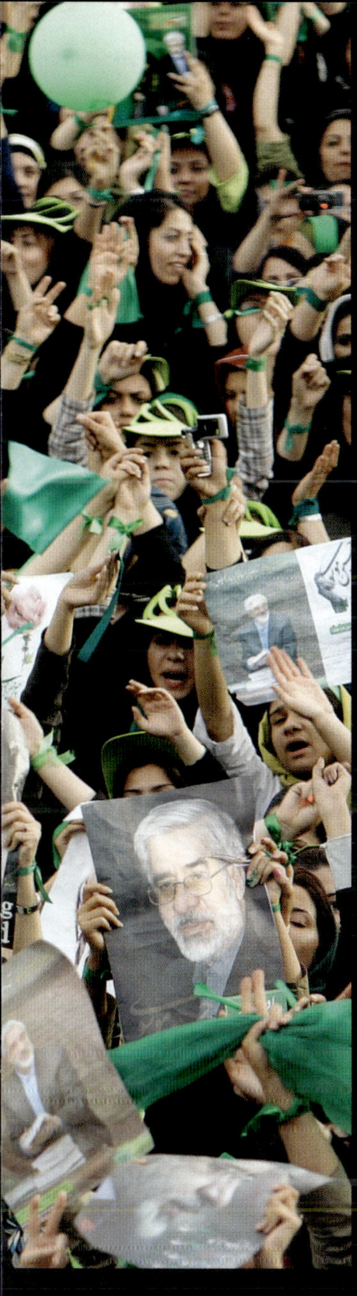

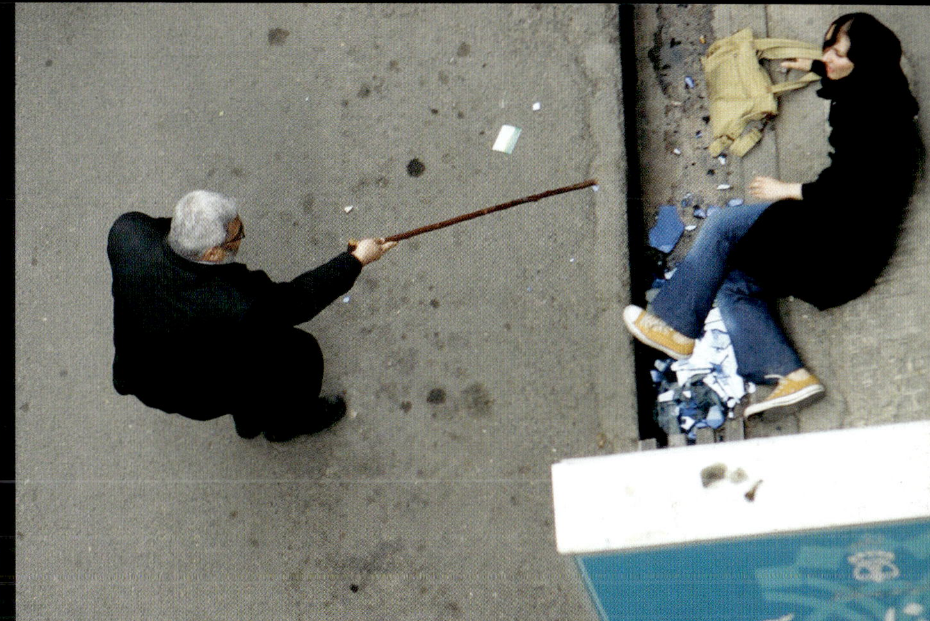

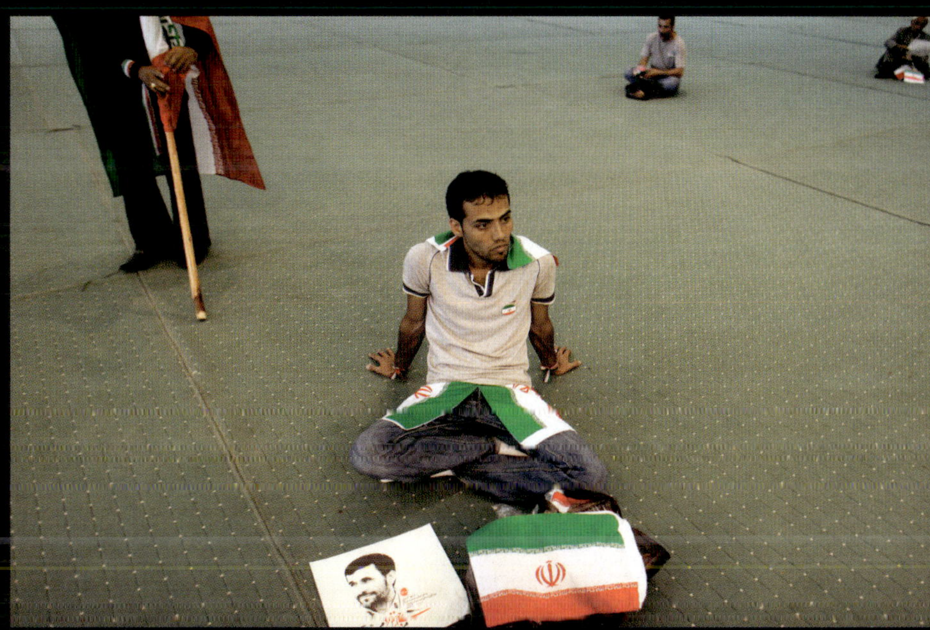

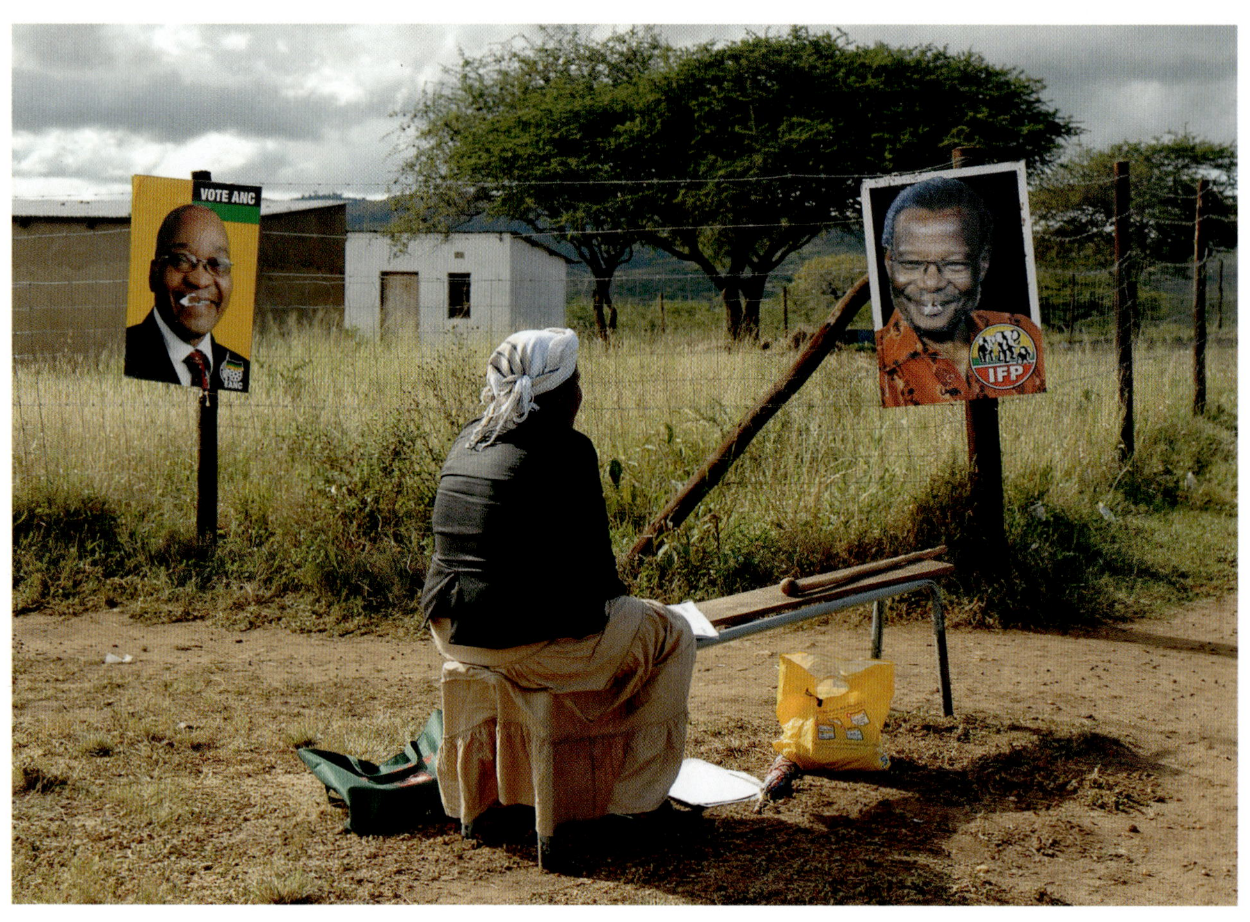

099 Nkandla, South Africa

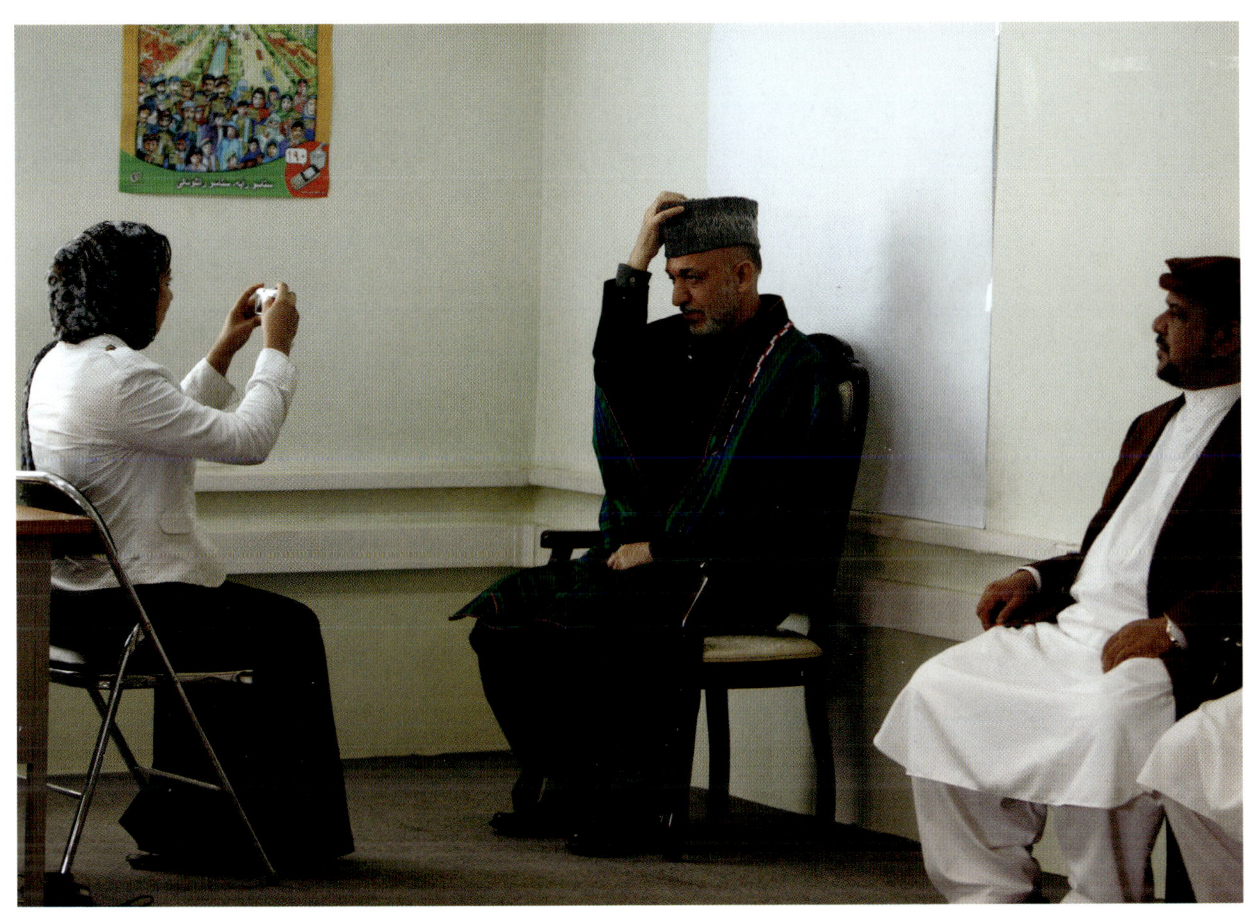

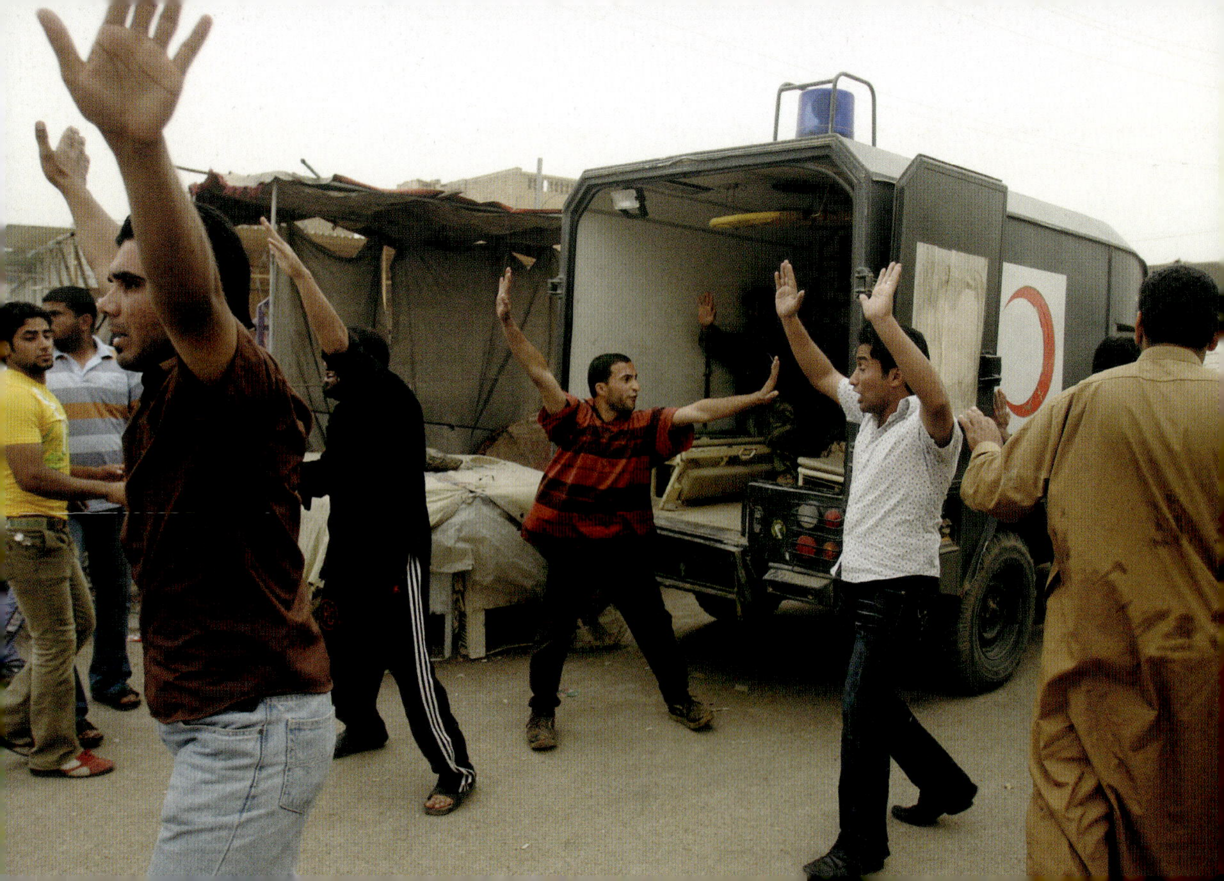

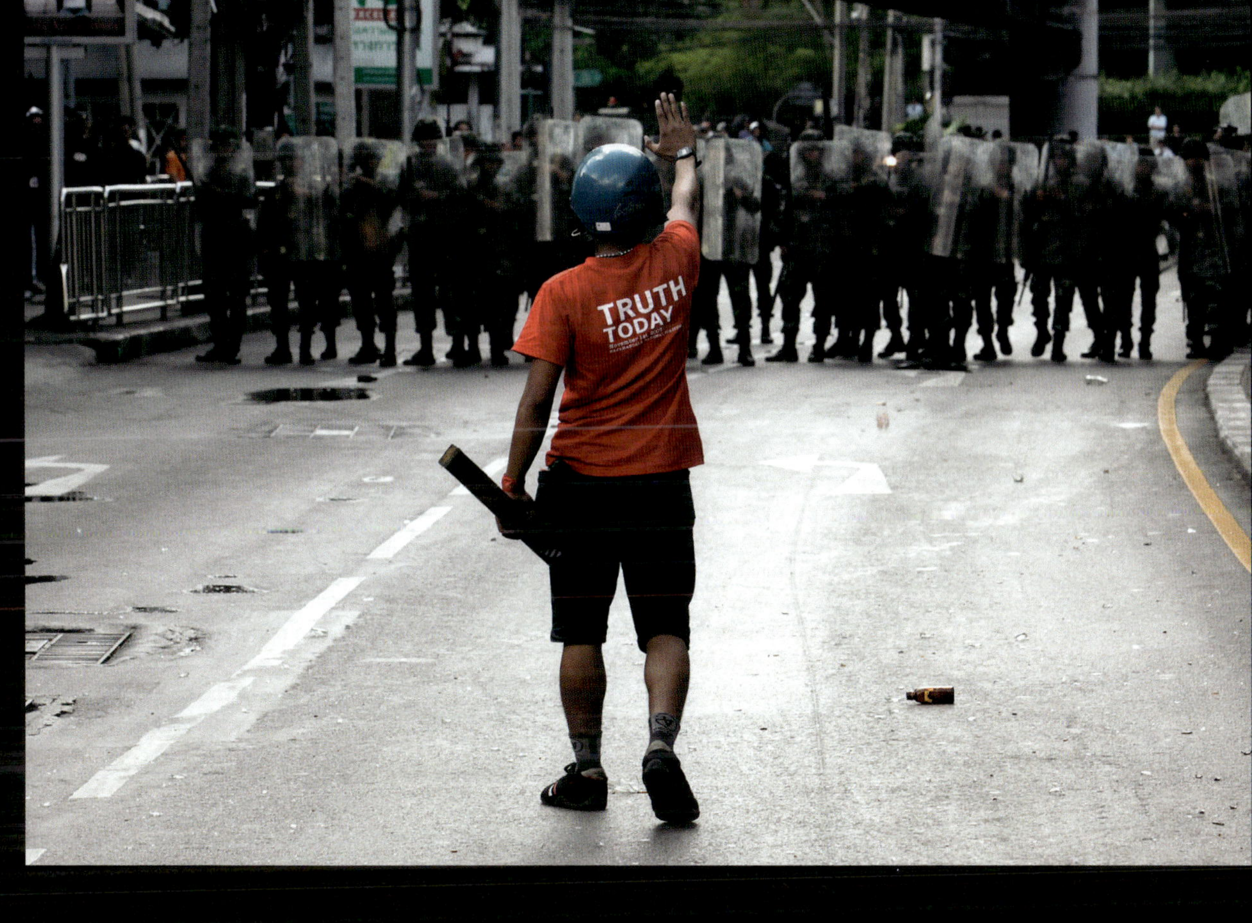
TRUTH
TODAY

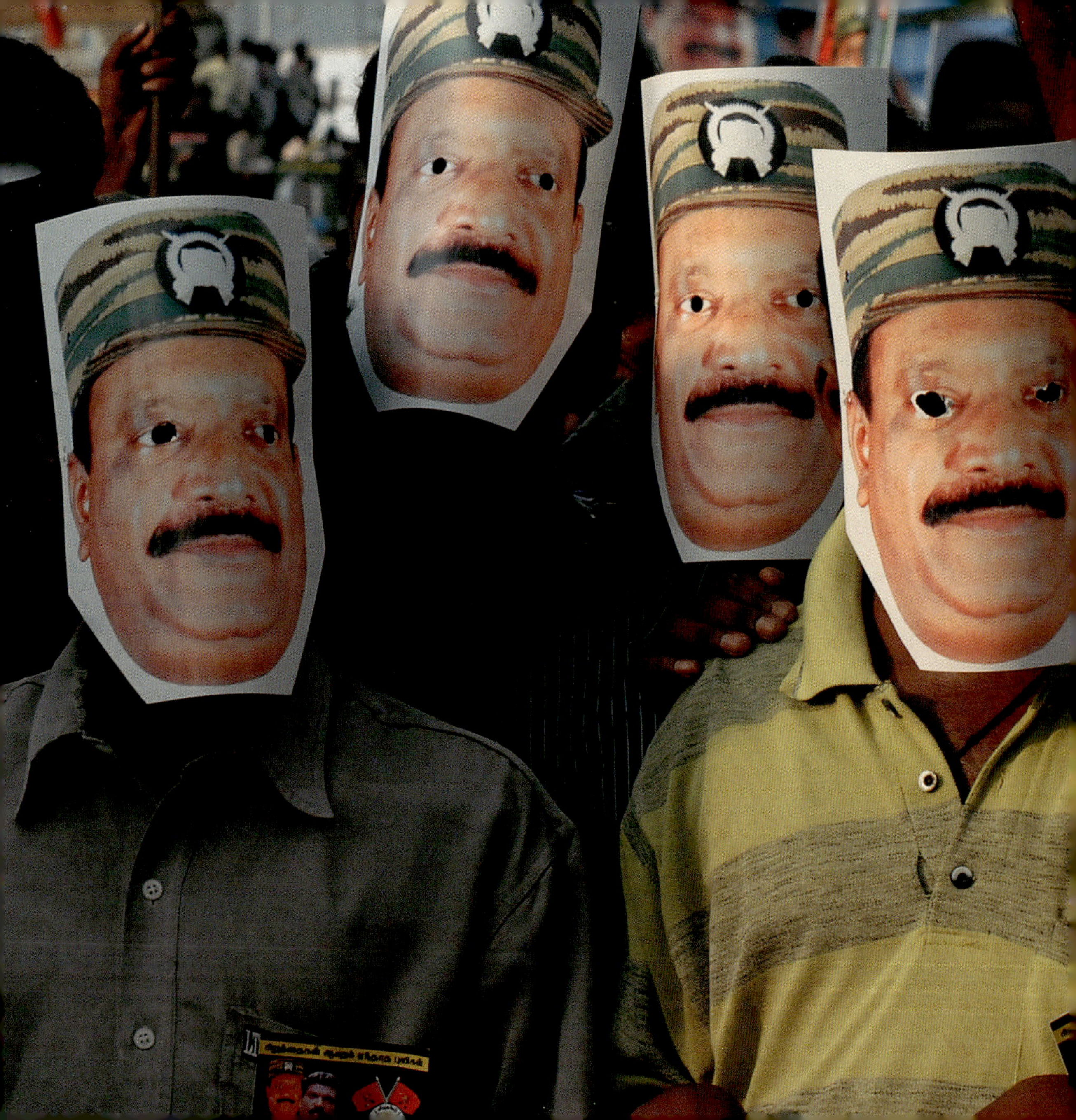

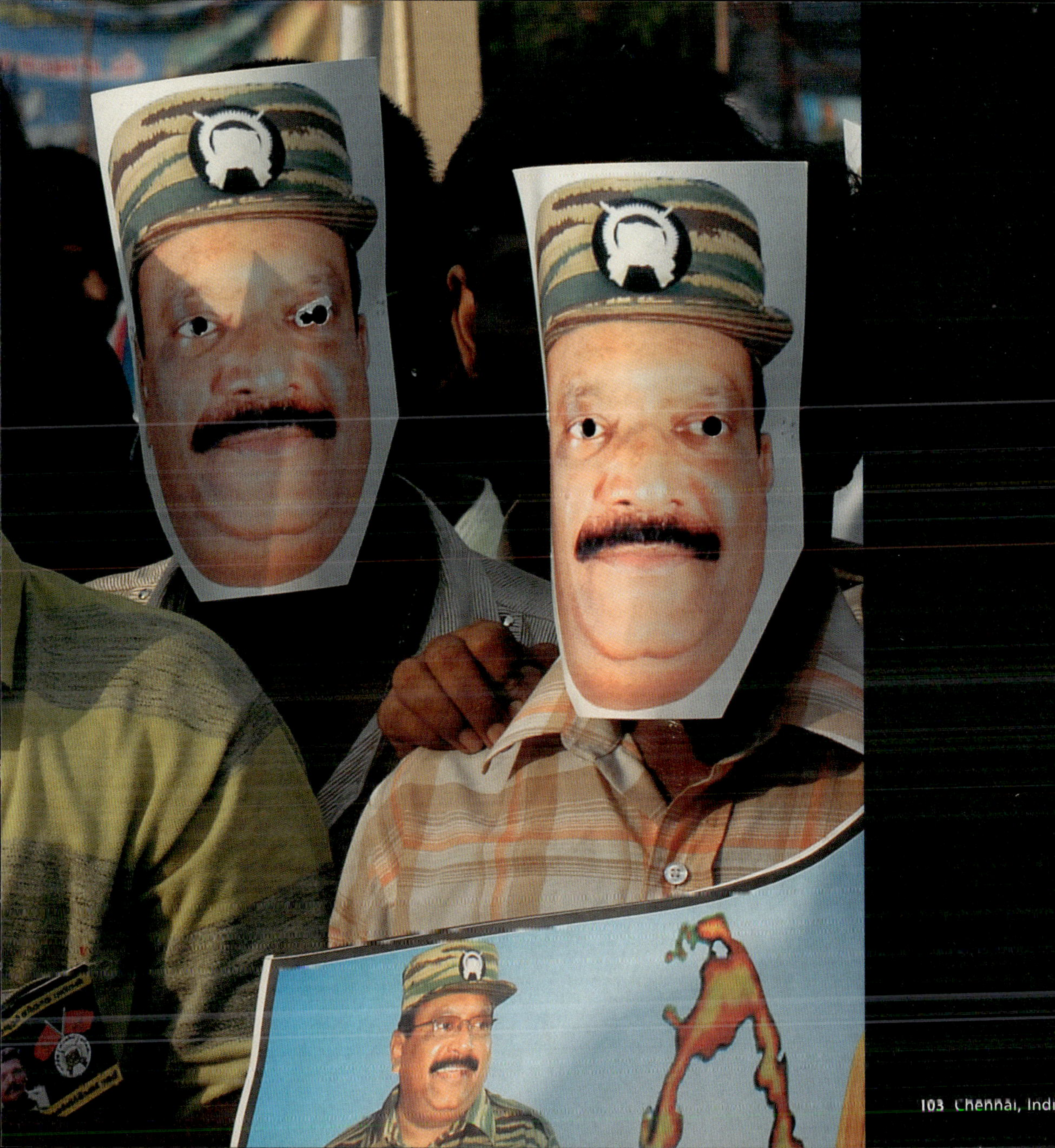
103 Chennai, India

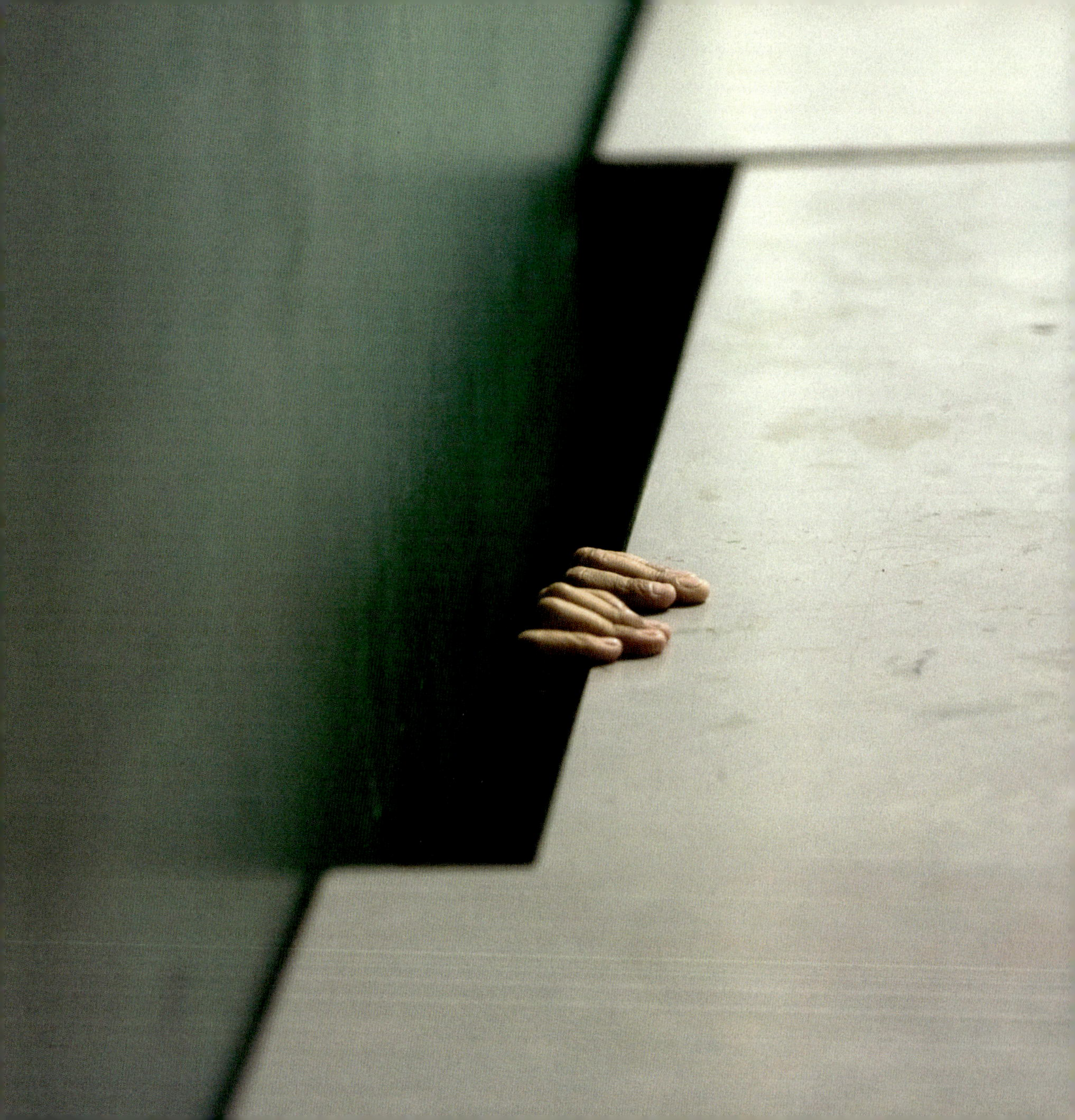

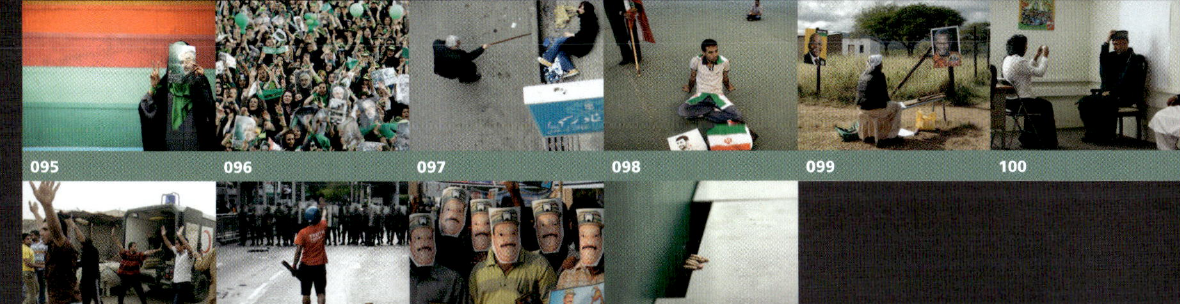

095 A supporter of Iran's presidential election candidate Mirhossein Mousavi covers her face with his picture during a pre-election gathering at a stadium in Tehran. 9 June 2009. Tehran, Iran. Damir Sagolj.

096 Supporters of Mirhossein Mousavi attend a campaign rally in Tehran. 9 June 2009. Tehran, Iran. Ahmed Jadallah.

097 A man gestures towards a woman on the ground during post-election protests in central Tehran. Disputed results plunged Iran into its deepest internal crisis since the 1979 Islamic revolution. Defeated candidate Mirhossein Mousavi said the poll was rigged to secure hardline President Mahmoud Ahmadinejad's re-election. Iranian authorities rejected the charge despite huge opposition protests. 14 June 2009. Tehran, Iran.

098 Supporters of Iranian President Mahmoud Ahmadinejad arrive for a final pre-election gathering in Tehran. 8 June 2009. Tehran, Iran. Damir Sagolj.

099 A South African election official waits for voters at a polling station in Nkandla. The ruling African National Congress won a sweeping election victory despite the strongest opposition challenge since the end of apartheid 15 years earlier. Party leader Jacob Zuma was sworn in as president on 9 May. 22 April 2009. Nkandla, South Africa. Rogan Ward.

100 Afghan President Hamid Karzai adjusts his hat as he is photographed during his registration to stand for re-election. 4 May 2009. Kabul, Afghanistan. Ahmad Masood.

101 Residents seek to prevent people from throwing stones at the Iraqi army at the site of a bomb attack in Baghdad's predominantly Shi'ite Sadr City neighbourhood. Over 50 people were killed and over 75 injured in twin car bomb blasts in a busy market, Iraqi police said. 29 April 2009. Baghdad, Iraq. Kahtan al-Mesiary.

102 A supporter of ousted Thai Prime Minister Thaksin Shinawatra gestures at riot troops guarding a road as the Thai army cracked down on anti-government protesters. Soldiers fired warning shots at activists who responded by hurling petrol bombs. 13 April 2009. Bangkok, Thailand. Sukree Sukplang.

103 Protesters wear masks depicting Vellupillai Prabhakaran, slain leader of the Liberation Tigers of Tamil Eelam (LTTE), during a protest rally against Sri Lanka's President Mahinda Rajapaksa in the southern Indian city of Chennai. Prabhakaran and his son Charles Anthony were killed on 18 May in a climactic gunbattle that resulted in the defeat of the LTTE and the end of Sri Lanka's 25-year civil war. 28 May 2009. Chennai, India. Babu.

104 An Israeli boy takes cover under a desk in a bomb shelter at a school in Jerusalem during a nationwide civil defence drill. 2 June 2009. Jerusalem. Ronen Zvulun.

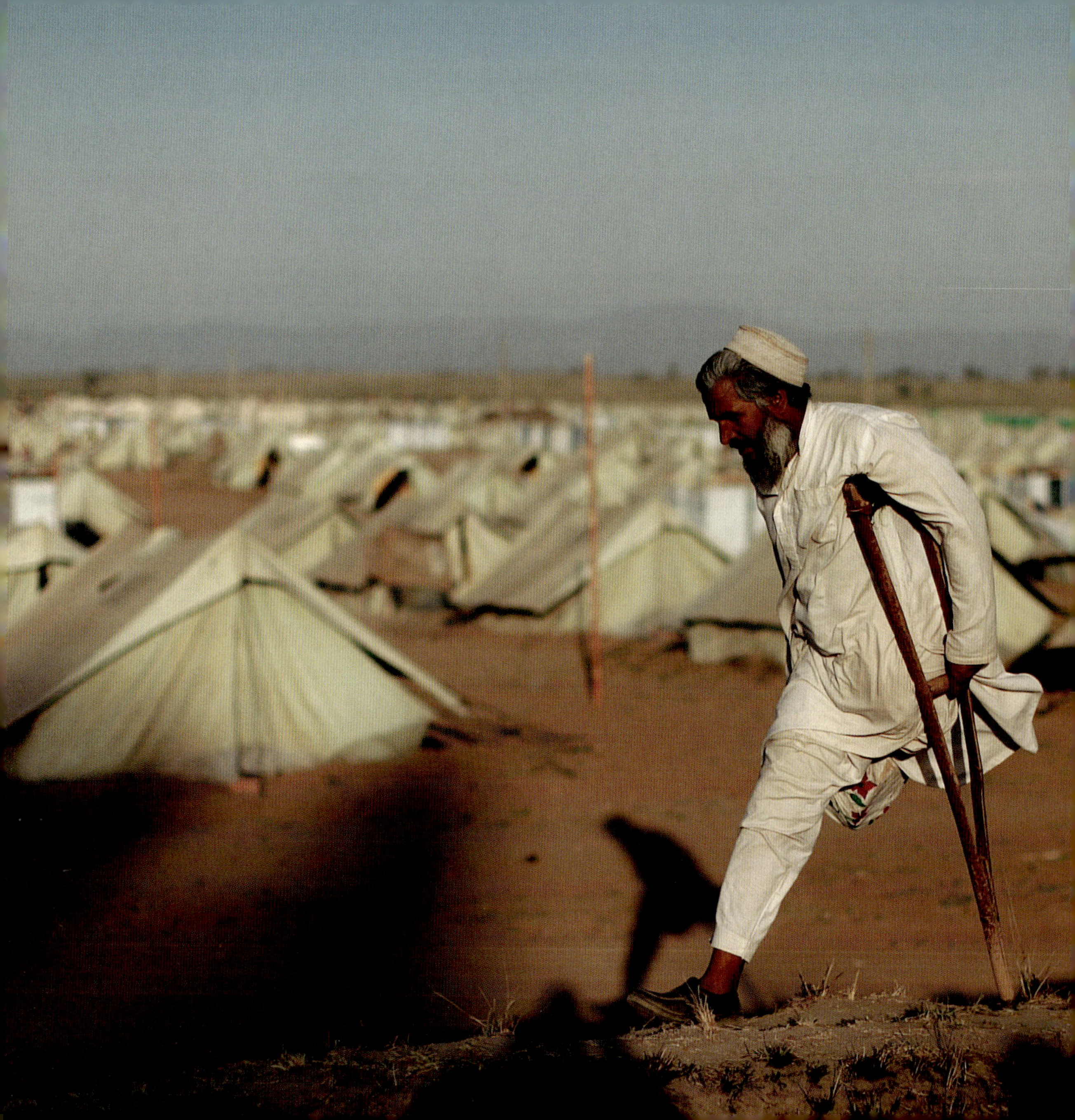

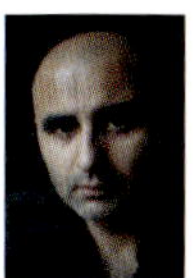

ADREES LATIF
Photographer
Born: 1973, Lahore, Pakistan
Based: Pakistan
Nationality: Pakistani/American

Refuge from Swat Valley

A cloud of red dust engulfed our car as we approached a UNHCR camp in Swabi, Pakistan, where residents of the scenic Swat Valley were taking refuge after a military offensive against the Taliban forced nearly two million people from their homes. Camps started filling in early May, and by June had grown into settlements of thousands under a baking sun. There was little privacy for a people traditionally very conservative and reserved.

As I wandered the maze of tents searching for photos, I realized I was being watched intently. Although Pakistani born, I stuck out as an outsider from head to toe – glasses, clothes, cameras and shoes.

On the horizon I saw two girls of about 12 with empty steel bowls heading to a camp kitchen for a nightly handout of bread and broth. I saw my foreground and background coming together. But after shooting an initial frame, I heard a man screaming in Pashto. He seized me tightly by my shirt and shook me. 'I have been watching you,' he said in broken Urdu. 'I have been watching your eyes. You have been hunting! With whose permission are you taking photographs of our girls?'

Within seconds, 100 or more onlookers had gathered. I gripped my aggressor's bicep, if only to keep my balance as he shoved me from side to side. 'You are right sir,' I said. 'I am hunting for an image that will show the world what is happening here. I am a Pakistani and I am Muslim! If you do not trust me to take a picture, who will you trust?'

A few men in the crowd nodded and I sensed my opportunity to escape. Still gripping his arm, I pulled him to me. 'I am your brother, I will pray for you,' I said before breaking away.

I returned to the camp almost a month later, after the Pakistani military announced Swat to be cleared of militants. The inhabitants were eager to head home. Camp authorities had told people to prepare to leave, but when transport did not arrive as scheduled, frustrated residents attacked staff and helped themselves to supplies. Uproar ensued.

In the mêlée of baton-charging policemen and fleeing villagers, I came eye-to-eye with the man who had accosted me before. He grabbed me momentarily by my wrist. 'Thank you for coming. I now understand why you are here,' he said, before running off with a bag of supplies.

105 Displaced Swat Valley resident Phakher Khan walks along a canal running through the UNHCR Yar Hussain camp. 14 July 2009. Swabi, Pakistan.

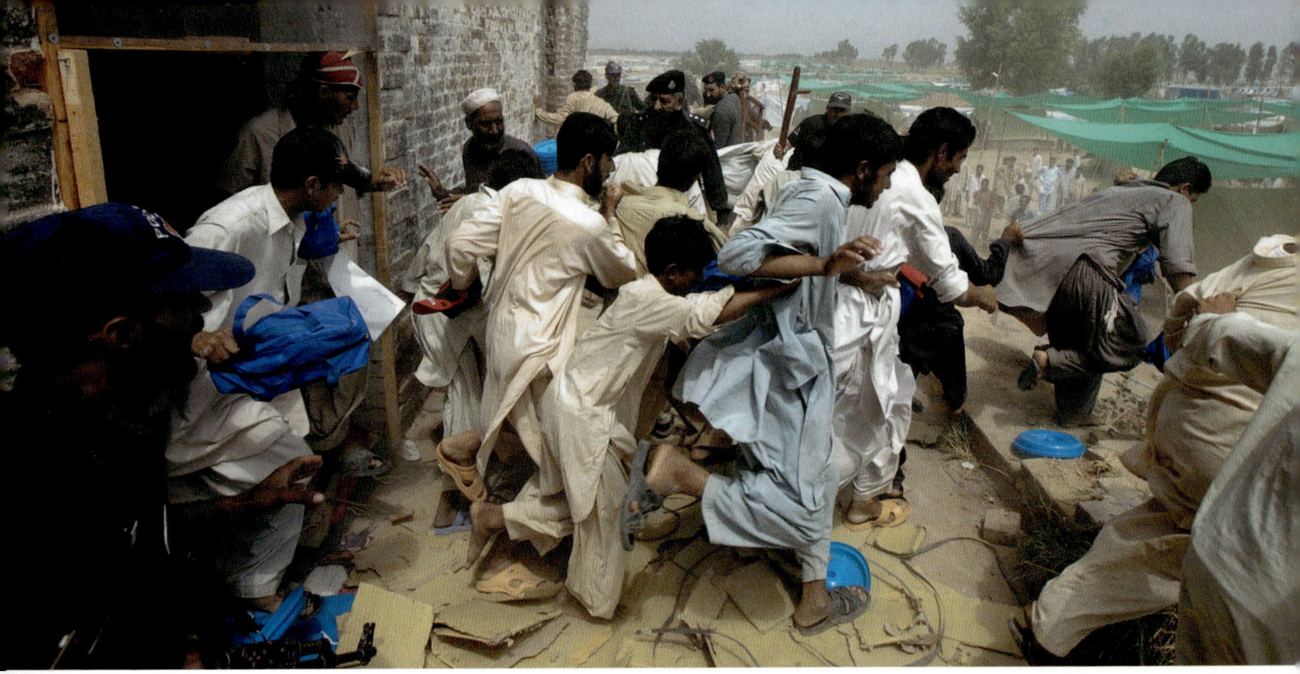

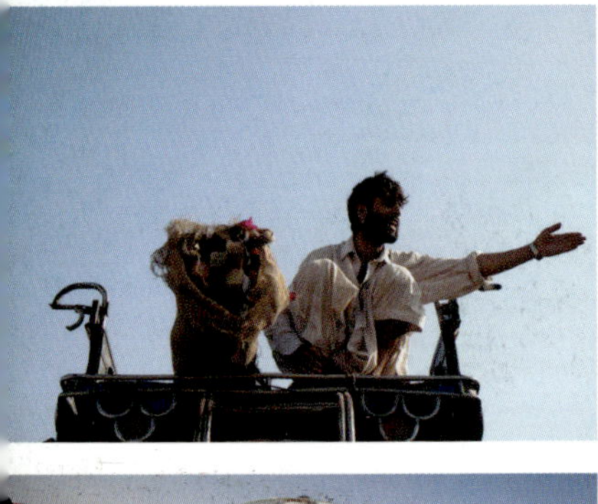
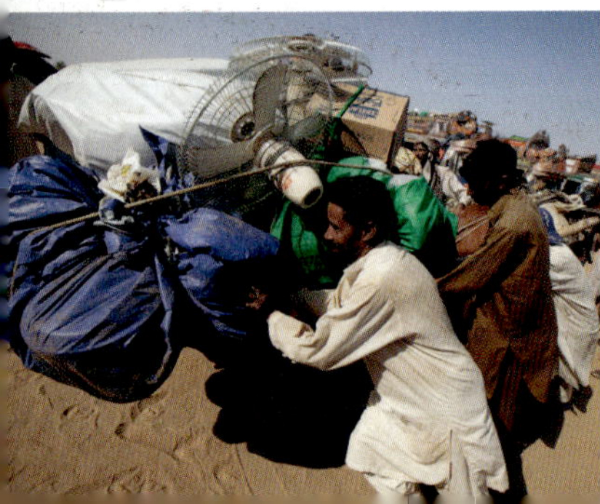
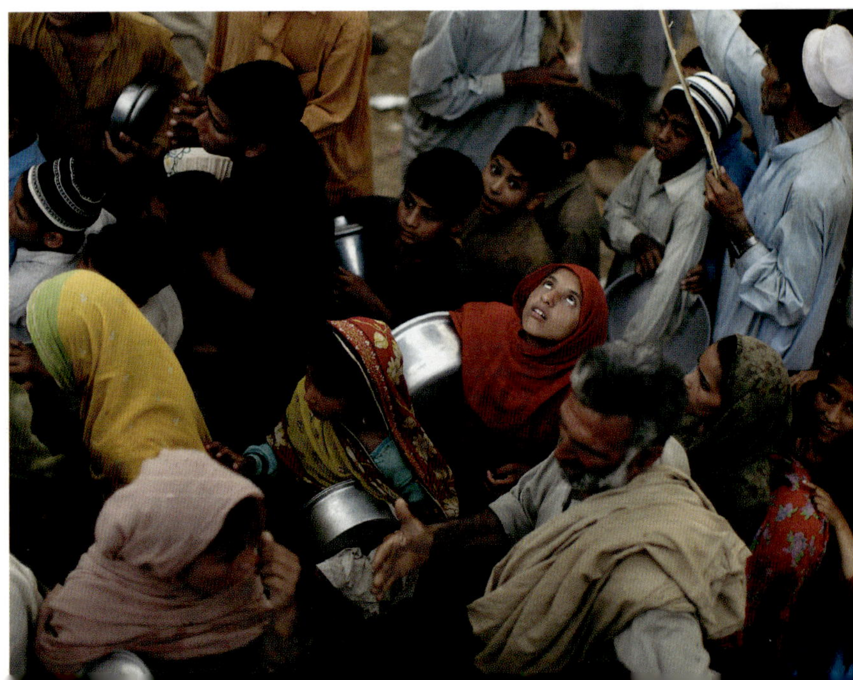

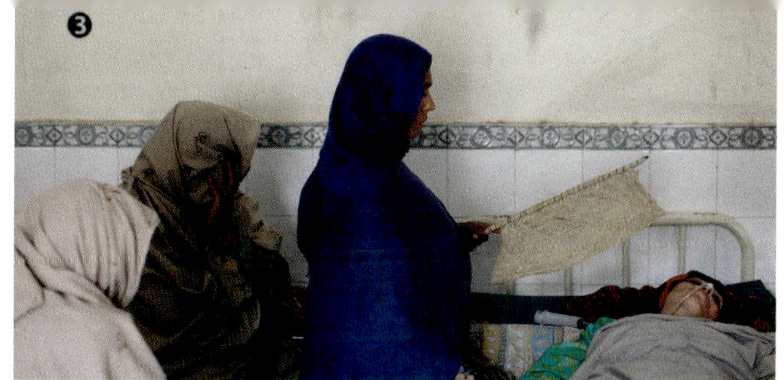

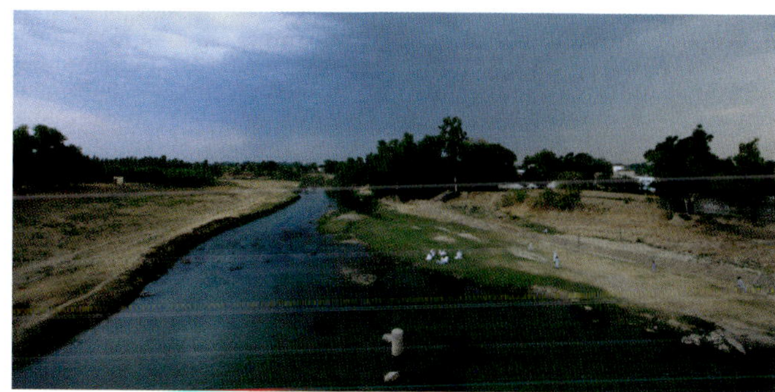

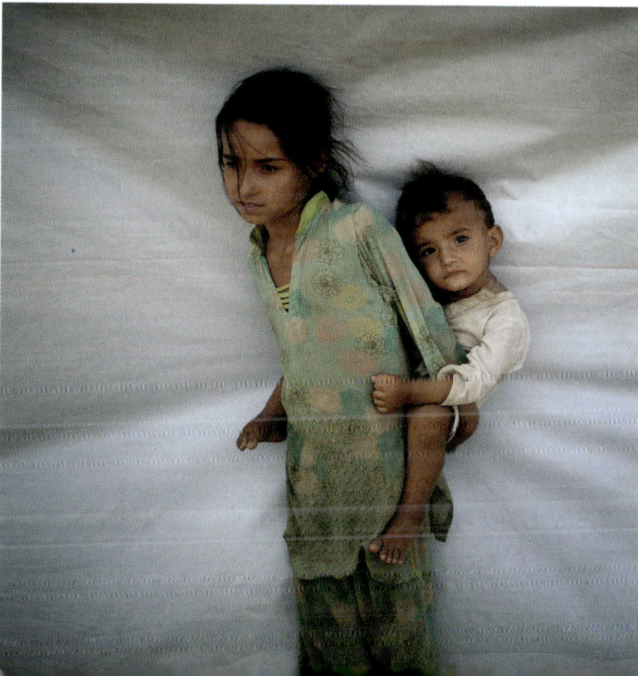

106 Internally displaced people flee after looting a supply room as police arrive on the scene at the UNHCR Yar Hussain camp in Swabi district, about 120 km (75 miles) northwest of Islamabad. 13 July 2009. Swabi, Pakistan. 107 A man helps others load their belongings onto a bus scheduled to take them home to the Swat Valley region. 14 July 2009. Swabi, Pakistan. 108 Men push a horse cart loaded with their belongings towards a bus scheduled to take them home. 14 July 2009. Swabi, Pakistan. 109 A girl looks up towards rain clouds while standing in line for curry and bread at the Yar Hussain camp. 1 June 2009. Swabi, Pakistan. 110 Family members stand over a woman awaiting medical treatment at a hospital in Daggar in Buner district, where the Pakistani army began its campaign against the Taliban. 21 June 2009. Daggar, Pakistan. 111 Men sit alongside a river running through Mardan district, about 150 km (95 miles) northwest of Islamabad. 19 June 2009. Mardan, Pakistan. 112 Sadaf, a six-year-old girl from Swat, holds her two-year-old brother Ali as they stand outside their family's tent at the Yar Hussain camp. 12 July 2009. Swabi, Pakistan. Adrees Latif.

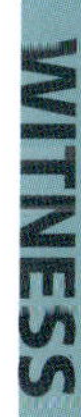

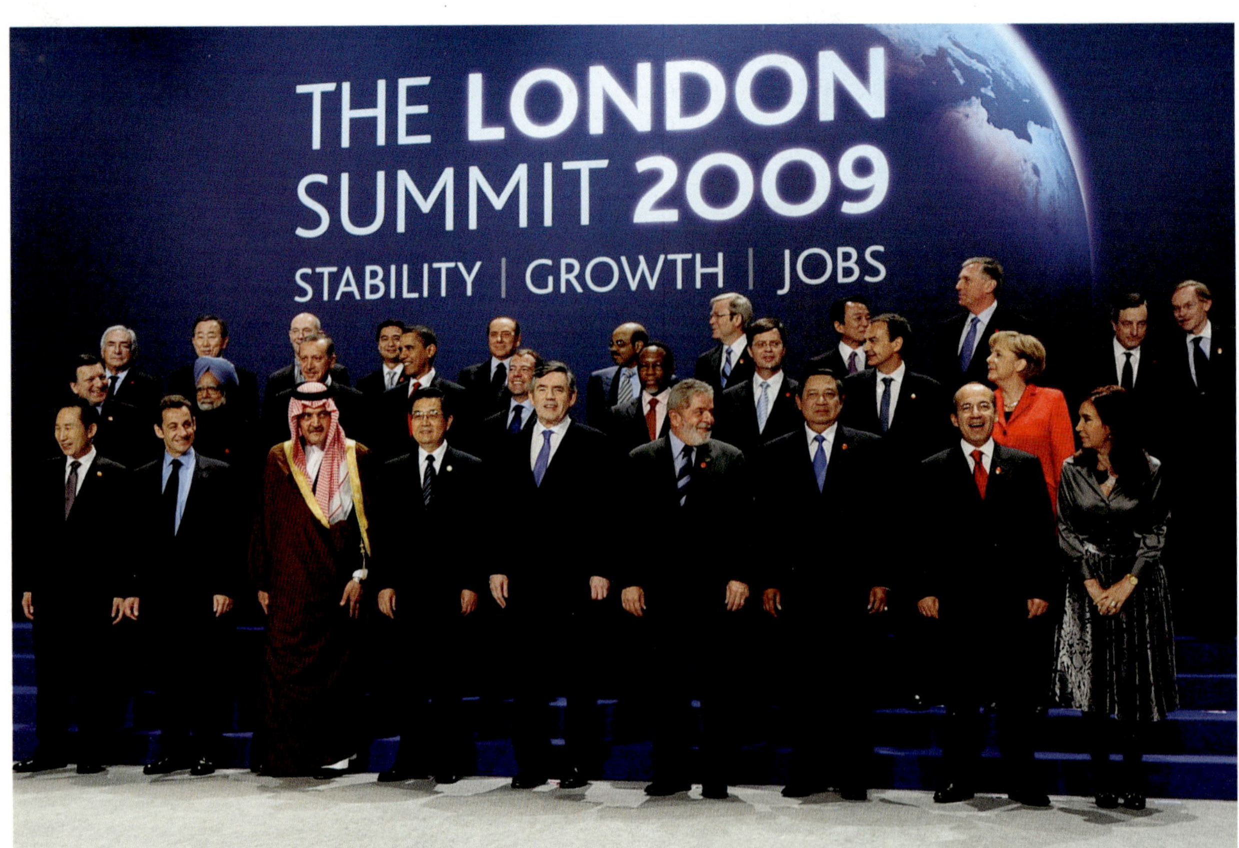

THE LONDON
SUMMIT 2009
STABILITY | GROWTH | JOBS

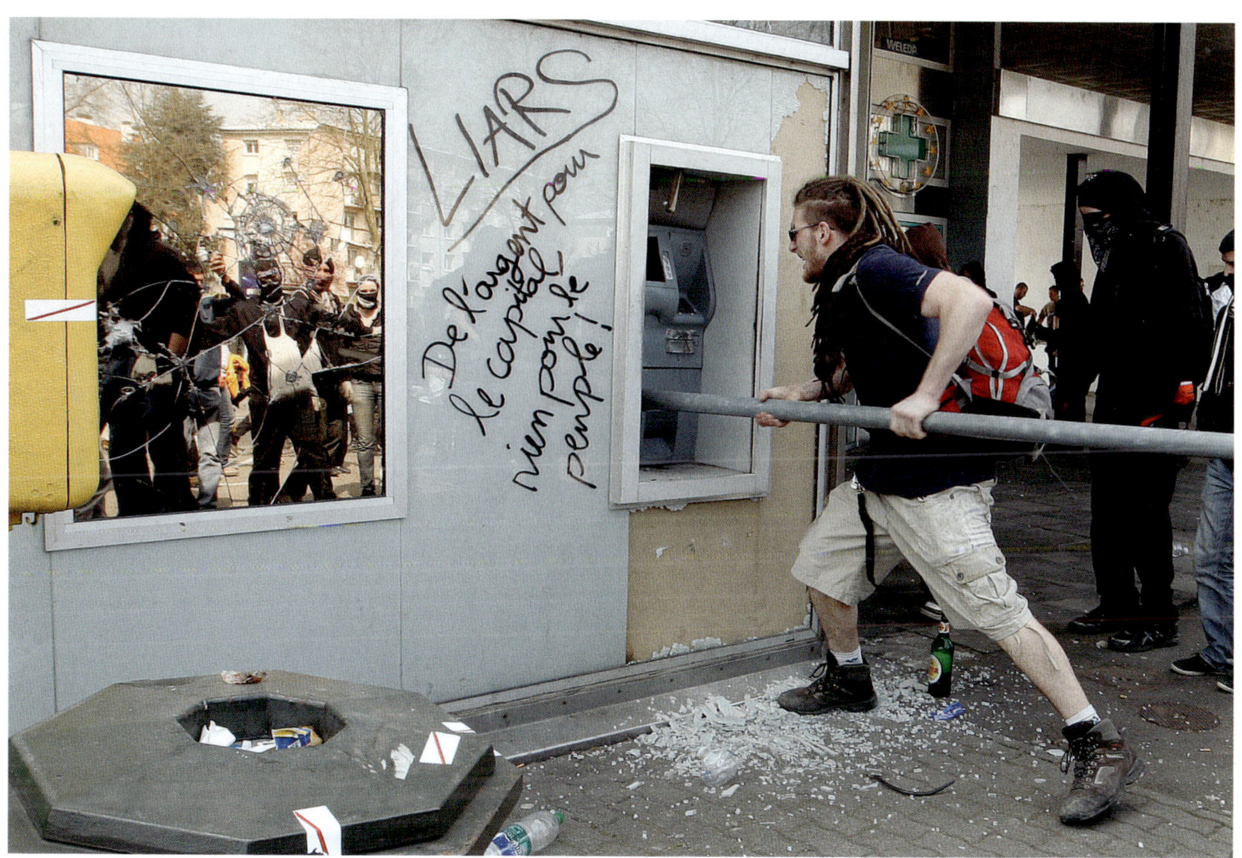

LIARS
De l'argent pour le capital! rien pour le peuple!

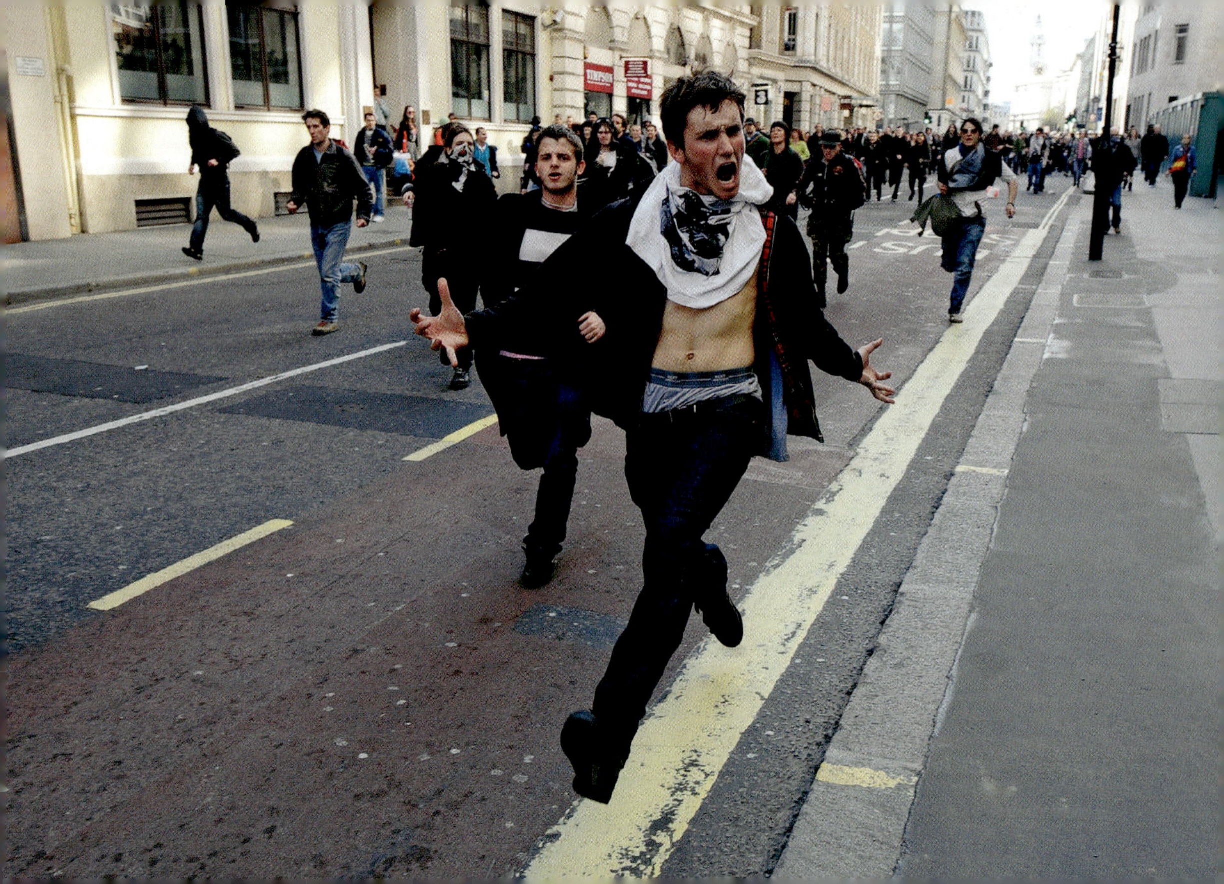

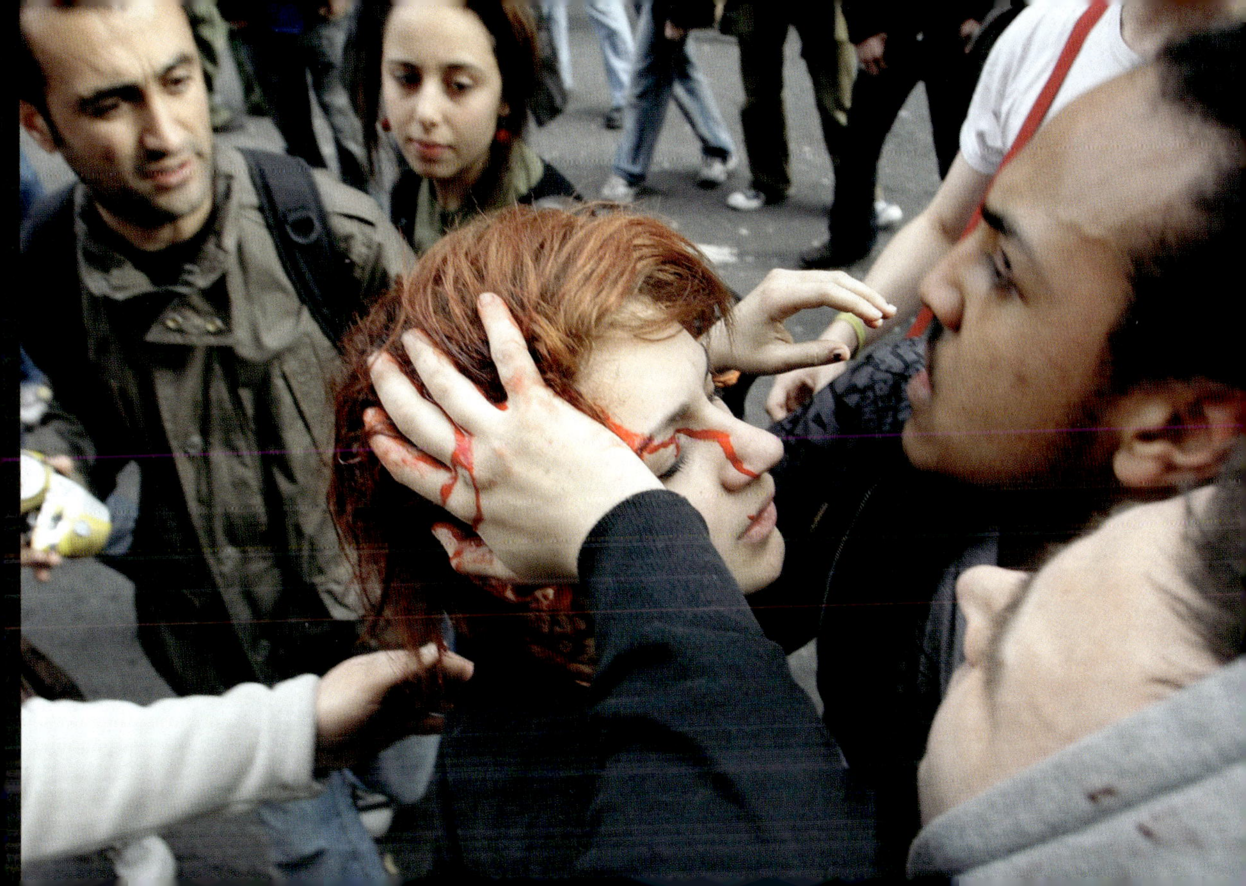

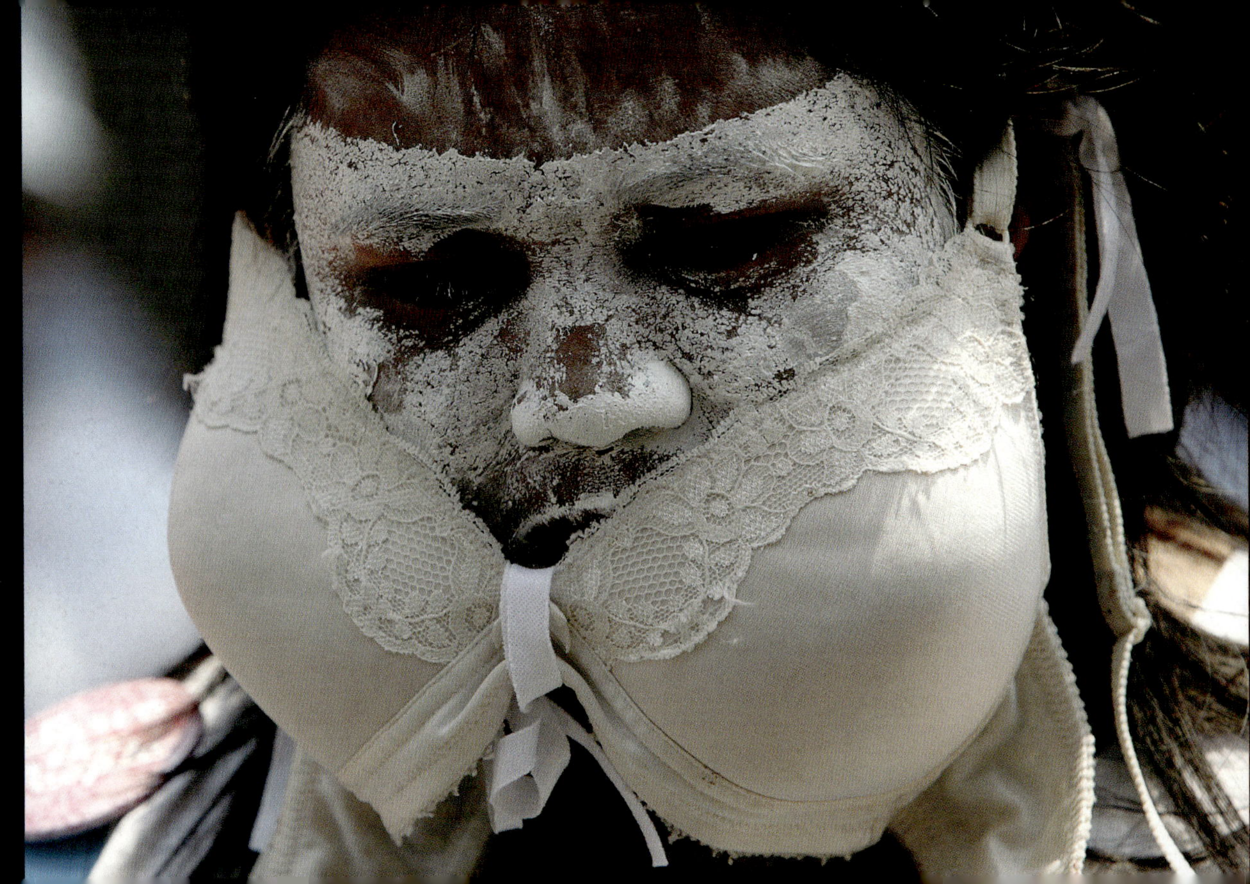

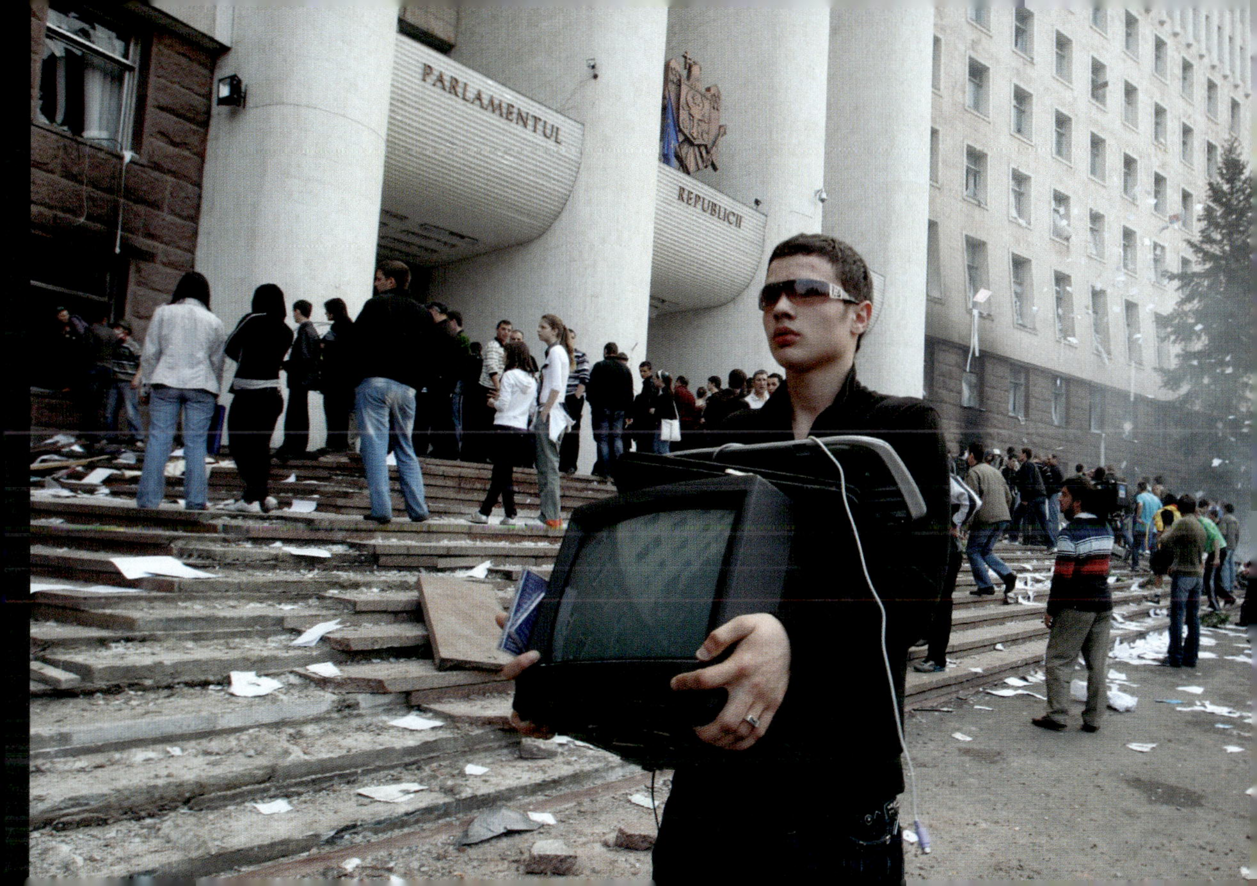

PARLAMENTUL
REPUBLICII

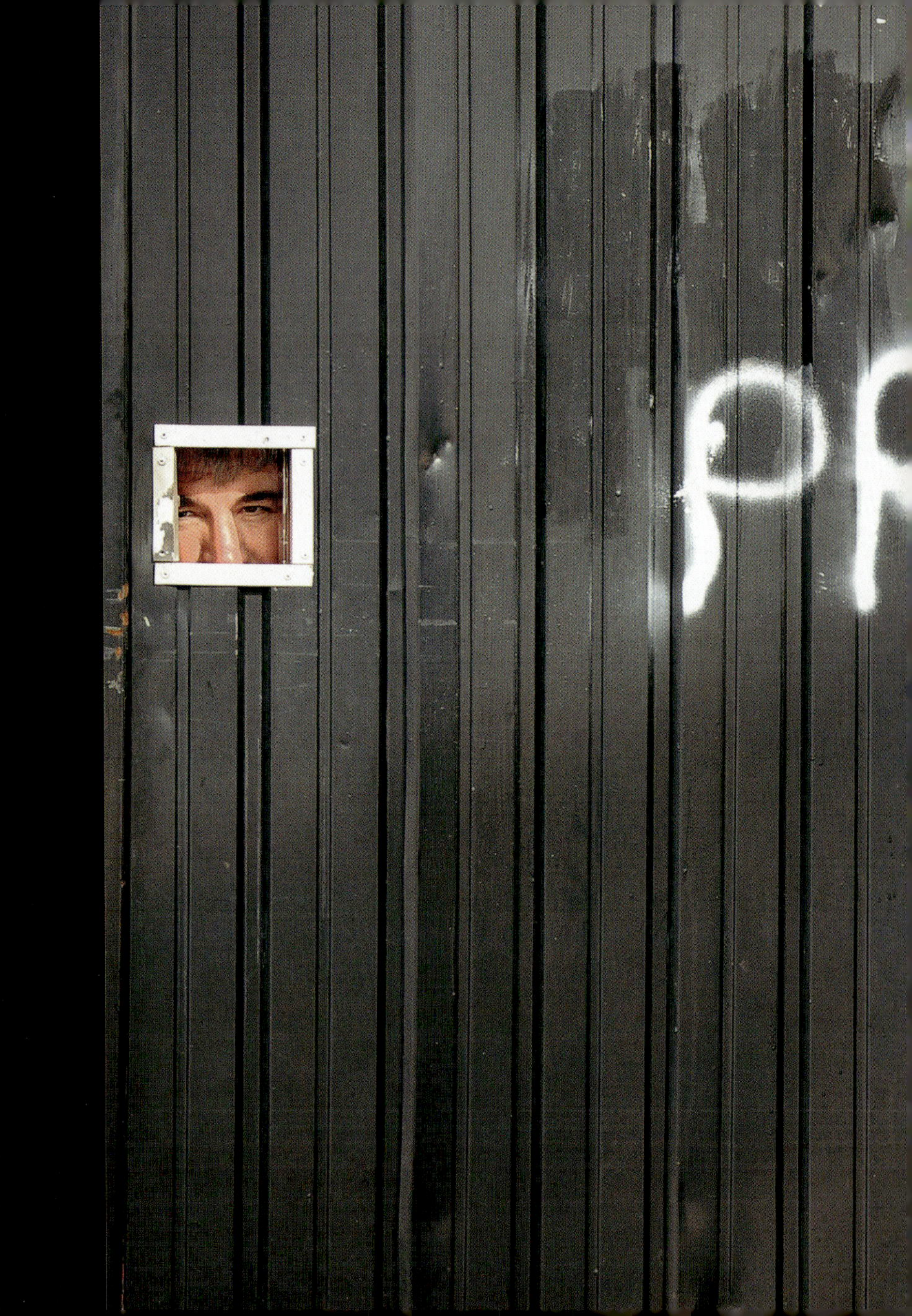

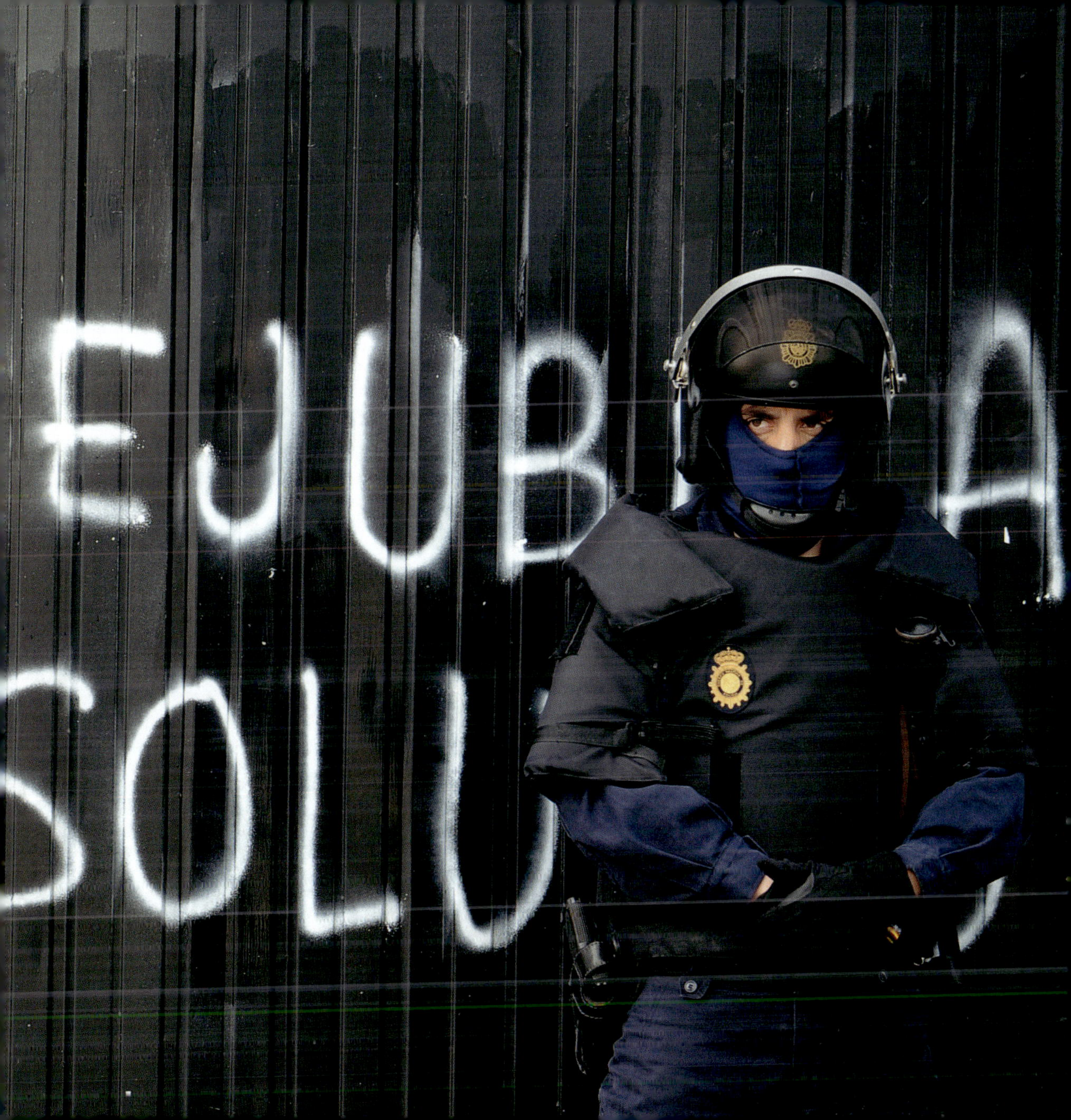

EJUB
SOLU

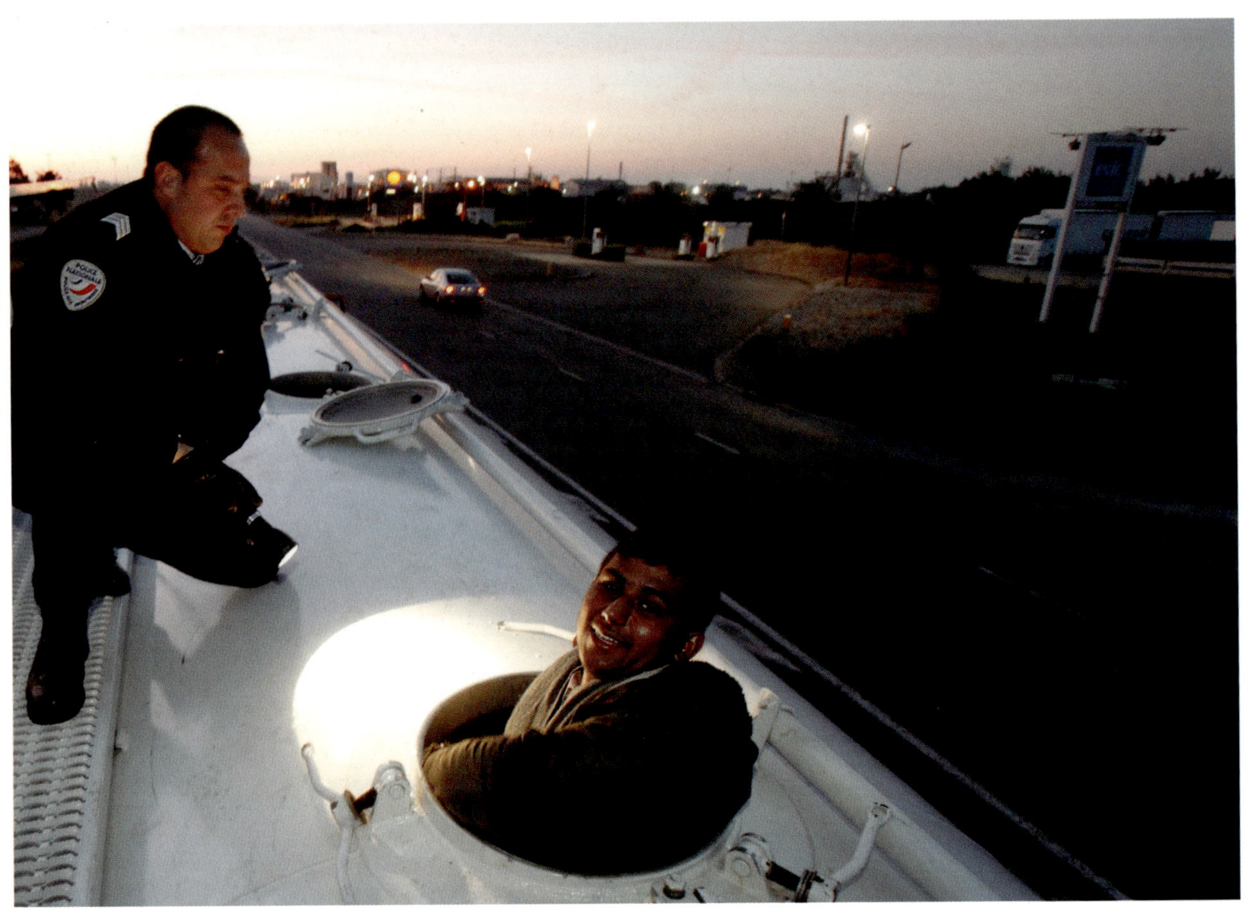

120 Calais, France

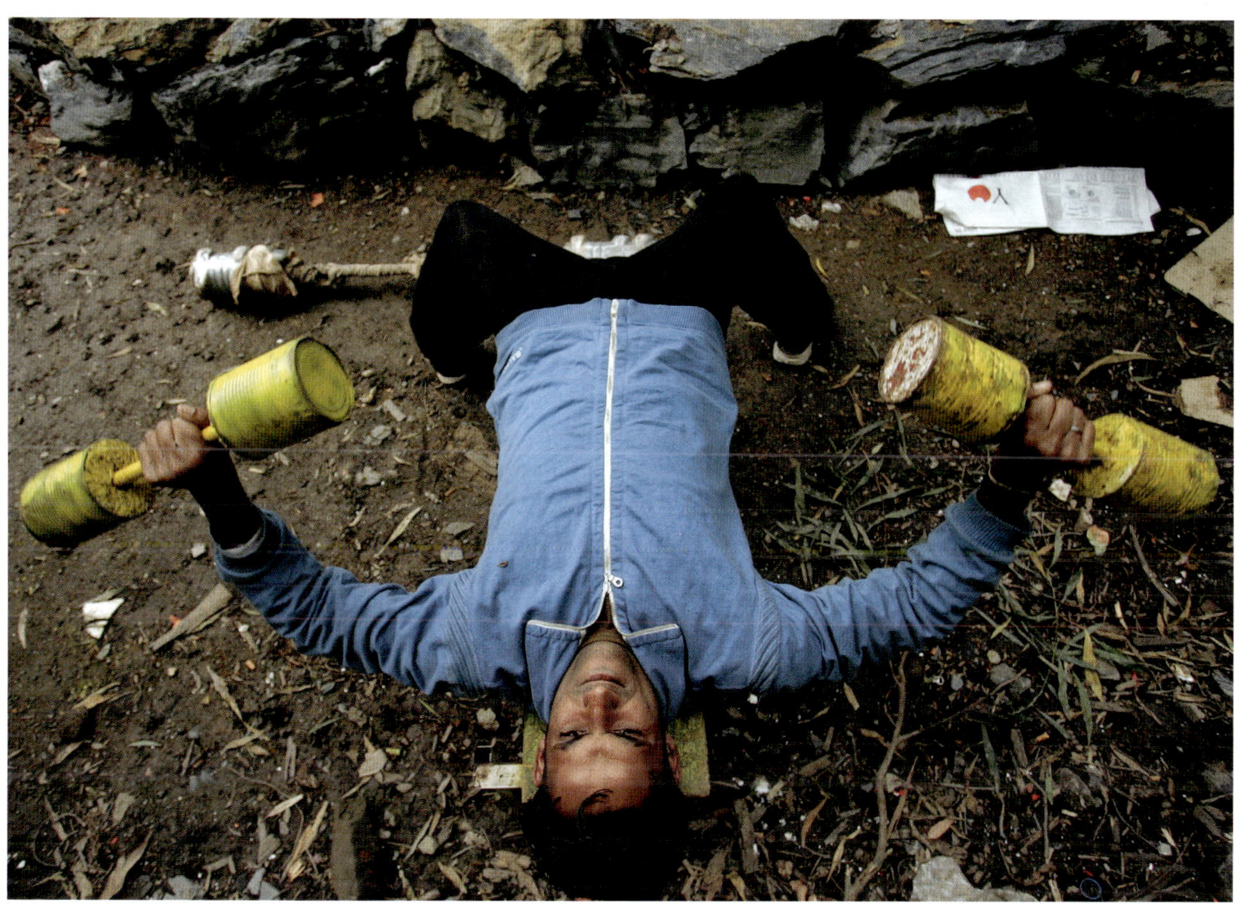

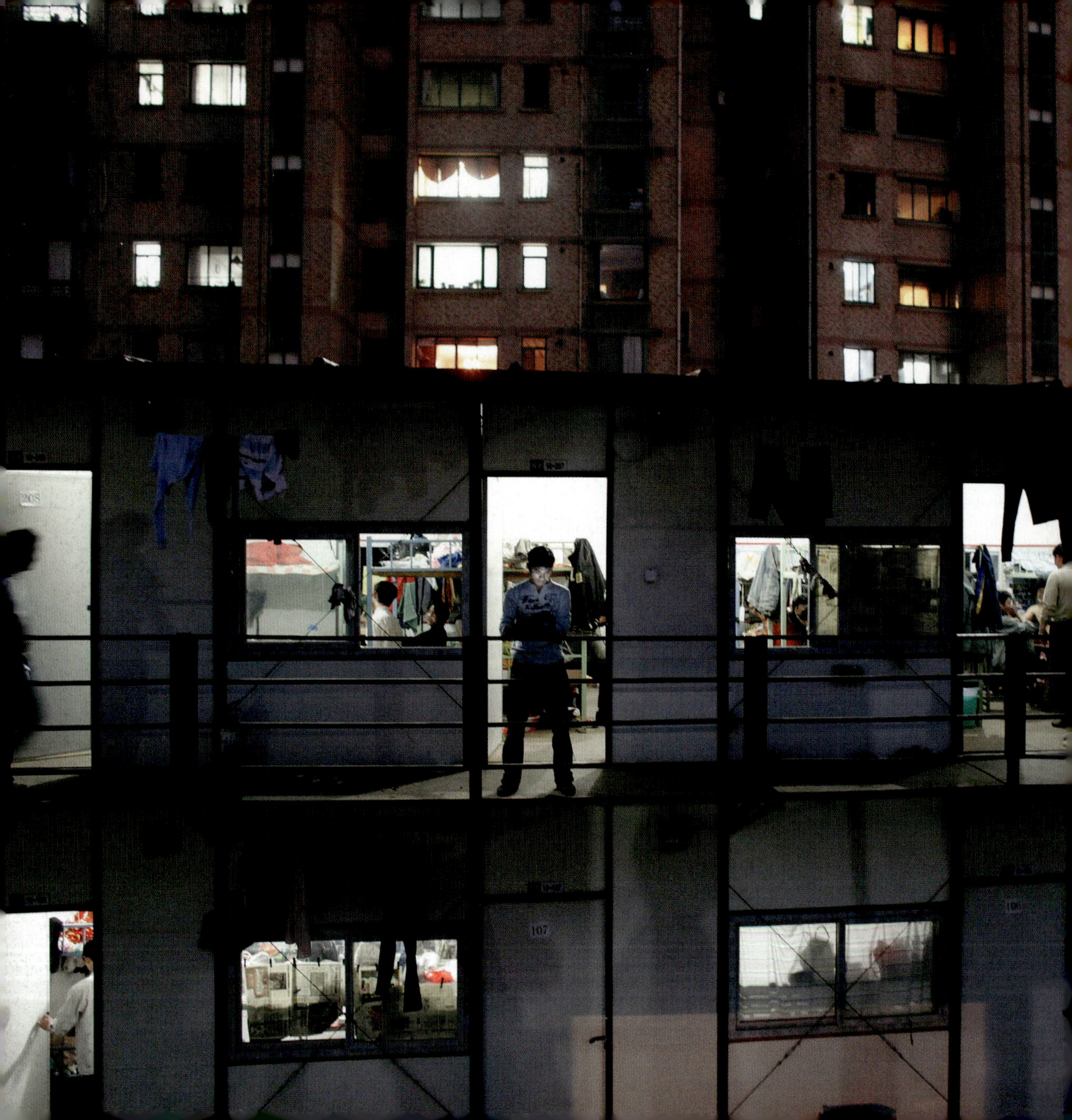

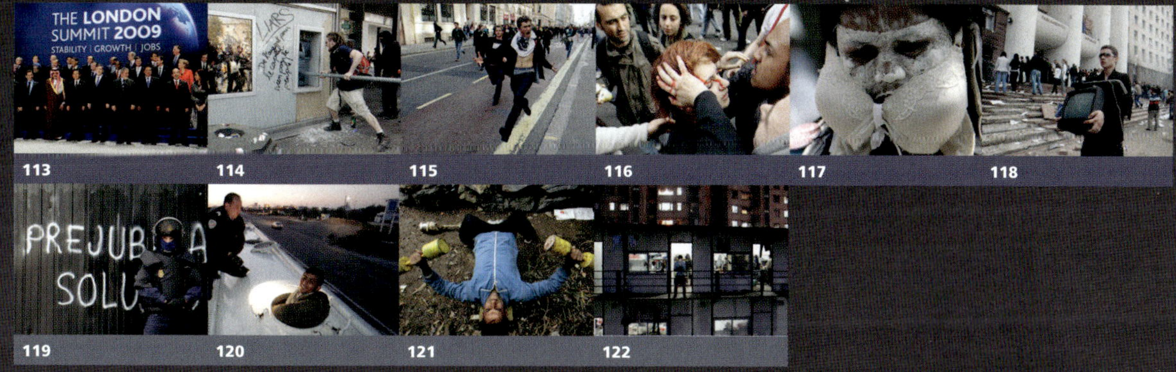

113 Heads of delegation pose for a group photograph at a G20 summit in London. 2 April 2009. London, Britain. Dylan Martinez.

114 Protesters attack a bank cash machine during anti-NATO demonstrations in a suburb outside Strasbourg as the military alliance celebrated its 60th anniversary at a summit co-hosted by Germany and France. The graffiti reads 'LIARS. Money for Capital, Nothing for the People'. 4 April 2009. Strasbourg, France. Vincent Kessler.

115 Demonstrators charge through a street in London during protests to coincide with a G20 summit meeting. Activists clashed with riot police and smashed bank windows in protest against a system they said had robbed the poor to benefit the rich. 1 April 2009. London, Britain. Dylan Martinez.

116 People carry an injured demonstrator during a protest near the Bank of England in London ahead of a G20 summit meeting in the city. 1 April 2009. London, Britain. Stefan Wermuth.

117 A dismissed employee of underwear manufacturer Triumph International demonstrates in front of Manila's Department of Labour and Employment. The company announced it was to close its Philippines operations with the loss of over 1,600 jobs, according to protest organizers. 30 June 2009. Manila, Philippines. Romeo Ranoco.

118 A looter carries a television out of the parliament building in the Moldovan capital Chisinau. Protesters denouncing a Communist election victory stormed the president's offices and broke into parliament, where they hurled furniture and computers into the street. 7 April 2009. Chisinau, Moldova. Gleb Garanich.

119 A policeman stands guard outside an occupied shipyard building in Gijón, northern Spain. The graffiti reads 'Solution for early retirement workers'. Former employees who had taken early retirement from shipbuilding company Naval Gijón occupied buildings and demanded assurances of their income after the forthcoming closure of the company. 19 May 2009. Gijón, Spain. Eloy Alonso.

120 A border policeman looks on as an asylum seeker emerges from the hatch of a tanker truck near the northern French port of Calais in the early morning. Hundreds of migrants, mostly from Iraq, Afghanistan and Eritrea, were living in a makeshift camp in woods near Calais and making nightly attempts to board trucks crossing the Channel by train or ferry. 17 June 2009. Calais, France. Pascal Rossignol.

121 An Indian immigrant exercises in his hiding place in the mountains near the Spanish city of Ceuta on the northern coast of Morocco. Illegal migrants see Spain's enclaves in Morocco as gateways to a better life in Europe, but many remain stranded there due to lack of proper immigration papers. 28 April 2009. Ceuta, Spain. Rafael Marchante.

122 A migrant construction worker checks his mobile phone outside his dormitory after a working shift at the World Expo 2010 construction site in Shanghai. 15 April 2009. Shanghai, China. Nir Elias.

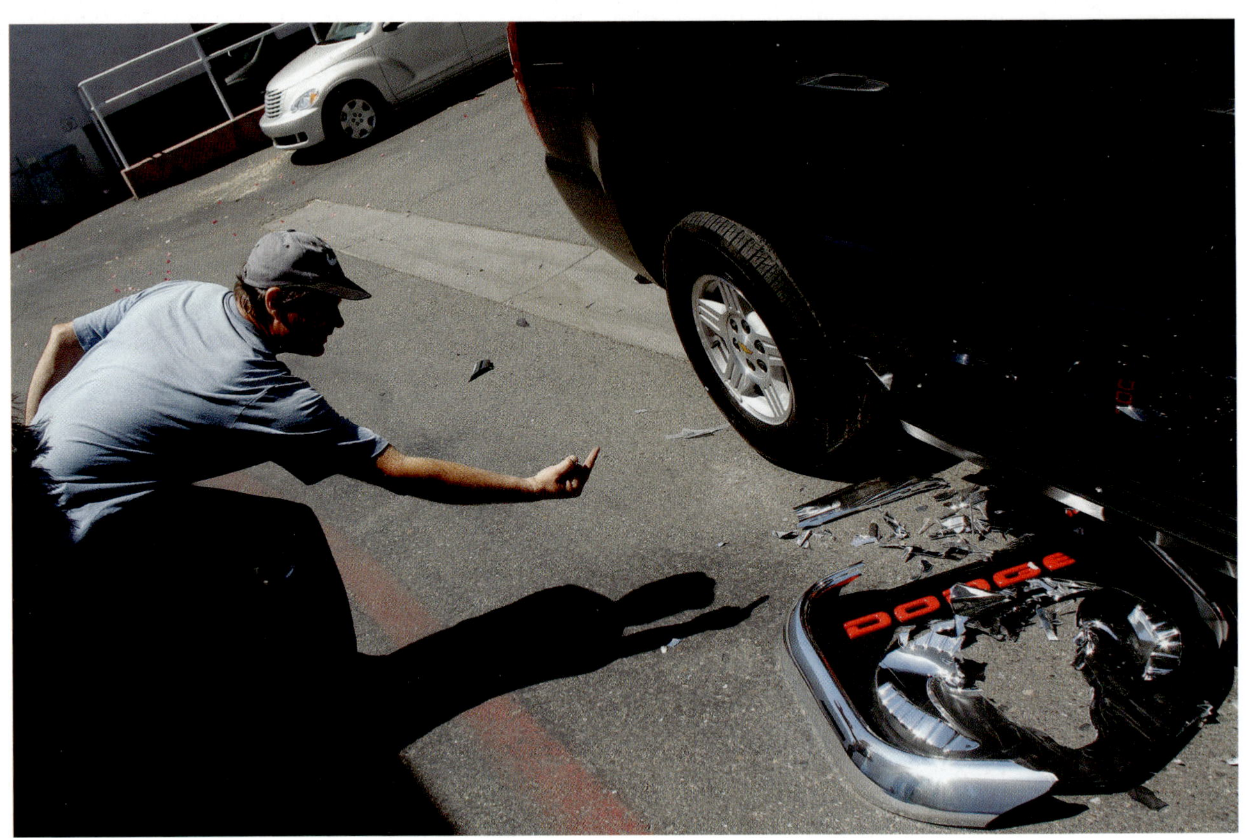
DODGE

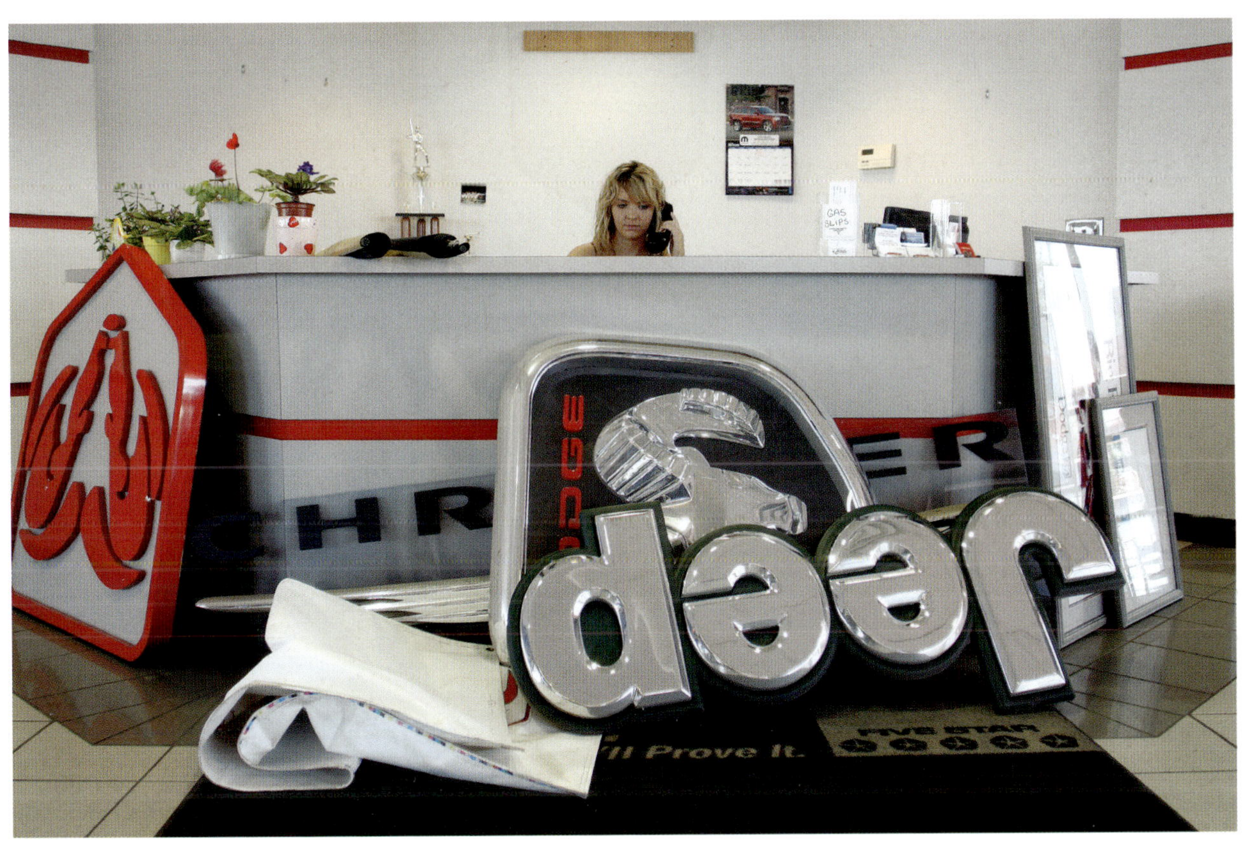
CHRYSLER
DODGE
deep
GAS
SLIPS
'll Prove It.
FIVE STAR

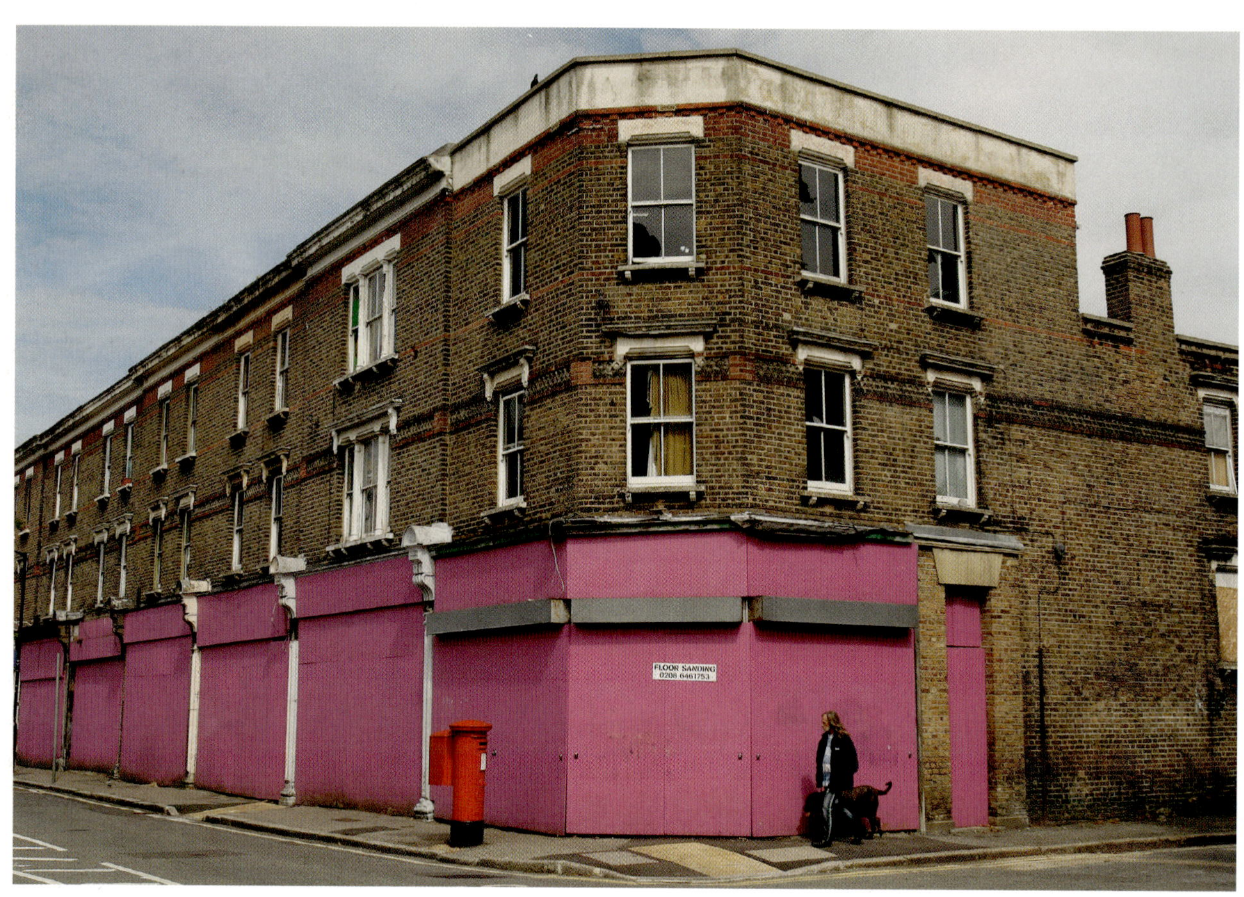

125 London, Britain

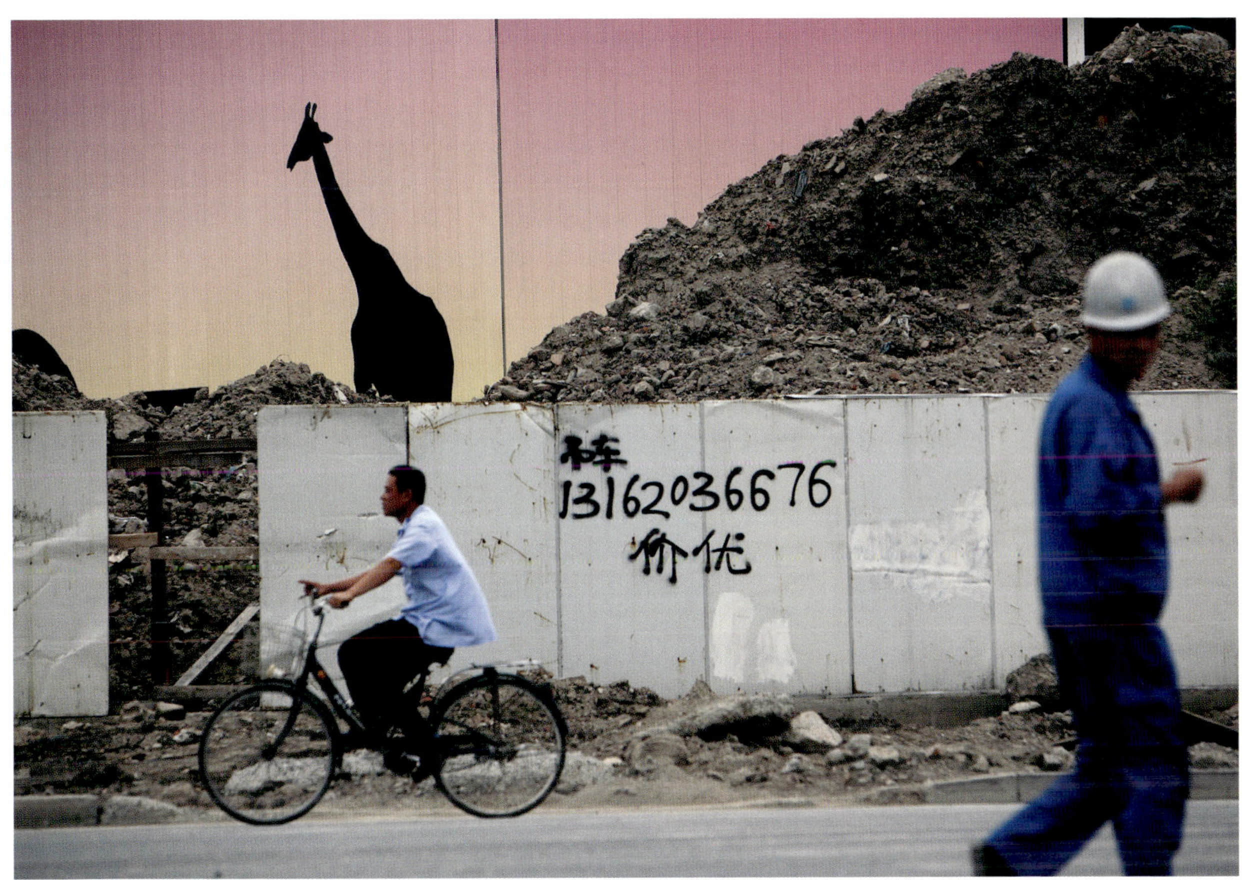13162036676

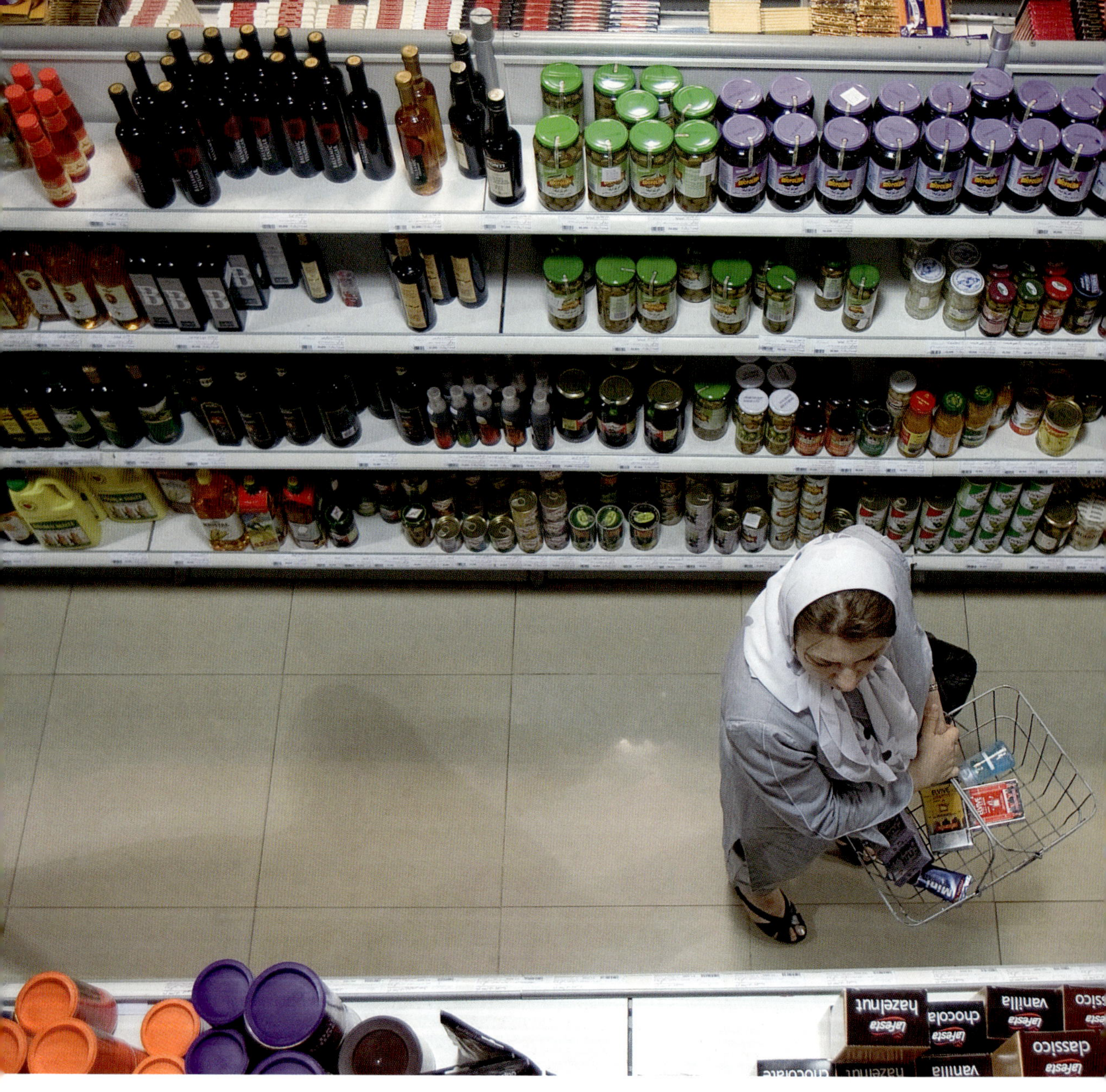

hazelnut
chocolat
vanilla
lassico
lafesta
lafesta
lafesta

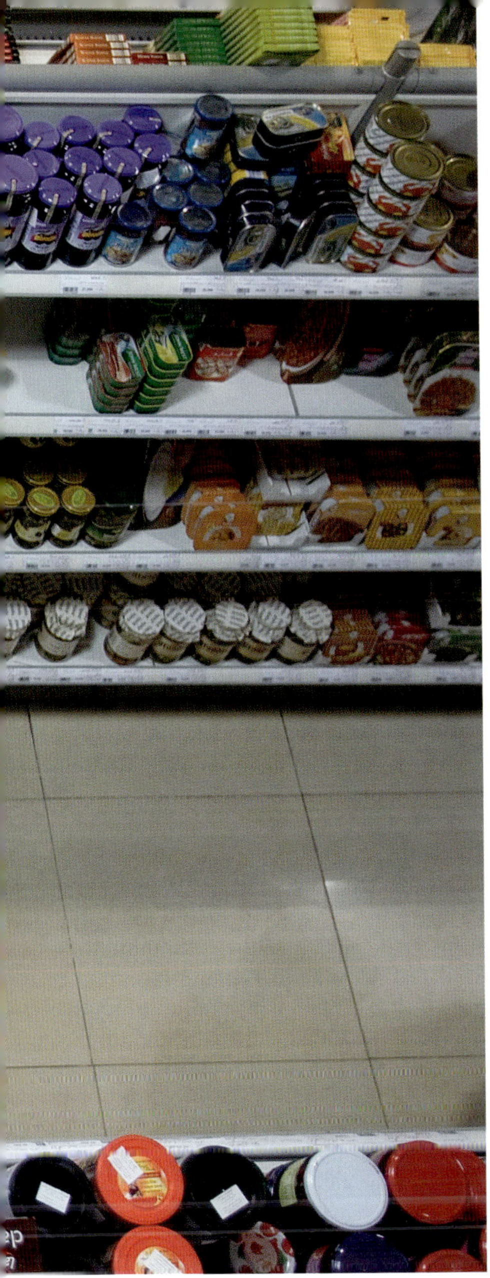

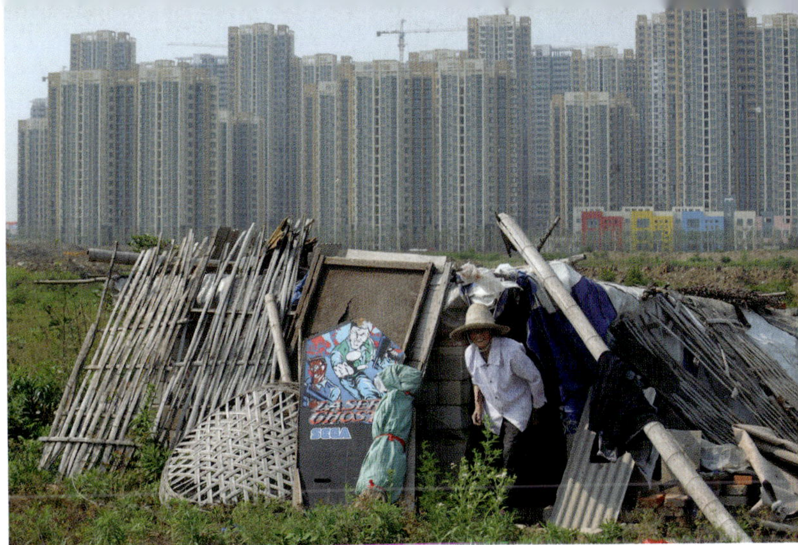

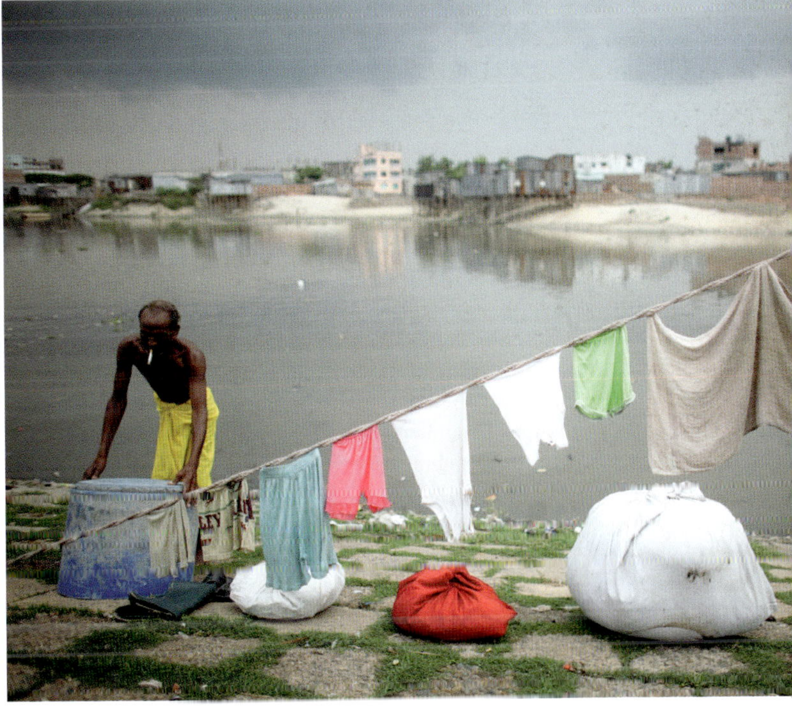

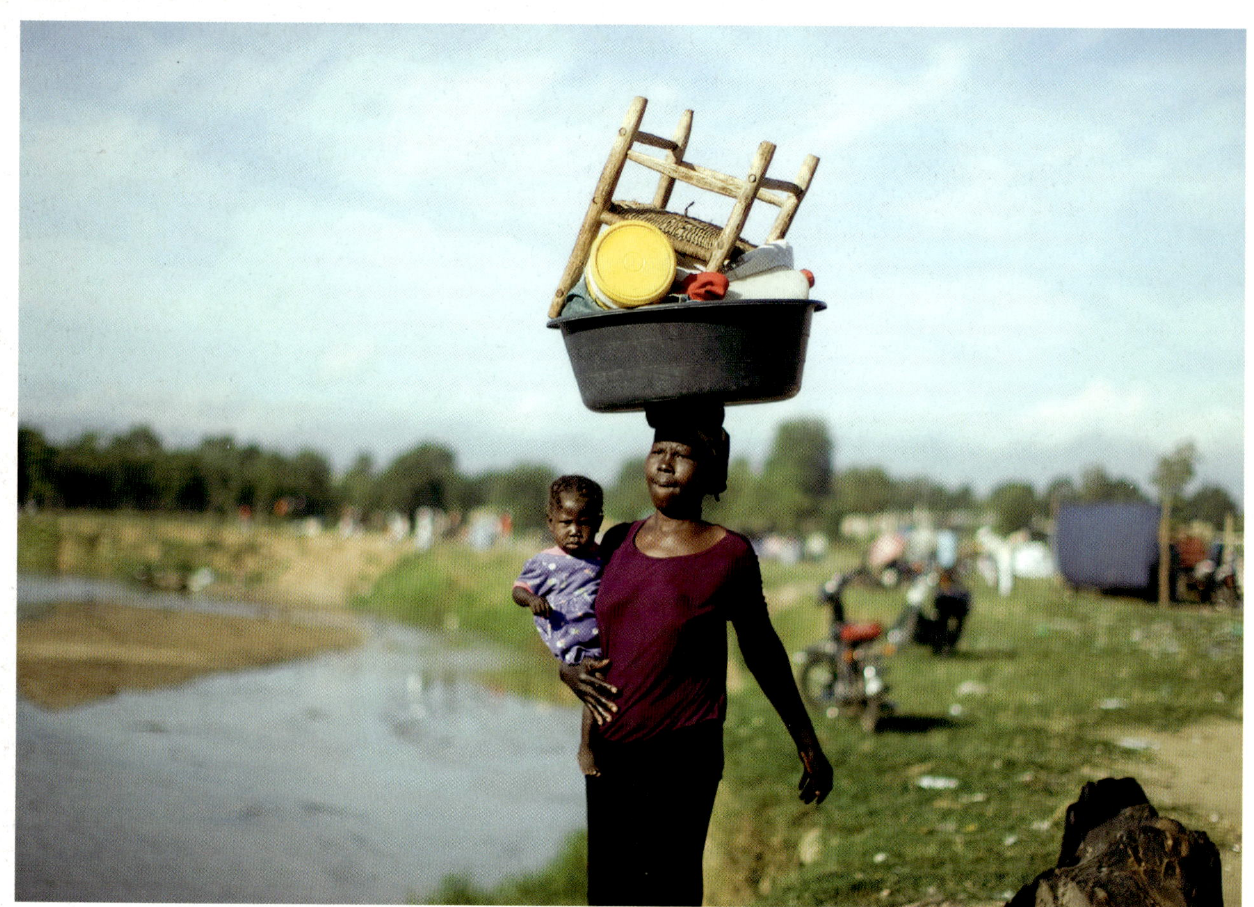

131 [OPPOSITE] New York, United States

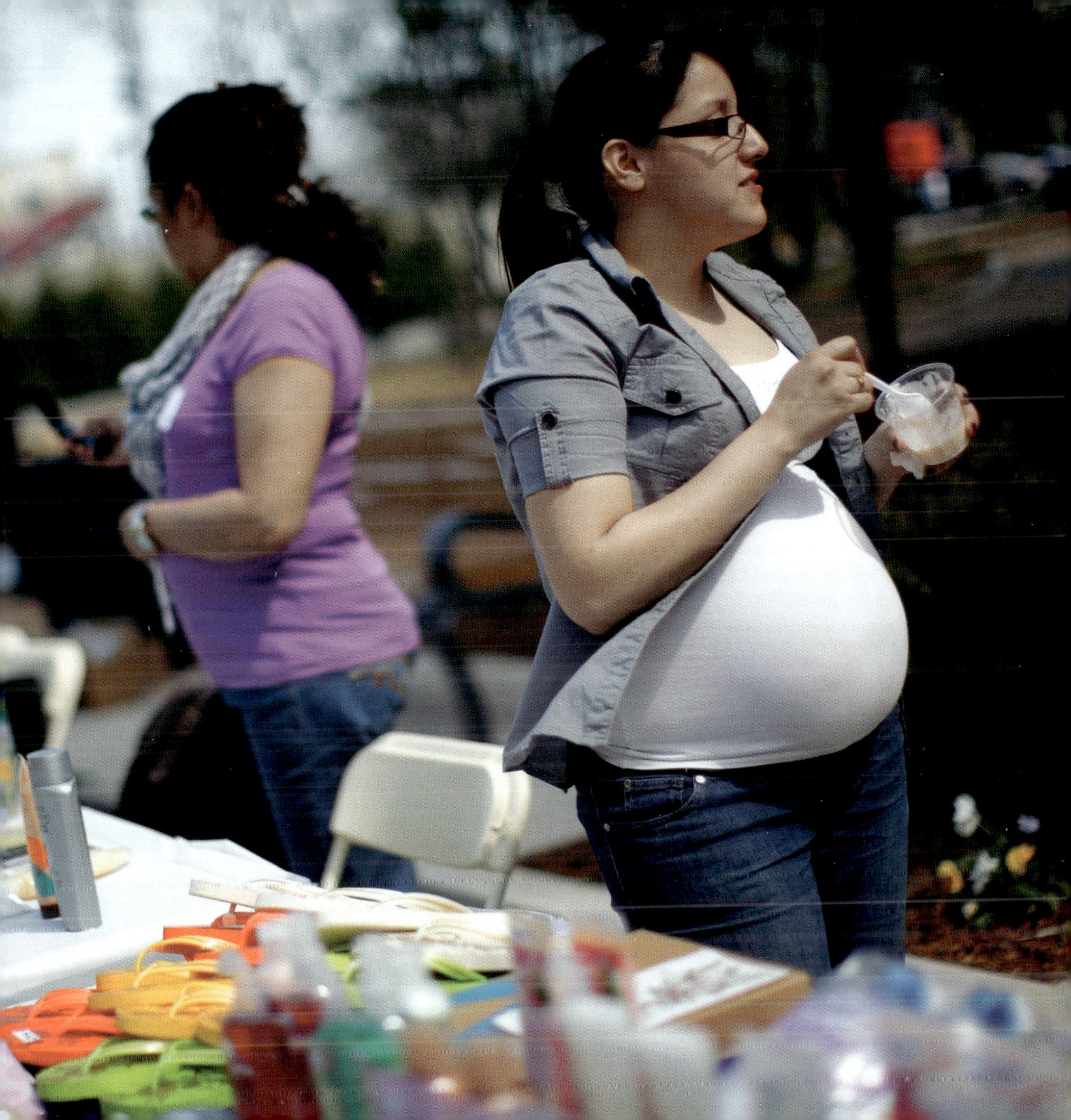

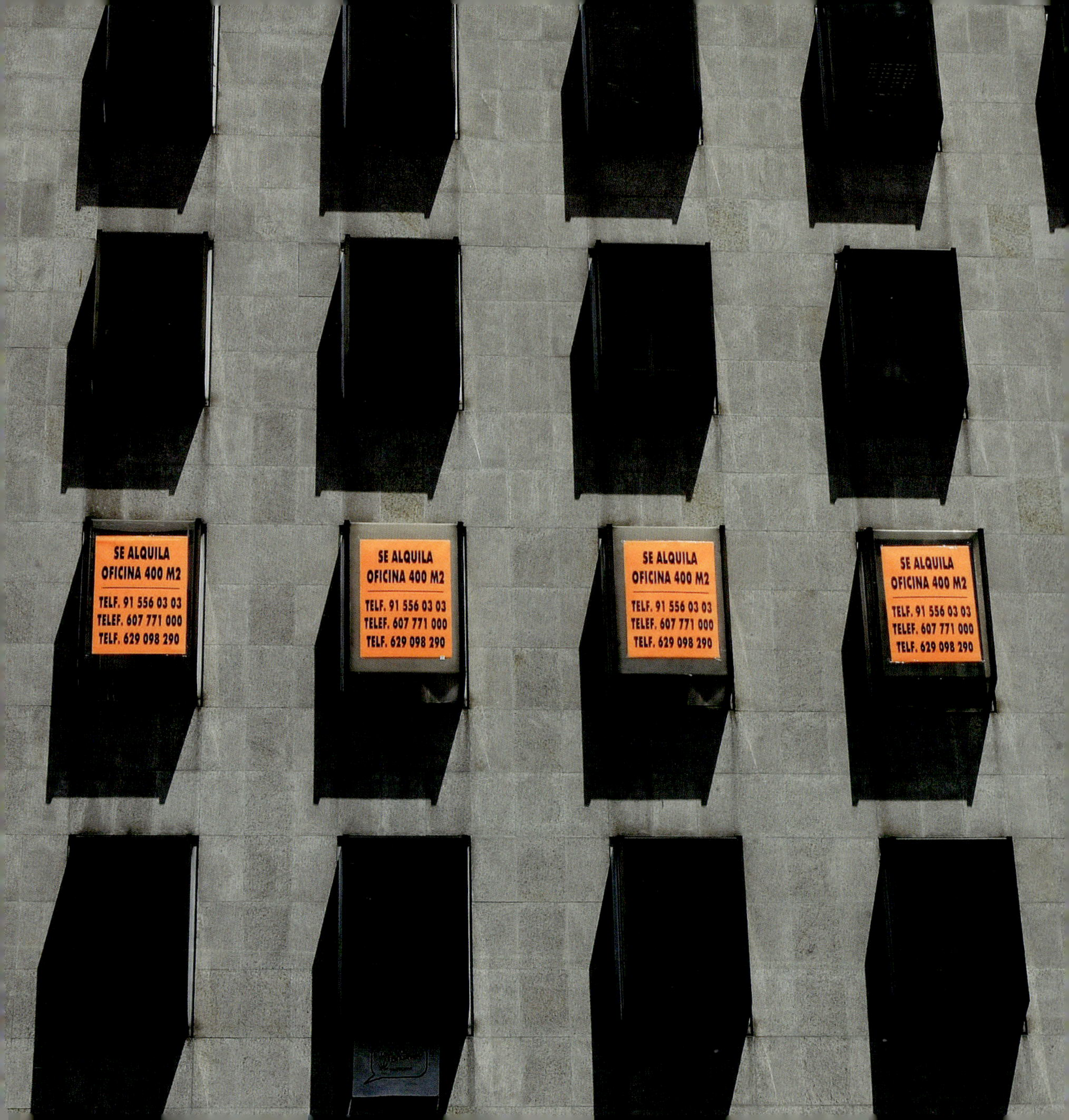

SE ALQUILA
OFICINA 400 M2
TELF. 91 556 03 03
TELEF. 607 771 000
TELF. 629 098 290

SE ALQUILA
OFICINA 400 M2
TELF. 91 556 03 03
TELEF. 607 771 000
TELF. 629 098 290

SE ALQUILA
OFICINA 400 M2
TELF. 91 556 03 03
TELEF. 607 771 000
TELF. 629 098 290

SE ALQUILA
OFICINA 400 M2
TELF. 91 556 03 03
TELEF. 607 771 000
TELF. 629 098 290

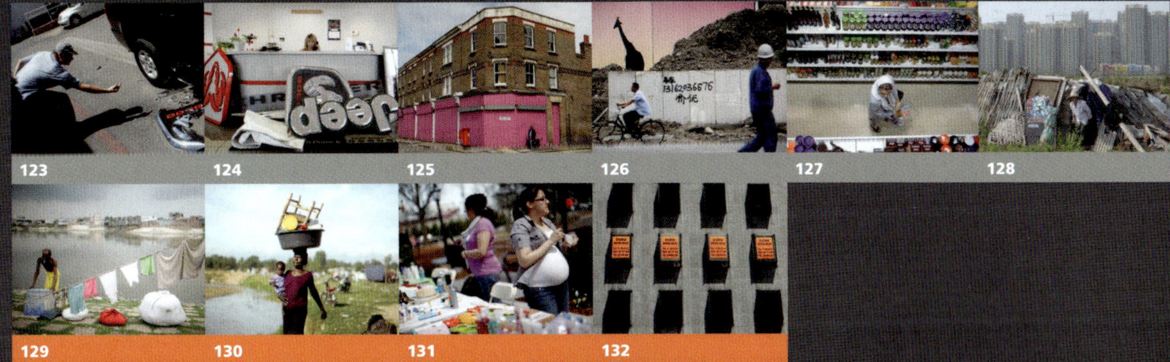

123 General manager Terry Lee drives his truck over a Dodge logo sign at Performance Chrysler Jeep Dodge dealership in Phoenix, Arizona, while his brother Jeff Lee (pictured) gestures. Theirs was one of 789 dealerships whose franchise agreement was terminated by Chrysler as the United States faced its worst recession in decades. 10 June 2009. Phoenix, United States. Joshua Lott.

124 Receptionist Michele Williams speaks on the phone at Performance Chrysler Jeep Dodge dealership. 10 June 2009. Phoenix, United States. Joshua Lott.

125 A man walks his dog past a row of boarded-up shops and homes in London. 12 June 2009. London, Britain. Luke MacGregor.

126 Workers walk by the African area of the World Expo 2010, under construction in Shanghai. 8 June 2009. Shanghai, China. Nir Elias.

127 A woman shops at a supermarket in northern Tehran. Rising consumer prices (inflation climbed to almost 30 percent in 2008) coupled with lack of jobs were among the loudest complaints in Iran as the Islamic Republic approached a presidential election. 26 May 2009. Tehran, Iran. Morteza Nikoubazl.

128 A woman steps out of her makeshift shelter in front of a row of newly built apartments in Hefei, Anhui province. 22 May 2009. Hefei, China. Jianan Yu.

129 A man washes clothes on the bank of the river Buriganga in Dhaka. Once the lifeline of the Bangladeshi capital, the Buriganga is now one of the country's most polluted rivers due to rampant dumping of industrial and human waste. 17 May 2009. Dhaka, Bangladesh. Andrew Biraj.

130 A Haitian woman in Ouanaminthe walks to cross the border into the Dominican Republic carrying goods for sale. Haiti is the western hemisphere's poorest nation, with a long history of violence and political unrest. 27 April 2009. Ouanaminthe, Haiti. Eduardo Munoz.

131 Karen Giral, 20, stands at her booth selling Avon products at a Grameen America event at St John's University, New York. Originally founded in Bangladesh, the non-profit microfinance organization Grameen has 600 borrowers in Queens, all women. The average loan is $2,200 and repayment rates are 99.6 percent. 18 April 2009. New York, United States. Eric Thayer.

132 Signs reading 'Office for rent' are displayed on a building in downtown Madrid. Thousands of new-build offices and homes stood empty across Spain in mid-2009 as the country experienced a property market collapse aggravated by chronic oversupply and surging unemployment. 21 May 2009. Madrid, Spain. Susana Vera.

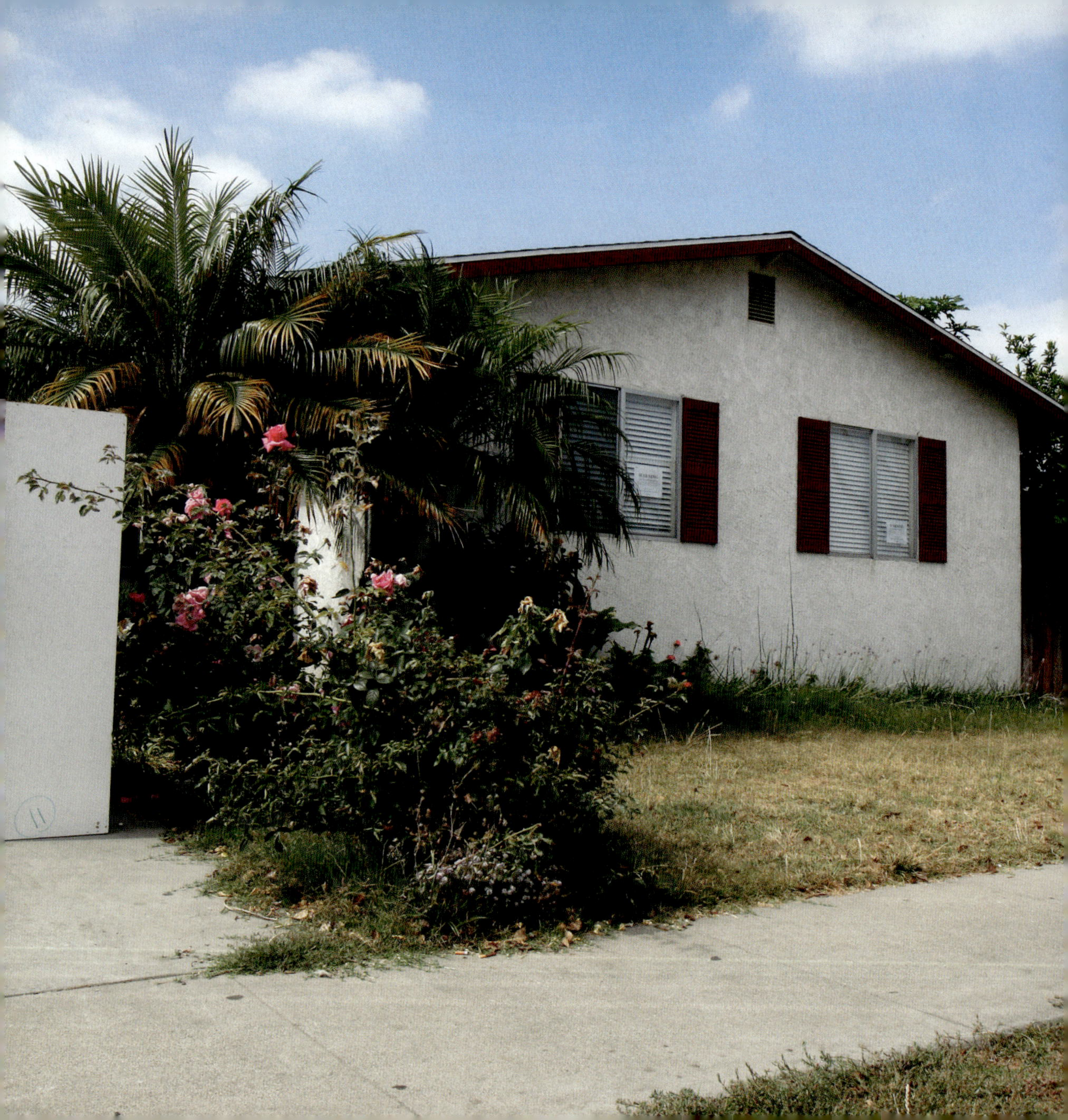

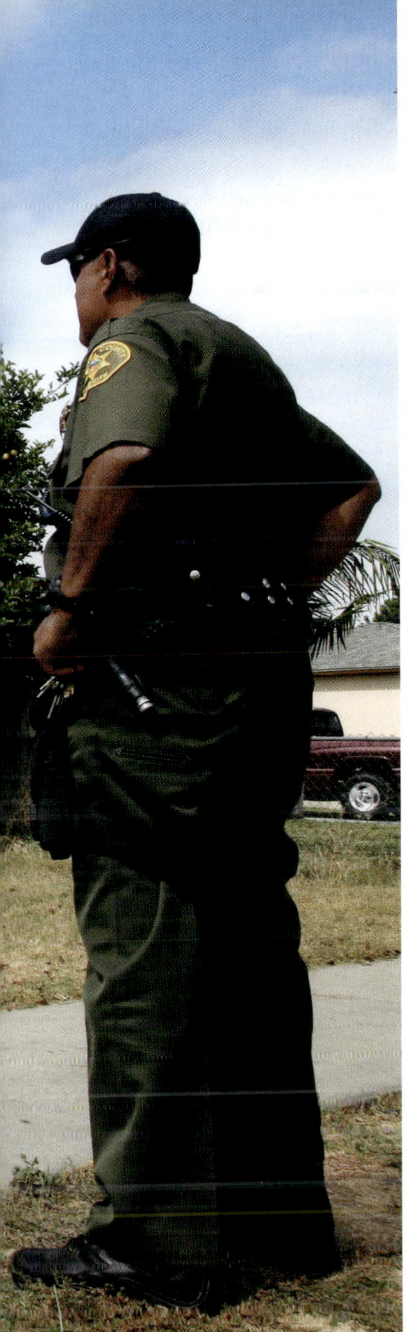

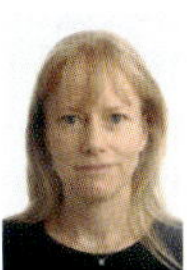

LUCY NICHOLSON
Photographer
Born: 1972, London, Britain
Based: Los Angeles, United States
Nationality: British/American

The human cost of the housing crisis

Tension mounted each time Orange County Sheriff's Deputy Dan Mendoza approached a home scheduled for repossession. He readied a hand on his gun. Trailing him with a camera, I kept a safe distance.

Many homes were already vacated, and Mendoza would walk through silent rooms, gun drawn, making sure nobody was there. But not all were empty. Mexican immigrant Aida Lemus, a frail 70-year-old, looked scared as she opened her front door and peered through the crack. Mendoza told her he was taking possession of her home for failure to pay the mortgage.

Aida opened the door. Family photos lined the walls of a well-kept living room, reminding me of childhood visits to my grandparents' home. She spoke little English. Mendoza found a bilingual neighbour to explain that she needed to gather a few belongings and leave so that he could change the locks. She began to cry and clutch her stomach as she talked about her grandchildren's bottled milk. Paramedics came to check on her. She eventually picked up her handbag and a towel and left her home, sobbing quietly. Mendoza and I were silent as we drove to the next property.

California led the United States when housing prices soared early in the decade, spurred by public policy incentives to encourage home ownership. The boom fuelled a frenzy of lending and spending that drove the U.S. economy. But California also proved to have been the epicentre of reckless lending that pushed the U.S. housing market over a cliff in 2007, and it became one of the states hit hardest by mortgage foreclosures.

Mendoza told me about finding senior citizens, pitbulls, even small children left behind in properties. His colleague, Sheriff's Deputy Ramona Figueroa, said many homes were in an appalling state: mould eating through the roof, meat rotting in the refrigerator and animal faeces soiling the carpet. One man took his life when a deputy arrived. Many vacated houses that we visited contained a scattering of forgotten belongings – a baby's sweater, a plate of uneaten food – that hinted at the lives of their former occupants and the haste with which they had apparently departed.

133 Sheriff's Deputy Dan Mendoza views a foreclosed home upon which he has to enforce an eviction order in Orange County, California. 23 June 2009. Fullerton, United States.

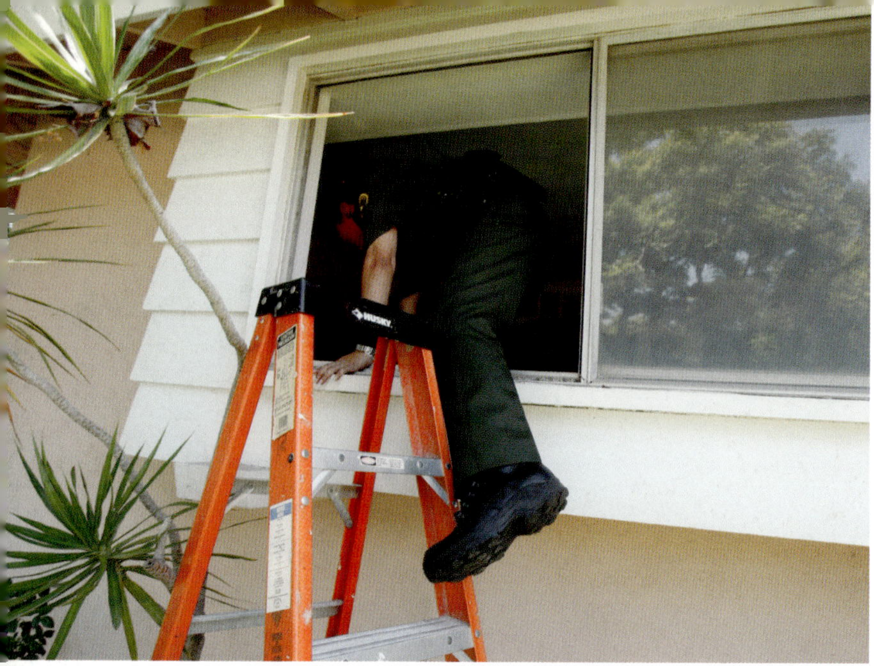

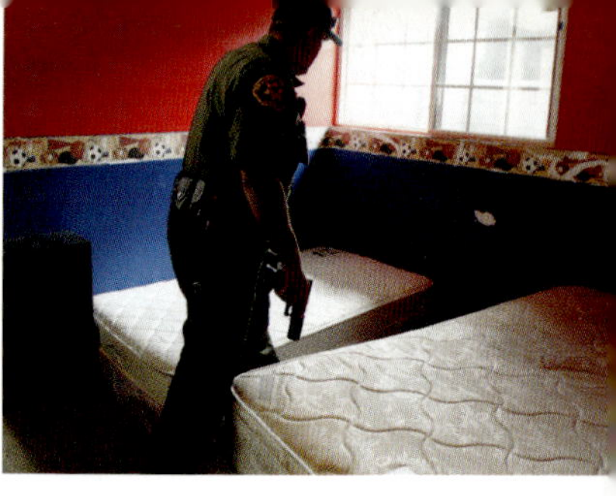
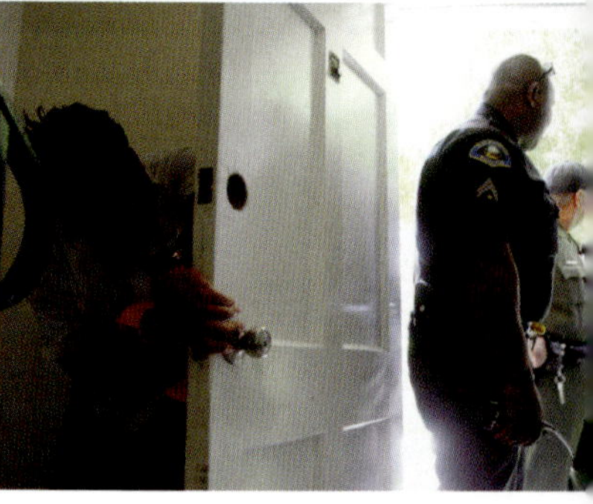
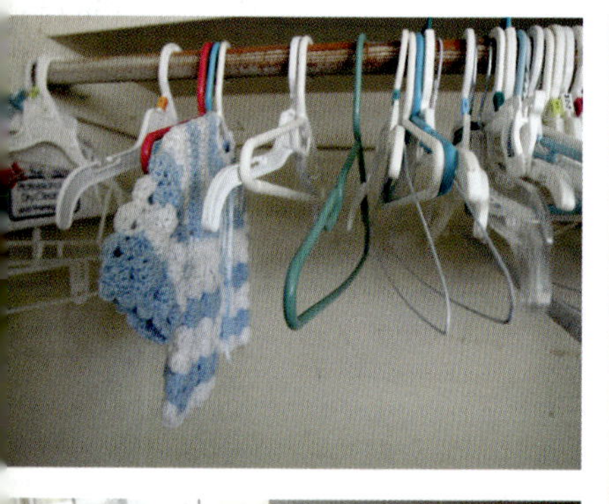
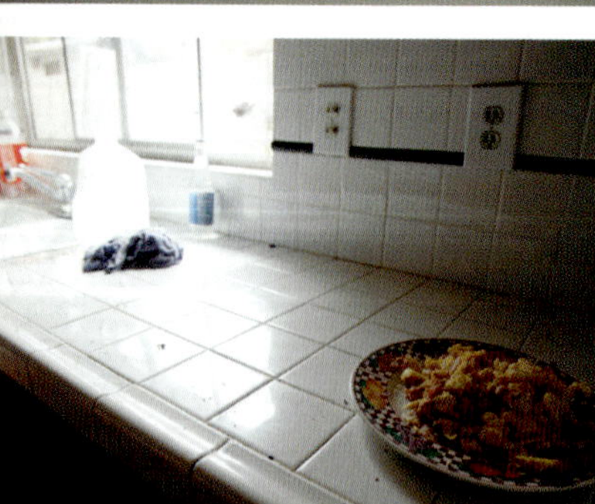
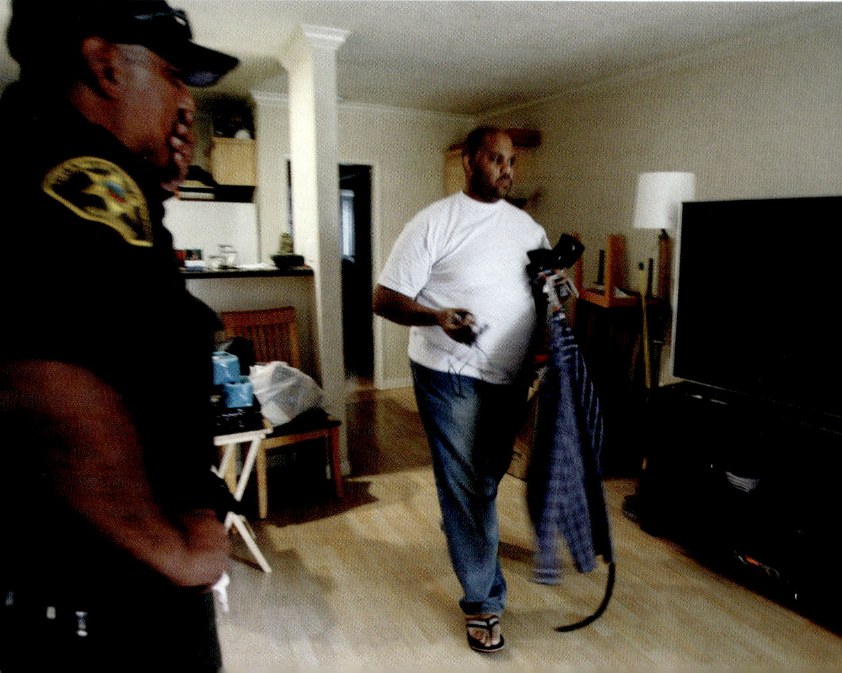

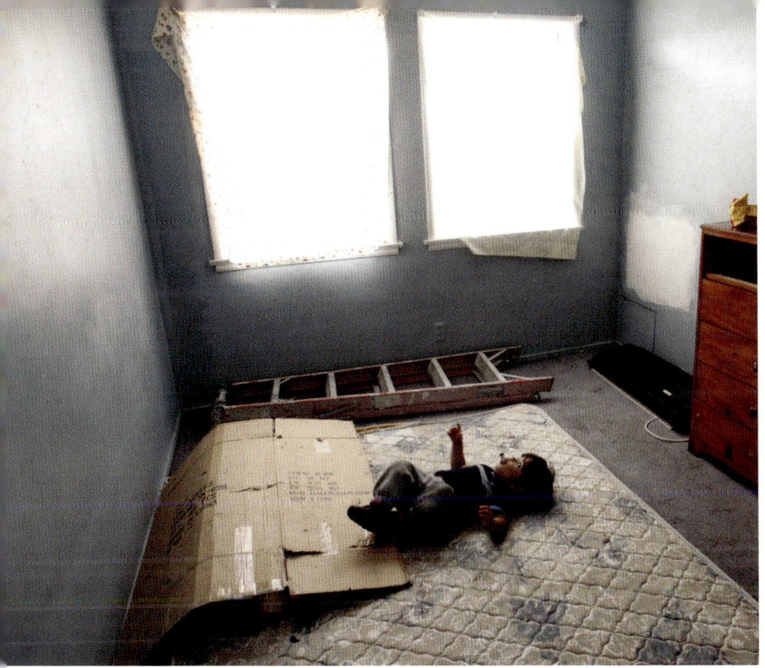

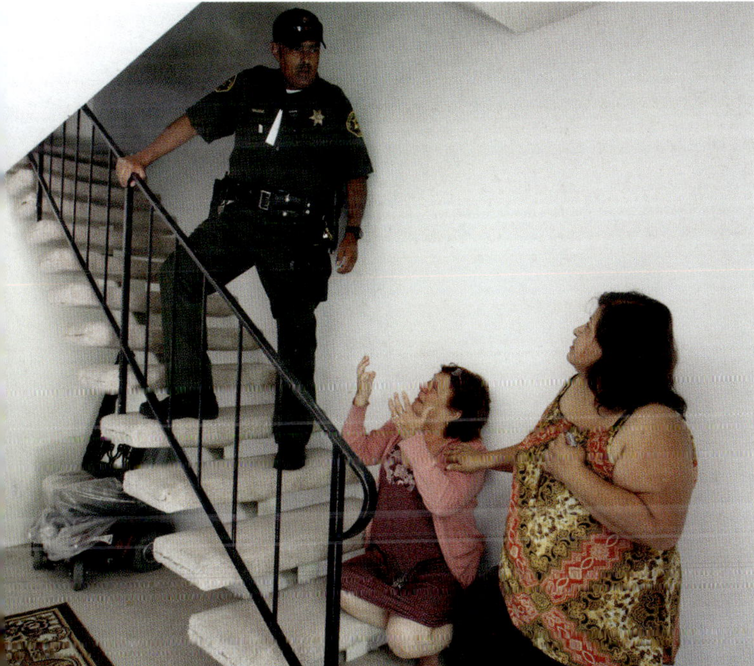

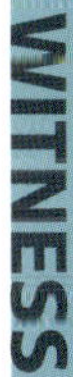

134 Orange County Sheriff's Deputy Ramona Figueroa climbs through a window to enforce an eviction order on a foreclosed home. 18 June 2009. Fullerton, United States. **135** Orange County Sheriff's Deputy Dan Mendoza searches a children's bedroom as he enforces an eviction order on a foreclosed home. 18 June 2009. Fullerton, United States. **136** A locksmith changes the locks on a house after Sheriff's Deputy Dan Mendoza (right) and Anaheim police officer Chris Ned (centre) enforced an eviction order. 23 June 2009. Anaheim, United States. **137** A baby's sweater remains hanging in a cupboard otherwise emptied of clothes. 18 June 2009. Fullerton, United States. **138** A plate of uneaten food is seen in a vacated home. 18 June 2009. Fullerton, United States. **139** Dante Jones glances at his flat-screen television as he is evicted from his apartment by Sheriff's Deputy Dan Mendoza. 18 June 2009. Fullerton, United States. **140** Angel Guevara, 2, lies in a bedroom as his family is evicted from their Los Angeles apartment. Tenants of this apartment building had been paying their rent, but were evicted after the owner failed to pay the mortgage. 11 June 2009. Los Angeles, United States. **141** Sheriff's Deputy Dan Mendoza talks to Aida Lemus, 70 (centre), as he enforces an eviction order on her foreclosed condominium. At right is neighbour Gloria Naranjo. 23 June 2009. Anaheim, United States. Lucy Nicholson.

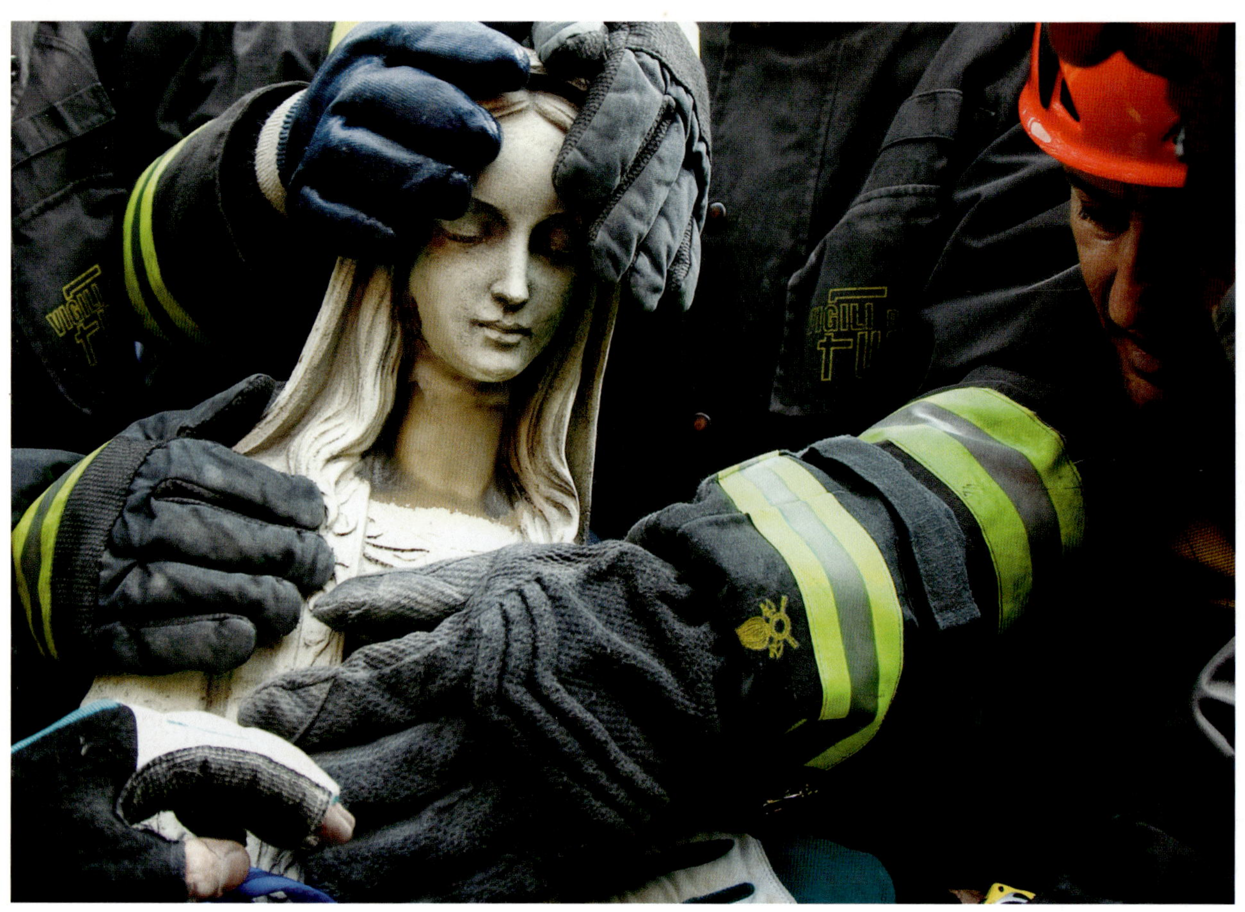

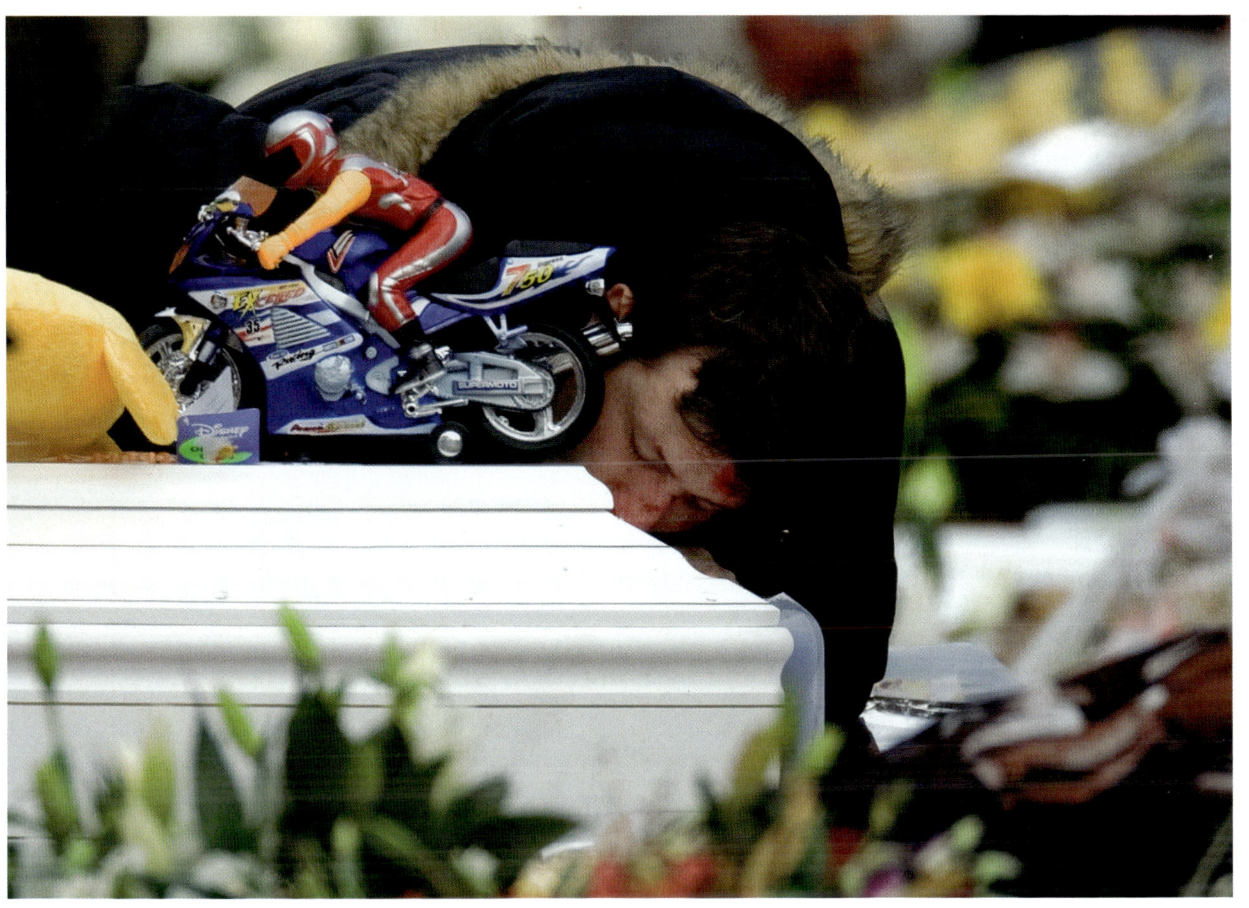

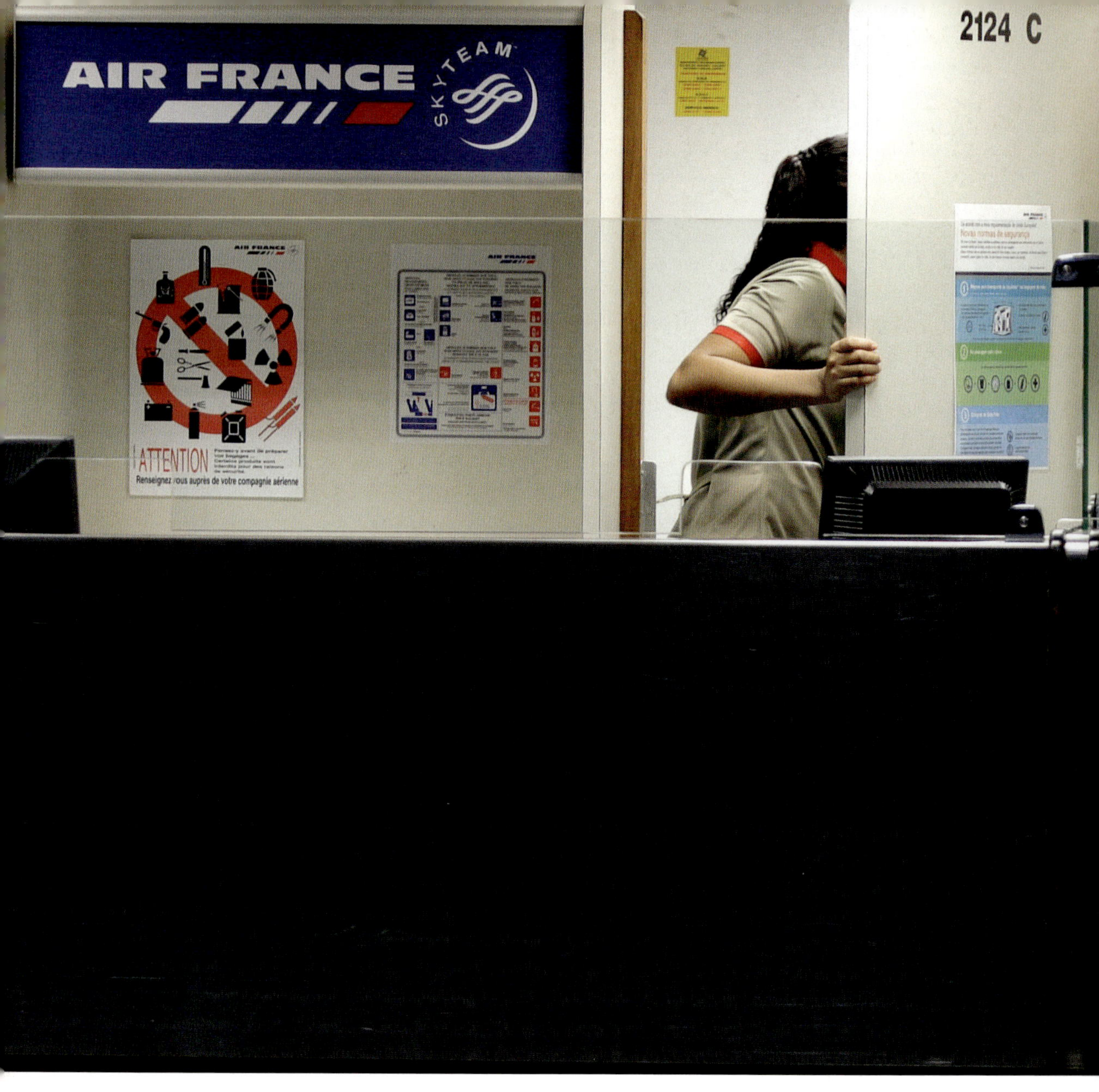

AIR FRANCE
SKYTEAM
2124 C
ATTENTION
Renseignez-vous auprès de votre compagnie aérienne
Novas normas de segurança

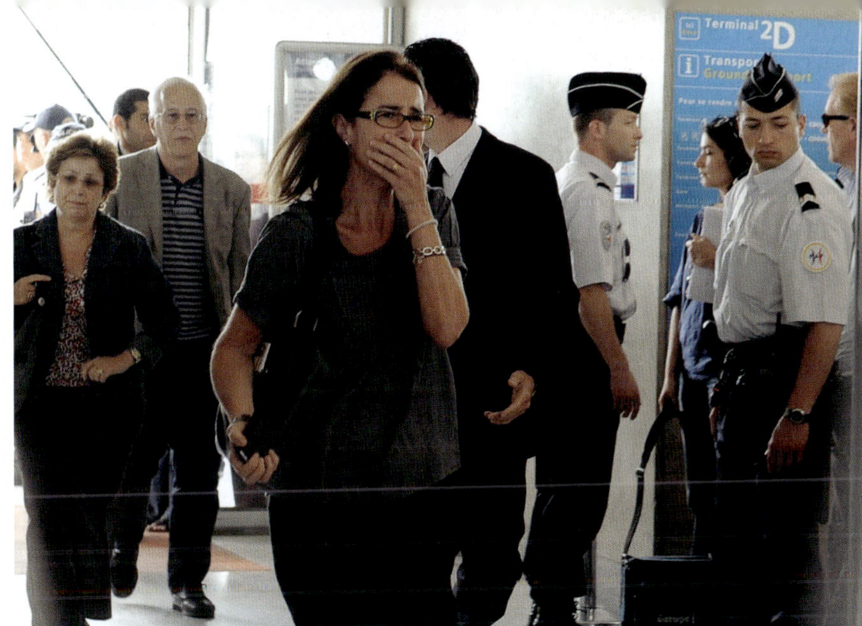

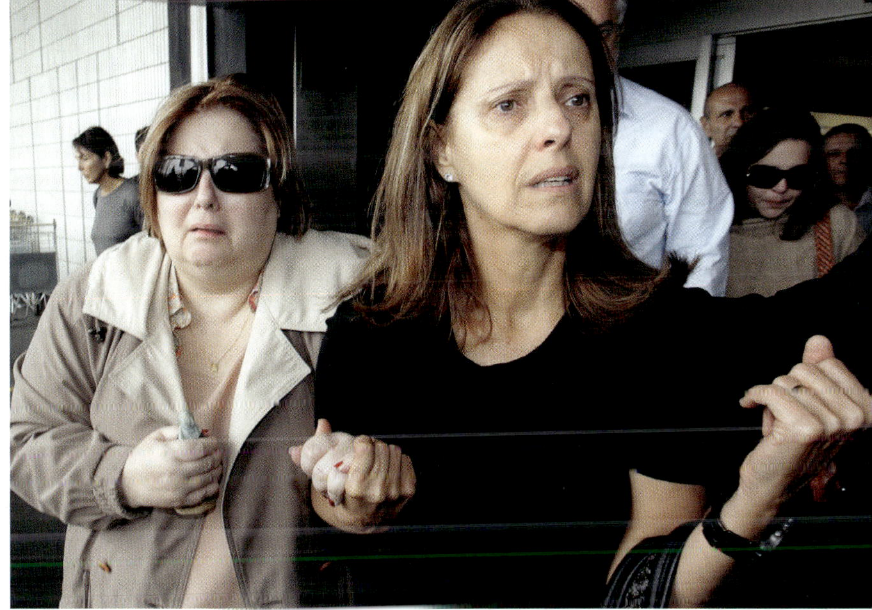

145 [TOP] Paris, France   **146** [ABOVE] Rio de Janeiro, Brazil

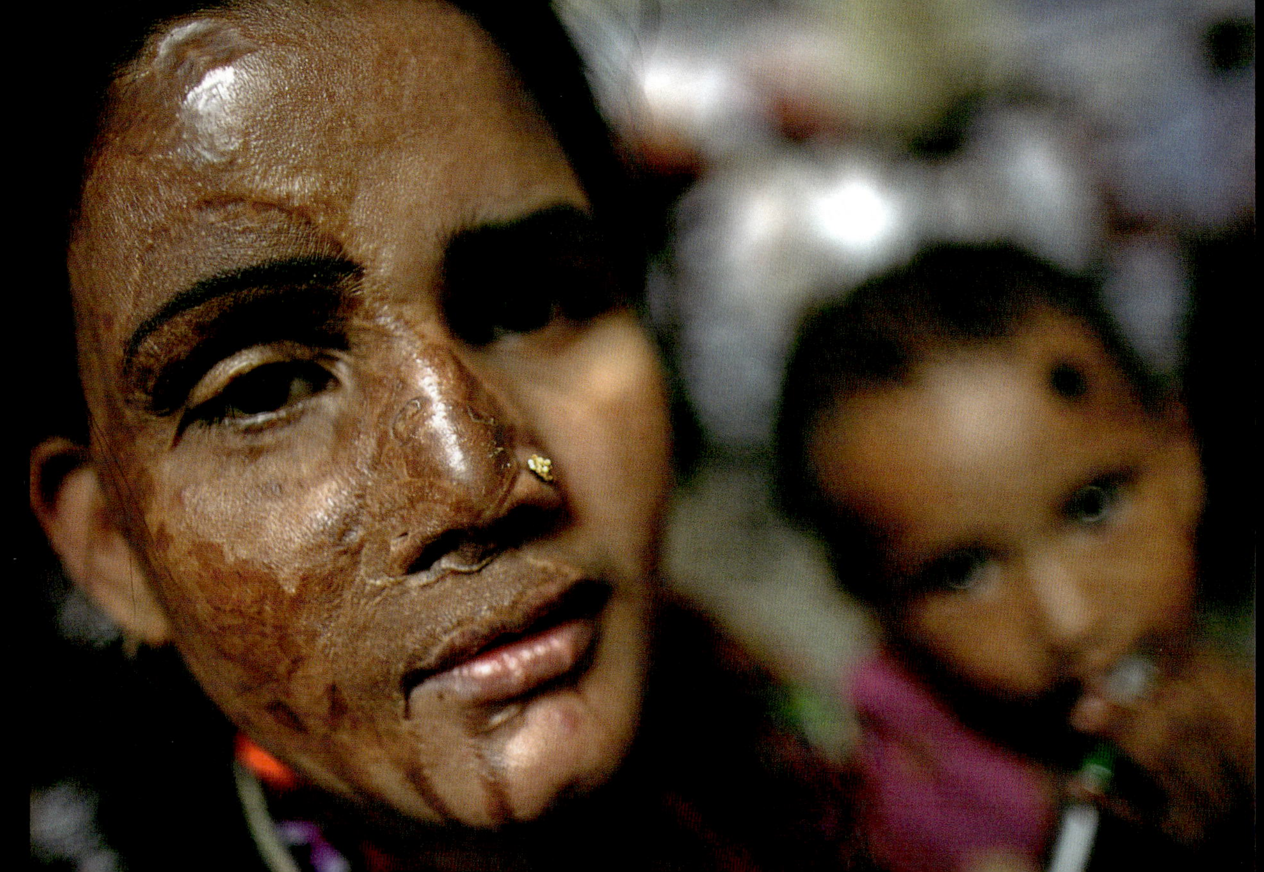

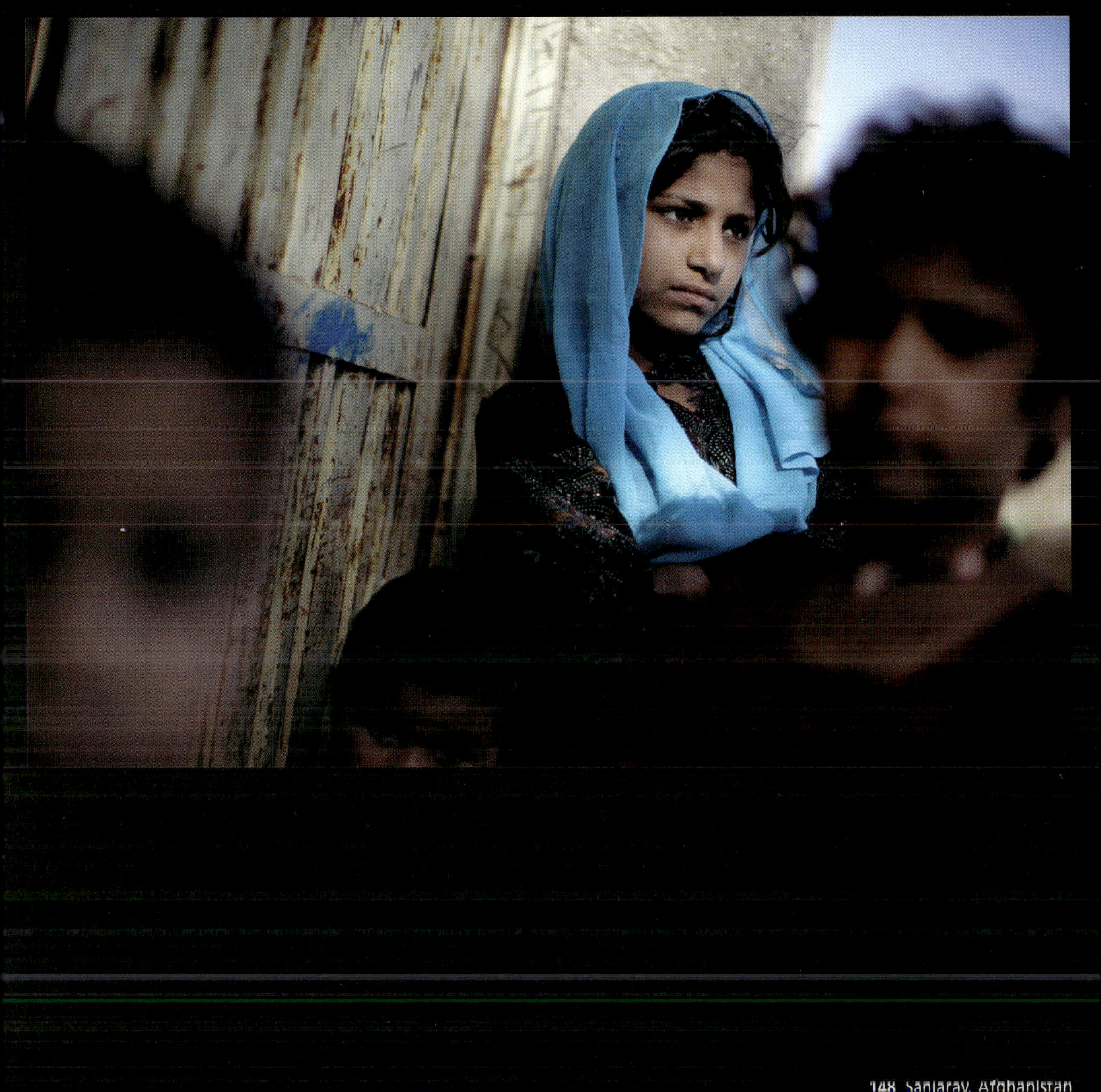

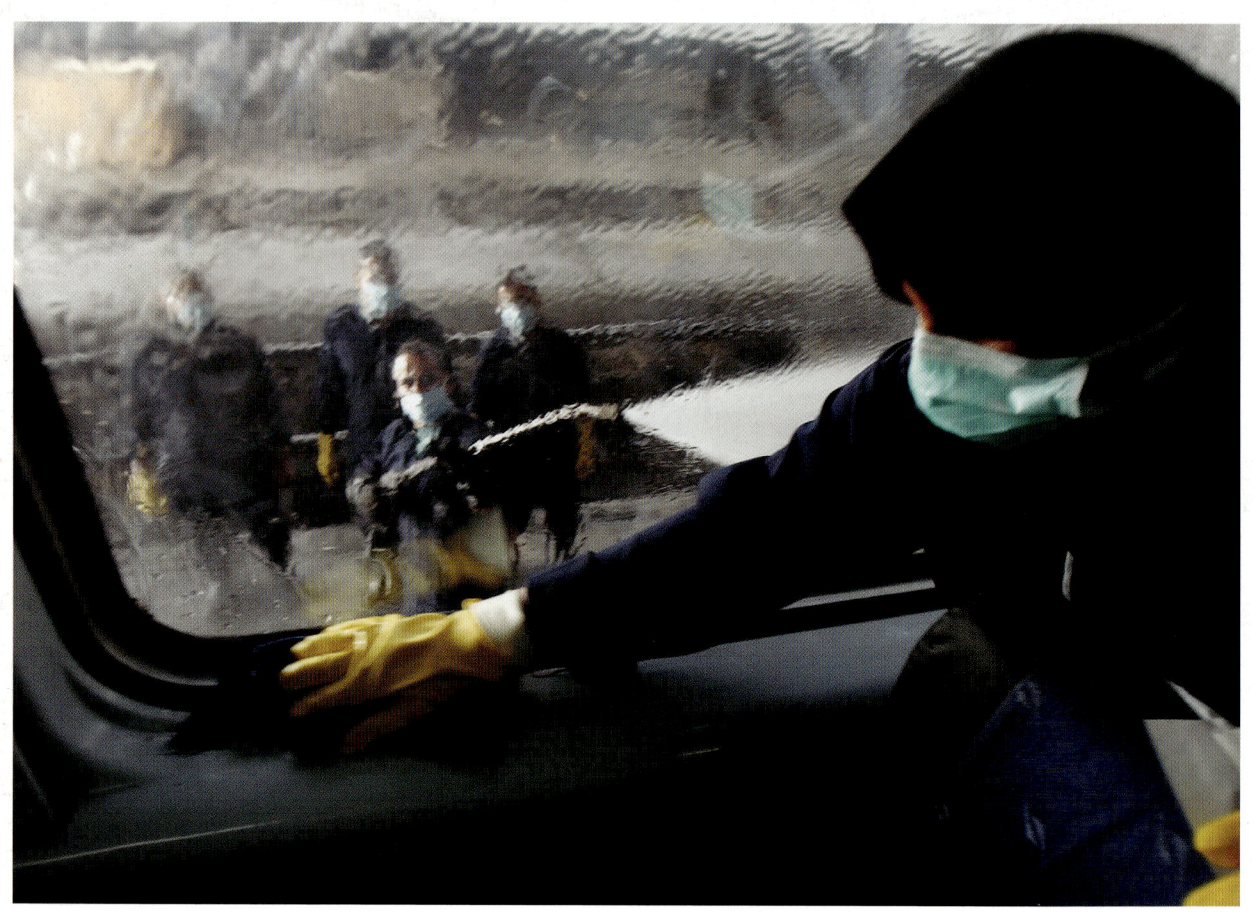

149 Cairo, Egypt

150 [OPPOSITE] Mexico City, Mexico

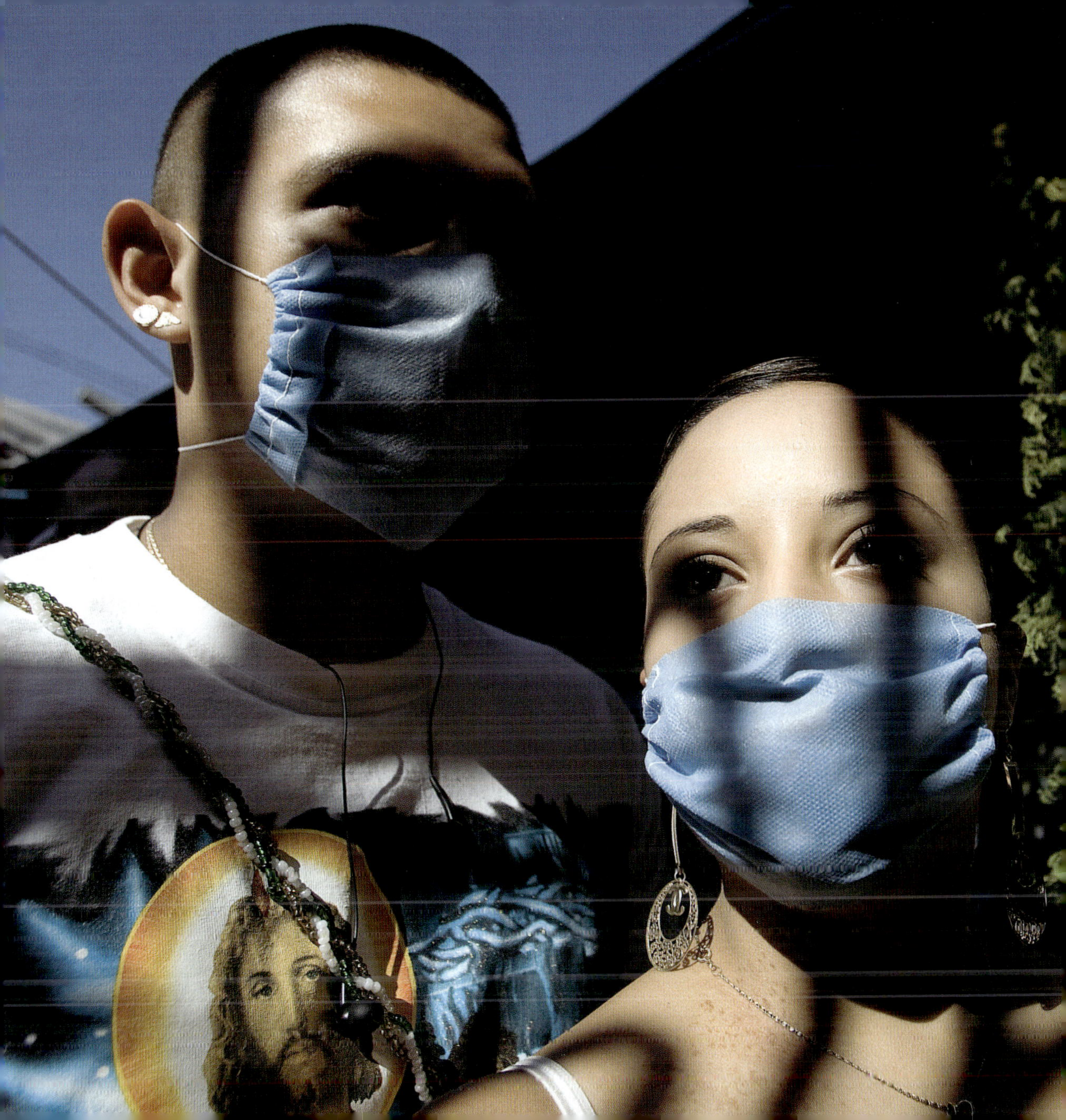

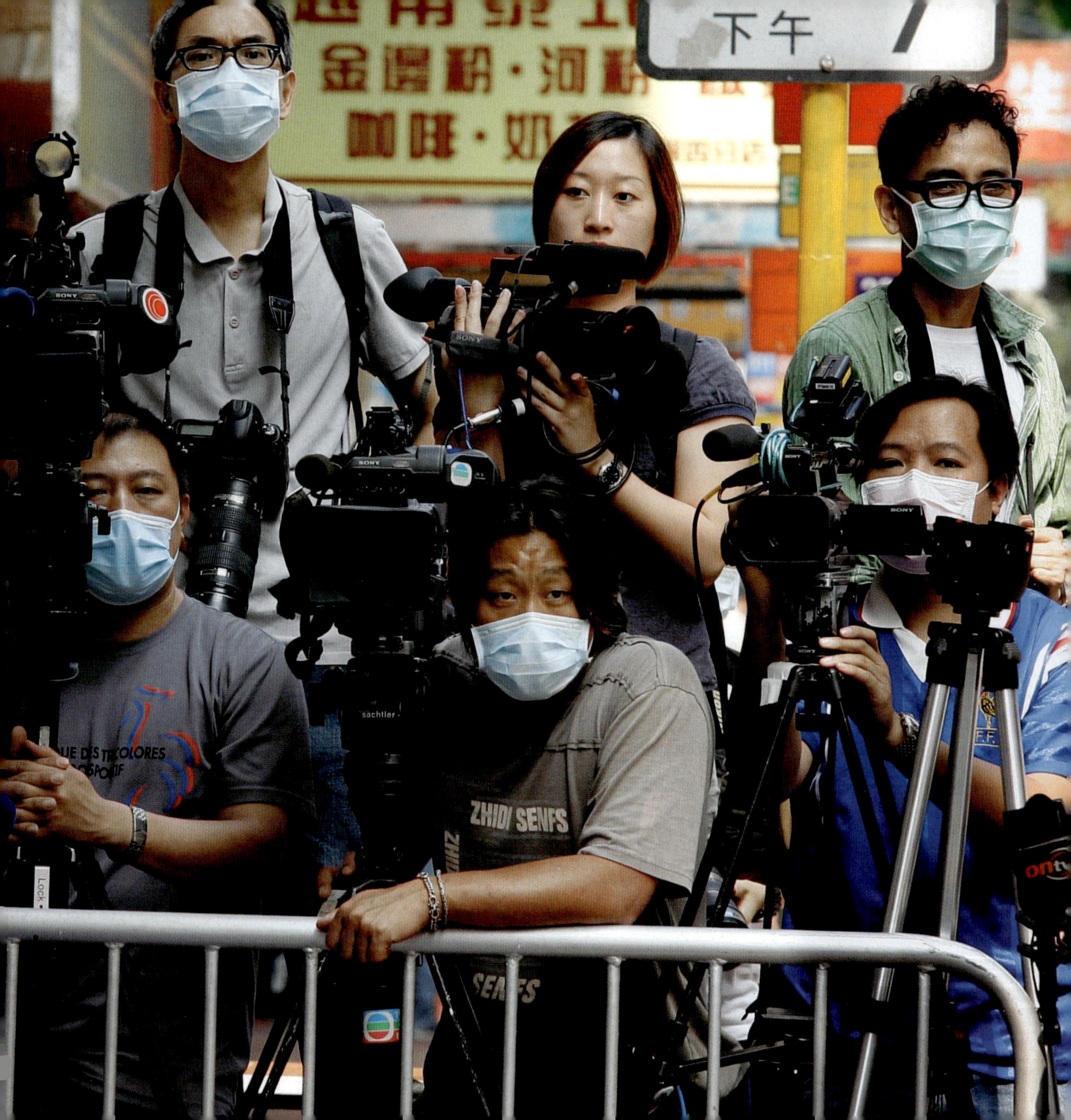

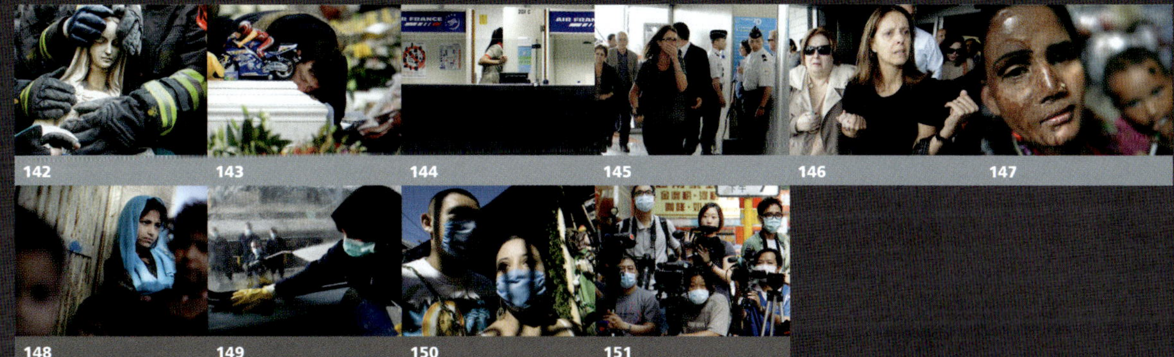

142 Firemen touch a marble statue of the Madonna after removing it from the top of the church in Paganica, near L'Aquila. The church was damaged in a 6.3 magnitude earthquake that hit Italy's Abruzzo region in the early hours of 6 April. 13 April 2009. Paganica, Italy. Max Rossi.

143 A man kisses his son's coffin during a state funeral for earthquake victims in L'Aquila. The medieval city of 68,000 bore the brunt of the disaster in which many of its buildings and centuries-old churches crumbled to the ground, killing 300 people. Authorities said poor building standards were to blame for the high death toll. 10 April 2009. L'Aquila, Italy. Chris Helgren.

144 An Air France employee mans the check-in counter at the Tom Jobim International airport in Rio de Janeiro. Air France flight AF447 from Rio to Paris disappeared from radar screens early on 1 June 2009 after it crashed into the Atlantic Ocean, killing all 228 people aboard. 1 June 2009. Rio de Janeiro, Brazil. Sergio Moraes.

145 Distraught relatives and friends of passengers on Air France flight AF447 arrive at a crisis centre at Charles de Gaulle airport near Paris. 1 June 2009. Paris, France. Gonzalo Fuentes.

146 Relatives and friends of passengers on Air France flight AF447 leave a crisis centre at the Tom Jobim International airport in Rio de Janeiro. 1 June 2009. Rio de Janeiro, Brazil. Sergio Moraes.

147 A survivor of an acid attack attends a rally with her child in Dhaka. Some 600 acid attack victims from Bangladesh, Pakistan, India, Cambodia, Uganda and Nepal participated in an international conference to mark the 10th anniversary of the Acid Survivors Foundation of Bangladesh. The attacks mostly result from refusal of sexual advances, demand for dowry or disputes over land. 12 May 2009. Dhaka, Bangladesh. Andrew Biraj.

148 Afghan children stand at the door of their home during an anti-Taliban operation in Sanjaray, Kandahar province. More than 1,000 soldiers from the Canadian, U.S. and Afghan armies took part. 16 May 2009. Sanjaray, Afghanistan. Jorge Silva.

149 A worker uses disinfectant to clean the interior of a train in a Cairo trainyard. Egypt detected its first H1N1 (swine flu) case in early June in a 12-year-old American girl who arrived for a holiday. 15 June 2009. Cairo, Egypt. Amr Abdallah Dalsh.

150 Devotees wear surgical masks to ward off swine flu infection as they participate in a pilgrimage to the shrine of San Judas Tadeo (St Jude the Apostle), the patron saint of lost causes, at San Hipólito church in Mexico City. The emergence of the H1N1 virus in Mexico and the United States and its fast international spread led the World Health Organization to declare in June that a pandemic was under way. 28 April 2009. Mexico City, Mexico. Jorge Dan.

151 Journalists wearing surgical masks wait behind a fence outside a Hong Kong hotel in which 200 guests and 100 staff were quarantined for a week after a Mexican guest tested positive for H1N1 (swine flu). 4 May 2009. Hong Kong, China. Bobby Yip.

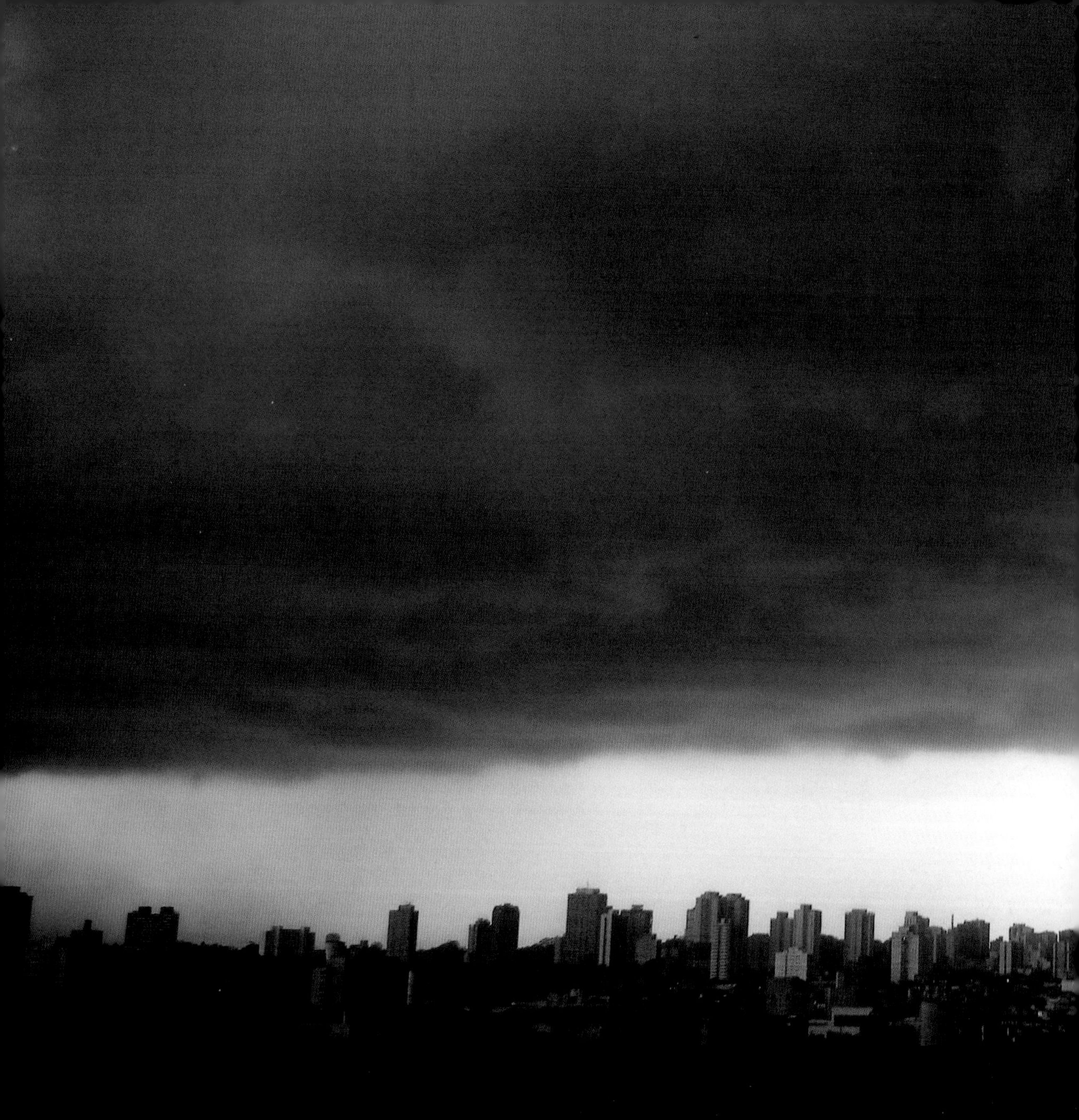

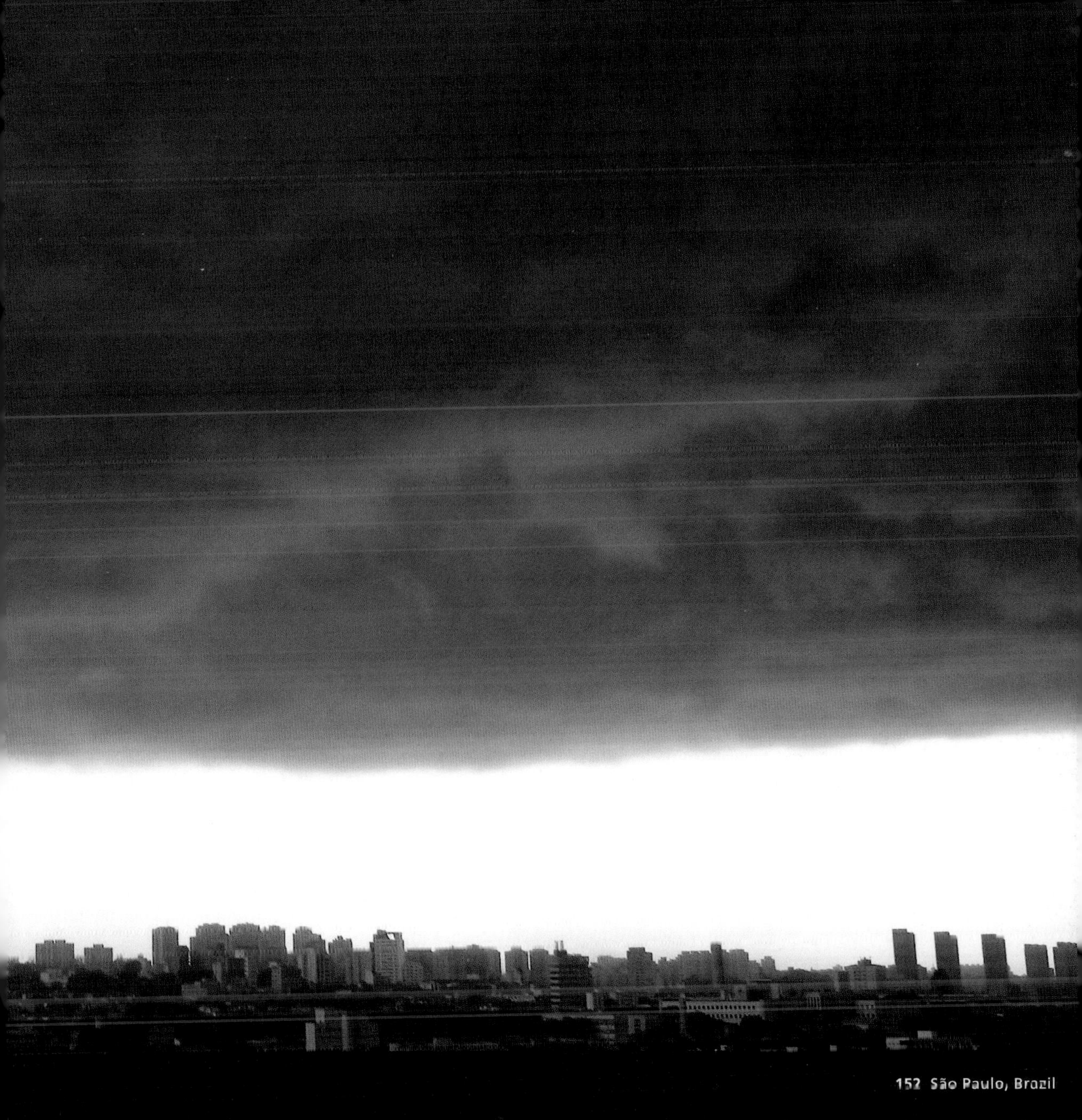

152 São Paulo, Brazil

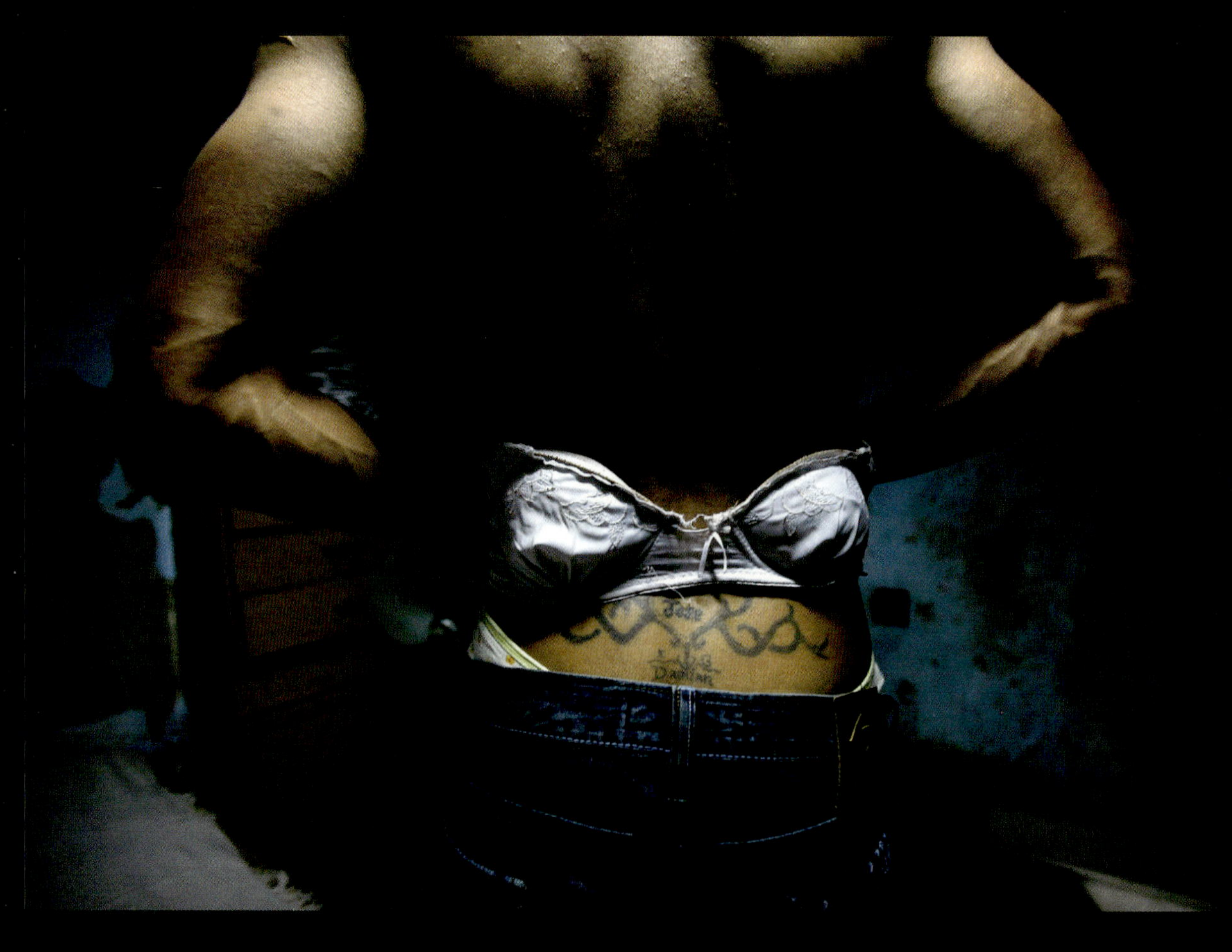

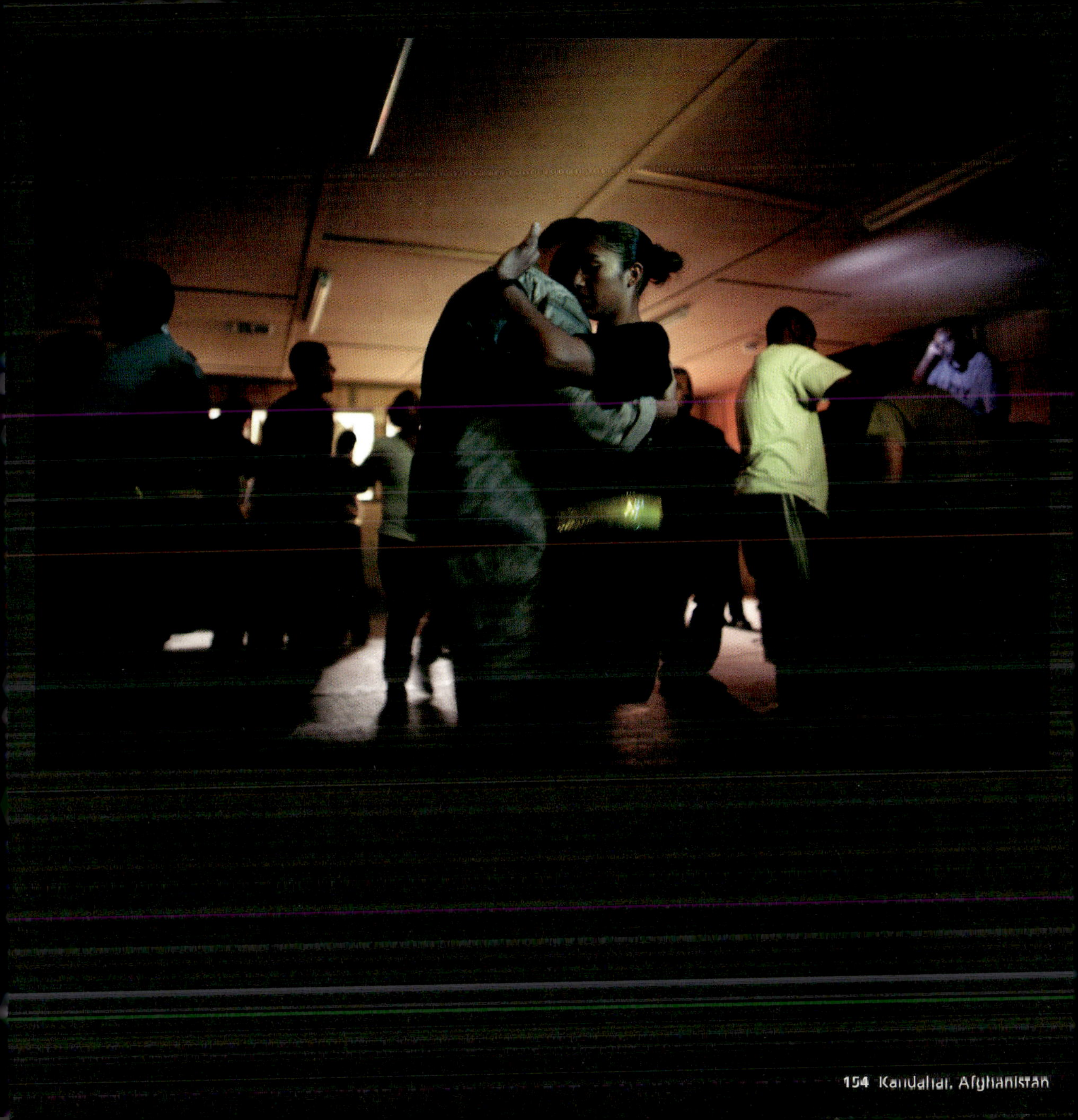

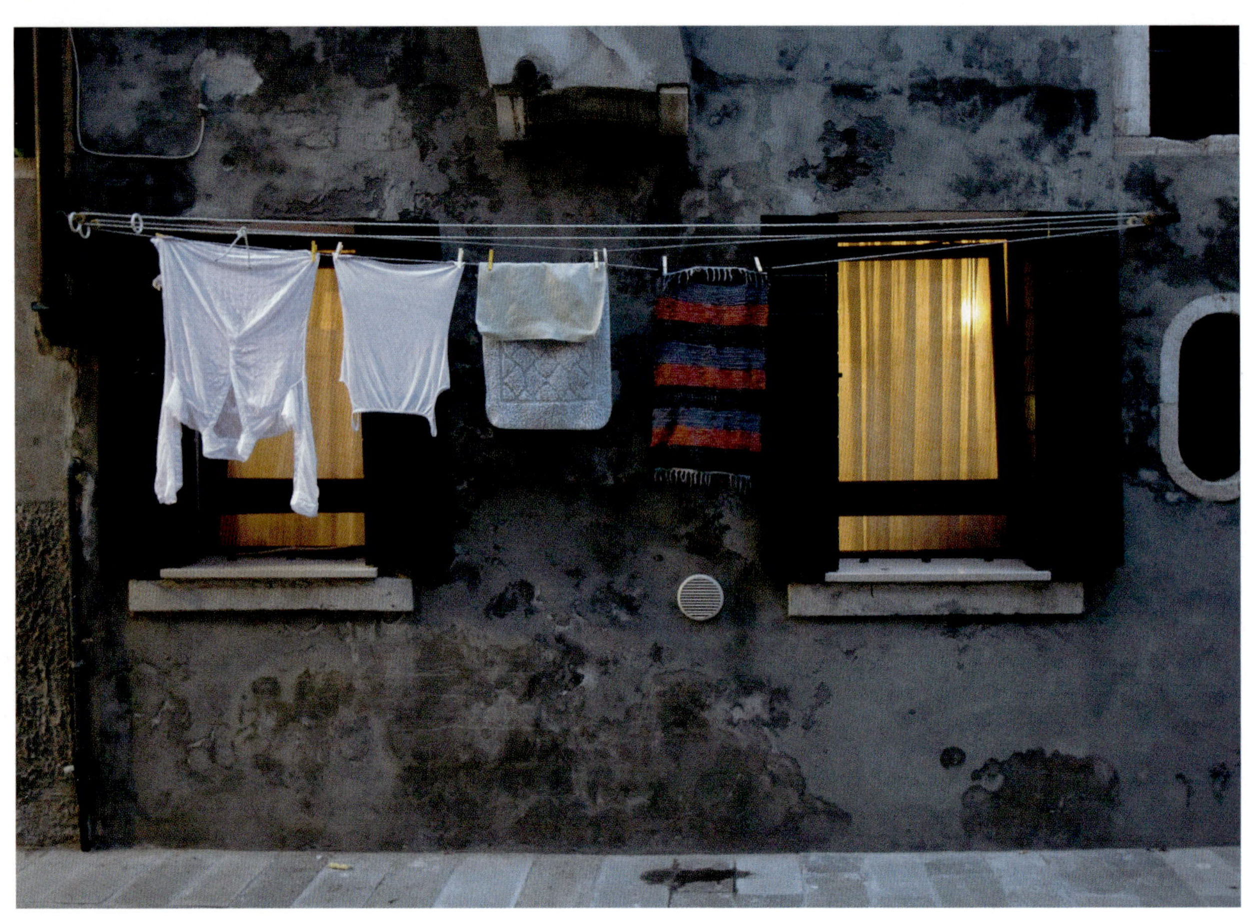

155 Venice, Italy

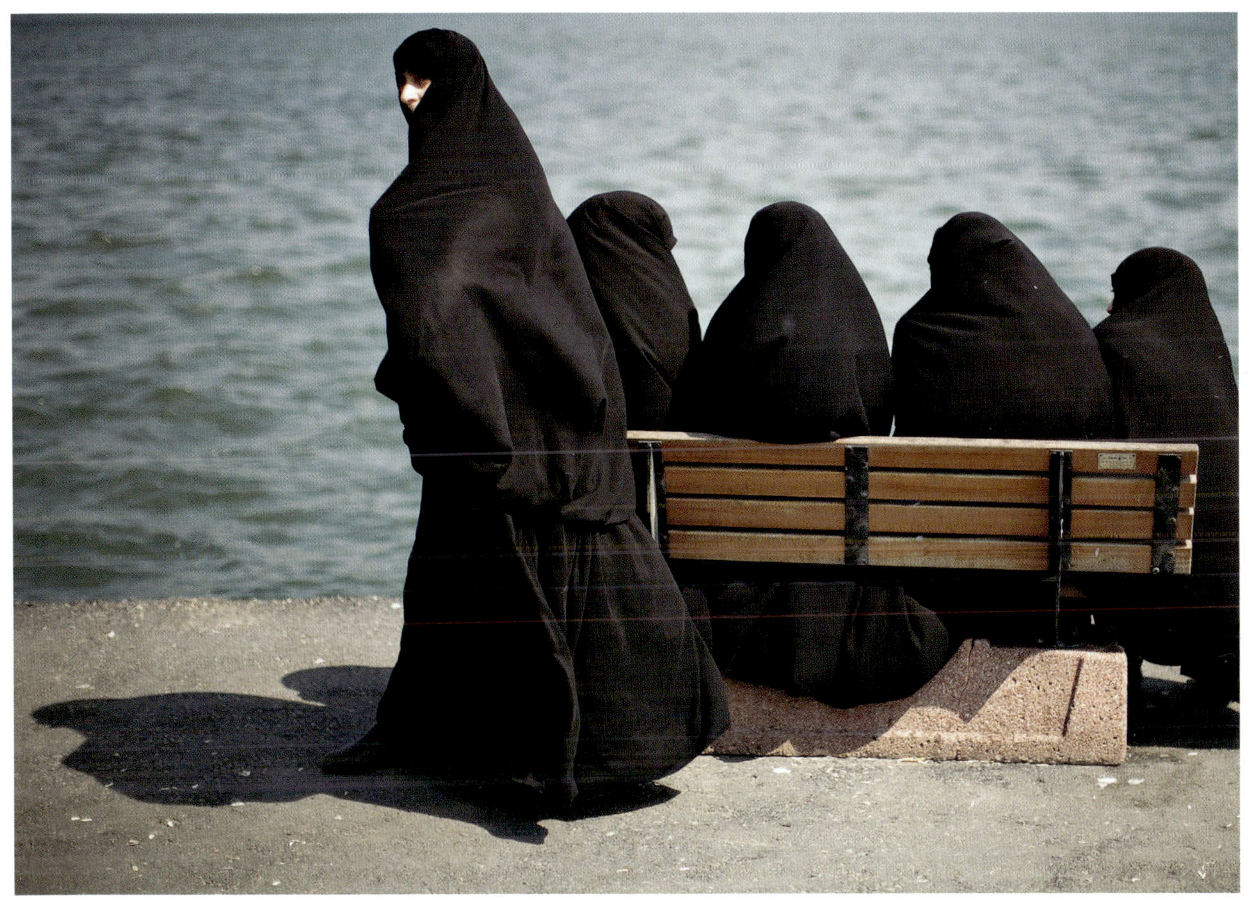

156 Istanbul, Turkey

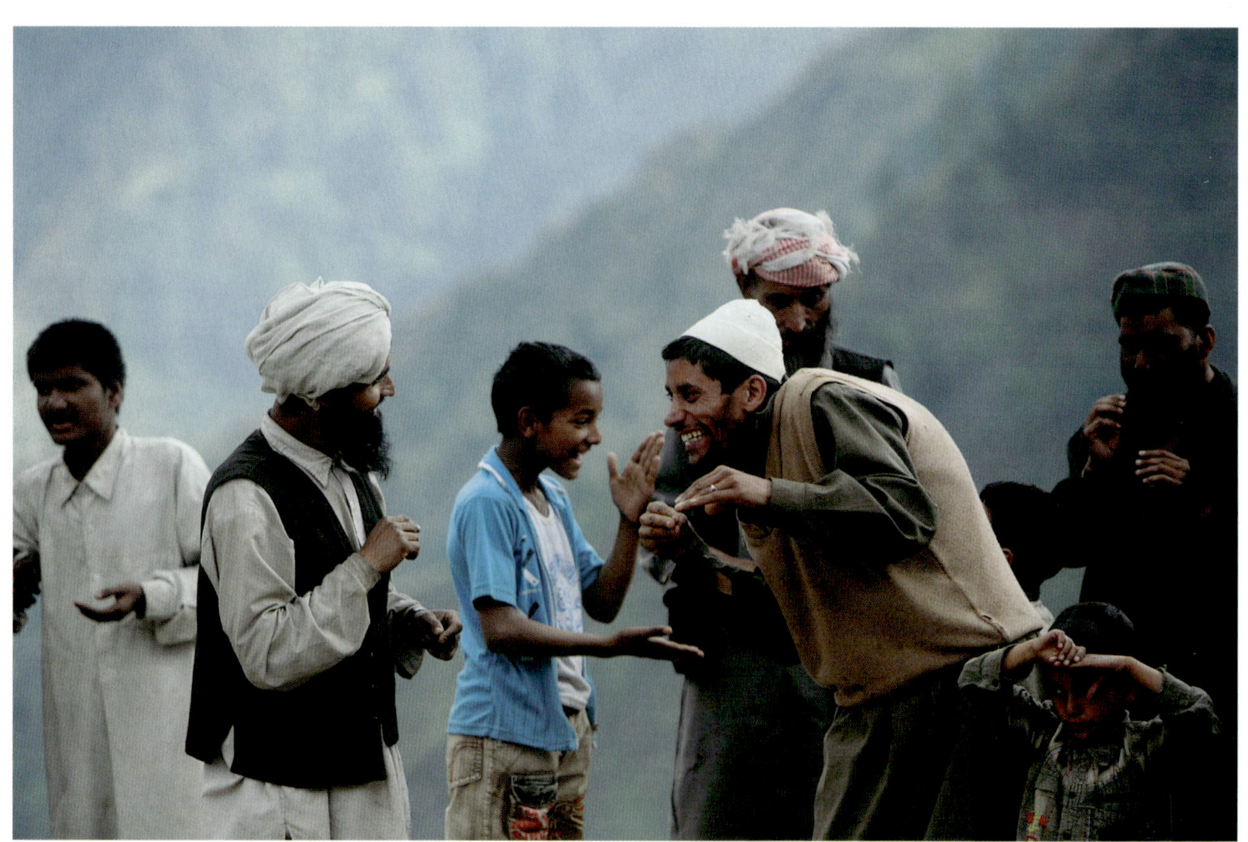

157 Dadhkai, India

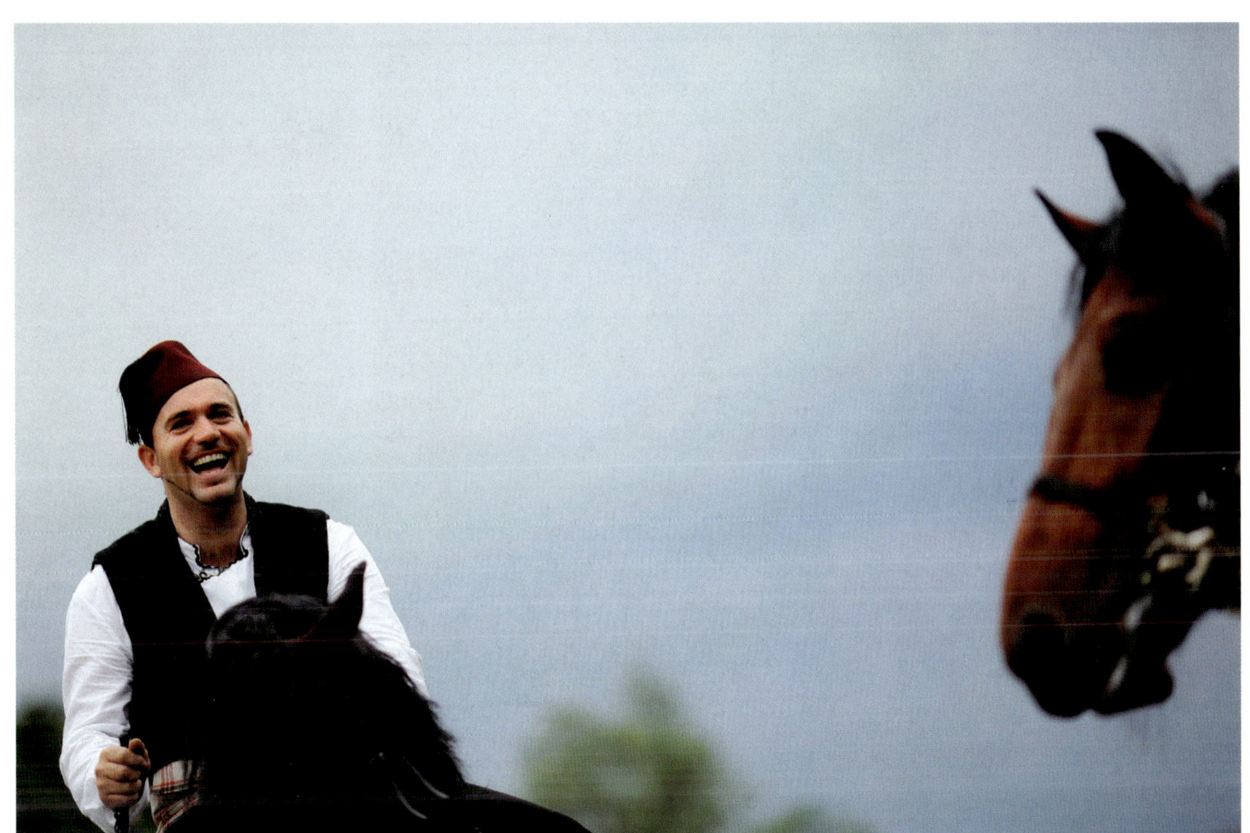

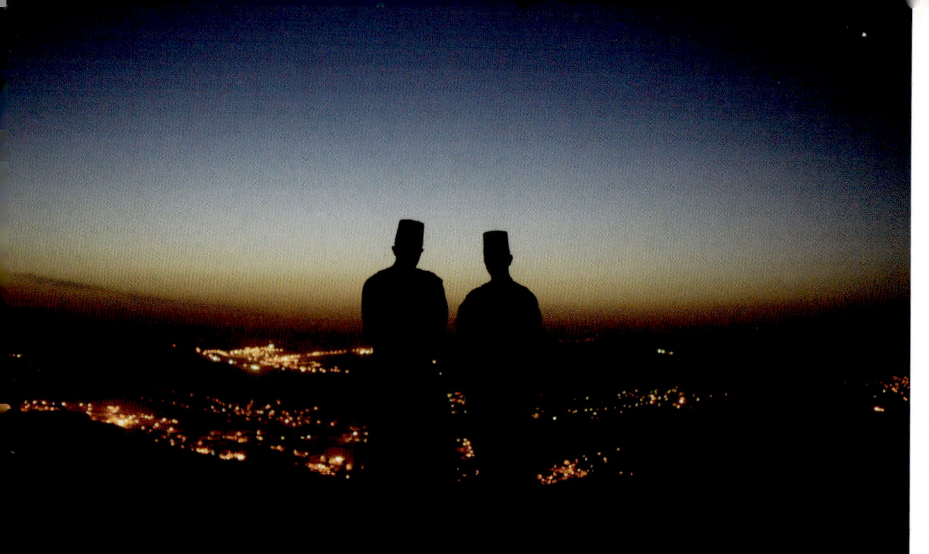

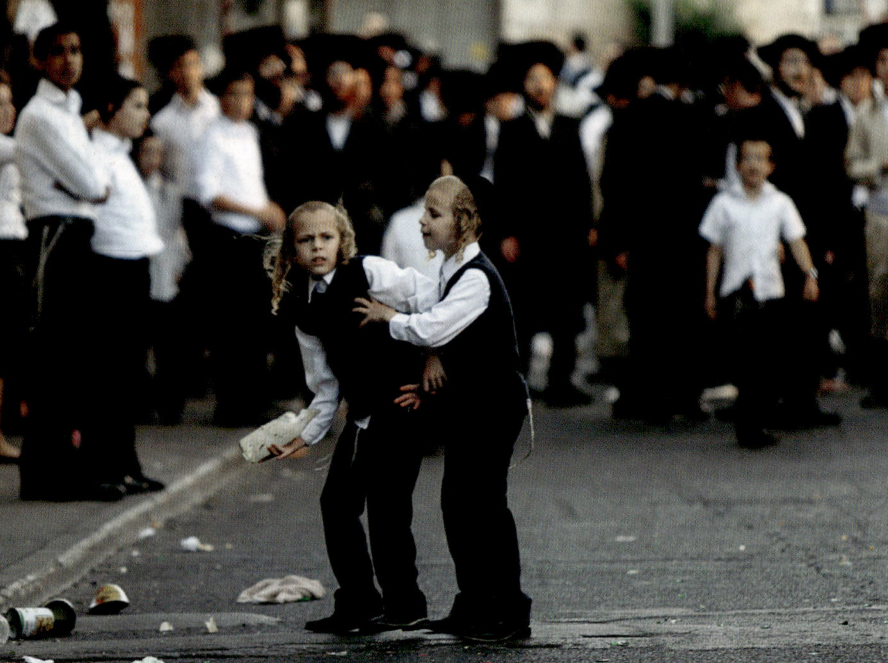

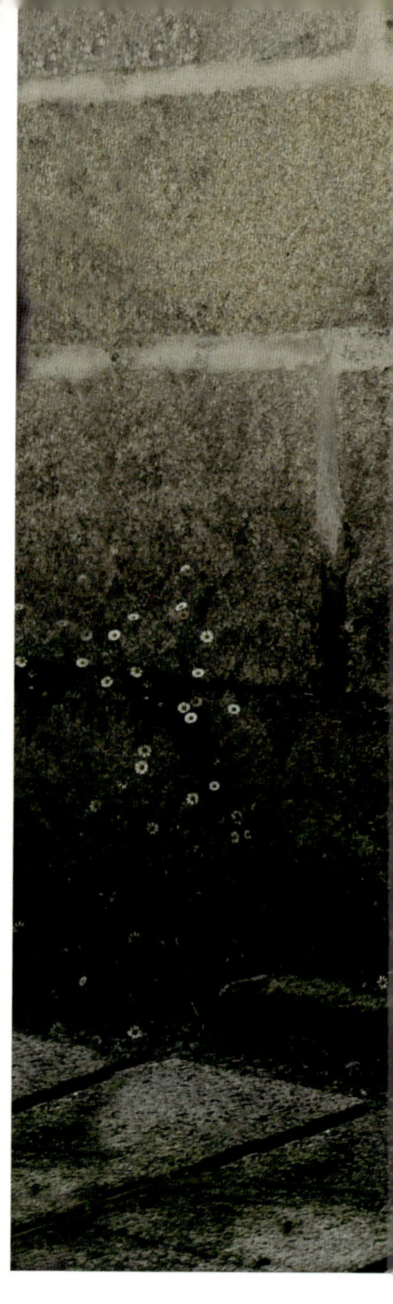

159 [TOP] Mount Gerizim, West Bank   **160** [ABOVE] Jerusalem

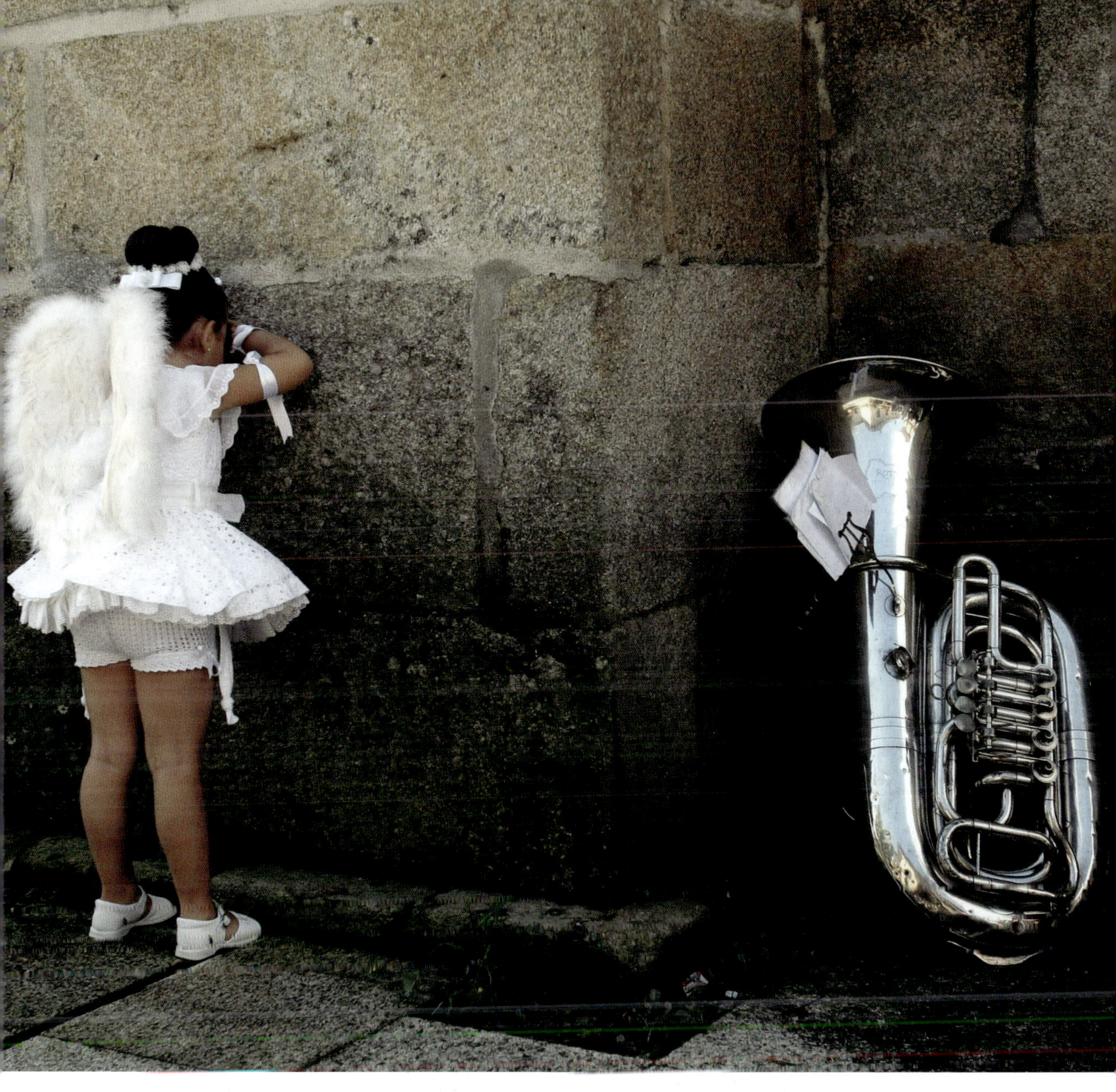

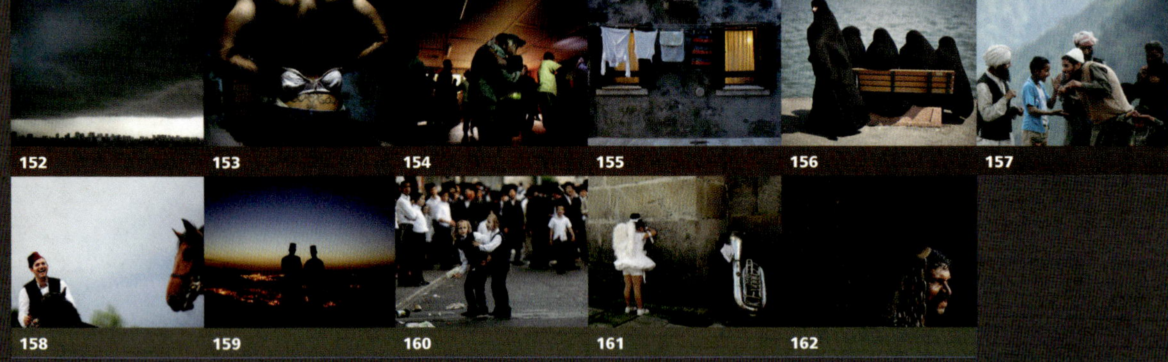

152 Rain clouds gather over the city of São Paulo. 4 May 2009. São Paulo, Brazil. Alex Almeida.

153 Transsexual Julio Yoaris Alvarez dresses at home in Havana on International Day Against Homophobia. Alvarez was awaiting a sex-change operation, available free of charge under the Cuban health care system. 16 May 2009. Havana, Cuba. Claudia Daut.

154 U.S. army soldiers dance during their time off at Kandahar Airfield. 6 June 2009. Kandahar, Afghanistan. Jorge Silva.

155 Clothes hang outside a traditional house in downtown Venice. 2 June 2009. Venice, Italy. Tony Gentile.

156 Muslim women sit on a park bench overlooking the Golden Horn on the Sea of Marmara in Istanbul. 3 April 2009. Istanbul, Turkey. Finbarr O'Reilly.

157 A group of deaf and mute villagers communicate using sign language at Dadhkai village in northern India's Jammu district. Each of the 47 families in this Himalayan village has at least one member who can neither hear nor speak. The first reported case dates back to 1931 and numbers have now swelled to 82. 18 June 2009. Dadhkai, India. Mukesh Gupta.

158 A Bosnian Muslim wearing traditional costume arrives in the central Bosnian village of Prusac for the annual pilgrimage to Ajvatovica. Tens of thousands of Muslims climb the mountain each year to pray at the site where, according to tradition, a huge rock divided in half to release spring water after a holyman prayed in front of it. The pilgrimage, the biggest for Muslims in Europe, has a 499-year-old tradition. 27 June 2009. Prusac, Bosnia. Damir Sagolj.

159 Members of the Samaritan sect look towards the West Bank city of Nablus as they stand atop Mount Gerizim during the traditional pilgrimage marking the holiday of Shavuot. The Samaritans, who trace their roots to the biblical Kingdom of Israel in what is now the northern occupied West Bank, observe religious practices similar to those of Judaism. 31 May 2009. Mount Gerizim, West Bank. Darren Whiteside.

160 Ultra-Orthodox Jews protest against the opening of a Jerusalem parking lot on the Jewish sabbath. Secular protesters held a counter demonstration in support of the move. 27 June 2009. Jerusalem. Baz Ratner.

161 A four-year-old girl plays during the traditional 'Coca' celebration in Redondela in rural northeastern Spain. 11 June 2009. Redondela, Spain. Miguel Vidal.

162 A keeper stands between ceremonial elephants after they were blessed by a Buddhist monk as part of New Year celebrations in Colombo. 15 April 2009. Colombo, Sri Lanka. David Gray.

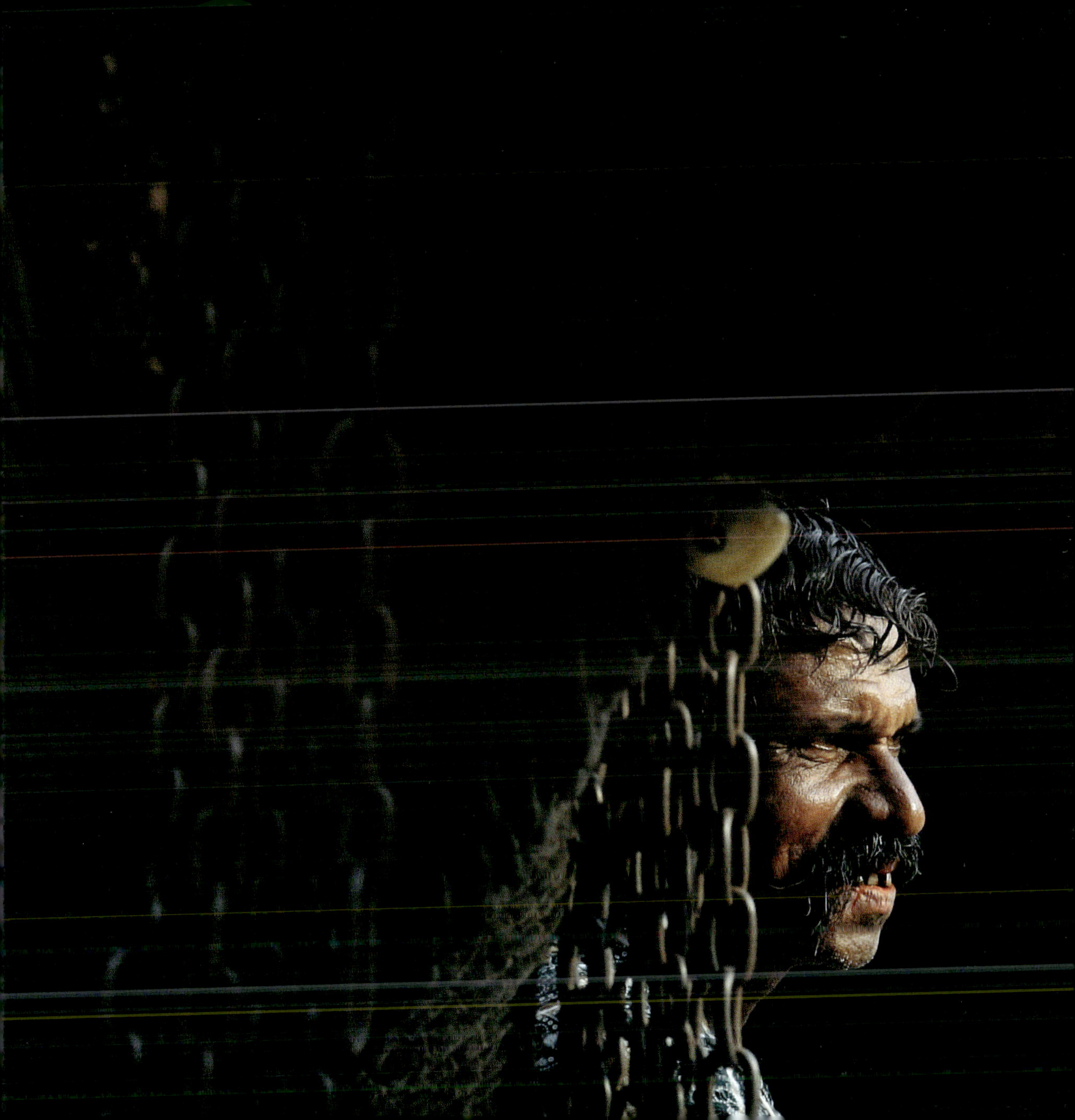

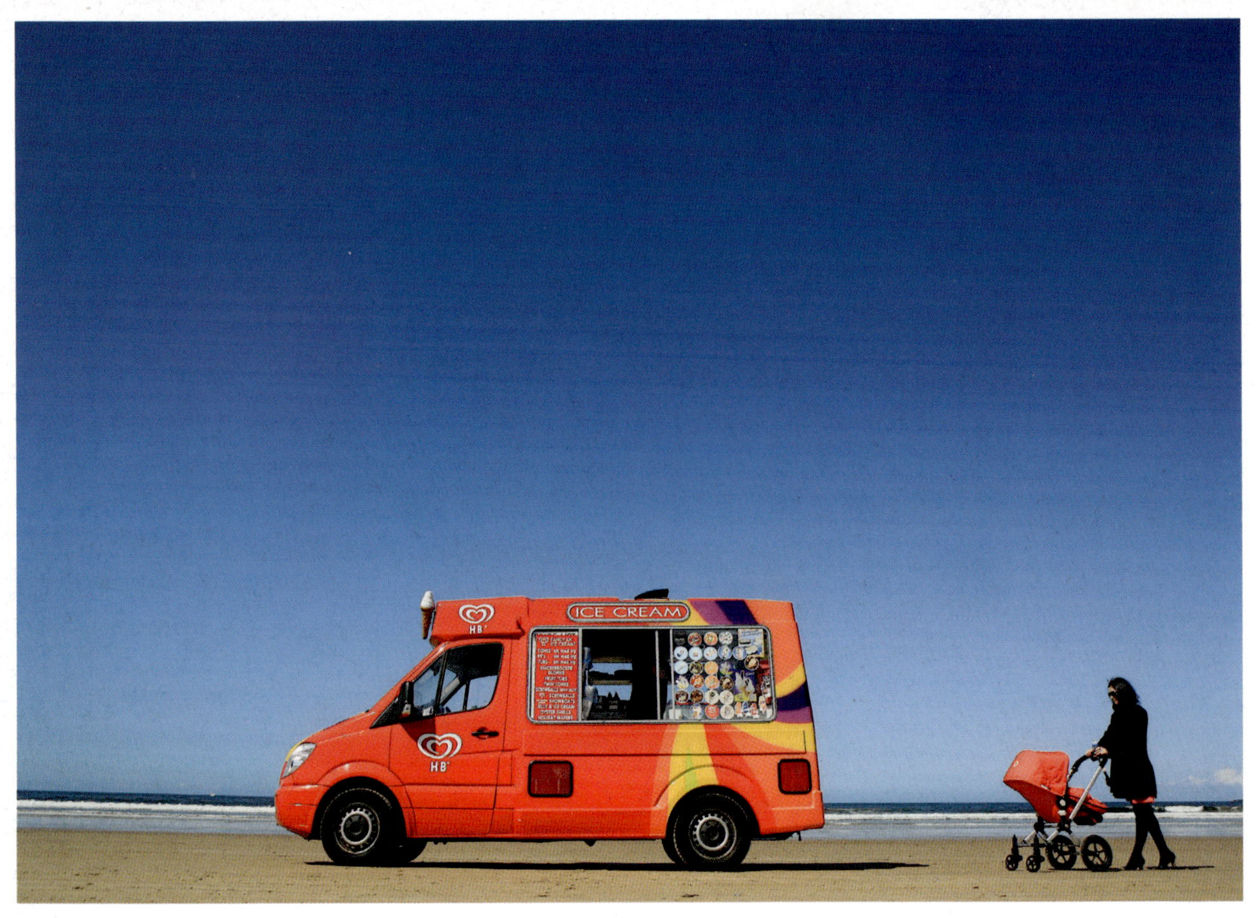

163 Portstewart, Northern Ireland

164 [OPPOSITE] Horsham, Britain

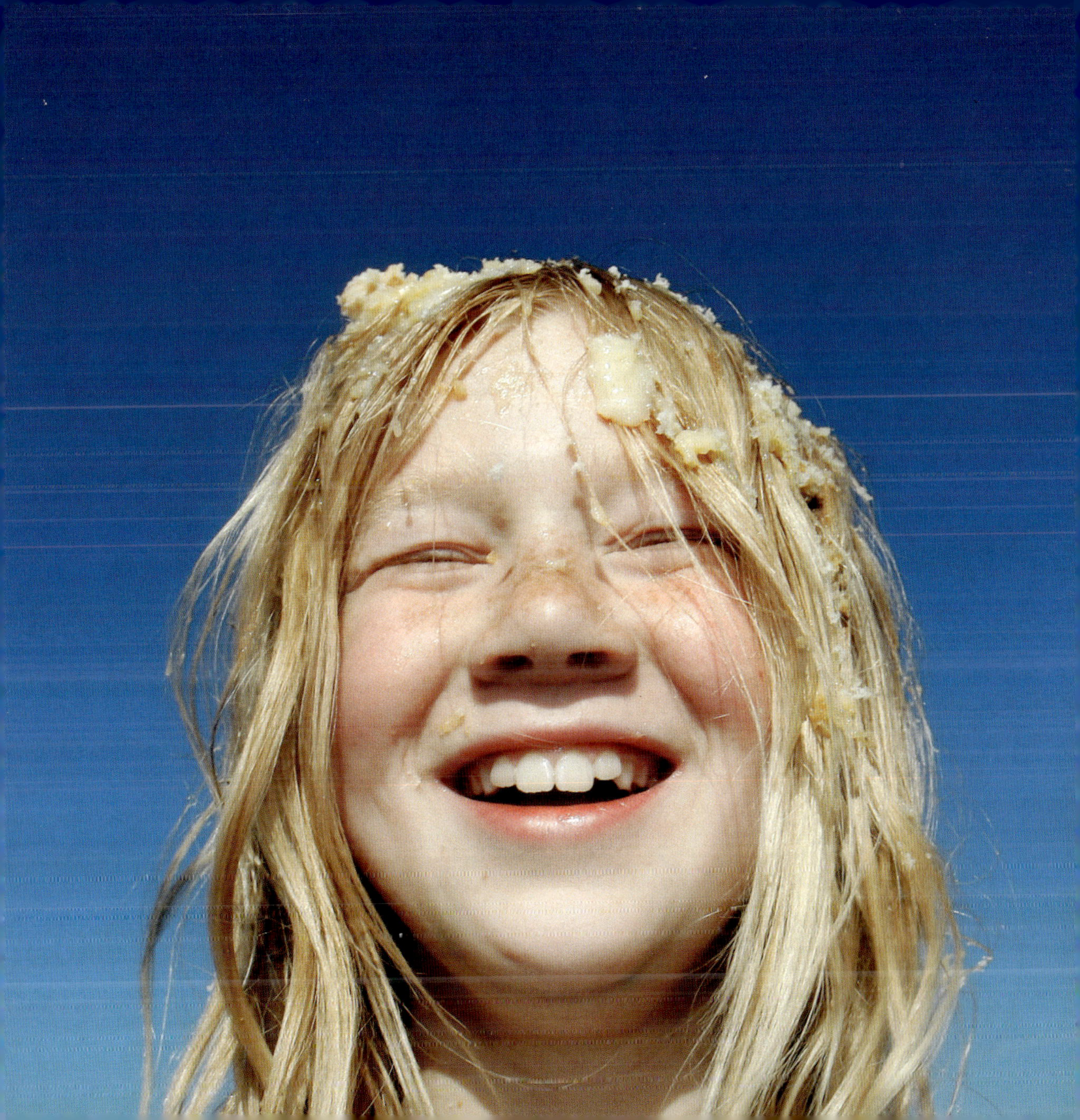

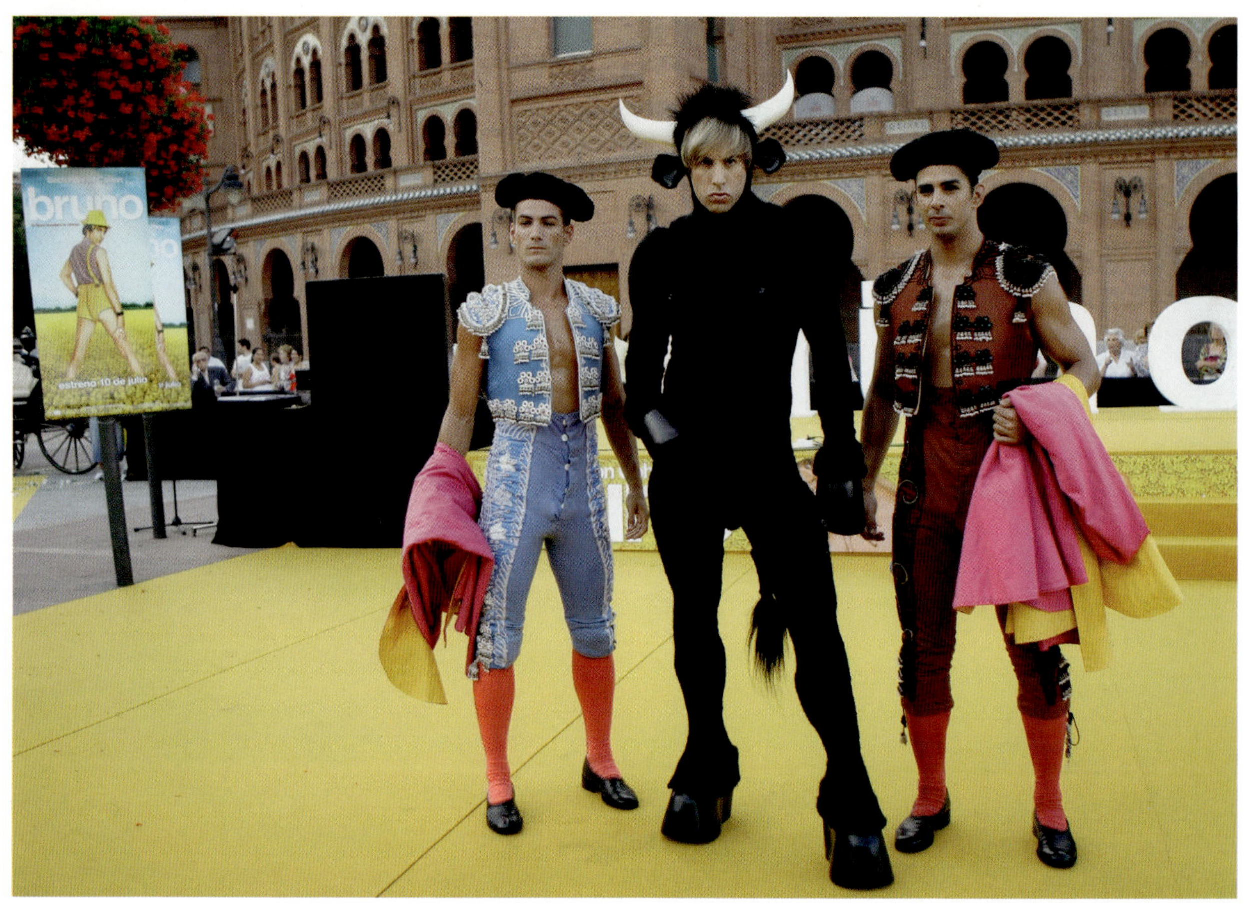
bruno
estreno 10 de julio

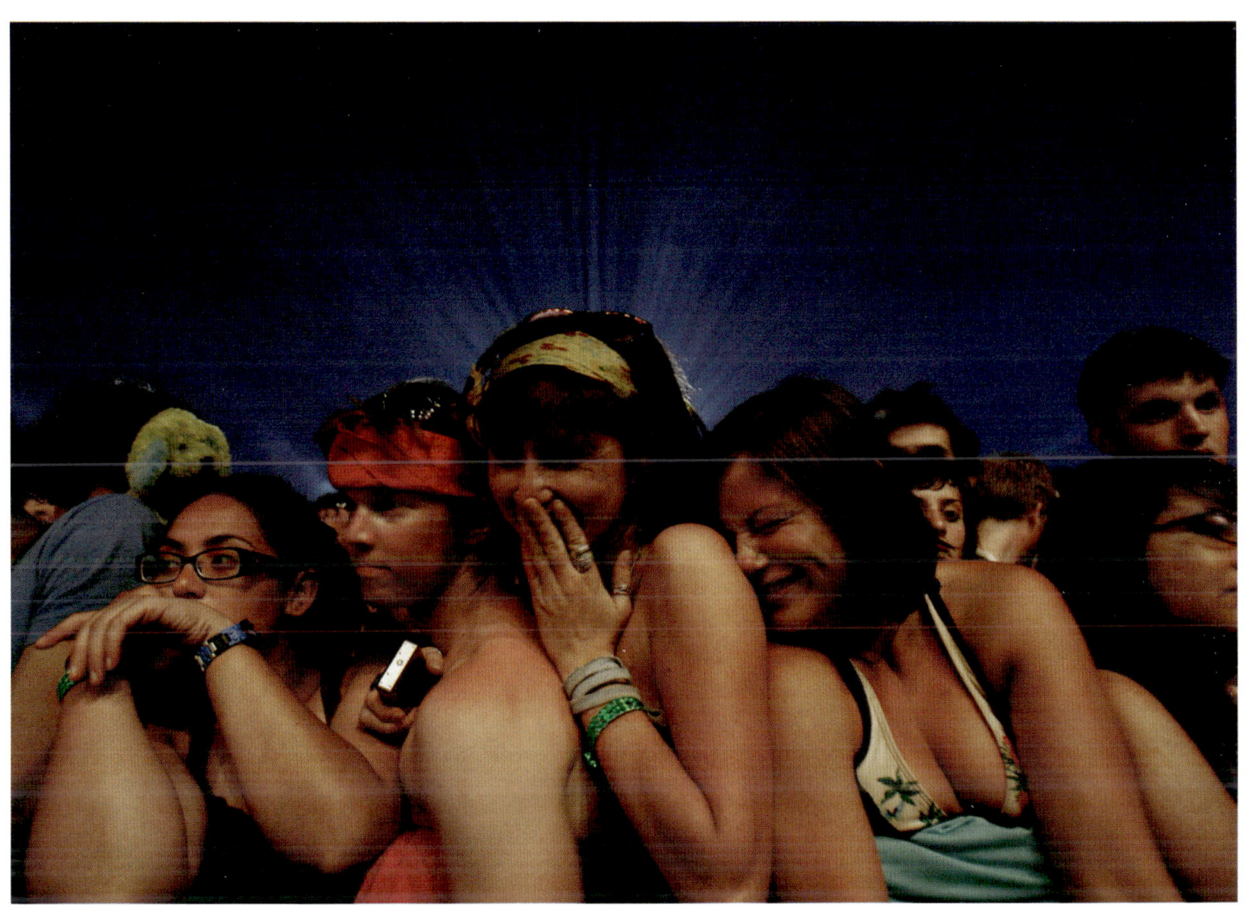

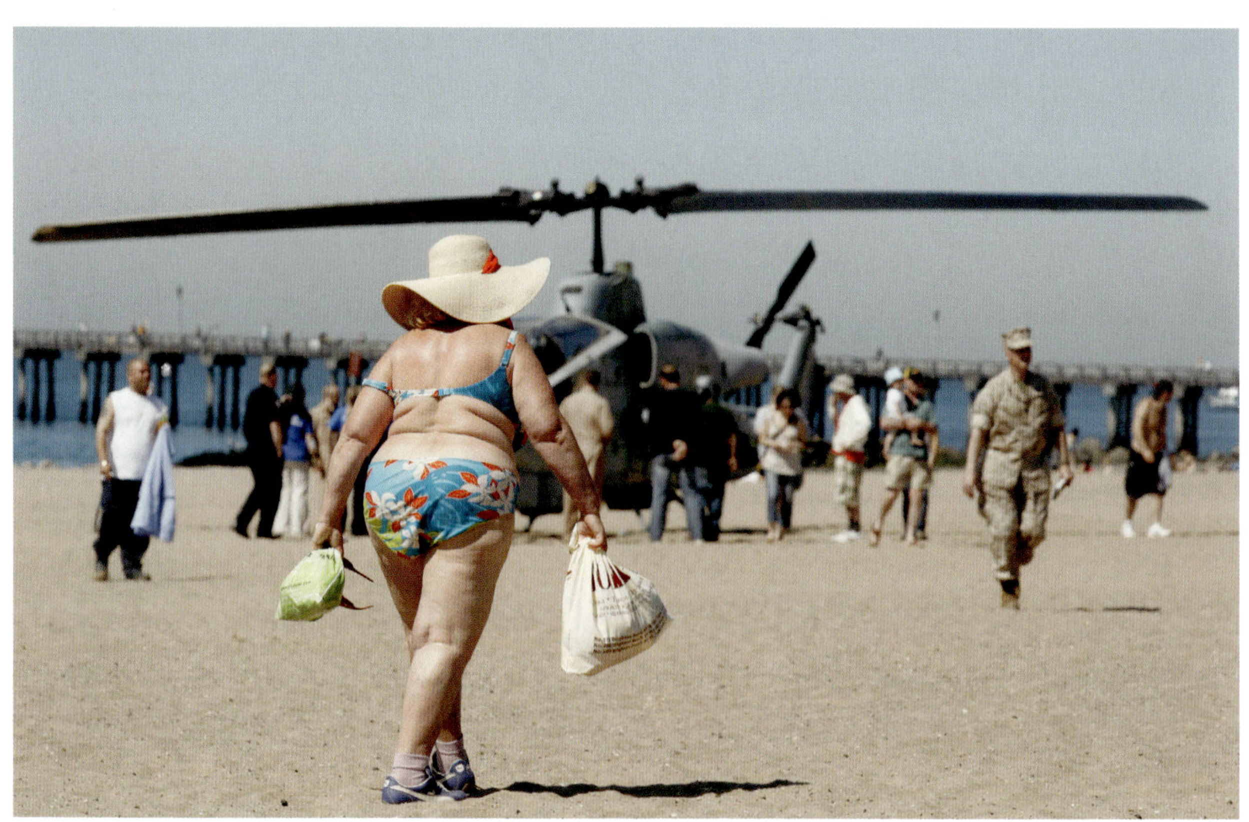

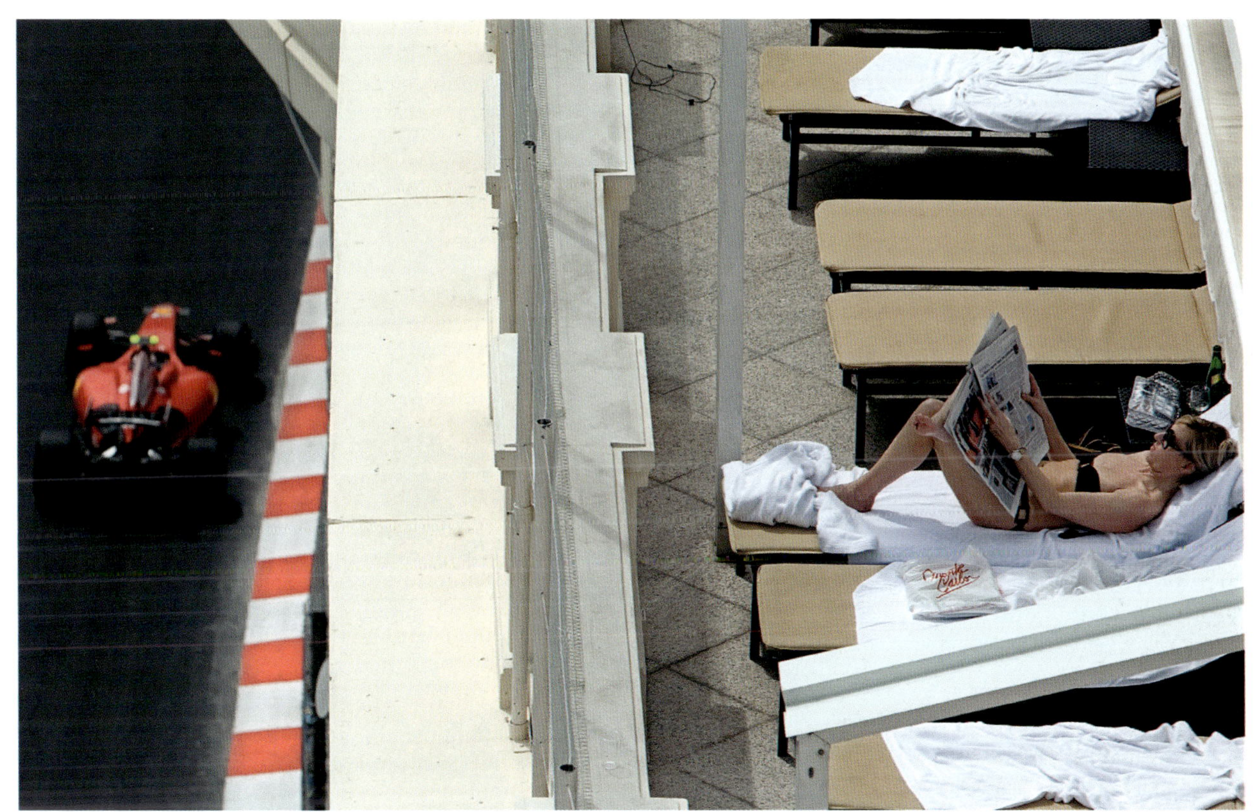

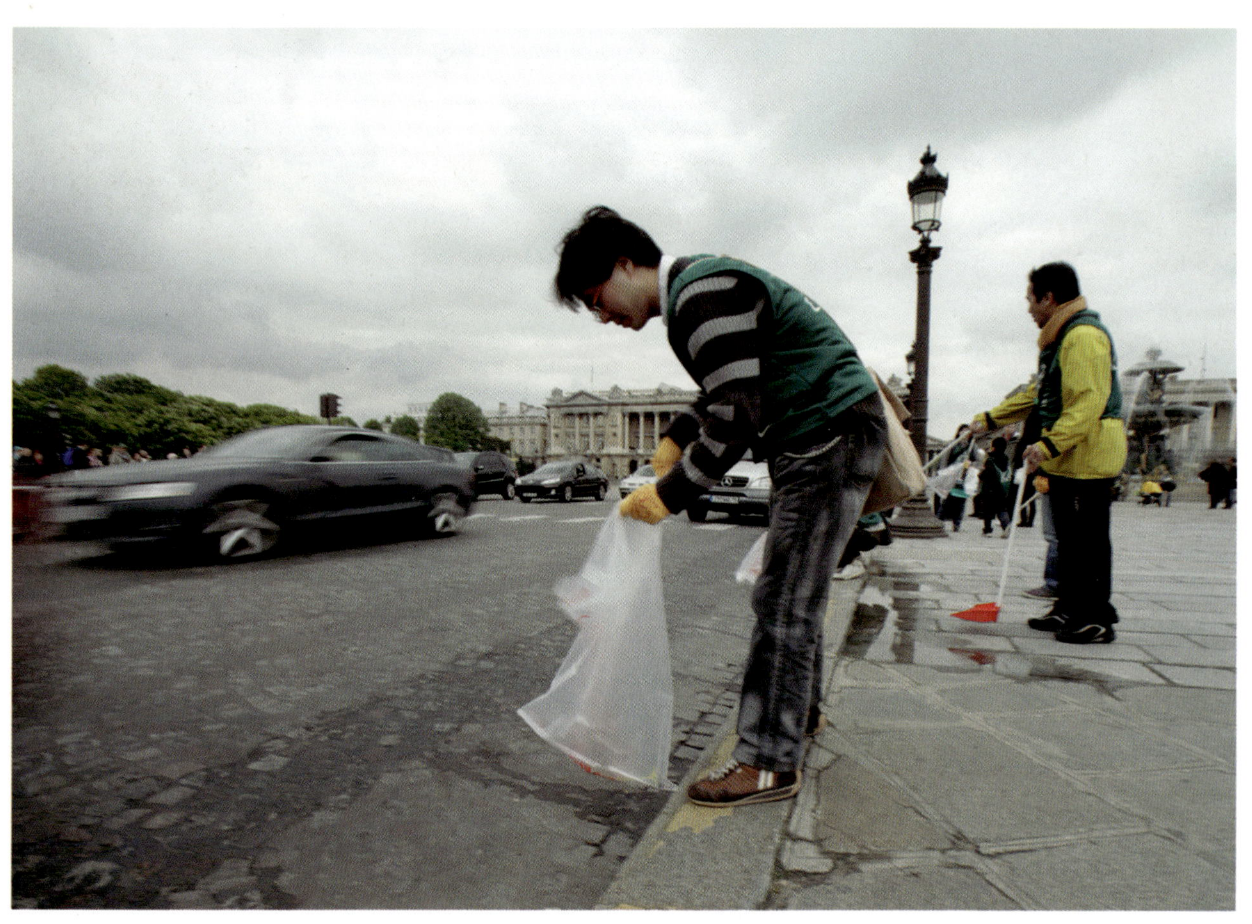

169 Paris, France

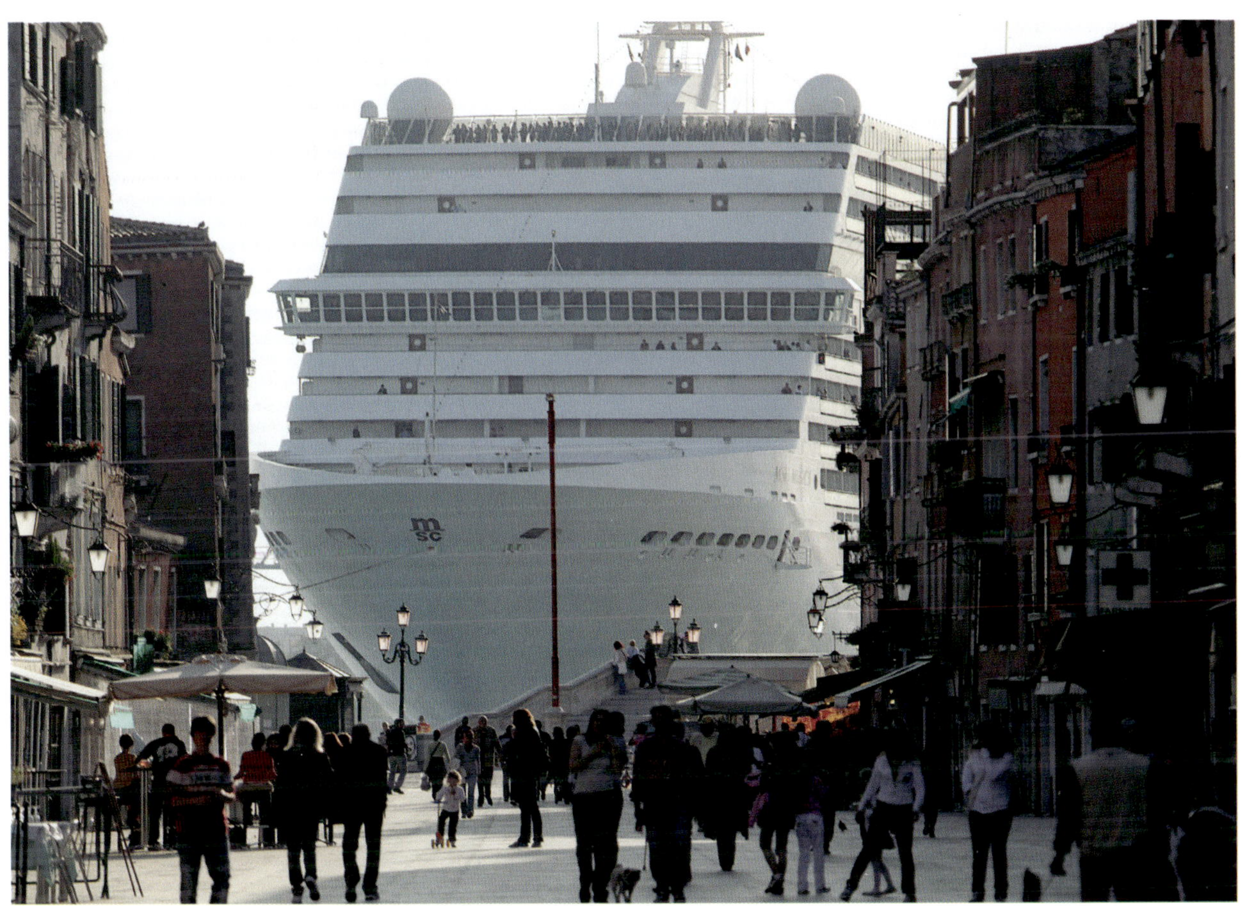

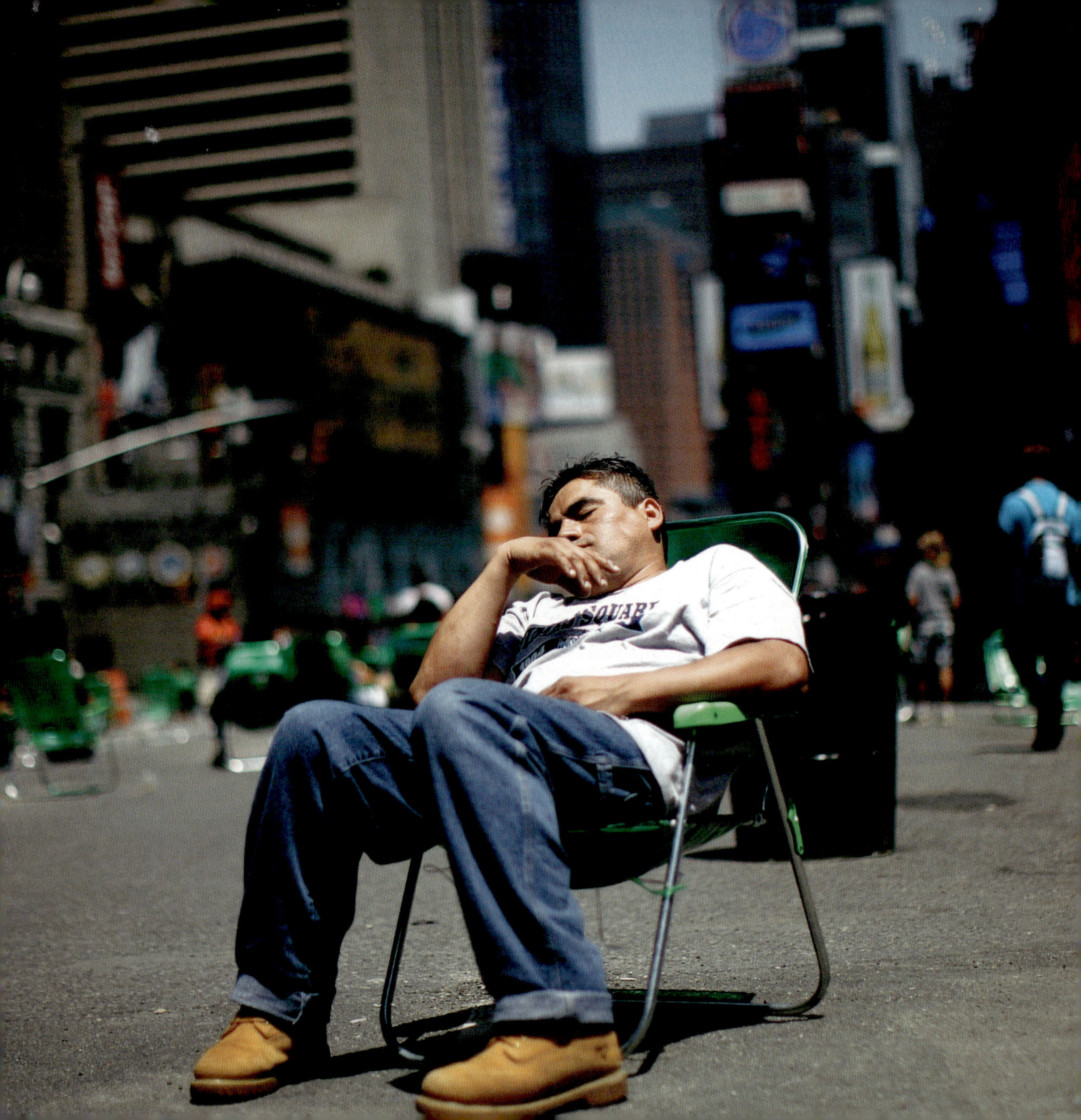

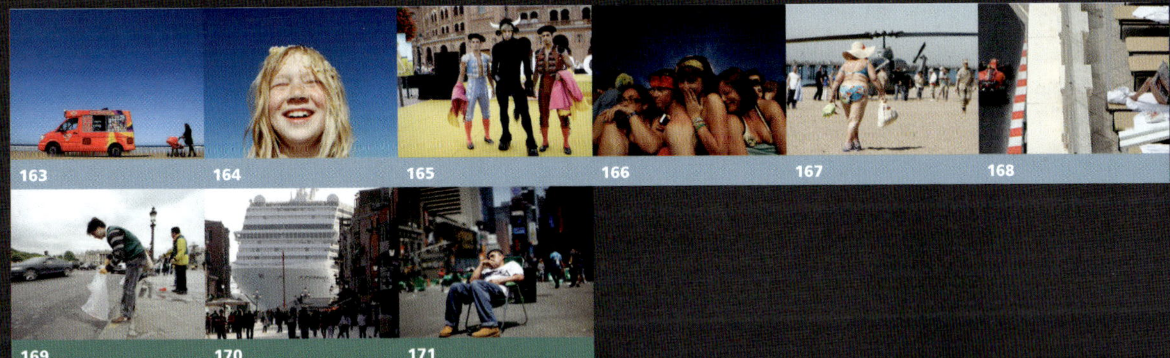

163 A woman pushes her pram towards an ice cream vendor on Portstewart Strand beach, Northern Ireland. 10 May 2009. Portstewart, Northern Ireland. Cathal McNaughton.

164 A girl laughs as she takes part in a successful attempt at the world record for the largest custard pie fight staged at the Kidz Stuff Festival in Horsham, southeast England. 31 May 2009. Horsham, Britain. Luke MacGregor.

165 British actor Sacha Baron Cohen, dressed as a bull, poses during the Spanish premiere of his film *Brüno* outside Madrid's Las Ventas bullring. 18 June 2009. Madrid, Spain. Juan Medina.

166 Concert-goers wait for the band My Bloody Valentine to take the stage at the Coachella Music Festival in California. 19 April 2009. Indio, United States. Mario Anzuoni.

167 A woman walks on the beach at Coney Island, New York, past an AH-1 Cobra helicopter. 21 May 2009. New York, United States. Lucas Jackson.

168 A woman sunbathes as Ferrari Formula One driver Kimi Räikkönen of Finland takes part in the second practice session of the Monaco F1 Grand Prix. 21 May 2009. Monte Carlo, Monaco. Max Rossi.

169 Japanese Greenbird Paris volunteers clear litter from Place de la Concorde. The group of Japanese expatriates staged the clean-up action as part of a monthly campaign to make the French capital a cleaner place for the many thousands of Japanese tourists who visit. 19 April 2009. Paris, France. Thomas White.

170 The cruise ship MSC Musica dwarfs Via Garibaldi as it arrives in Venice. The ship, owned by the Mediterranean Shipping Company, is 294 m (965 ft) long. 4 May 2009. Venice, Italy. Manuel Silvestri.

171 A man sleeps in a chair on a closed portion of Broadway in Times Square. A five-block section of the busy New York thoroughfare was closed to traffic for use as a pedestrian promenade on an experimental basis through summer 2009. 7 June 2009. New York, United States. Eric Thayer.

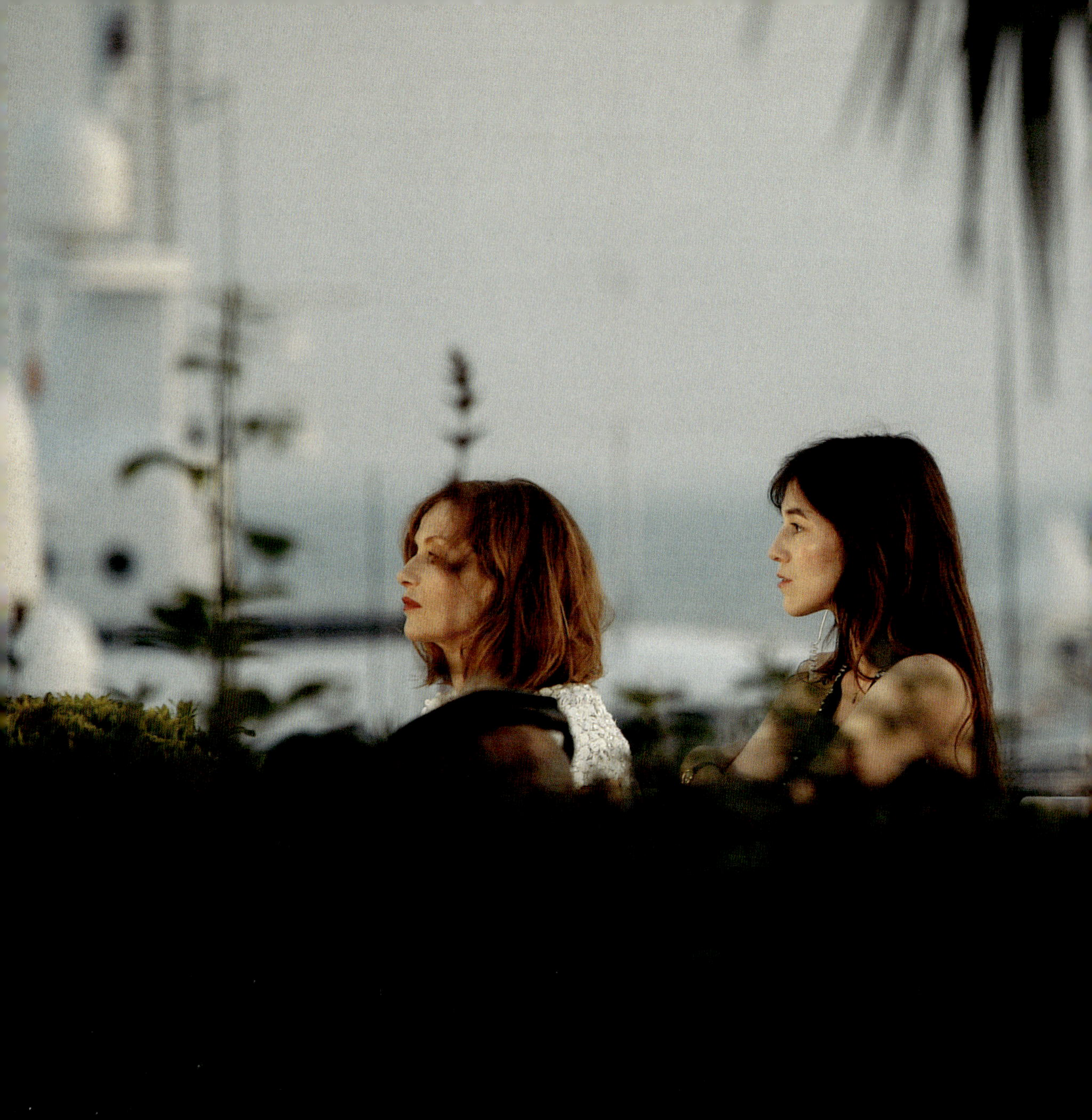

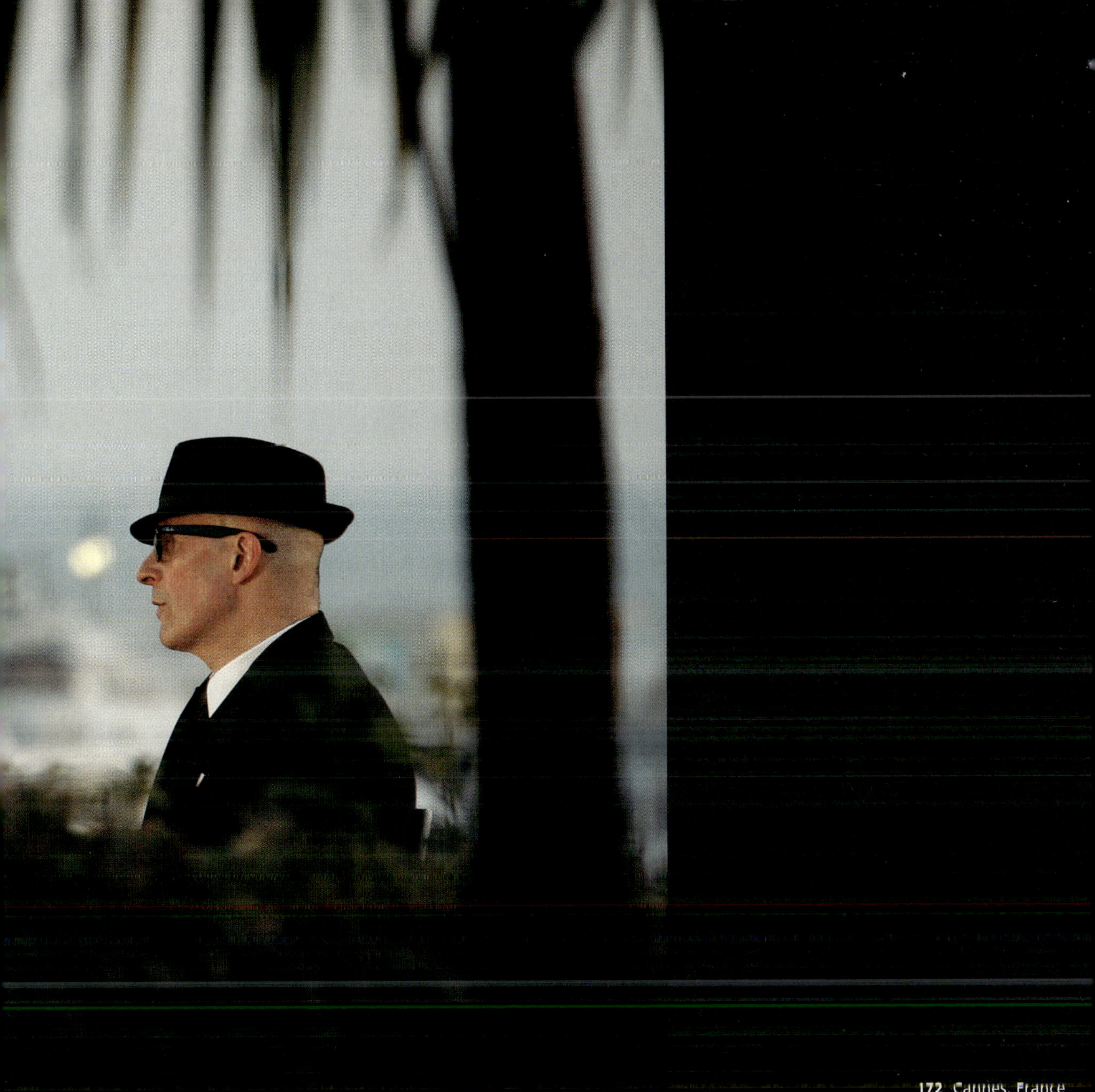

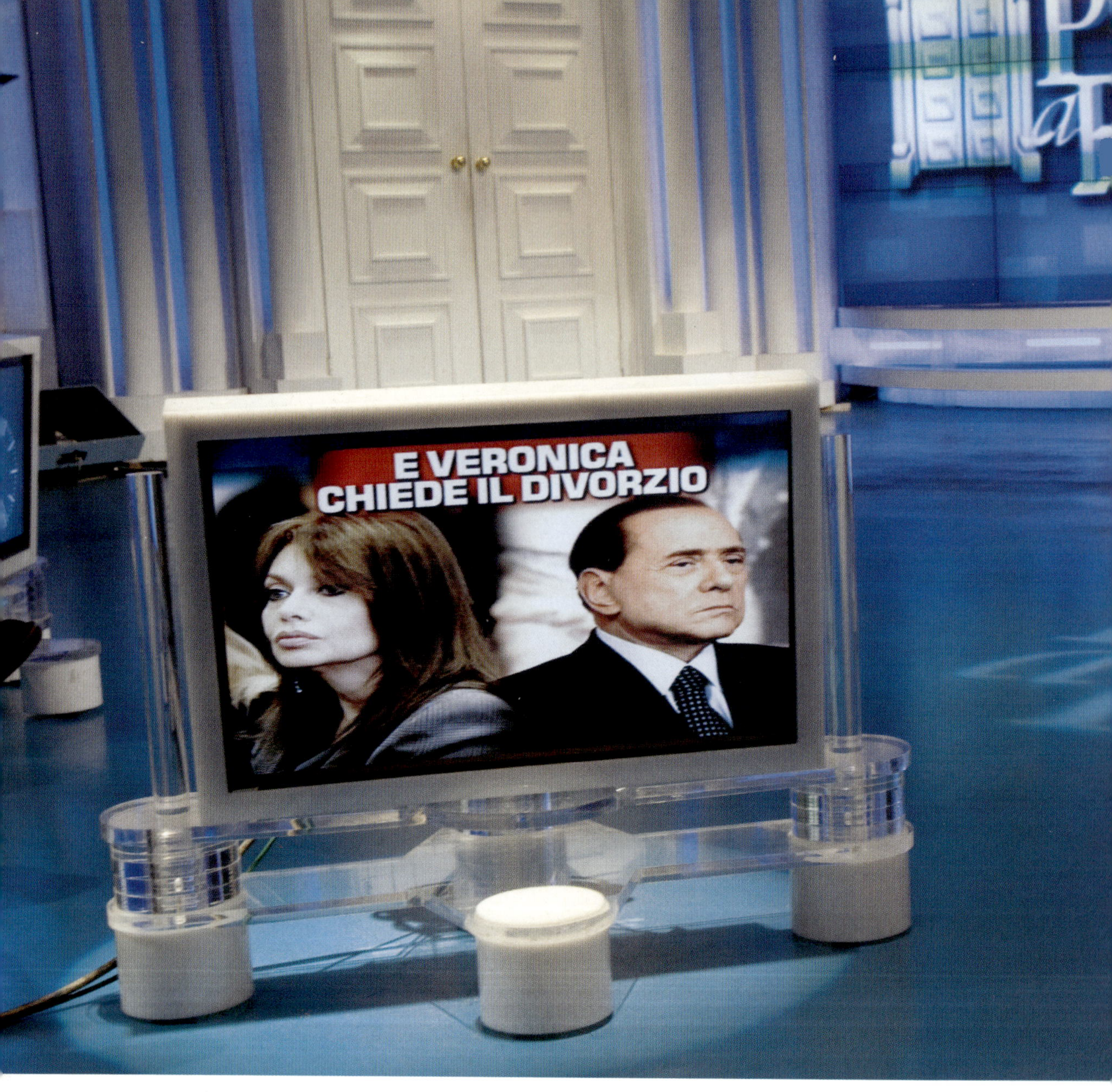
E VERONICA
CHIEDE IL DIVORZIO

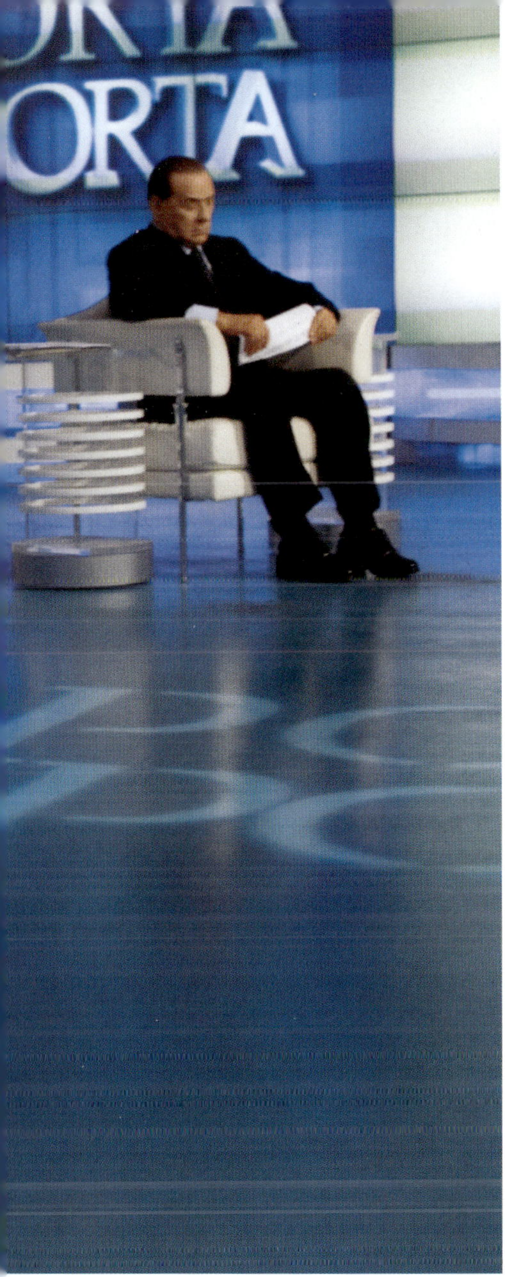

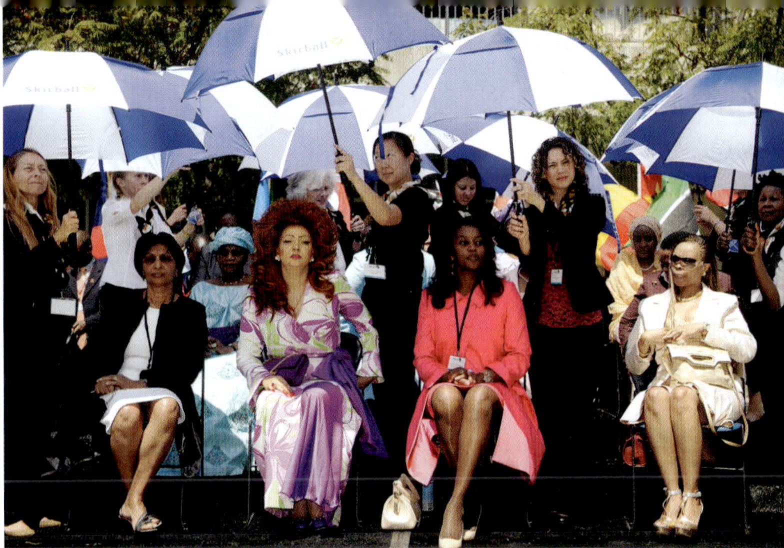

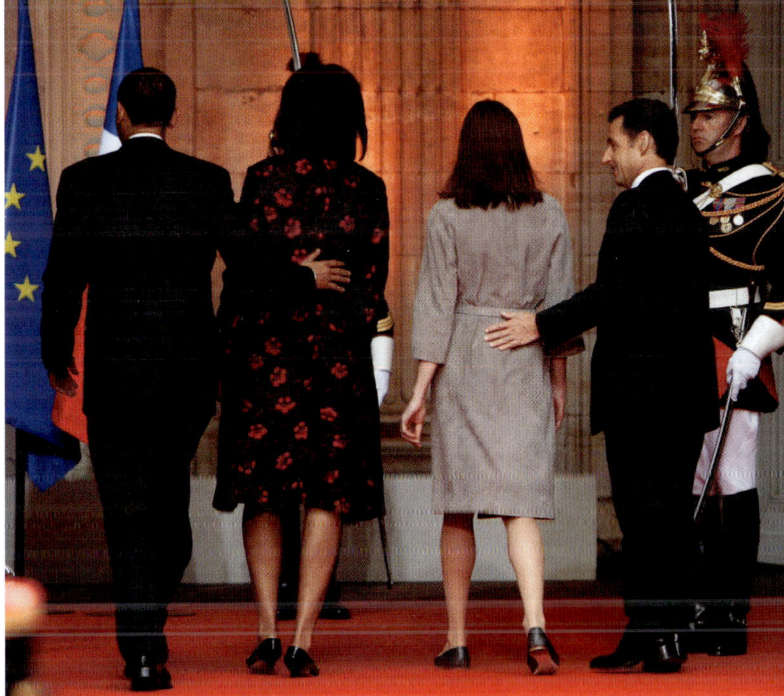

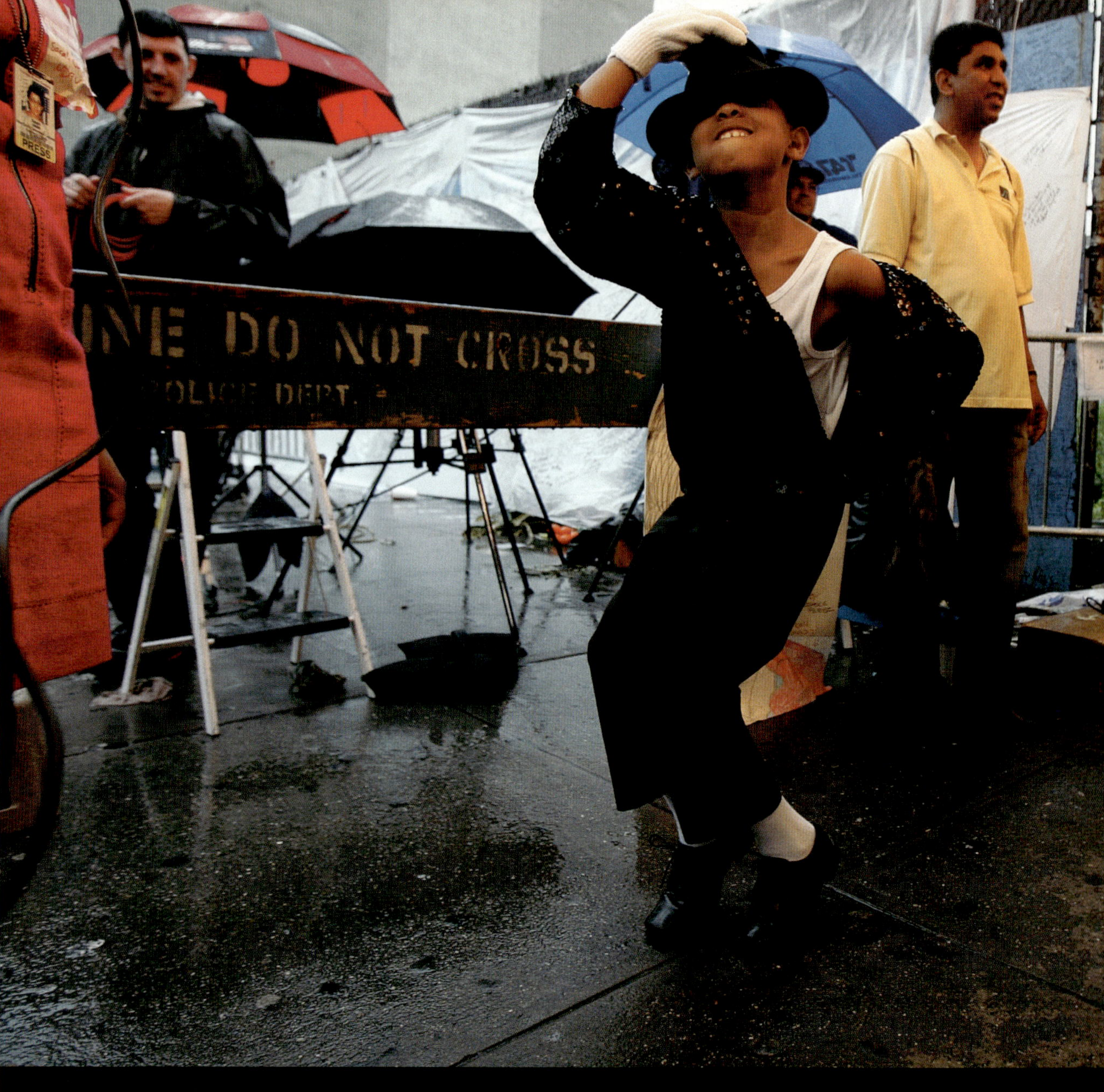
NE DO NOT CROSS
POLICE DEPT.
PRESS

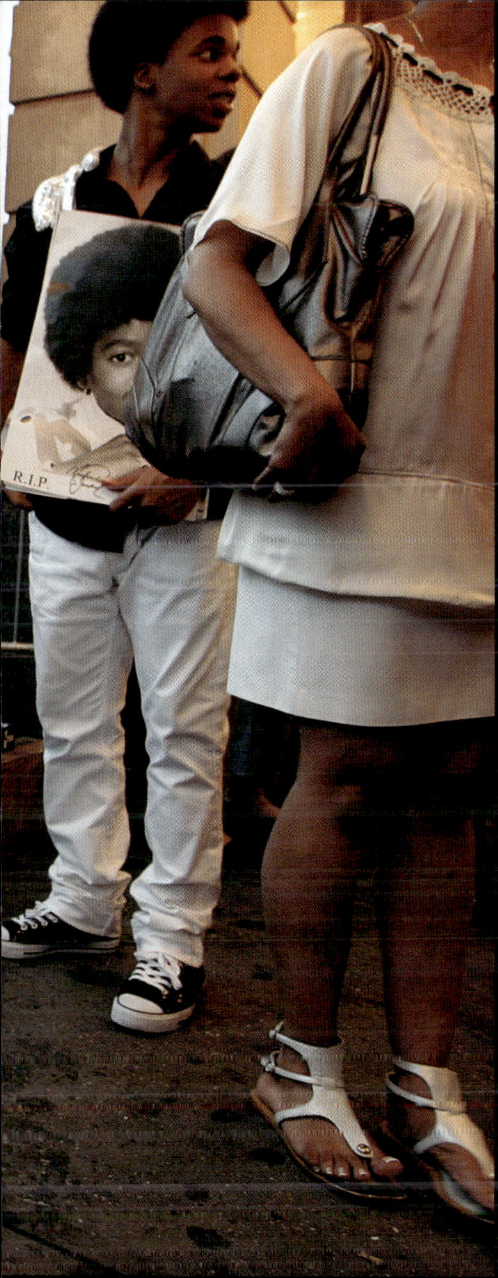

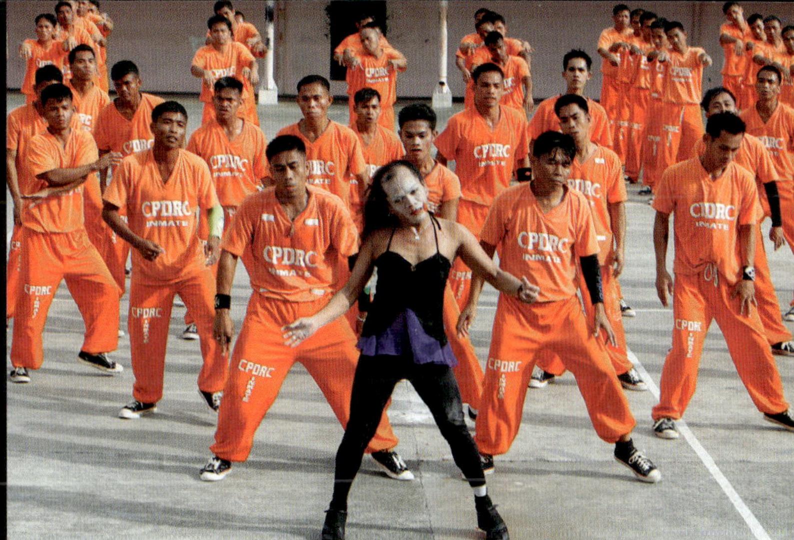

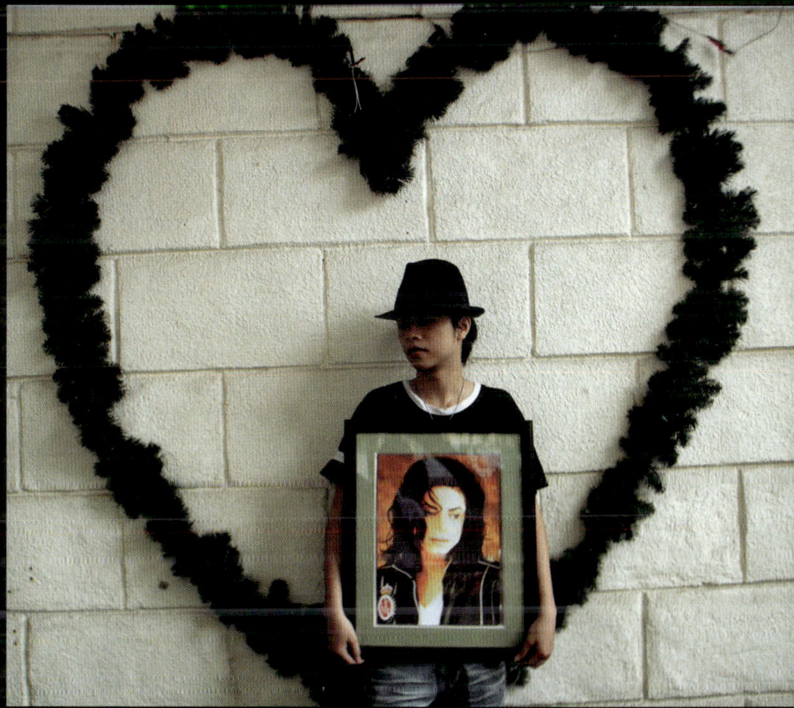

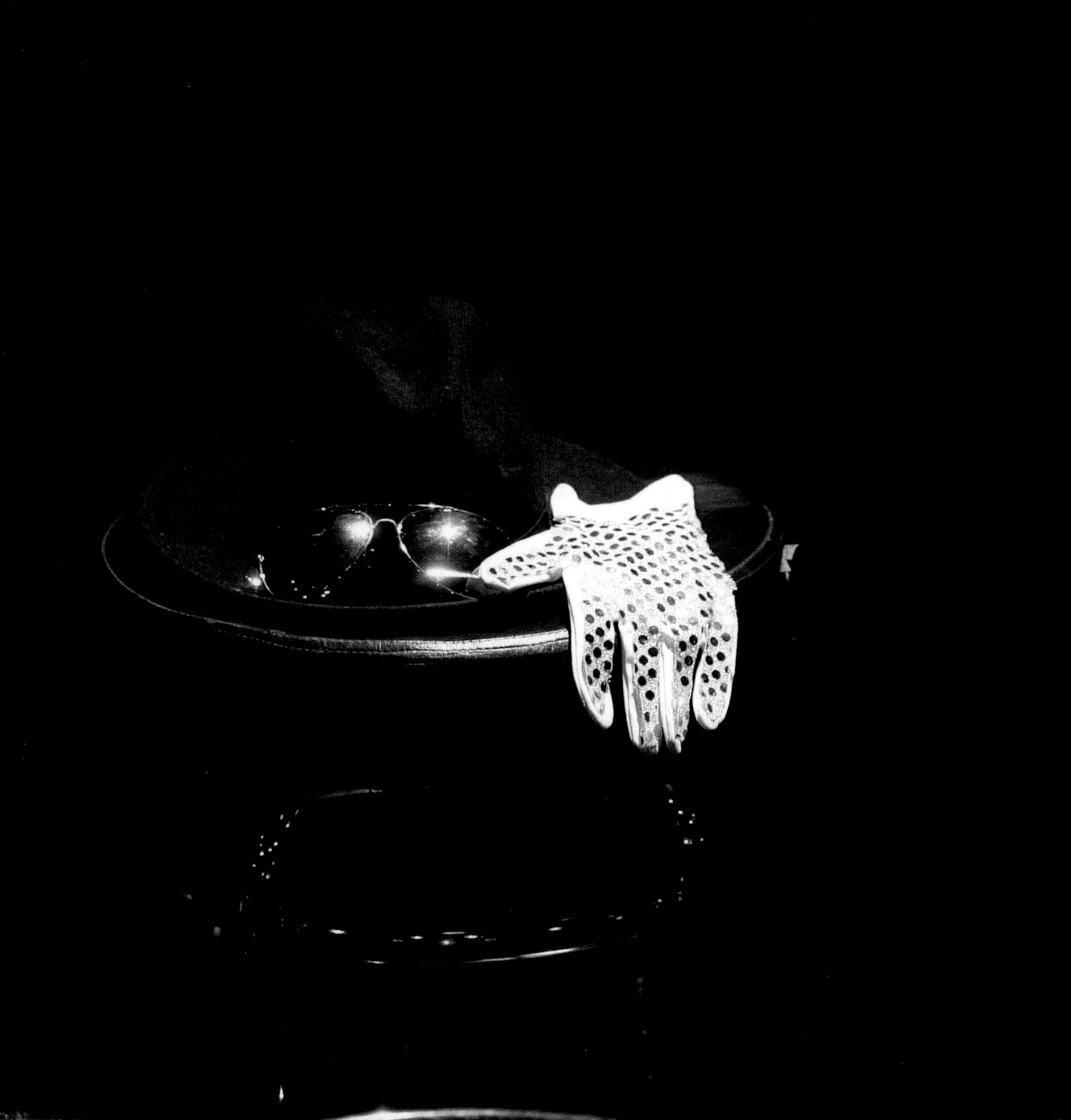

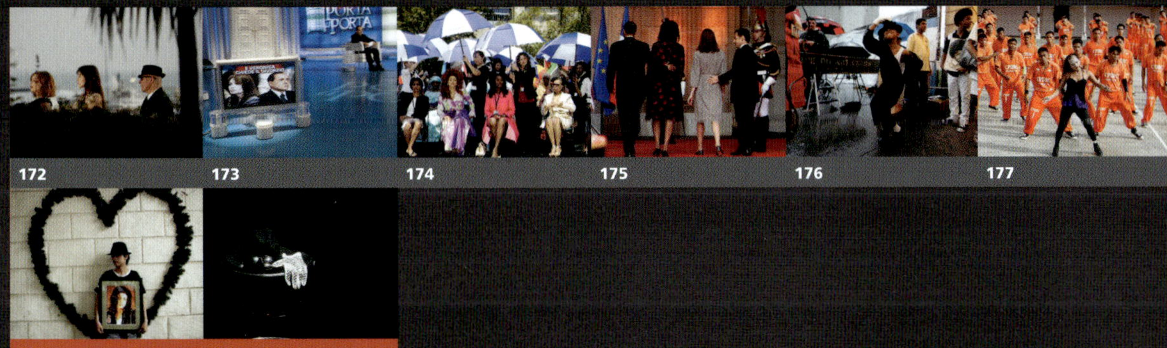

172 Jury President Isabelle Huppert, actress Charlotte Gainsbourg and director Jacques Audiard await a photocall after the award ceremony at the 62nd Cannes Film Festival. 24 May 2009. Cannes, France. Vincent Kessler.

173 Italy's Prime Minister Silvio Berlusconi sits in a television studio during the taping of talk show *Porta a Porta*. A nearby monitor shows images of him and his wife Veronica Lario, with a headline that reads 'And Veronica asked for divorce'. Italian media reported in May that Berlusconi's wife planned to file for divorce, days after she criticized him for attending the birthday party of an 18-year-old aspiring model. 5 May 2009. Rome, Italy. Remo Casilli.

174 Volunteers hold umbrellas over (left to right) Adélcia Barreto Pires of Cape Verde, Chantal Biya of Cameroon, Ana Paula Dos Santos of Angola, and Queen Inkhosikati LaMbikiza of Swaziland during the African First Ladies Health Summit in Los Angeles. 20 April 2009. Los Angeles, United States. Phil McCarten.

175 U.S. President Barack Obama and first lady Michelle Obama take part in a welcoming ceremony with France's President Nicolas Sarkozy and first lady Carla Bruni-Sarkozy in Strasbourg, France, ahead of a summit marking the 60th anniversary of the NATO military alliance. 3 April 2009. Strasbourg, France. Jim Young.

176 A young fan dances as he waits to enter the Apollo Theater in New York for a public memorial to Michael Jackson. The 50-year-old pop star was pronounced dead on 25 June in Los Angeles after going into cardiac arrest. 30 June 2009. New York, United States. Lucas Jackson.

177 More than 1,500 prison inmates perform a tribute to Michael Jackson at prison grounds in Cebu city in central Philippines. The prisoners' 'Thriller' dance, part of a physical fitness and stress-relief regime established in 2007, became a YouTube hit attracting over 23 million views. 27 June 2009. Cebu, Philippines. Erik de Castro.

178 A member of Michael Jackson's Fan Club in Vietnam poses with a portrait of the star during a memorial tribute at a café in Hanoi. Jackson's death dominated news bulletins, radio airwaves and websites the world over as tributes poured in for a man dubbed the 'King of Pop'. 27 June 2009. Hanoi, Vietnam. Kham.

179 A hat, a pair of glasses and a glove sit on a chair at the Michael Jackson public memorial at New York's Apollo Theater. 30 June 2009. New York, United States. Lucas Jackson.

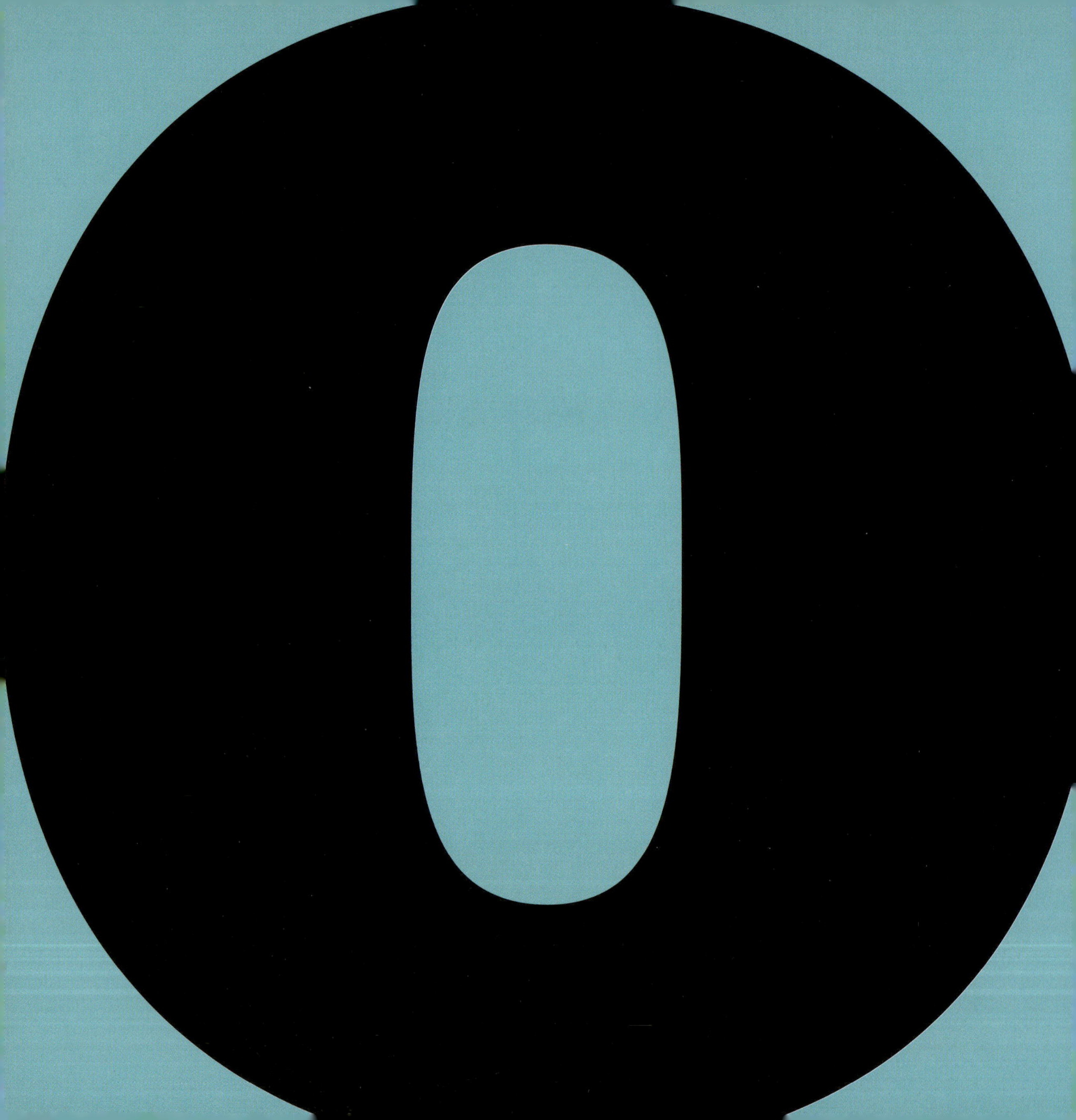

3

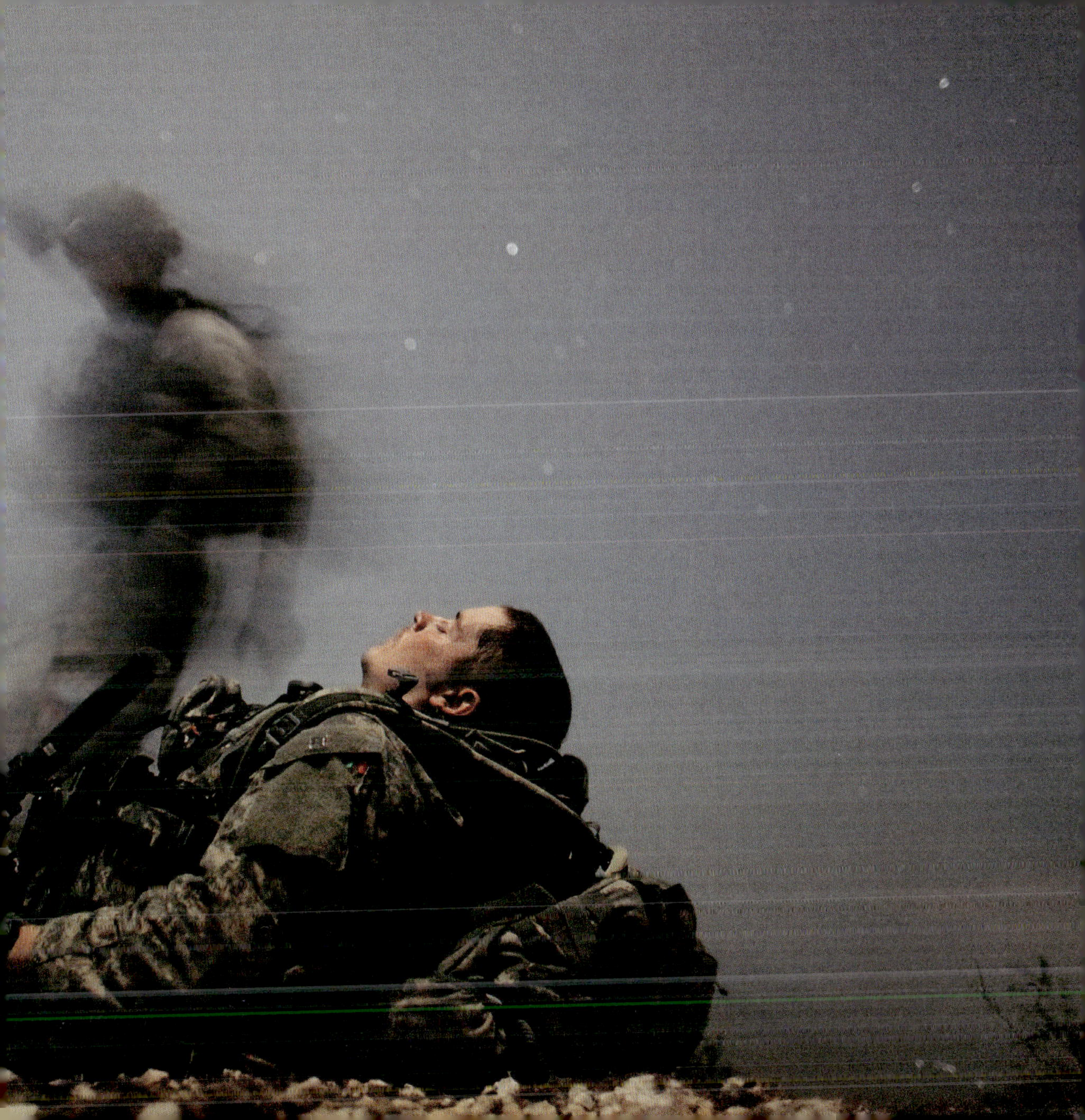

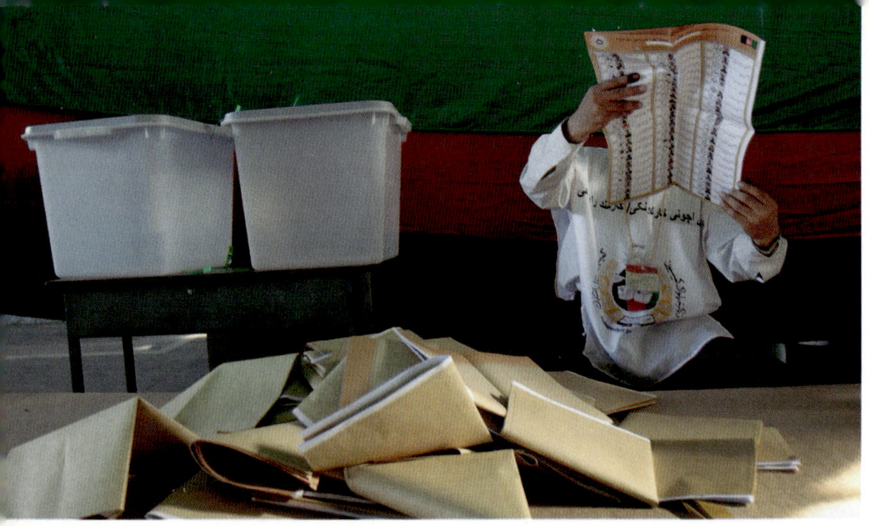

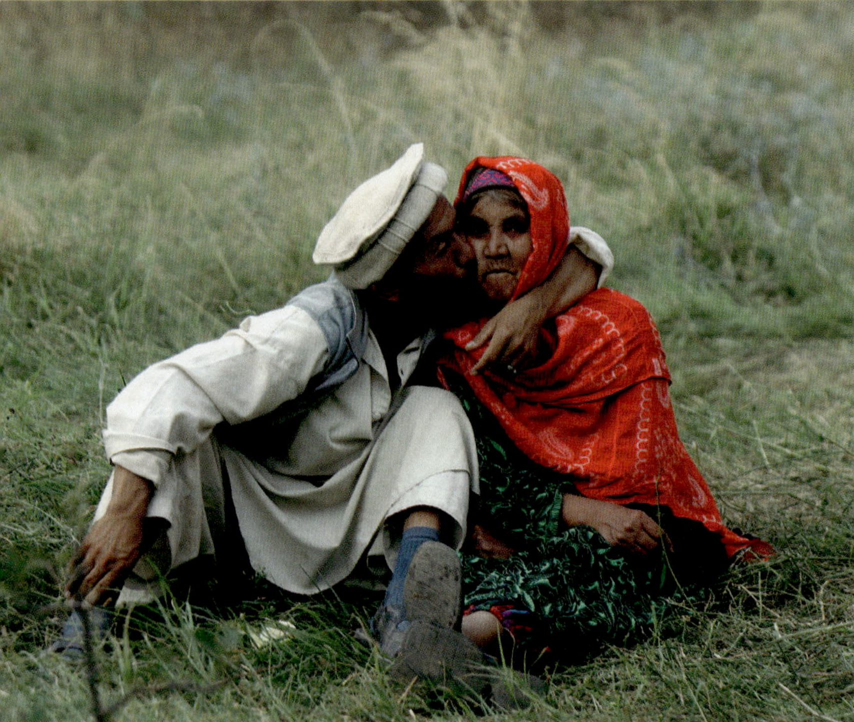

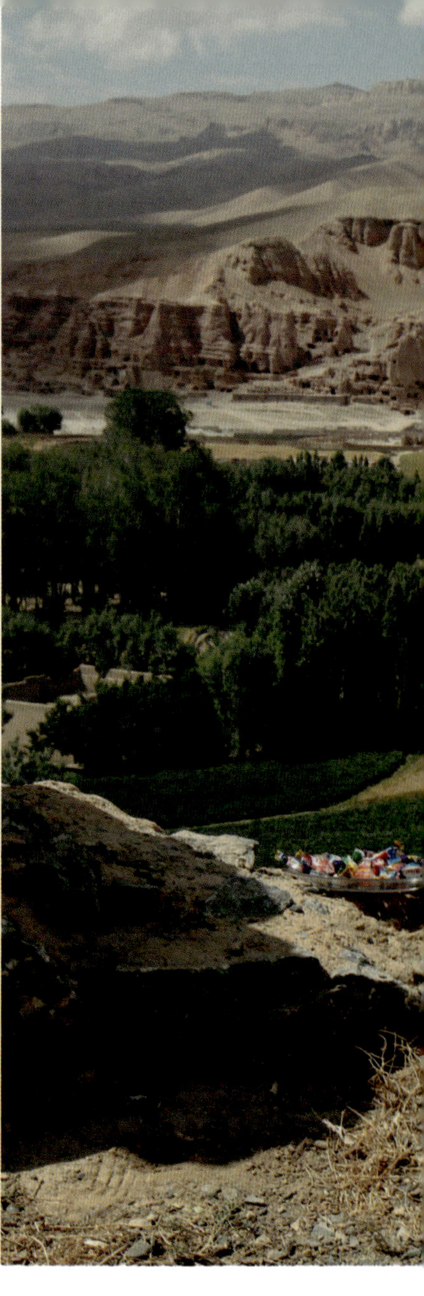

181 [TOP] Kabul, Afghanistan   **182** [ABOVE] Daraye Kaihan Valley, Afghanistan

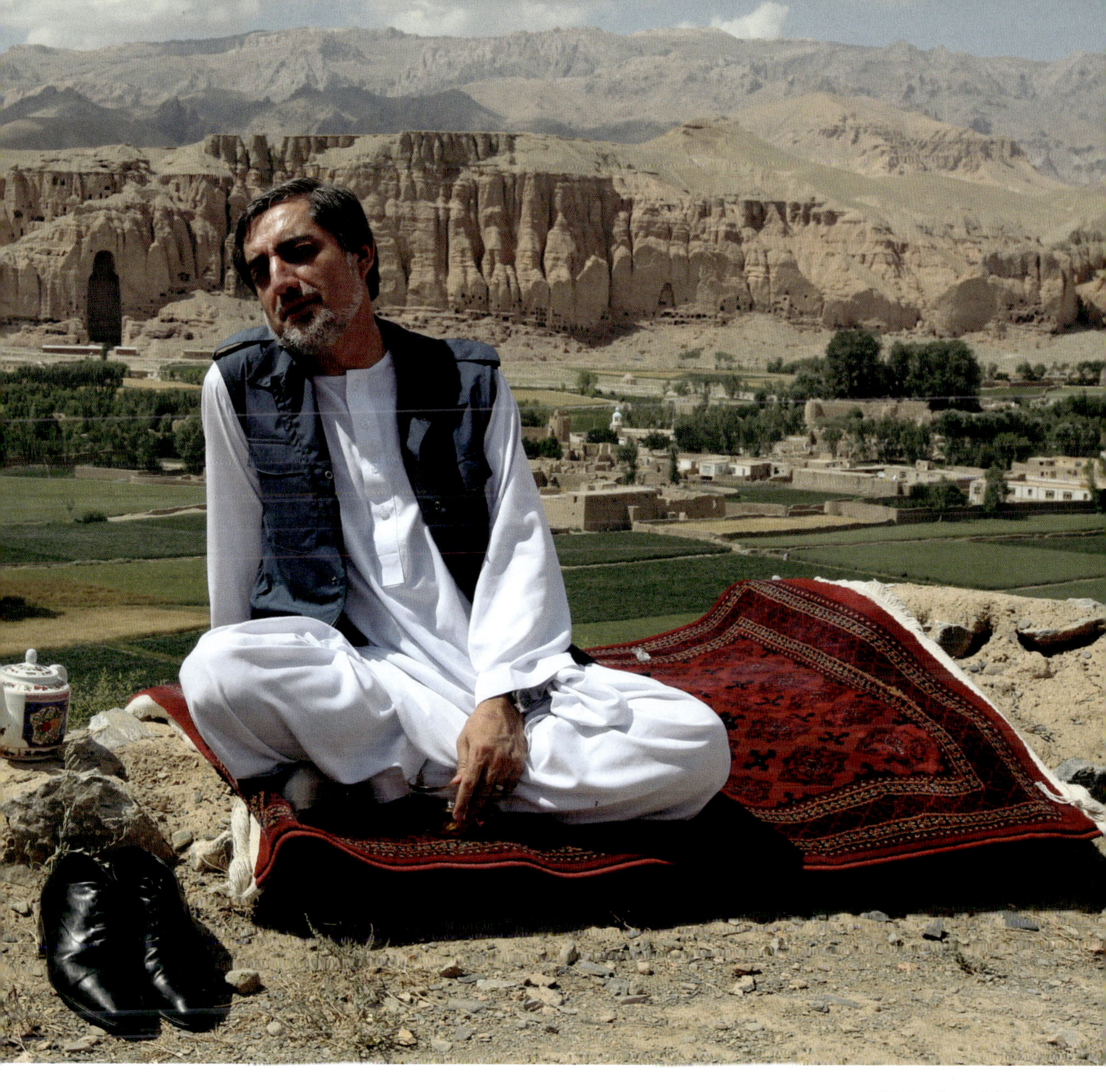

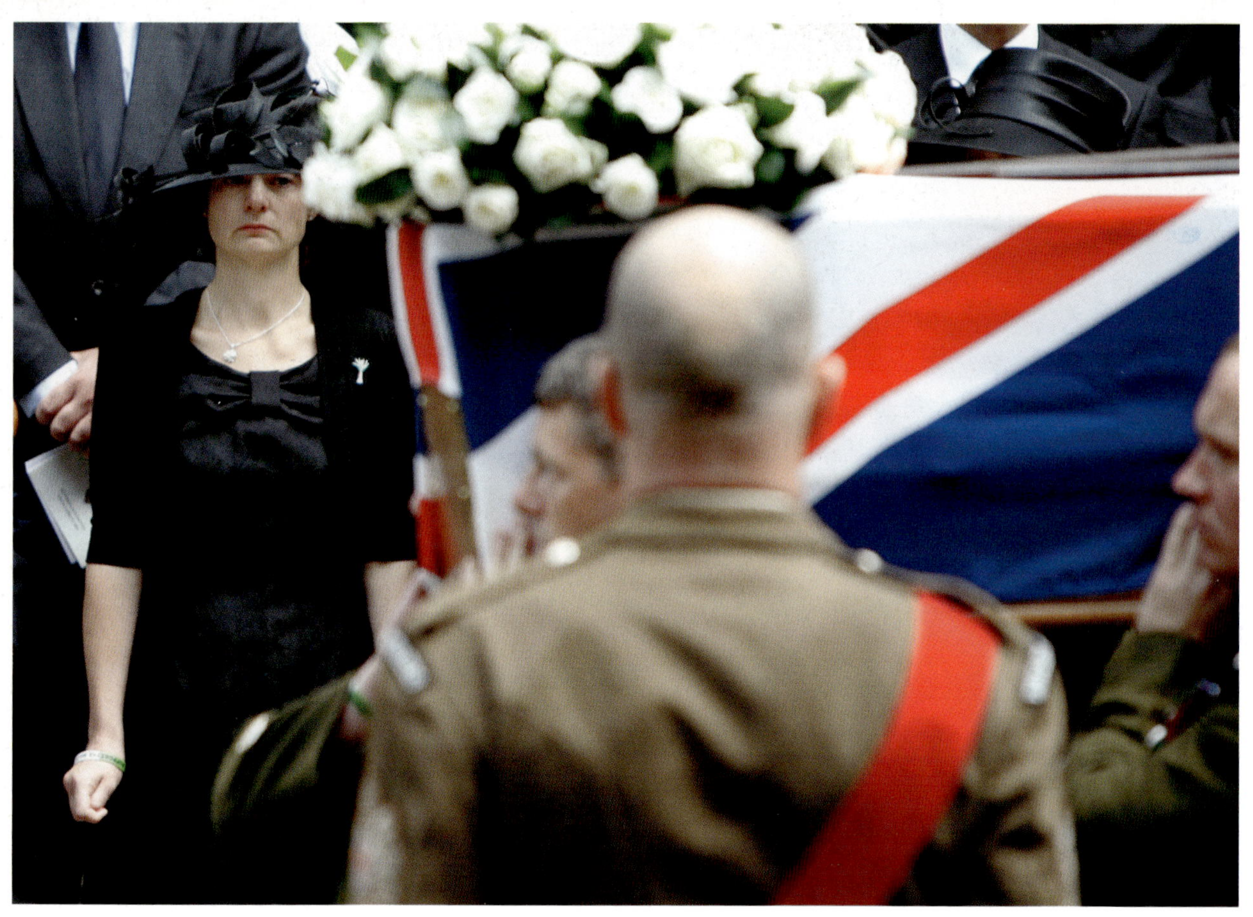

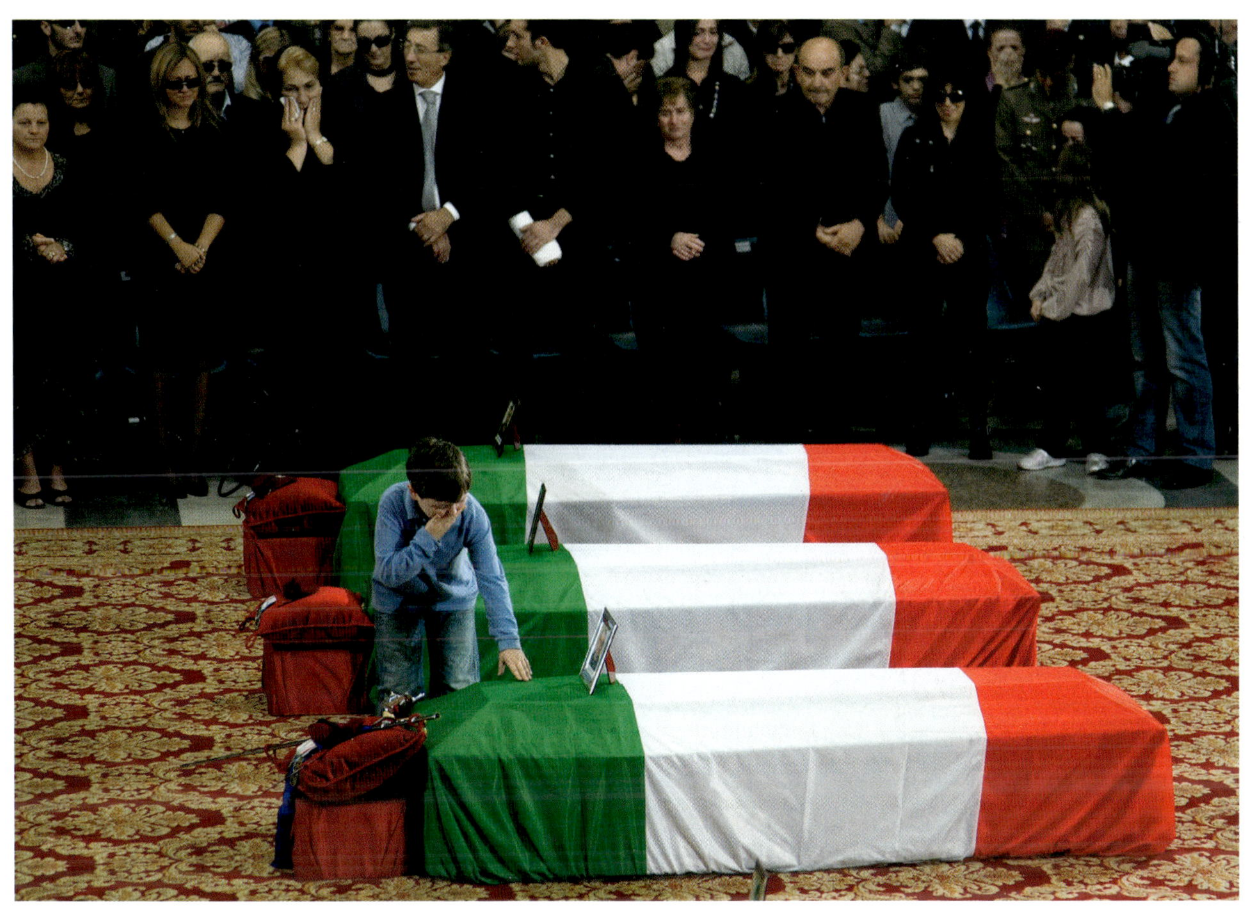

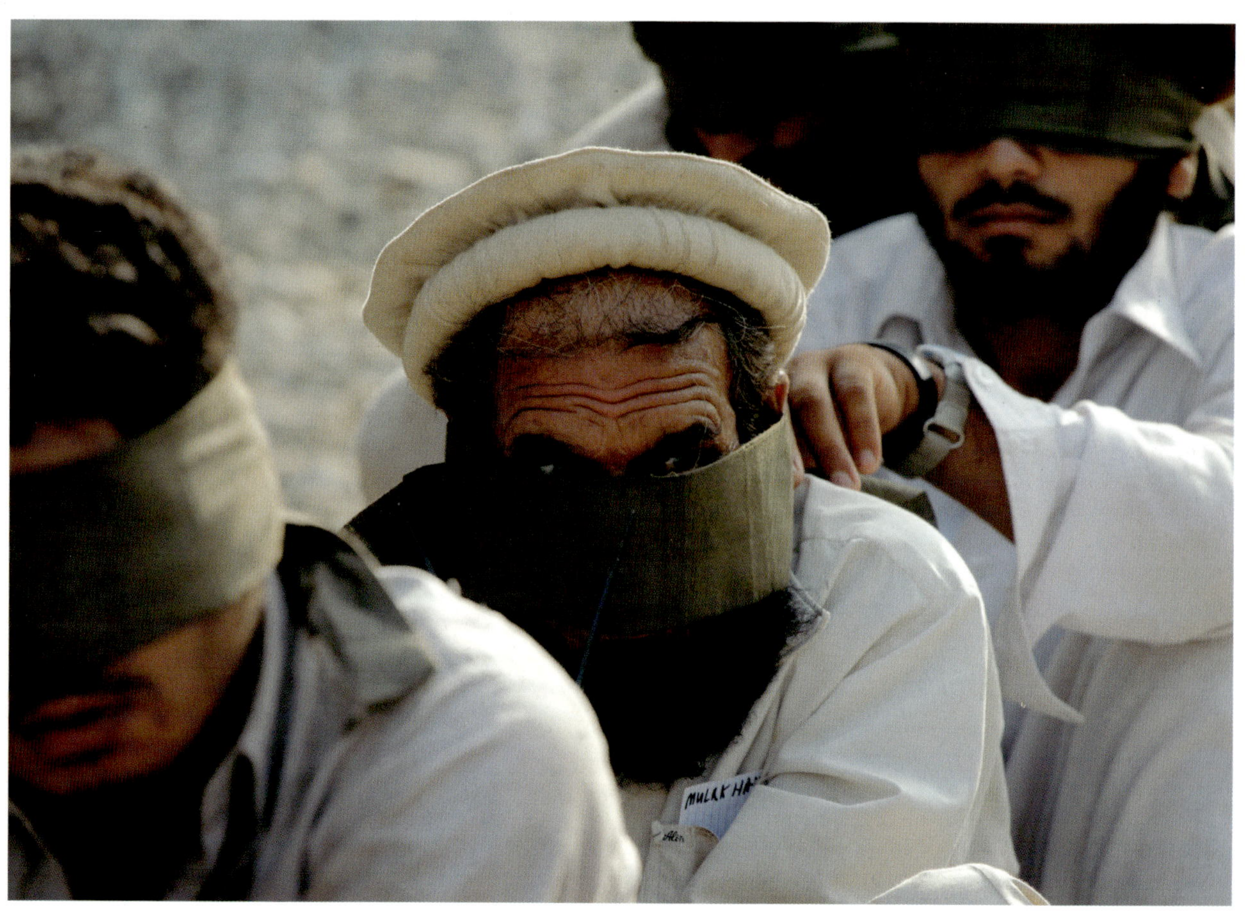

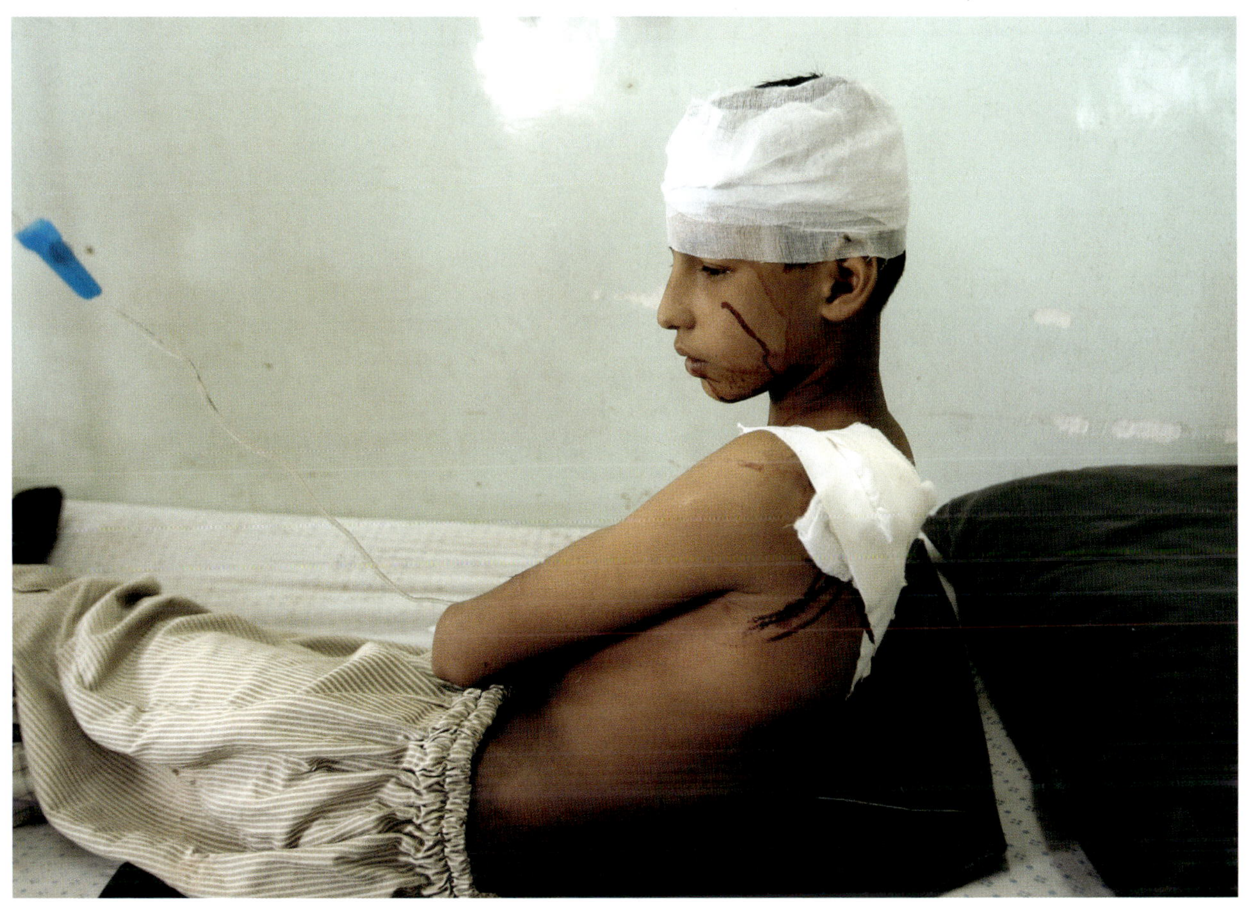

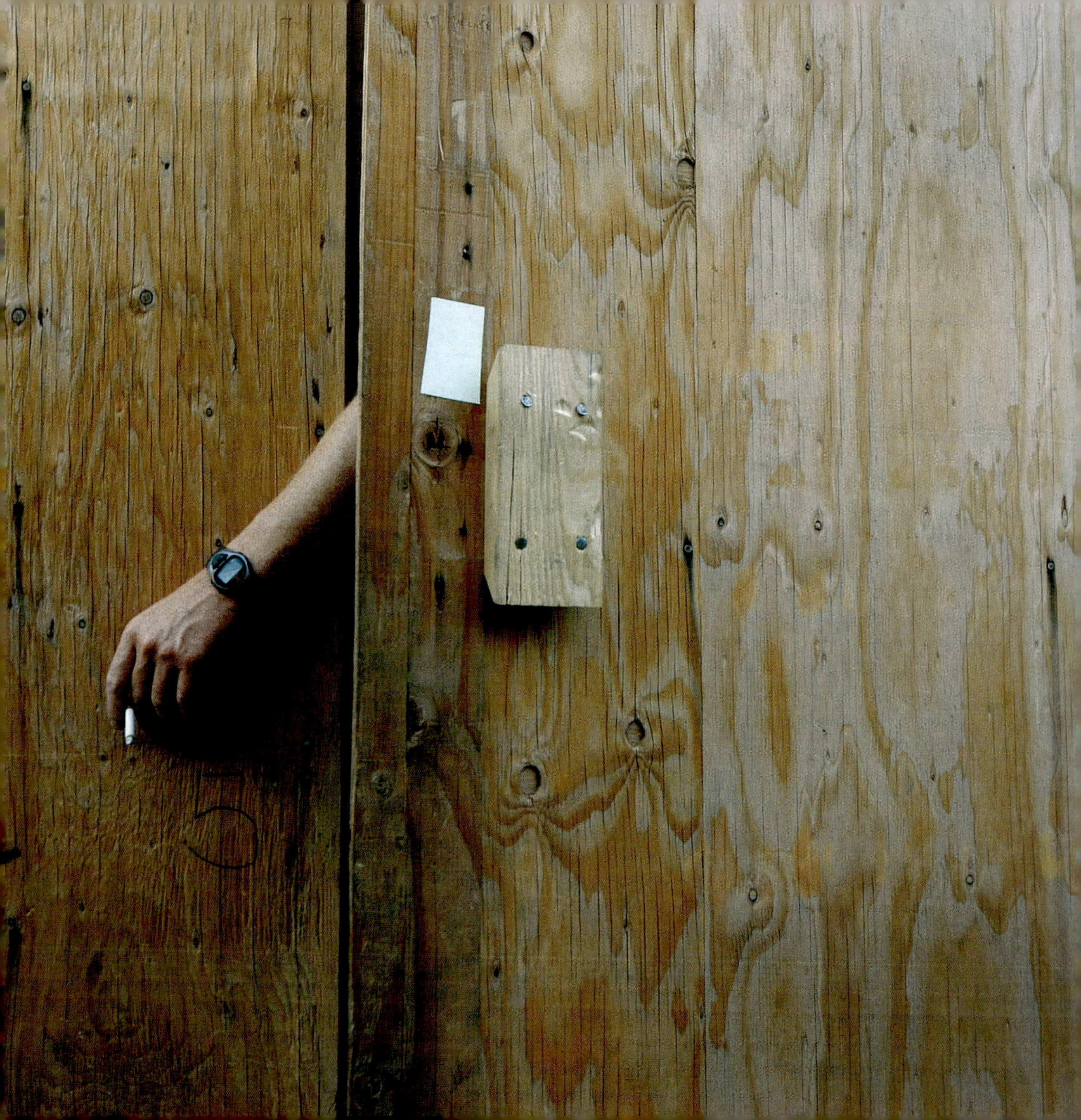

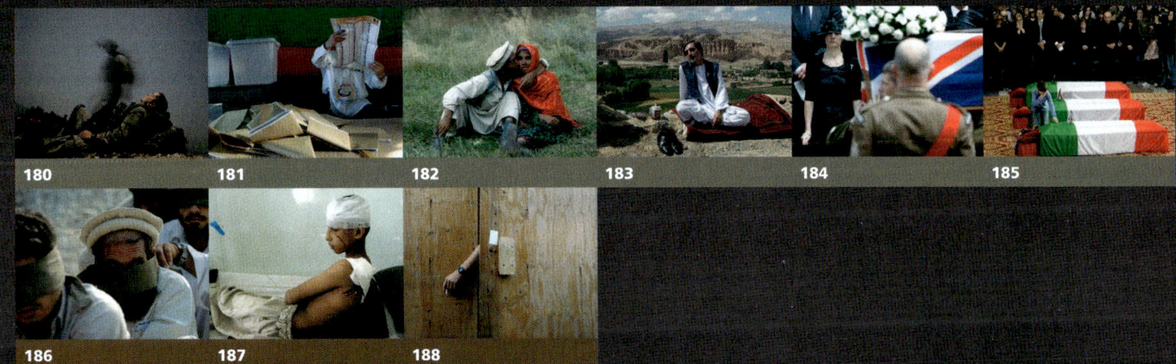

180 A U.S. soldier of 2-12 Infantry 4BCT-4ID Task Force Mountain Warrior takes a break during a night mission near Honaker Miracle camp in the Pesh Valley, in Afghanistan's Kunar province. 12 August 2009. Pesh Valley, Afghanistan. Carlos Barria.

181 An Afghan election worker sorts through ballots in Kabul. The August election was marred by widespread fraud and was followed by weeks of political uncertainty before incumbent Hamid Karzai was declared victor on 2 November. 20 August 2009. Kabul, Afghanistan. Adrees Latif.

182 An Afghan man kisses his mother during an election campaign rally in Daraye Kaihan Valley in Baghlan province. 31 July 2009. Daraye Kaihan Valley, Afghanistan. Omar Sobhani.

183 Afghan presidential candidate Abdullah Abdullah speaks with the media at the end of an election rally in Bamiyan province. 29 July 2009, Bamiyan, Afghanistan. Ahmad Masood.

184 The coffin of Lieutenant Colonel Rupert Thorneloe, the highest ranking British soldier to be killed in the conflict in Afghanistan to date, is carried past his widow Sally after his funeral service at Wellington Barracks in Westminster, central London. 16 July 2009. London, Britain. Stephen Hird.

185 Martin Fortunato, the son of slain captain Antonio Fortunato, cries as he touches the coffin of one of six Italian soldiers during a state funeral service at St Paul's basilica in Rome. The soldiers were killed in a 17 September bomb attack in Kabul, the deadliest on Italian forces in Afghanistan to date. Their deaths reignited debate over Italy's peacekeeping mission in the region and prompted a key government ally to call for all troops to be brought home. 21 September 2009. Rome, Italy. Alessandro Bianchi.

186 A man arrested by U.S. forces peers out from a loose blindfold as he sits with other suspected Taliban militants in Combat Main camp in the Pesh Valley in Kunar Province. 14 August 2009. Pesh Valley, Afghanistan. Carlos Barria.

187 An Afghan boy awaits medical attention at a hospital in Kabul after being injured in a suicide bomb blast that hit an Italian military convoy in the centre of Kabul. Six Italian soldiers and 10 Afghan civilians died in the attack, which occurred within walking distance of the presidential palace. 17 September 2009. Kabul, Afghanistan. Omar Sobhani.

188 A U.S. soldier from 2-12 Infantry, 4th Brigade holds his cigarette outside the door of living quarters at Michigan Base in the Pesh Valley in Kunar province. 3 August 2009. Pesh Valley, Afghanistan. Tim Wimborne.

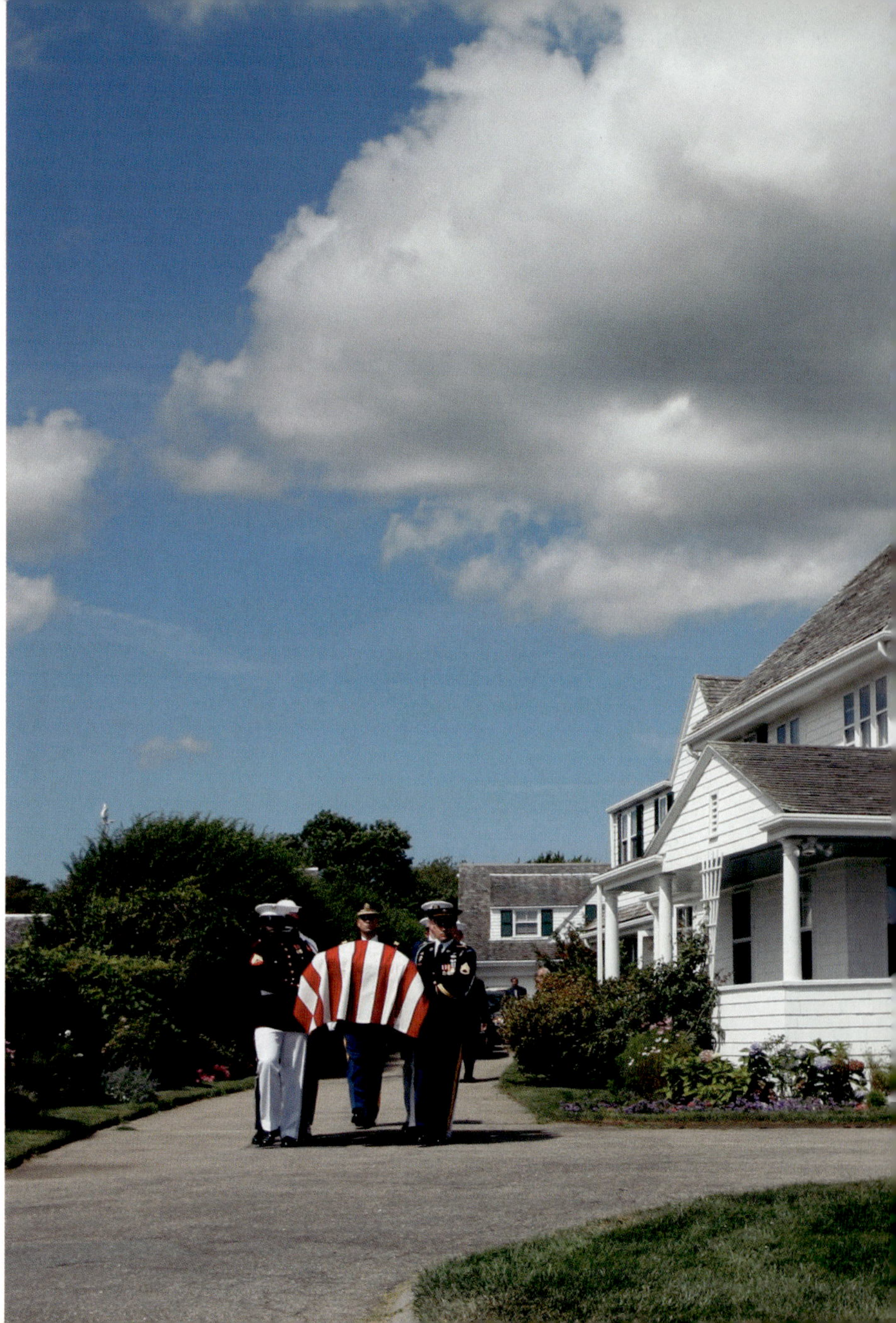

189 Hyannis Port, United States

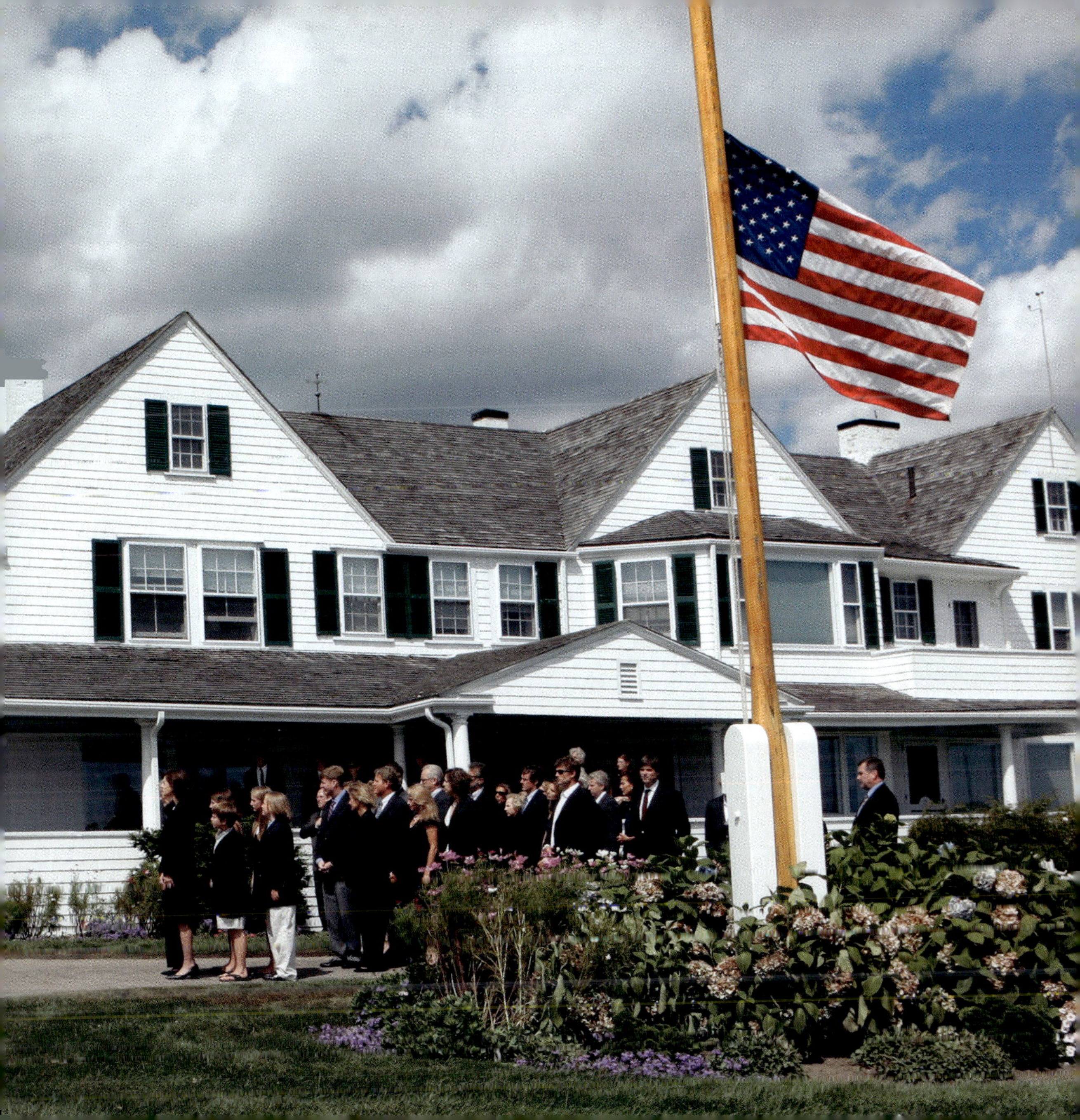

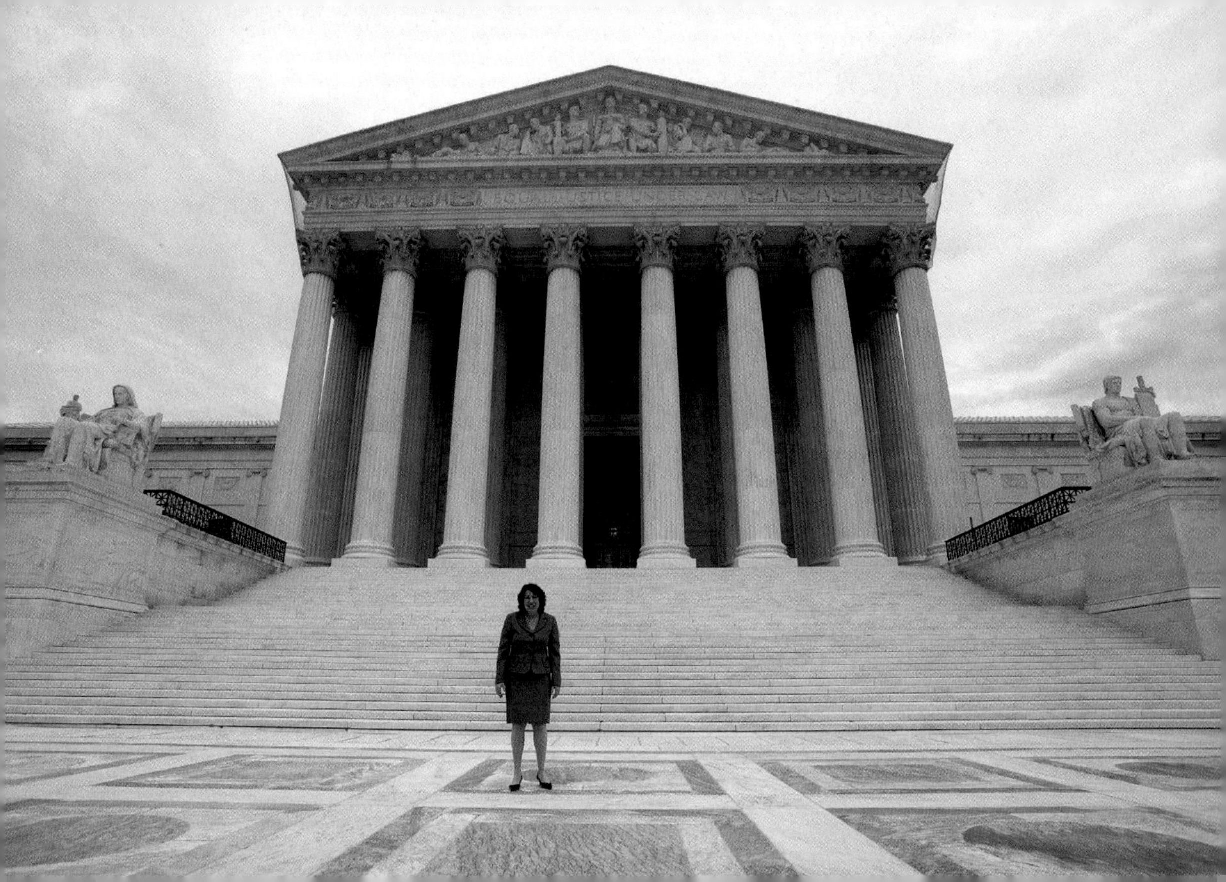

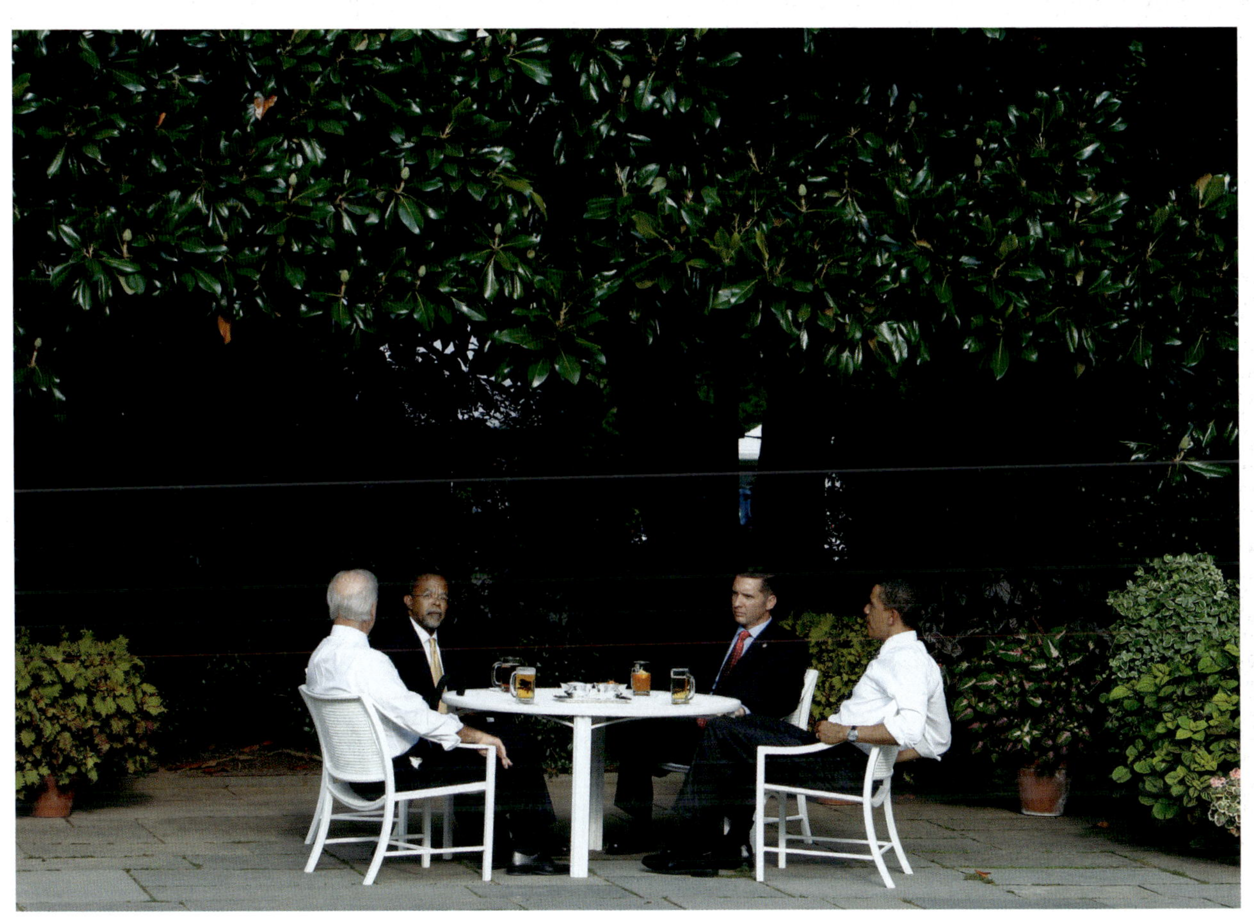

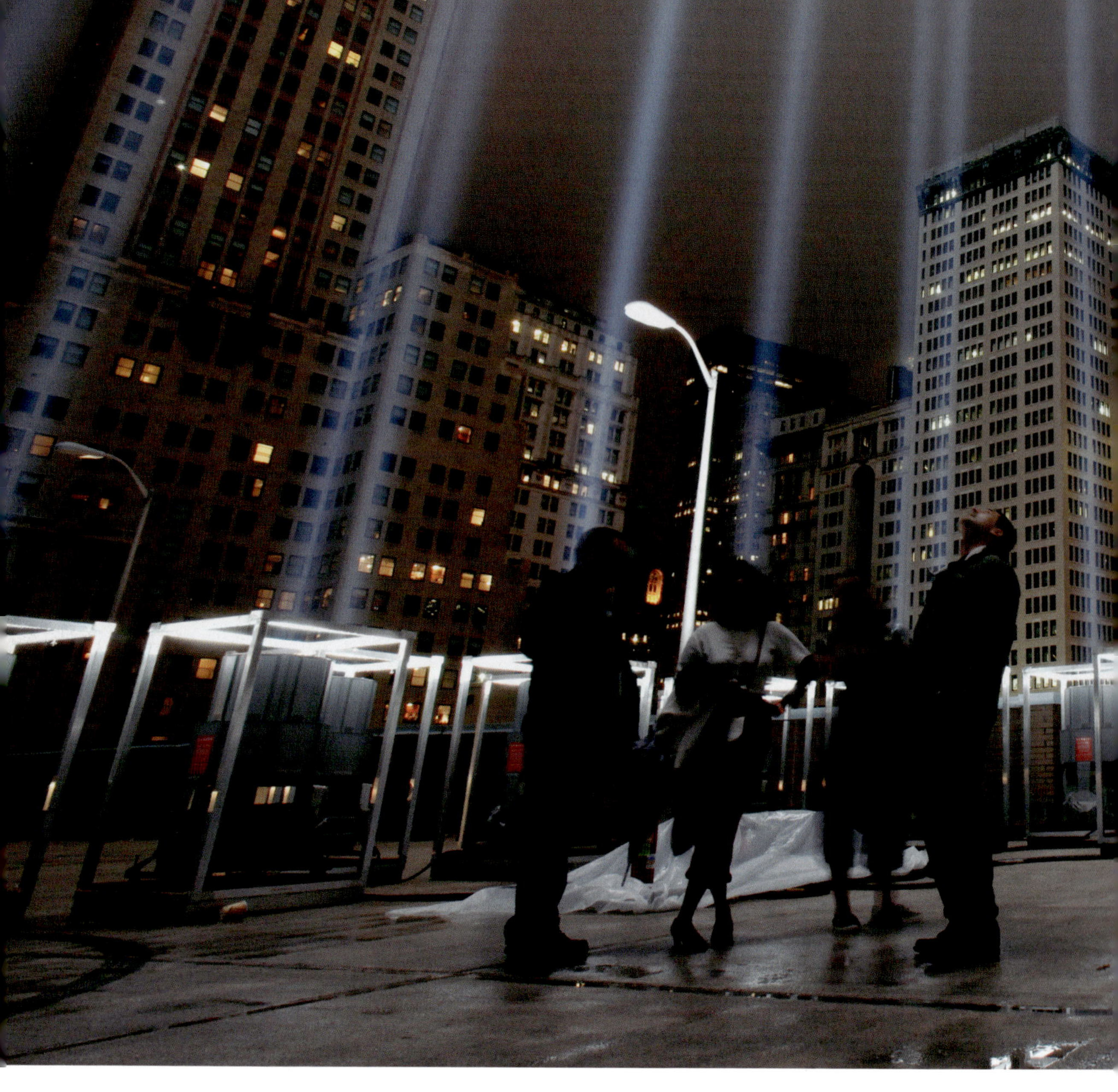

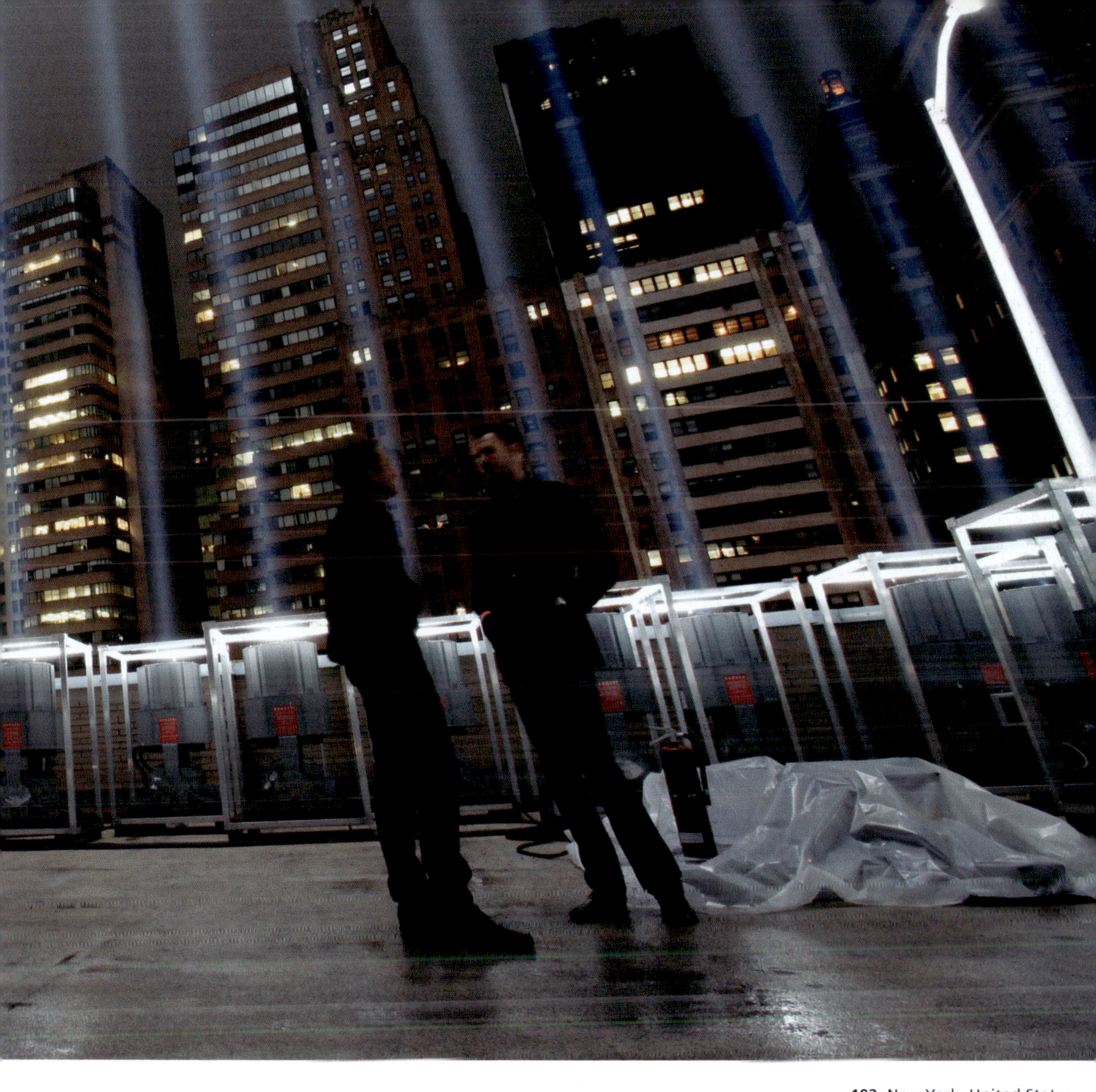

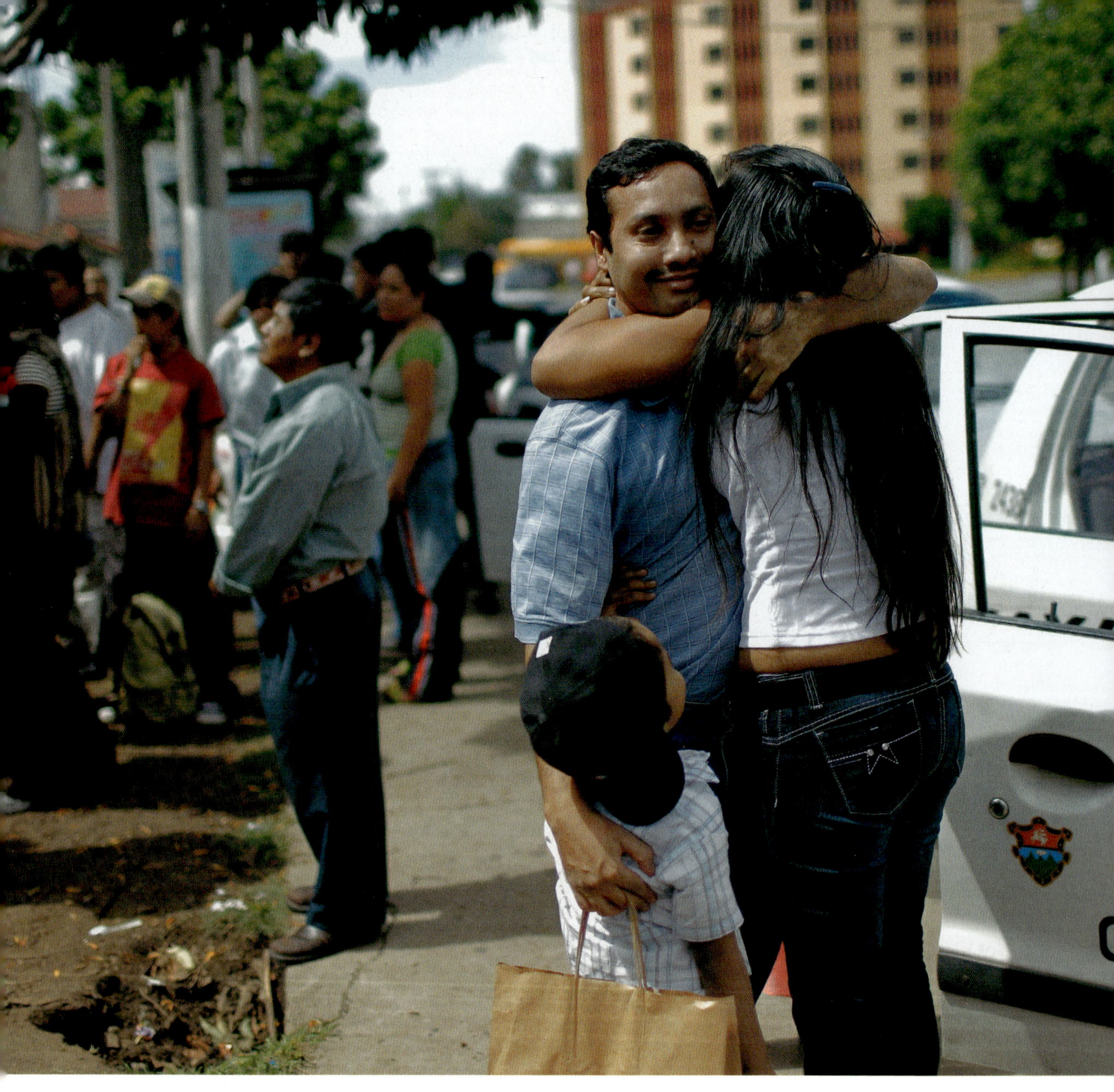

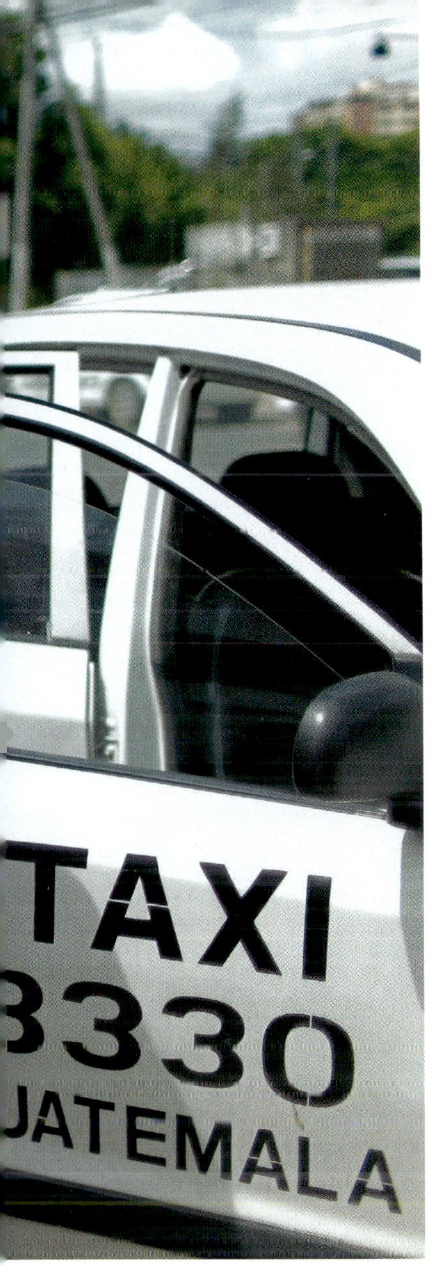

TAXI
3330
JATEMALA

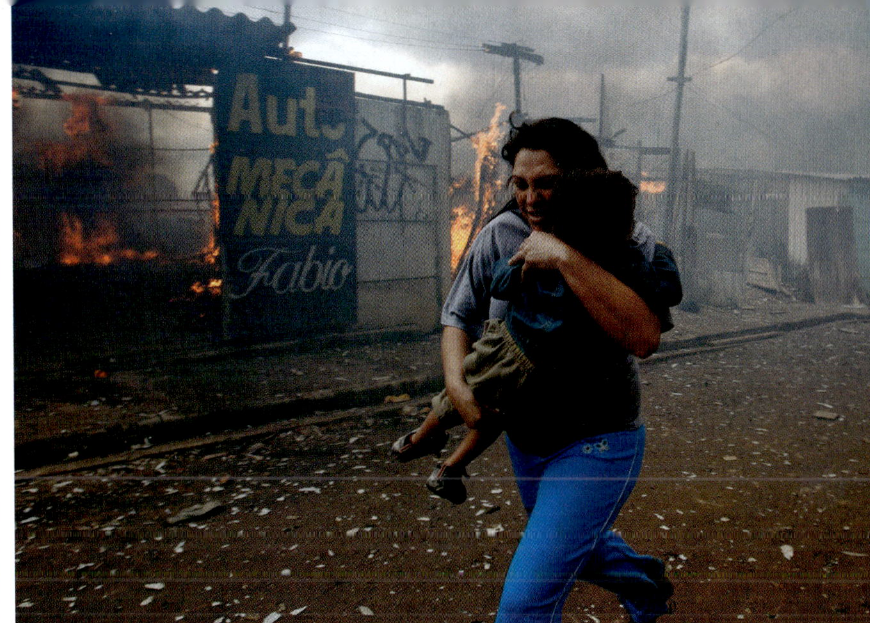

Auto
MECÂ
NICA
Fabio

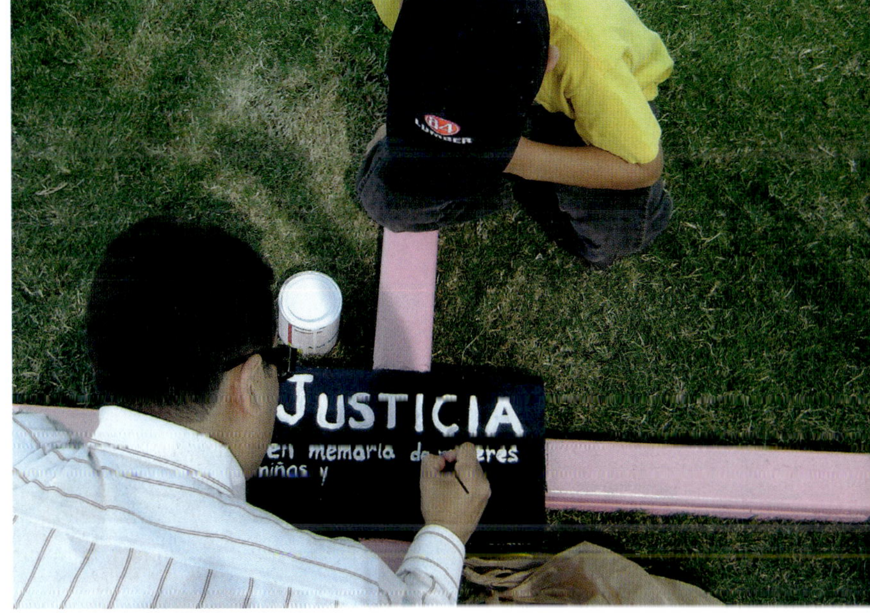

JUSTICIA
en memoria de mujeres
niñas y

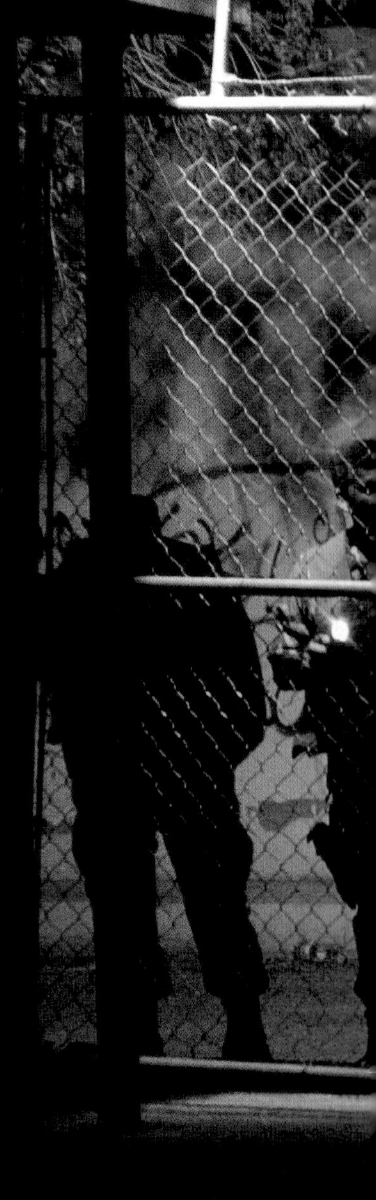

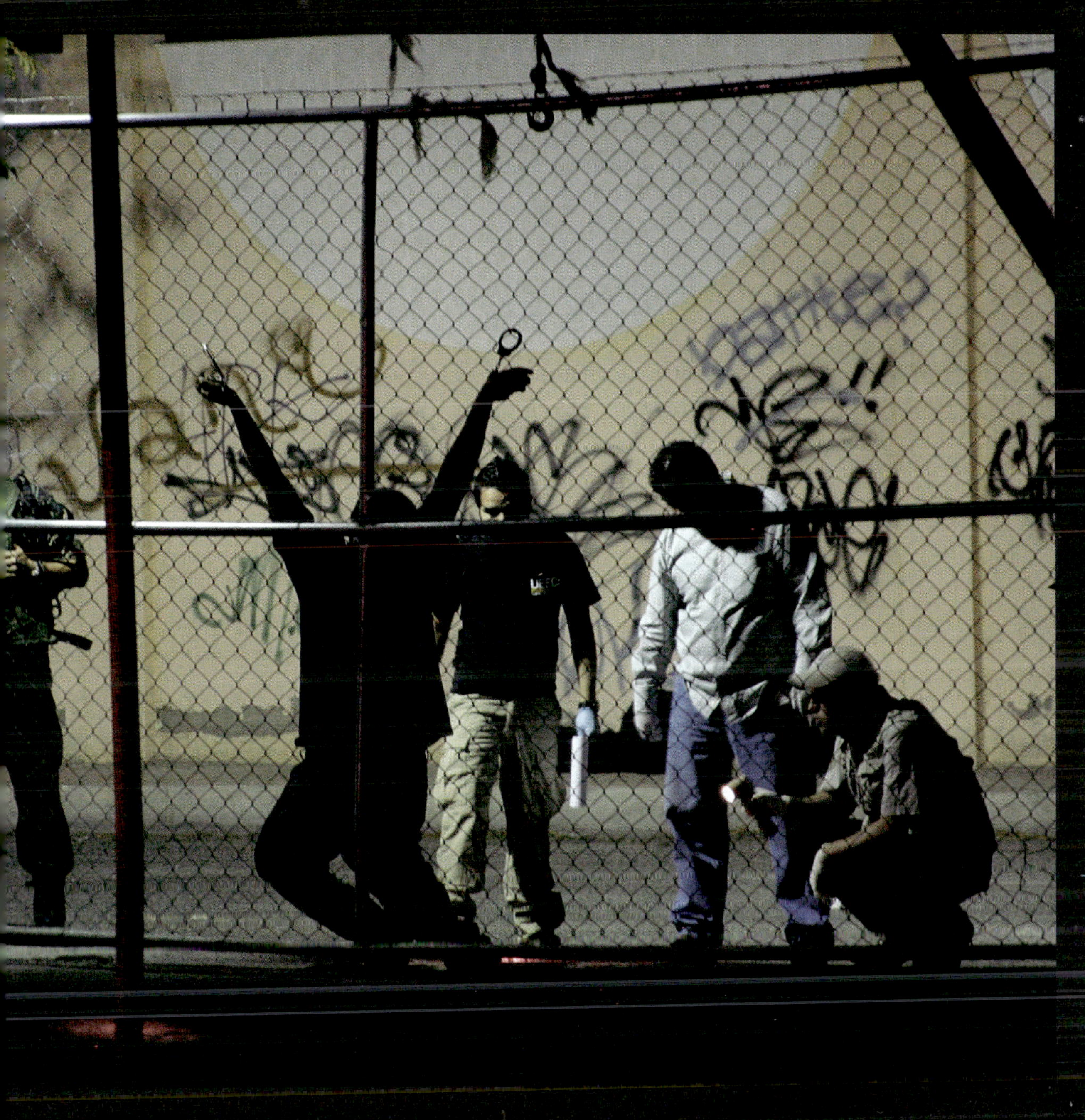

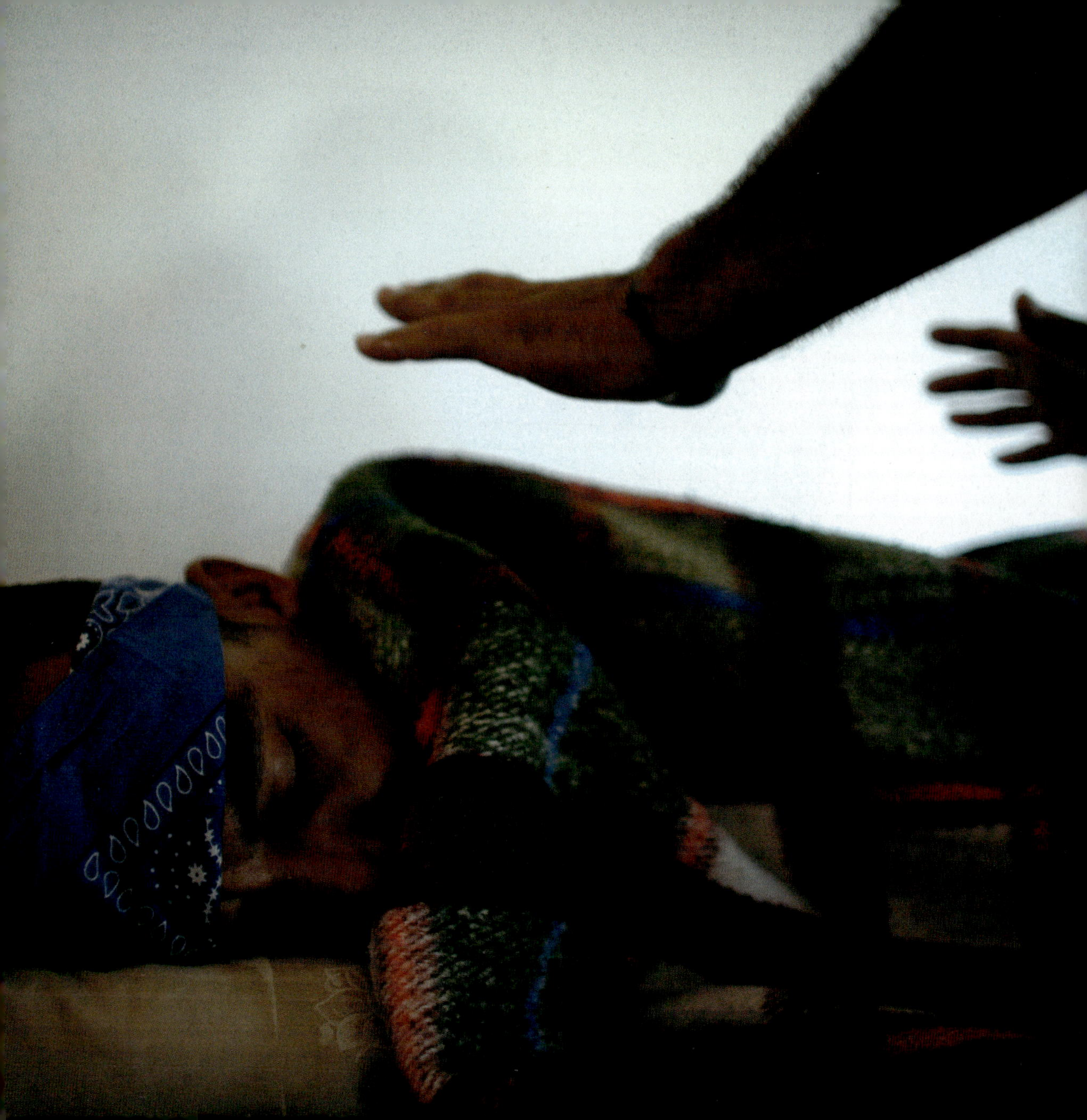

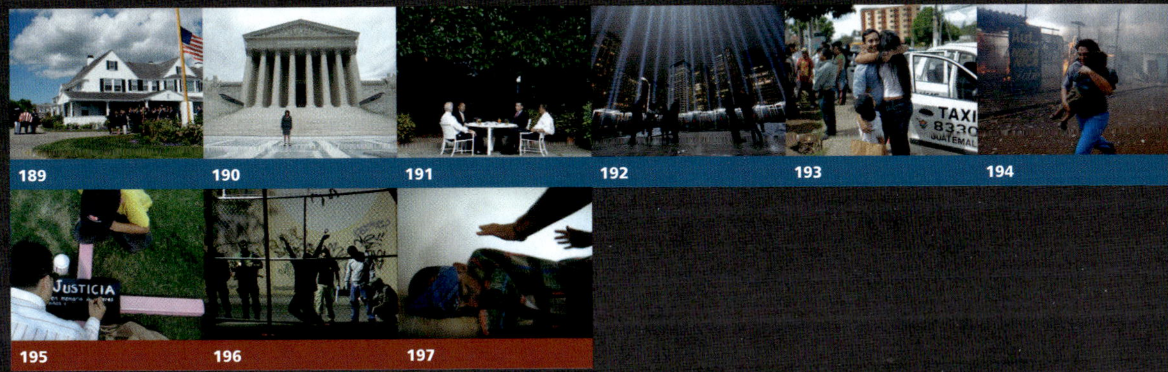

189 The casket of U.S. Senator Edward Kennedy is carried out of the family complex by a military honour guard in Hyannis Port, Massachusetts. Kennedy died on 25 August aged 77 after a year-long battle with cancer. 27 August 2009. Hyannis Port, United States. Mike Segar.

190 Newly appointed Associate Justice Sonia Sotomayor poses in front of the Supreme Court building. Sotomayor became the first Hispanic and only the third woman to serve on the U.S. high court. 8 September 2009. Washington, DC, United States. Jason Reed.

191 U.S. President Barack Obama sits with Harvard scholar Henry Louis Gates (second left), police Sergeant James Crowley (second right) and Vice President Joe Biden. Crowley arrested Gates for disorderly conduct on the porch of his own home in Cambridge, Massachusetts, during an investigation into a burglary. Obama plunged into a charged racial debate when he accused police of acting stupidly. He later expressed regret for his remarks and invited the professor and police officer to the White House for what was dubbed a 'beer summit'. 30 July 2009. Washington, DC, United States. Jim Young.

192 Onlookers stand inside the 'Tribute in Lights' in Manhattan on the eighth anniversary of the attacks on the World Trade Center. 11 September 2009. New York, United States. Lucas Jackson.

193 Erwin Baches Chavez, an illegal immigrant deported from the United States, embraces his son and wife in Guatemala City. Almost 12 million illegal immigrants live and work in the United States. U.S. Immigration and Customs Enforcement, pursuing a policy begun under former President George W. Bush, deported an average of 4,200 unauthorized migrants a week through the first half of 2009, up from 3,700 in 2008. 10 July 2009. Guatemala City, Guatemala. Carlos Barria.

194 A woman runs with her child past a house on fire at Capão Redondo slum in the outskirts of São Paulo. Residents set fire to houses in protest after police and officials removed 800 families from the slum, which had been illegally occupied since 2007. 24 August 2009. São Paulo, Brazil. Paulo Whitaker.

195 A man writes 'Justice in memory of women and girls' on a cross during a memorial event for murder victims in the Mexican border city of Ciudad Juárez. The appointment of Arturo Chavez as attorney general sparked protests from opposition parties and human rights activists, who accuse him of negligence during a decade of unsolved murders in the state of Chihuahua, where he was state attorney general between 1996 and 1998. More than 400 young women were killed in Ciudad Juárez between 1993 and 2003. 14 September 2009. Ciudad Juárez, Mexico. Alejandro Bringas.

196 Military and forensic experts inspect a body outside a nightclub in Ciudad Juárez. The man was handcuffed to a fence and shot by drug hitmen, local media reported. 31 August 2009. Ciudad Juárez, Mexico. Alejandro Bringas.

197 Ricardo, a recovered heroin addict and volunteer of the 'Outcry in the Barrio' ministry, prays over a heroin addict. The ministry in Ciudad Juárez helps drug addicts, alcoholics and prostitutes to transform their lives. 9 September 2009. Ciudad Juárez, Mexico. Tomas Bravo.

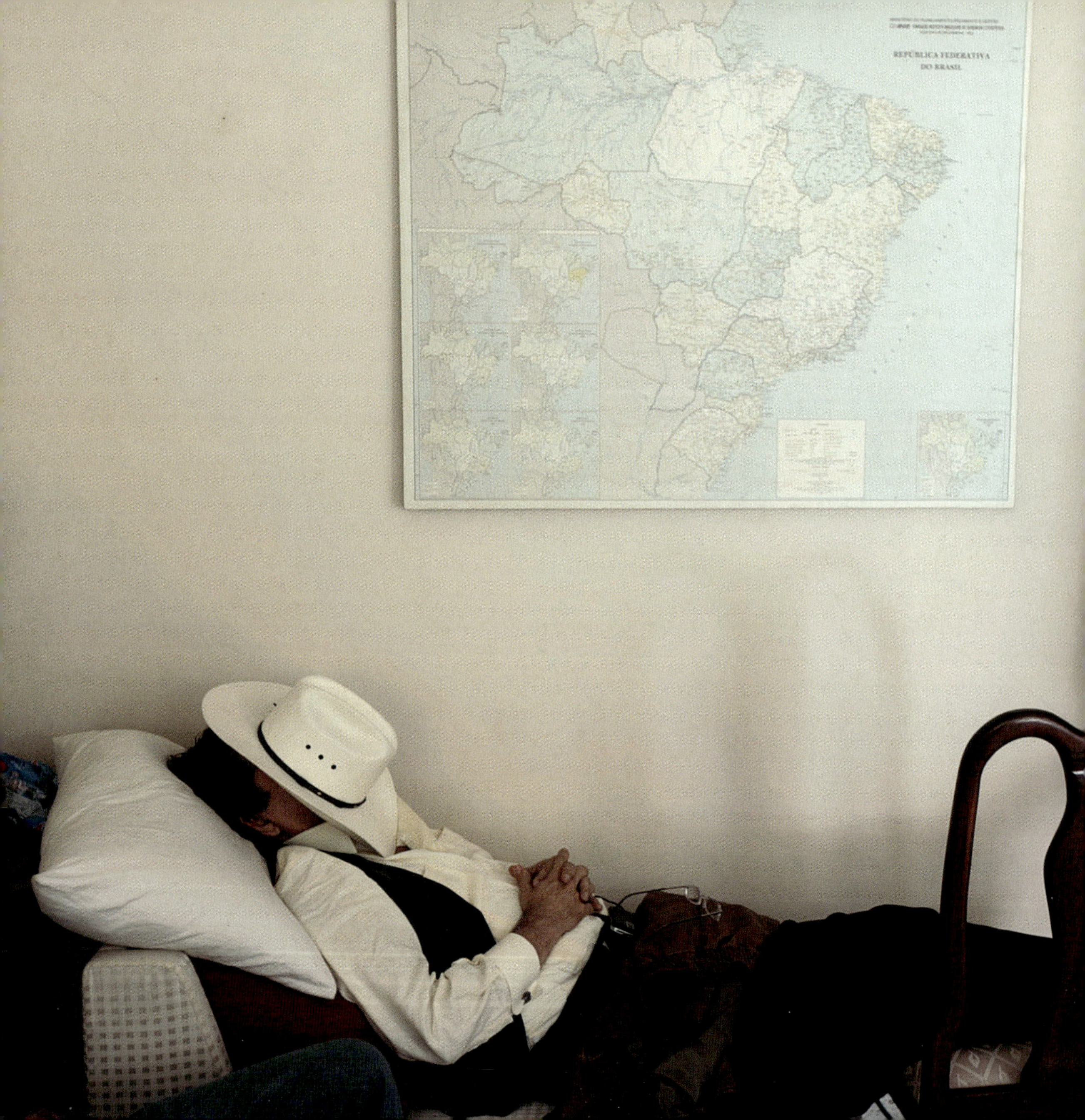

REPÚBLICA FEDERATIVA
DO BRASIL

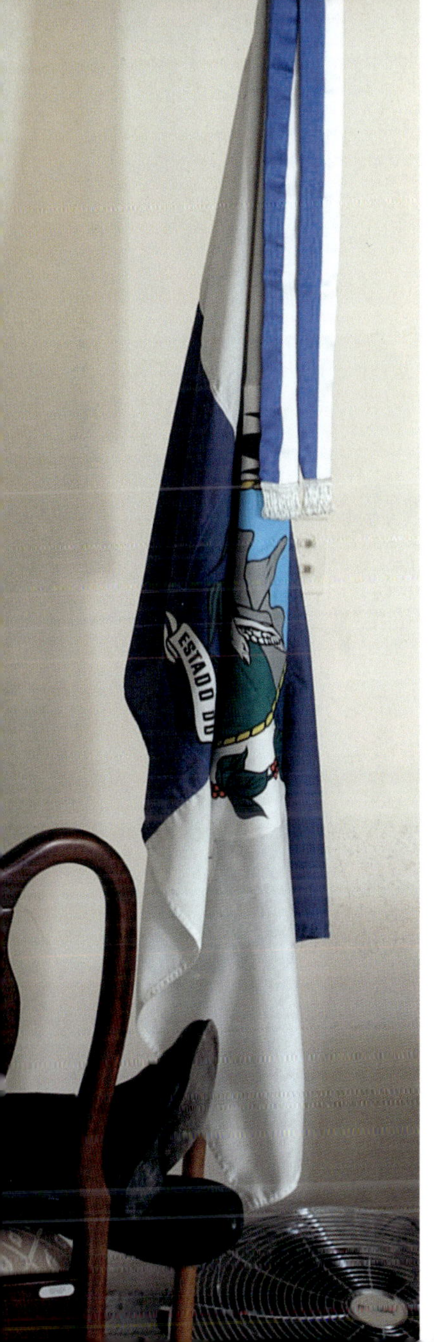

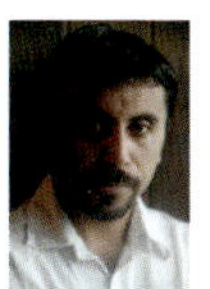

EDGARD GARRIDO
Photographer
Born: Puerto Varas, Chile, 1975
Based: Tegucigalpa, Honduras
Nationality: Chilean

Deadlock in Honduras

News flash! Ousted Honduran President Manuel Zelaya has returned to the country after 82 days in exile.

Fifteen minutes later I was there as 50 Zelaya supporters cheered outside the U.N. building in the capital Tegucigalpa. His closest allies appeared, making gestures of triumph, but it was soon apparent that Zelaya wasn't really here. The lie was a strategy to confuse the security forces that had blocked his previous attempts to return since being ousted in a June coup. Suddenly one demonstrator screamed, 'To the Brazilian embassy!' I joined a rush of followers and reporters. A crush at the door, and I was inside.

I was told Zelaya was in the next room, but I still couldn't be certain. Then a door opened and I saw him: I snapped two photos and sent my first dispatch.

Zelaya decided to camp right where he was. The de facto government was quick to respond, with soldiers and police breaking up pro-Zelaya demonstrations outside the embassy and turning on a high-frequency acoustic device to harass those inside. We worried there might be a military operation to seize control of the building.

With a cement floor as my mattress and a backpack as pillow, I got little sleep amid the screams and chanting. After two days in the embassy, there was no food, no telephone, no bath and no clean clothes. It became a war of nerves. Stones hit the roof as the Honduras national anthem was blasted out on powerful sound systems. At night soldiers banged on their riot shields.

Then came allegations of a gas attack. Zelaya said he believed mercenaries were trying to force him out using toxic gas. Many inside complained of a burning sensation in their throats, while others showed what seemed to be traces of blood in their saliva. Officials outside said the odours were from a cleaning crew nearby. It was unclear what was really happening.

As time went on and the political impasse continued, the pressure tactics eased and I was able to receive food, fresh clothes and an inflatable mattress from my colleagues on the outside, although part of one food package was eaten by the policeman who had promised to pass it in.

At the end of each day I received a phone call from my wife, 'Our baby son is fine, we'll see you soon,' she said. Little did we anticipate that it would be 47 days before we were reunited. I left the embassy with Zelaya still holed up inside and no end in sight to the political deadlock.

198 Ousted Honduran President Manuel Zelaya sleeps inside the Brazilian embassy in the Honduran capital Tegucigalpa. 22 September 2009.

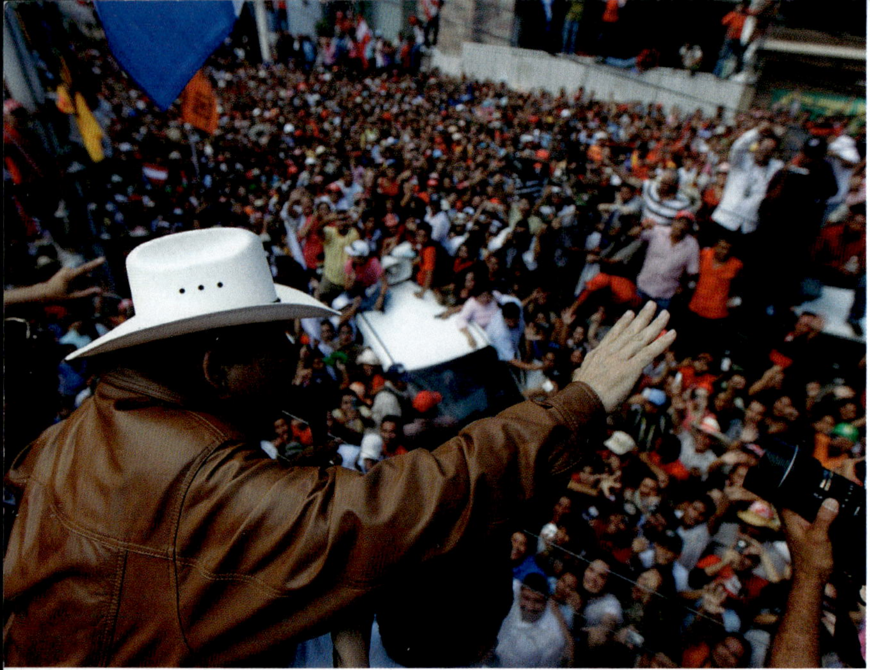

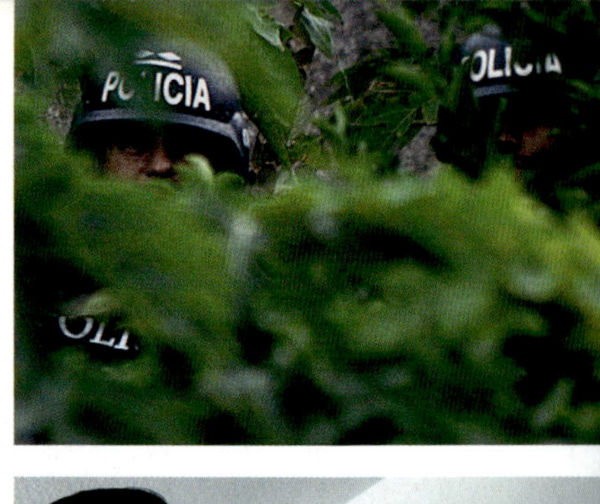
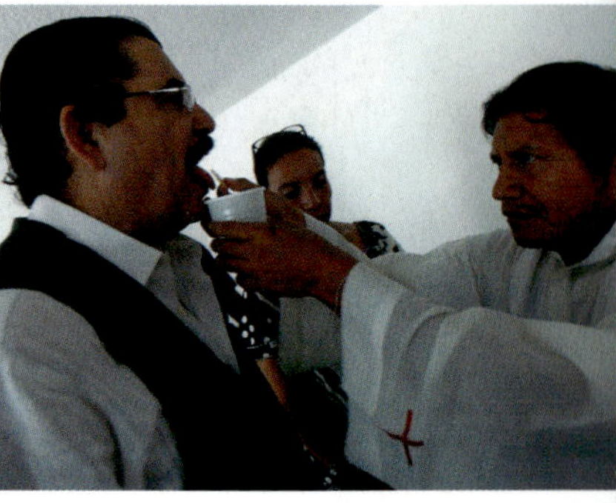
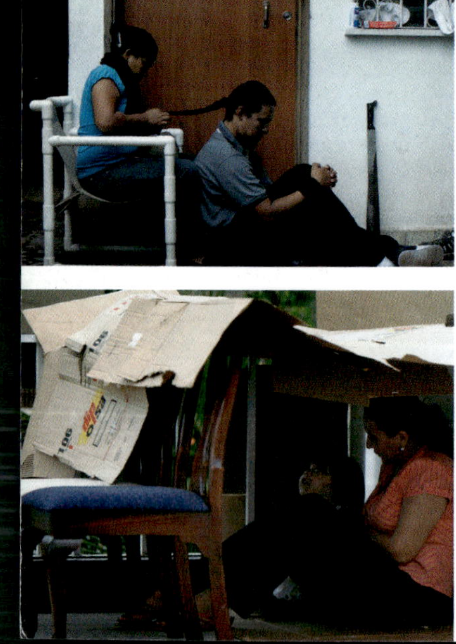
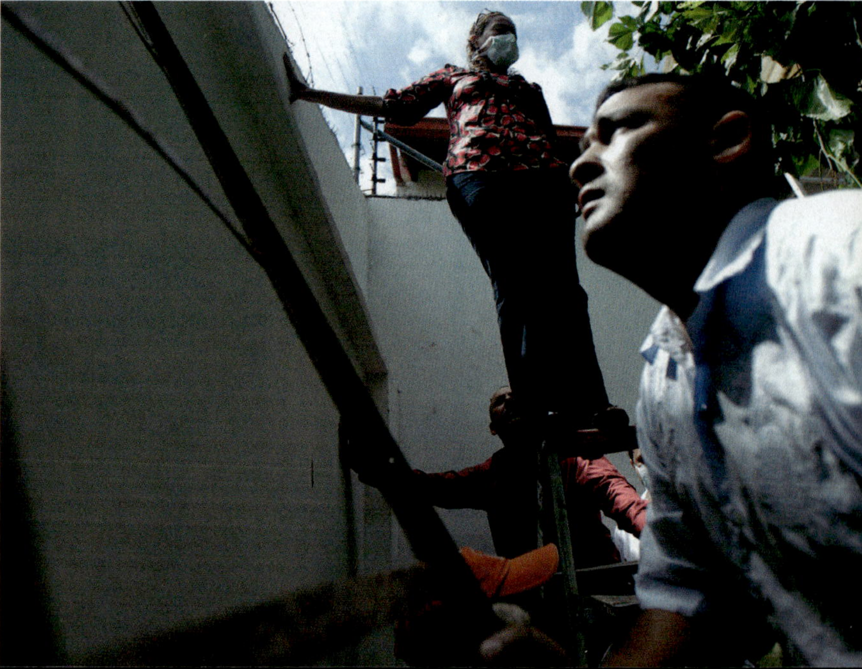

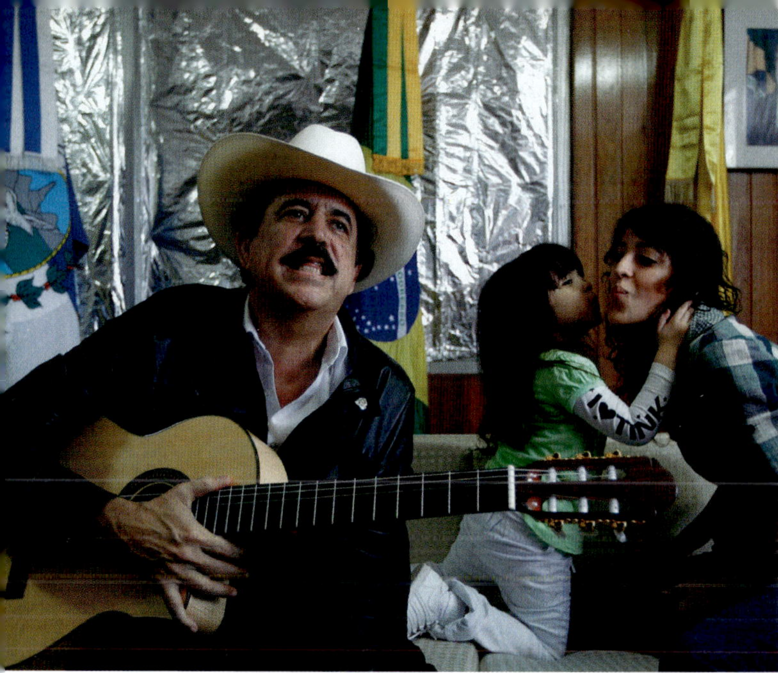

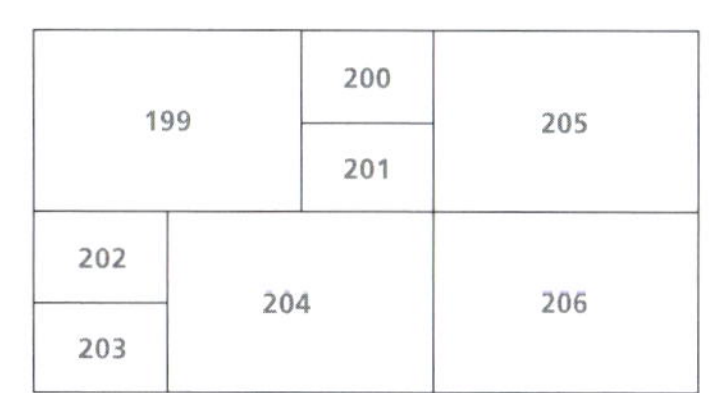

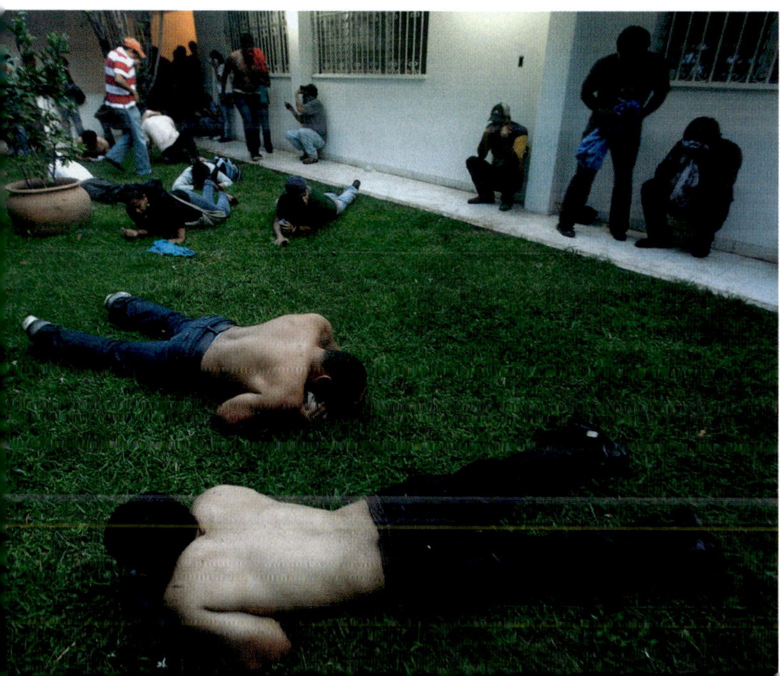

199 Ousted Honduran President Manuel Zelaya greets supporters from inside the Brazilian embassy in Tegucigalpa. Zelaya sneaked back into Honduras on 21 September almost three months after he was toppled in a coup, and took refuge in the Brazilian embassy to avoid arrest. 21 September 2009. **200** Police officers keep watch in a neighbourhood near the embassy. 26 September 2009. **201** A priest gives Zelaya a communion wafer as he conducts mass inside the embassy. 4 October 2009. **202** A supporter of Zelaya braids another's hair inside the embassy. 27 September 2009. **203** Xiomara Castro Zelaya, wife of Zelaya, plays with her granddaughter Irene Melara during a visit at the embassy. 25 October 2009. **204** Xiomara Castro Zelaya stands on a ladder to argue with soldiers after Zelaya accused the de facto government of injecting 'toxic gas' into the embassy building. 25 September 2009. **205** Zelaya plays guitar alongside his granddaughter Irene Melara and daughter Xiomara. 1 November 2009. **206** Supporters of Zelaya inside the embassy react to teargas fired by police. 22 September 2009. Edgard Garrido.

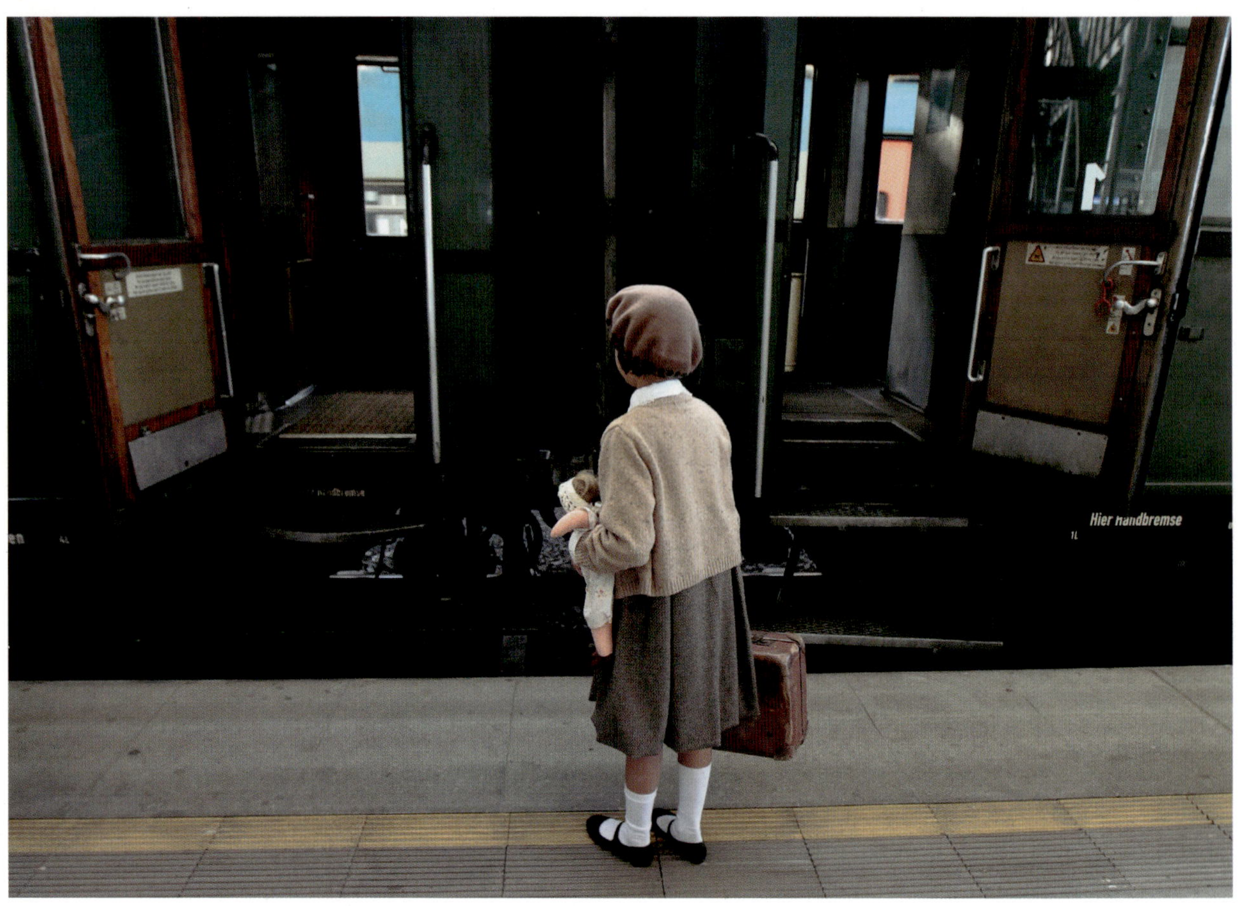

207 Prague, Czech Republic

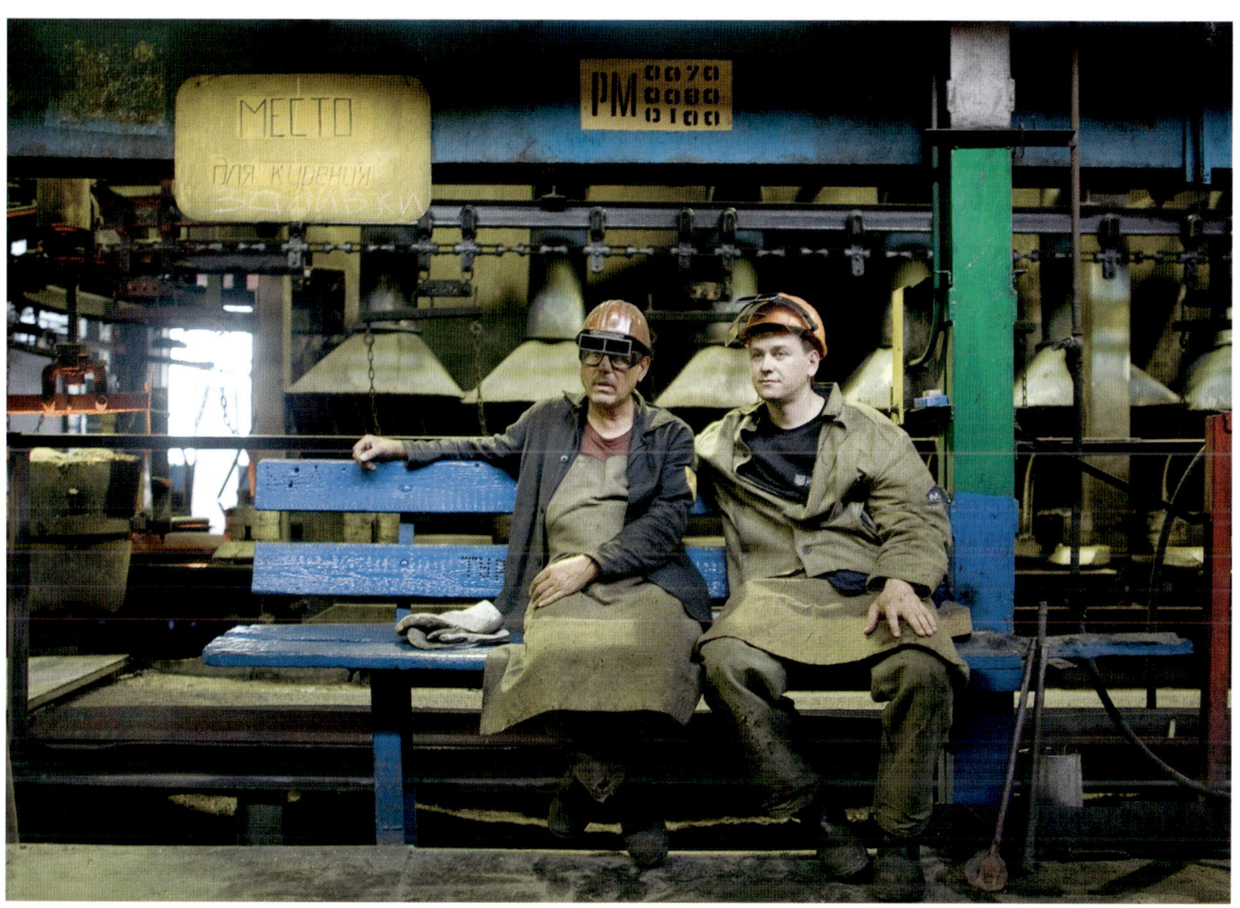
МЕСТО
ДЛЯ КУРЕНИЯ

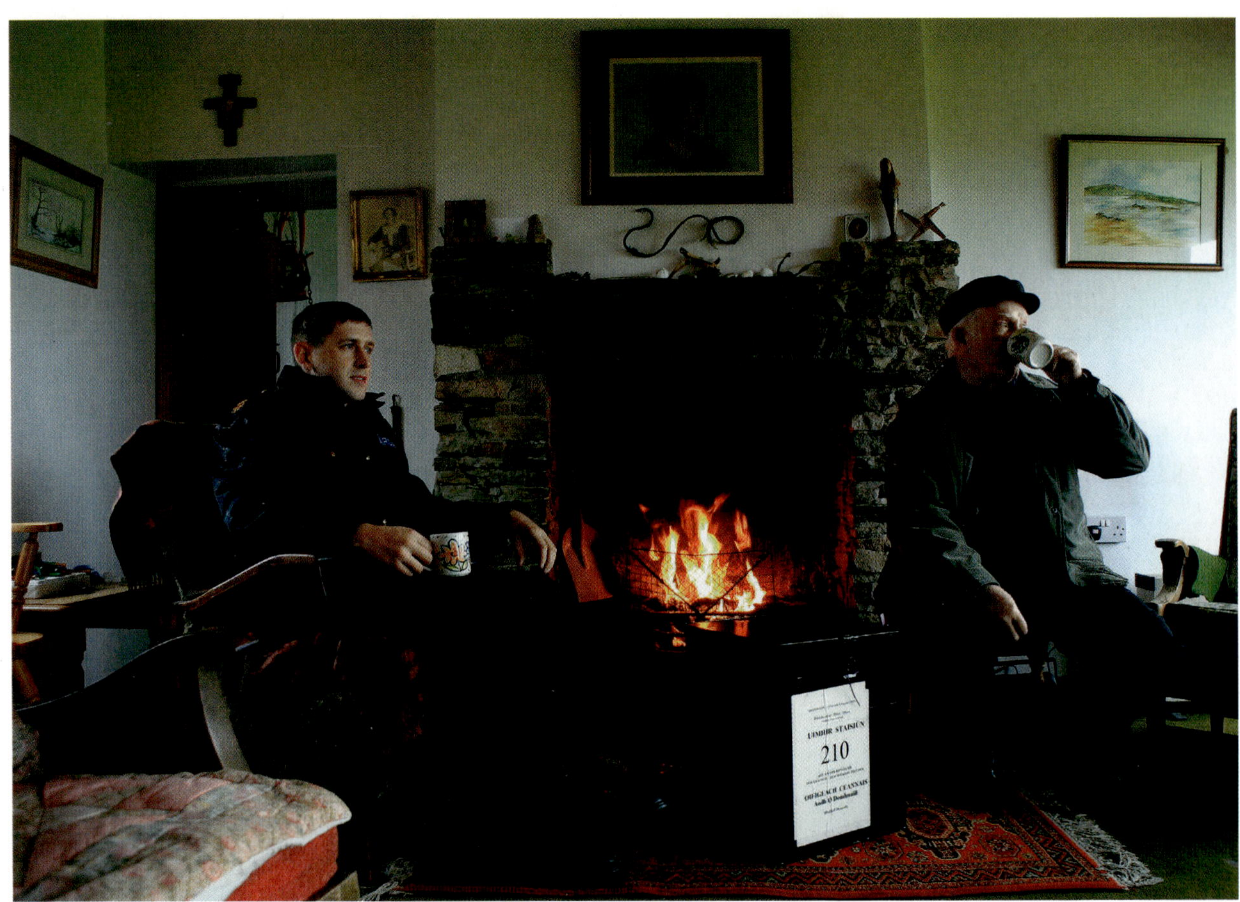

209 Inishfree, Ireland

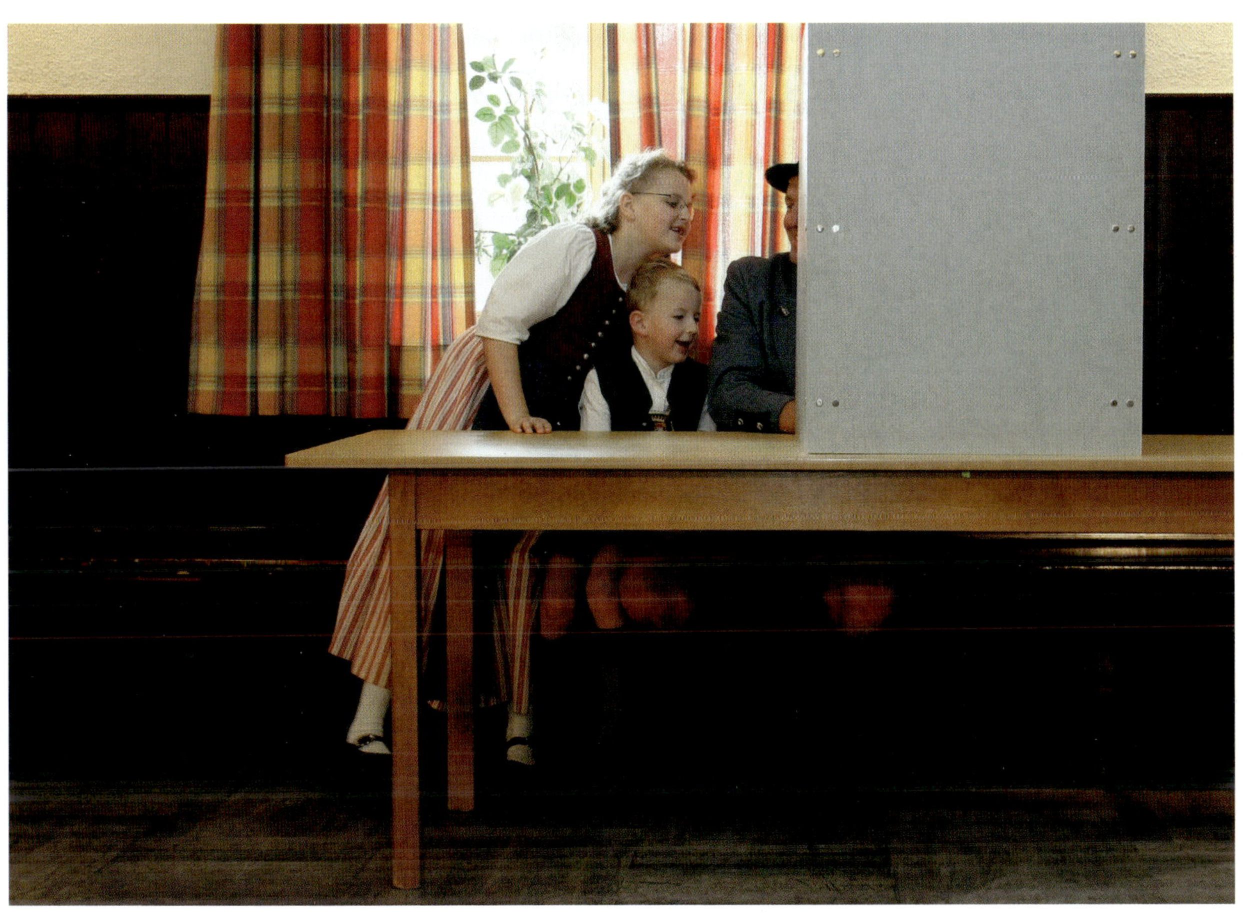

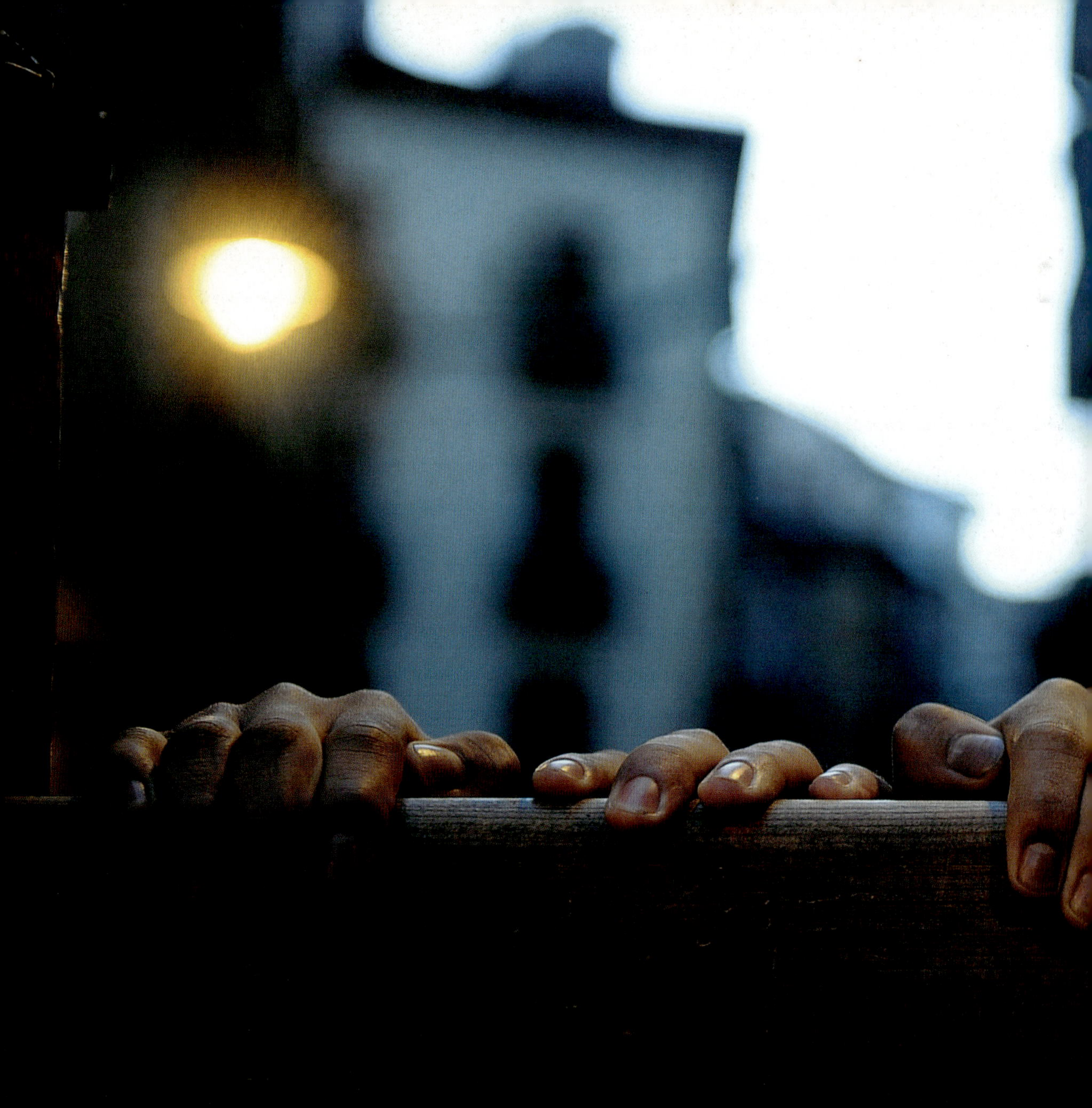

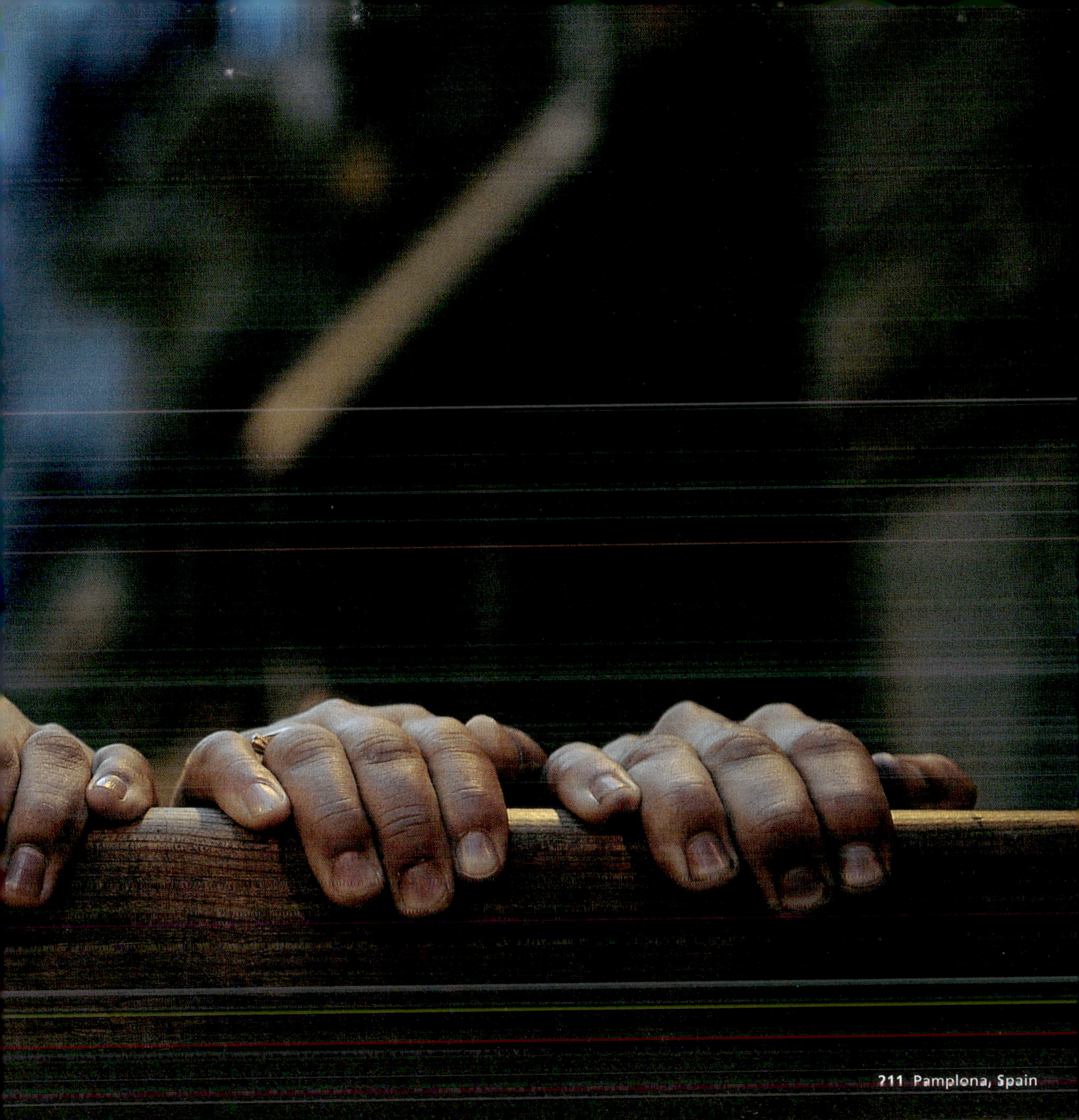

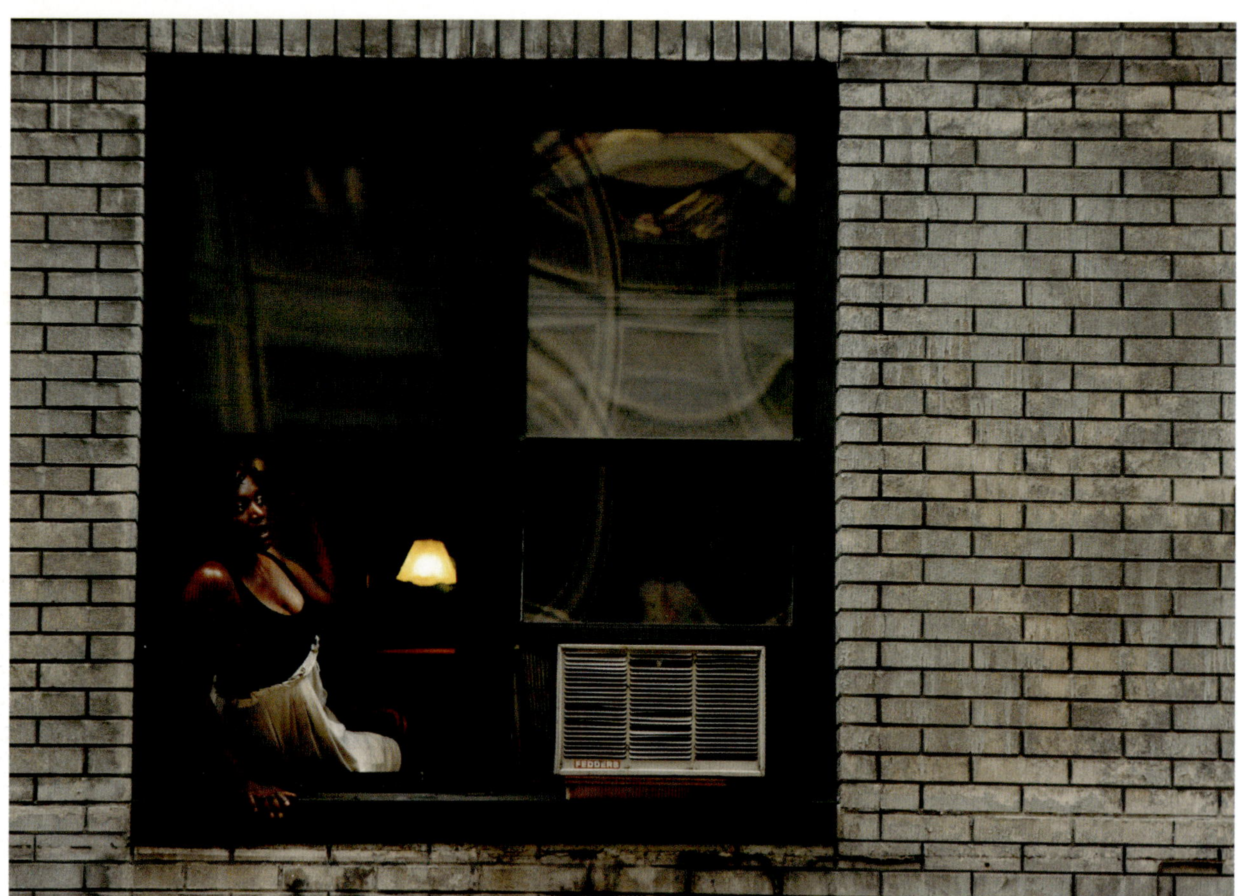

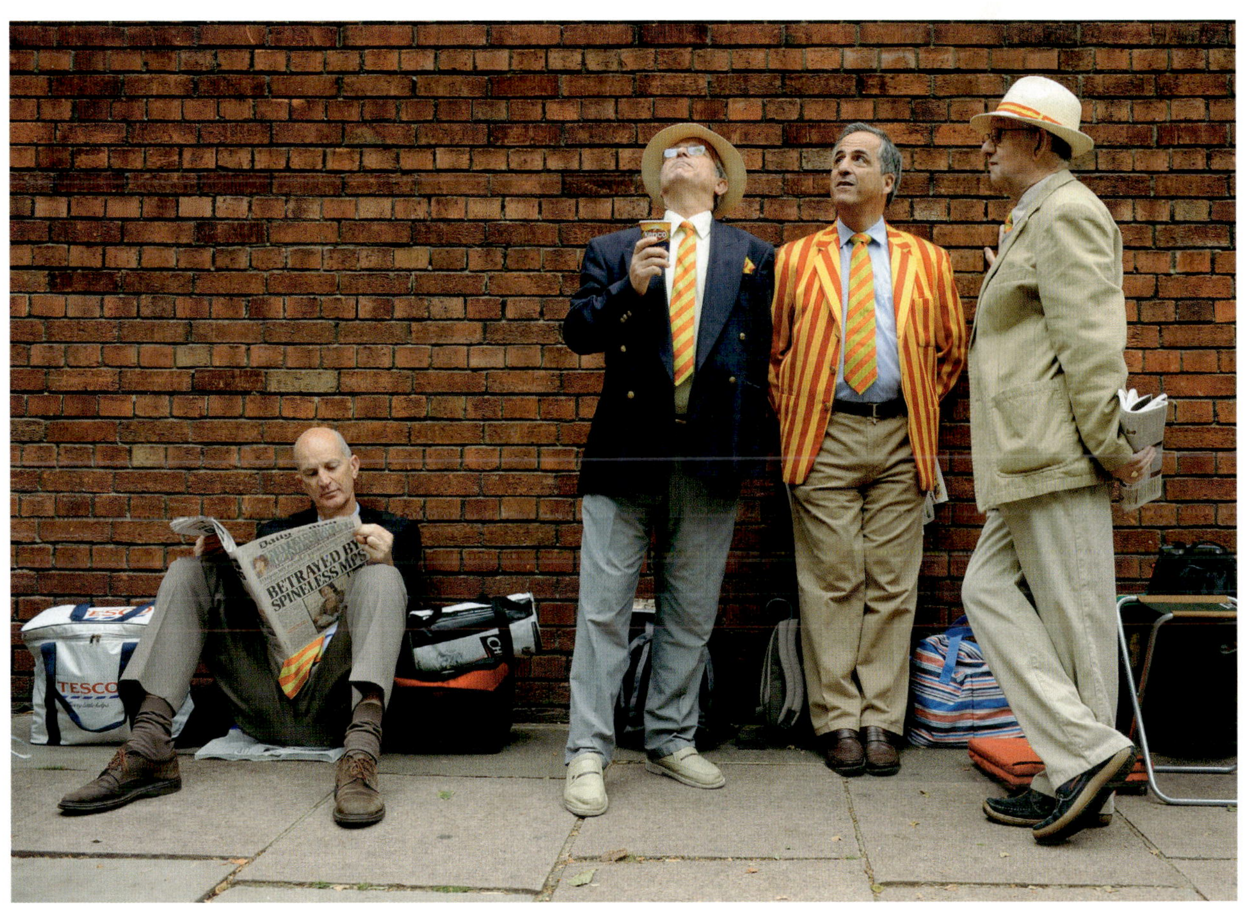
BETRAYED BY
SPINELESS MPs

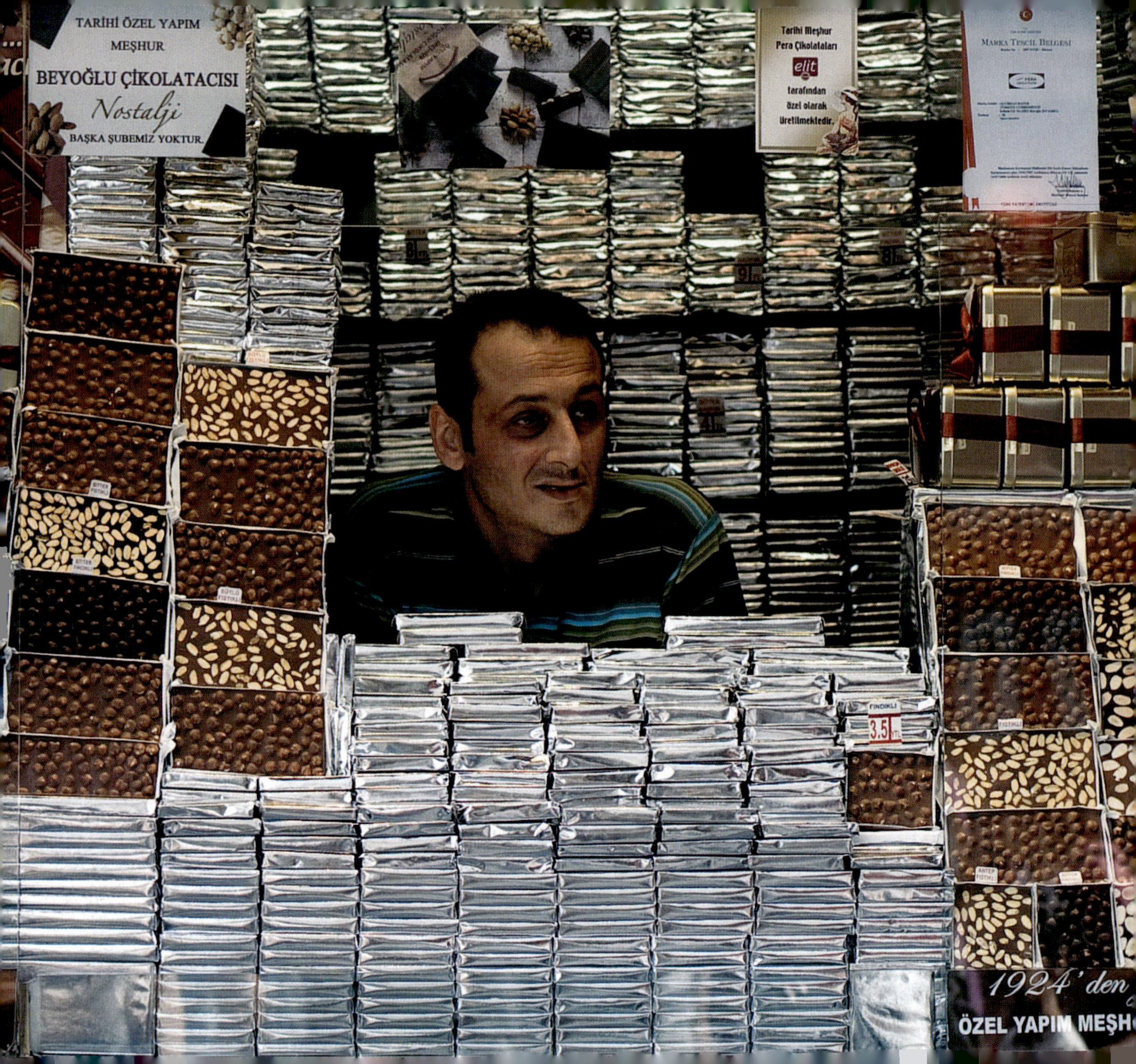

TARİHİ ÖZEL YAPIM
MEŞHUR
BEYOĞLU ÇİKOLATACISI
Nostalji
BAŞKA ŞUBEMİZ YOKTUR.
Tarihi Meşhur
Pera Çikolataları
elit
tarafından
özel olarak
Üretilmektedir.
MARKA TESCİL BELGESİ
FINDIKLI
3.5 YTL
1924'den
ÖZEL YAPIM MEŞH

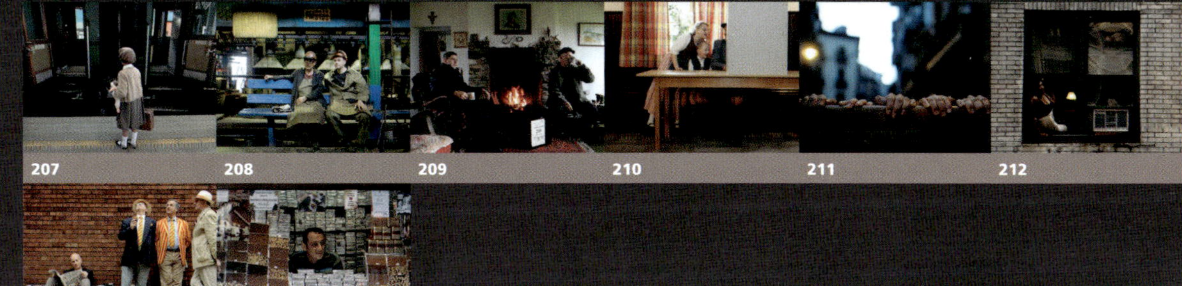

207 In a re-enactment of events 70 years ago, a girl stands in front of a vintage train before its departure from Prague with survivors and descendants of the so-called 'Winton's children' on board. Sir Nicholas Winton organized the evacuation by train of 669 mostly Jewish children from Nazi-occupied Czechoslovakia in 1939. Dubbed the 'English Schindler', he turned 100 in May 2009 and was present to meet the group at London's Liverpool Street Station at the end of the last leg of their journey. 1 September 2009. Prague, Czech Republic. Petr Josek.

208 Foundry workers rest in the Minsk Automobile Factory. 27 August 2009. Minsk, Belarus. Vasily Fedosenko.

209 Presiding officer Hugh O'Donnell (right) and police (Gardaí) officer Barry McCann take a break after carrying the ballot box to be used on the Island of Inishfree, off the coast of Donegal, where a total of six people are registered to vote. Irish voters approved the European Union's Lisbon Treaty by a resounding margin in a referendum on 2 October. 30 September 2009. Inishfree, Ireland. Cathal McNaughton.

210 Children watch as a man dressed in traditional Bavarian costume casts his vote in the German federal election. Chancellor Angela Merkel won a second term in office with a slim but clear centre-right majority. 27 September 2009. Baiernrain, Germany. Michaela Rehle.

211 Festival-goers hold on to a barrier on the sixth day of the traditional Running of the Bulls at the San Fermín festival in Pamplona. San Fermín was made famous by Ernest Hemingway's novel *The Sun Also Rises*, and the week-long fiesta now attracts hundreds of runners from around the world. One participant was gored to death in 2009, and dozens more were injured. 12 July 2009. Pamplona, Spain. Eloy Alonso.

212 A woman leans out of a window on Broadway to watch Paul McCartney perform with his band atop the Ed Sullivan Theater while appearing on the *Late Show with David Letterman*. 15 July 2009. New York, United States. Mike Segar.

213 Marylebone Cricket Club members wait in a queue outside Lord's Cricket Ground before the second Ashes test cricket match between England and Australia. 16 July 2009. London, Britain. Philip Brown.

214 A chocolate seller waits in his booth for customers. 22 September 2009. Istanbul, Turkey. Morteza Nikoubazl.

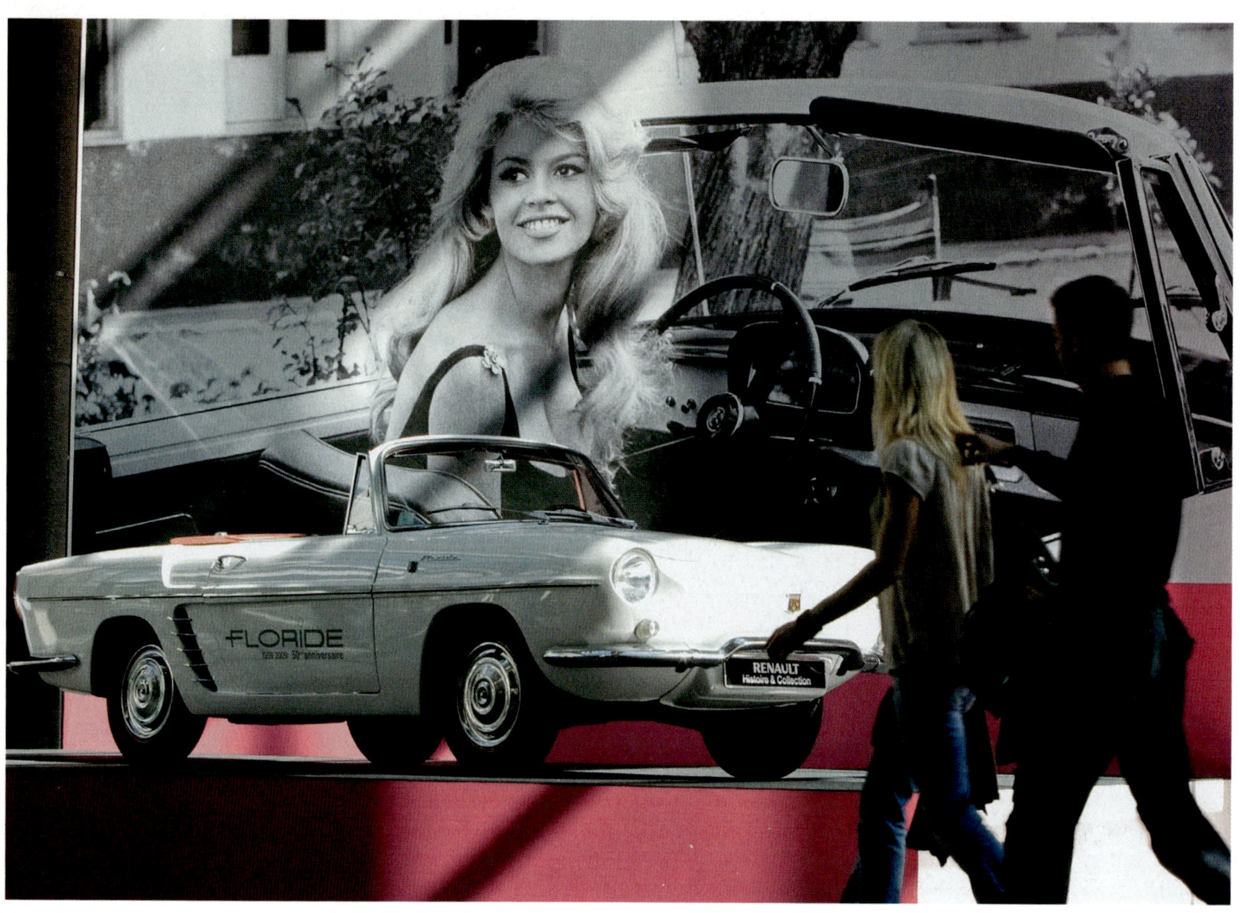
FLORIDE
1959 2009 50e anniversaire
RENAULT
Histoire & Collection

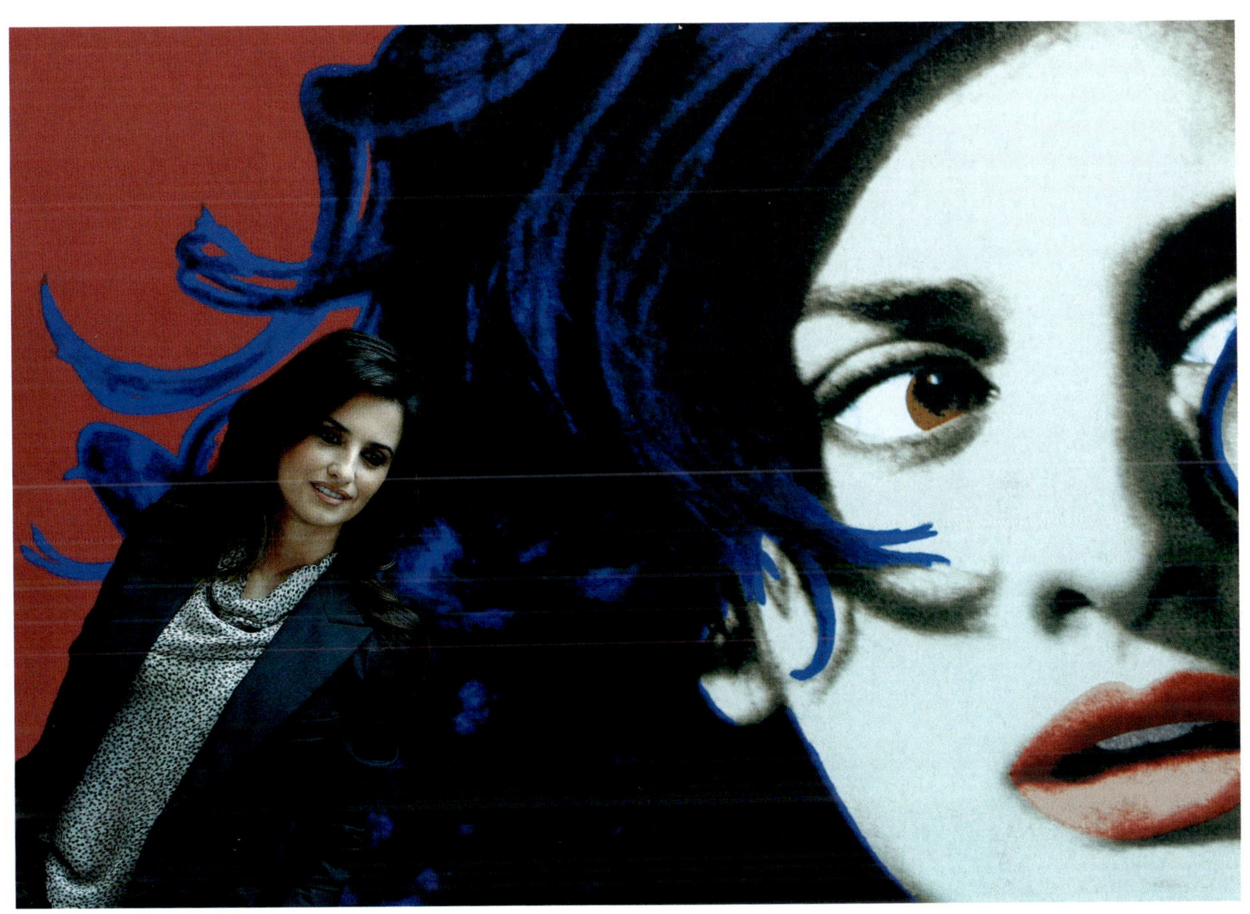

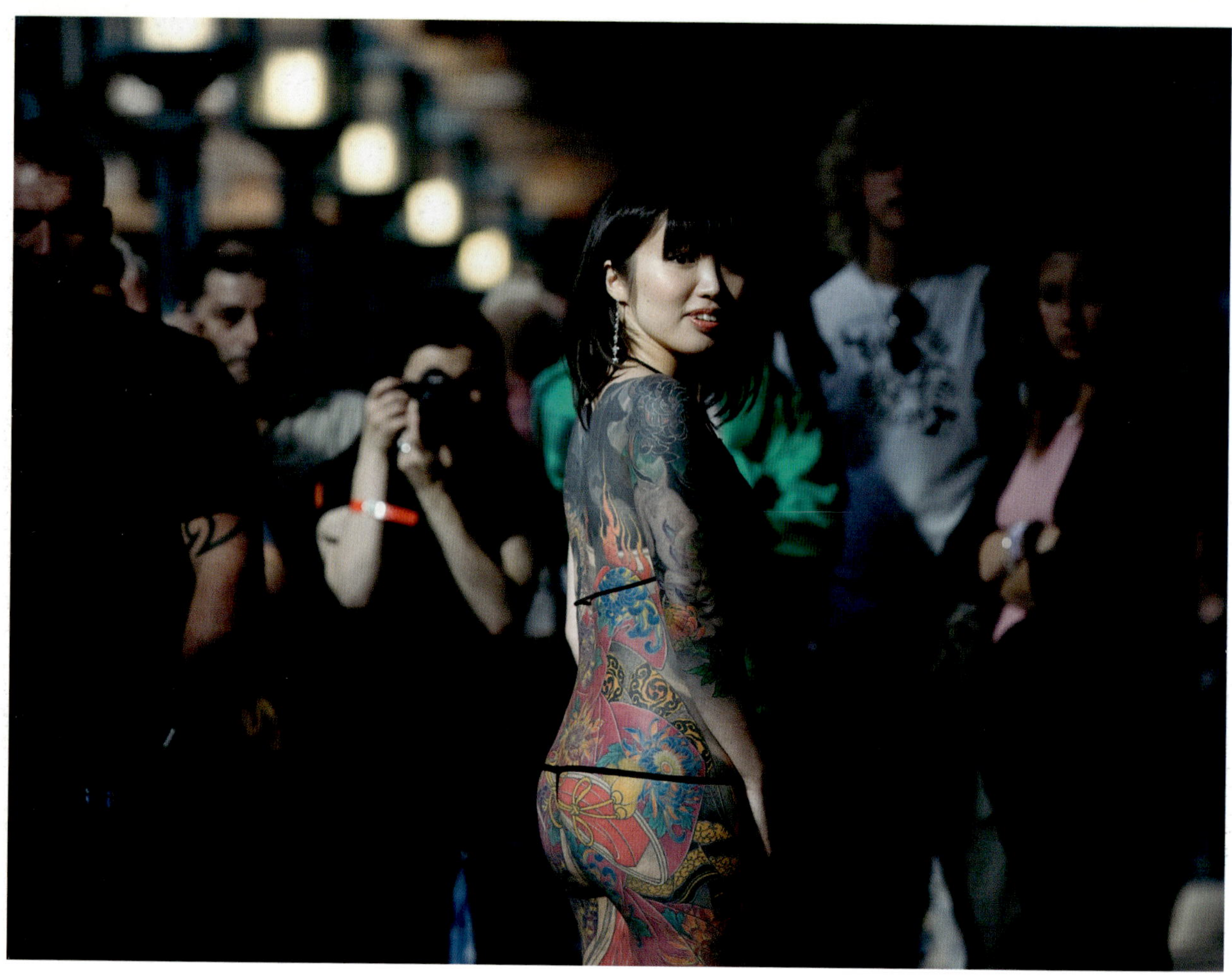

217 London, Britain

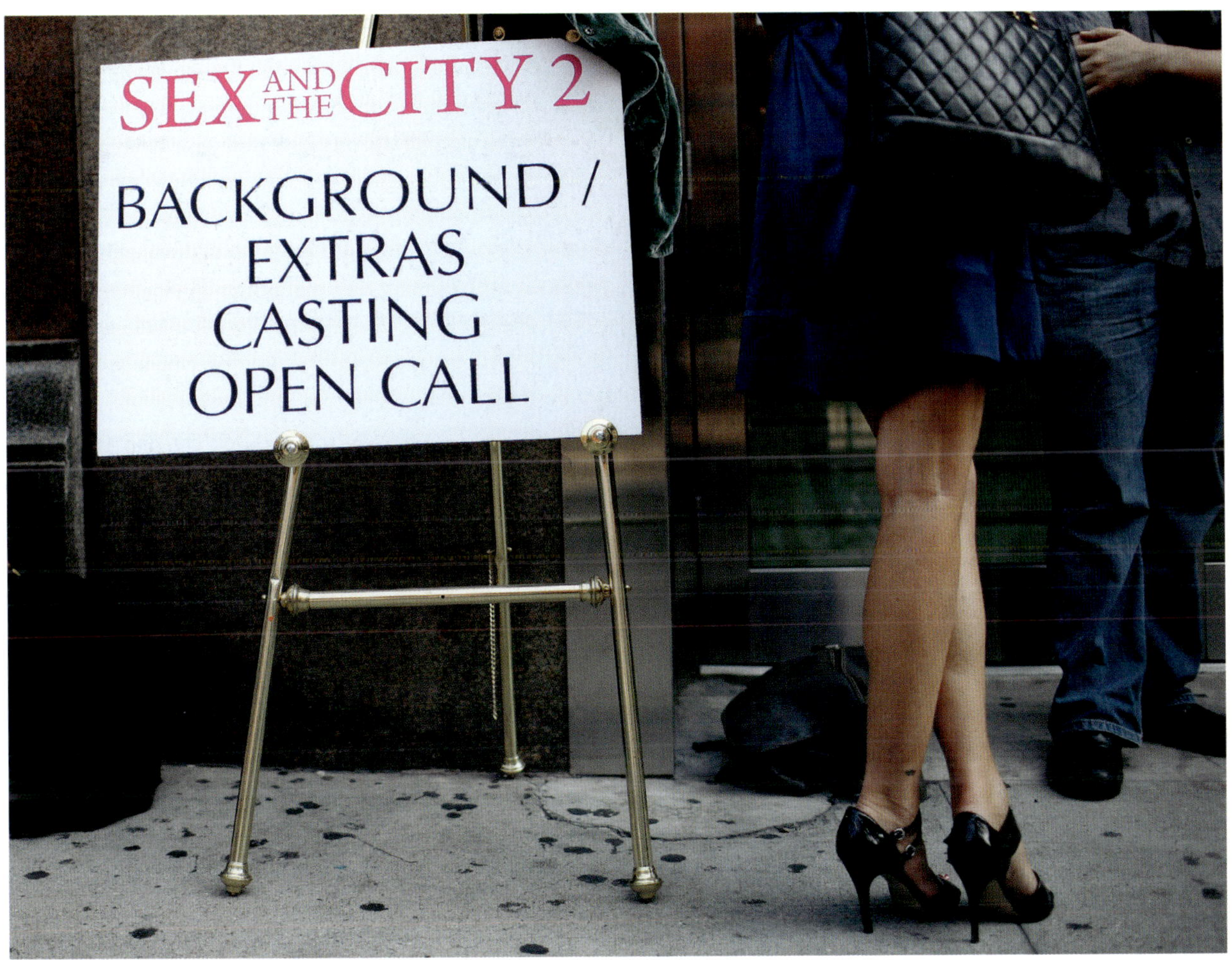
SEX AND THE CITY 2
BACKGROUND /
EXTRAS
CASTING
OPEN CALL

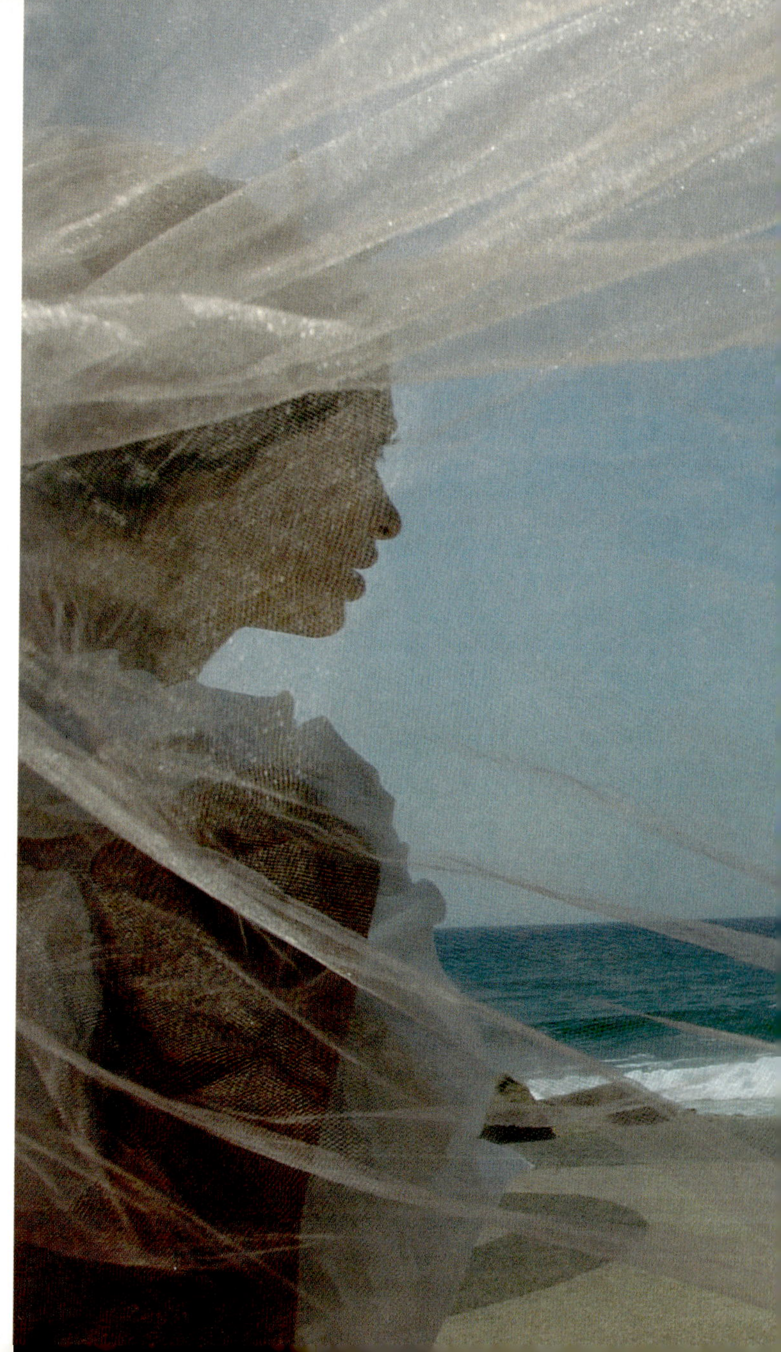

219 Tel Aviv, Israel

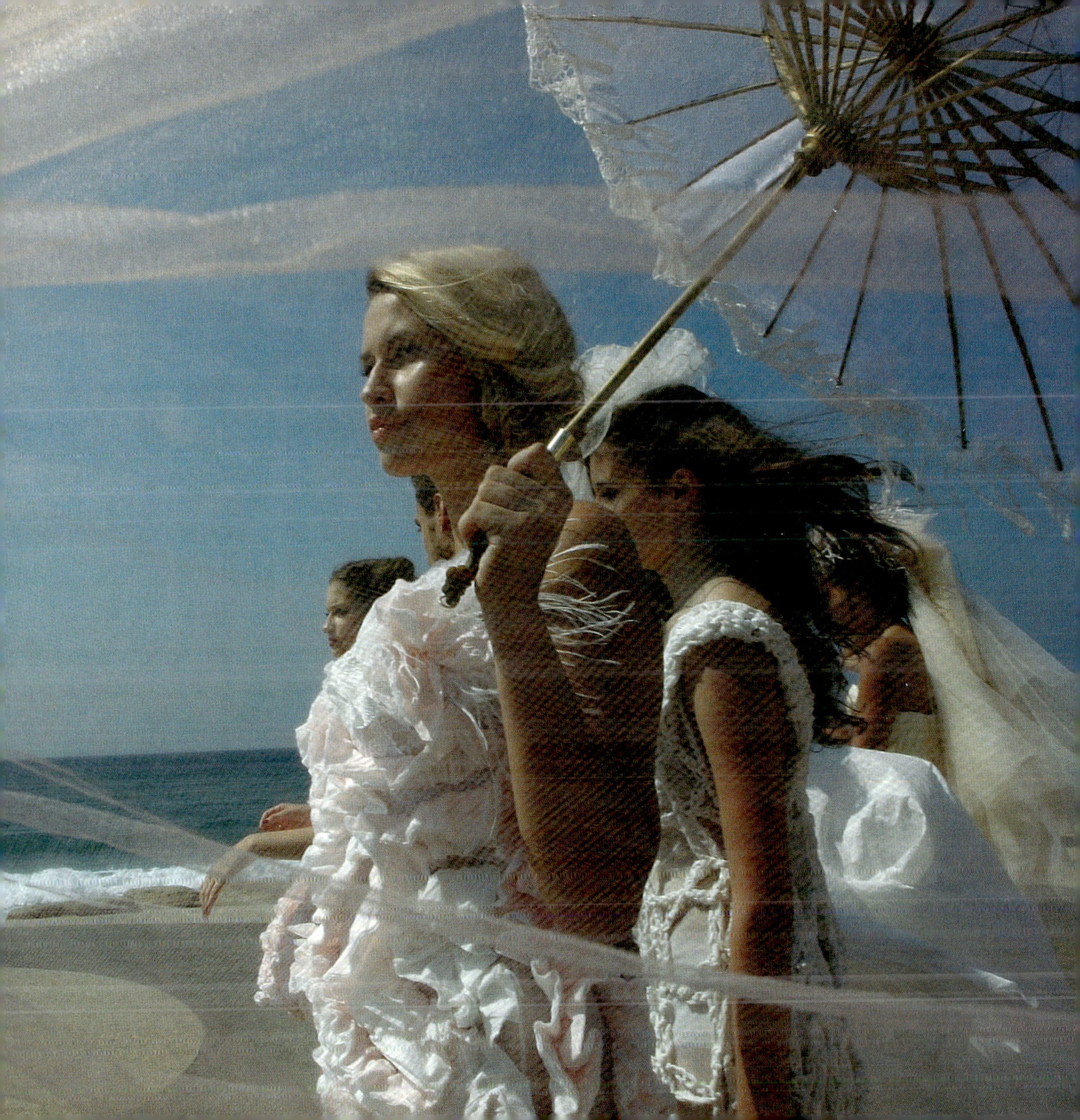

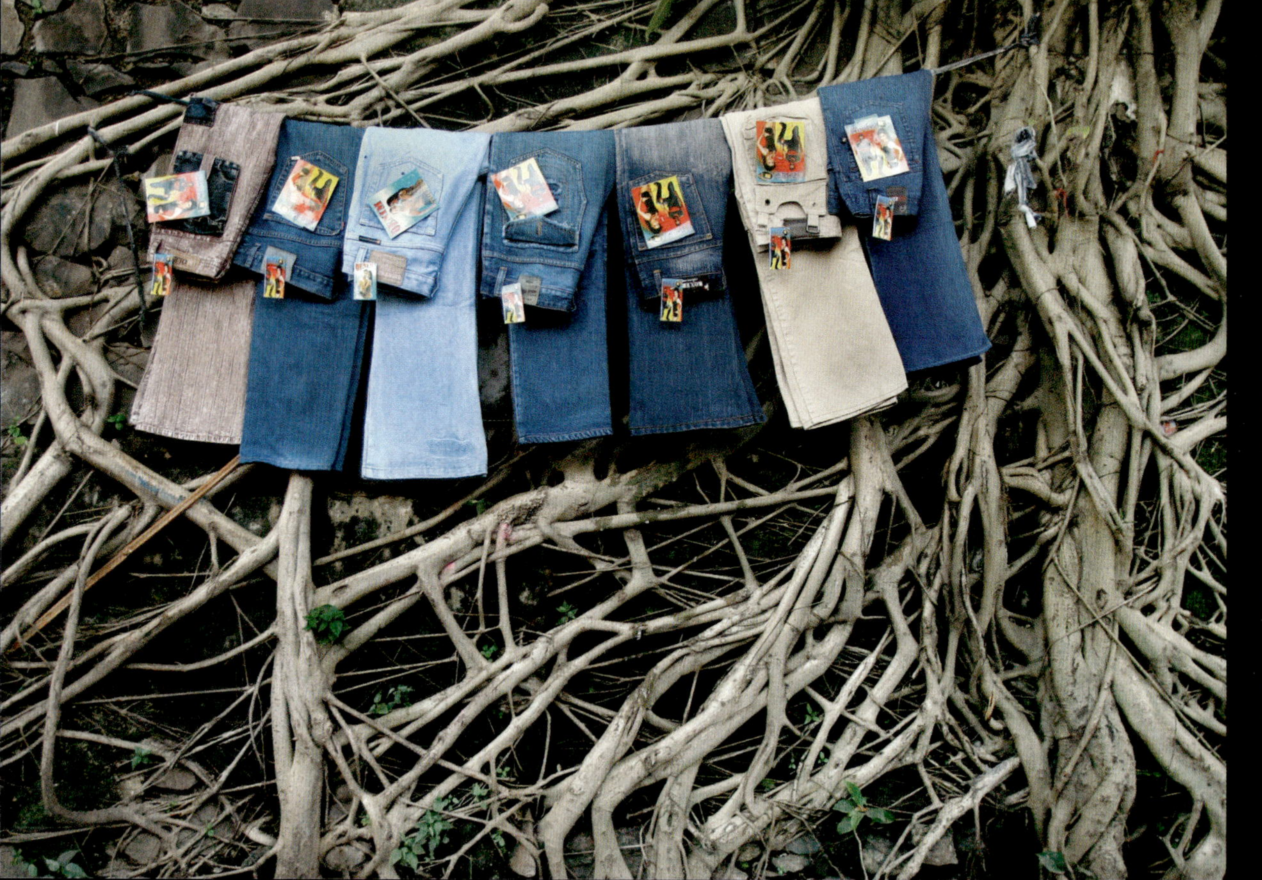

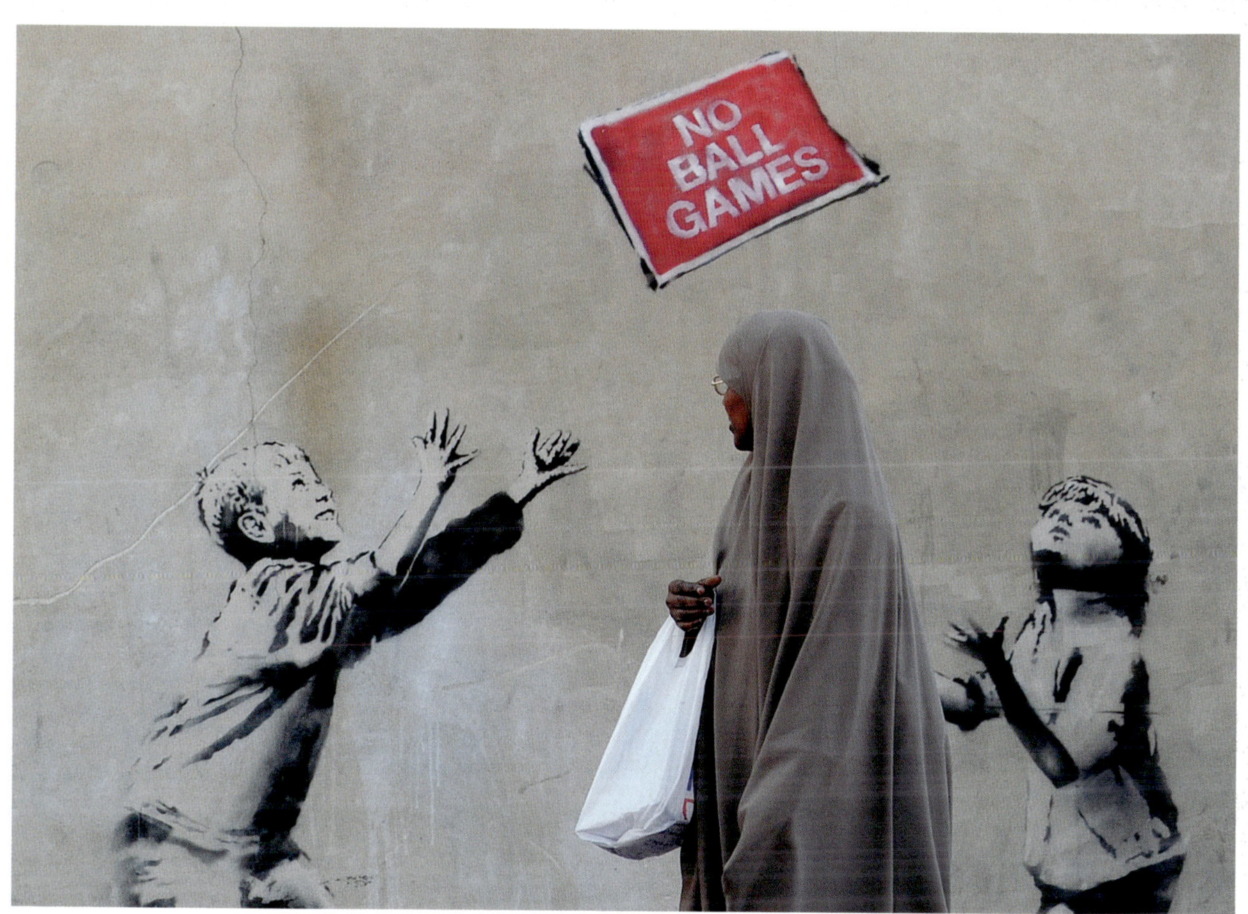

NO
BALL
GAMES

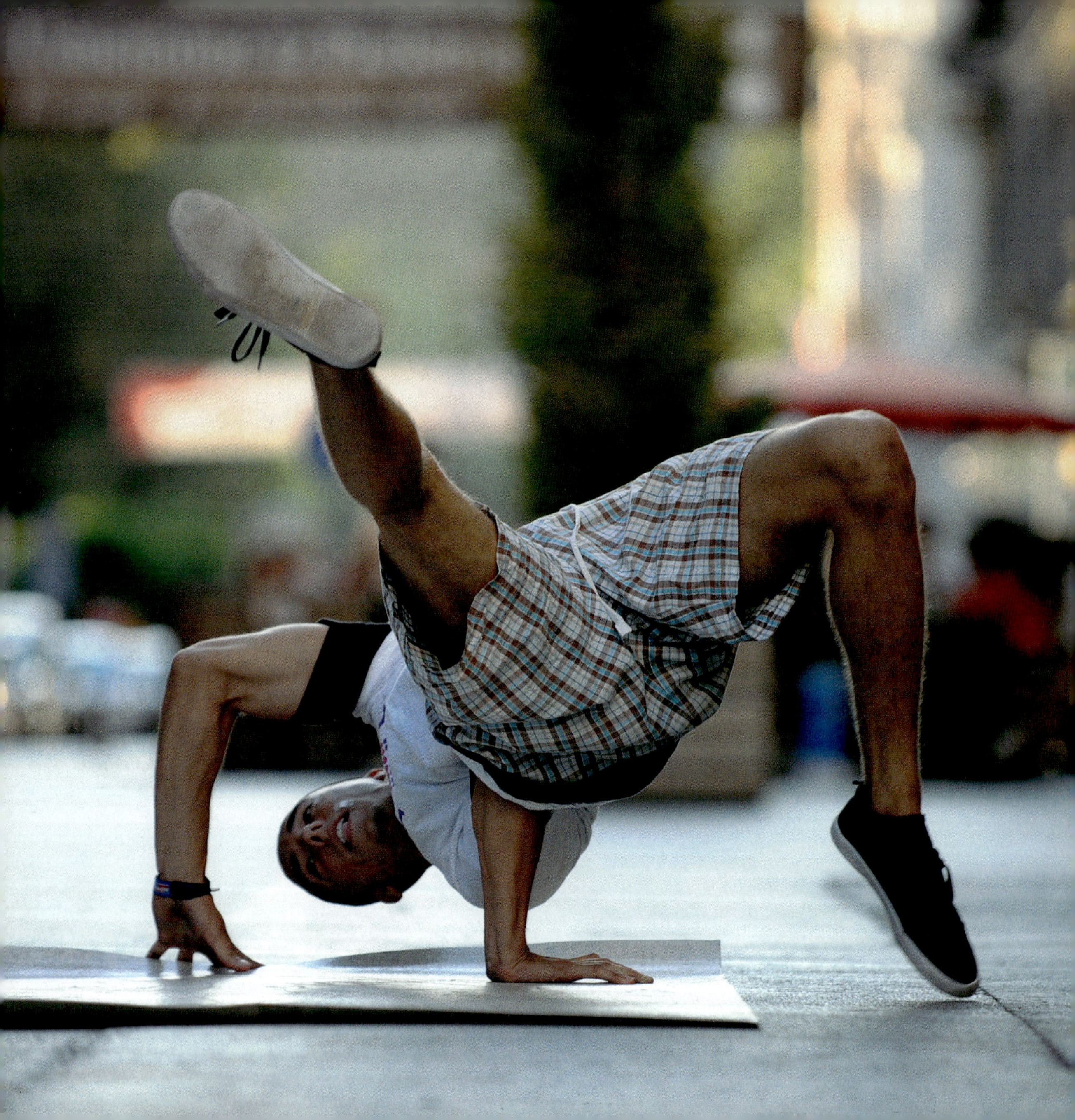

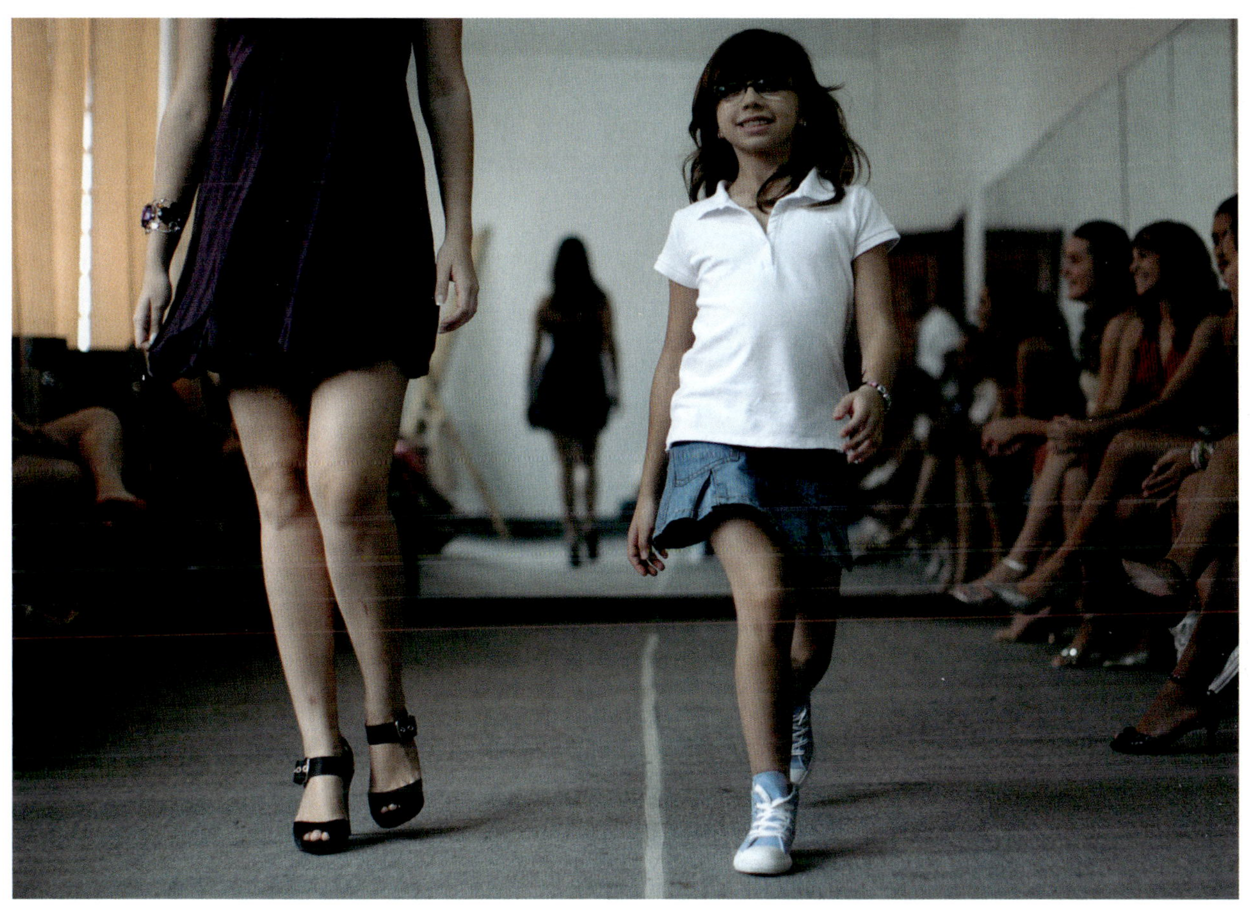

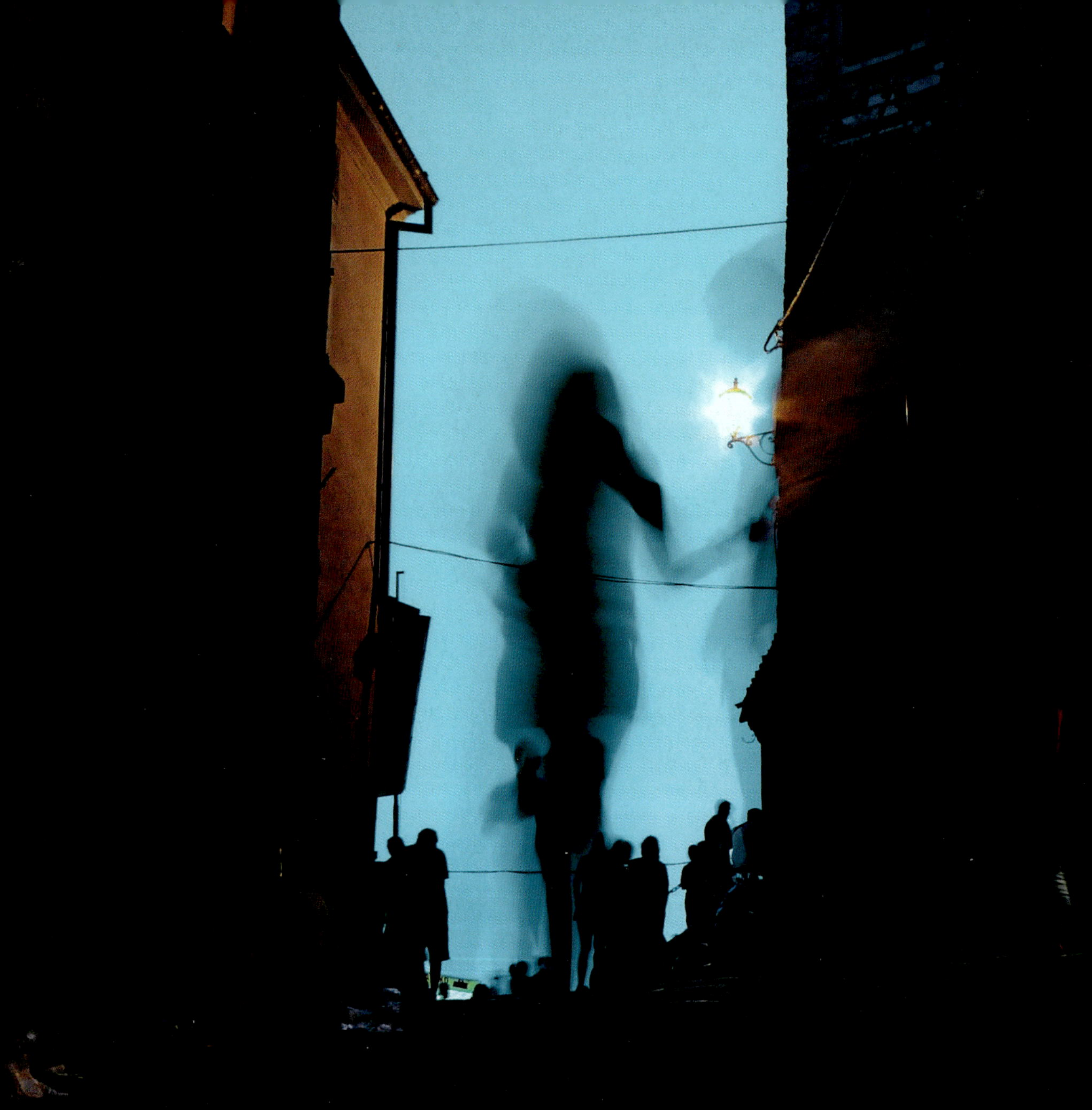

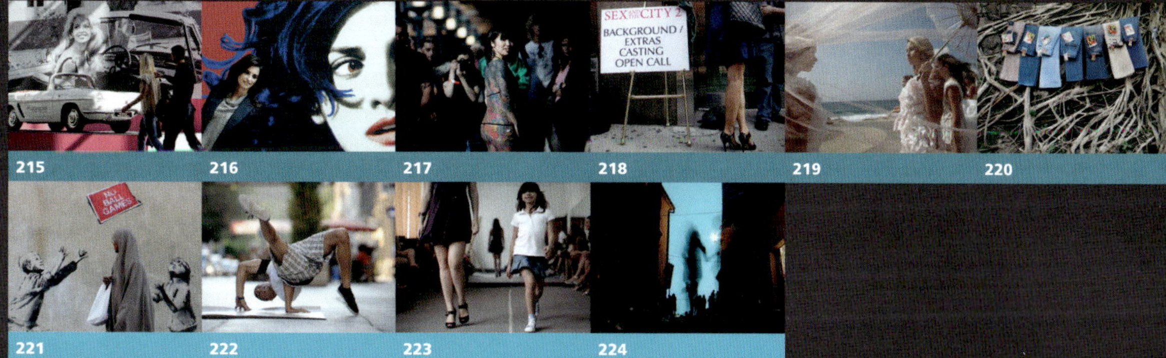

215 Visitors pass by a car that belonged to former actress Brigitte Bardot at an exhibition devoted to the French star in Boulogne-Billancourt, Paris. 25 September 2009. Paris, France. Charles Platiau.

216 Spanish actress Penélope Cruz poses during a photocall to promote the film *Broken Embraces*, directed by Pedro Almodóvar. 3 August 2009. Berlin, Germany. Fabrizio Bensch.

217 Rie Gomita from Osaka, Japan, shows off her tattoos at a London tattoo convention. 25 September 2009. London, Britain. Andrew Winning.

218 A woman waits in line during an open casting call for background performers in the movie *Sex and the City 2*. The all-day casting call drew hundreds of hopefuls. 4 August 2009. New York, United States. Mike Segar.

219 Israeli models display wedding dresses made mostly from toilet paper. Seven designers created the gowns for an advertising campaign for an Israeli toilet paper brand to mark 9 September 2009 (09/09/09), a popular date for weddings. 8 September 2009. Tel Aviv, Israel. Gil Cohen Magen.

220 Jeans on sale are hung from the roots of a banyan tree growing out of a Mumbai streetside wall. 11 September 2009. Mumbai, India. Arko Datta.

221 A pedestrian passes graffiti art on a wall in north London. British media attributed the new work to secretive British street artist Banksy. 24 September 2009. London, Britain. Toby Melville.

222 A boy breakdances on a street in the old quarter of Ljubljana. 1 September 2009. Ljubljana, Slovenia. Bor Slana.

223 A girl practises walking at a modelling school in Caracas. The title of Miss Universe was awarded for the sixth time and the second consecutive year to Miss Venezuela on 23 August. The oil-producing South American country is famous for its beauty queens. 27 August 2009. Caracas, Venezuela. Jorge Silva.

224 A visitor returns home at the end of the 11th Motovun Film Festival on the Croatian Adriatic peninsula of Istria. 1 August 2009. Motovun, Croatia. Nikola Solic.

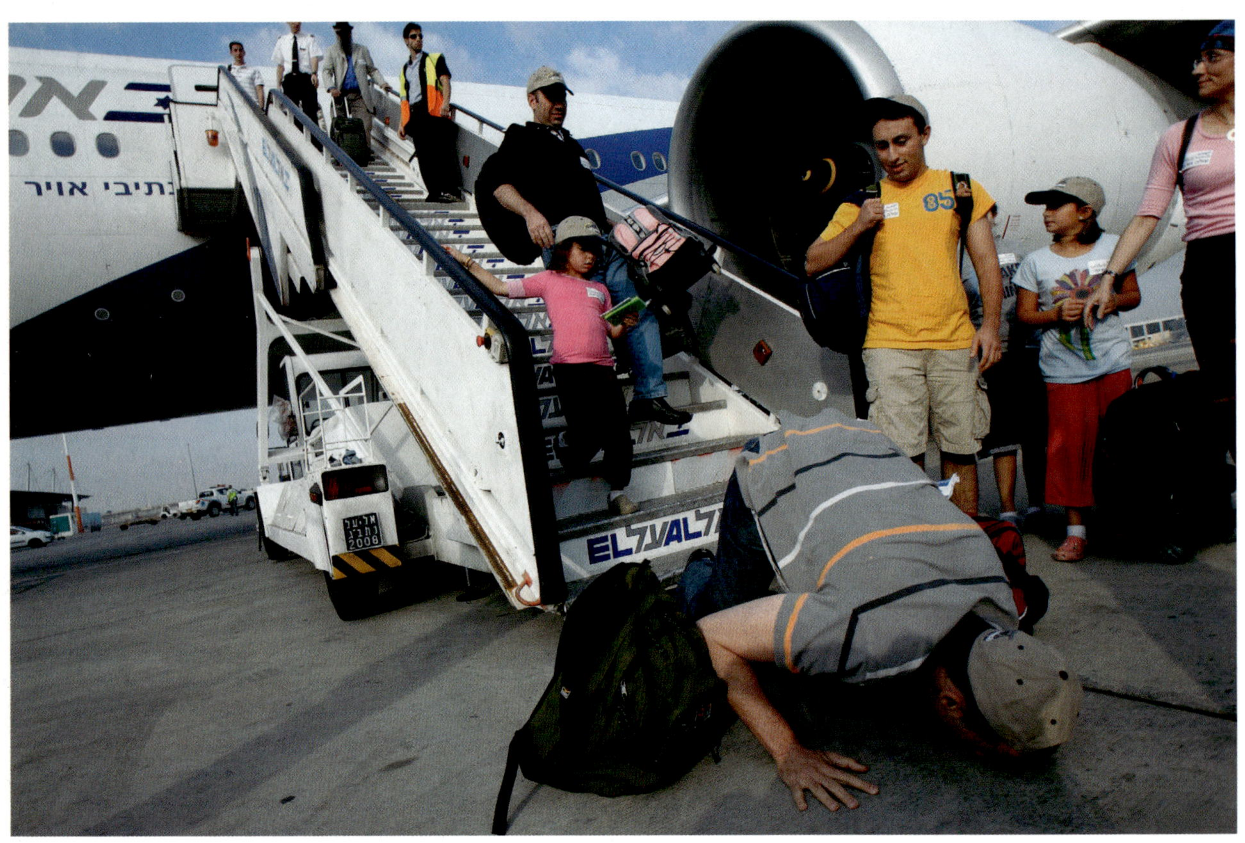

225 Tel Aviv, Israel

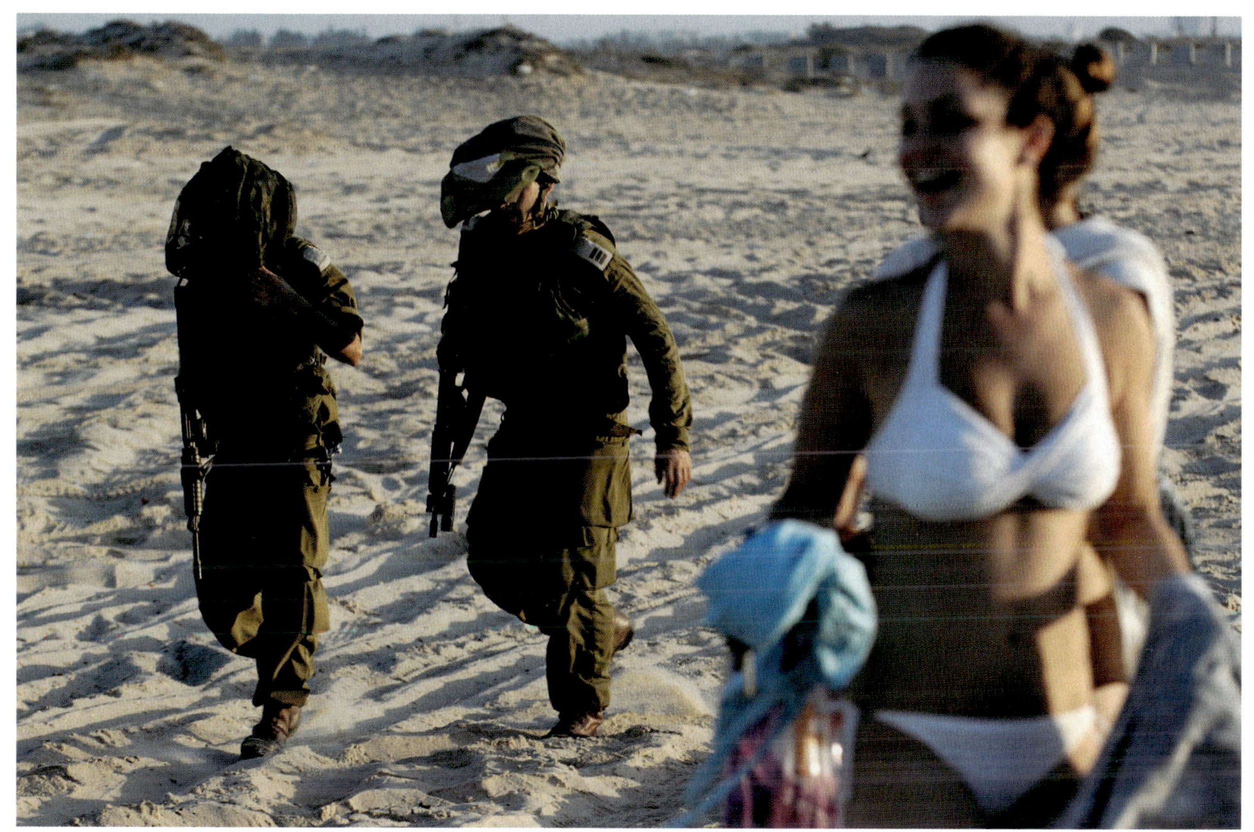

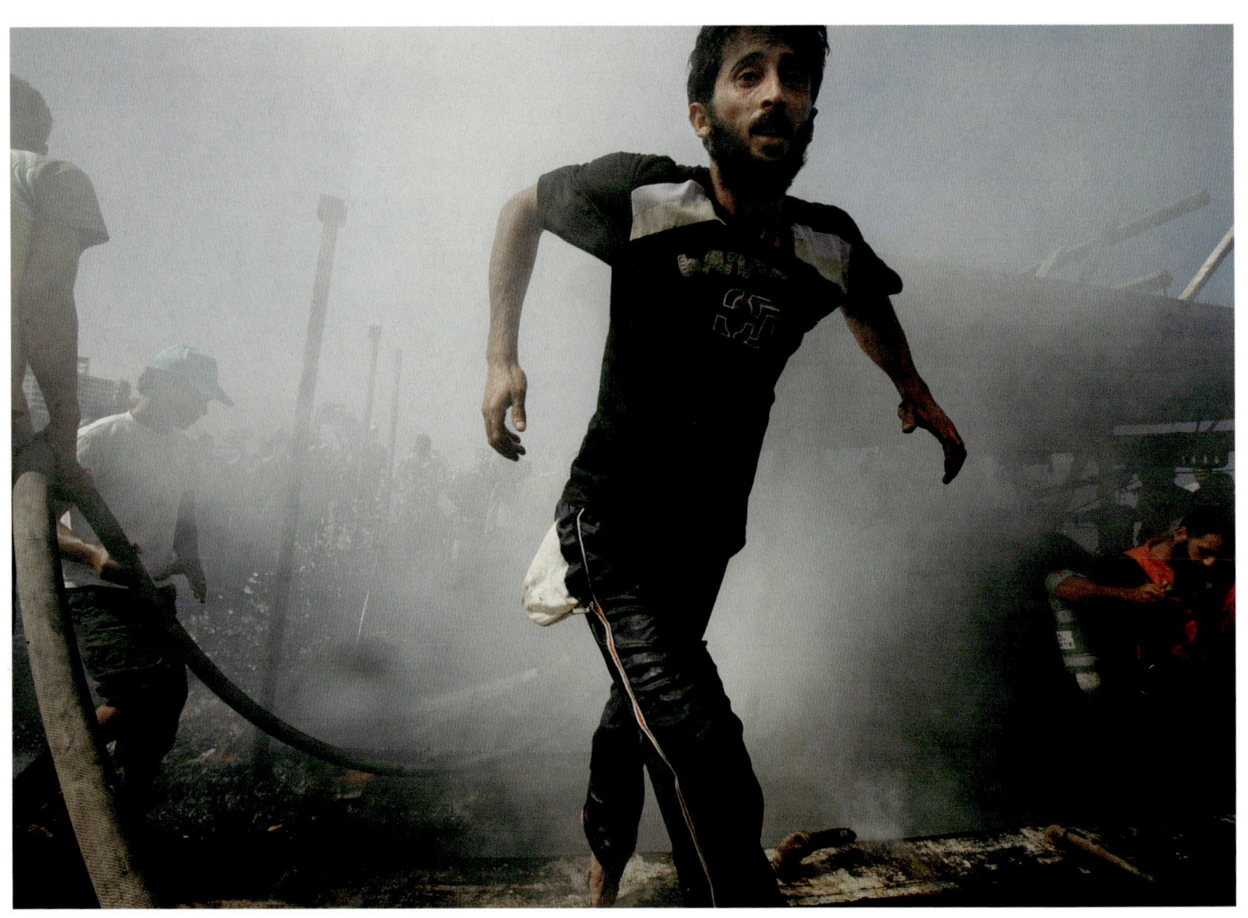

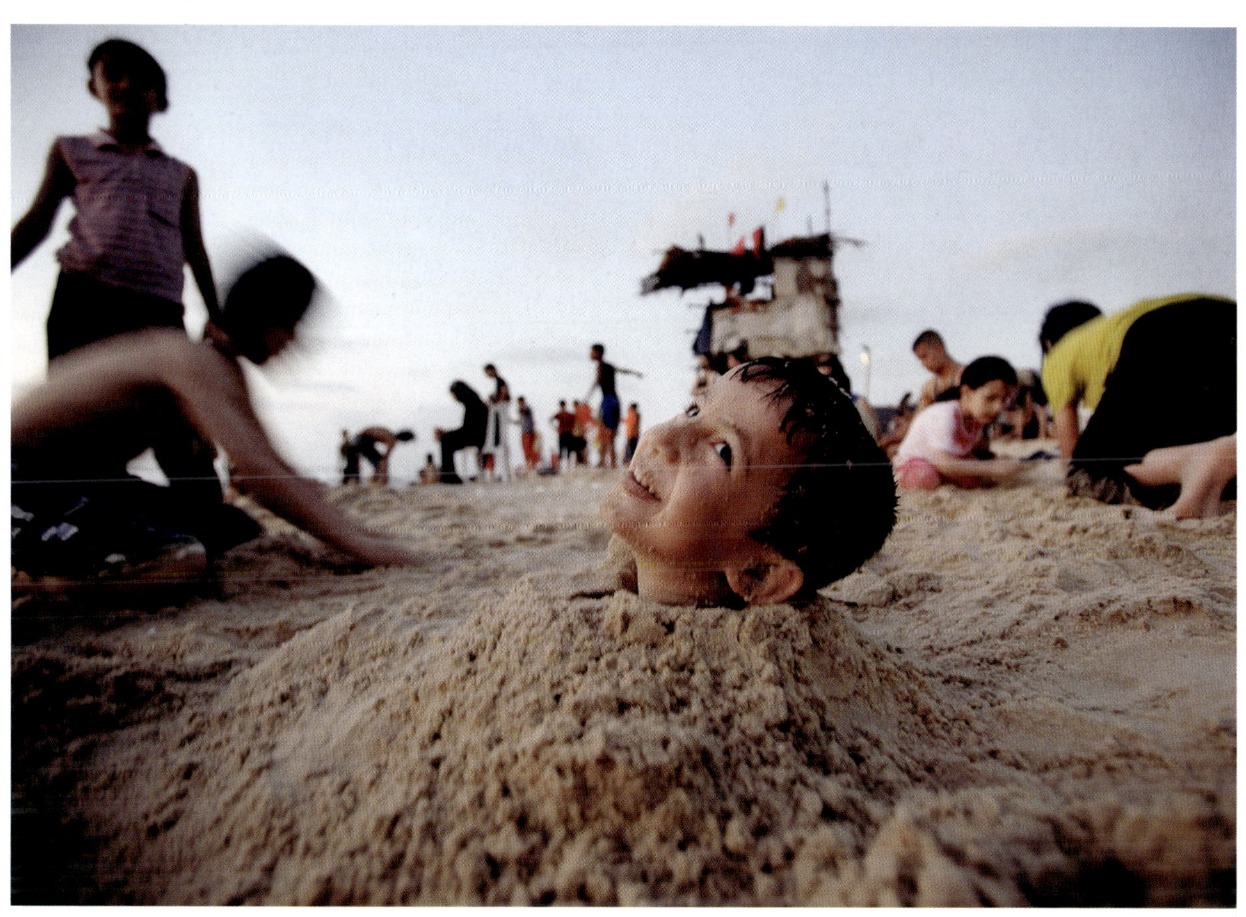

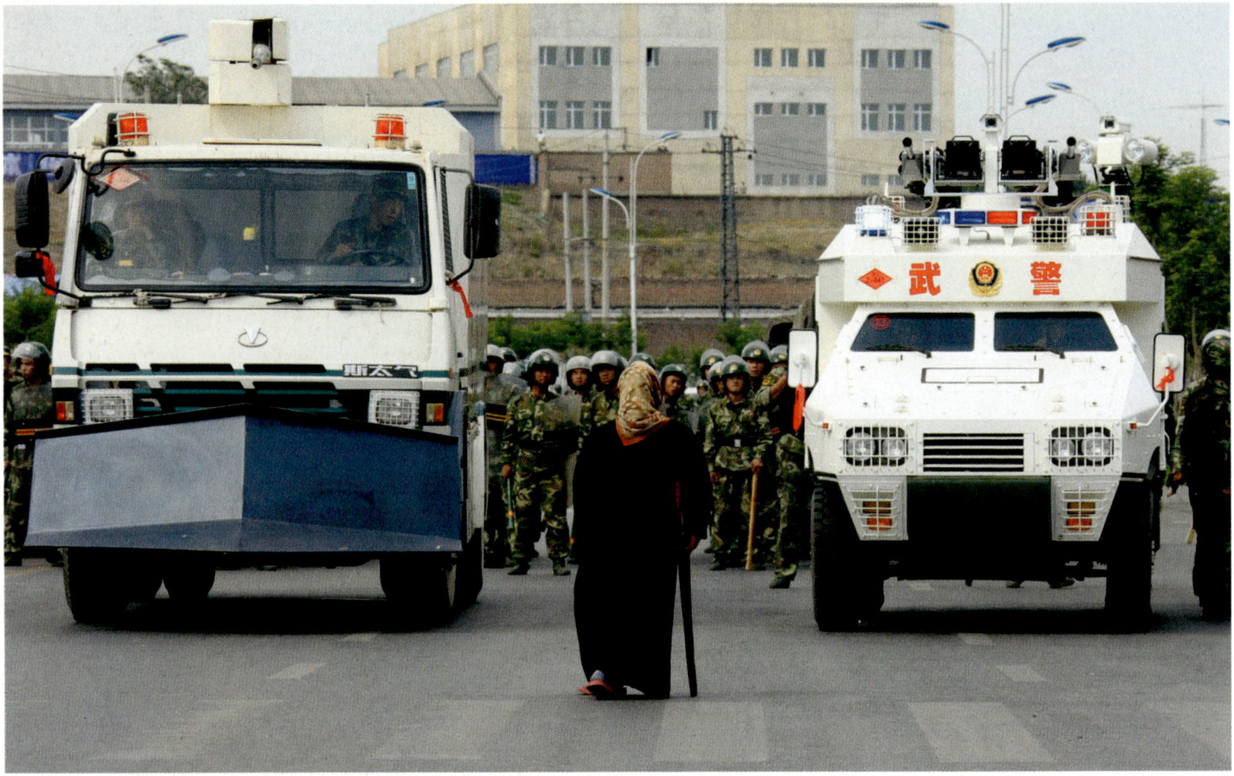

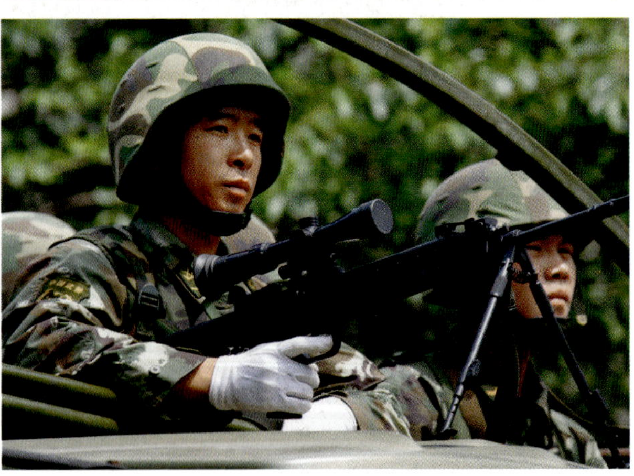
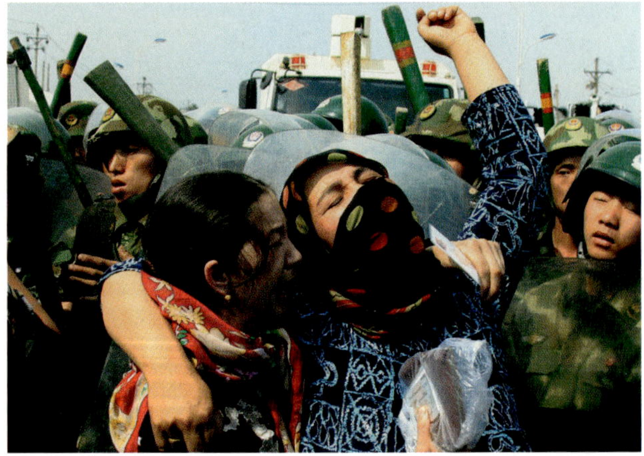

229 [TOP]   230 [ABOVE]   231 [ABOVE RIGHT]   Urumqi, China

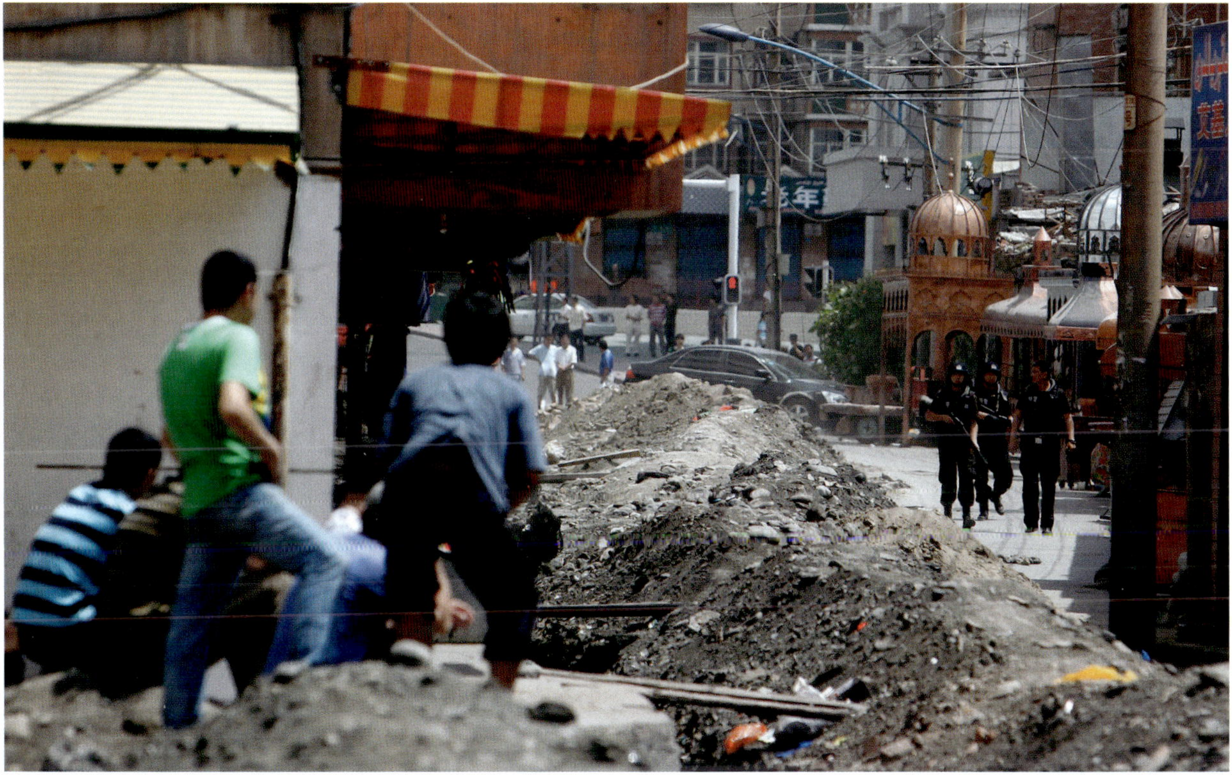

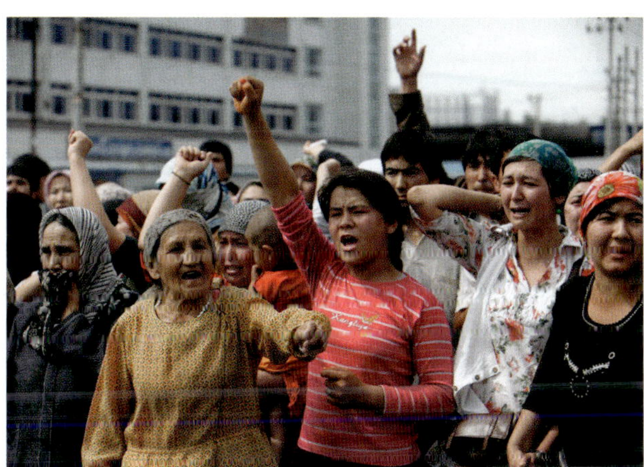

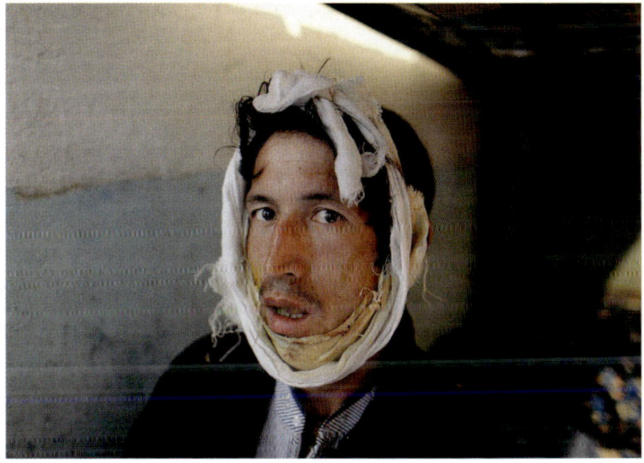

232 [TOP] 233 [ABOVE LEFT] 234 [ABOVE] Urumqi, China

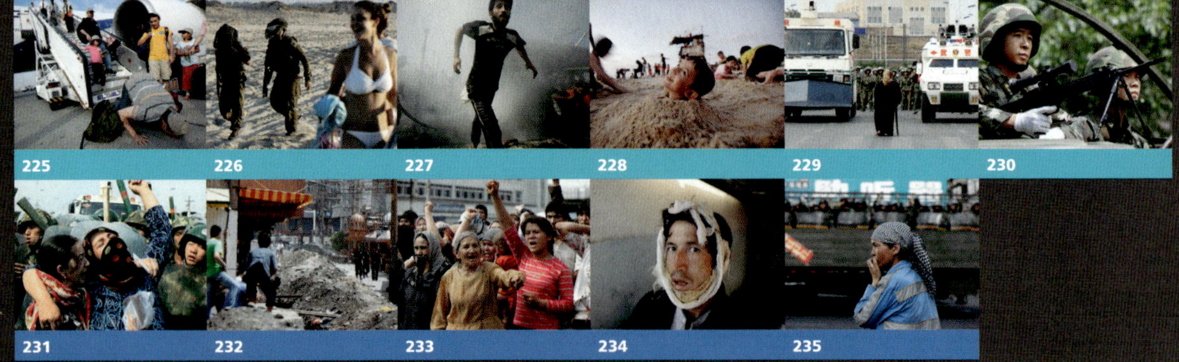

225 A Jewish immigrant from North America kisses the ground on arrival at Ben Gurion International airport near Tel Aviv. 4 August 2009. Tel Aviv, Israel. Gil Cohen Magen.

226 Israeli soldiers patrol along a beach after mortar bombs fired by Palestinian militants in Gaza landed near Kibbutz Zikim, just outside the northern Gaza Strip. 24 August 2009. Near Kibbutz Zikim, Israel. Amir Cohen.

227 A Palestinian fisherman runs out of a fishing boat after it was hit by Israeli army fire at Gaza's seaport. The Israeli army said the boat had violated security boundaries, crossing into an area outside of a permitted fishing zone. 31 August 2009. Gaza. Suhaib Salem.

228 Palestinian children play on the beach in the northern Gaza Strip. 31 July 2009. Gaza. Suhaib Salem.

229 A woman confronts armoured personnel carriers and soldiers in the city of Urumqi in China's far western Xinjiang region. Riots swept Urumqi in July, killing at least 197 people, mostly Han Chinese, and wounding more than 1,600. The riots began after police stopped Uighurs, a Muslim people native to the energy-rich region, demonstrating against the deaths of Uighur factory workers attacked by Han Chinese co-workers. 7 July 2009. Urumqi, China. David Gray.

230 A Chinese paramilitary policeman rides a truck along a main street in Urumqi. Security forces massed in Uighur neighbourhoods in the aftermath of the riots as officials set stability as their top priority. 16 July 2009. Urumqi, China. David Gray.

231 Women gesture in front of Chinese soldiers as a crowd of angry locals confront security forces on a street in Urumqi. Many Uighurs resent government restrictions on their religion and culture and a massive influx of Han Chinese settlers which has in some areas reduced them to a minority in their own land. 7 July 2009. Urumqi, China. David Gray.

232 Ethnic Uighurs look on as Chinese security forces stand by the entrance to the Uighur neighbourhood in Urumqi. 8 July 2009. Urumqi, China. Nir Elias.

233 Uighur protesters shout slogans during a demonstration in Urumqi. 7 July 2009. Urumqi, China. Nir Elias.

234 Ahmmad Ji, 28, an ethnic Uighur, wears bandages over injuries he says were inflicted by Han Chinese during riots in Urumqi. 8 July 2009. Urumqi, China. Nir Elias.

235 An ethnic Uighur woman stands on the side of a road as Chinese army troops ride on a truck on a main street in Urumqi. Along with Tibet, Xinjiang is one of the most politically sensitive regions in China, but has received less international attention. 9 July 2009. Urumqi, China. Nir Elias.

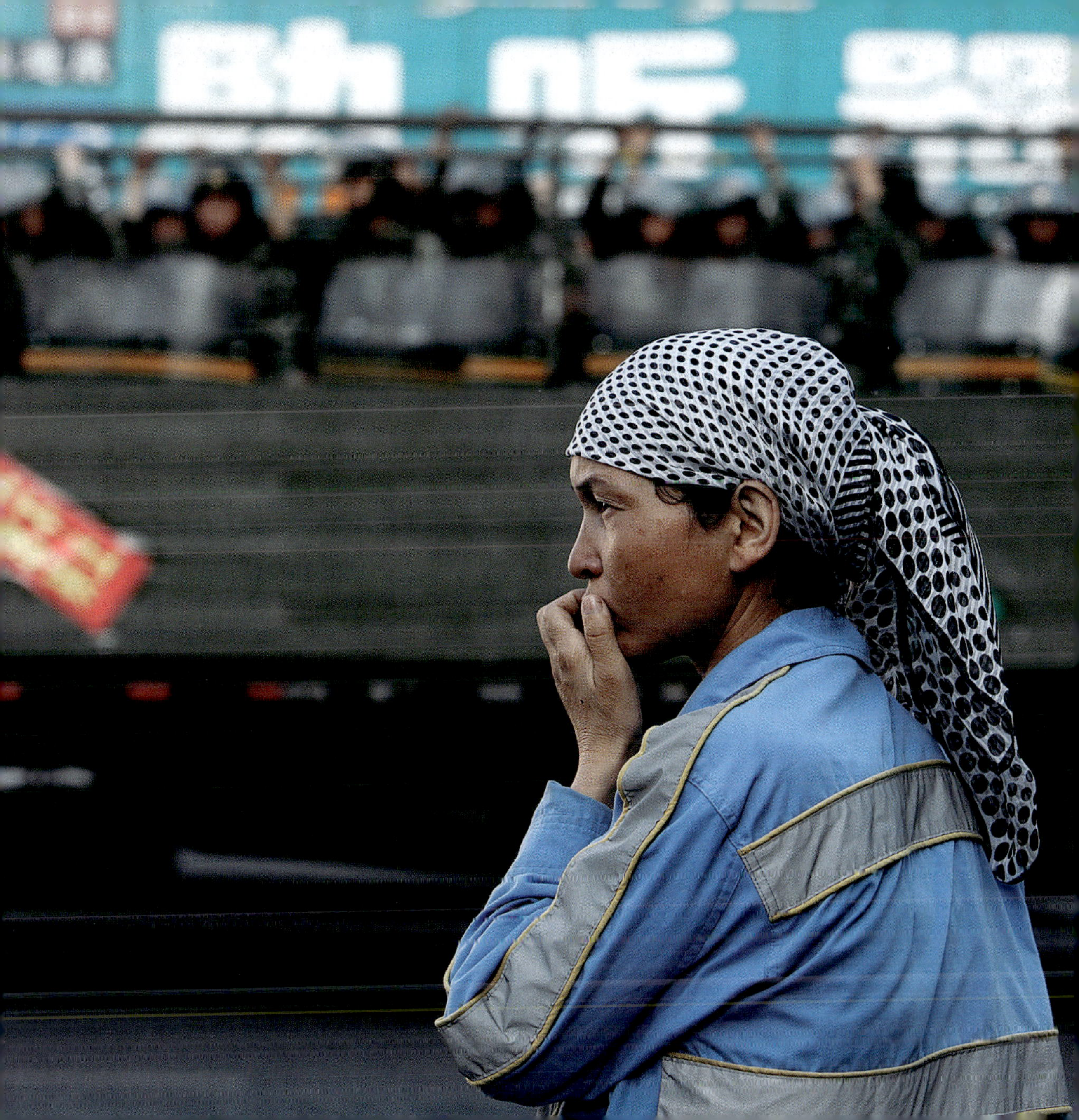

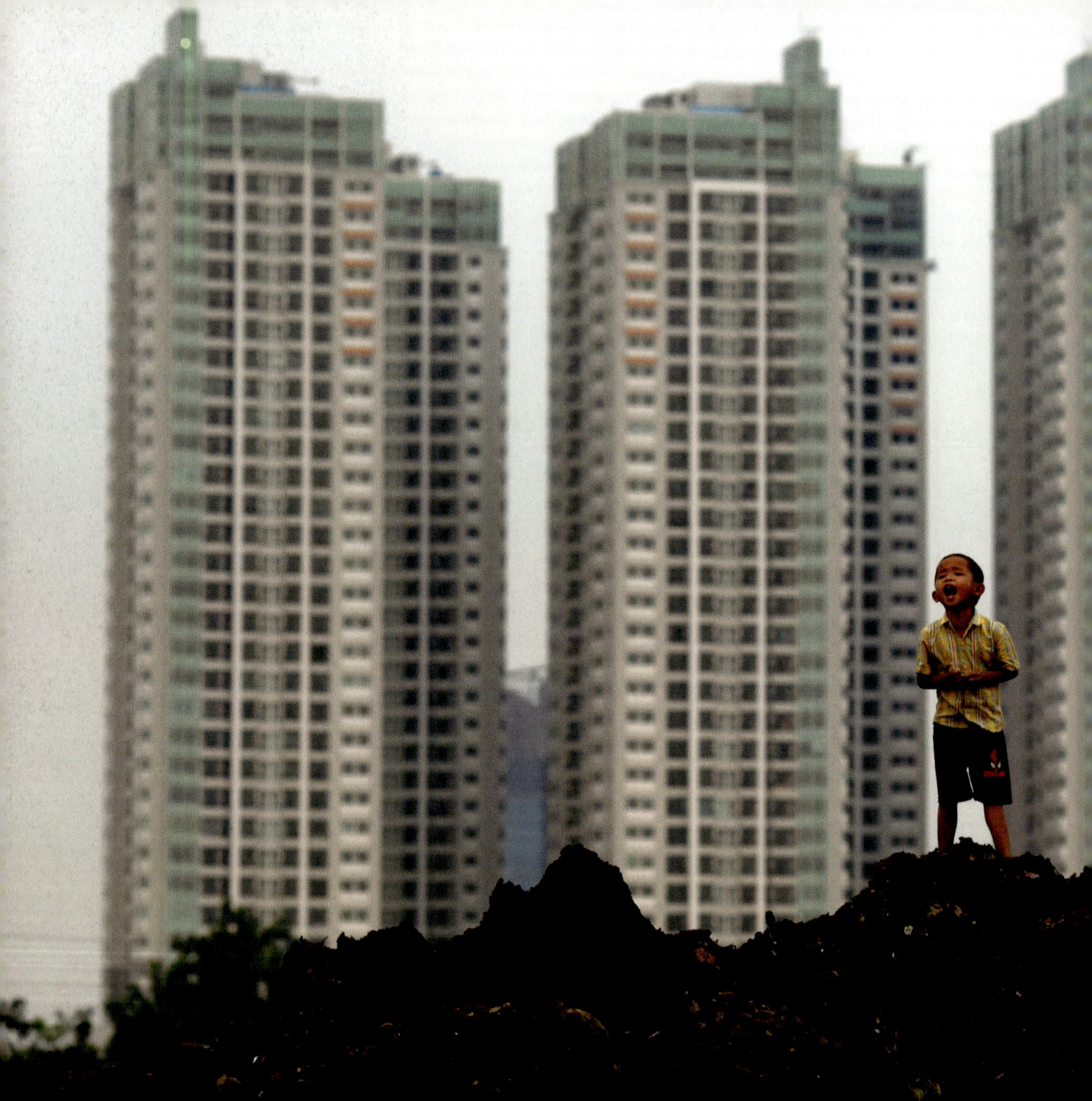

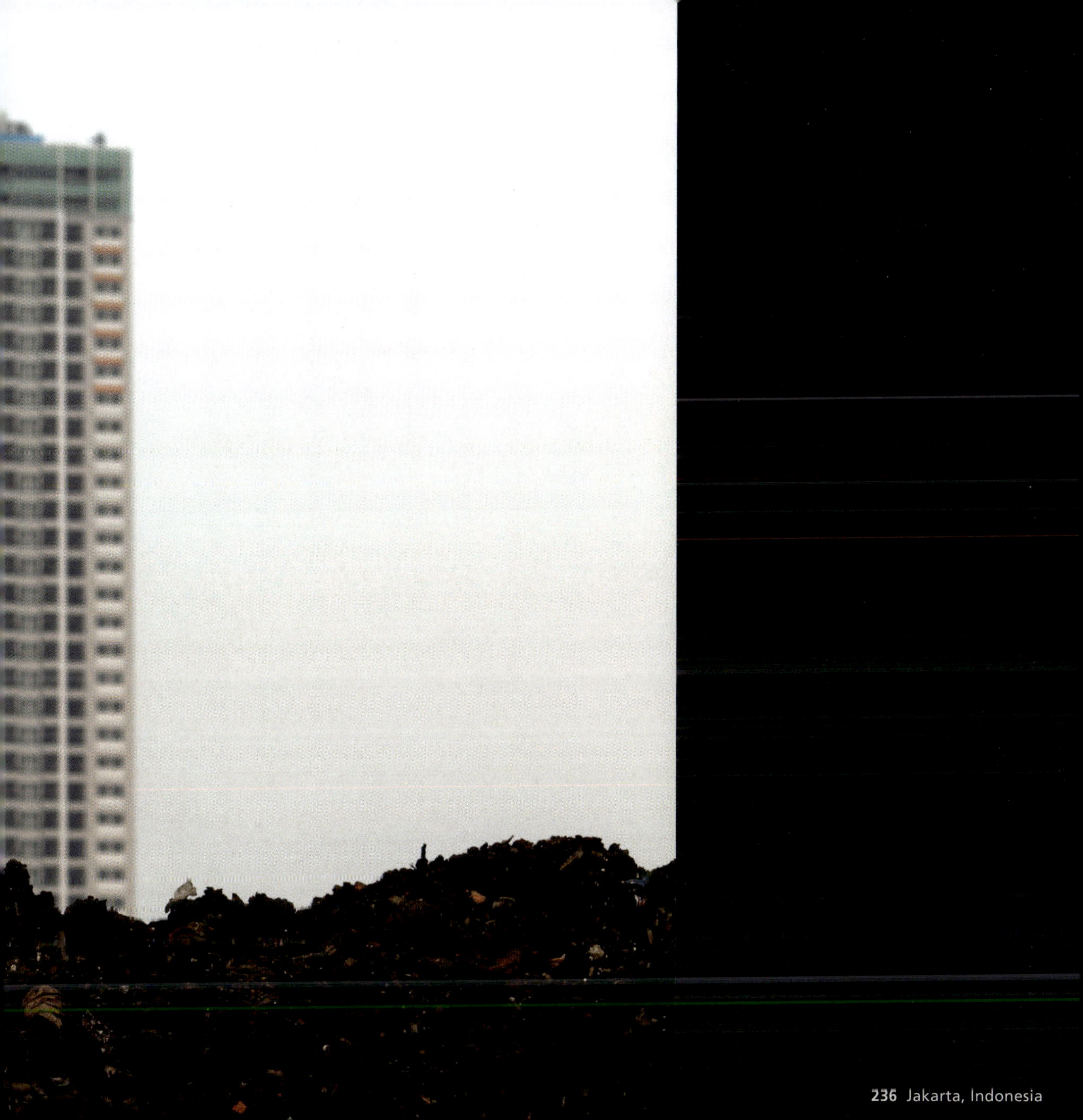

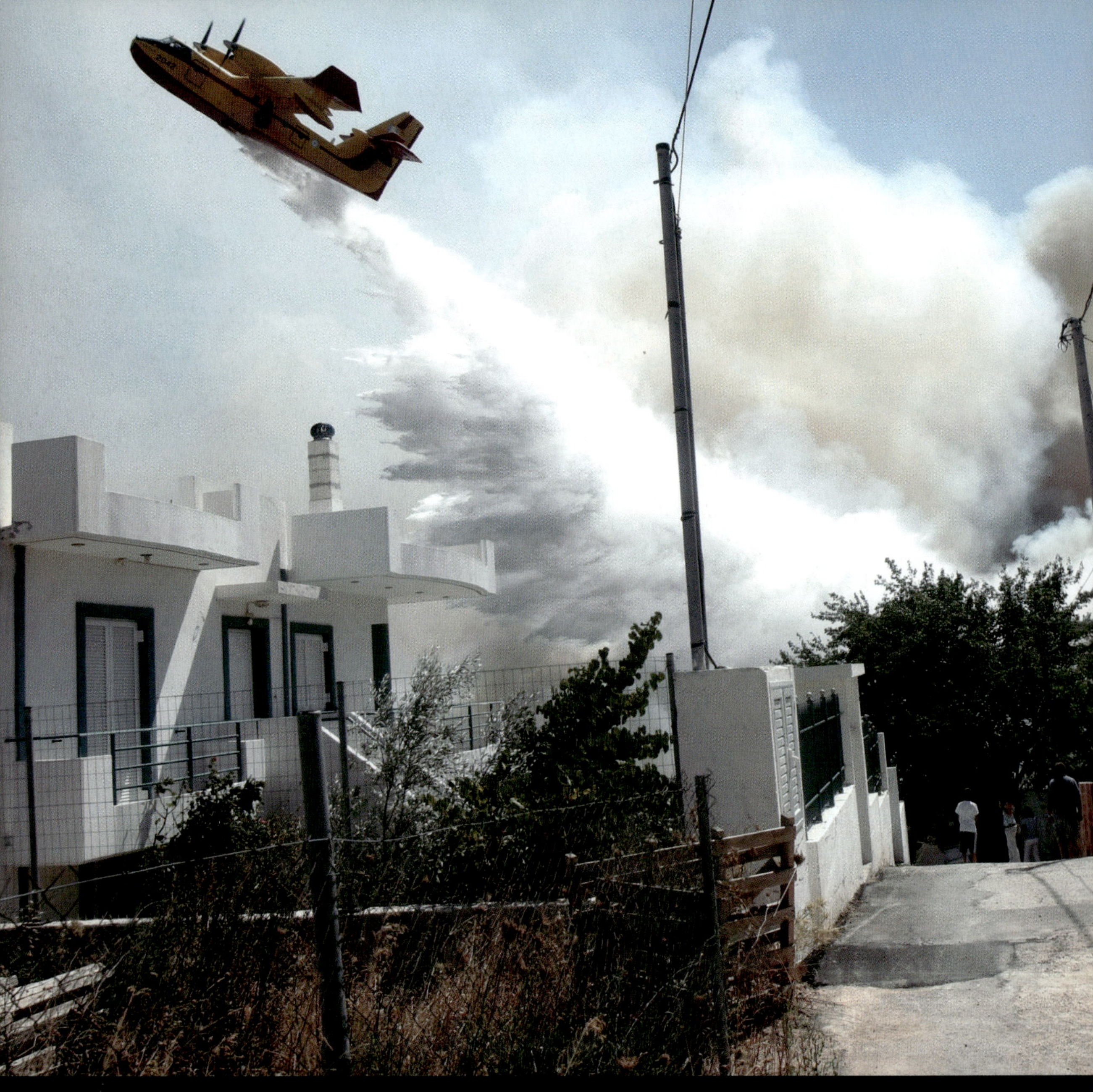

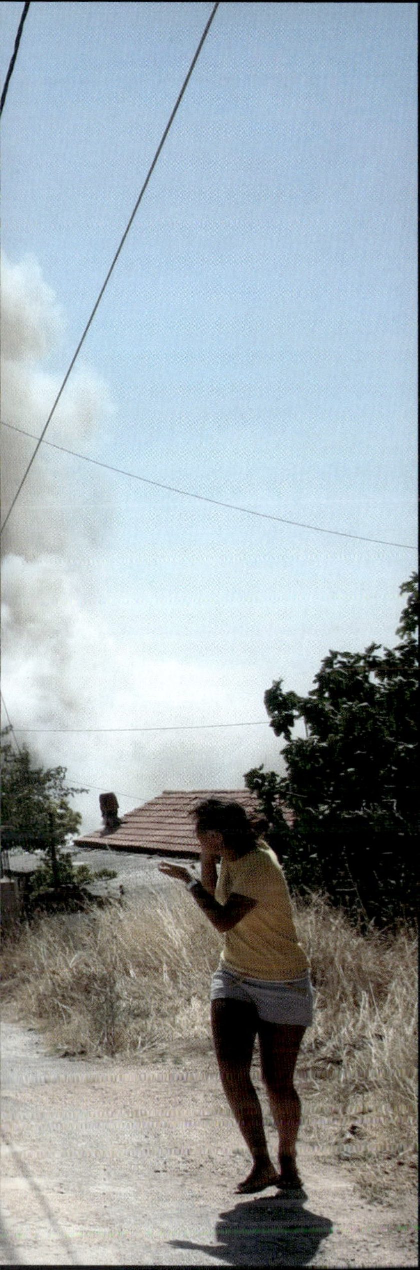

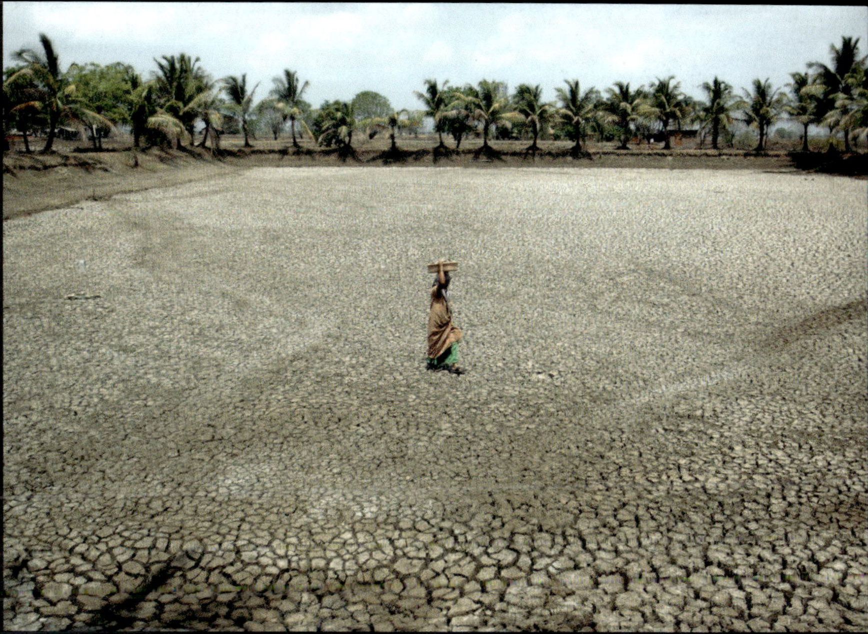

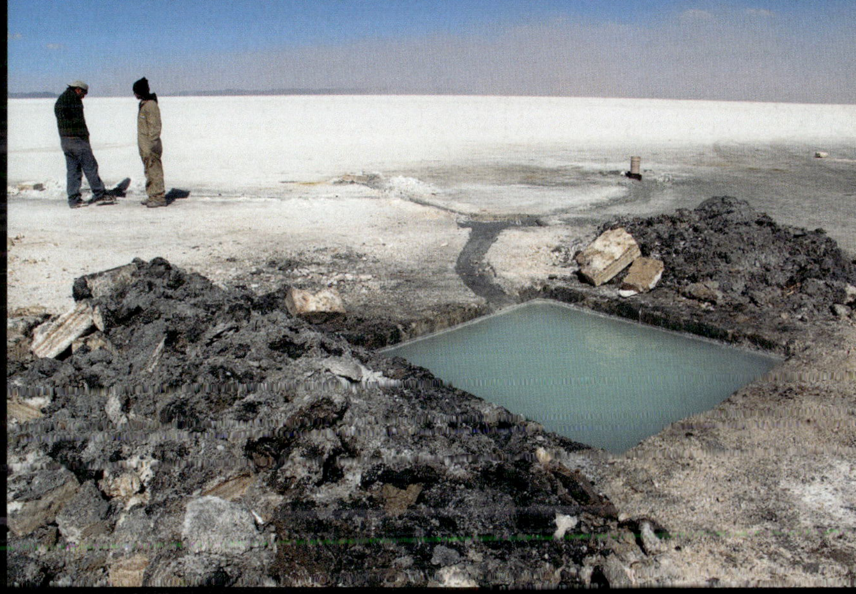

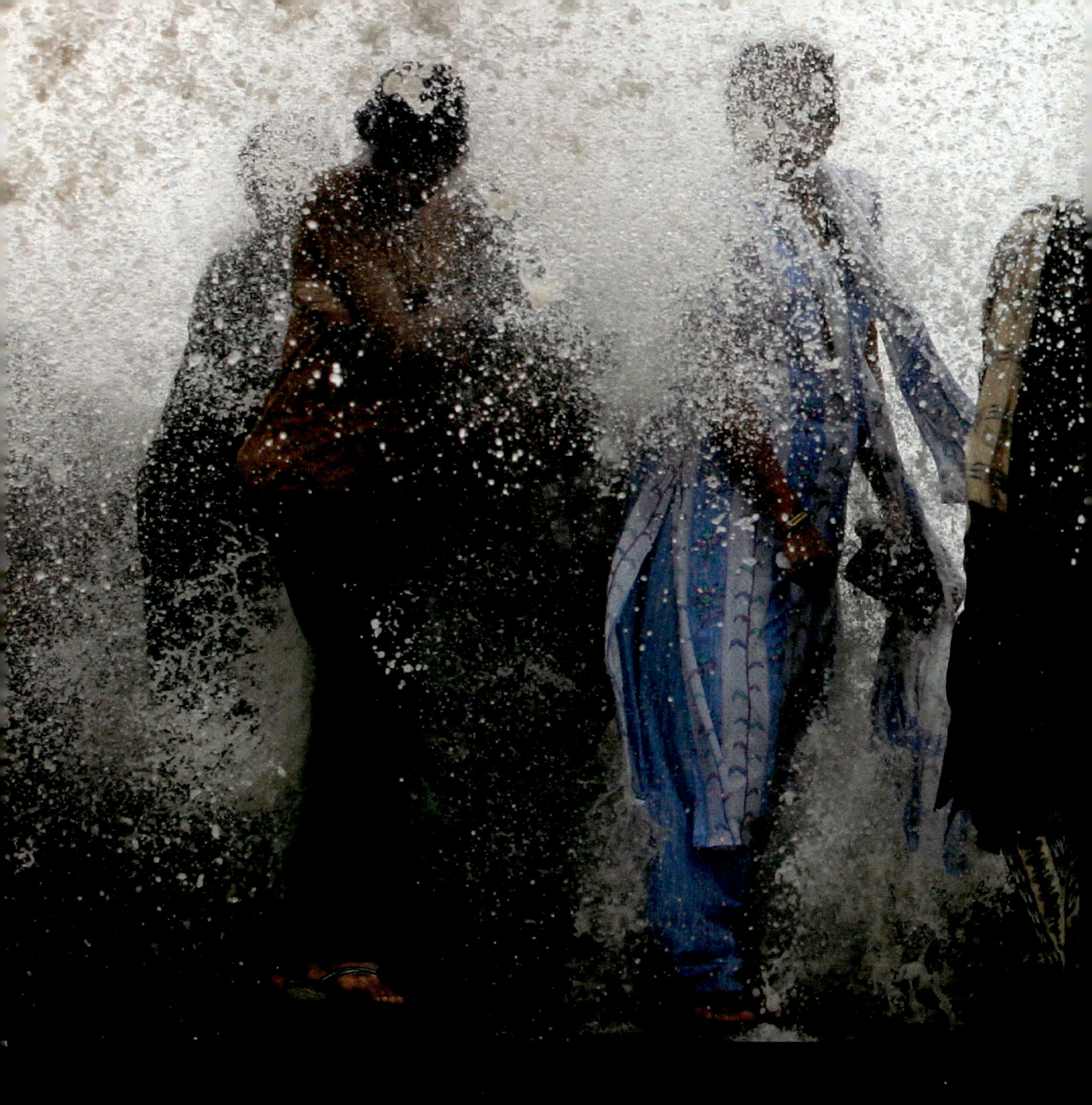

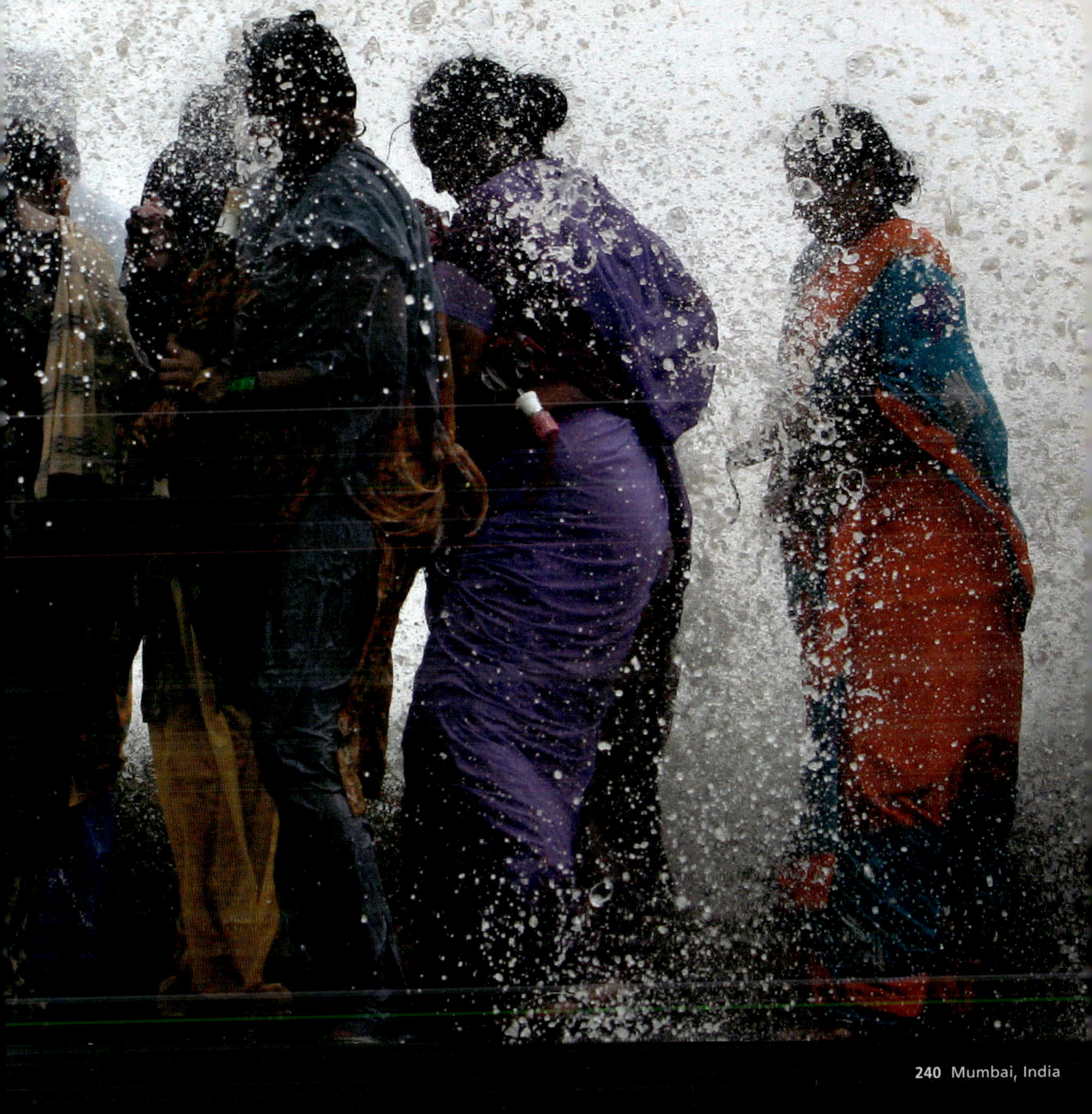

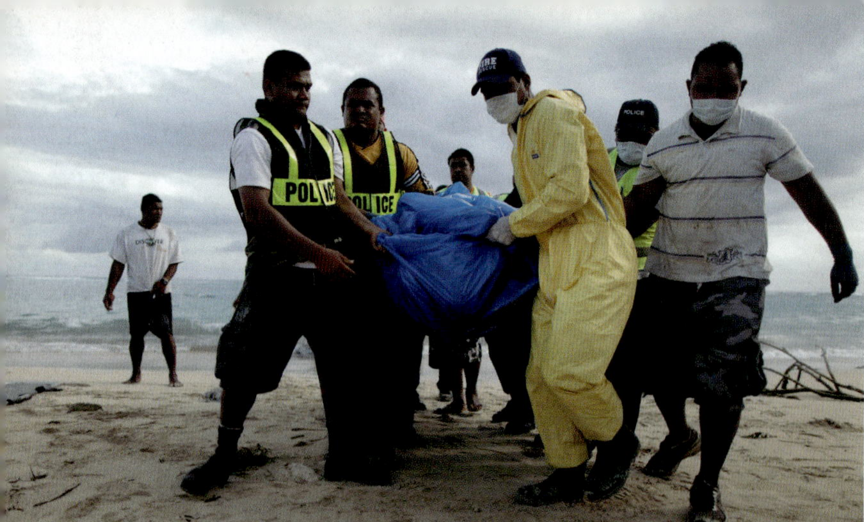

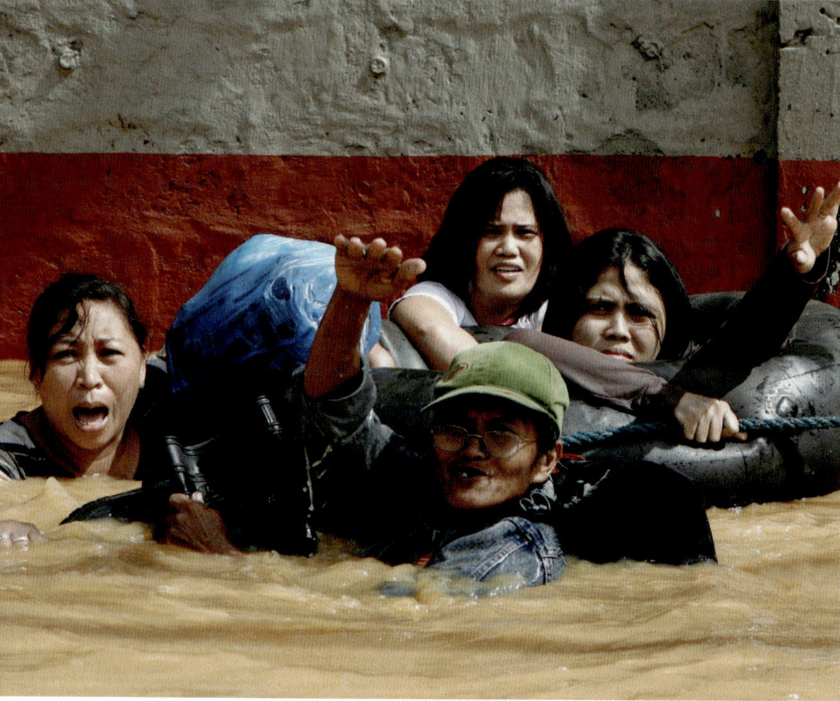

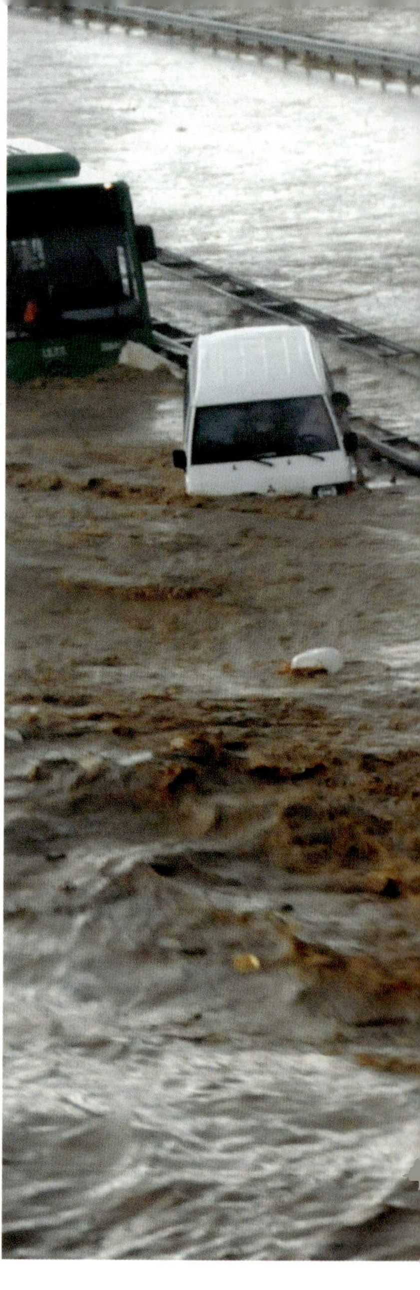

241 [TOP] Matavai, Samoa   **242** [ABOVE] Cainta, Philippines

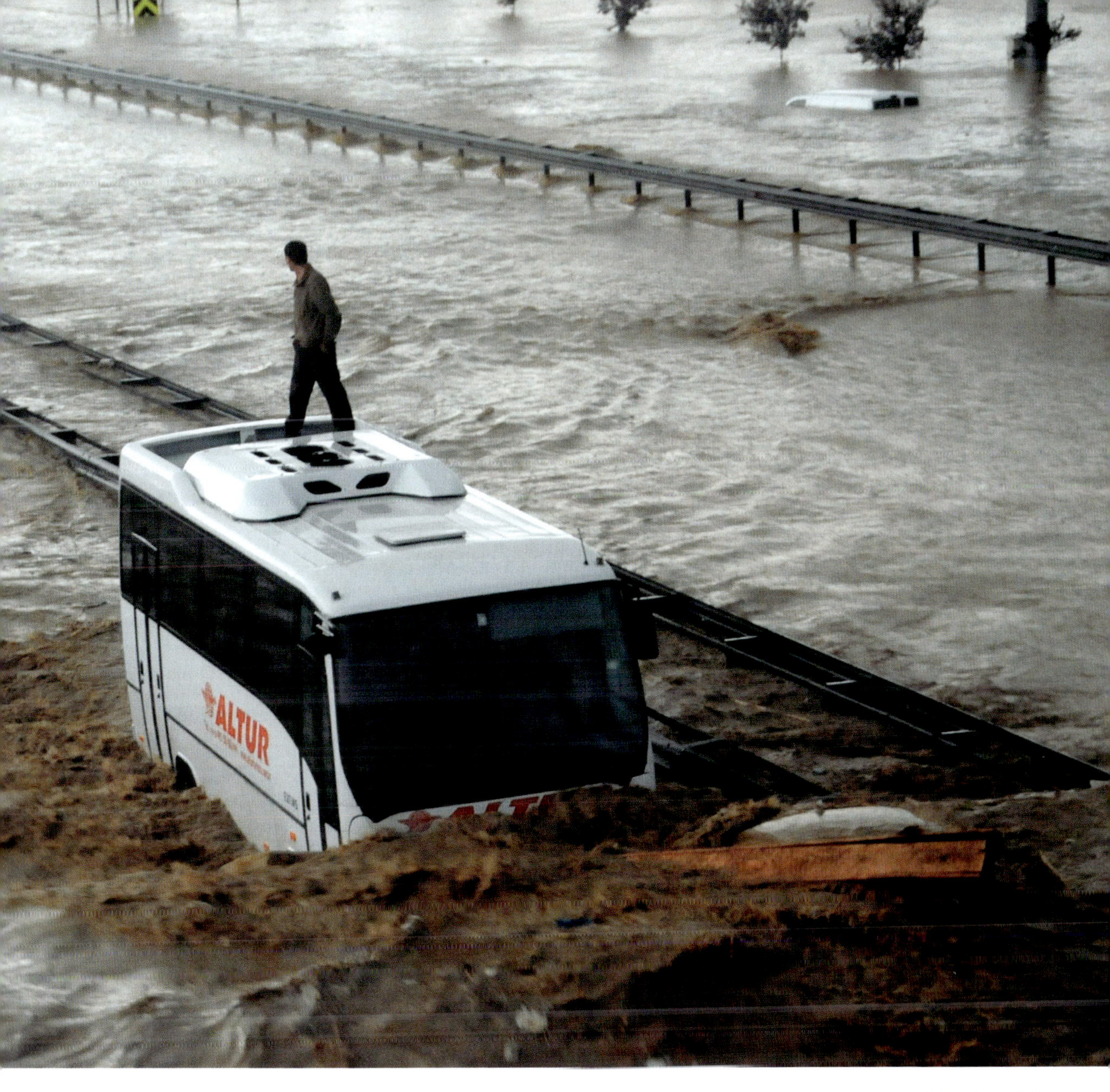

ALTUR

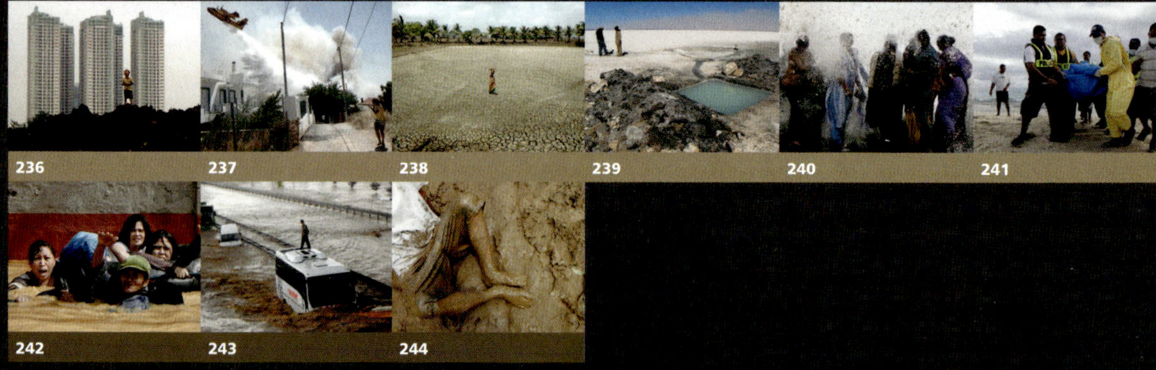

236

237

238

239

240

241

242

243

244

236 A child stands near a new apartment complex in Jakarta. 9 July 2009. Jakarta, Indonesia. Beawiharta.

237 A fire-fighting plane drops water over a forest fire in Varnava village, northeast of Athens. Fire raged in east Attica for three days, devouring about 30,000 hectares (75,000 acres) of forest, farming land and olive groves, and destroying about 150 homes, before being brought under control. 22 August 2009. Athens, Greece. Yiorgos Karahalis.

238 A worker walks through a dry fish pond in a field earmarked for a Special Economic Zone in Pen, about 70 km (45 miles) east of Mumbai. India's hopes of replicating China's export success through the establishment of tax-free Special Economic Zones were checked in 2009 by the economic crisis and a rising tide of protests from environmentalists and farmers. 28 June 2009. Pen, India. Punit Paranjpe.

239 Bolivian workers stand near a brine pool used to extract lithium from Salar de Uyuni, a huge salt lake that holds the world's largest reserves of lithium, about 500 km (300 miles) south of La Paz. The government of Evo Morales wants to build a large plant to extract lithium, which is used to produce rechargeable batteries for laptops and cell phones. 3 September 2009. Salar de Uyuni, Bolivia. David Mercado.

240 People are drenched by a large wave on Mumbai's seafront during high tide as meteorologists predicted some of the highest tides of the season, with waves expected to reach 5 metres (16 feet). 23 July 2009. Mumbai, India. Arko Datta.

241 Samoan police carry the body of a tsumani victim found in the waters near Matavai on the southern coast of Samoa. The Pacific island nation was hit on 29 September by four tsunamis triggered by a powerful 8.0 earthquake, killing some 200 people across the region, flattening villages and leaving thousands homeless. 30 September 2009. Matavai, Samoa. Tim Wimborne.

242 Residents await evacuation from floods caused by Typhoon Ketsana (locally known as Ondoy) in Cainta, Rizal province, east of Manila. More than 400 people were killed, Manila was blacked out and airline flights were suspended as the powerful typhoon battered the main Philippines island of Luzon, officials said. 27 September 2009. Cainta, Philippines. Erik de Castro.

243 A man on a partially submerged bus awaits evacuation on a highway in Istanbul. Thirty-two people were killed when flash floods swept the city, swamping houses, turning highways into fast-flowing rivers and drowning seven women in a minibus that was taking them to work. 9 September 2009. Istanbul, Turkey.

244 A man sits on a muddy street after Typhoon Ketsana hit Montalban in Rizal province, east of Manila. 28 September 2009. Montalban, Philippines. Romeo Ranoco.

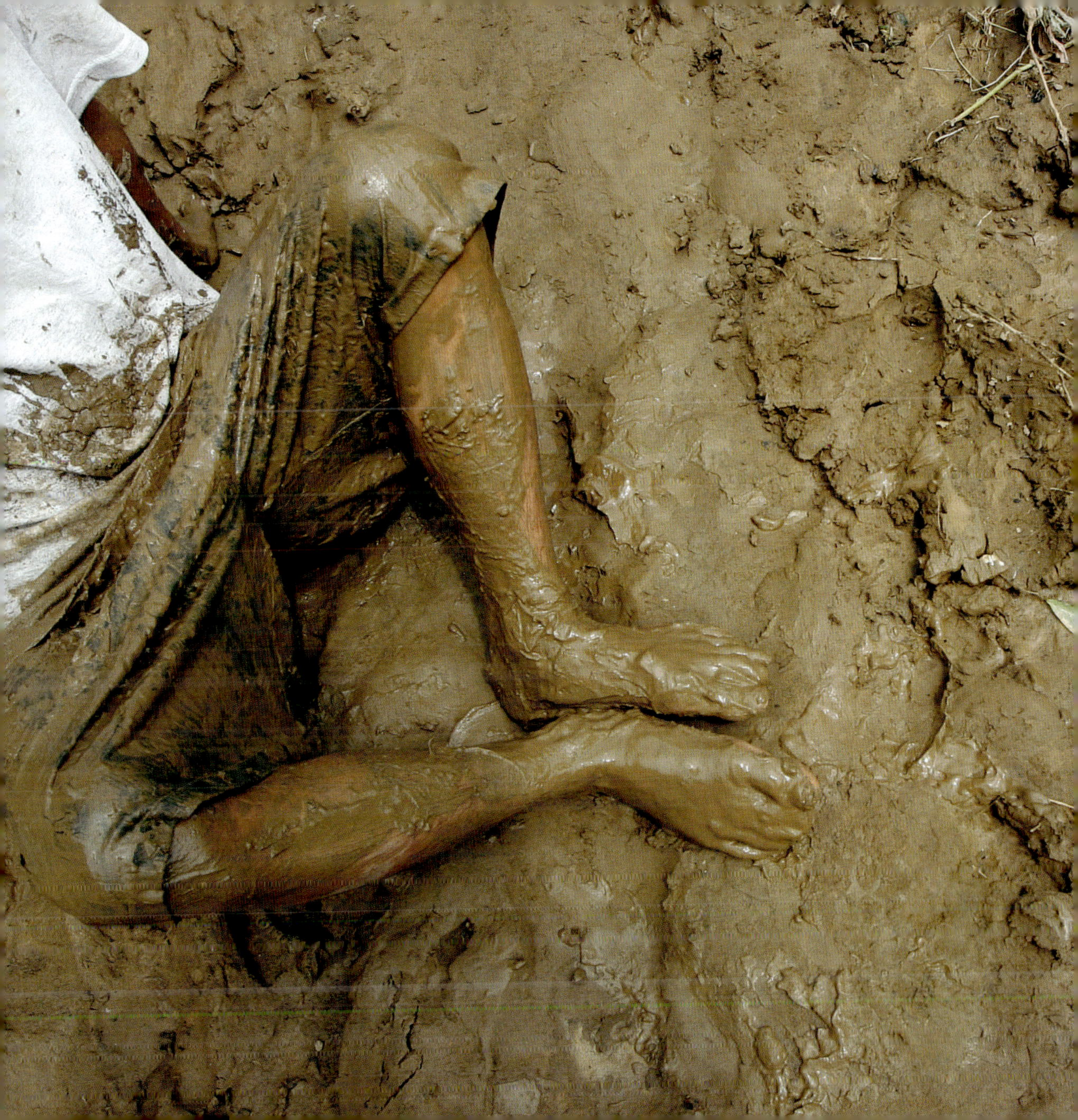

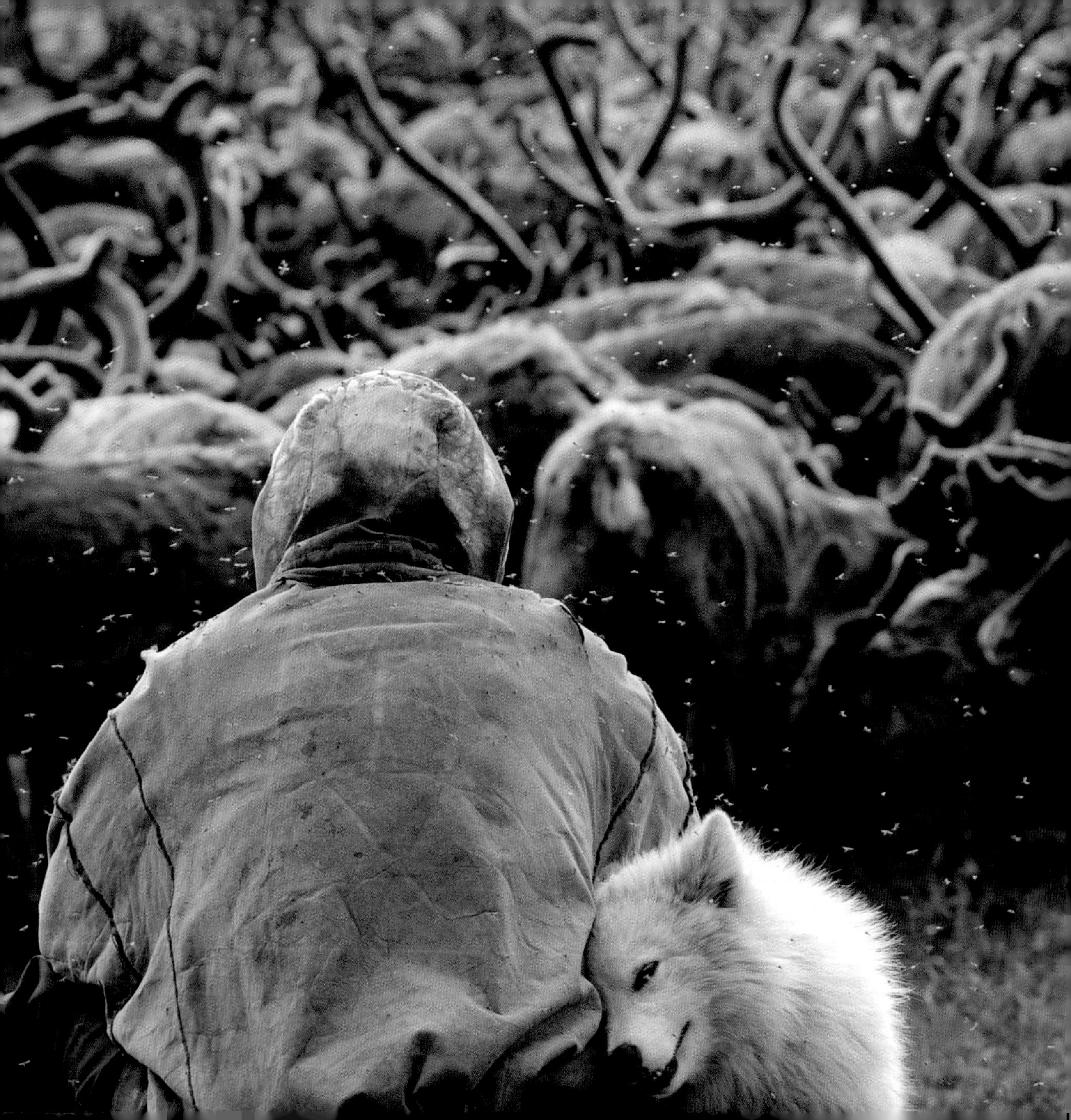

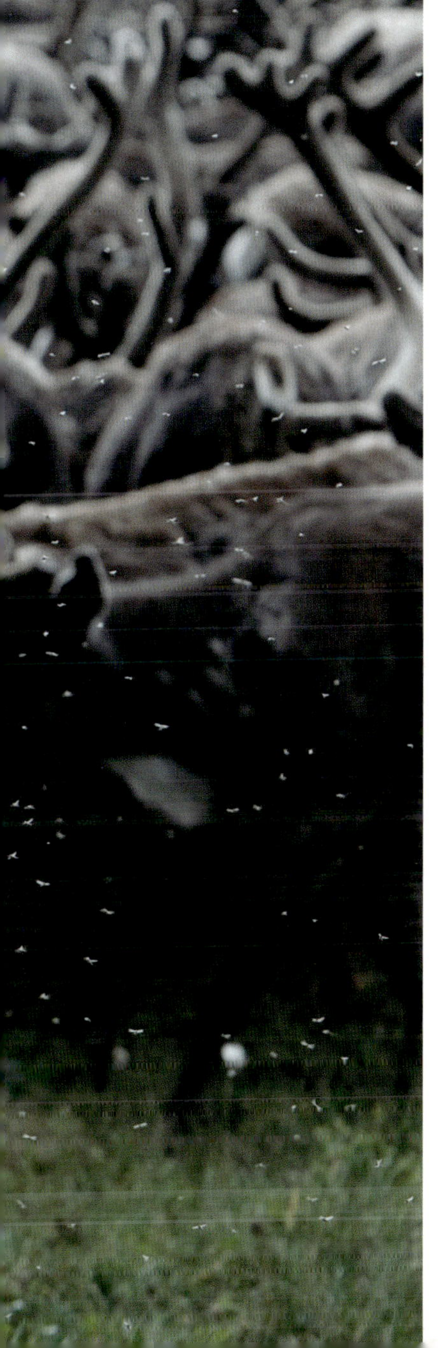

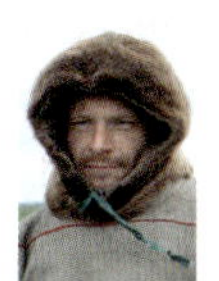

DENIS SINYAKOV
Photographer
Born: Obninsk, Russia, 1977
Based: Moscow, Russia
Nationality: Russian

Challenging times in Russia's Arctic north

The Nenets tribespeople of Russia's frozen Yamal peninsula have survived the age of the Tsars, the Bolshevik revolution and the chaotic 1990s, but now confront their biggest challenge to date. For under the Nenets' fur-bundled feet lie reserves of 16 trillion cubic metres of gas. Yamal already accounts for more than 90 percent of Russian state energy giant Gazprom's gas output. The government is keen to develop the region, and has proposed tax breaks to entice foreign firms to drill the frozen land.

Yamal lies within the Arctic circle, 2,000 km (1,250 miles) northeast of Moscow. Two of the three weeks of our expedition were spent getting from Moscow to Yamal and back, by plane, ship, motor boat and cross-country vehicle.

Numbering around 42,000, the Nenets are animists whose way of life has scarcely changed in a millennium. They migrate over 150 km (100 miles) every year, spending only a few days in one place, living off reindeer and fish, and lugging their tents, kerosene lamps and wood-fired stoves on reindeer-drawn sleighs across the flat marshy tundra.

This is a place of endless sunrise and sunset, where plans are forever thwarted by constant changes in the weather. It takes most of a day to pack up camp, but the Nenets never seem to be in a hurry, spending hours drinking tea and talking in their tents. Time here has a different quality.

Some state benefits are welcomed by the Nenets – helicopters transport them to towns of a few hundred people an hour's flight away and children attend Russian-language schools, living in town with other Nenets families.

But experts and the Nenets say industry will damage and pollute the tundra. Already a new railway, opened in September 2009, runs around two-thirds of the 700 km (430 mile) peninsula. It will serve Russia's biggest gas field Bovanenkovo at the top of Yamal, which will feed the Nord Stream pipeline to Germany from 2012.

'I just pray Gazprom won't change us,' said Valentina, 52. 'I want my grandchildren to see our land as it is: beautiful, fresh, full of berries and deer.'

245 A Nenets tribesman sits in front of a herd of reindeer on Russia's Yamal peninsula, which lies north of the Arctic Circle. 4 August 2009.

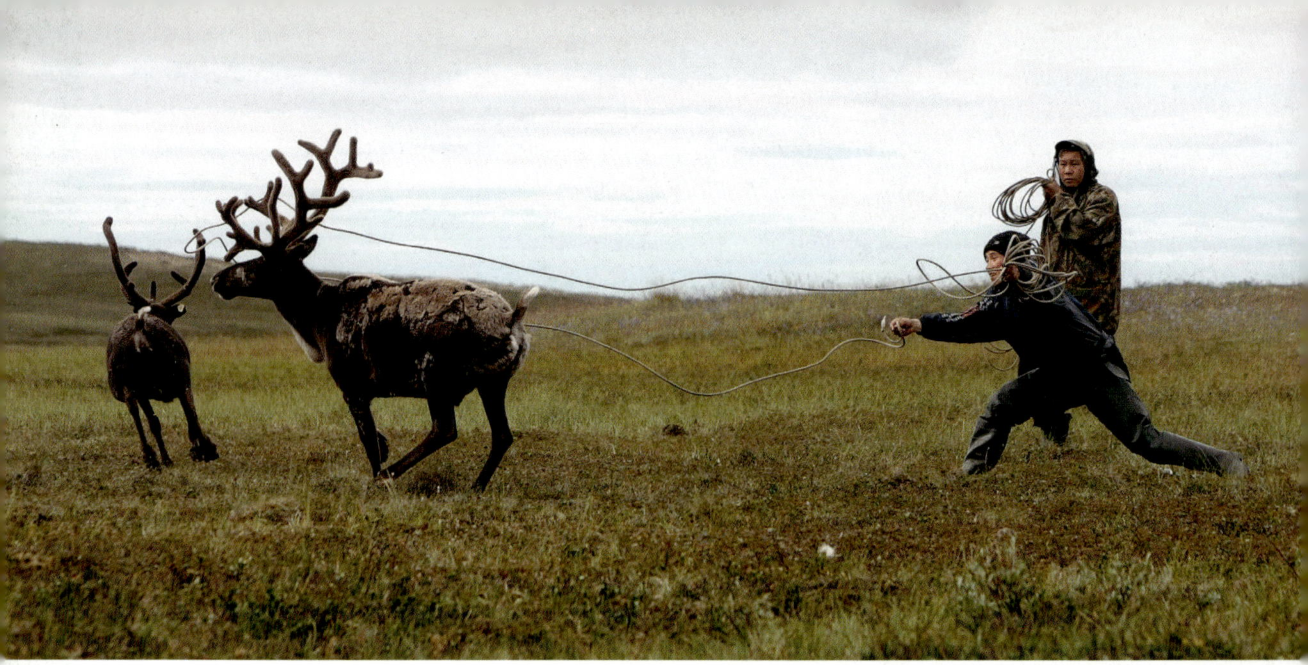

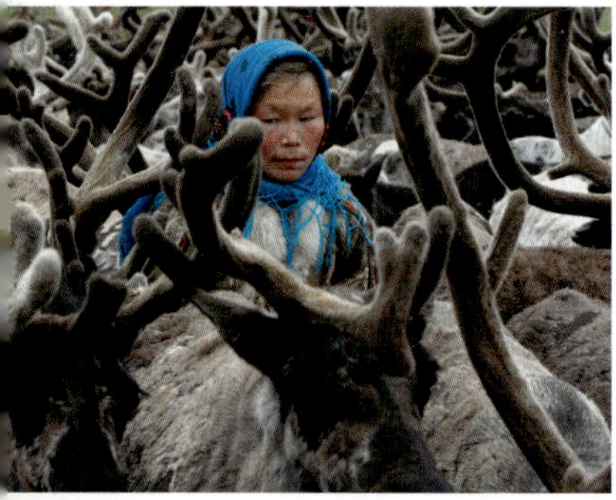

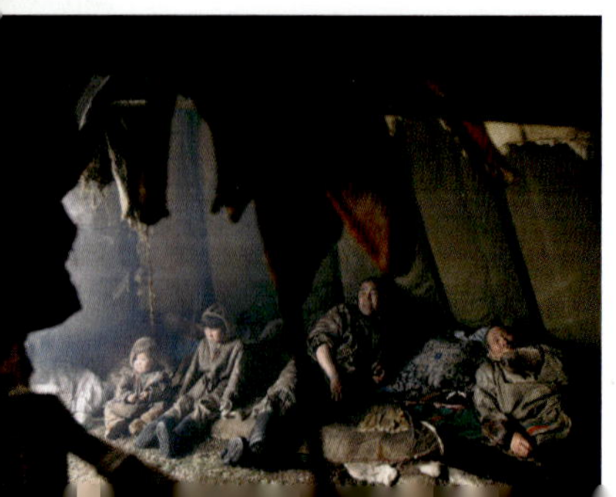
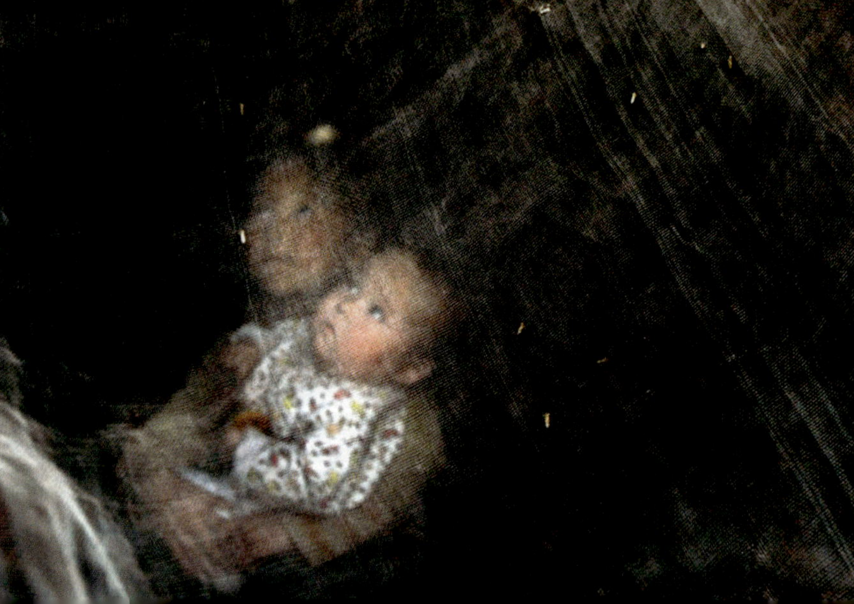

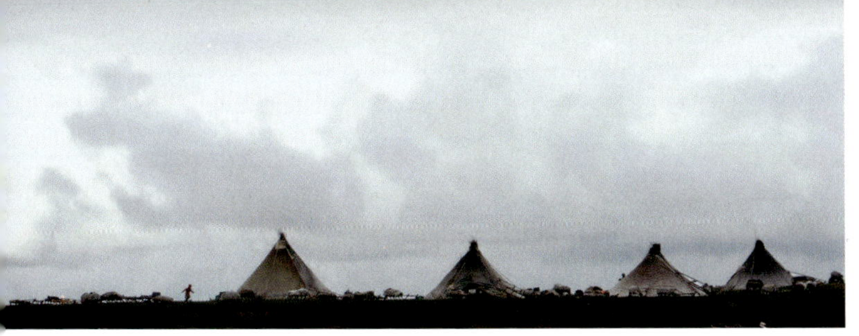

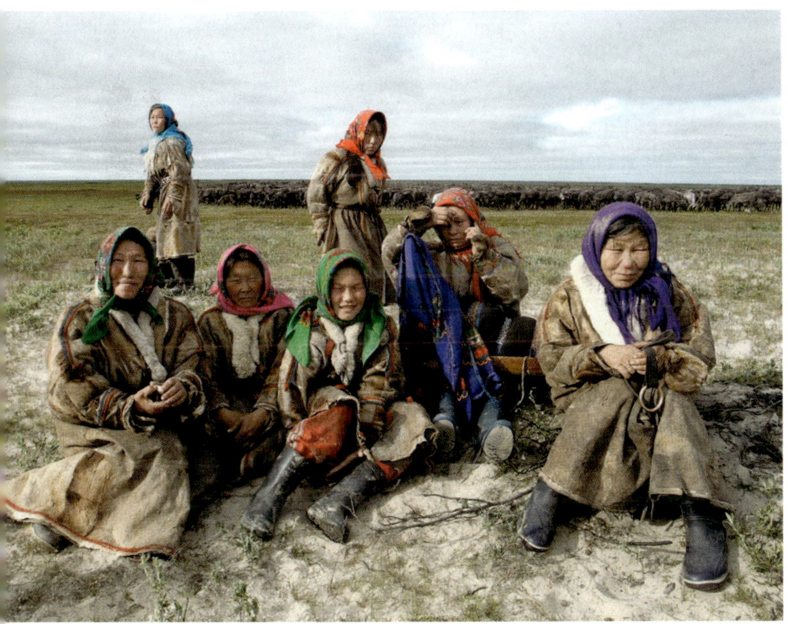

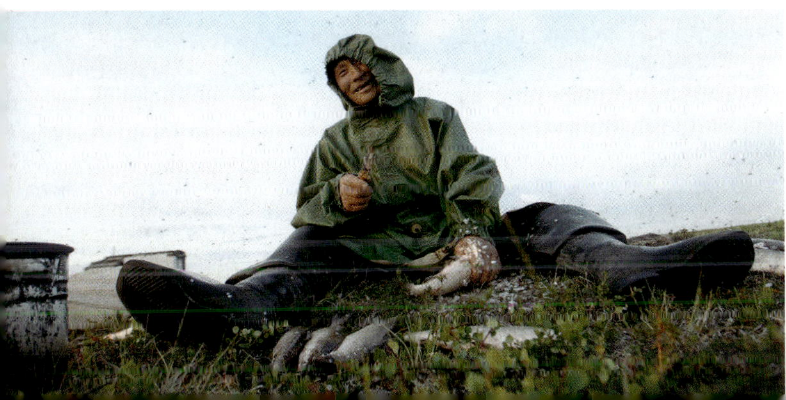

246 Nenets catch reindeer with a lasso on Russia's Yamal peninsula, north of the Arctic Circle. **247** A woman stands among reindeer. **248** Nenets rest in a traditional tent. **249** Children rest in a tent. **250** Traditional tents are seen on the skyline. **251** Women pose for a picture. **252** A man prepares fish for cooking. 4 August 2009. Denis Sinyakov.

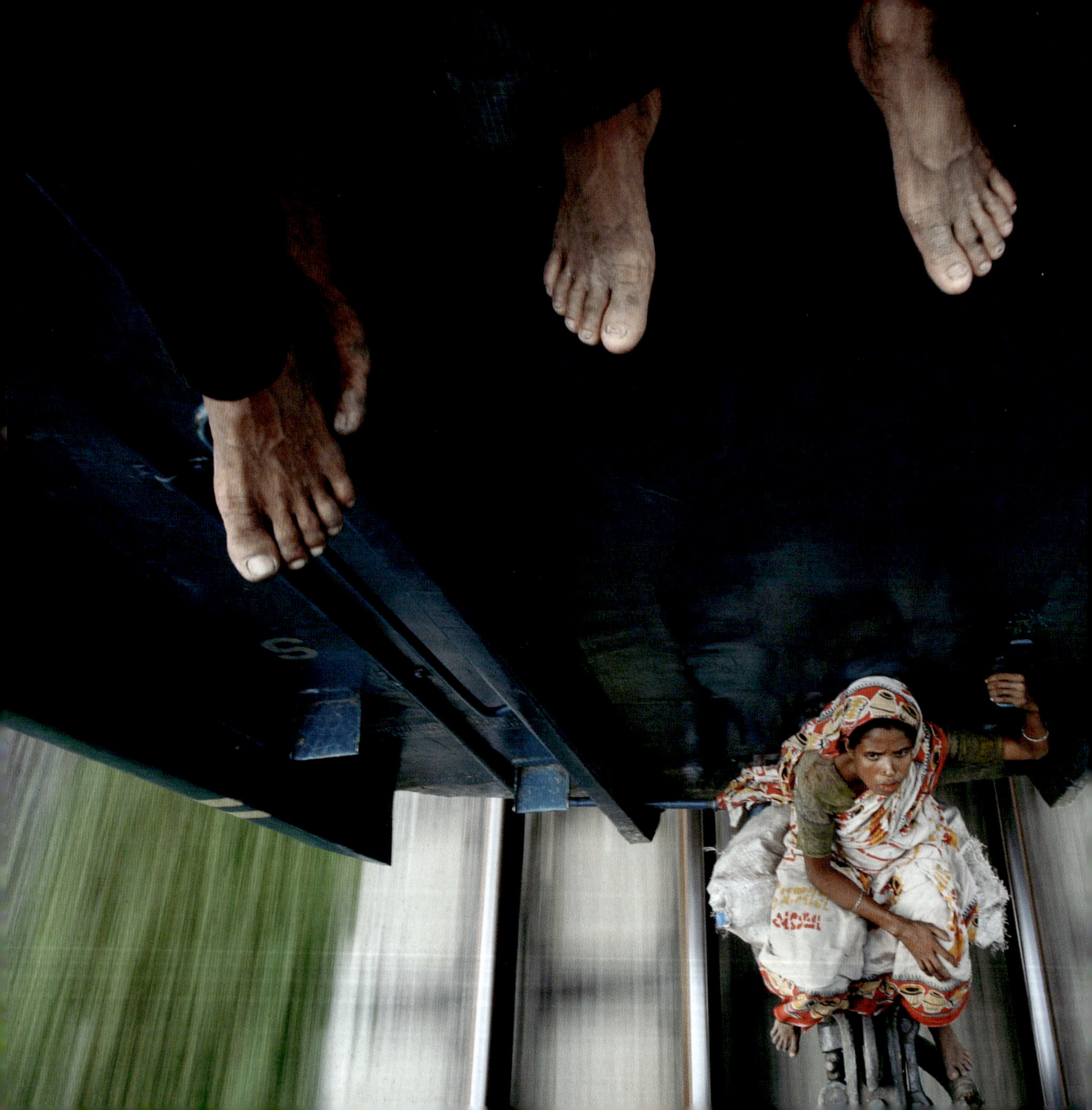

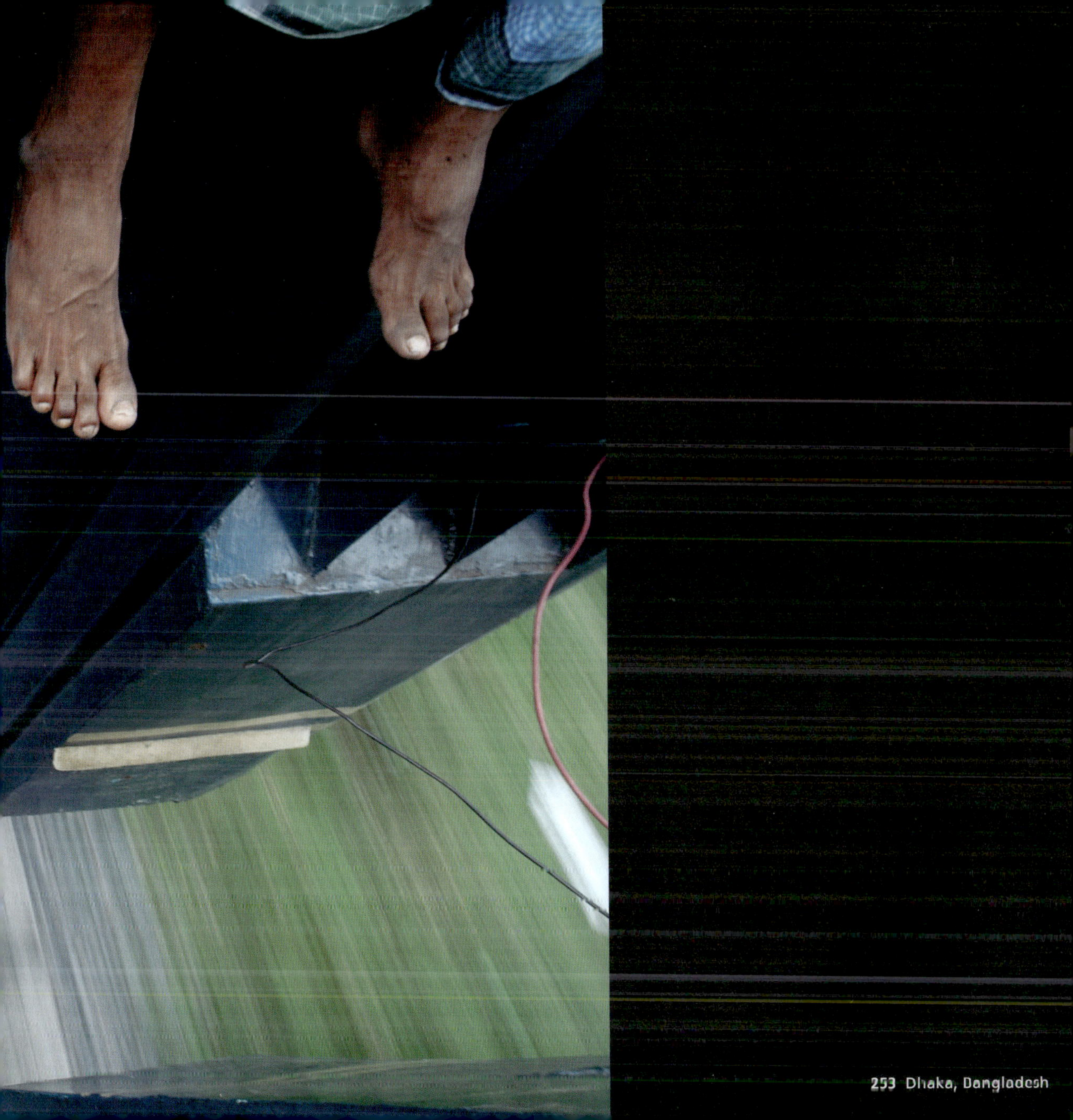

253 Dhaka, Bangladesh

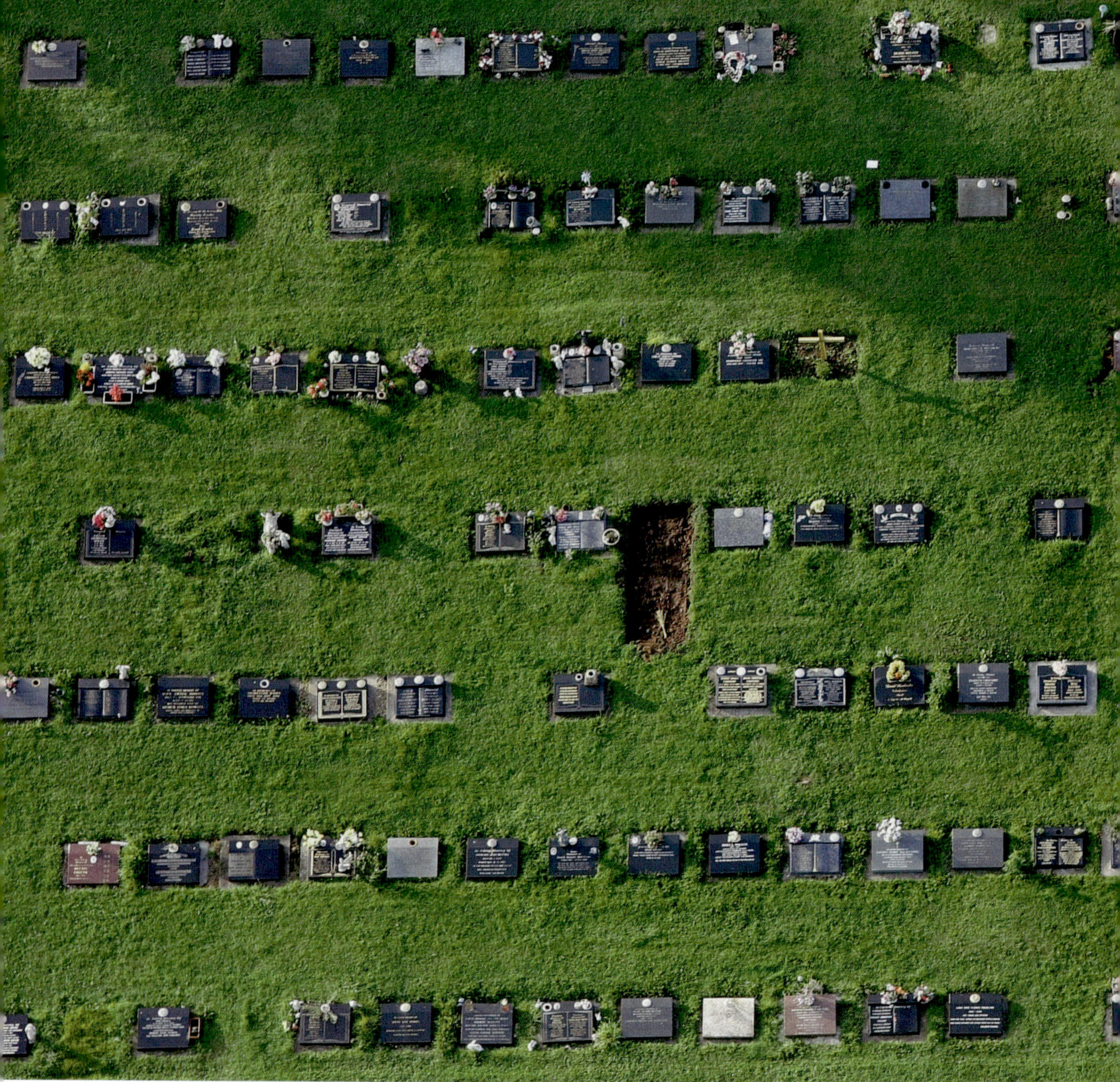

254 Bristol, Britain

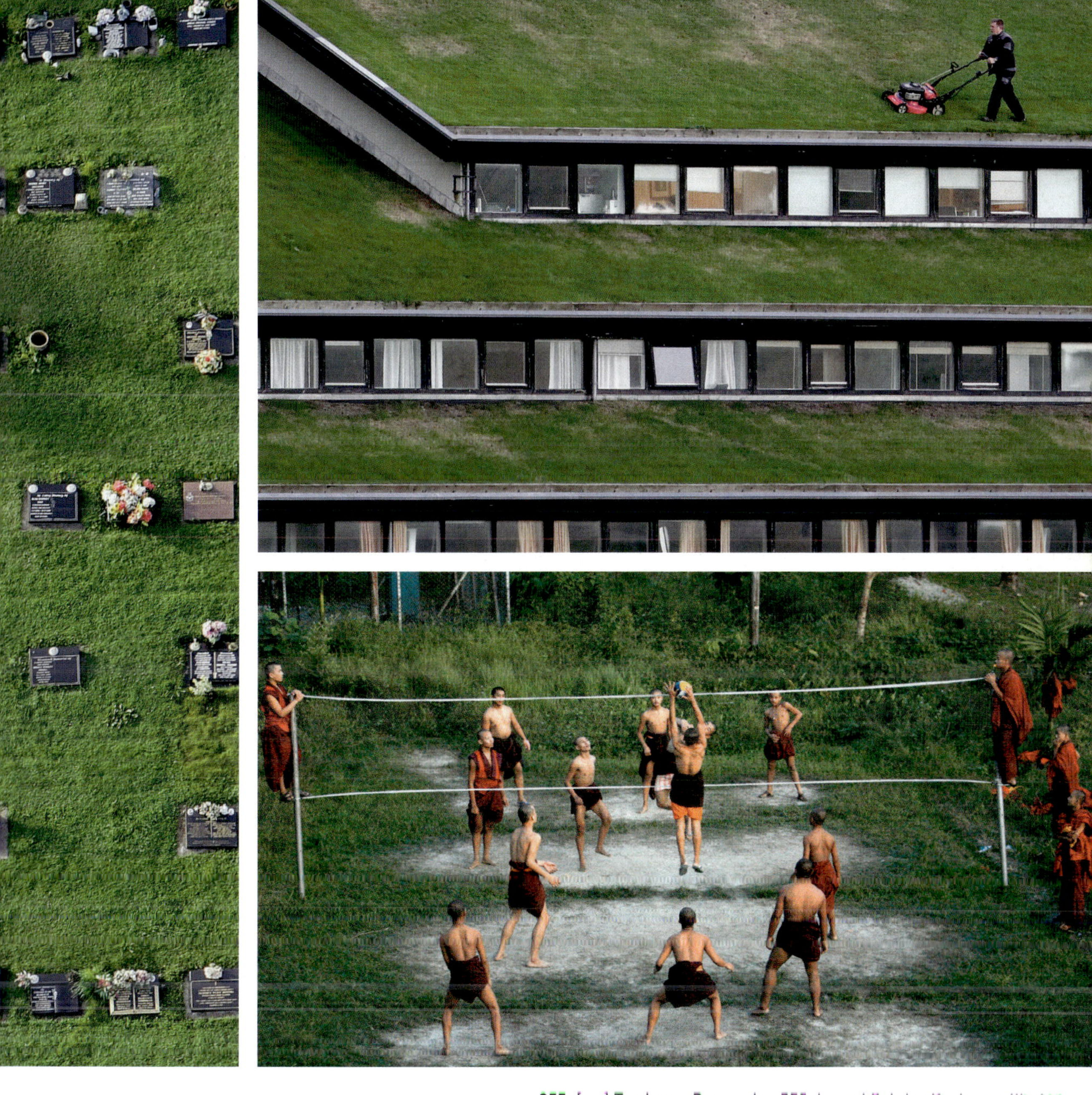

255 [TOP] Torshavn, Denmark   **256** [ABOVE] Rabdey Dratsang, Bhutan

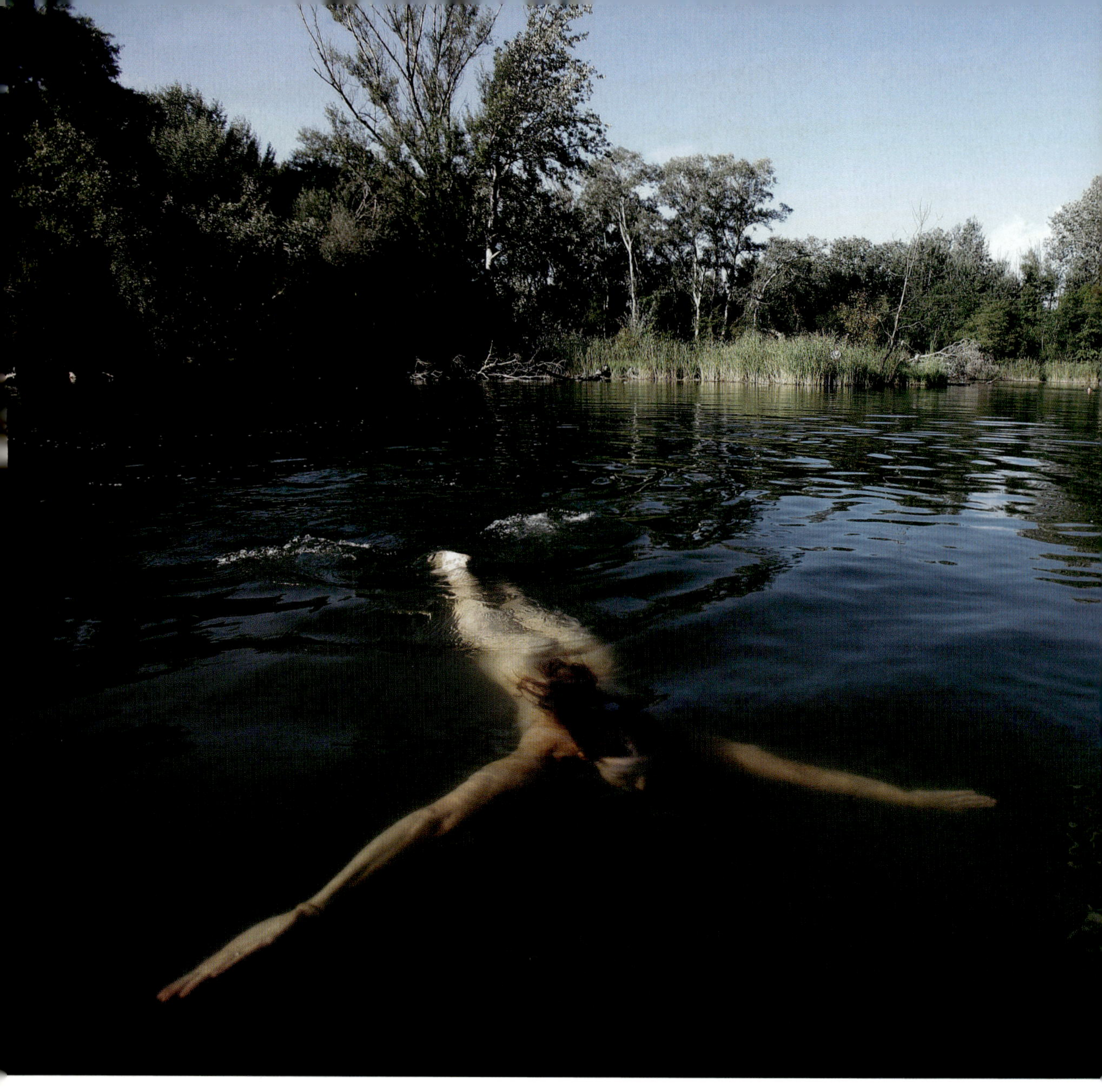

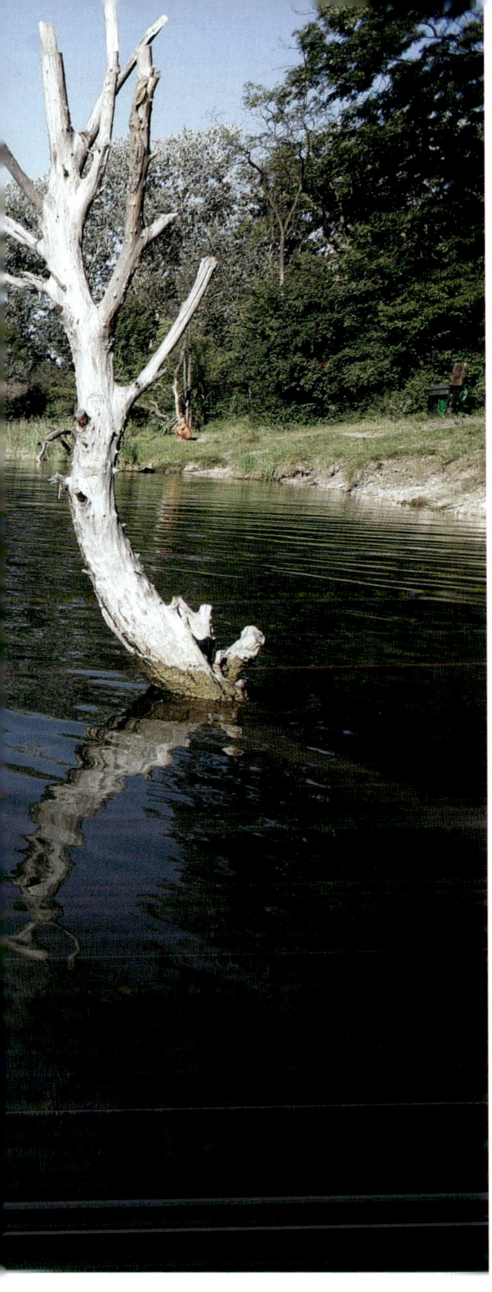

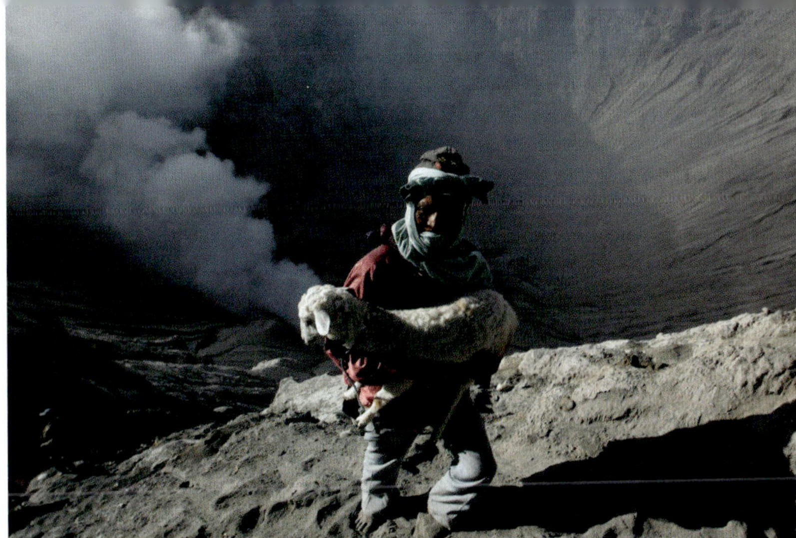

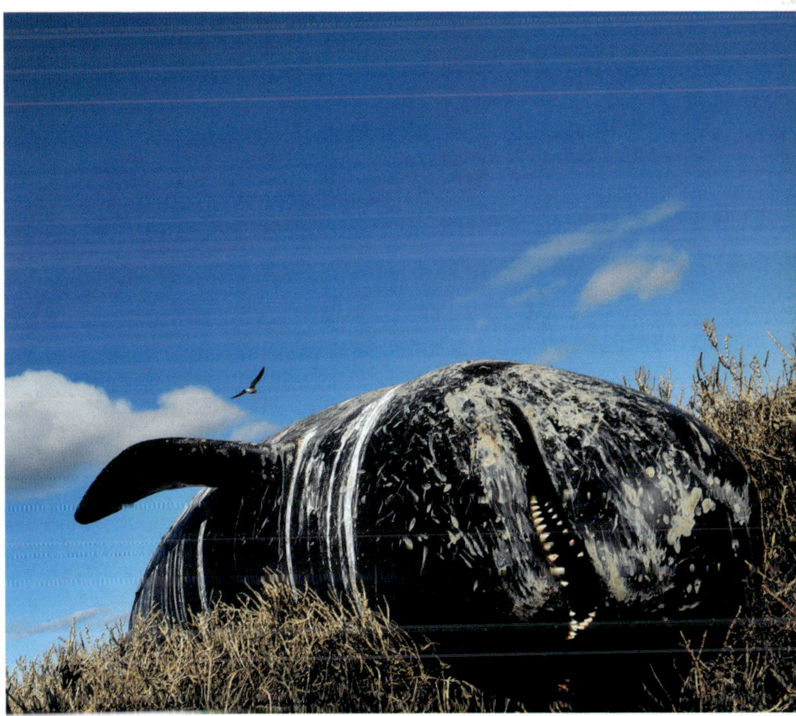

260 Sydney, Australia

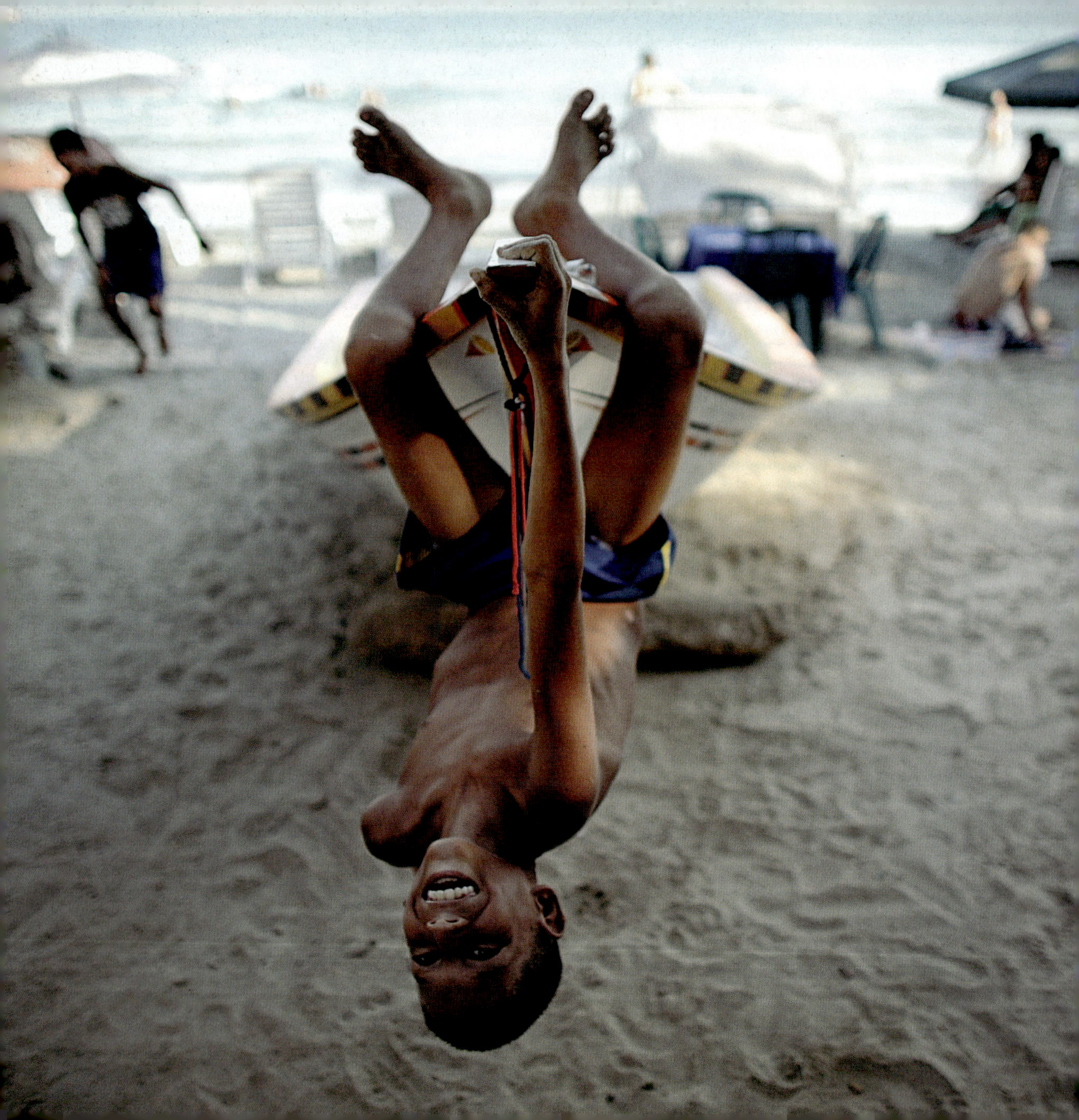

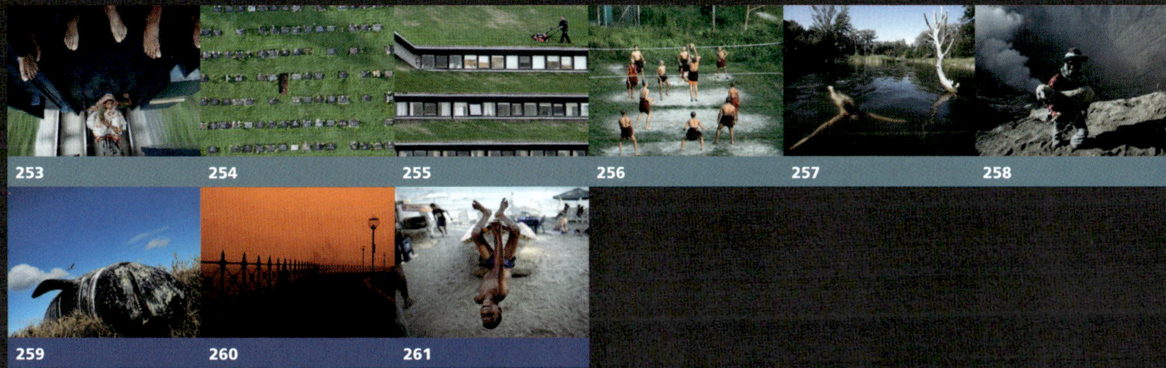

253 254 255 256 257 258

259 260 261

253 A woman sits between carriages on a crowded train travelling from Dhaka to Mymensingh. Millions of Bangladeshis made the journey home from the capital city to celebrate the Muslim Eid al-Fitr holiday, which marks the end of the fasting month of Ramadan. 20 September 2009. Dhaka, Bangladesh. Andrew Biraj.

254 A cemetery near Bristol in western England is seen from a hot air balloon. 7 August 2009. Bristol, Britain. Stefan Wermuth.

255 A workman mows the grass roof of a Danish government building near Torshavn, capital of the Faroe Islands. 13 August 2009. Torshavn, Denmark. Bob Strong.

256 Buddhist monks play volleyball in Rabdey Dratsang in Bhutan's southeastern district of Samdrup Jongkhar. 3 September 2009. Rabdey Dratsang, Bhutan. Singye Wangchuk.

257 A woman swims in a lake in the Lobau area, the floodplain forest along the Danube river near Vienna, as she enjoys the last days of summer. 7 September 2009. Vienna, Austria. Herwig Prammer.

258 A villager carries a lamb retrieved after it was thrown by worshippers into a volcanic crater during a ritual to mark the Kasada festival at Mount Bromo in East Java. Offerings are thrown into the crater to give thanks to the Hindu gods. 6 September 2009. Mount Bromo, Indonesia. Sigit Pamungkas.

259 The body of a stranded pilot whale is seen on a beach in Bustamante Bay in the Patagonian province of Chubut. This was one of 40 whales that beached themselves over a weekend in the Argentine bay, the location of a similar occurrence in 1991 involving over 400 pilot whales. 14 September 2009. Bustamante Bay, Argentina. Maxi Jonas.

260 Sydney's iconic Opera House is seen at sunrise during a huge dust storm that swept eastern Australia, disrupting transport, forcing people indoors and stripping thousands of tonnes of valuable farmland topsoil. 23 September 2009. Sydney, Australia. Tim Wimborne.

261 A boy hangs upside down from a boat on Pampatar beach on Margarita Island in northwestern Venezuela, near the venue of a summit of African and South American leaders. 25 September 2009. Margarita Island, Venezuela. Jorge Silva.

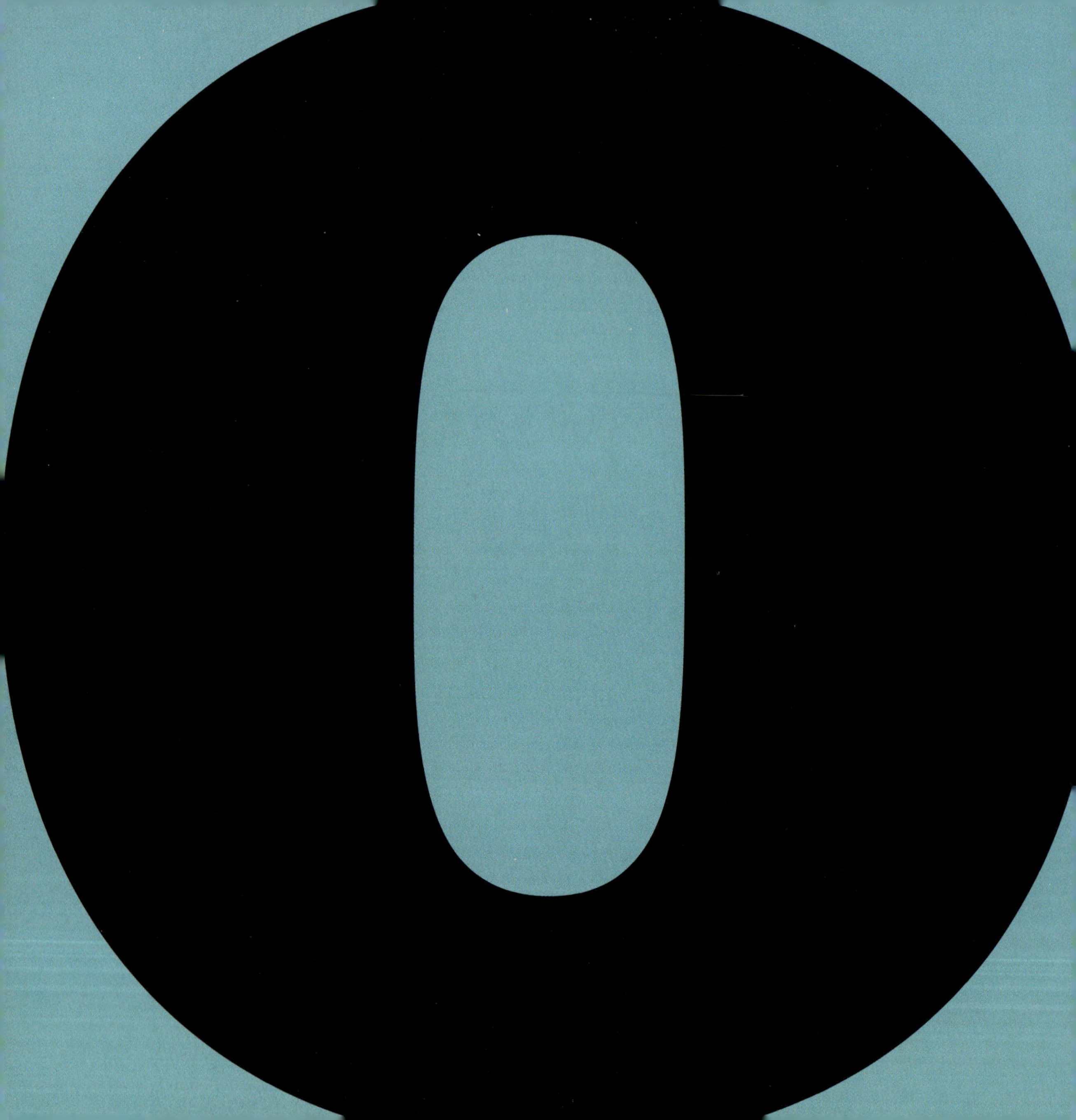

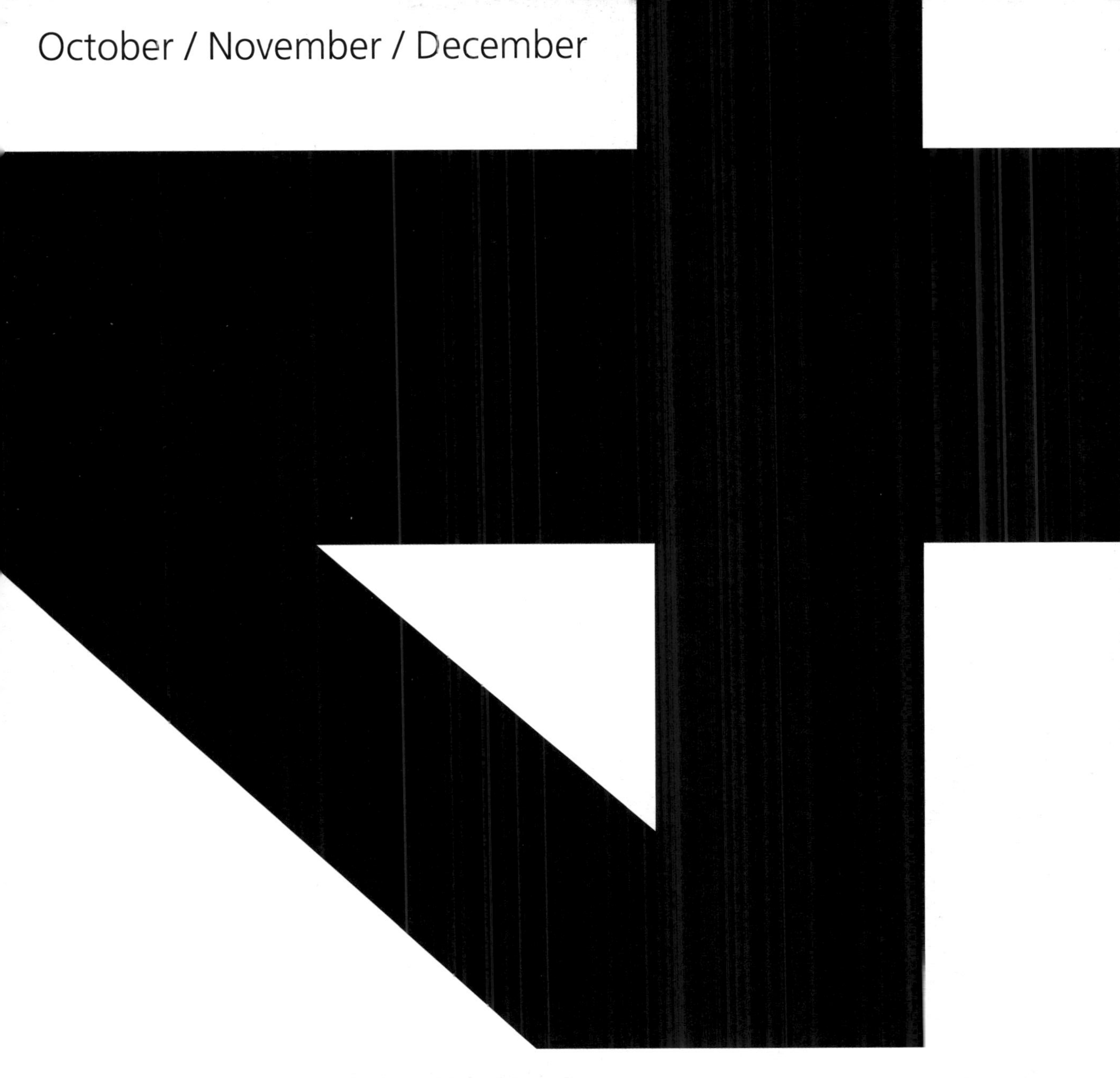

October / November / December

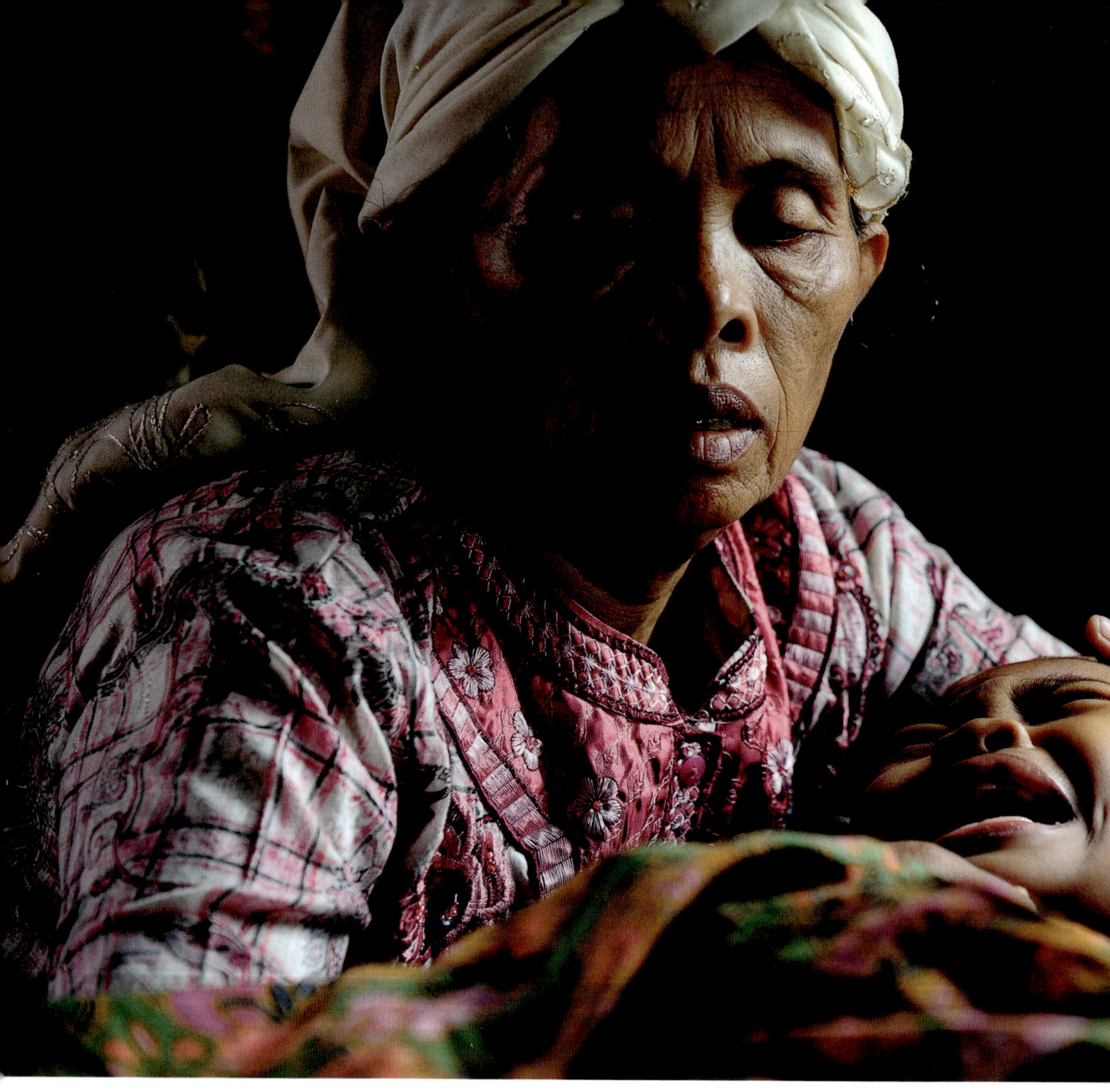

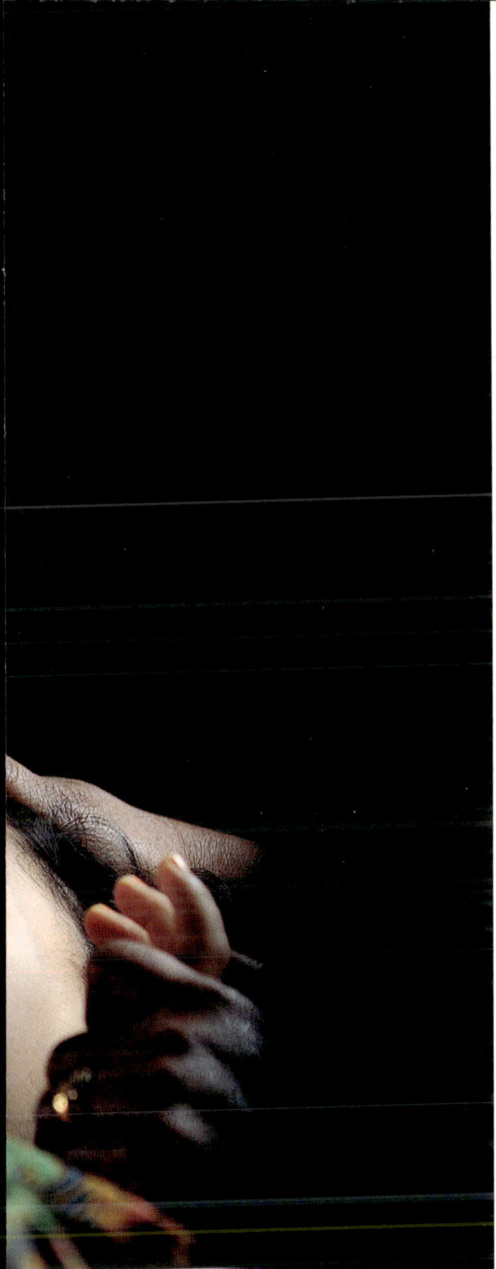

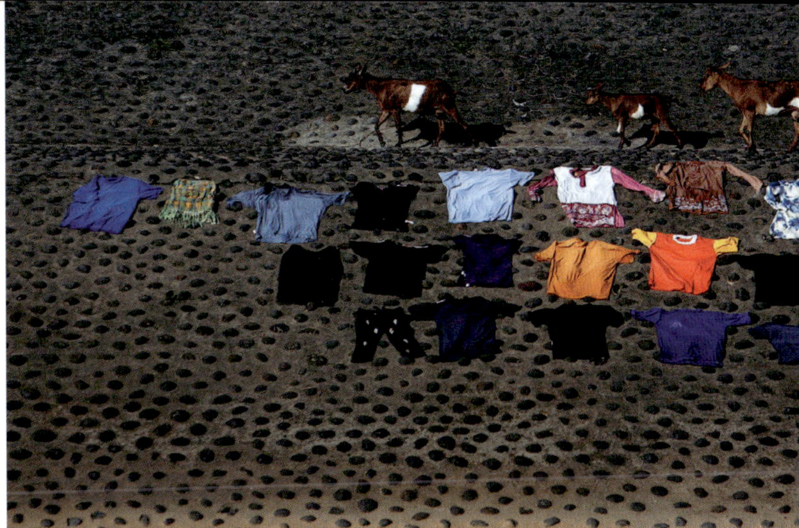

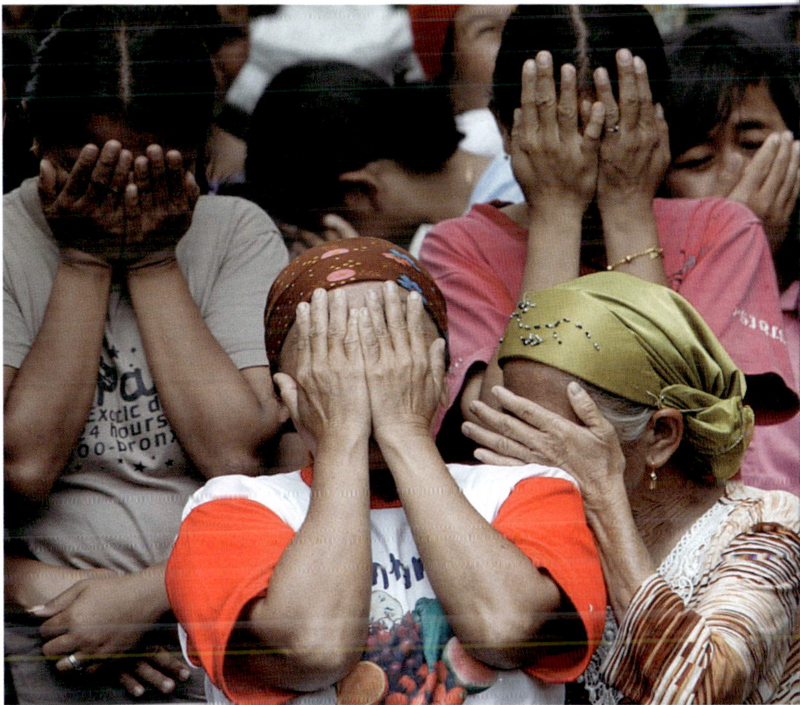

263 [TOP] Padang, Indonesia   264 [ABOVE] Padang Pariaman, Indonesia

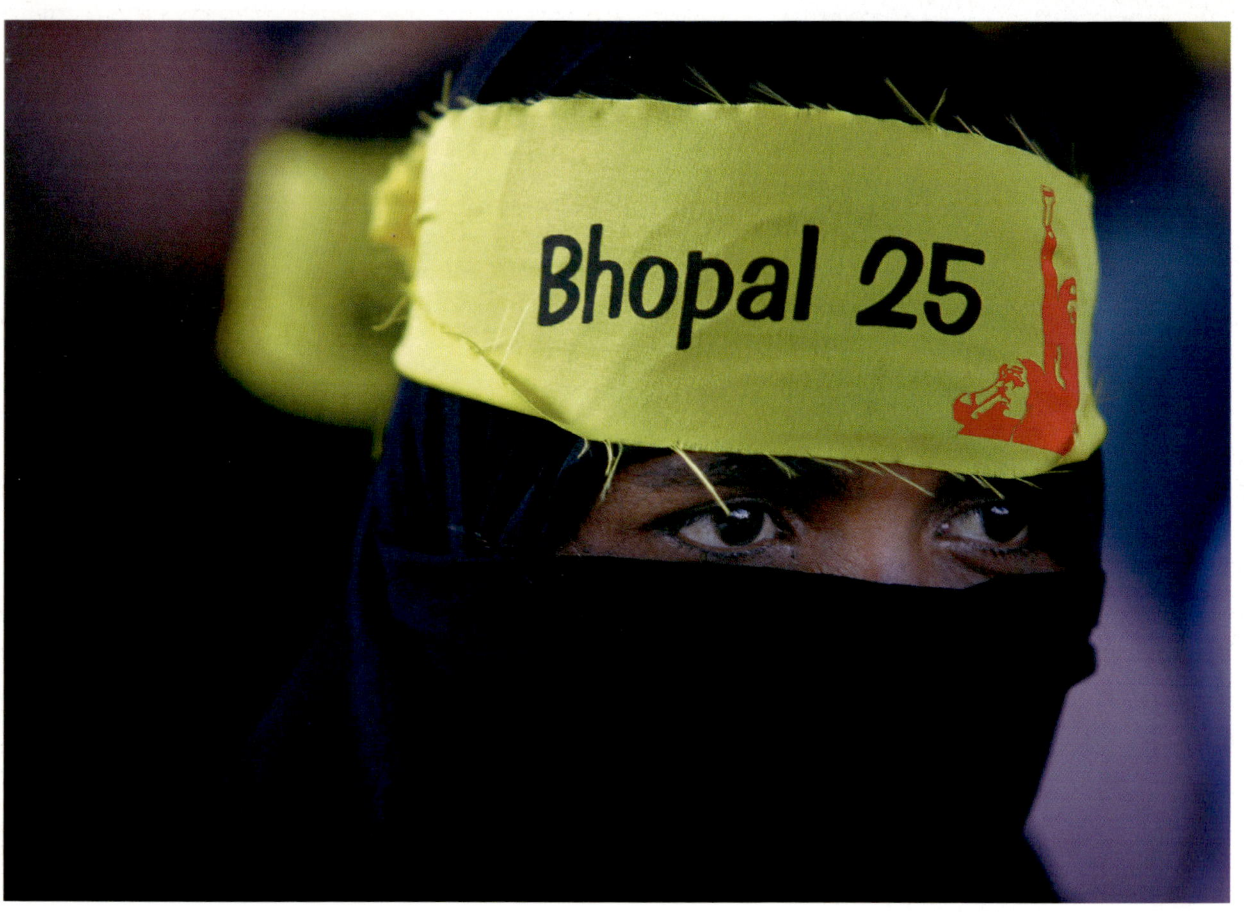

Bhopal 25

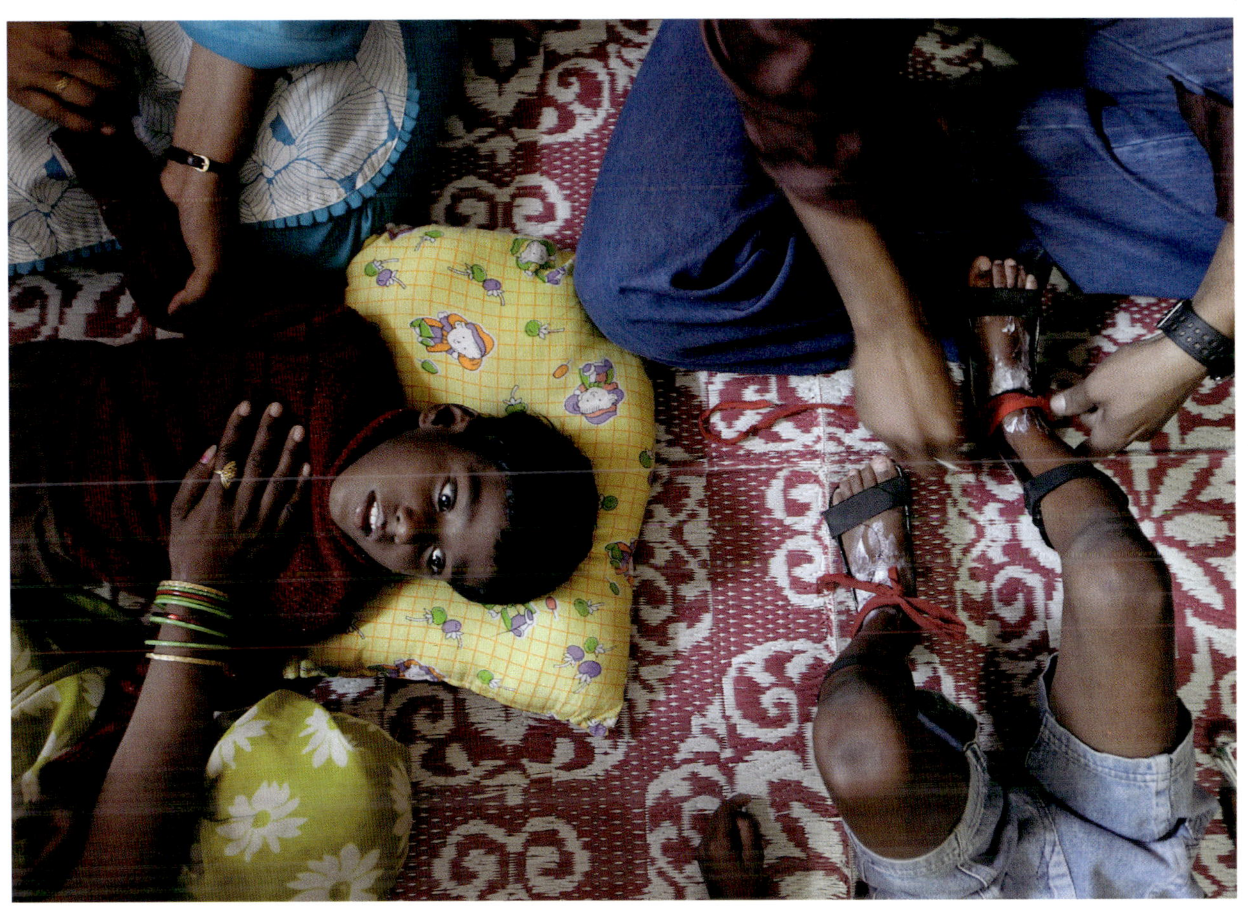

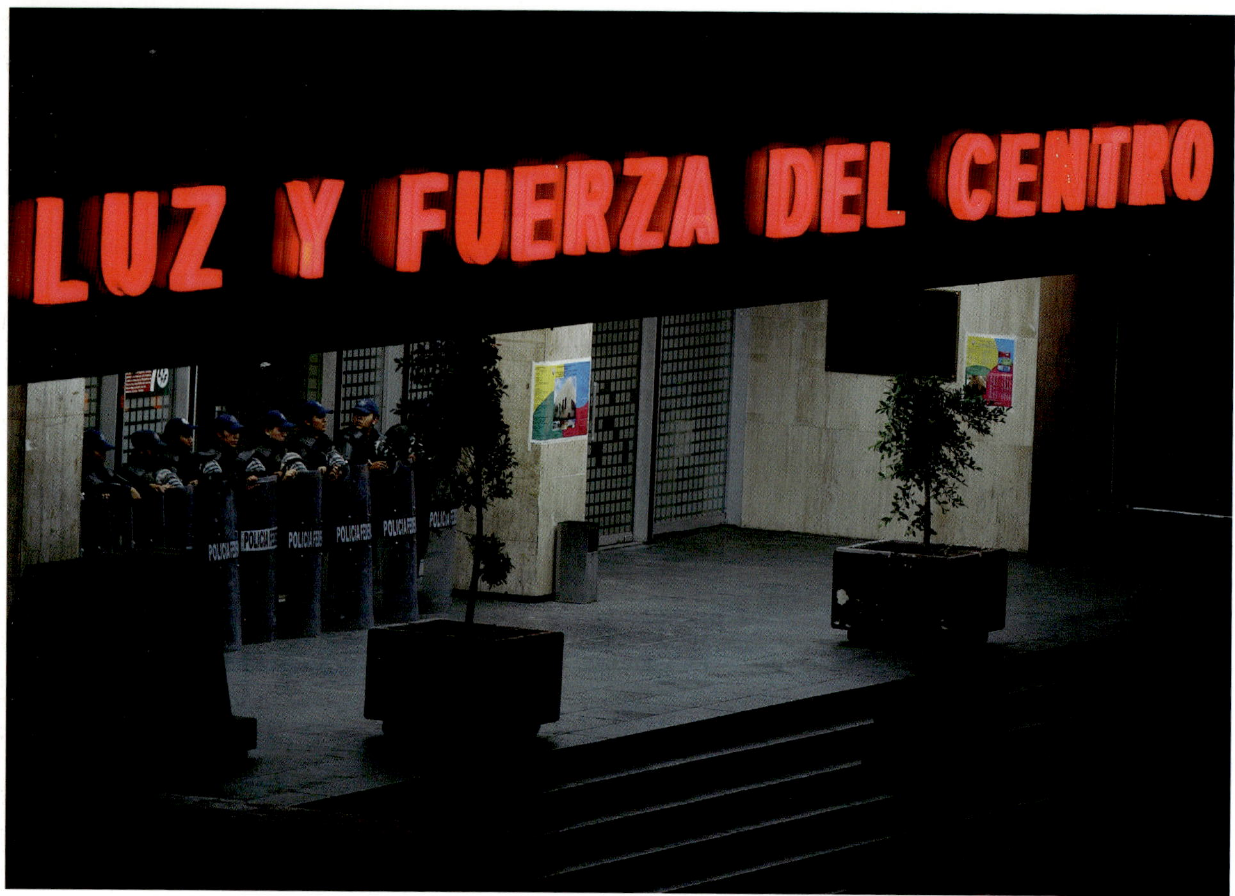

LUZ Y FUERZA DEL CENTRO
POLICIA FEDERAL

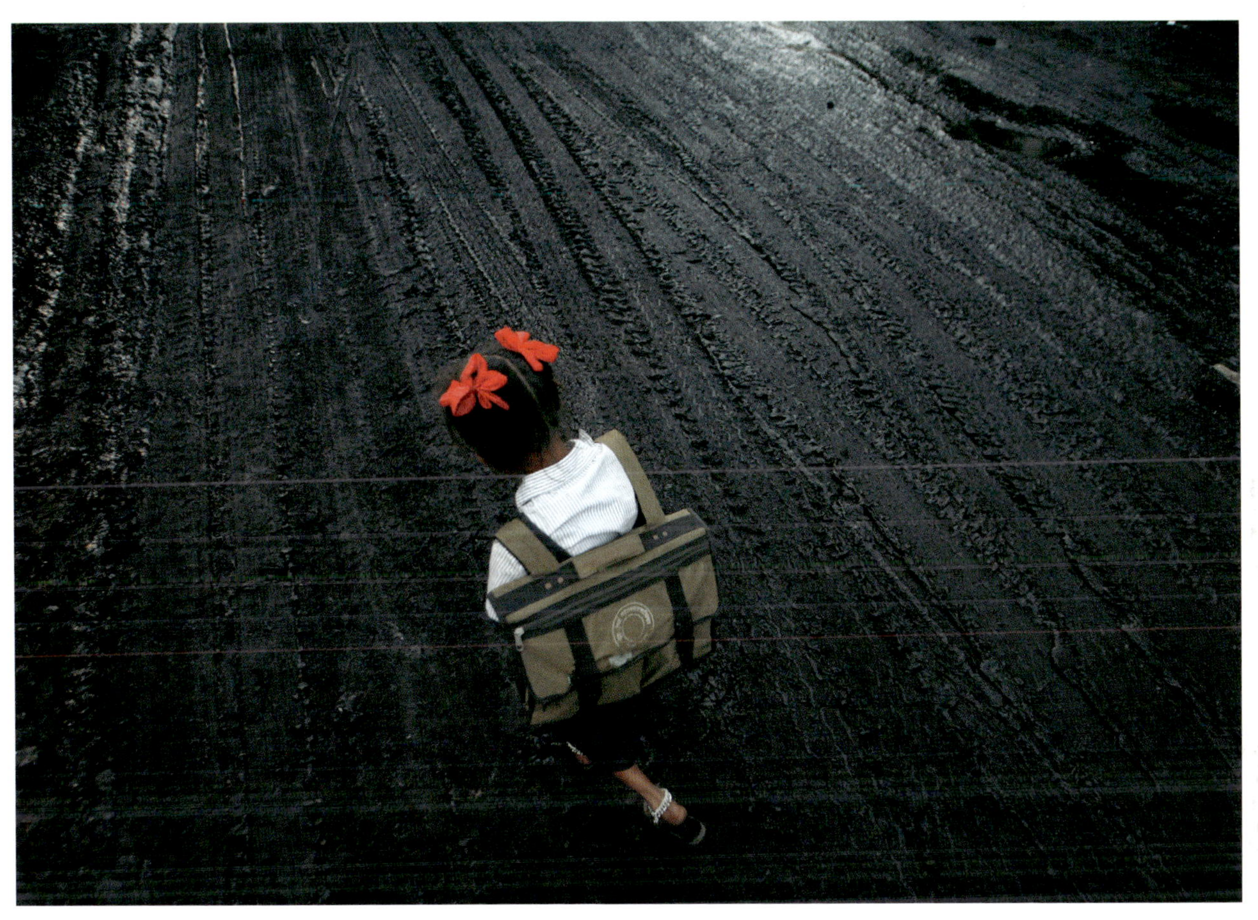

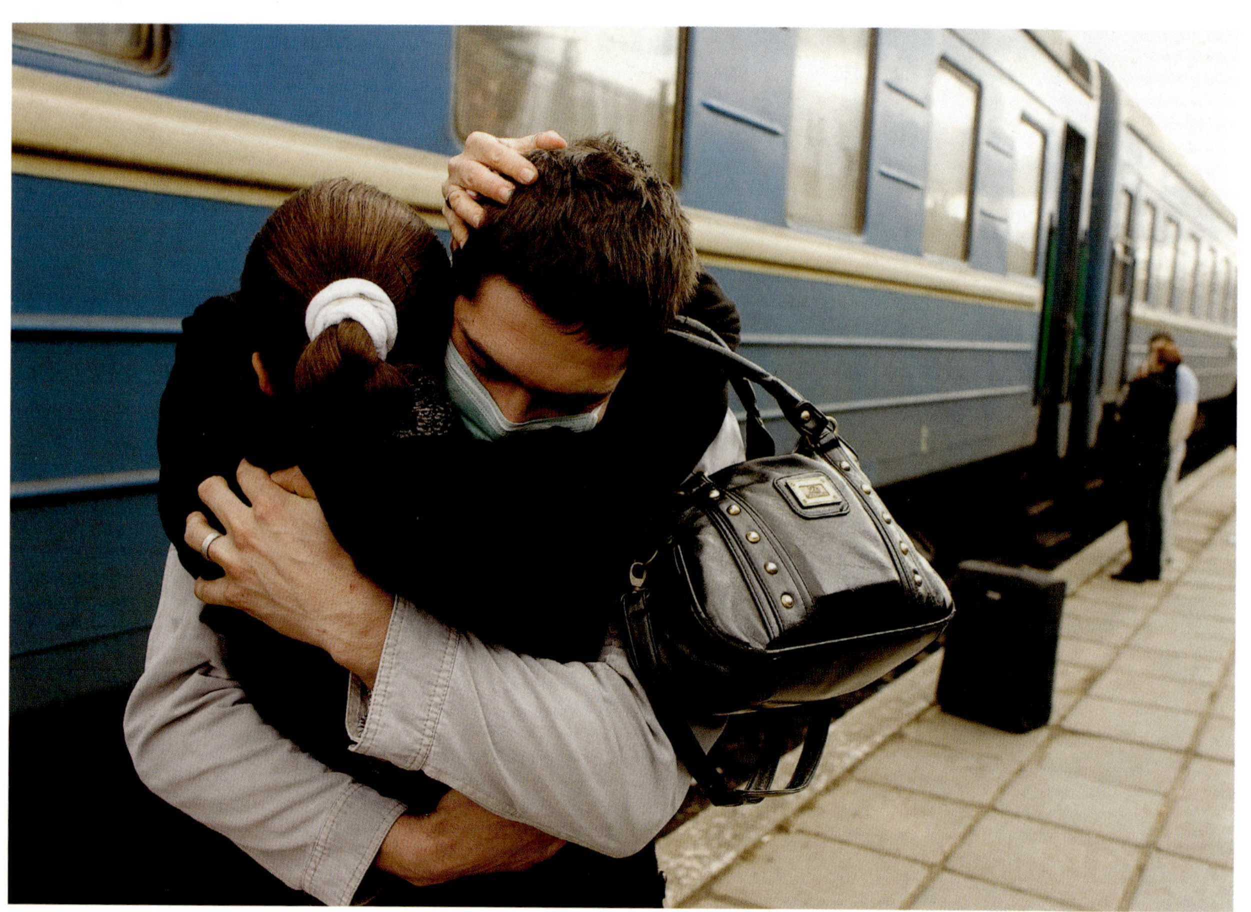

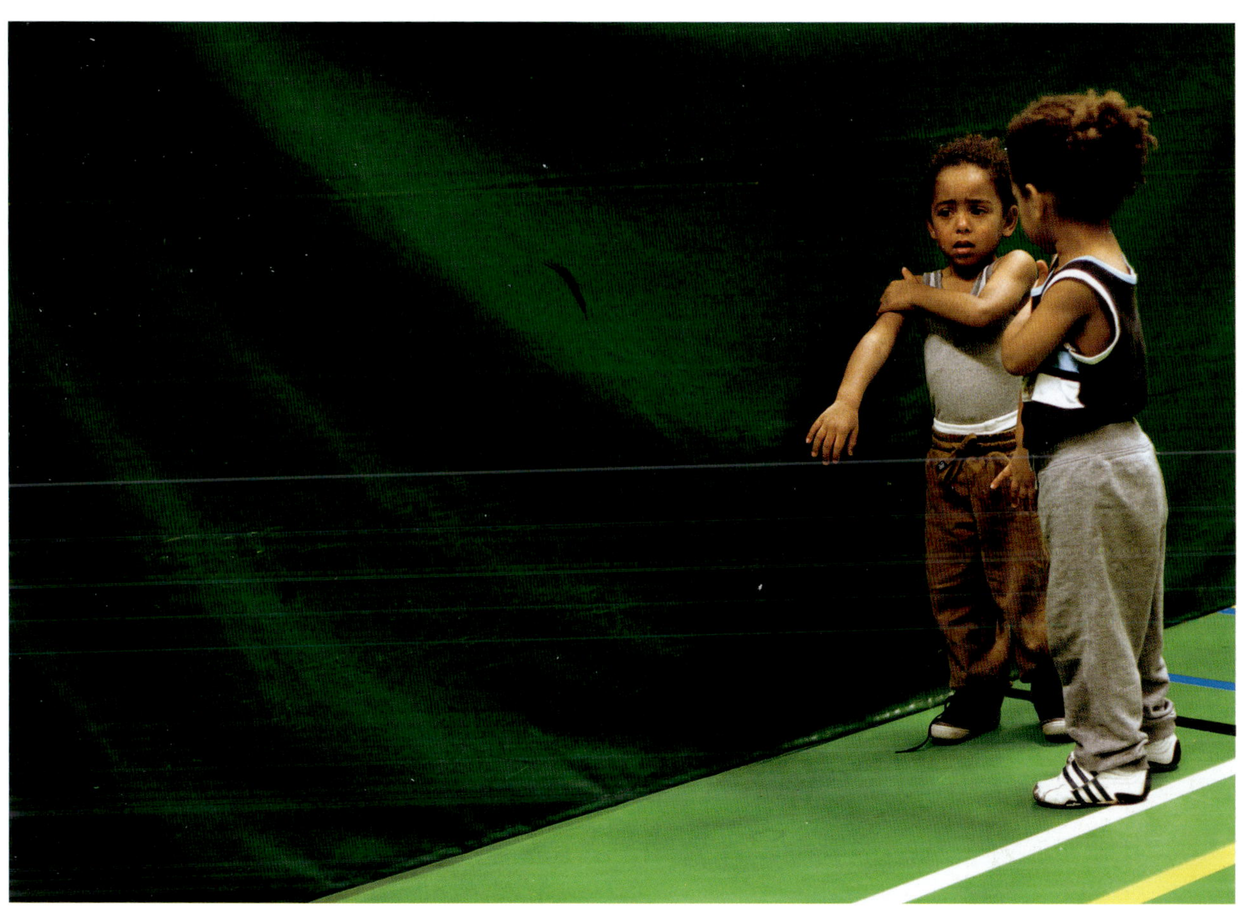

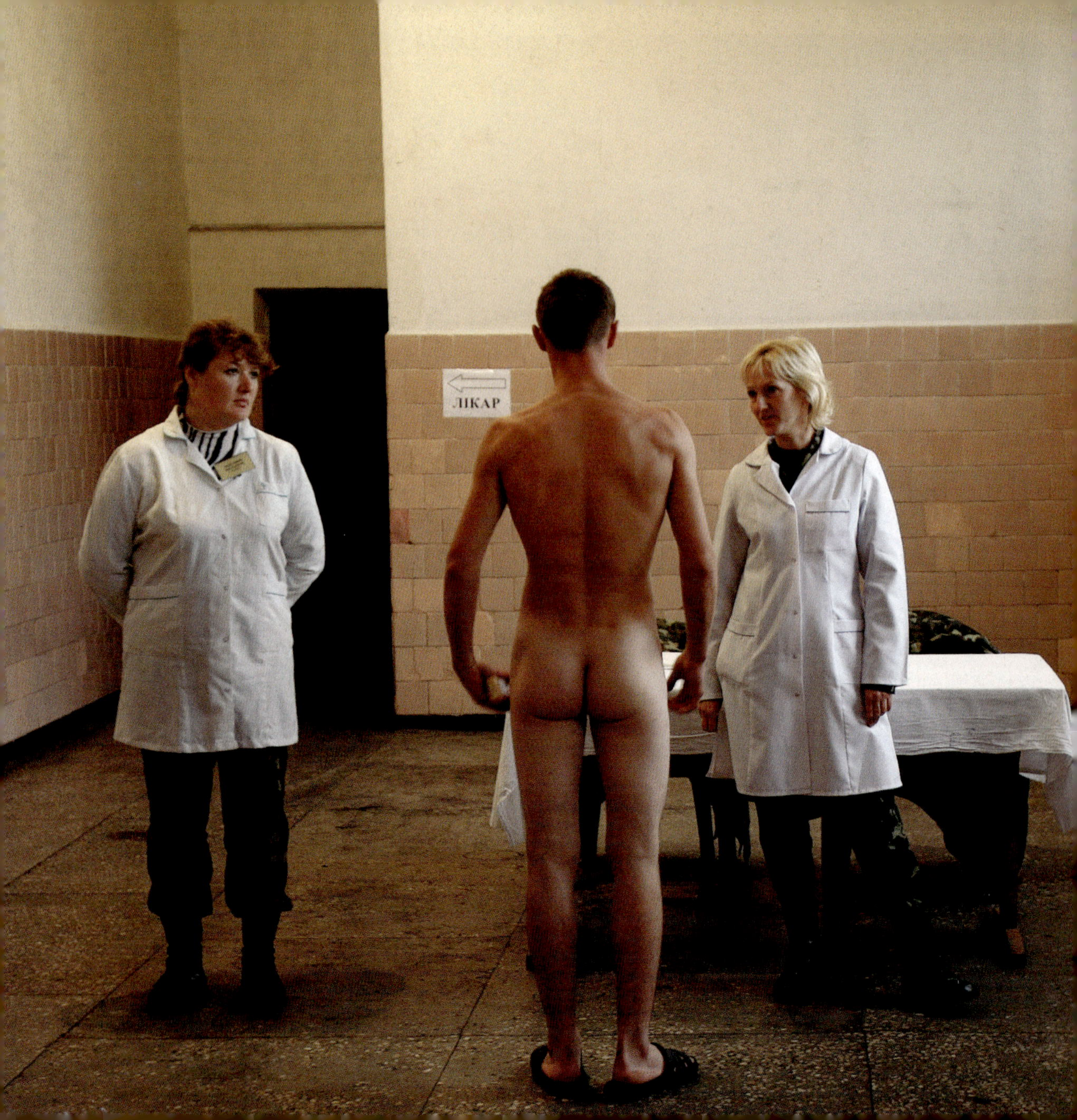

ЛІКАР

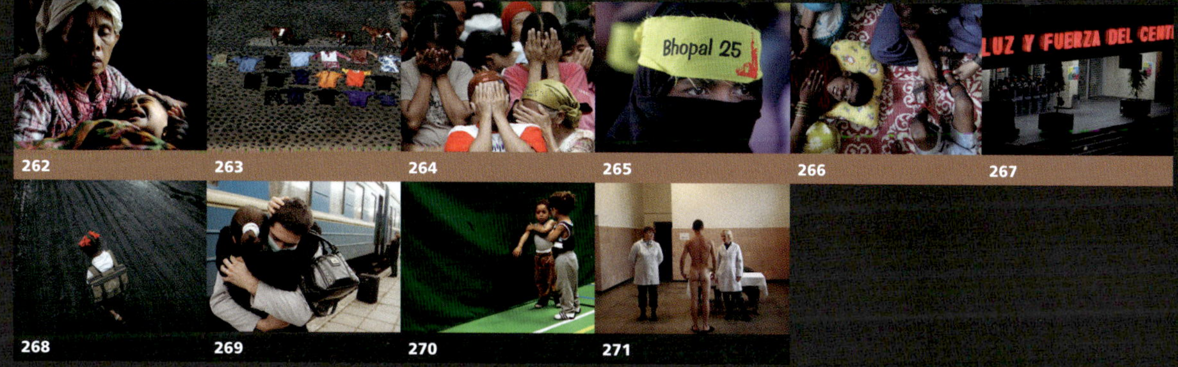

262 Nine-year-old Indah, who has two broken legs, is consoled by her grandmother in a makeshift tent outside the partially destroyed M Djamil hospital in Padang, West Sumatra. The area was hit by a 7.6 magnitude earthquake on 30 September, killing more than 1,000 people. 3 October 2009. Padang, Indonesia. Dylan Martinez.

263 Animals walk past an earthquake survivor's laundry laid out to dry on a riverbank in Padang, West Sumatra. 7 October 2009. Padang, Indonesia. Nicky Loh.

264 Villagers react as a helicopter lands to distribute aid in earthquake-hit Lima Koto Timur district, West Sumatra. 7 October 2009. Padang Pariaman, Indonesia. Crack Palinggi.

265 An activist attends a demonstration on the 25th anniversary of the gas disaster in the Indian city of Bhopal. On 3 December 1984 some 40 tonnes of toxic gas leaked from a plant owned by Union Carbide Corp., now part of Dow Chemical Co. The gas killed thousands in the surrounding slums and injured many more. 3 December 2009. Bhopal, India. Reinhard Krause.

266 Six-year-old Sneha Shahu (left) receives treatment in a rehabilitation centre for children born with mental and physical disabilities in Bhopal. Activists and health workers calculate that 25,000 people died from exposure to the gas either immediately after the leak or in the years that followed, and that many more continue to suffer today. Sicknesses range from cancer, blindness, respiratory difficulties, immune and neurological disorders, reproductive disorders and birth defects. 2 December 2009. Bhopal, India. Reinhard Krause.

267 Federal police take control of the Central Light and Power Company headquarters in Mexico City. Mexico's government announced the closure of the power company because of inefficiency and massive operating losses that were costing it almost as much as Mexico's army. With a workforce of 47,000 employees set to lose their jobs, union leaders promised widespread protests. 11 October 2009. Mexico City, Mexico. Daniel Aguilar.

268 A schoolgirl walks on a road covered with oil and soot in an industrial area of Mumbai. 3 December 2009. Mumbai, India. Arko Datta.

269 A man in a protective mask hugs a woman in the western Ukrainian town of Rovno. Ukraine closed schools, restricted travel and banned public meetings, including presidential election rallies, on 30 October for a three-week period after confirming its first death from H1N1 swine flu. 31 October 2009. Rovno, Ukraine. Vasily Fedosenko.

270 Two children in Schiedam discuss their vaccination against the H1N1 swine flu virus. Many European countries launched vaccination programmes in autumn 2009 to try to halt the spread of the H1N1 virus. 31 October 2009. Schiedam, Netherlands. Jerry Lampen.

271 Medical officers review a conscript at a military training centre, the biggest in the former Soviet Union, in the village of Oster in Ukraine. Around 19,500 recruits were called up to the Ukrainian army in autumn 2009. 29 October 2009. Oster, Ukraine. Gleb Garanich.

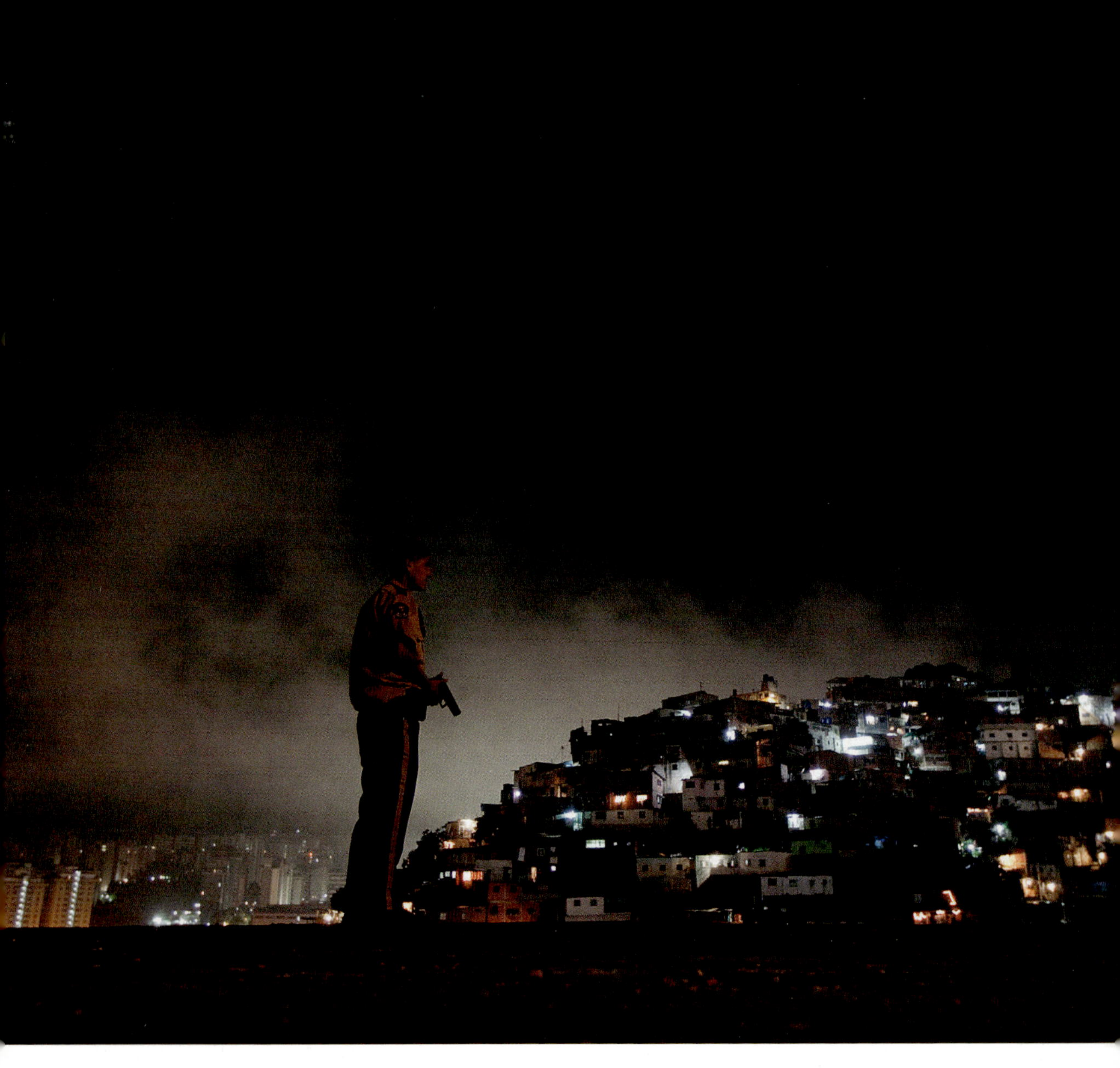

 Caracas, Venezuela

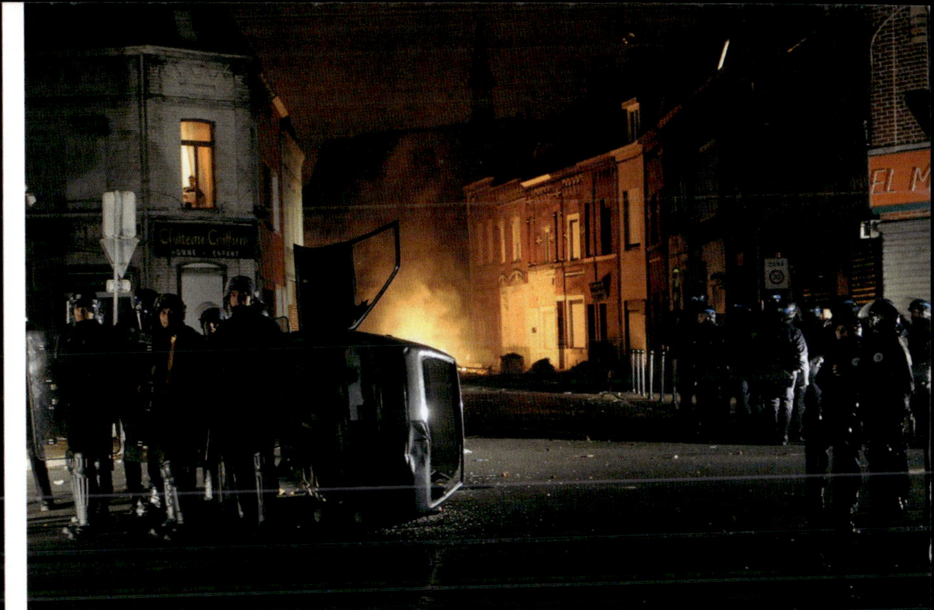

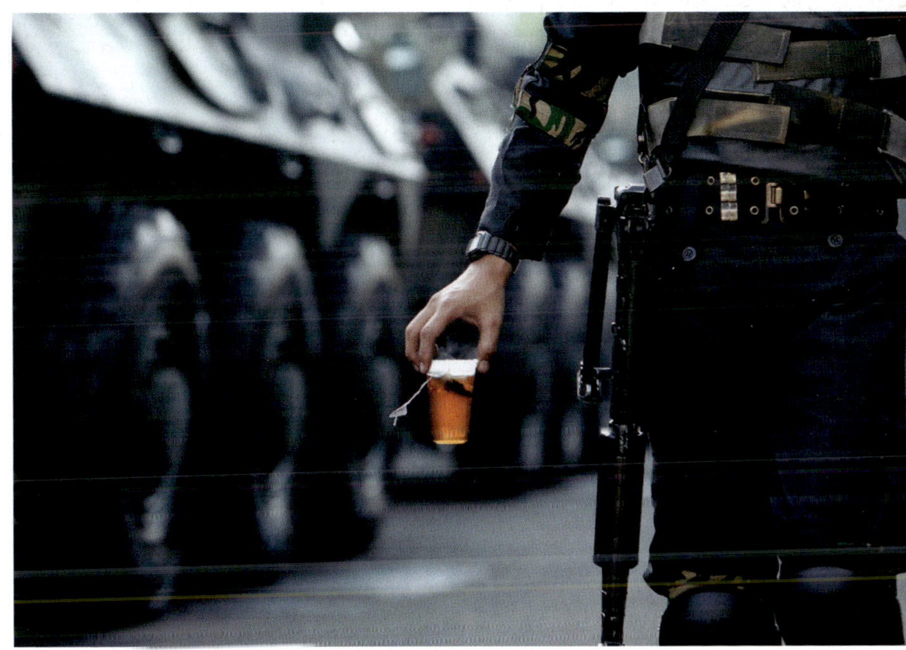

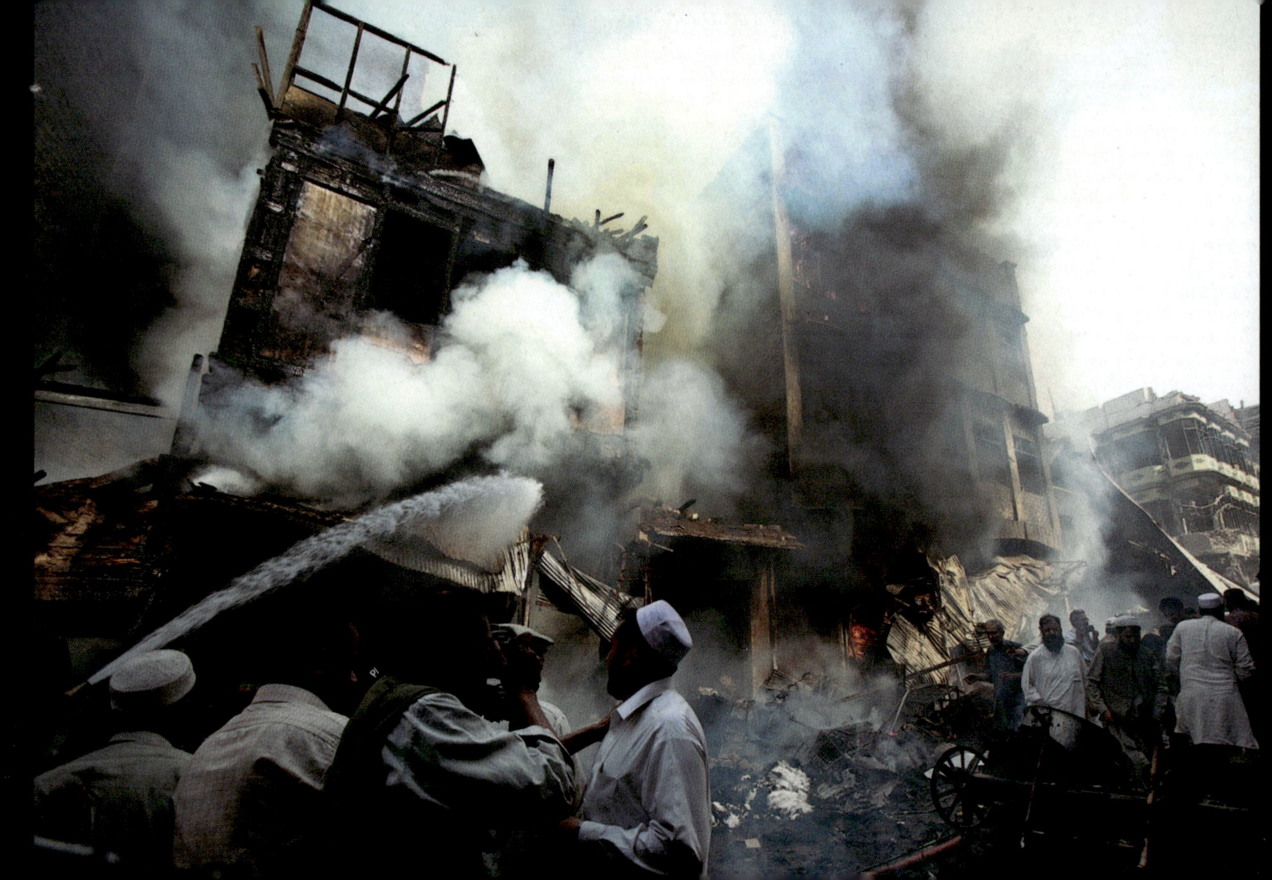

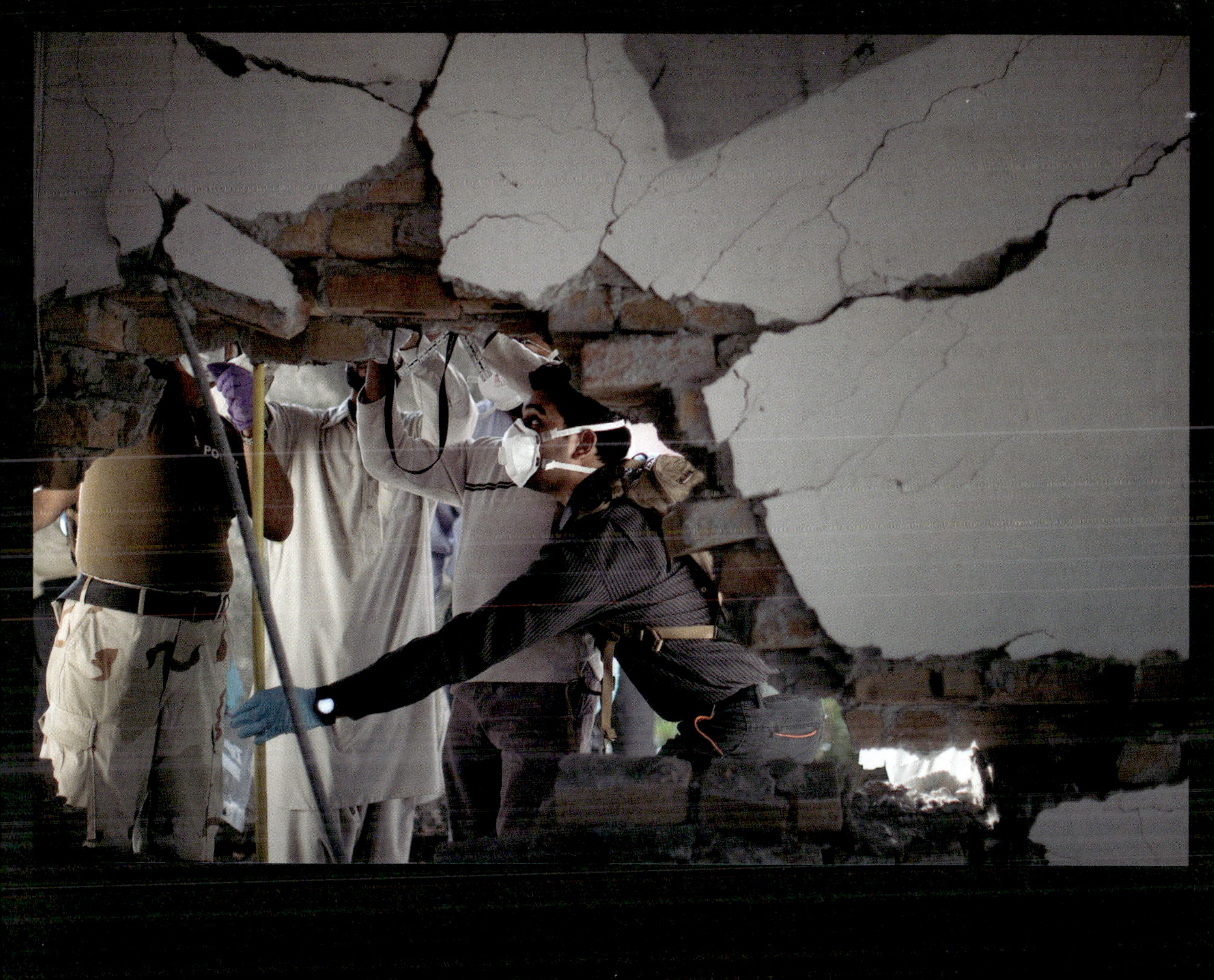

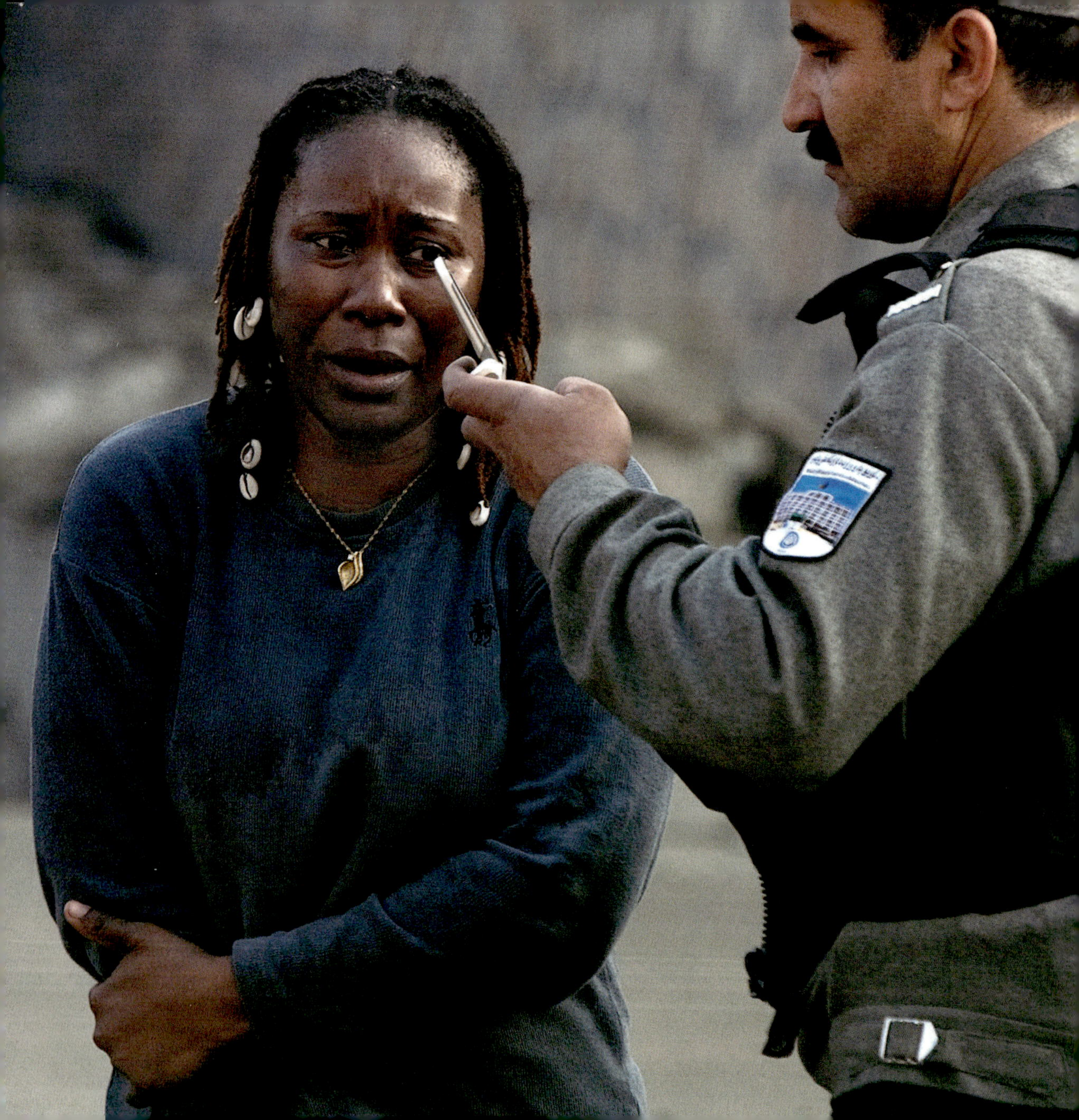

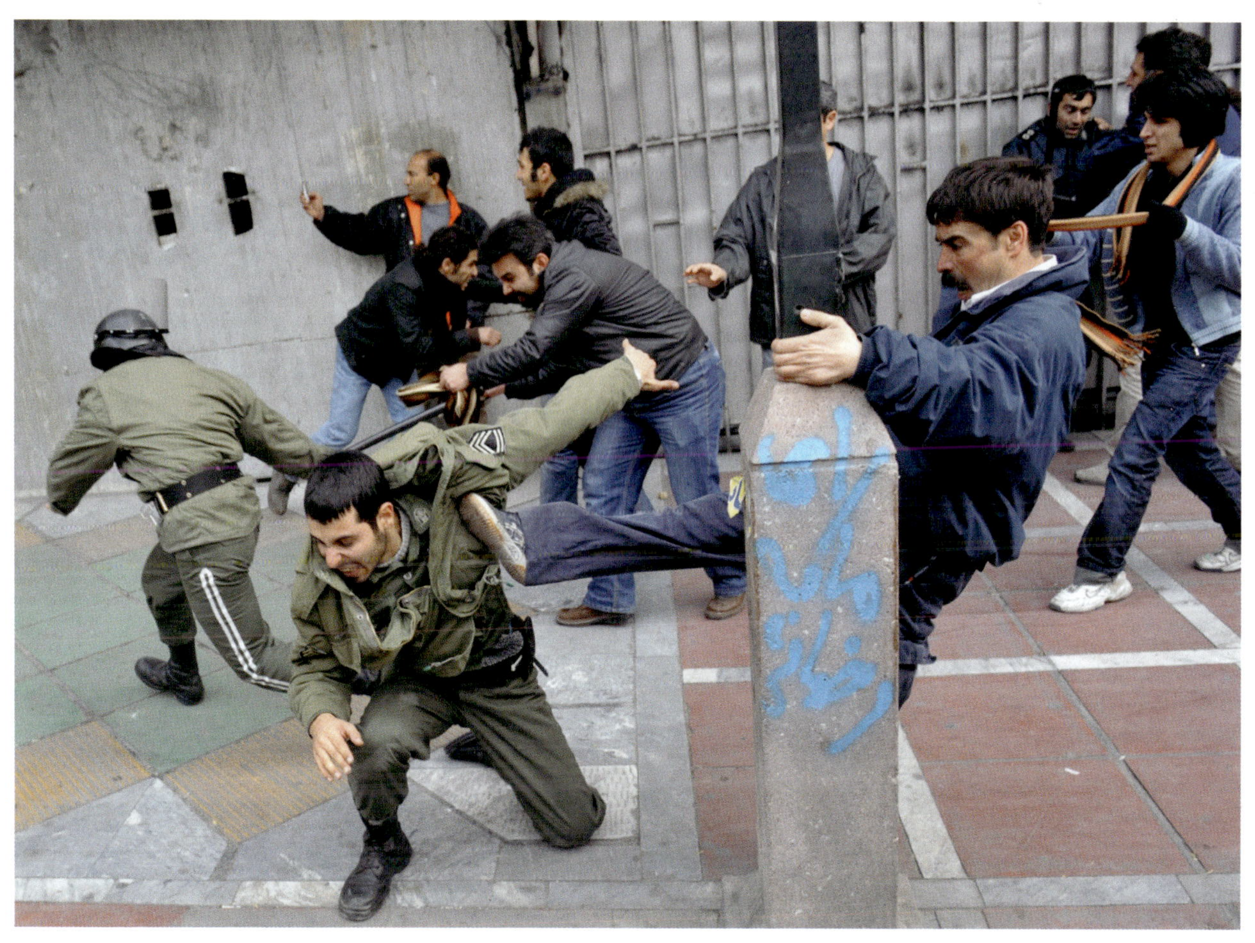

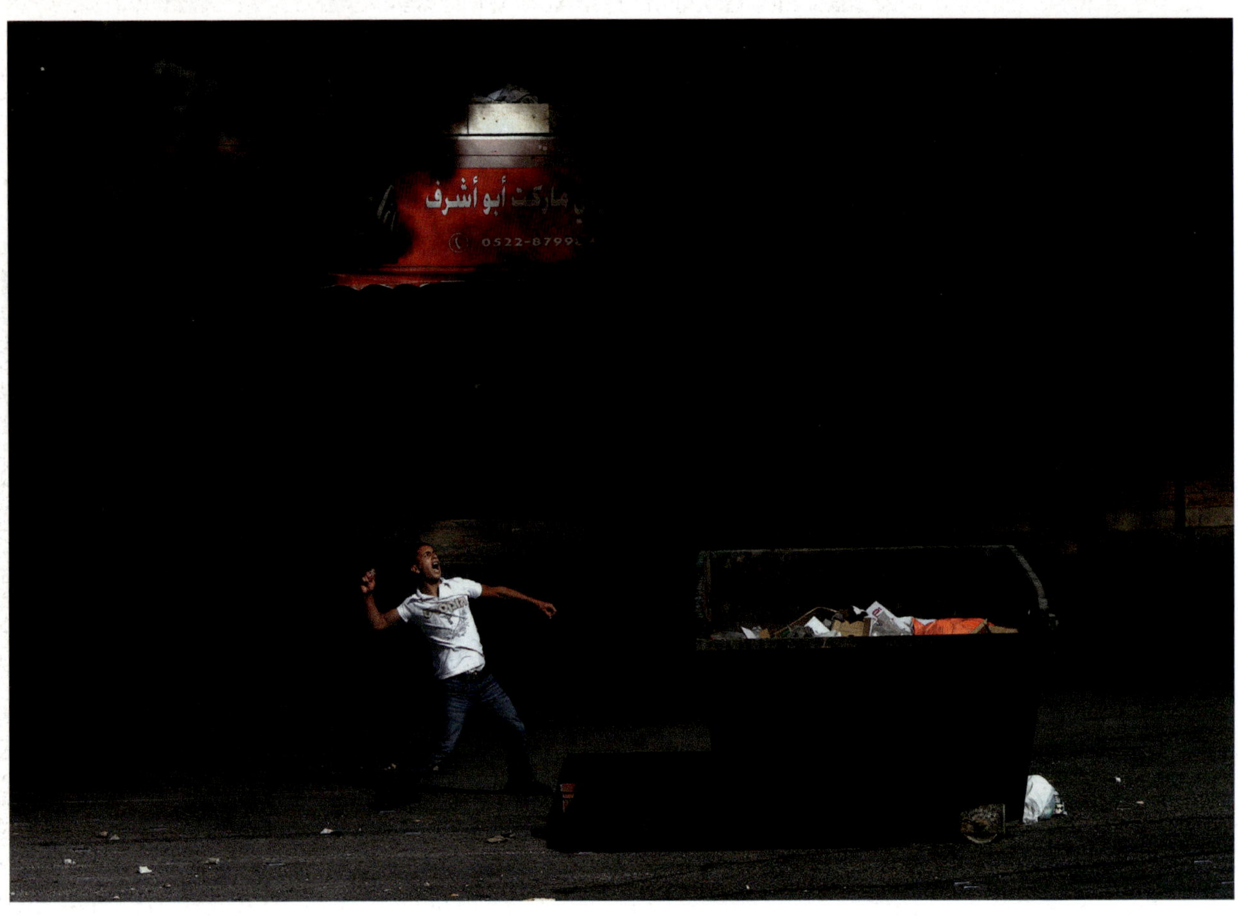

279 Ramallah, West Bank

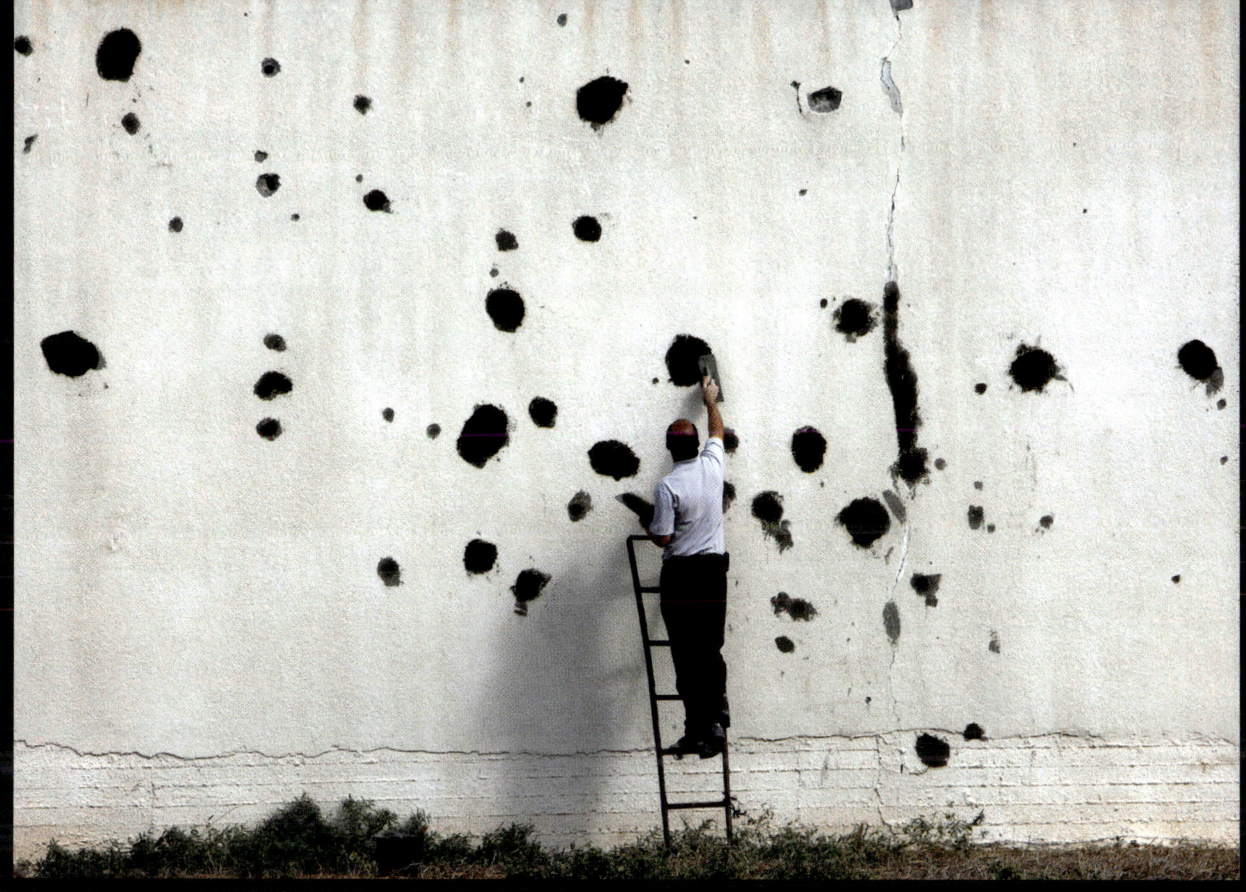

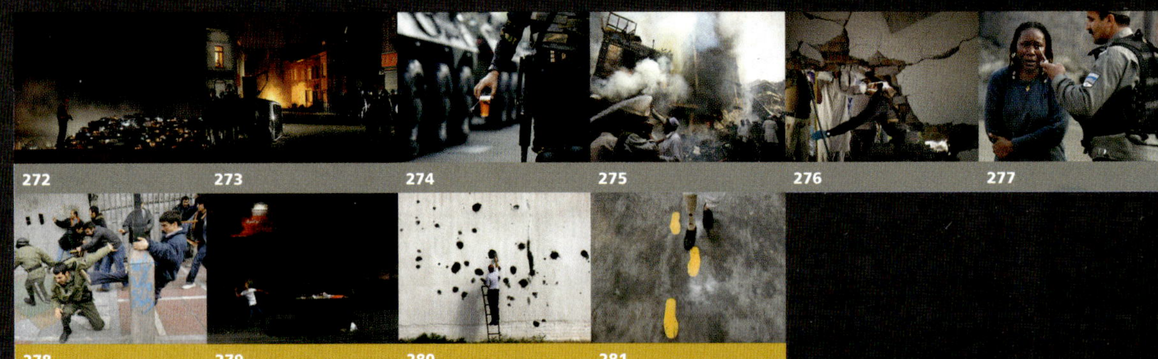

272 A policeman patrols the slum district of Petare in Caracas. The dozens of murders every weekend in Caracas are just the tip of a crime problem that polls show is Venezuelans' main concern. 21 November 2009. Caracas, Venezuela. Carlos Garcia Rawlins.

273 Riot policemen stand guard near a destroyed car at a street in Roubaix in northeastern France. Groups of people set fire to garbage cans and vehicles, plundered a store and threw stones at the fire brigade after Algeria beat Egypt to qualify for the 2010 soccer World Cup. 19 November 2009. Roubaix, France. Farid Allouache.

274 An Indonesian army soldier carries tea as he walks past an armoured car, part of security operations at the House of Representatives compound in Jakarta during the inauguration of President Susilo Bambang Yudhoyono. The president was sworn in for a second term with an agenda headed by the need to enact bureaucratic reforms, fix infrastructure, amend labour laws and attract investment. 20 October 2009. Jakarta, Indonesia. Beawiharta.

275 Firefighters work to extinguish fires after a bomb explosion in a crowded market in Peshawar, in Pakistan's restive North West Frontier Province. The blast, which killed more than 80 people, came just hours after U.S. Secretary of State Hillary Clinton arrived in the country, pledging a fresh start in relations. 28 October 2009. Peshawar, Pakistan. Fayaz Aziz.

276 Security forces measure a hole made by an explosion at the site of a bomb blast at the International Islamic University in Islamabad. Two suicide bomb blasts at the university killed six people and wounded at least 20. 20 October 2009. Islamabad, Pakistan. Adrees Latif.

277 A woman talks to a member of the security forces as they secure the area around an international guest house in Kabul after an attack by Taliban militants in which six U.N. foreign staff were killed. Rockets were also fired at a foreign-owned hotel in the Afghan capital, forcing 100 guests into a bunker. 28 October 2009. Kabul, Afghanistan. Ahmad Masood.

278 Iranian opposition supporters beat police officers during clashes in central Tehran. 27 December 2009. Tehran, Iran.

279 Smoke rises from burning tyres as a Palestinian throws a stone at Israeli soldiers during clashes at the Qalandiya checkpoint near the West Bank city of Ramallah. 9 October 2009. Ramallah, West Bank. Yannis Behrakis.

280 A Palestinian worker repairs a wall at a factory in the northern Gaza Strip that was damaged by bullets during the three-week offensive by Israel launched in December 2008. 2 November 2009. Gaza. Yannis Behrakis.

281 An Afghan man who lost his leg in an anti-personnel mine blast walks in the International Committee of the Red Cross orthopaedic centre in Herat. 5 November 2009. Herat, Afghanistan. Morteza Nikoubazl.

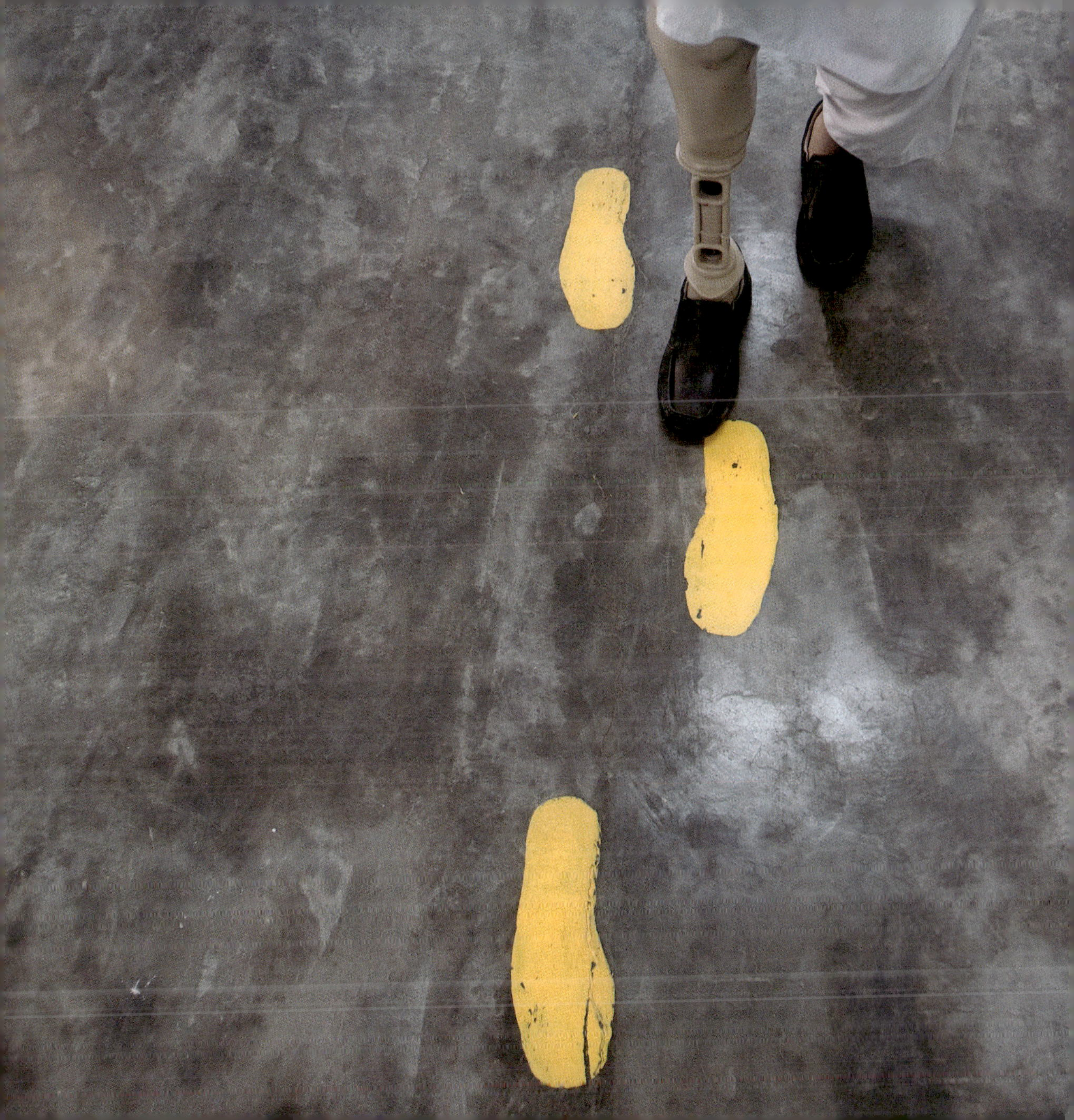

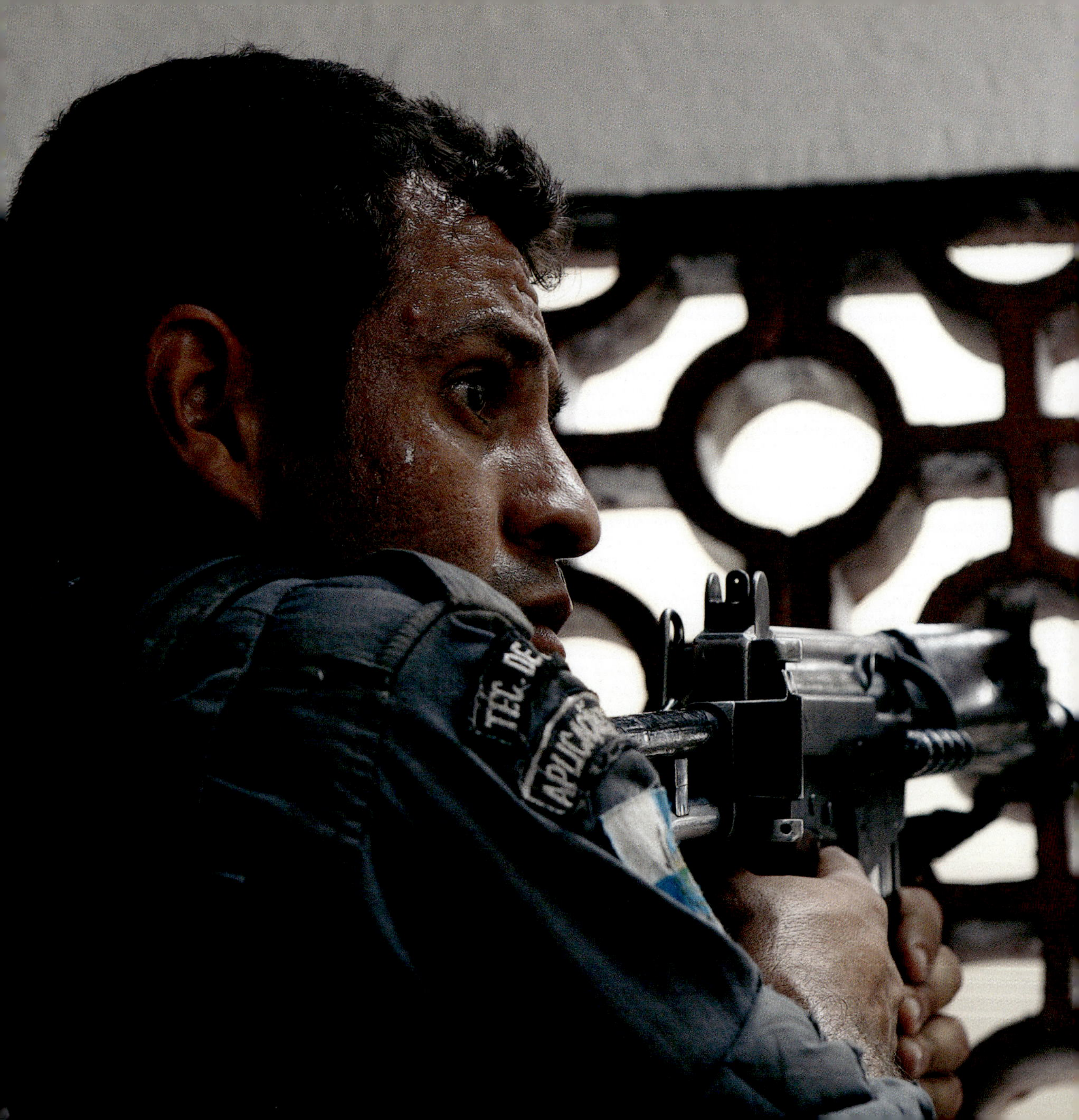

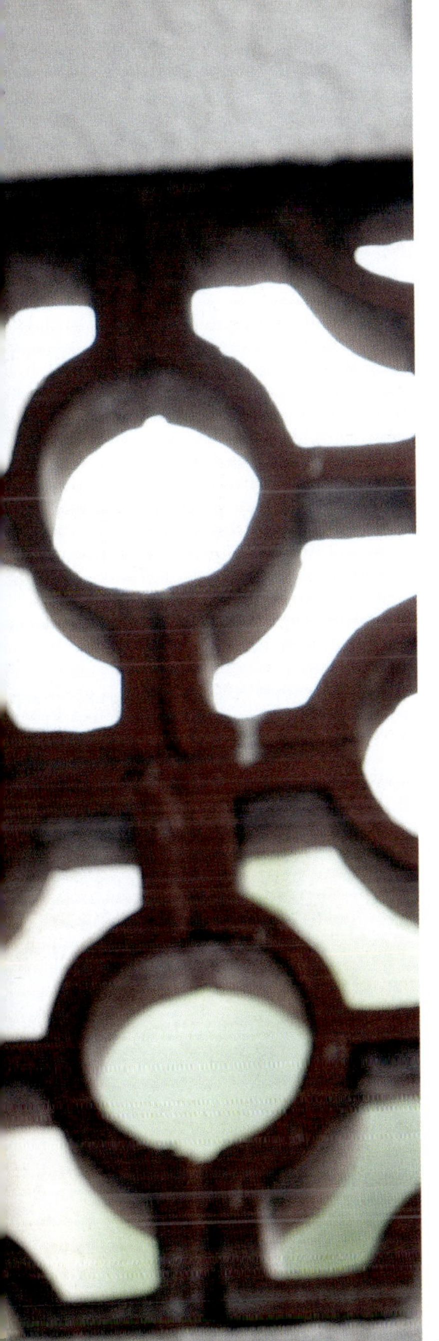

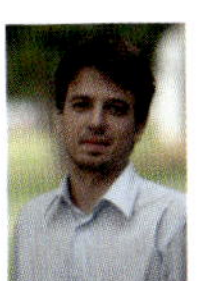

RICARDO MORAES
Photographer
Born: São Paulo, Brazil, 1984
Based: Brasilia, Brazil
Nationality: Brazilian

Rio, Olympic city in flames

The smouldering carcass of a police helicopter, panicked residents fleeing intense gunfights, buses ablaze under smoke-filled skies…. Two weeks after Rio de Janeiro was awarded the 2016 Olympics the city awoke in flames.

A Friday night of routine drug gang battles over control of Morro dos Macacos (Monkey Hill) turned into a Saturday like no other. A police helicopter that was trying to intervene was shot down, crashing in flames and killing three officers.

The conflict spread quickly. In a nearby slum, bandits set fire to buses to distract the police while they escaped. An armoured police vehicle circled. The atmosphere was tense. Police were determined to find the gang that brought down the chopper, and several thousand were mobilized. They surrounded the suspects' hideouts. The number of dead in Morro dos Macacos increased daily. It was there, while checking information about another victim, that I came across a dead youth dumped in a supermarket cart. Residents surrounded the scene, some laughing, others shocked.

Amidst that atmosphere of combat a superhero suddenly appeared in an alleyway. A woman pulled along a boy dressed as Batman. I imagined that he had been playing in the neighbourhood when the police arrived, and his mother took advantage of a lull in the gunfire to get him to safety.

Home to 6 million people, Rio is a city with a vibrant cultural heritage combined with a rare natural beauty that serves as backdrop to an endless war. Shootouts break out almost daily between police and the heavily armed gangs that control many of the city's roughly 1,000 slums or favelas. Gangsters are often better armed than the police.

Photojournalism in Rio is a high-risk profession. In 2008 a colleague investigating a slum under militia control was kidnapped and tortured by paramilitaries, and was subsequently forced to change both city and profession. Earlier in 2009, two cameramen were hit by shrapnel during a gun battle between police and drug bandits. Most recently, a photographer was killed in an attempted robbery in a Rio suburb.

The refrain most commonly heard during interviews with Rio slum dwellers is that of all civilians trapped in a war zone: 'We leave home, and don't know if we're coming back.'

282 A police officer takes a position in Rio's Cruzeiro slum. Violence left parts of the city looking like a war zone two weeks after It was awarded the 2016 Olympic Games. 21 October 2009. Rio de Janeiro, Brazil. Ricardo Moraes.

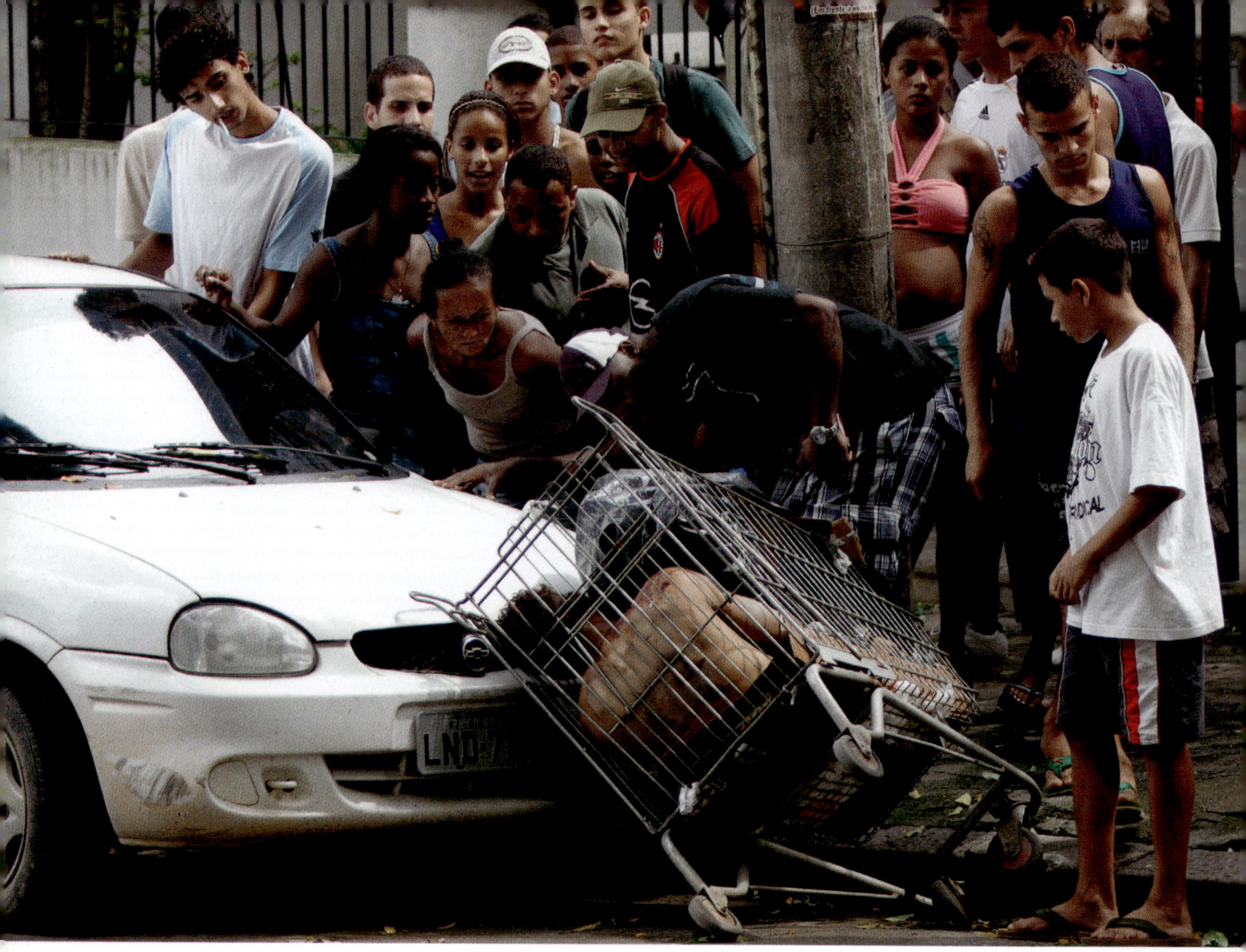

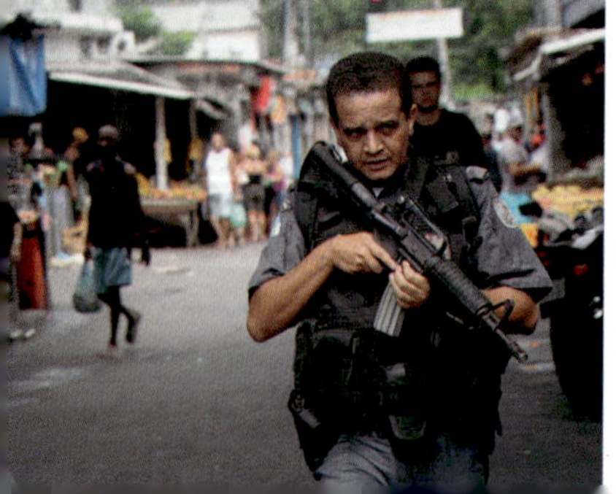

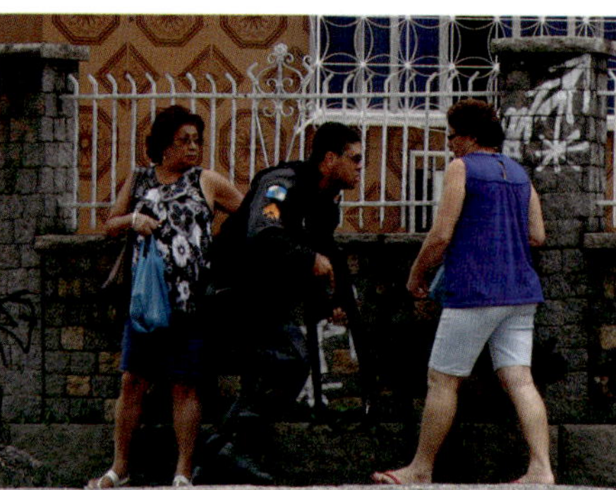

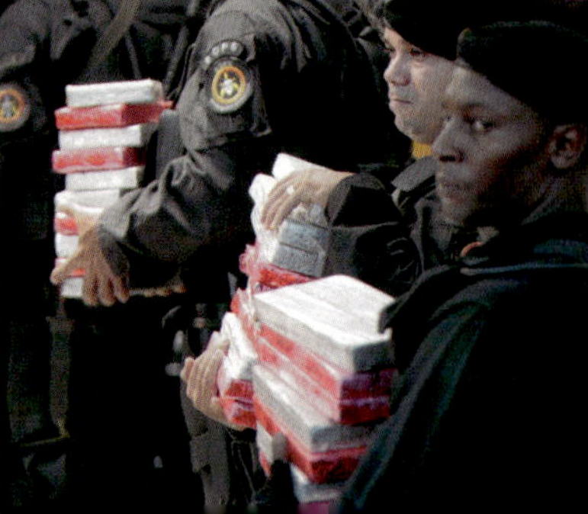

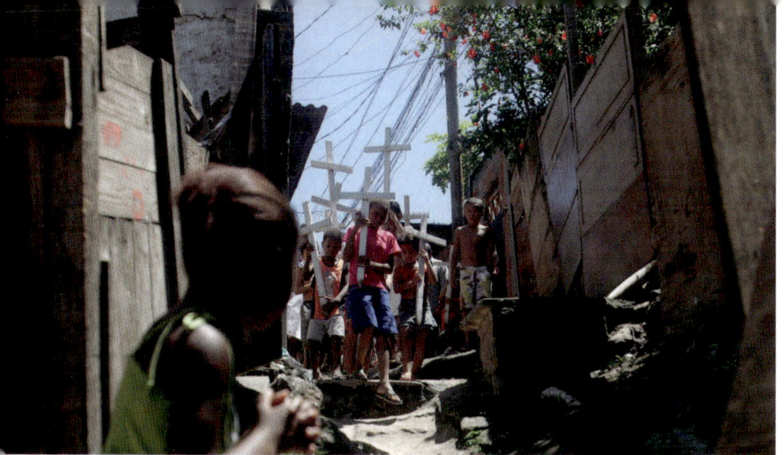

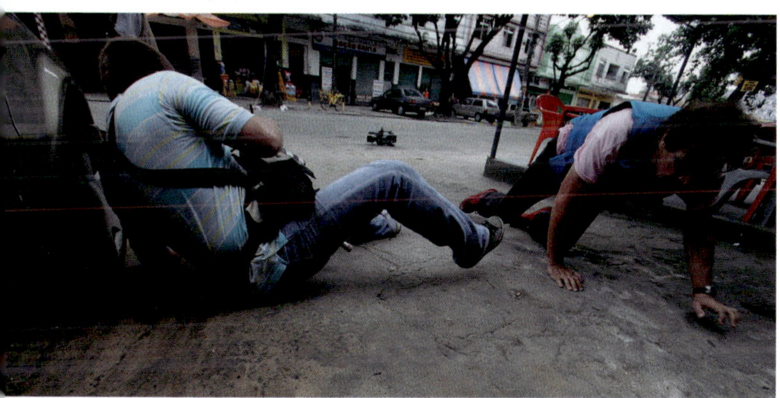

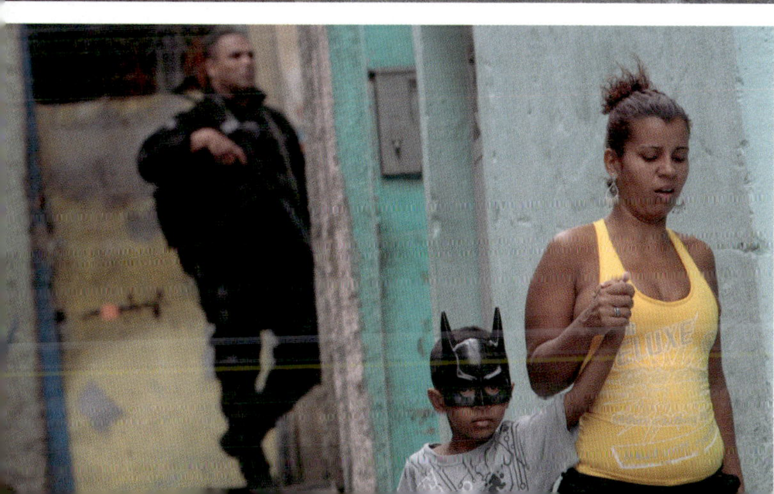

<table>
<tr><td rowspan="2" colspan="3">283</td><td>287</td></tr>
<tr><td>288</td></tr>
<tr><td>284</td><td>285</td><td>286</td><td>289</td></tr>
</table>

283 Residents look at a body left in a supermarket cart in the Morro dos Macacos slum in Rio de Janeiro. The man was suspected to have been killed by rival drug gangs. 20 October 2009. **284** Police patrol the Jacarezinho slum two days after drug traffickers shot down one of their crime-fighting helicopters, killing three officers. 19 October 2009. **285** A police officer runs past residents during a police operation near the Cruzeiro slum. 21 October 2009. **286** Policemen carry drugs confiscated in a raid on the Jacarezinho slum. 18 October 2009. **287** Children carry crosses during a demonstration against violence in Mandela slum, the week after a young student died during a shootout between policemen and drug dealers. 2 November 2009. **288** Journalists take cover during a police operation against drug dealers in the Vila Cruzeiro slum. 23 October 2009. **289** A police officer patrols Rio's Jacarezinho slum as a woman and child walk past. 18 October 2009. Ricardo Moraes

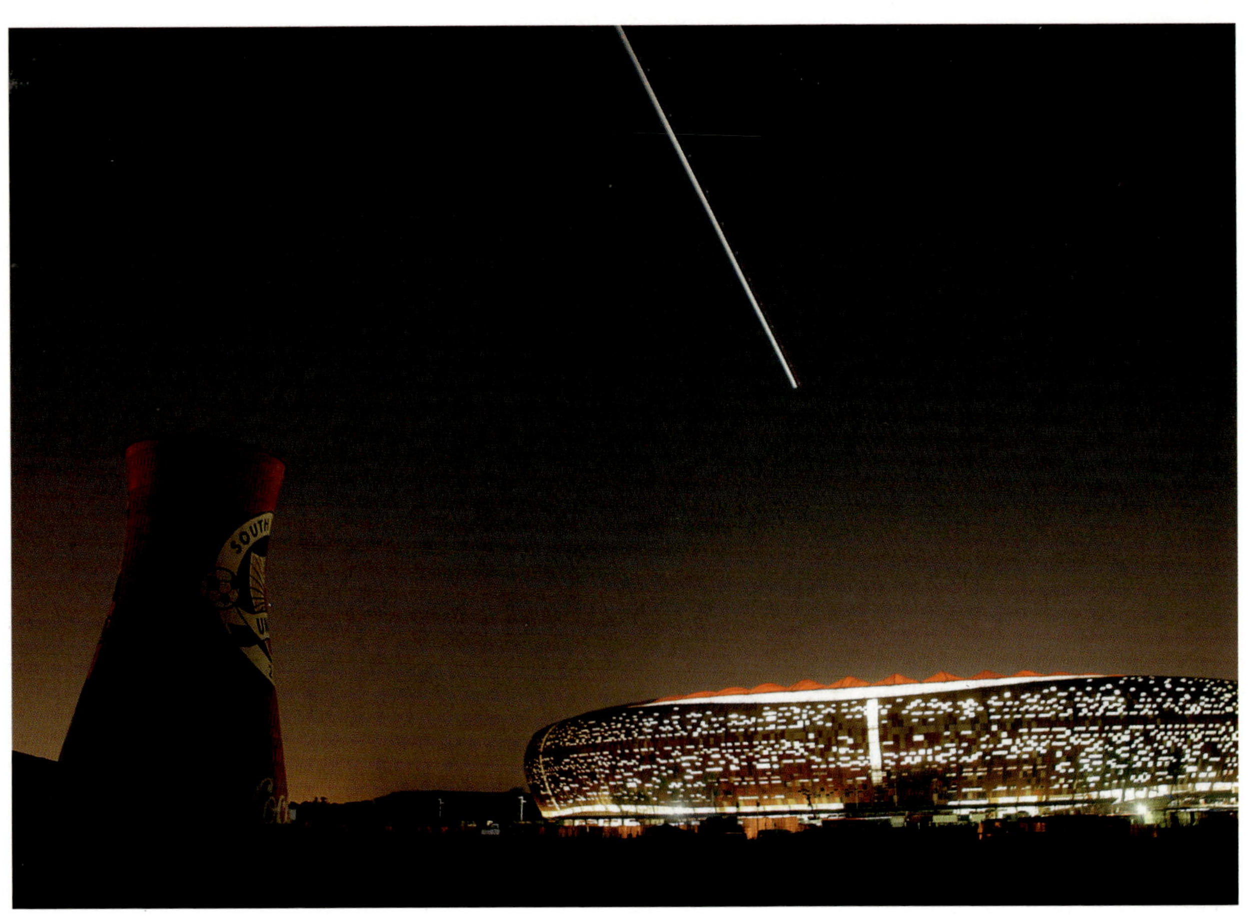

 Johannesburg, South Africa

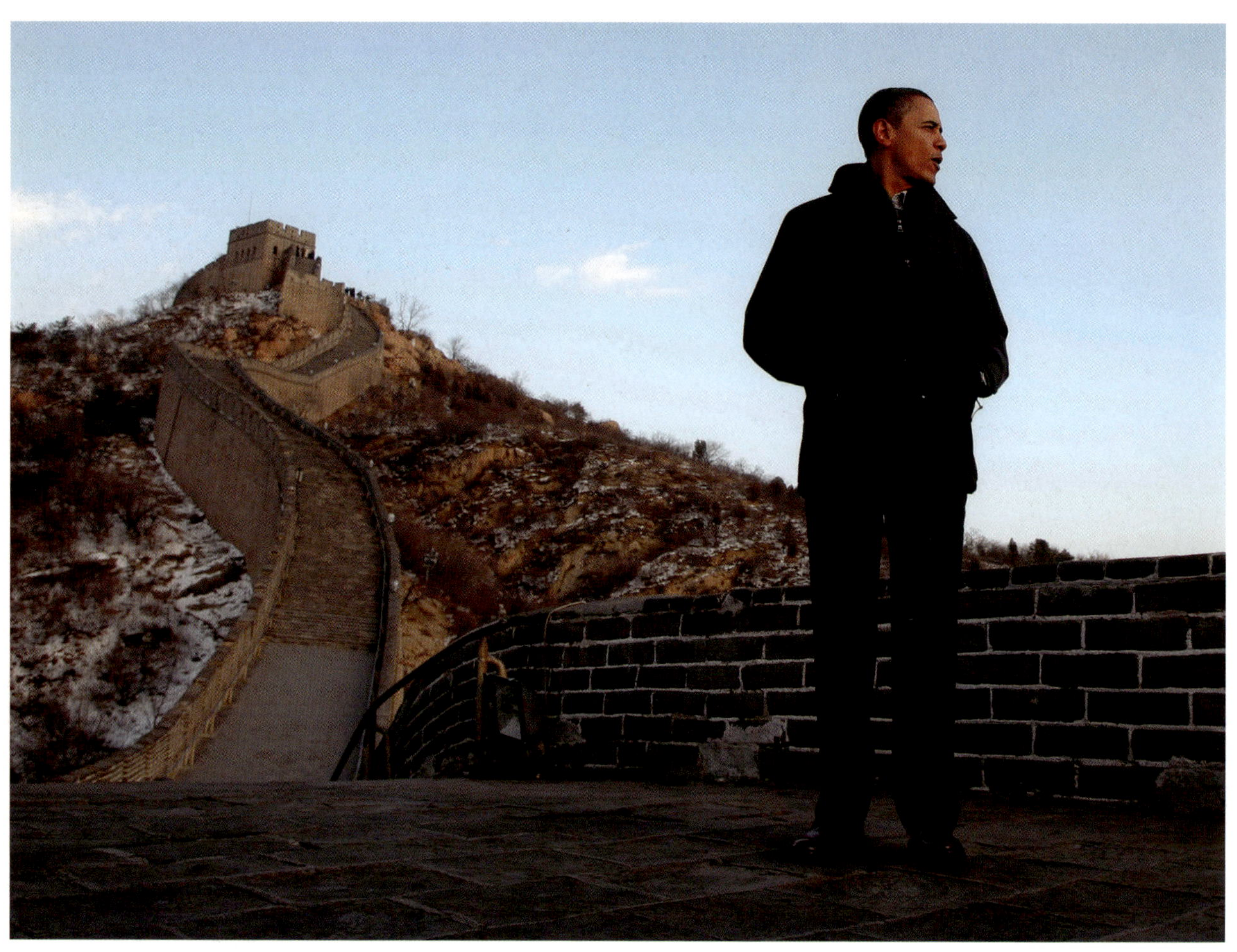

292 Badaling, China

 Anchorage, United States

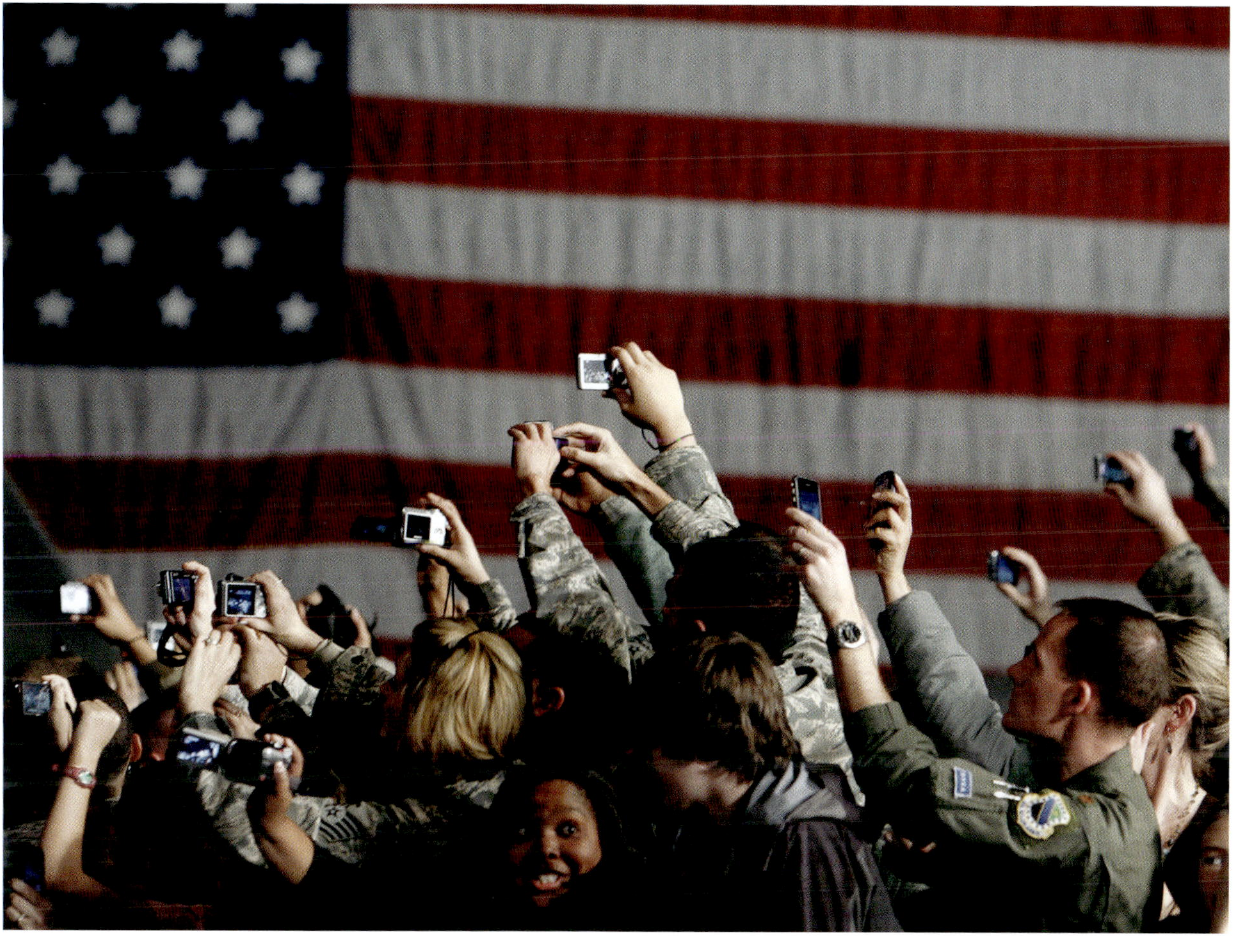

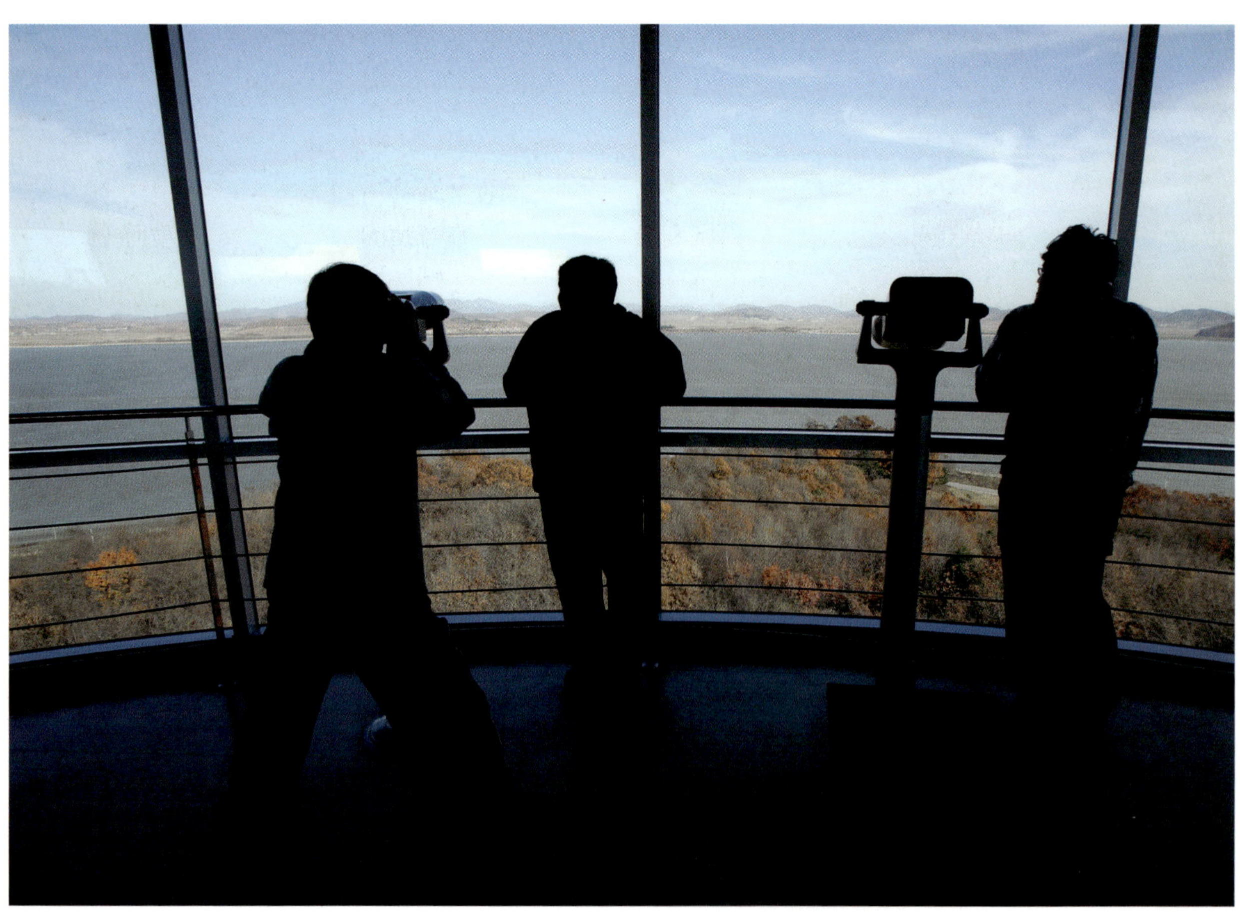

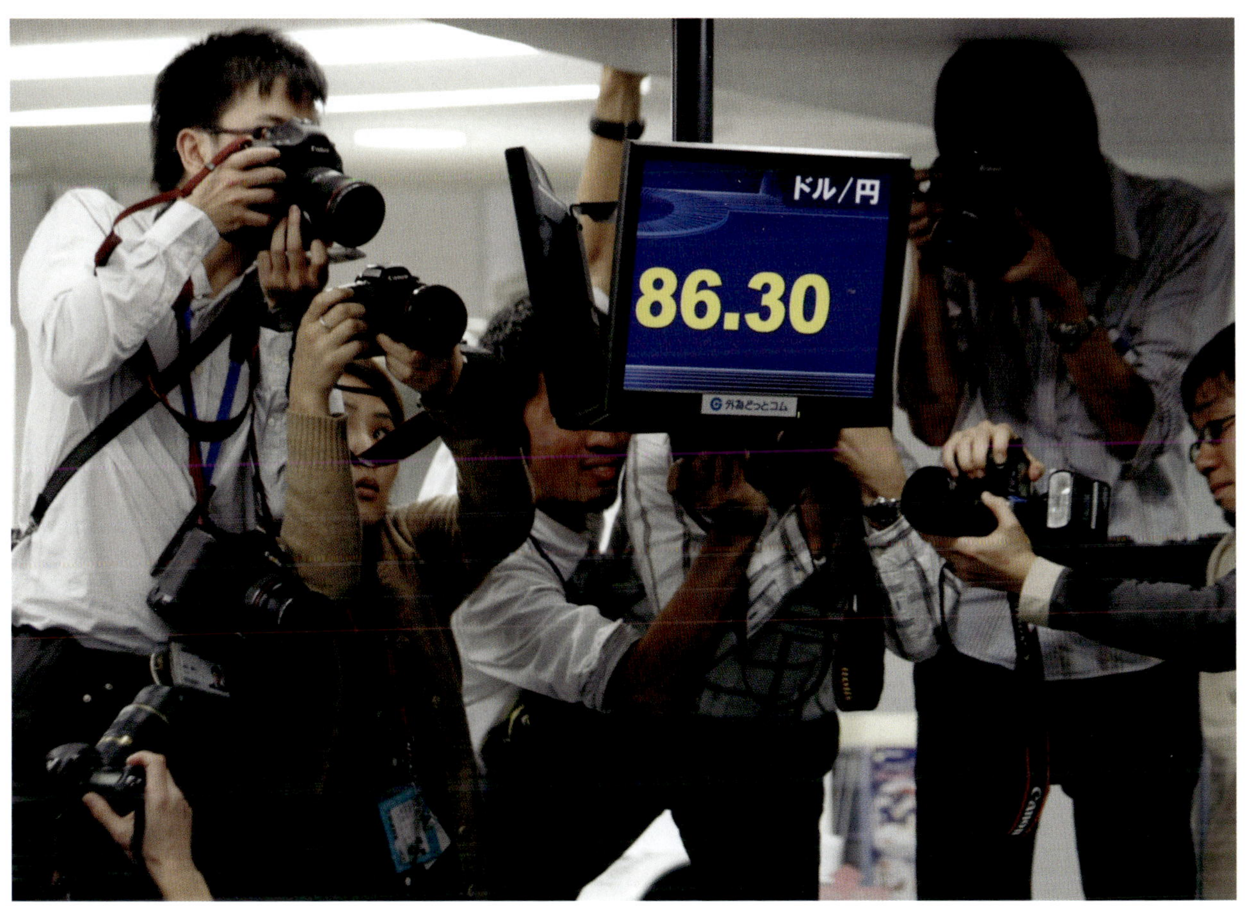

ドル/円
86.30
外為どっとコム

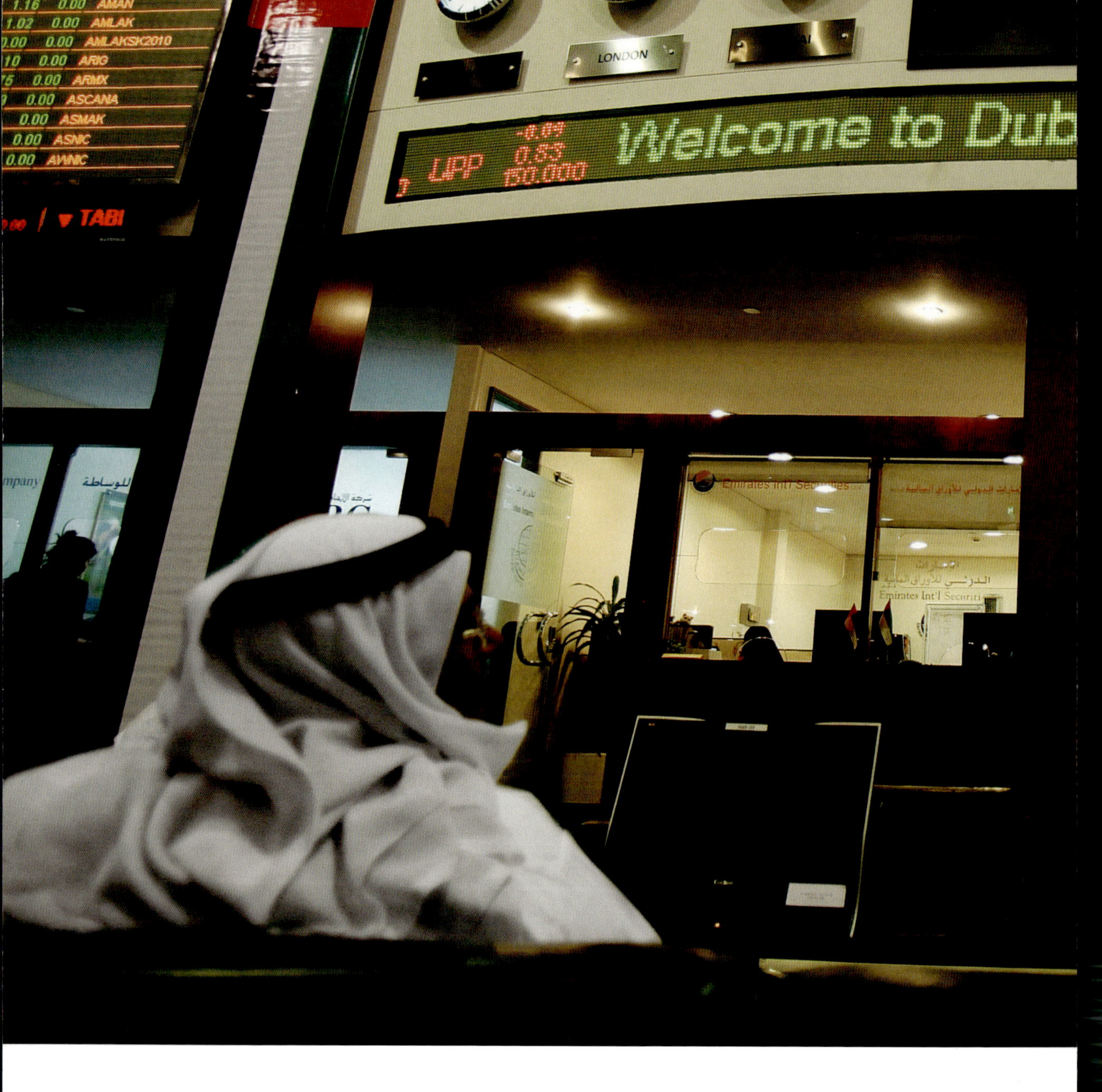

1.16   0.00 AMAN
1.02   0.00 AMLAK
0.00   0.00 AMLAKSK2010
10   0.00 ARIG
5   0.00 ARMX
0.00   ASCANA
0.00   ASMAK
0.00   ASNIC
0.00   AWNIC
TABI
LONDON
Welcome to Dub
UPP
Emirates Int'l Securities
Emirates Int'l Securiti

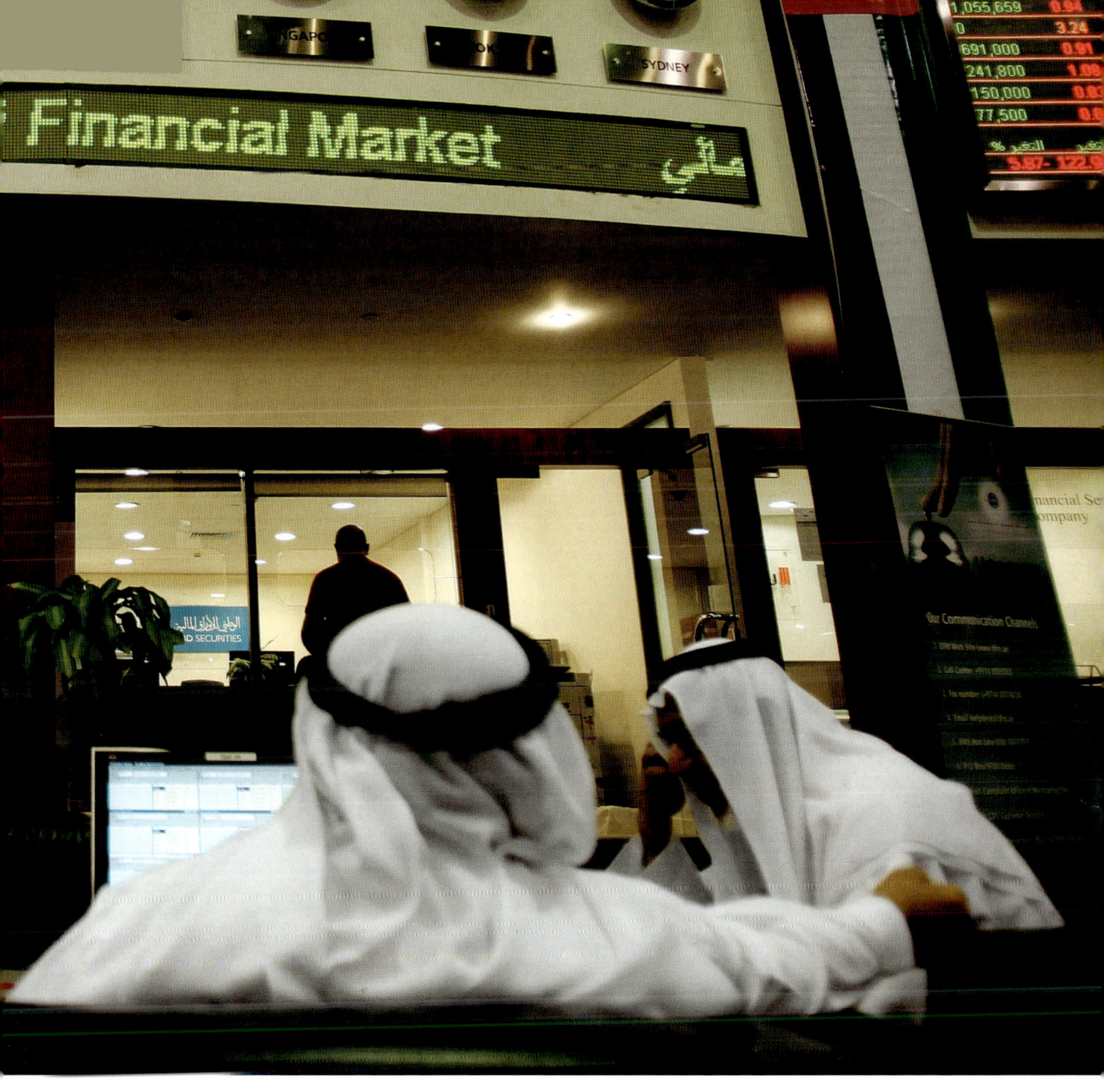

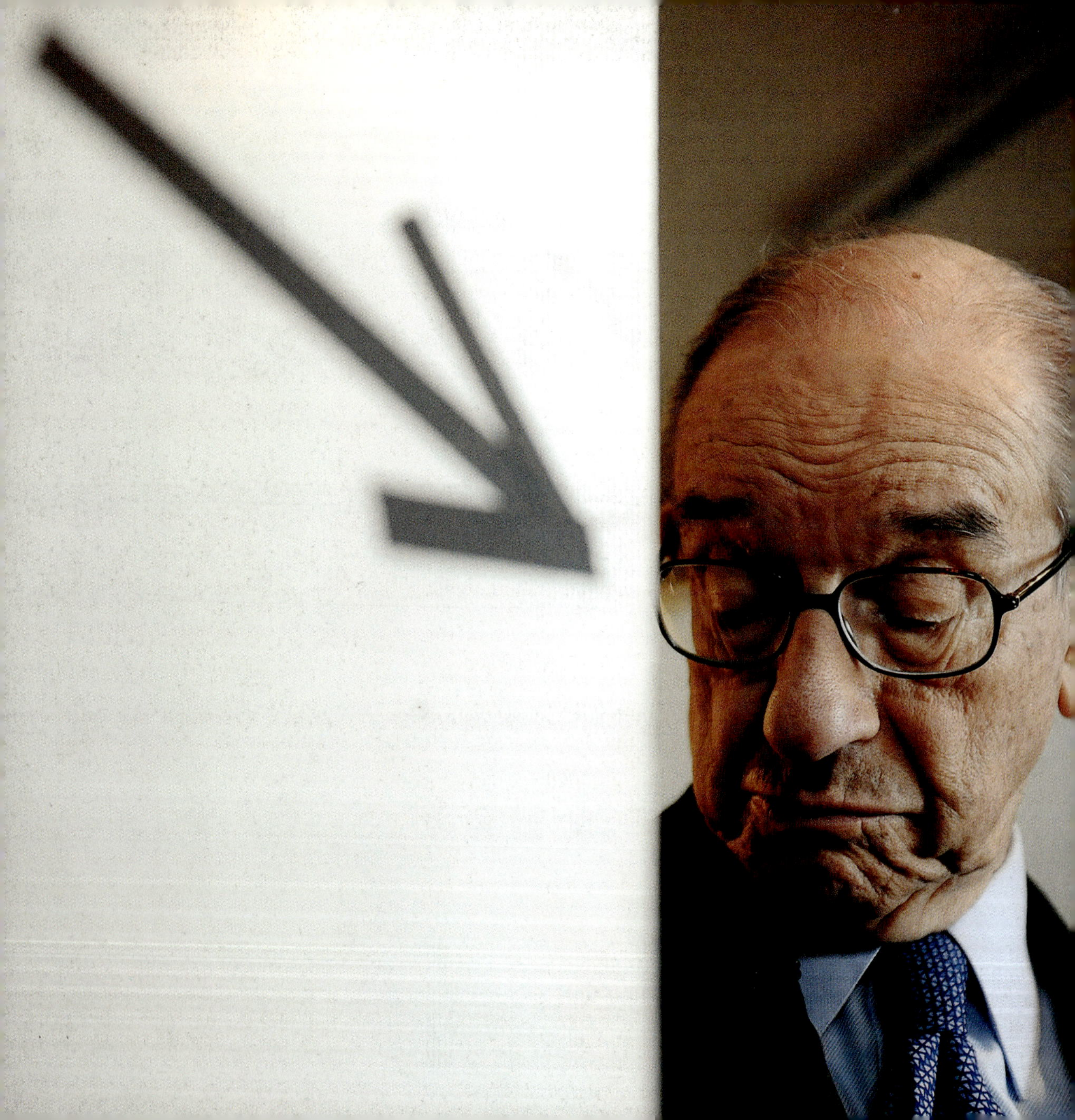

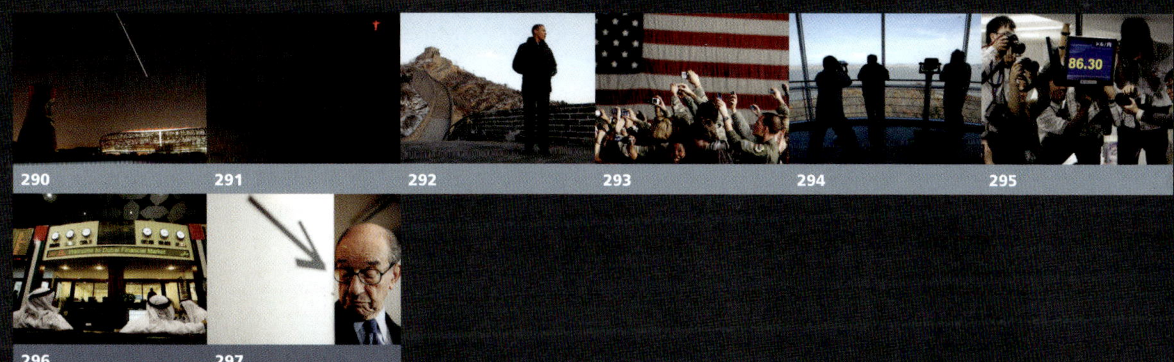

290 Vapour trails from a plane are seen in the sky over Johannesburg's Soccer City, also known as the FNB Stadium. The stadium is earmarked to host the opening and final soccer matches of the 2010 FIFA World Cup. 25 November 2009. Johannesburg, South Africa. Siphiwe Sibeko.

291 The statue of Christ the Redeemer atop Corcovado mountain in Rio is seen lit up in red during a World AIDS Day event. 1 December 2009. Rio de Janeiro, Brazil. Sergio Moraes.

292 U.S. President Barack Obama visits the Great Wall of China. 18 November 2009. Badaling, China. Jason Reed.

293 Military service personnel take pictures of U.S. President Barack Obama at Elmendorf Air Force Base near Anchorage, Alaska. Obama was en route to Tokyo to begin his first trip to Asia as president. 12 November 2009. Anchorage, United States. Jason Reed.

294 South Koreans look north at the Pyeonghwa (meaning 'peace') Observation Post in Ganghwa, near the Military Demarcation Line separating the two Koreas. The navies of the rival Koreas exchanged gunfire for the first time in seven years on 10 November, raising tension just days before U.S. President Barack Obama was scheduled to travel to Asia. 11 November 2009. Ganghwa, South Korea. Jo Yong-Hak.

295 Photographers take pictures of electronic boards showing the Japanese yen's exchange rate against the U.S. dollar at a trading room in Tokyo. 26 November 2009. Tokyo, Japan. Toru Hanai.

296 Investors attend the opening of the Dubai Financial Market. A shock announcement by Dubai on 25 November that it was seeking a repayment freeze on $26 billion worth of debt at troubled state conglomerate Dubai World battered investor confidence in the world's top oil-exporting region and sent shares across the Gulf tumbling. 30 November 2009. Dubai, United Arab Emirates. Ahmed Jadallah.

297 Former Federal Reserve Chairman Alan Greenspan waits to go onstage for an interview at the Newseum in Washington. The interview was part of the First Draft of History event, held by the *Atlantic* magazine and the Aspen Institute to bring together newsmakers, historians and journalists. 2 October 2009. Washington, DC, United States. Jonathan Ernst.

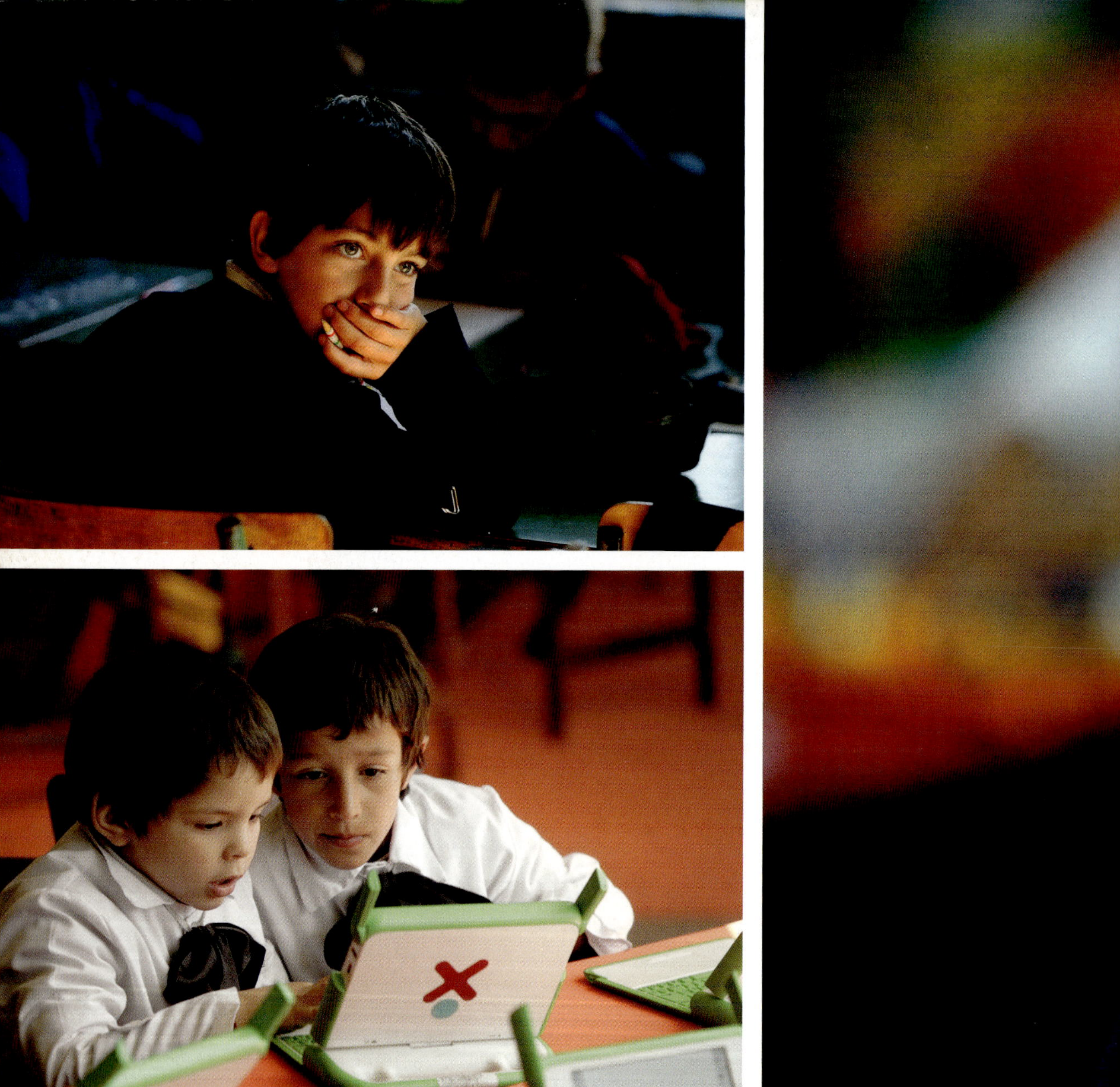

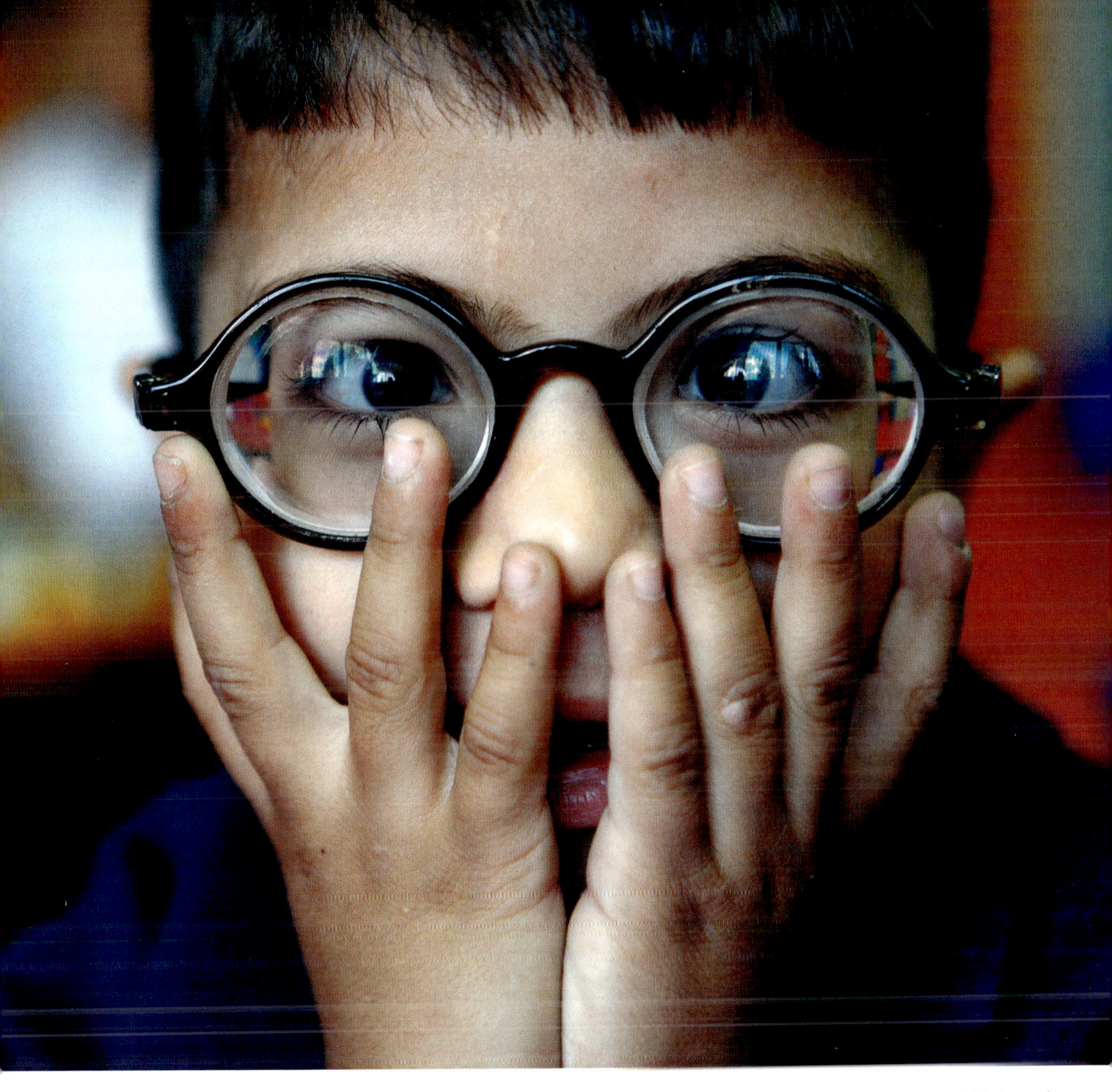

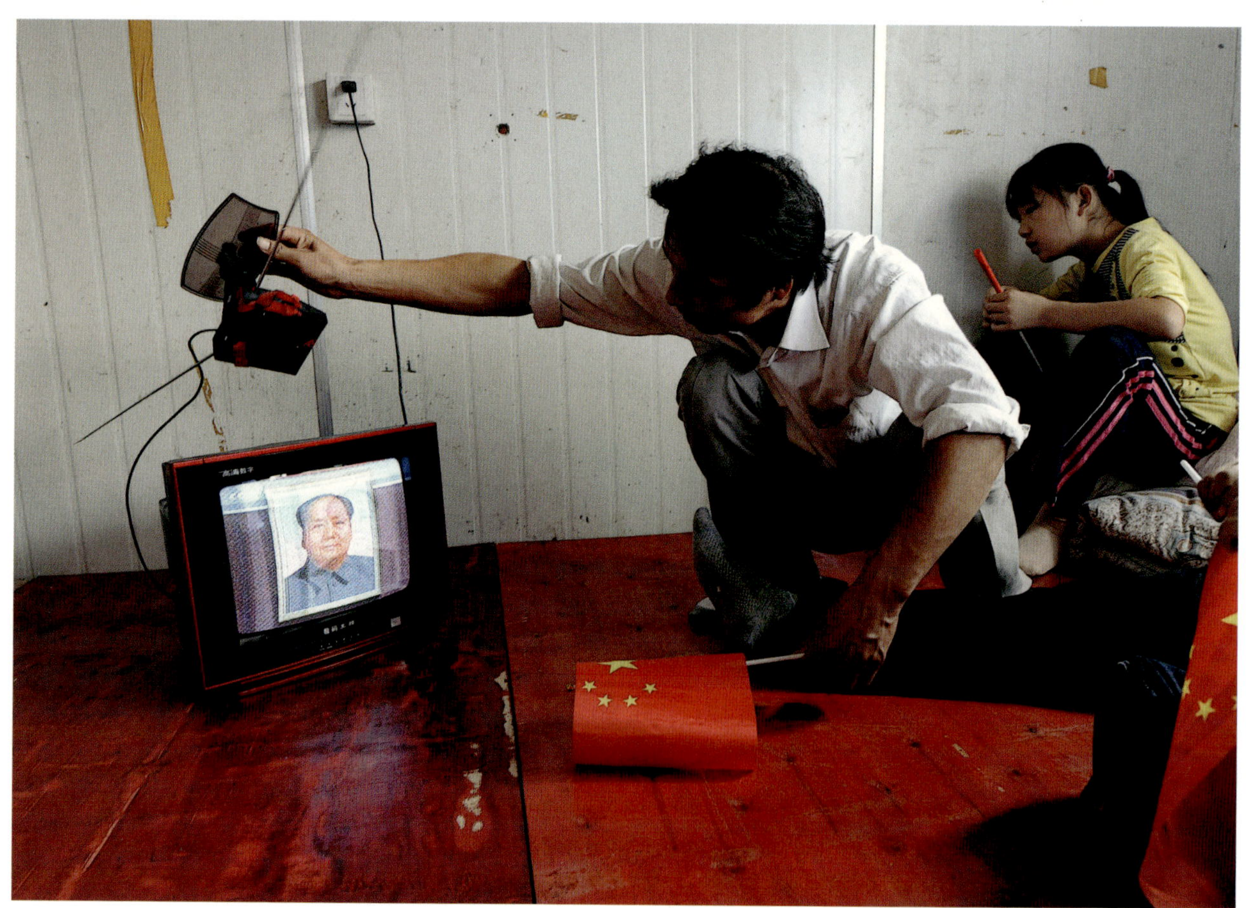

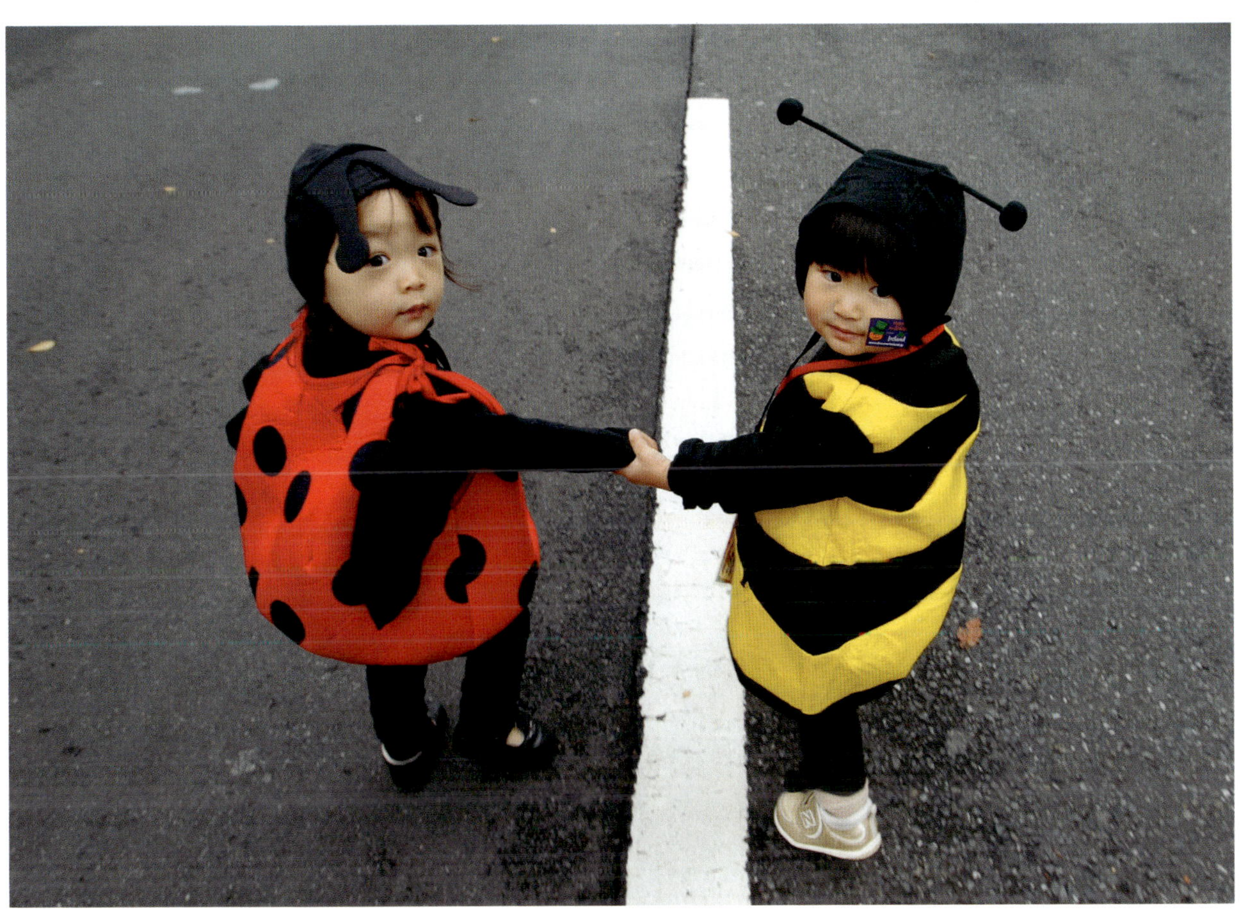

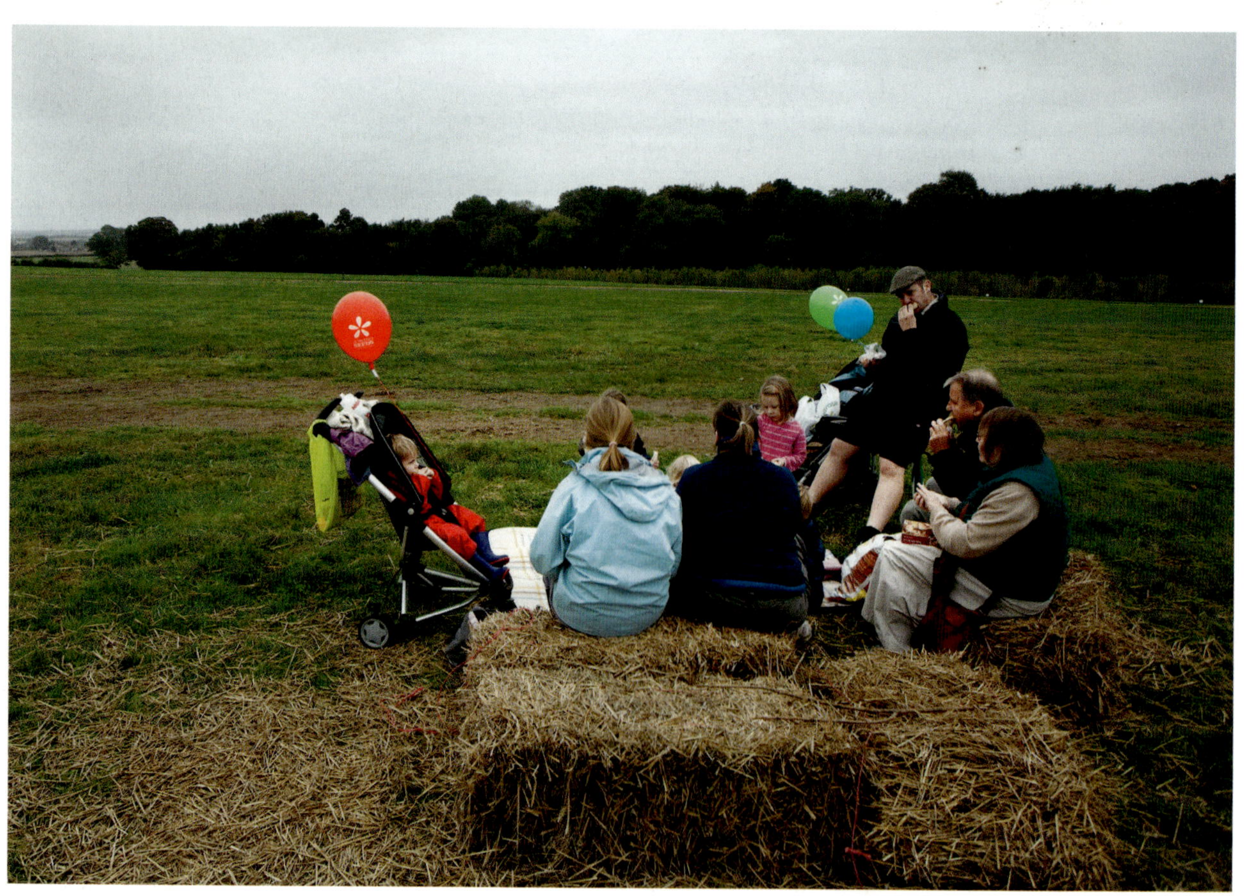

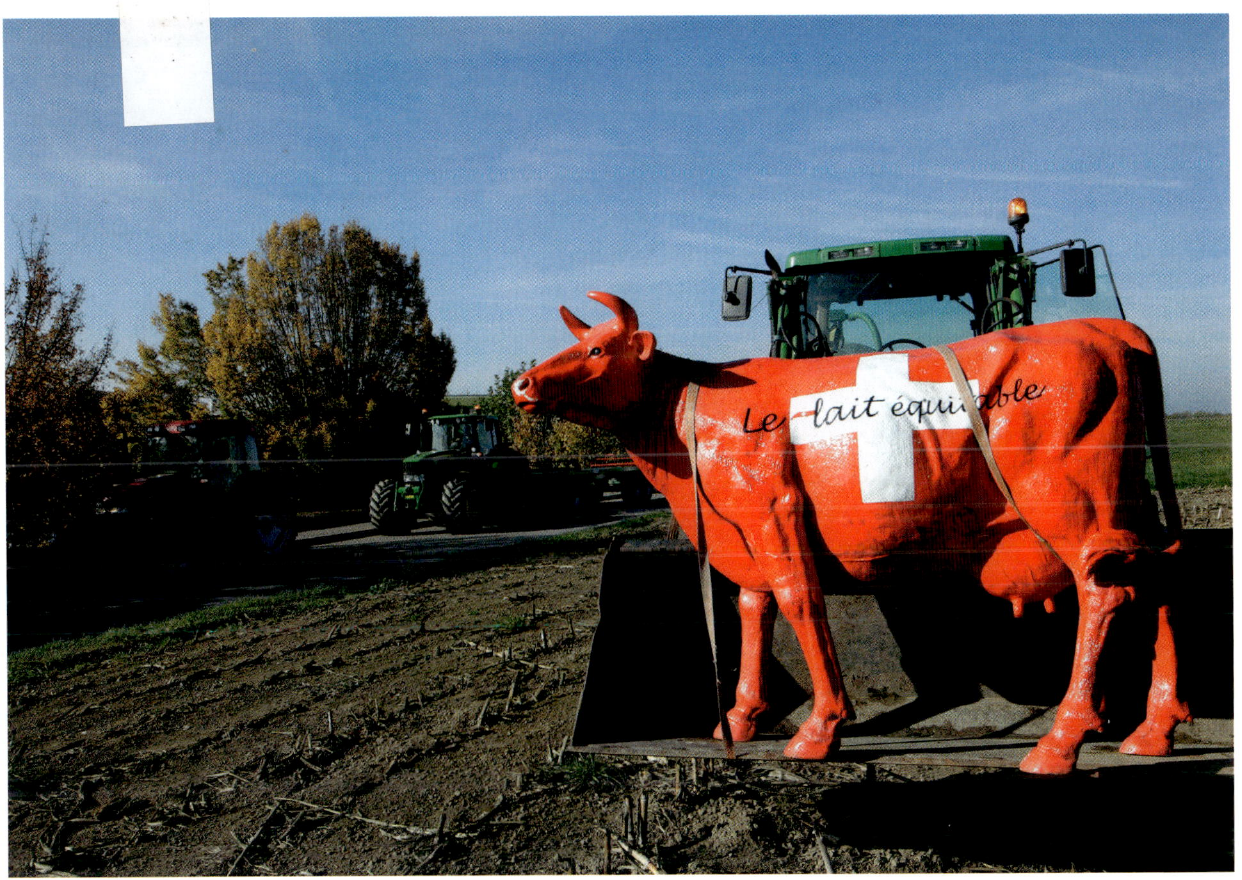
Le lait équitable

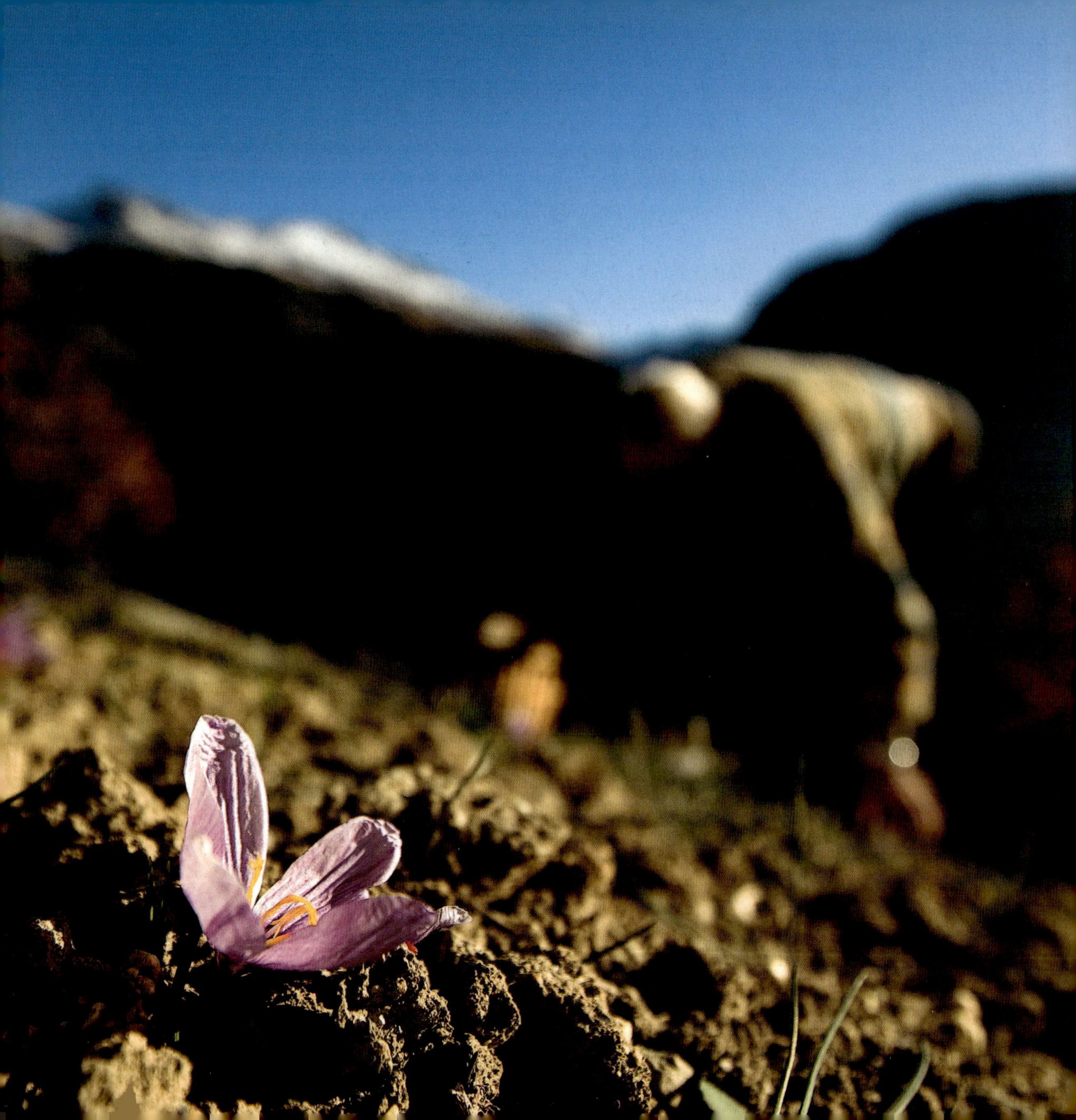

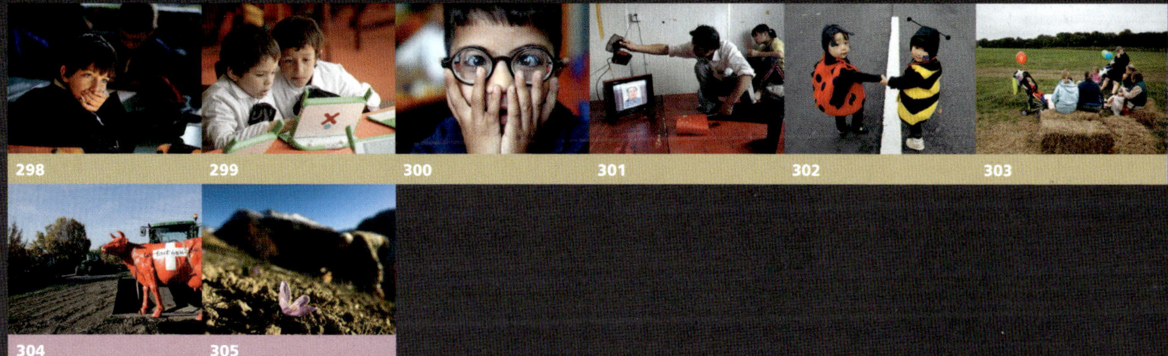

298   299   300   301   302   303   304   305

298   A boy sits in class at the Trifun Panovski elementary school in the village of Dihovo in southwestern Macedonia. The prime minister pledged a computer for every student in the landlocked Balkan country during an election campaign in 2009. Given the poor conditions and many basic needs in Macedonia's ageing schools, some question whether the 60-million euro ($90 million) programme is an appropriate allocation of resources. 18 November 2009. Dihovo, Macedonia. Ognen Teofilovski.

299   First graders work with XO laptop computers at a public school in Montevideo. The Uruguayan government has provided a low-cost XO to every public school child in the country under the 'Plan CEIBAL' programme. 13 October 2009. Montevideo, Uruguay. Andres Stapff.

300   Wadee Daoud, a 5-year-old visually impaired Palestinian boy, reacts to the light as a teacher opens the window blinds in his classroom at the Helen Keller Centre for blind and visually impaired children in the East Jerusalem neighbourhood of Beit Hanina. Dr Helen Keller visited the school in the 1950s and agreed for it to adopt her name. 10 September 2009. Jerusalem. Yannis Behrakis.

301   A migrant worker adjusts a television aerial at a dormitory in Hefei, Anhui province, to get a better reception of the live broadcast of the parade in Beijing to mark the 60th anniversary of the founding of the People's Republic of China. 1 October 2009. Hefei, China. Jianan Yu.

302   Children take part in a Halloween parade in Tokyo. 25 October 2009. Tokyo, Japan. Yuriko Nakao.

303   A family eat a picnic lunch sitting on hay bales at the Cranborne Chase Woodfair, a typical English country fair, at Tollard Royal in Dorset. 11 October 2009. Tollard Royal, Britain. Kevin Coombs.

304   A convoy of tractors belonging to Swiss milk producers arrives at the Cremo building in Le Mont near Lausanne, where farmers staged a demonstration against low milk prices. The slogan on the model cow reads 'Fair priced milk'. 28 October 2009. Le Mont, Switzerland. Denis Balibouse.

305   Otto Andres picks flowers of *Crocus sativus* near the Swiss mountain village of Mund. About 120 planters cultivate the saffron crocus in the region of Mund at an altitude of 1,200 metres (4,000 feet). It takes some 130,000 flowers or 390,000 stigmas to produce 1 kg (2.2 lb) of the dried spice, which is sold for a price of 15,000 Swiss francs ($14,500) per kilogram. 30 October 2009. Mund, Switzerland. Michael Buholzer.

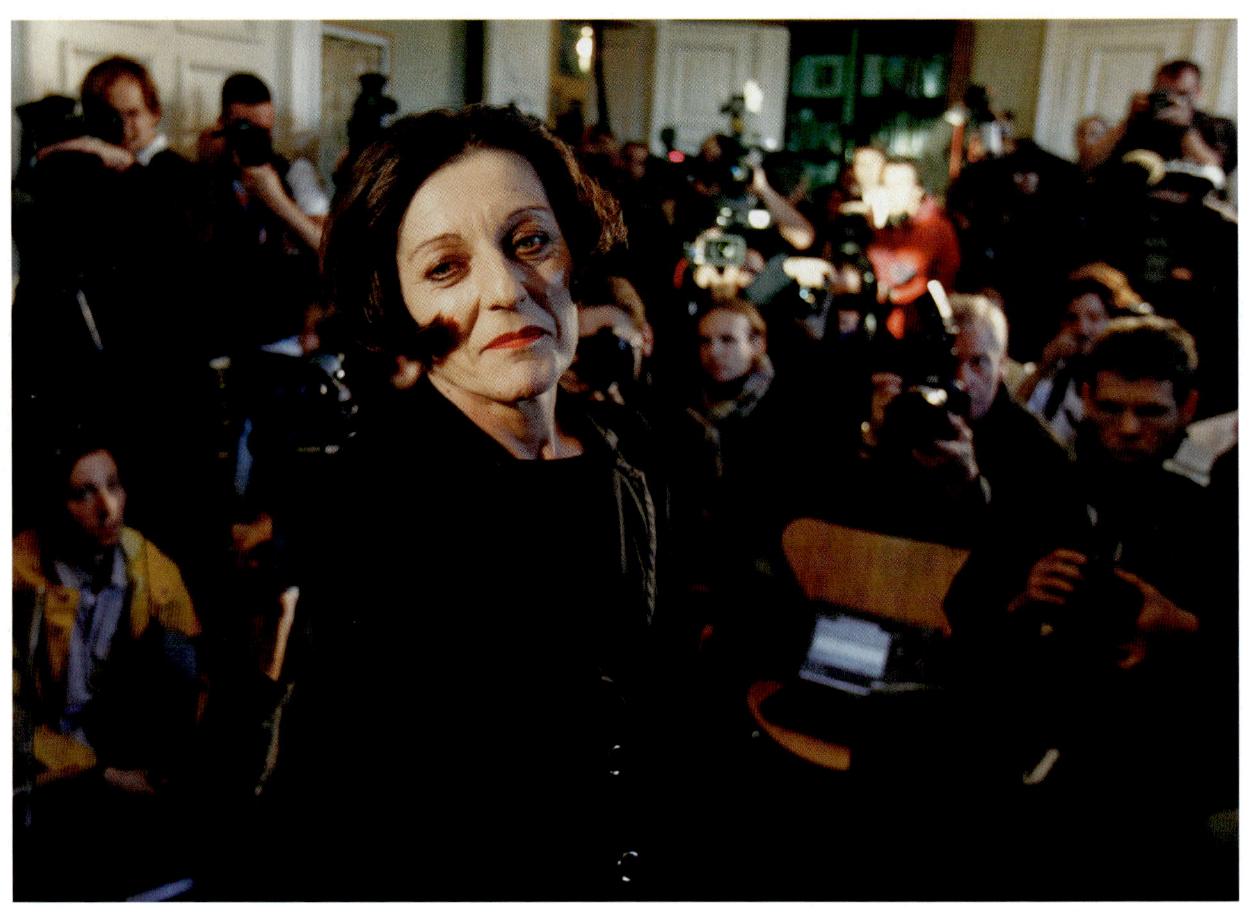

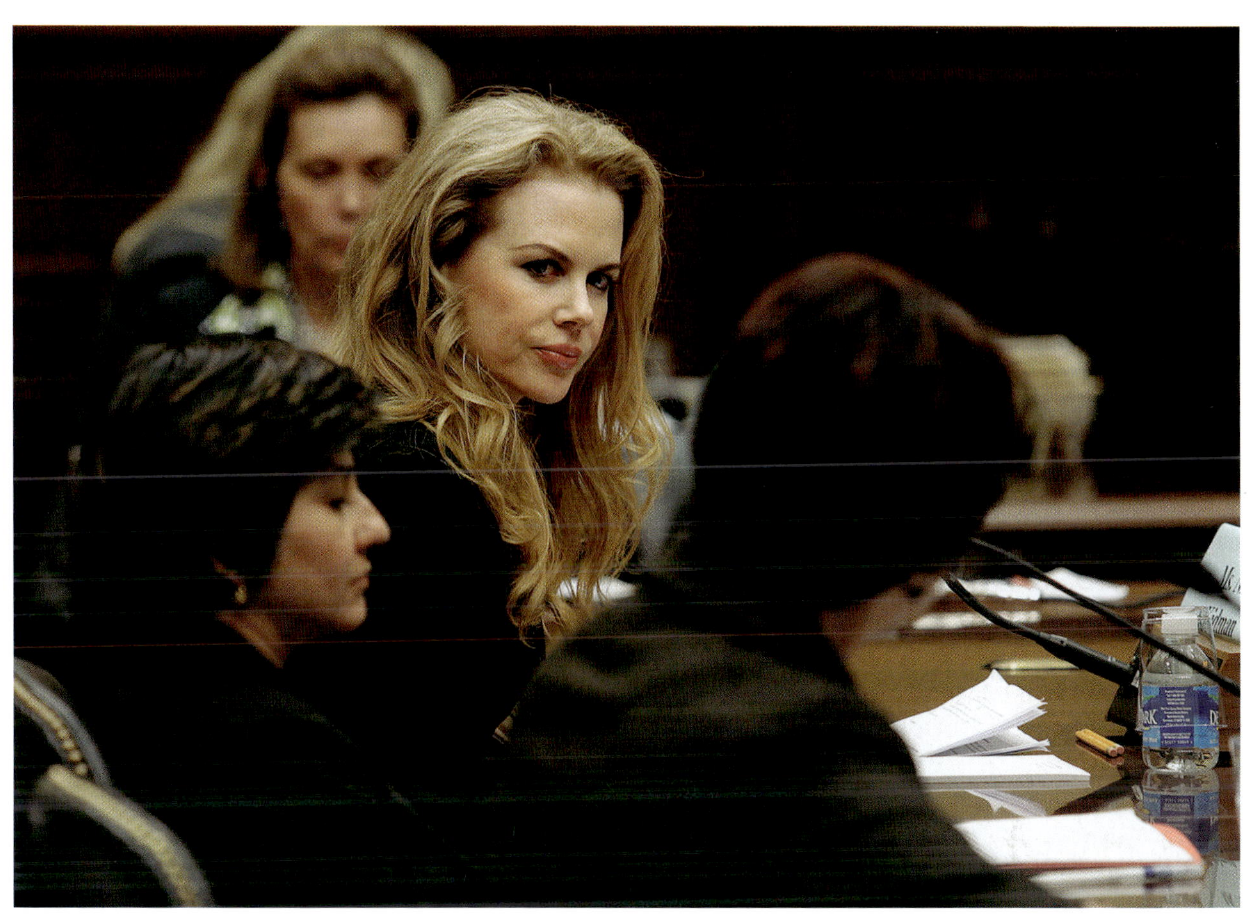

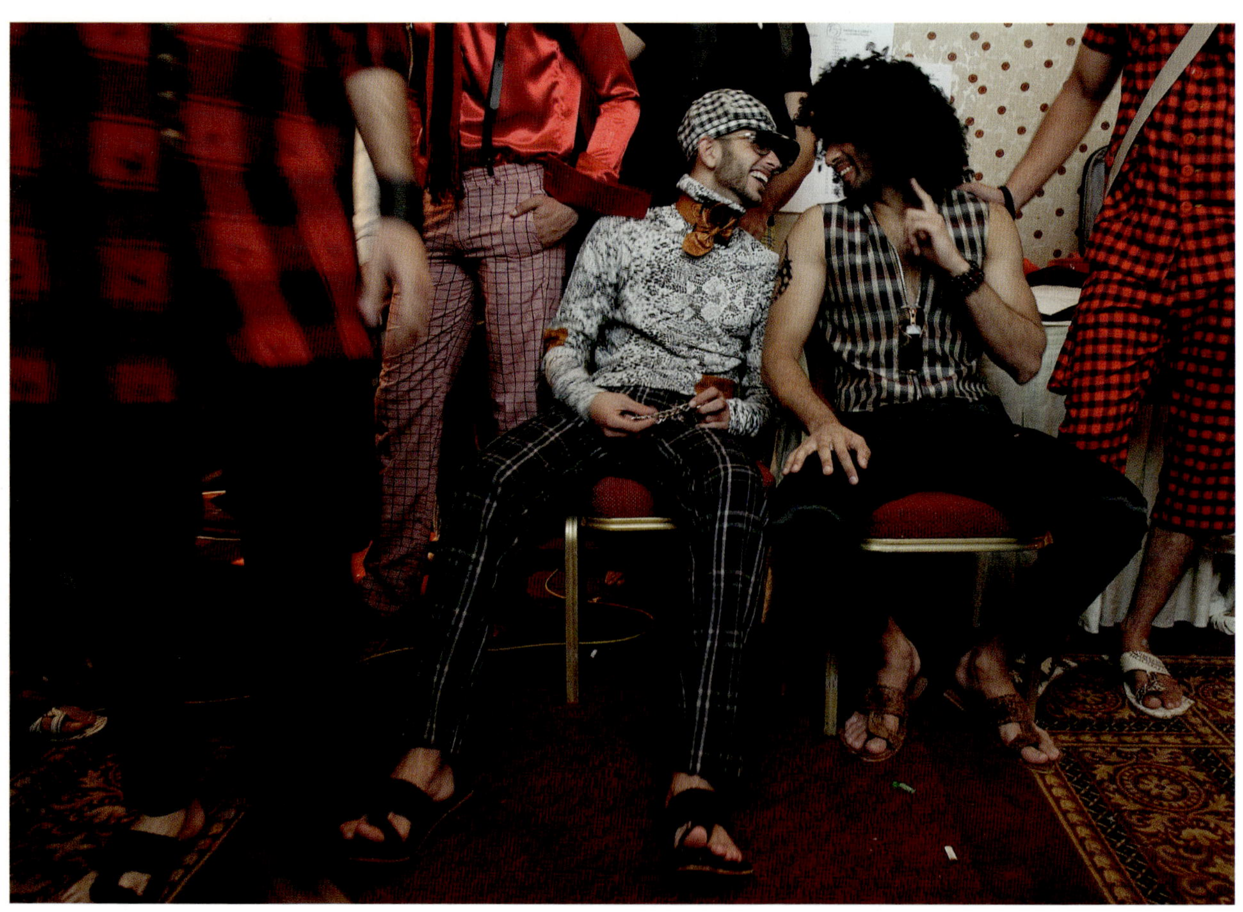

308 Karachi, Pakistan

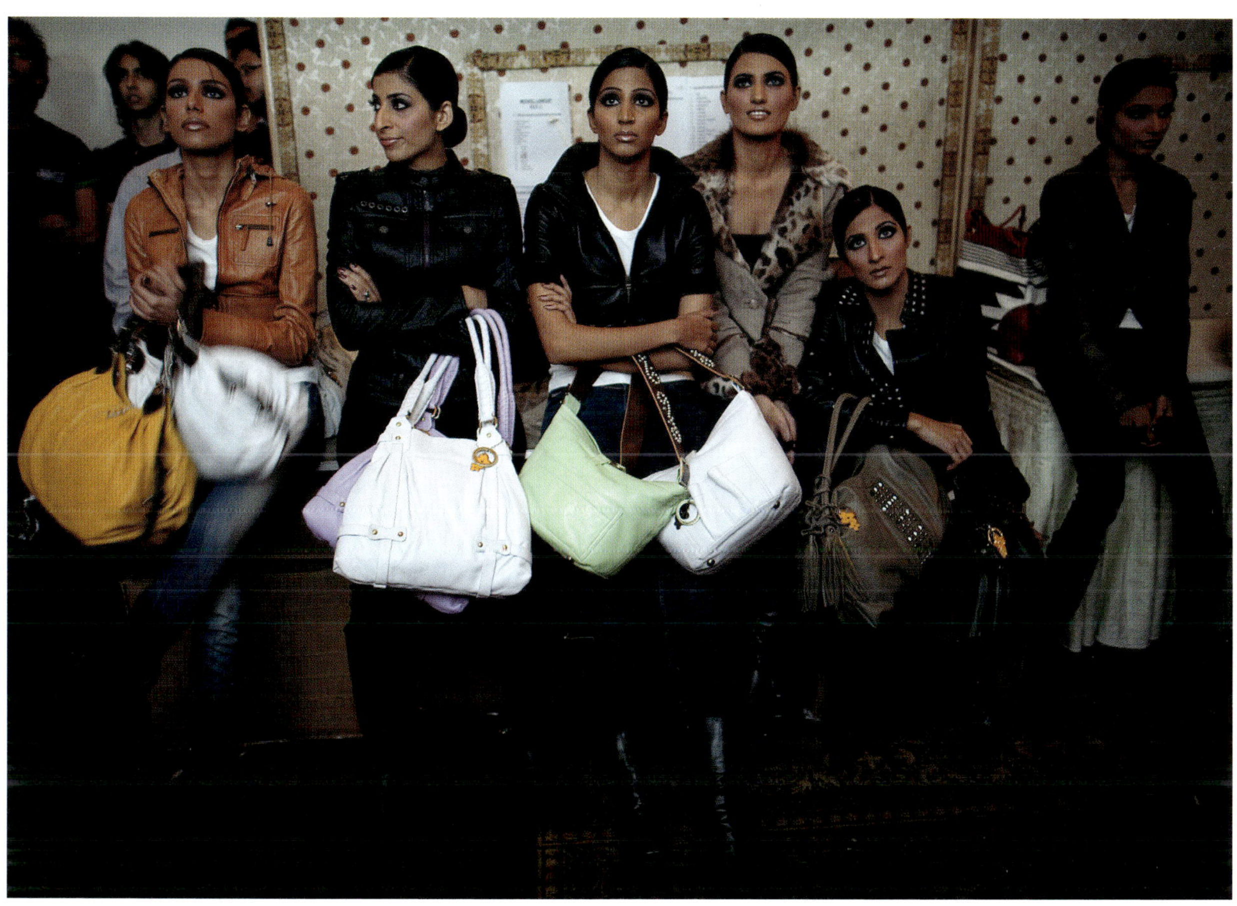

309 Karachi, Pakistan

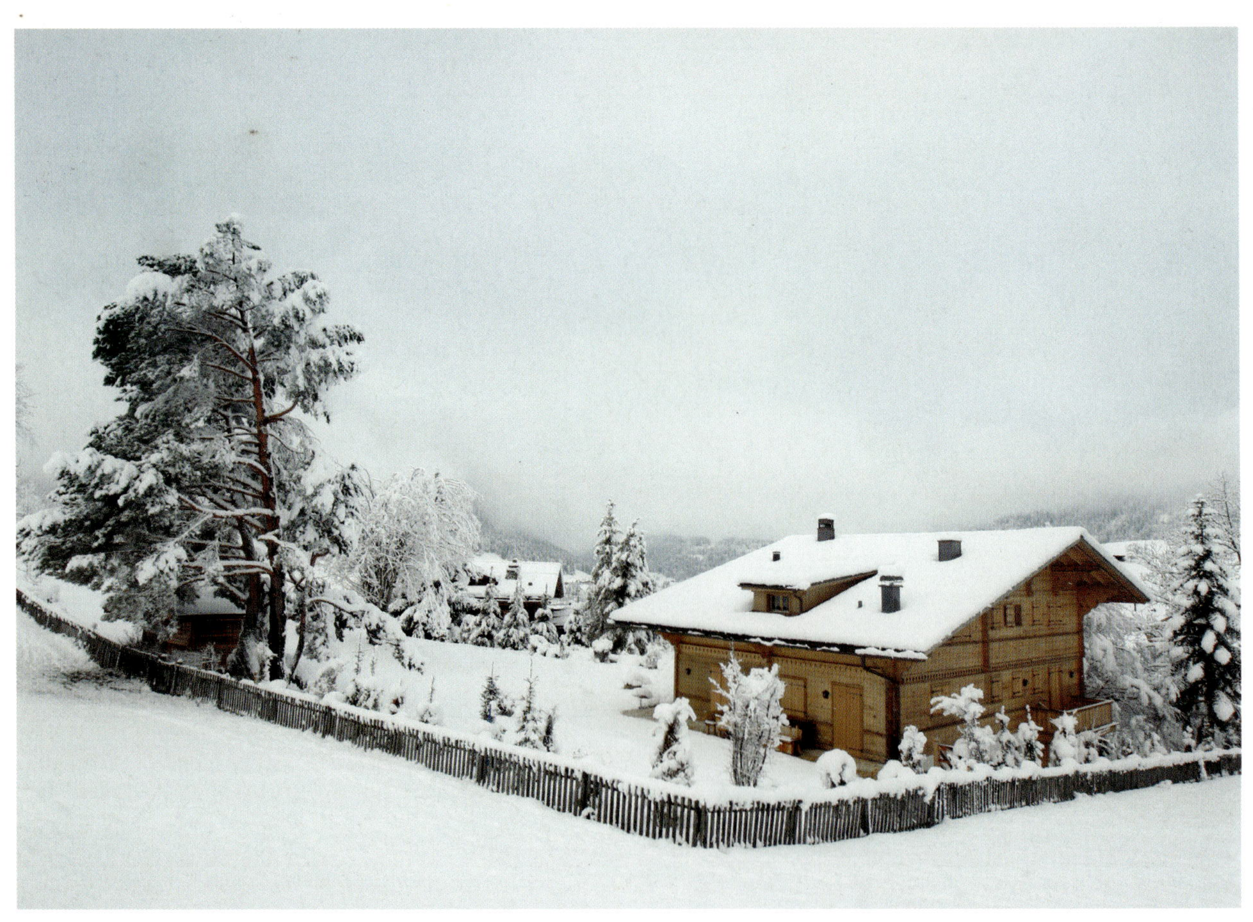

310 Gstaad, Switzerland

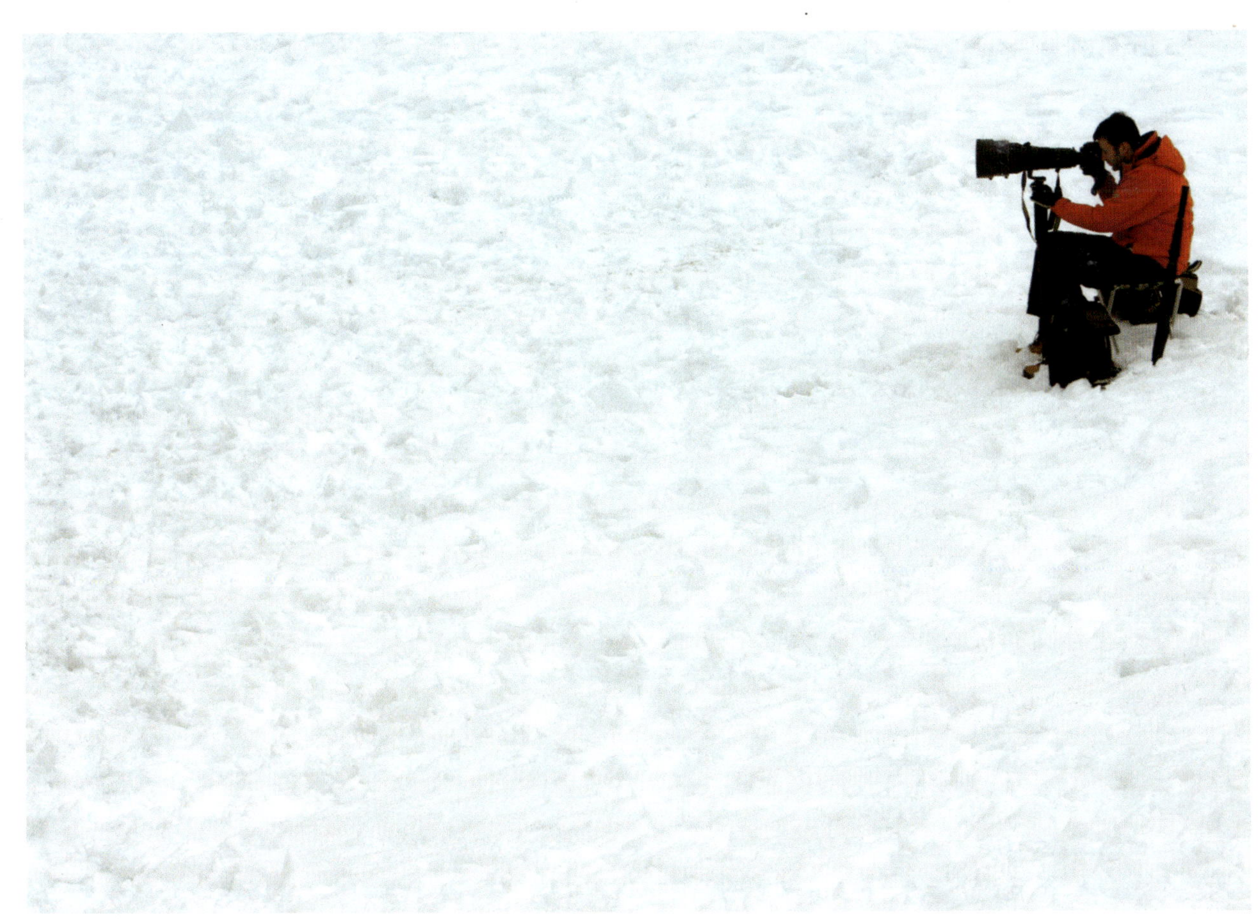

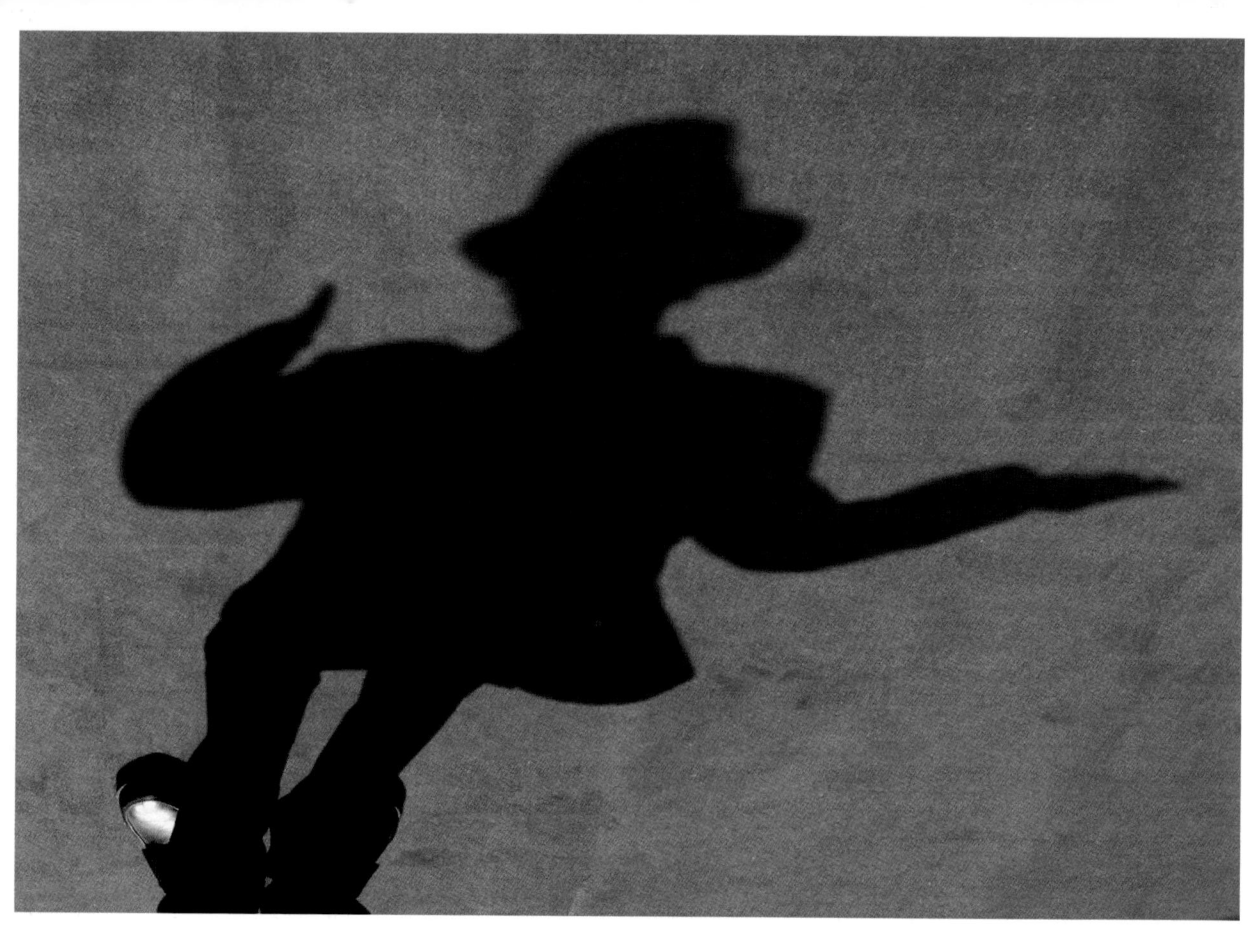

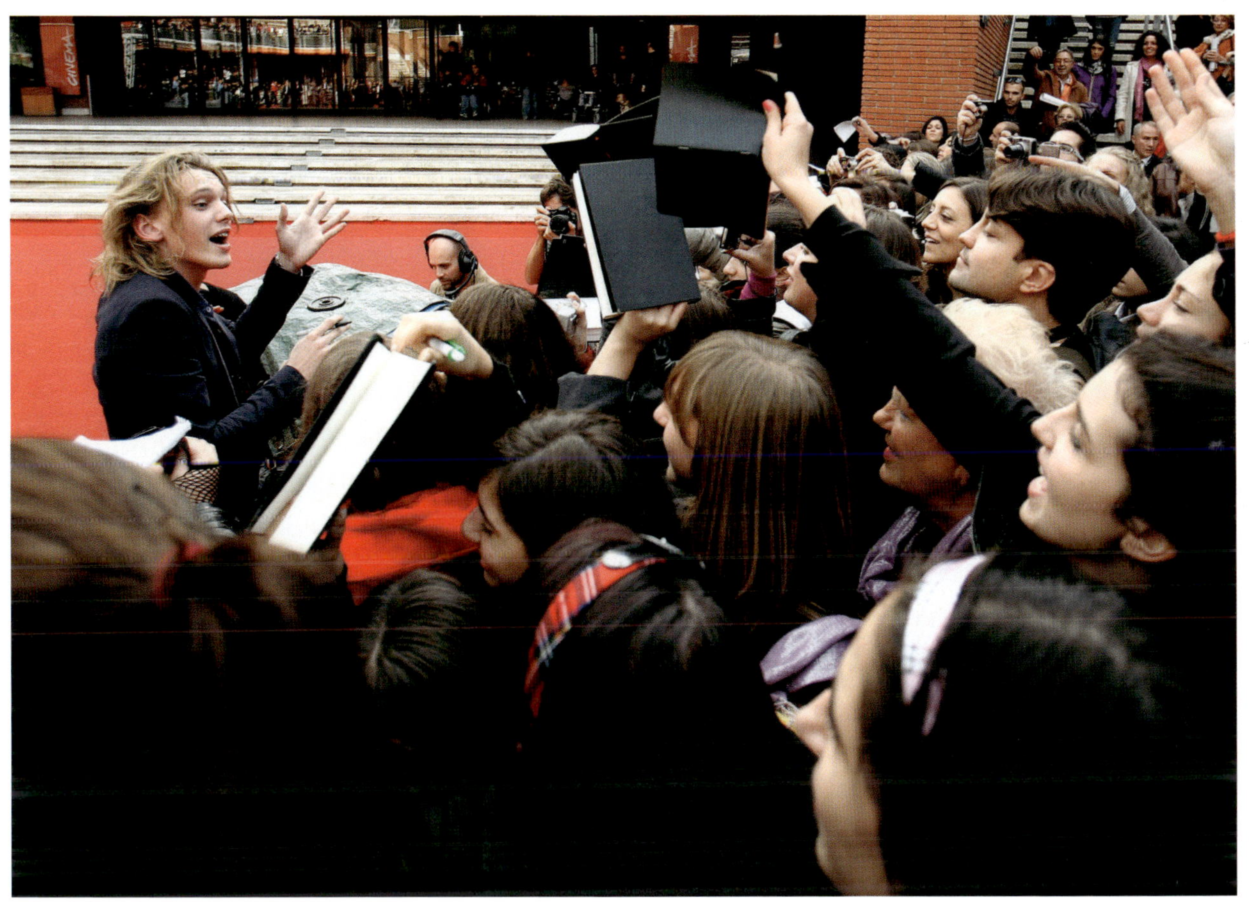

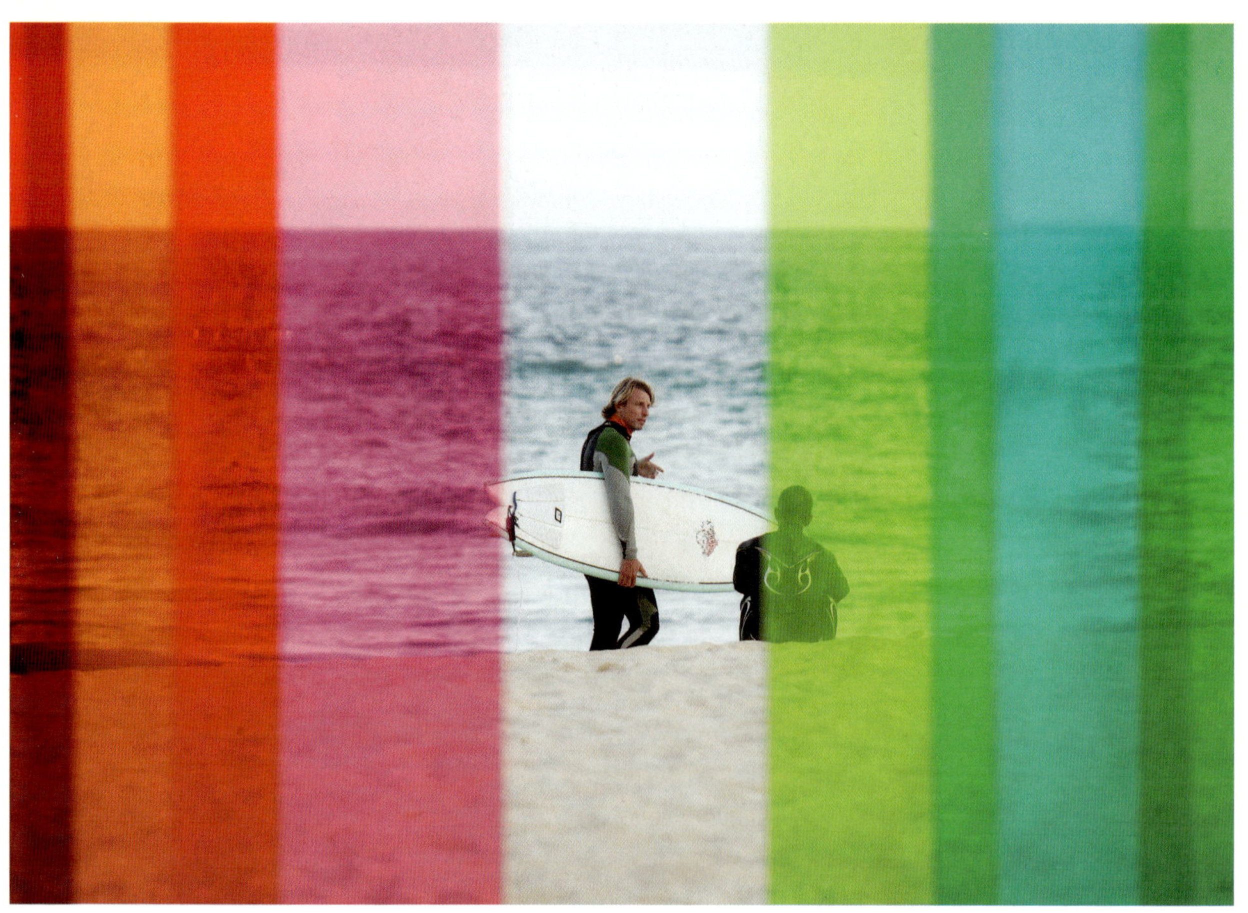

314 Sydney, Australia

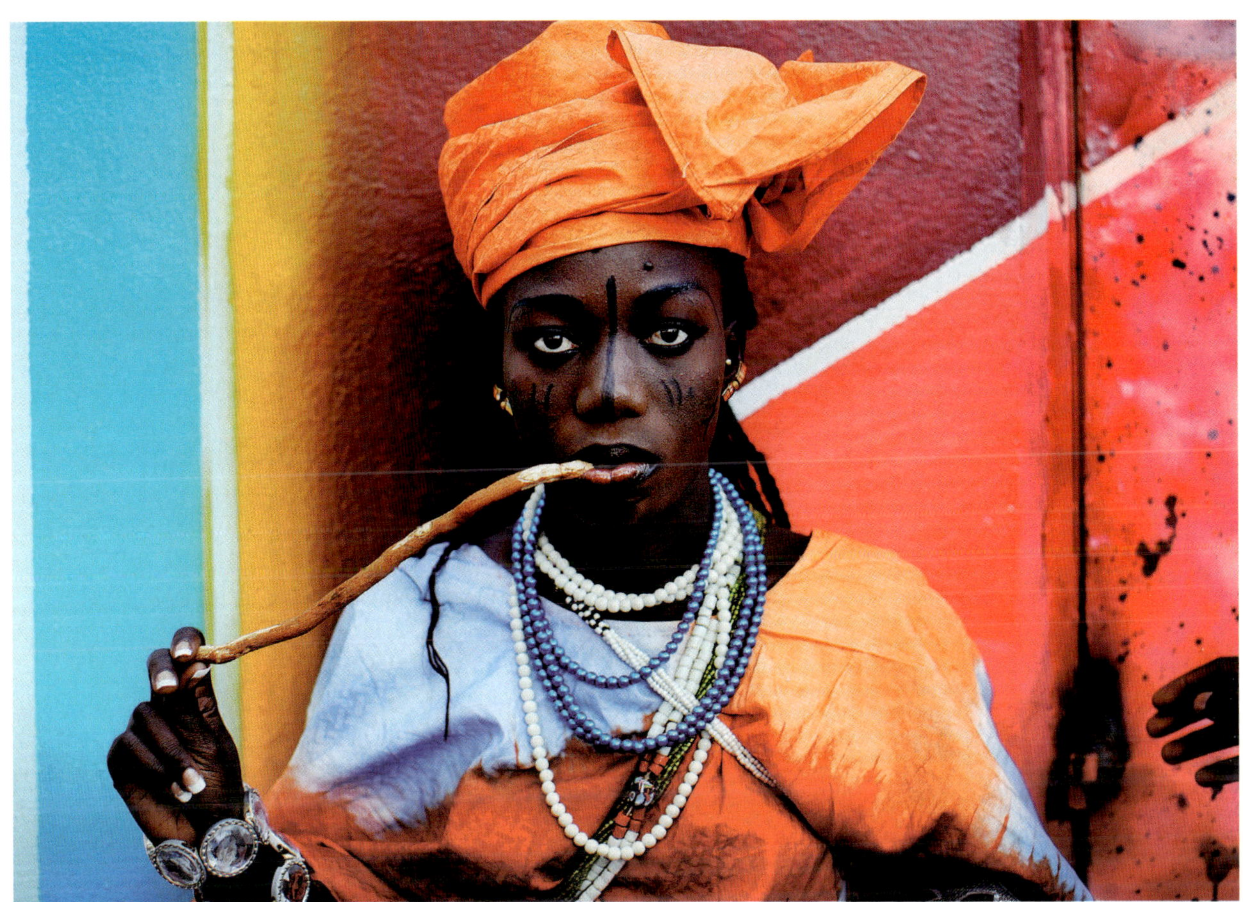

315 Dakar, Senegal

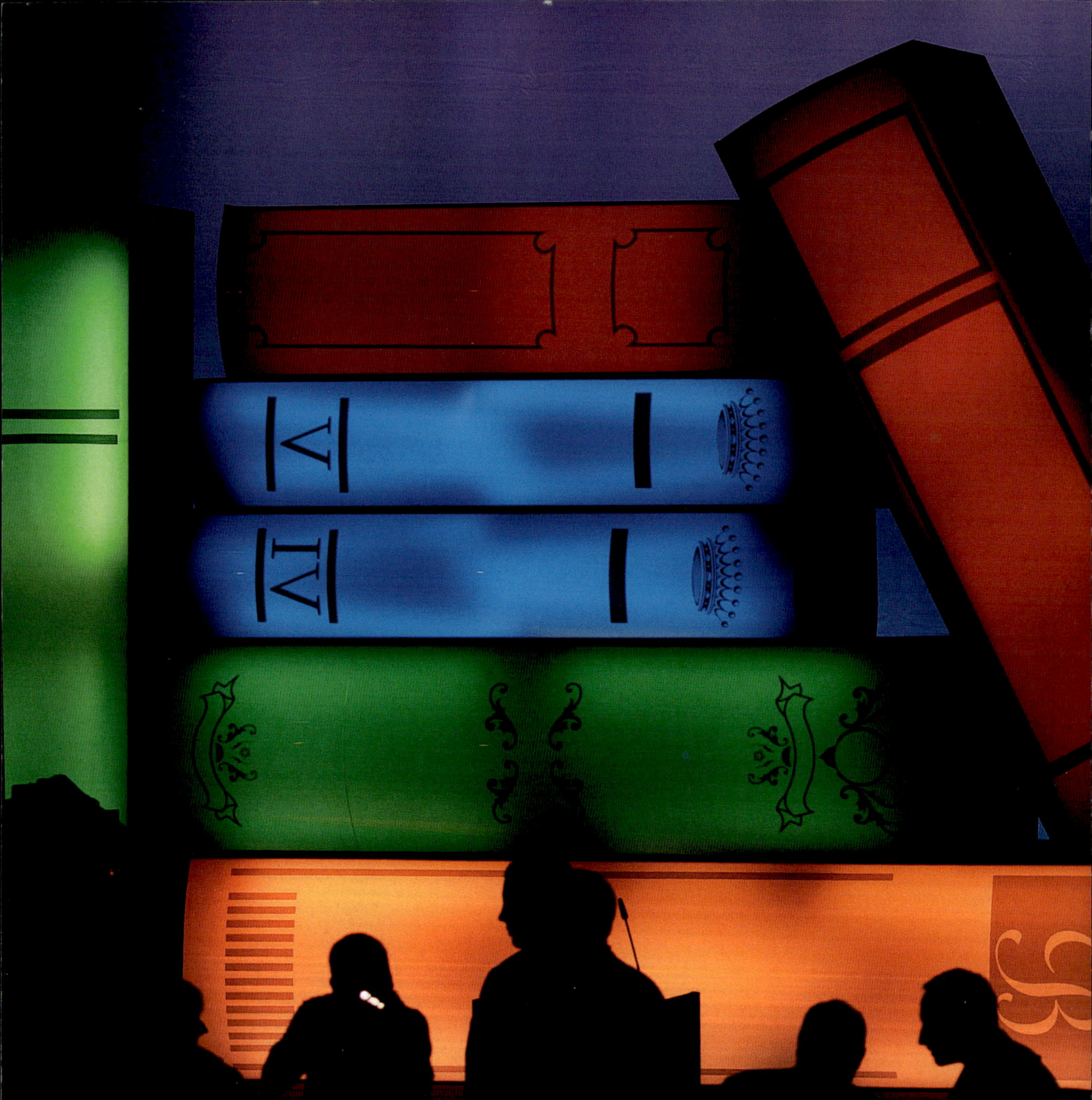

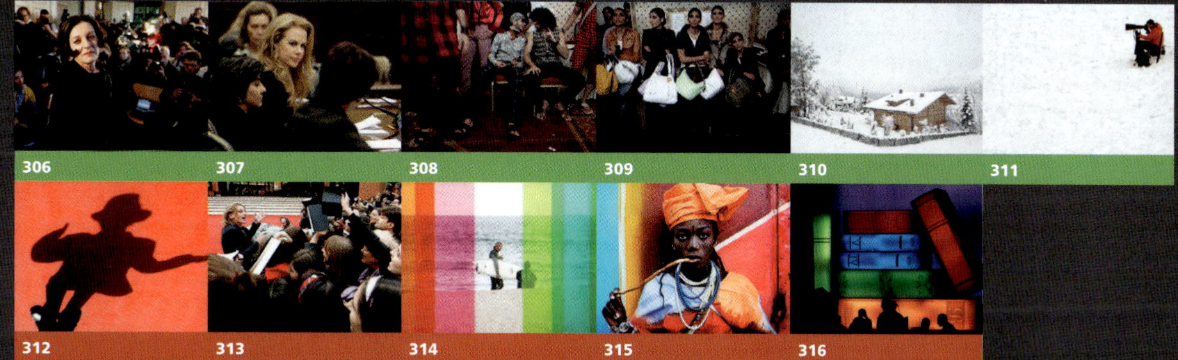

306 Herta Müller, winner of the 2009 Nobel Prize in Literature, stands before a news conference in Berlin. The Romanian-born German writer said that Nicolae Ceauşescu's brutal dictatorship had compelled her to write. 8 October 2009. Berlin, Germany. Fabrizio Bensch.

307 Actress Nicole Kidman prepares to testify on violence against women before the House Foreign Affairs committee on Capitol Hill in Washington. Kidman is a goodwill ambassador for UNIFEM, the U.N. Development Fund for Women. 21 October 2009. Washington, DC, United States. Yuri Gripas.

308 Male models, wearing creations by Pakistani designer Yazir Mirza, wait backstage during Fashion Pakistan Week in Karachi. The four-day event was rescheduled twice due to security concerns. 5 November 2009. Karachi, Pakistan. Adrees Latif.

309 Models sporting creations by Pakistani designer Ayesha await their turn to take the catwalk during Fashion Pakistan Week. 4 November 2009. Karachi, Pakistan. Adrees Latif.

310 The luxury chalet of Oscar-winning film director Roman Polanski is seen in the mountain resort of Gstaad. He was arrested on 26 September at the request of the United States upon his arrival in Switzerland to receive a lifetime achievement award at a film festival. The Swiss authorities released him into house arrest while he fought extradition. Polanski fled the United States in 1978 on the eve of his sentencing after pleading guilty to a charge of unlawful sex with a 13-year-old girl. 1 December 2009. Gstaad, Switzerland. Christian Hartmann.

311 A photographer sits in a meadow near the chalet belonging to film director Roman Polanski. 6 December 2009. Gstaad, Switzerland. Arnd Wiegmann.

312 A shadow of a dancer impersonating Michael Jackson is cast on the red carpet during the Taiwan premiere of Jackson's posthumous movie *This Is It*. The movie was culled from 80 hours of videotape taken of rehearsals for a series of London concerts that had been scheduled for July. 28 October 2009. Taipei, Taiwan. Nicky Loh.

313 Actor Jamie Campbell Bower signs autographs ahead of a 20-minute preview screening of the movie *The Twilight Saga: New Moon* at the Rome Film Festival. 22 October 2009. Rome, Italy. Alessia Pierdomenico.

314 Two surfers are seen behind Nicholas Elias's sculpture *A Symbolic Inscription of the Imaginary* as part of the 'Sculpture by the Sea' exhibition at Tamarama beach in Sydney. This free outdoor exhibition, in its 13th year, displays artworks along a 2 km (1.25 mile) stretch of Sydney's shore. 29 October 2009. Sydney, Australia. Daniel Munoz.

315 An actress from the Dseu Renaissance de Pikine theatre group, wearing traditional Toukouleur make-up and chewing a stick toothbrush, waits for a rehearsal to begin at a community centre in the slum neighbourhood of Pikine in Senegal's capital, Dakar. 7 November 2009. Dakar, Senegal. Finbarr O'Reilly.

316 People stand in front of the stage during the opening ceremony of the annual Frankfurt Book Fair. 13 October 2009. Frankfurt, Germany. Johannes Eisele.

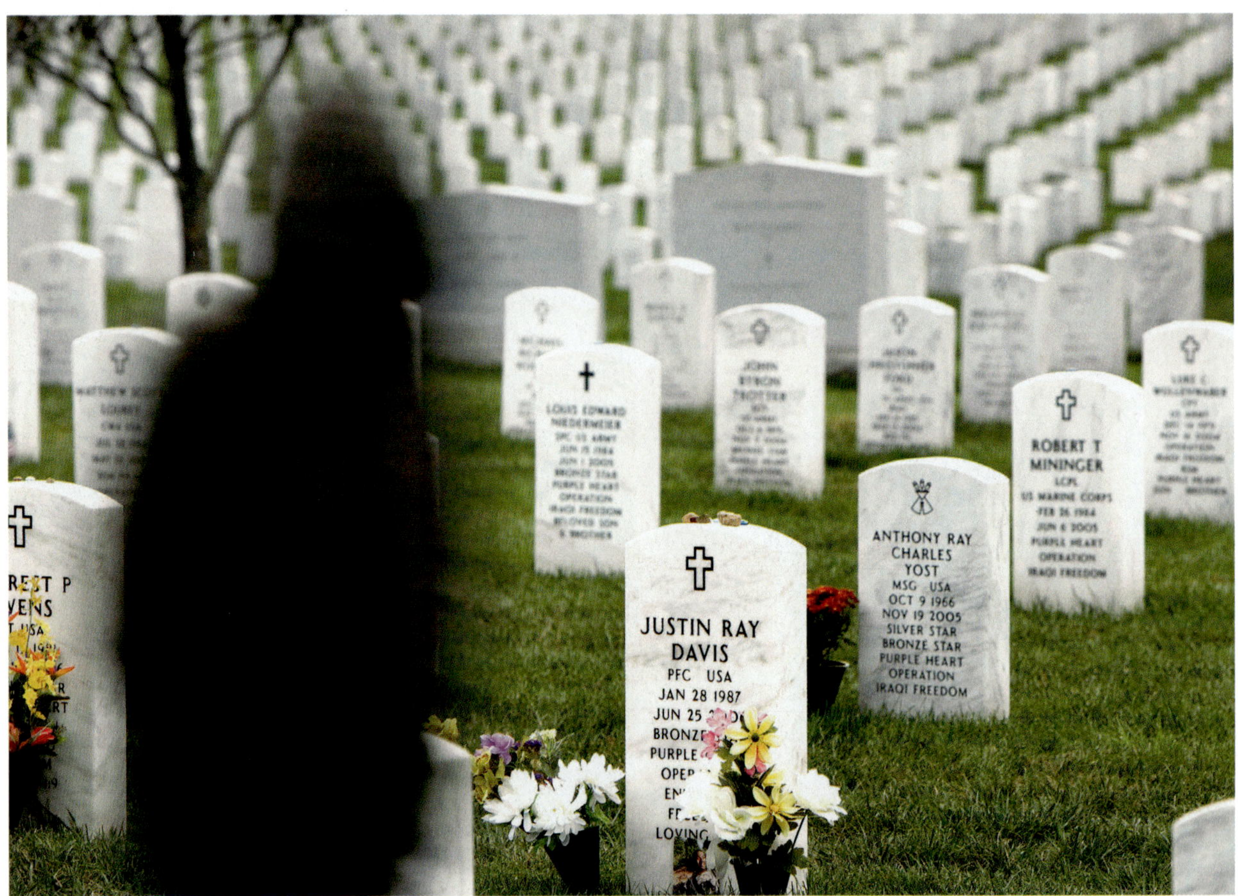

317 Washington, DC, United States

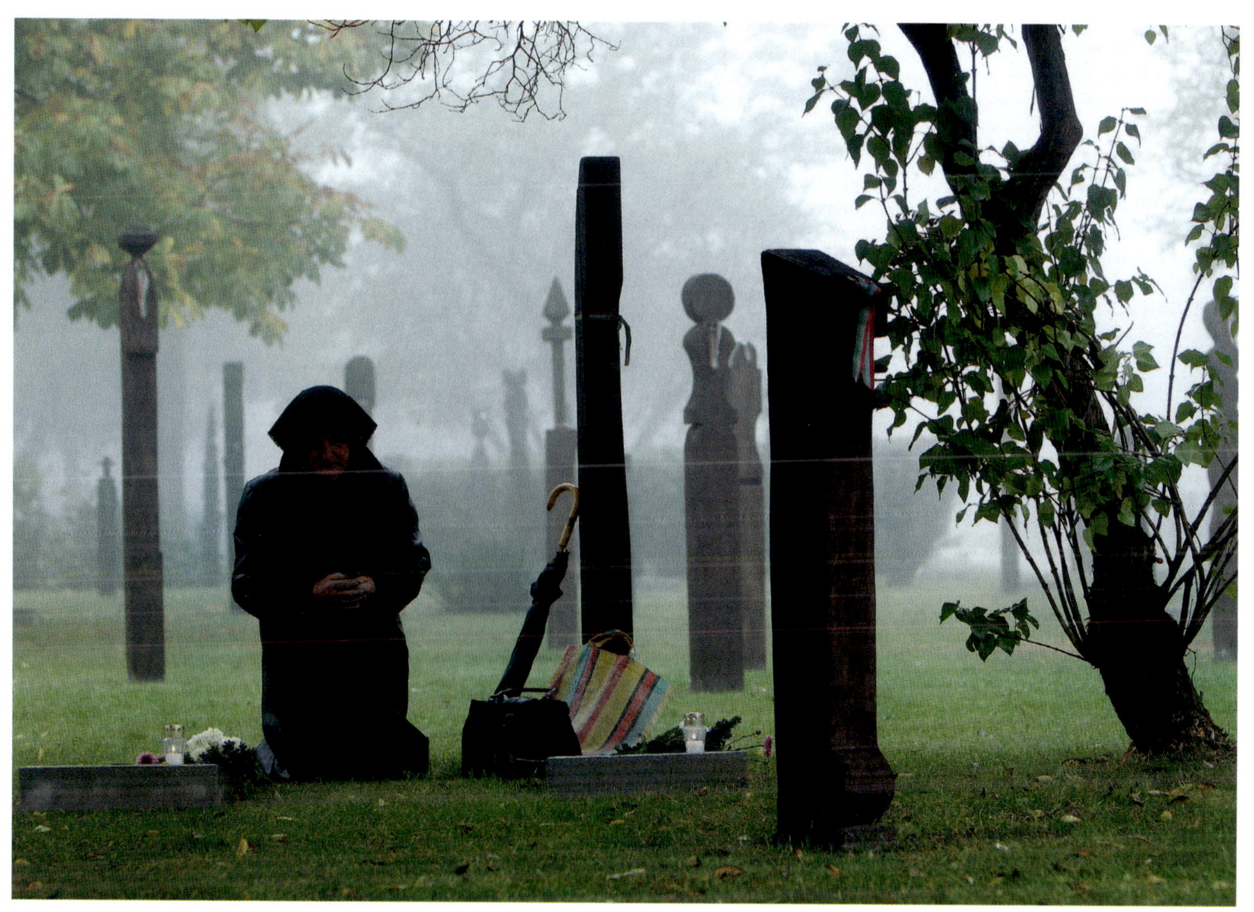

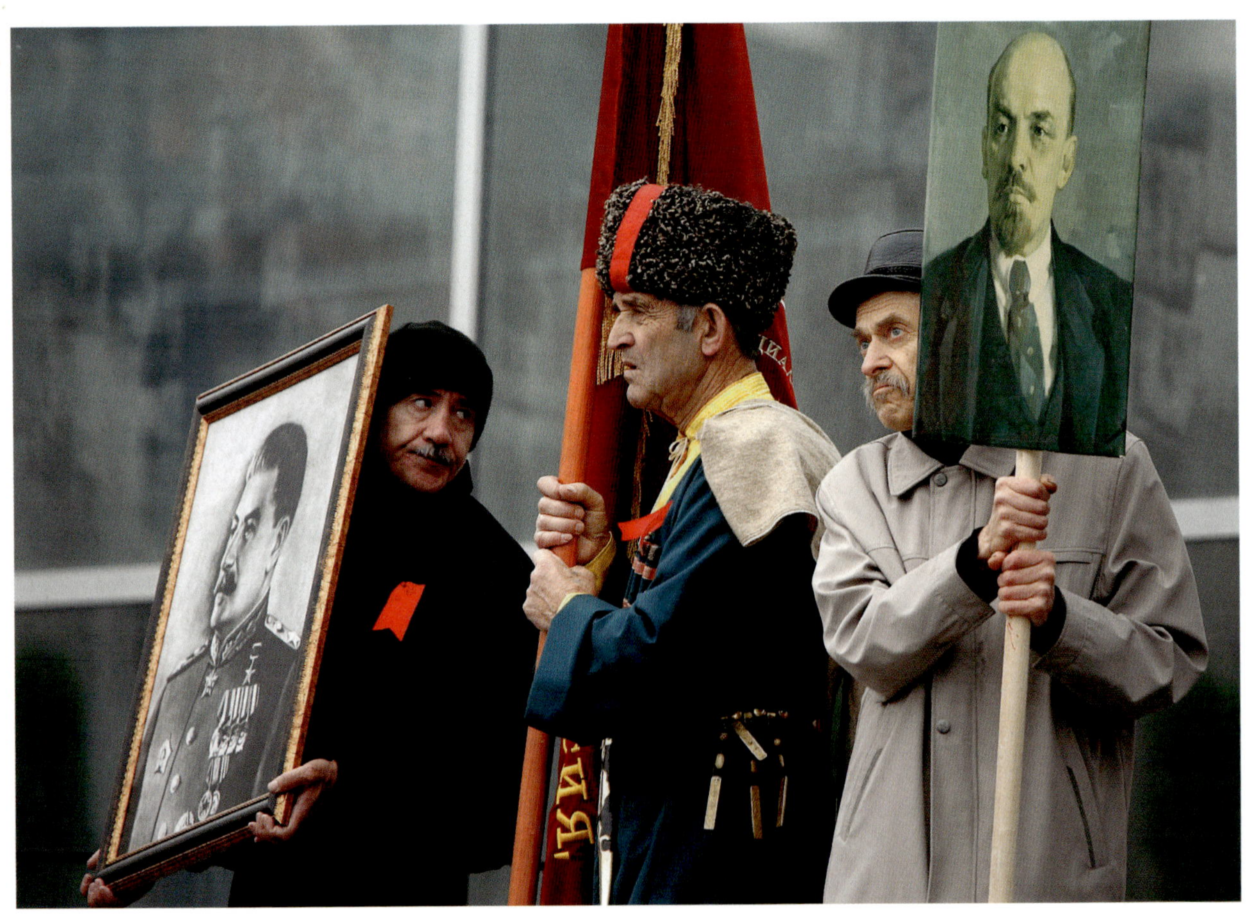

319 Vladikavkaz, Russia

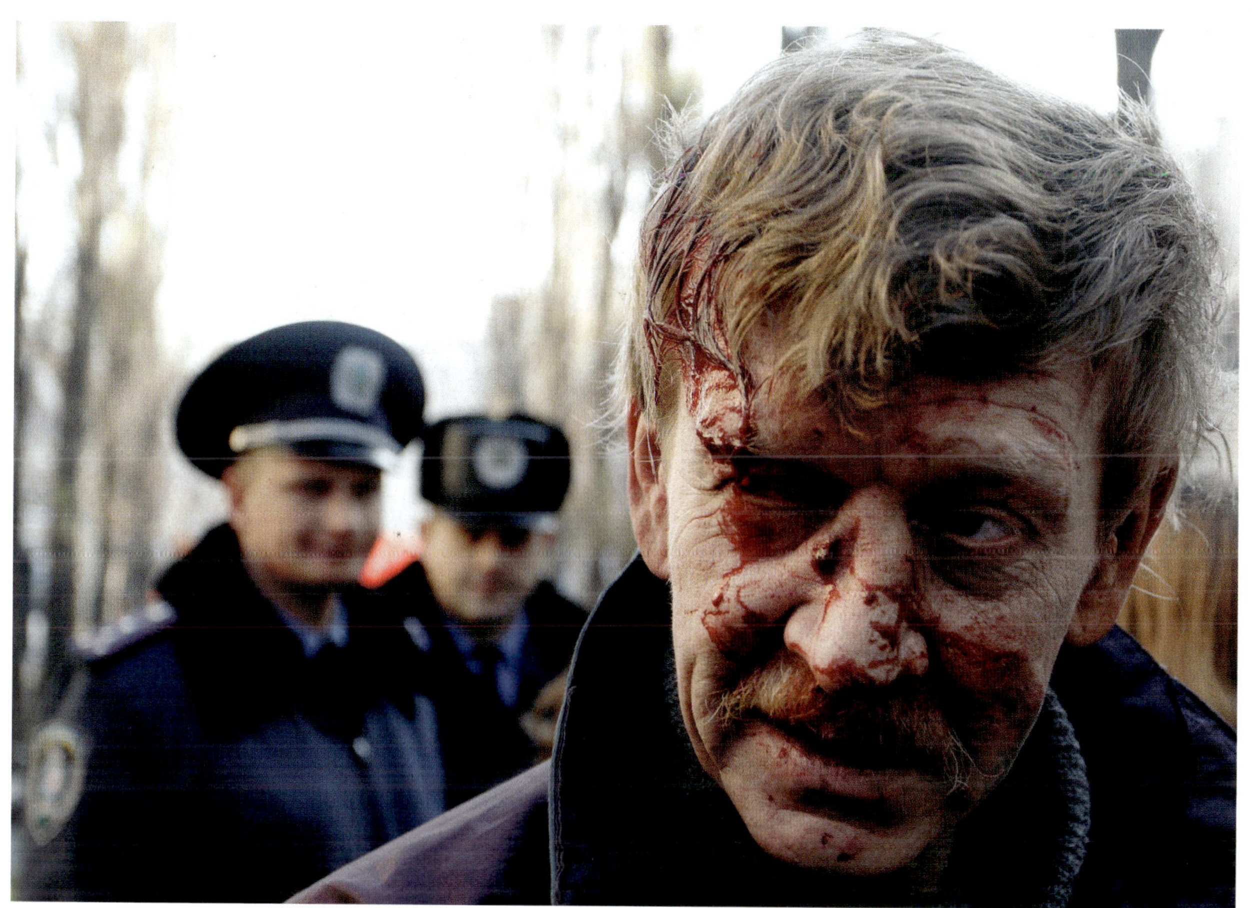

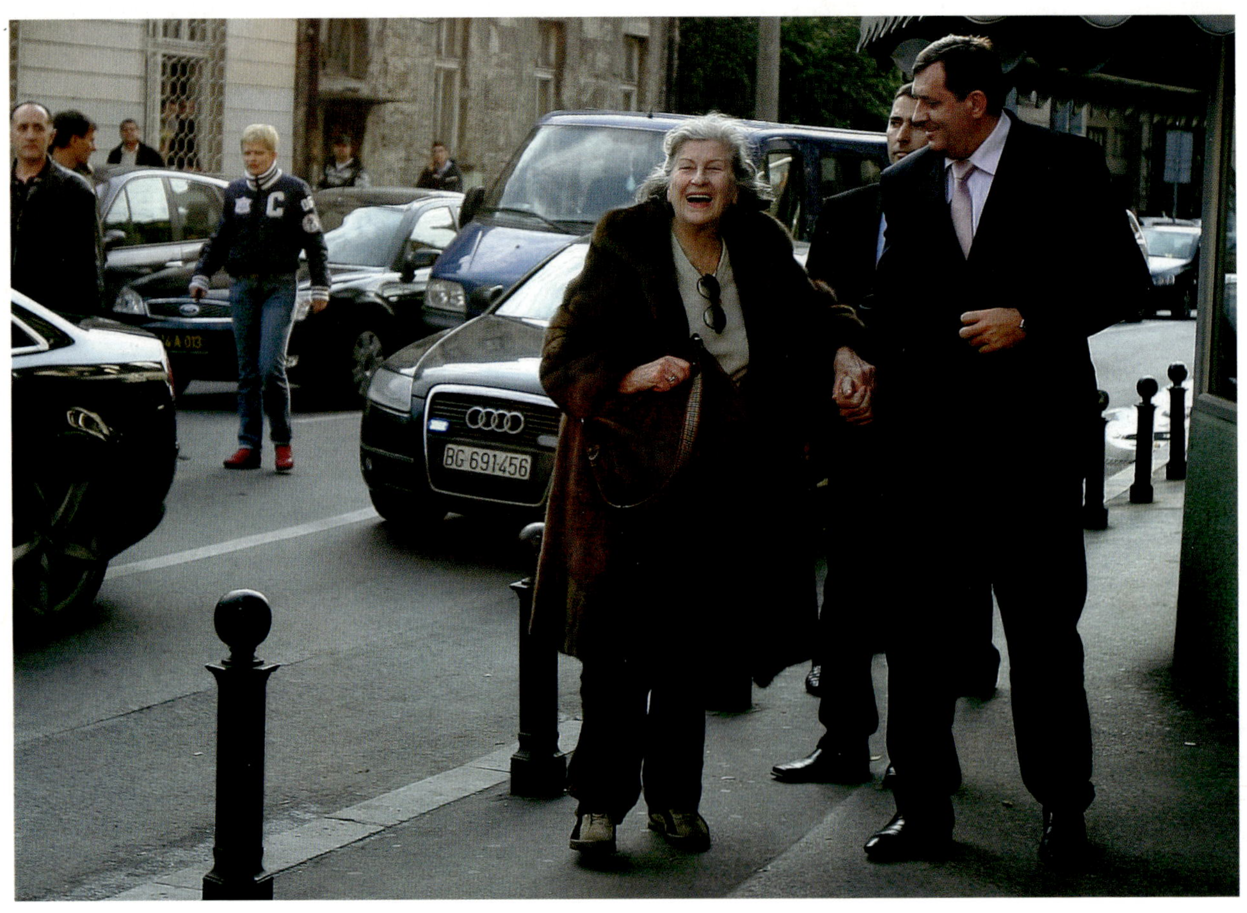

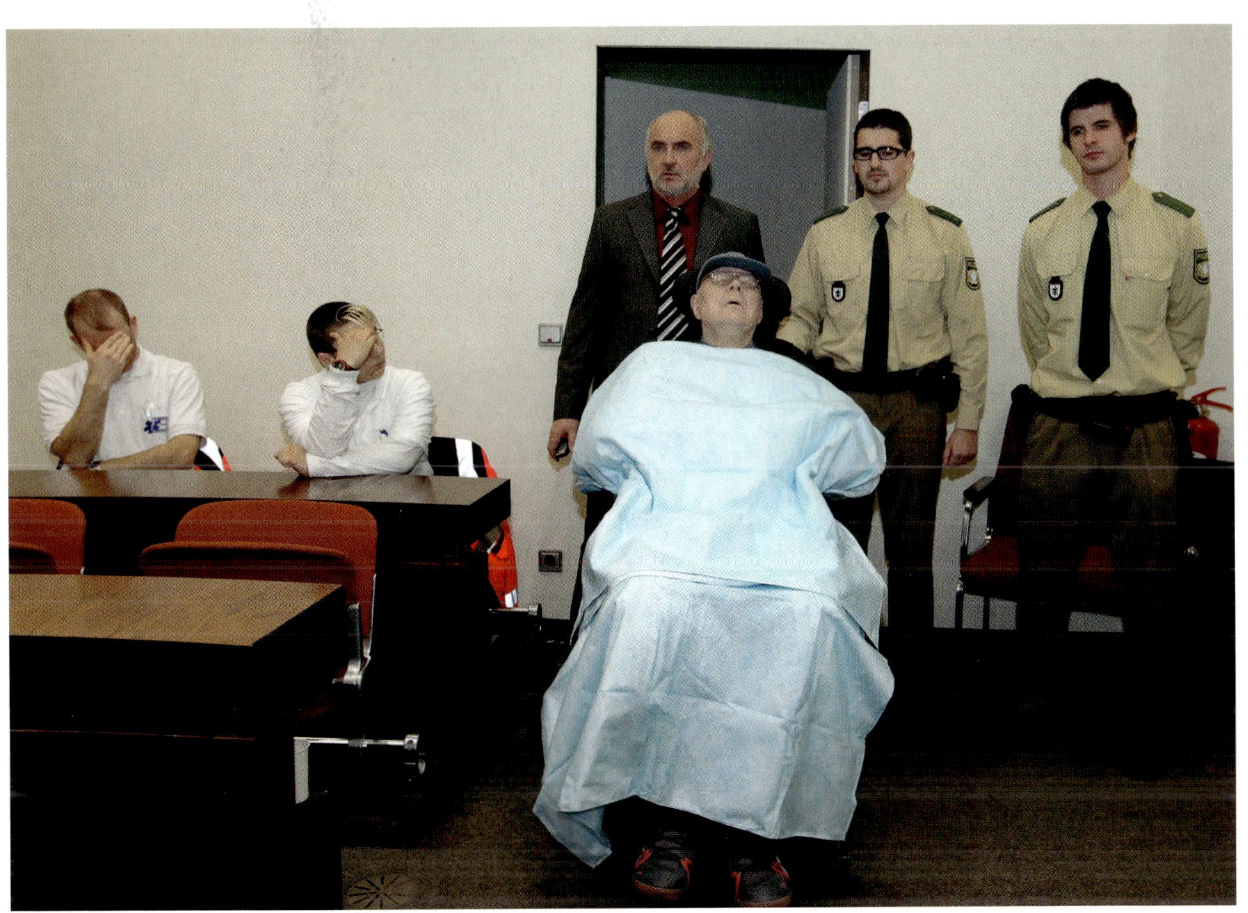

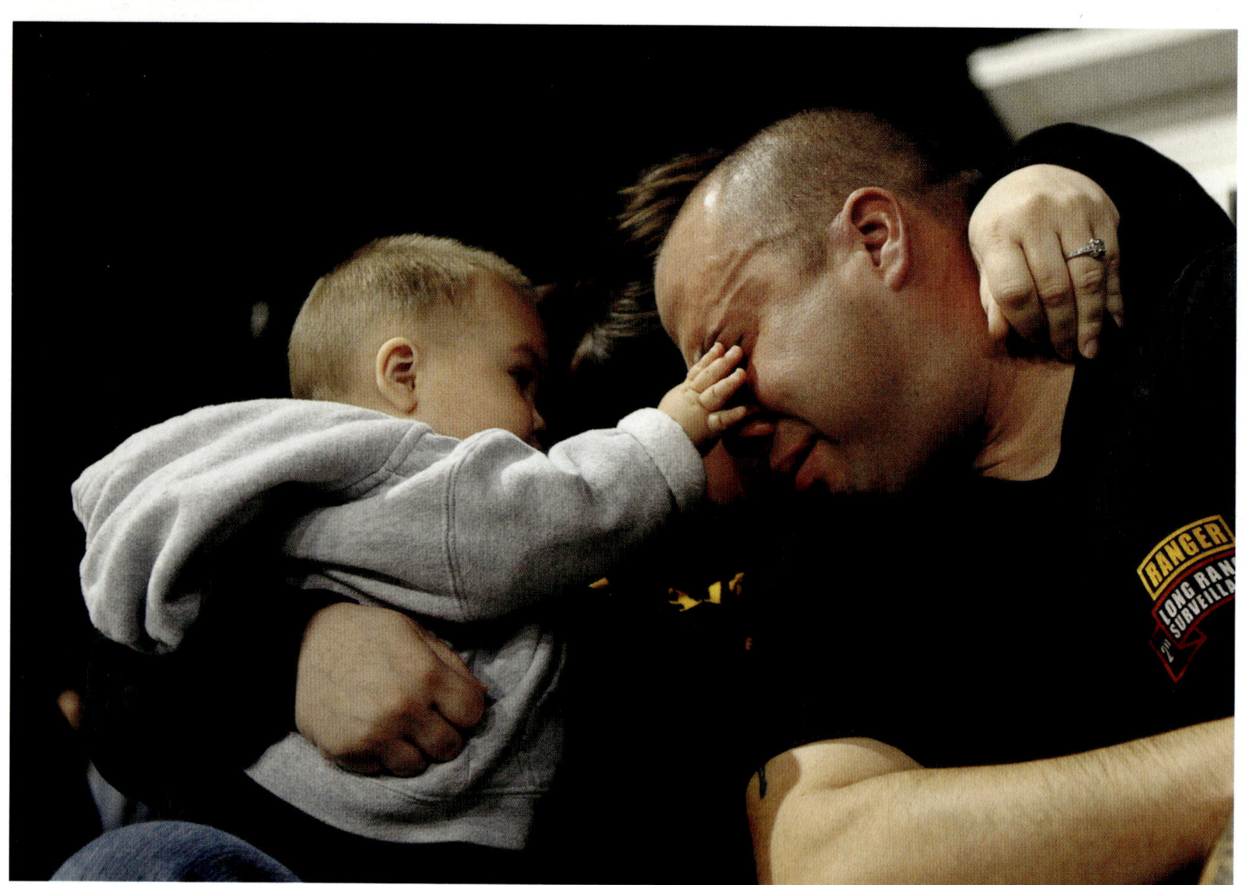

323 Fort Hood, United States

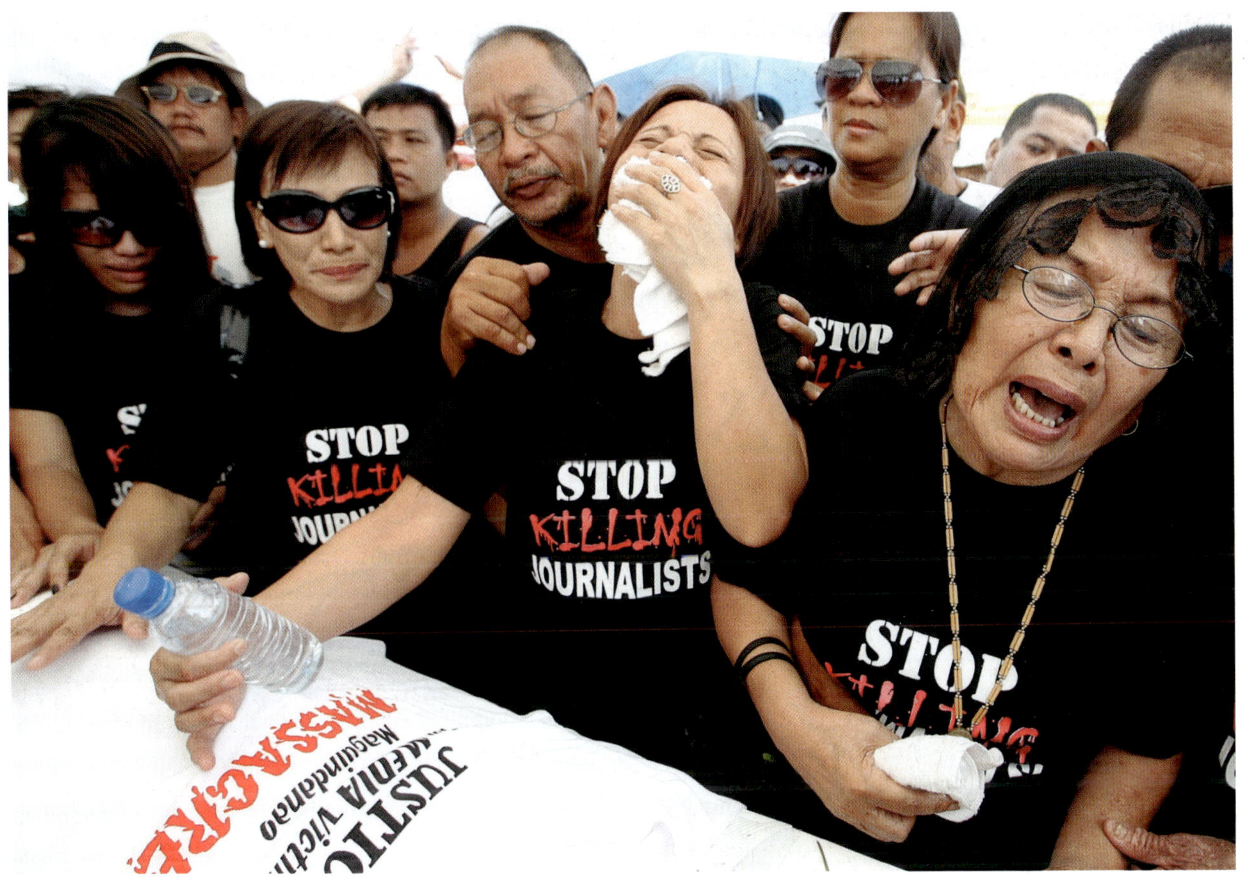

STOP
KILLING
JOURNALISTS
JUSTICE
MEDIA Victi
Maguindanao
MASSACRE

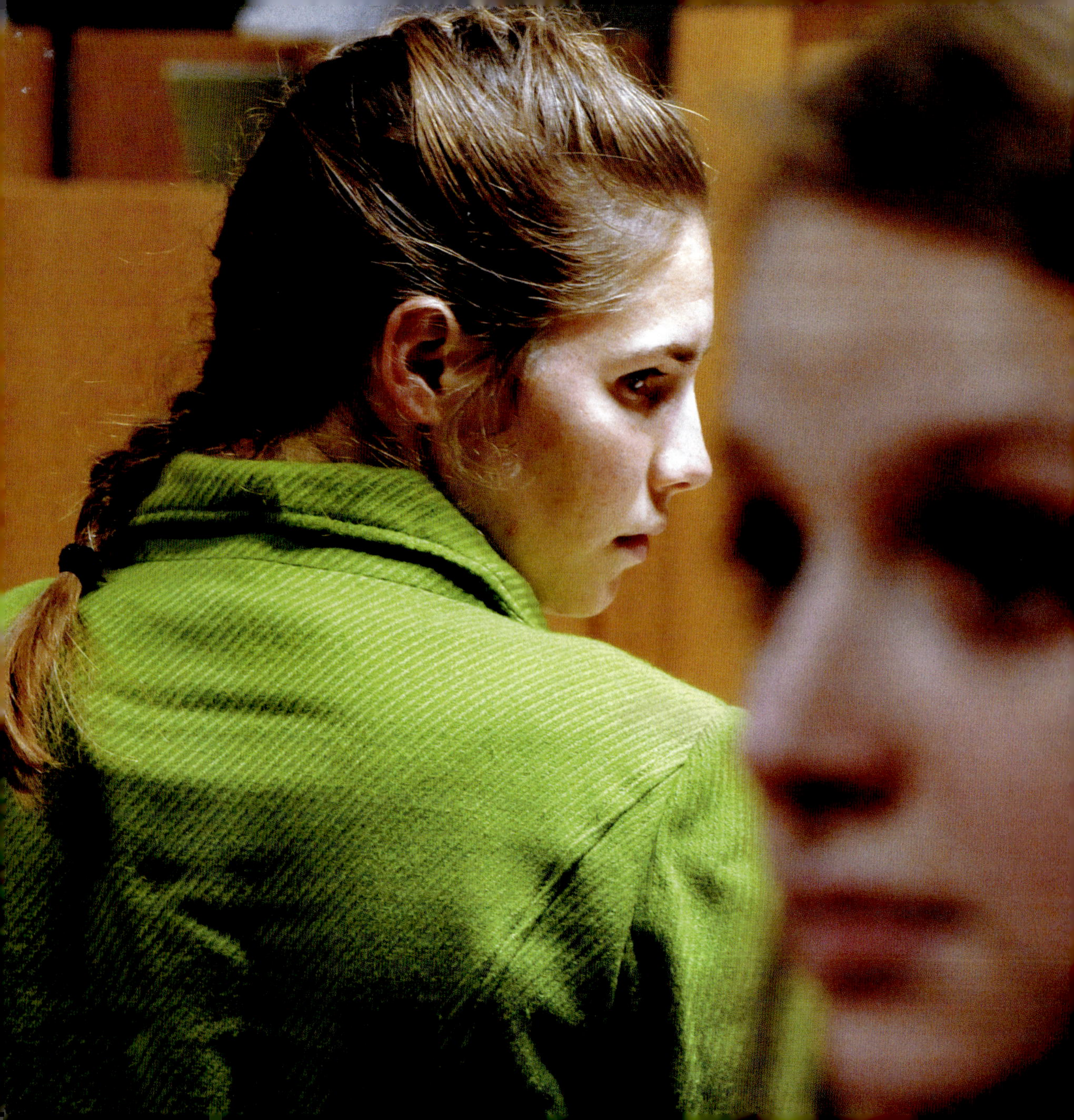

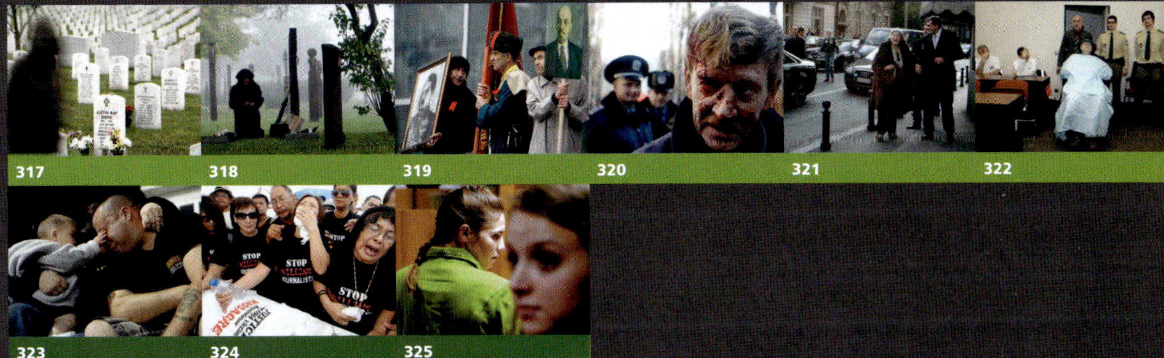

317 A visitor walks in Arlington National Cemetery outside Washington. 12 September 2009. Washington, DC, United States. Larry Downing.

318 On the anniversary of Hungary's 1956 uprising against Soviet rule, a woman prays in Budapest's central cemetery over the graves of relatives killed in those events. 23 October 2009. Budapest, Hungary. Laszlo Balogh.

319 Russian Communist supporters hold portraits of Soviet dictator Josef Stalin and Soviet state founder Vladimir Lenin as they take part in a rally in Russia's southern city of Vladikavkaz to mark the anniversary of the 1917 Bolshevik revolution. 7 November 2009. Vladikavkaz, Russia. Kazbek Basaev.

320 Police officers in Kiev detain a protester who was beaten by Communist supporters for throwing paint onto a monument of Bolshevik leader Vladimir Lenin. The statue had been newly unveiled following restoration after it was vandalized by members of a nationalist group in June. 27 November 2009. Kiev, Ukraine. Vladimir Sindeyev.

321 Former Bosnian Serb President Biljana Plavšić (centre) smiles with Bosnia's Serb Republic Prime Minister Milorad Dodik following her release by Sweden, two-thirds into an 11-year jail term for war crimes. Dubbed the Iron Lady of Bosnia's Serb Republic, Plavšić was the most senior politician to be sentenced by the Hague War Crimes tribunal. 27 October 2009. Belgrade, Serbia. Igor Pavicevic.

322 Accused Nazi death camp guard John Demjanjuk, in a wheelchair, attends court in Munich. The 89-year-old faced charges that he helped murder 27,900 Jews in Sobibor extermination camp in 1943. 30 November 2009. Munich, Germany. Michael Dalder.

323 Owen Rabago wipes a tear from the face of his father, Specialist Sheldon Rabago, during a candlelit vigil at Hood Stadium on the Fort Hood Army Post in Texas. Army psychiatrist Nidal Malik Hasan, a Muslim born in the United States, is accused of killing 13 people and wounding dozens in a 5 November shooting rampage at the base ahead of his deployment to Afghanistan. 6 November 2009. Fort Hood, United States. Jessica Rinaldi.

324 Family members cry during a funeral for journalists killed in the Maguindanao massacre in General Santos City in southern Philippines. Fifty-seven people, including 30 journalists, were killed after they were stopped at a checkpoint while on their way to file a candidate's nomination for elections. The killings led to a crackdown in the generally lawless southern Philippines and the imposition of martial law in Maguindanao. 4 December 2009. General Santos City, Philippines. Erik de Castro.

325 U.S. university student Amanda Knox is pictured during a break in her murder trial in Perugia as her sister Deanna (right) looks on. On 5 December an Italian court sentenced Knox to 26 years in prison and jailed her ex-boyfriend Raffaele Sollecito for 25 years after they were found guilty of murdering Knox's British roommate Meredith Kercher during a drunken sex game. 3 December 2009. Perugia, Italy. Alessandro Bianchi.

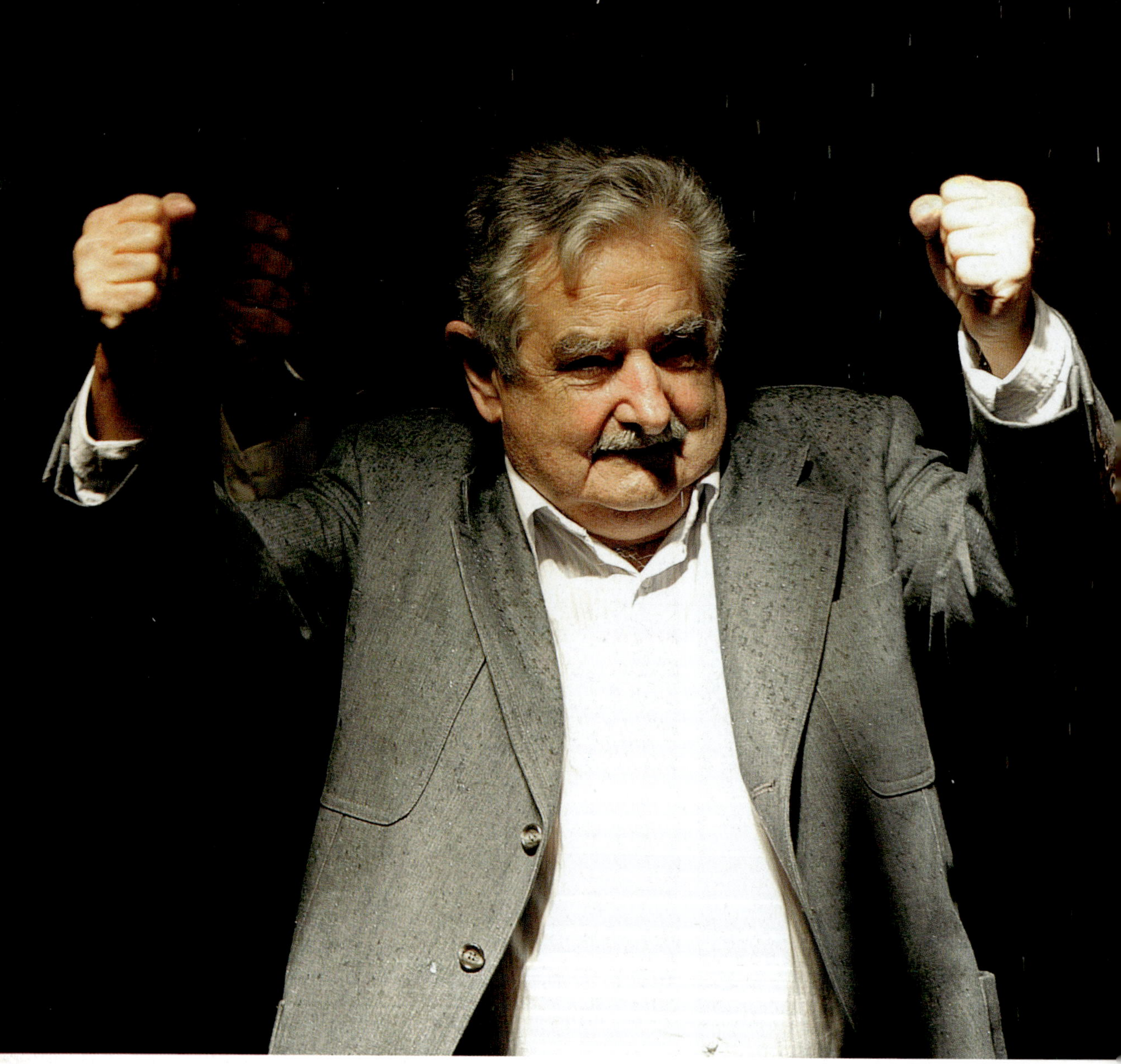

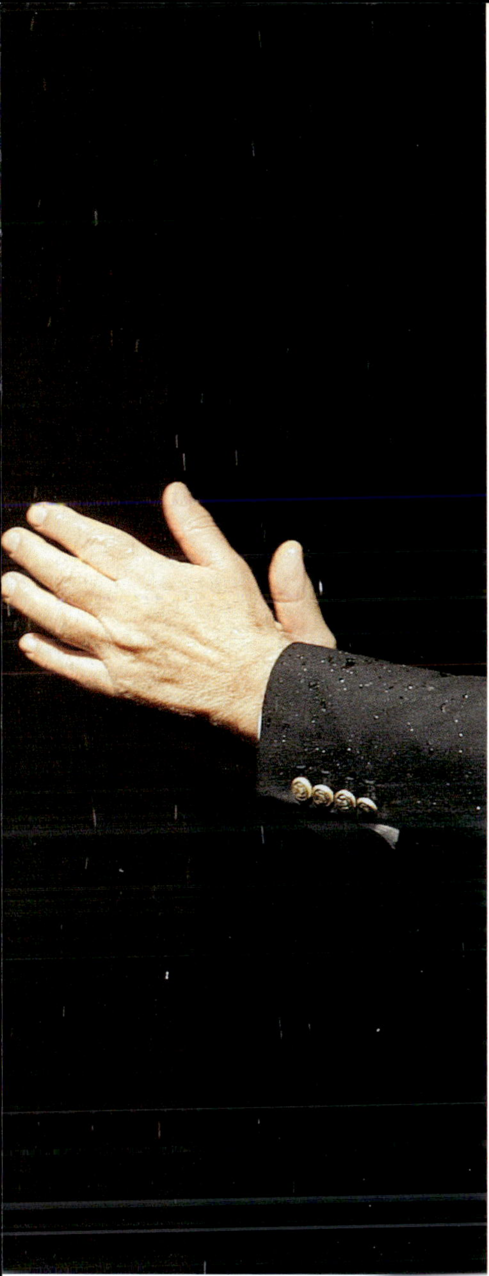

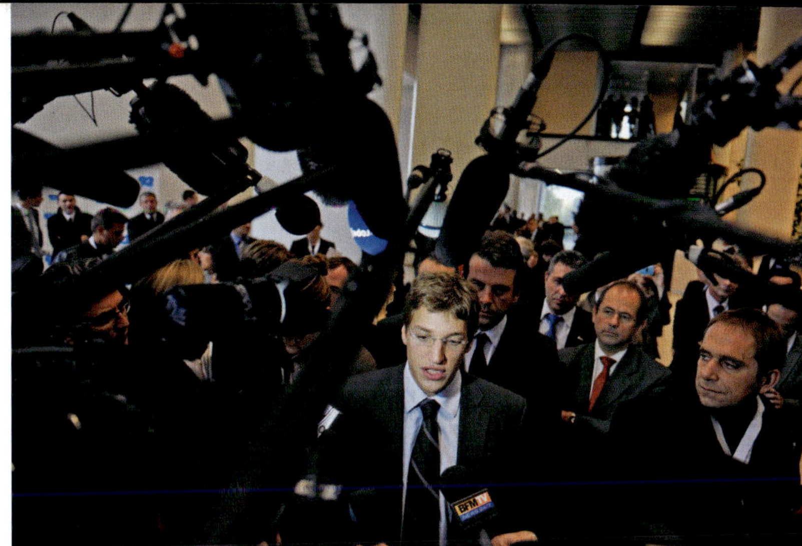

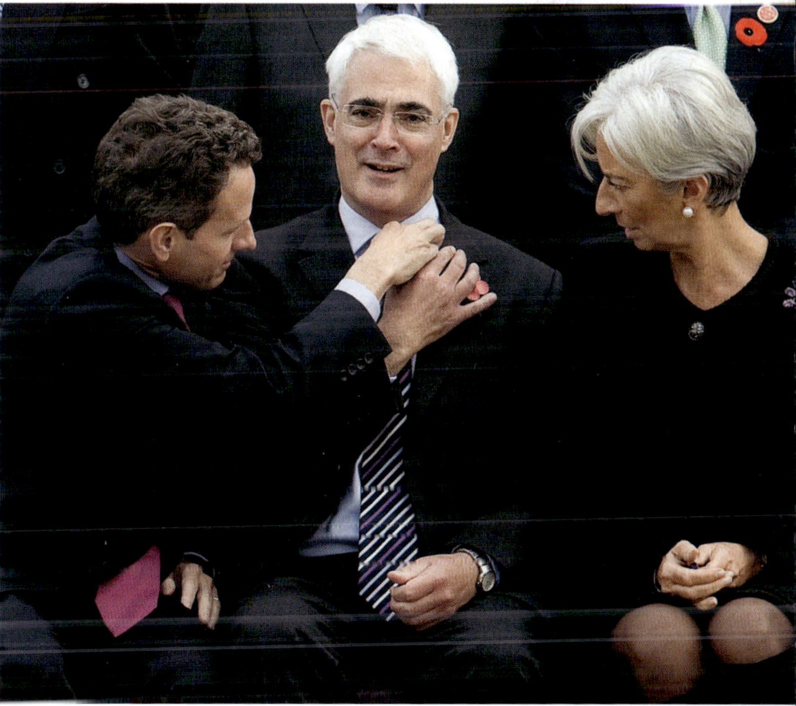

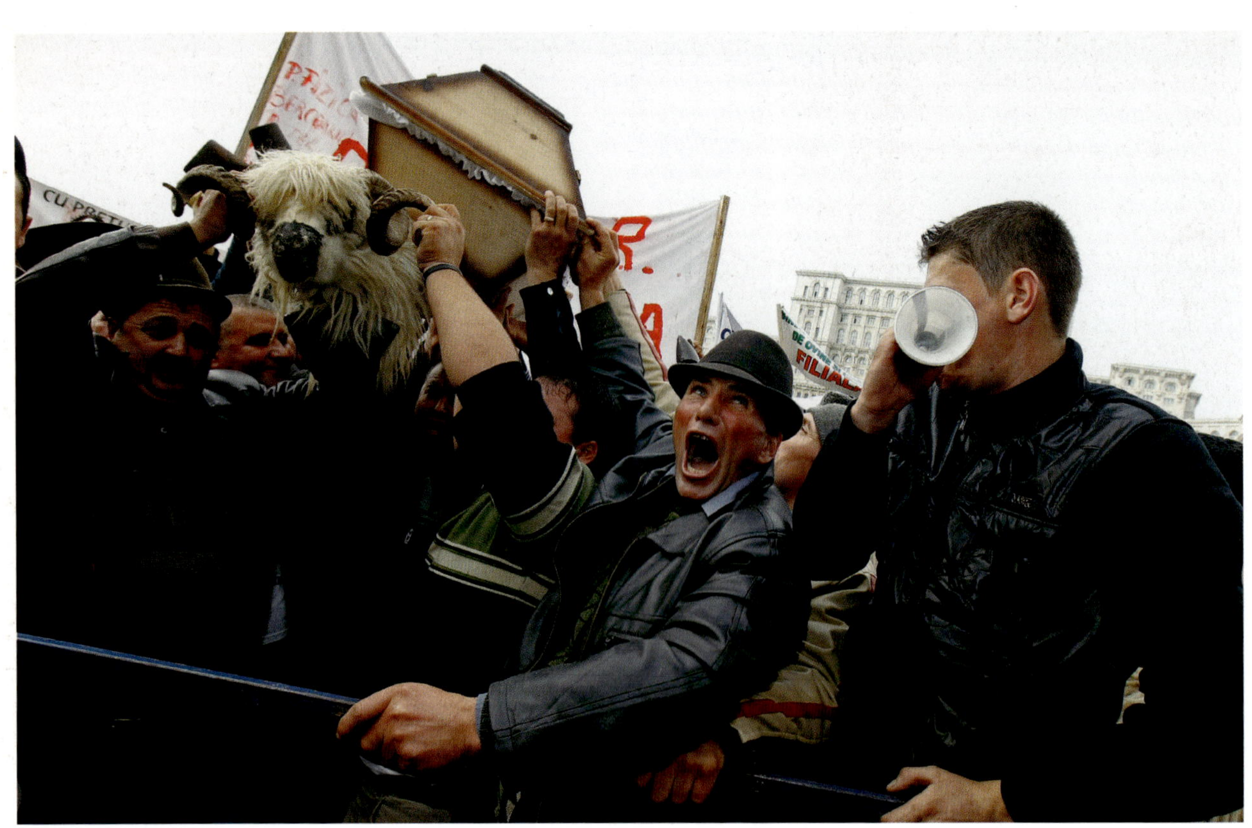

329 Bucharest, Romania

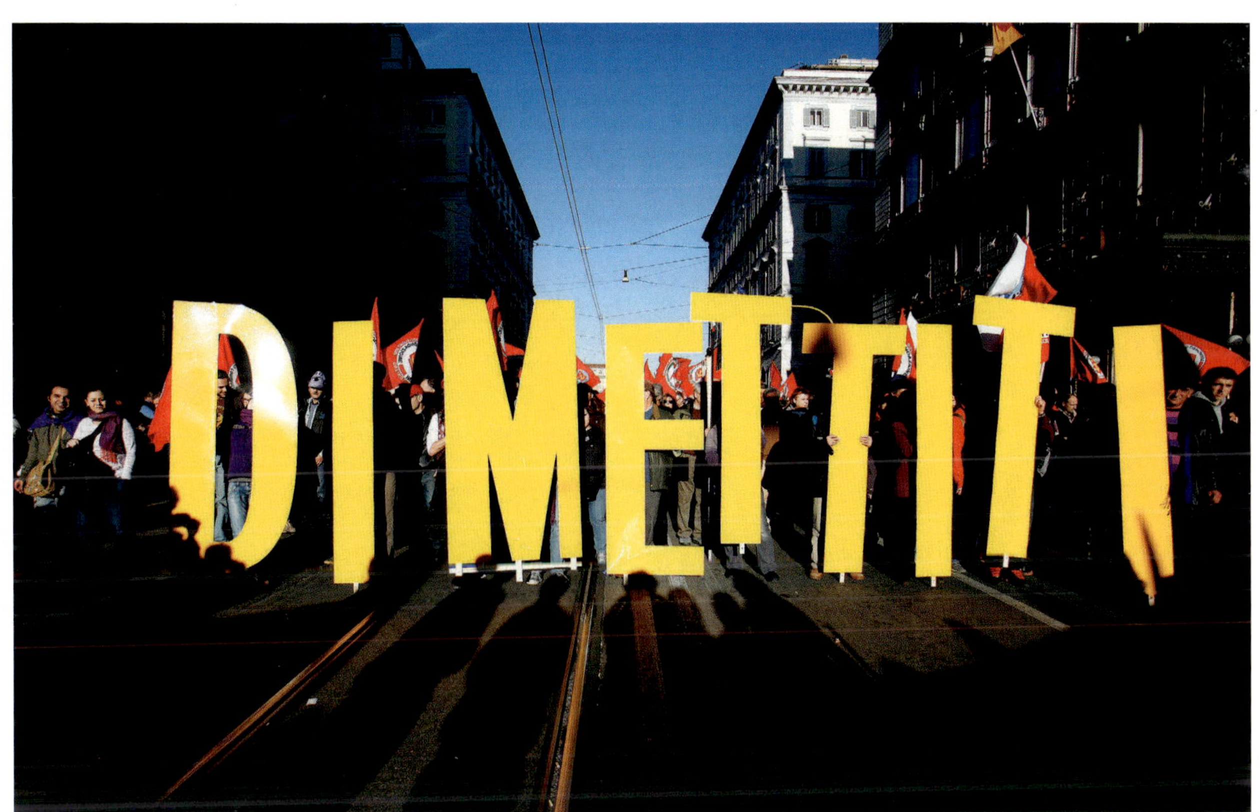

DIMETTITI

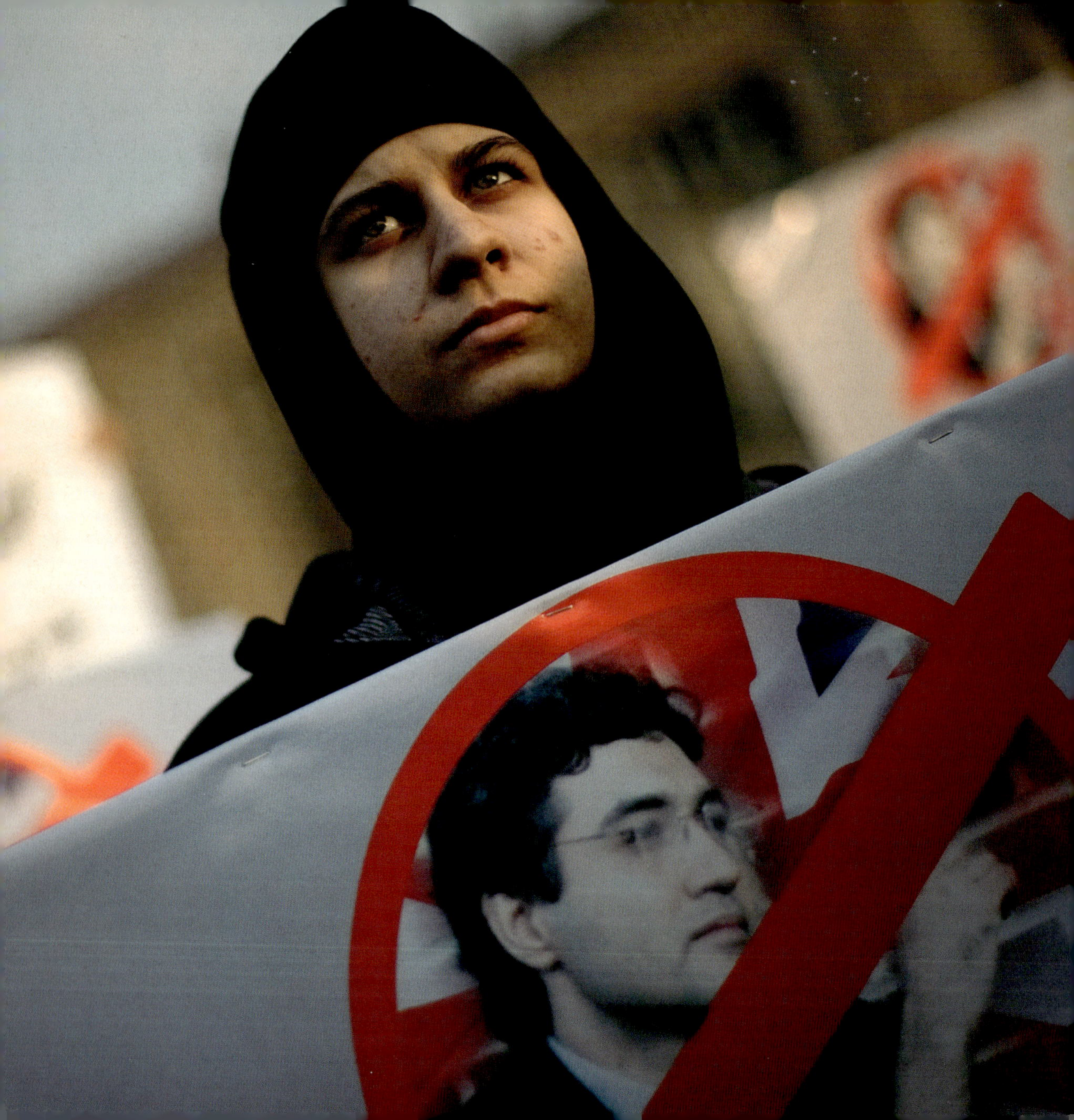

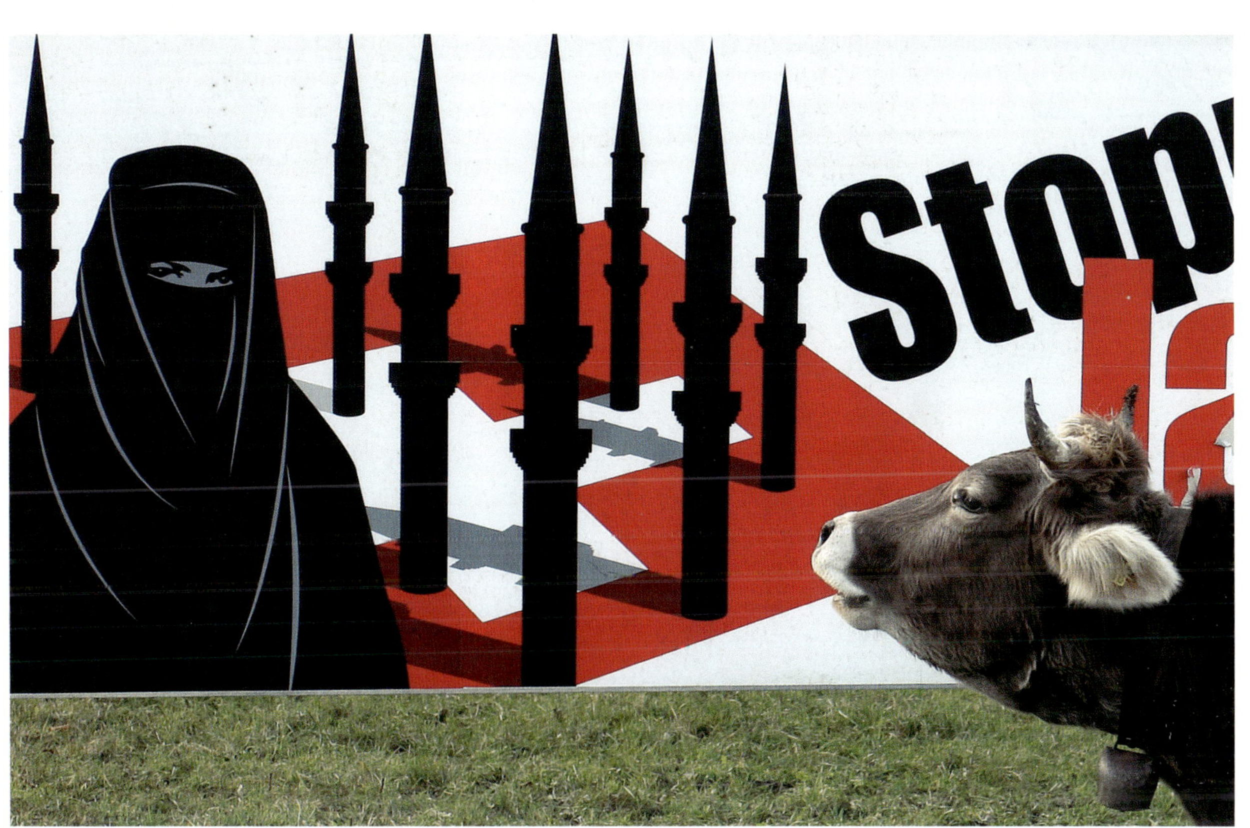

331 [OPPOSITE] Tehran, Iran   332 Zwillikon, Switzerland

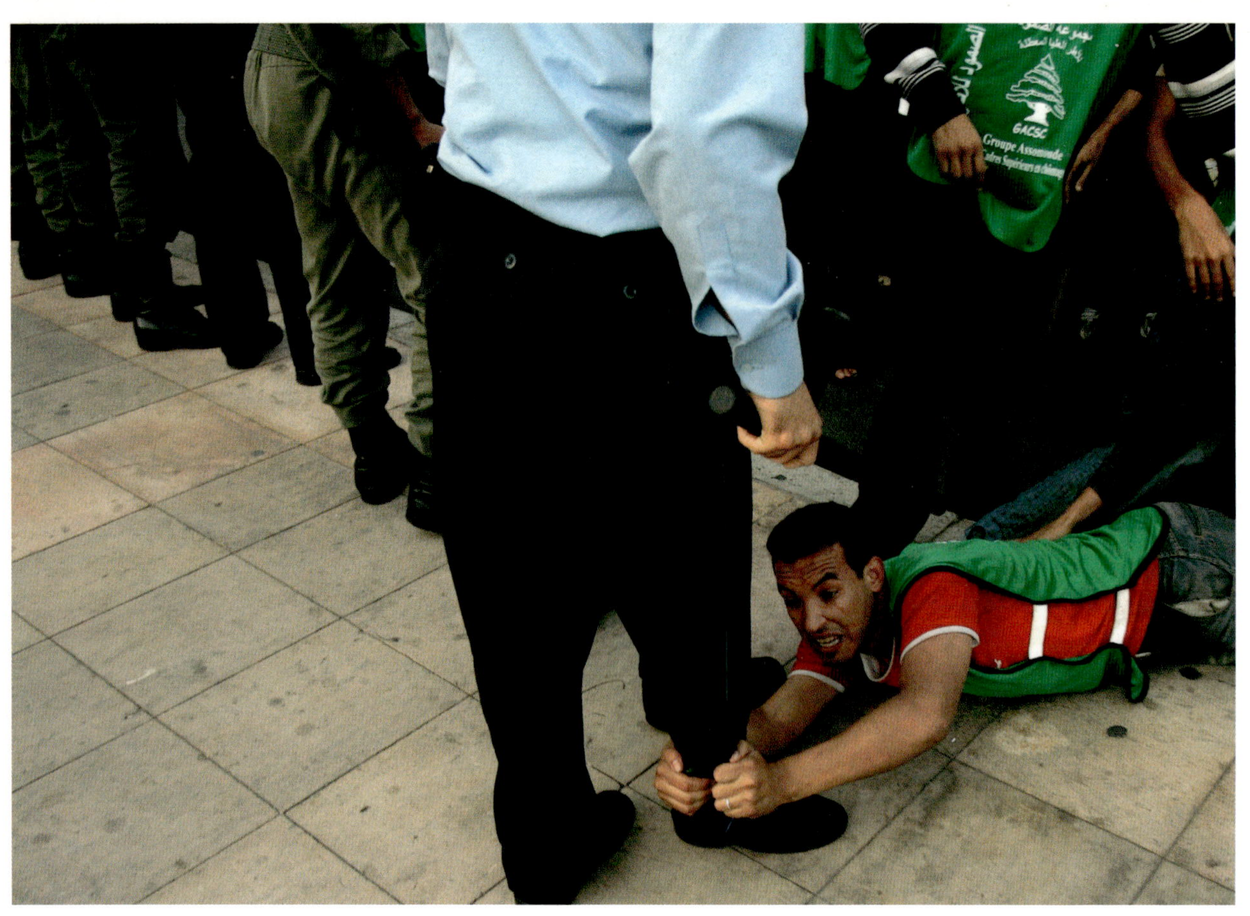

333 Rabat, Morocco

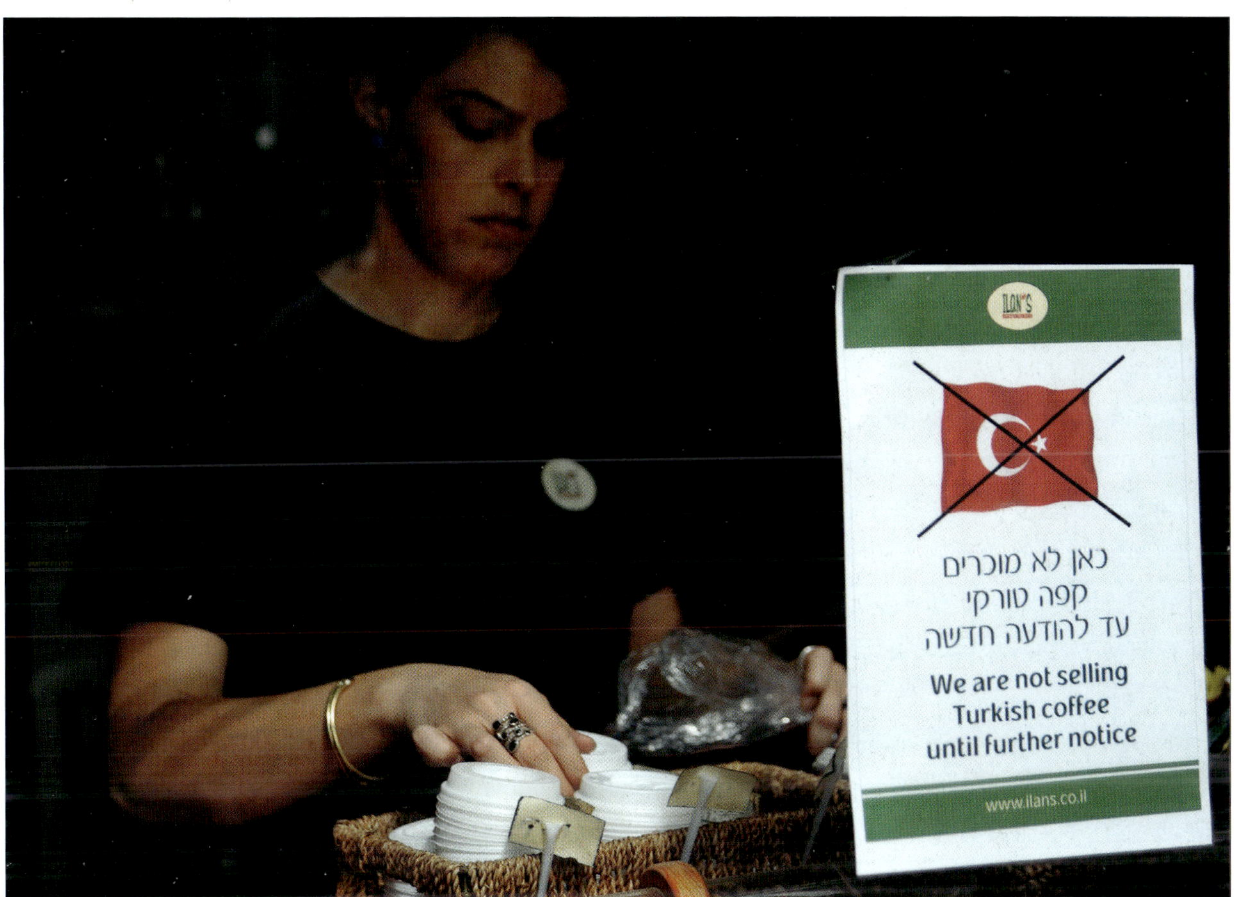
ILAN'S
נאן לא מוכרים
קפה טורקי
עד להודעה חדשה
We are not selling
Turkish coffee
until further notice
www.ilans.co.il

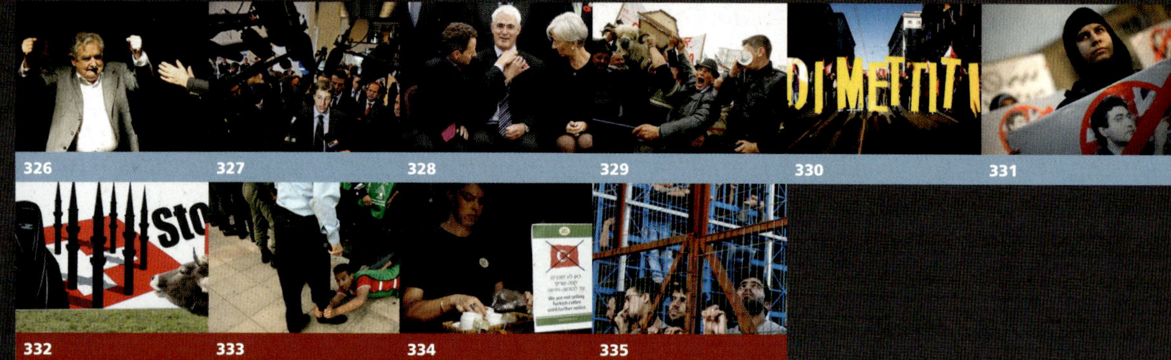

326 Uruguay's president-elect, former leftist guerrilla fighter José Mujica, celebrates his victory as Uruguay's President Tabaré Vázquez (right) applauds in Montevideo. 29 November 2009. Montevideo, Uruguay. Andres Stapff.

327 Jean Sarkozy, 23-year-old son of French President Nicolas Sarkozy, leaves the Hauts-de-Seine general council in Nanterre, west of Paris. Jean Sarkozy announced he was dropping a bid to run the EPAD agency which oversees Paris's wealthy business district of La Défense, saying he wanted to remove any suspicion of nepotism. The younger Sarkozy is a councillor in the wealthy Hauts-de-Seine department, where his father built his own political career. 23 October 2009. Nanterre, France. Philippe Wojazer.

328 Britain's Chancellor of the Exchequer Alistair Darling (centre) has his collar adjusted by U.S. Treasury Secretary Timothy Geithner as France's Finance Minister Christine Lagarde looks on during the family photo at the G20 finance ministers meeting in St Andrews. 7 November 2009. St Andrews, Britain. Andrew Winning.

329 Farmers carry a coffin with a sheep's head to symbolize the death of the Romanian farming system as they demonstrate in Bucharest to demand greater state subsidies for the agricultural sector. 28 October 2009. Bucharest, Romania. Bogdan Cristel.

330 Demonstrators hold placards reading 'Resign' during a 'No-Berlusconi Day' rally in Rome. 5 December 2009. Rome, Italy. Alessia Pierdomenico.

331 A woman attends a protest outside the British embassy in Tehran to demand the return of Arash Hejazi, who fled to London after being identified as a witness in the death of Neda Agha-Soltan. Graphic footage of her death in June during clashes following disrupted elections was seen around the world on the Internet. 2 December 2009. Tehran, Iran. Morteza Nikoubazl.

332 A cow stands next to a campaign poster in Zwillikon, Switzerland, promoting a ban on the construction of new minarets in the country. Switzerland is home to more than 300,000 Muslims but has just four minarets. 13 November 2009. Zwillikon, Switzerland. Dario Bianchi.

333 A demonstrator grabs the foot of a policeman during a protest in Rabat calling for more public sector jobs. 14 October 2009. Rabat, Morocco. Rafael Marchante.

334 An employee stands behind a sign depicting a crossed-out Turkish flag taped to the window of a coffee shop in Tel Aviv. A manager at the establishment said the decision not to sell Turkish coffee was made in protest at Turkish criticism of Israel over its military offensive in Gaza launched in December 2008. 27 October 2009. Tel Aviv, Israel. Amir Cohen.

335 Would-be migrants to Europe lean on fences during unrest in Pagani detention centre, on the eastern Aegean Greek island of Lesvos. Unrest has frequently broken out in the camp, originally designed for about 250 people but which now holds around 800. Campaigners say conditions in many Greek immigrant detention centres are appalling. 19 October 2009. Lesvos, Greece. John Kolesidis.

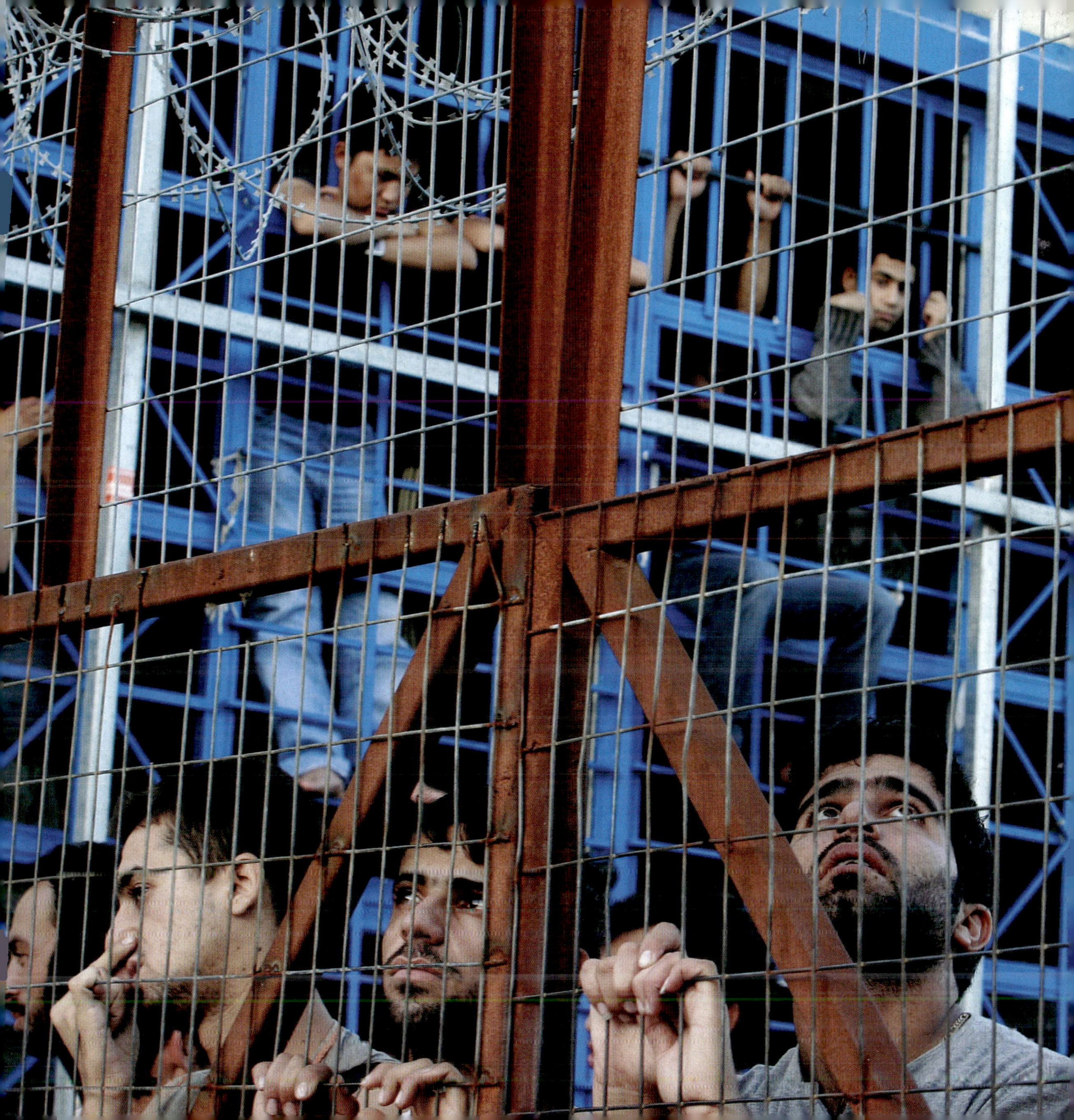

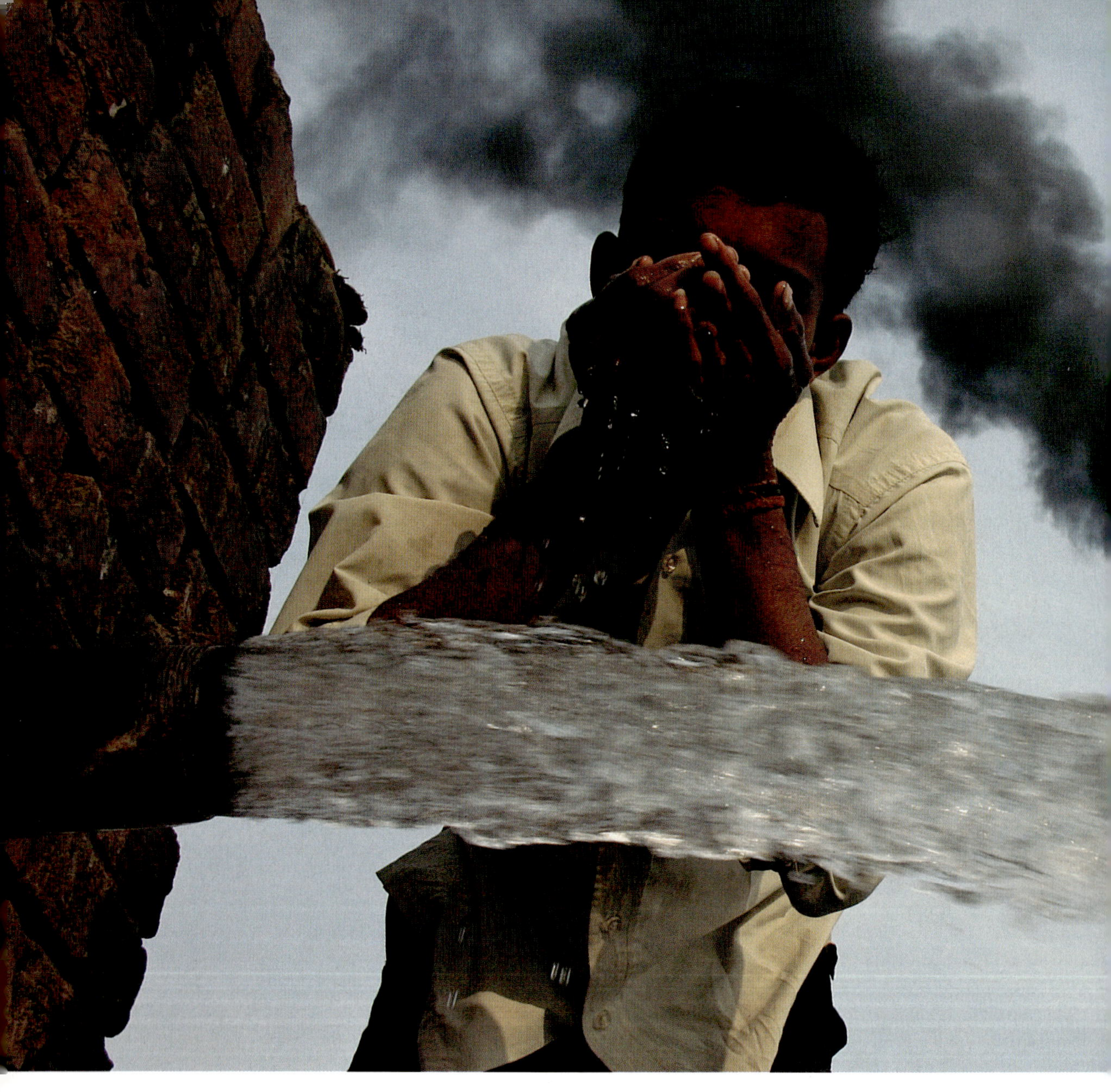

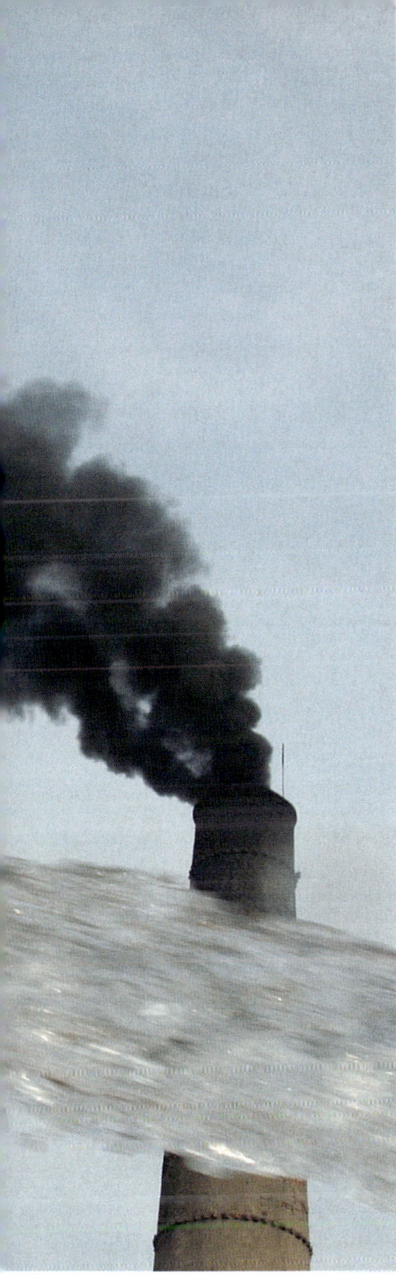

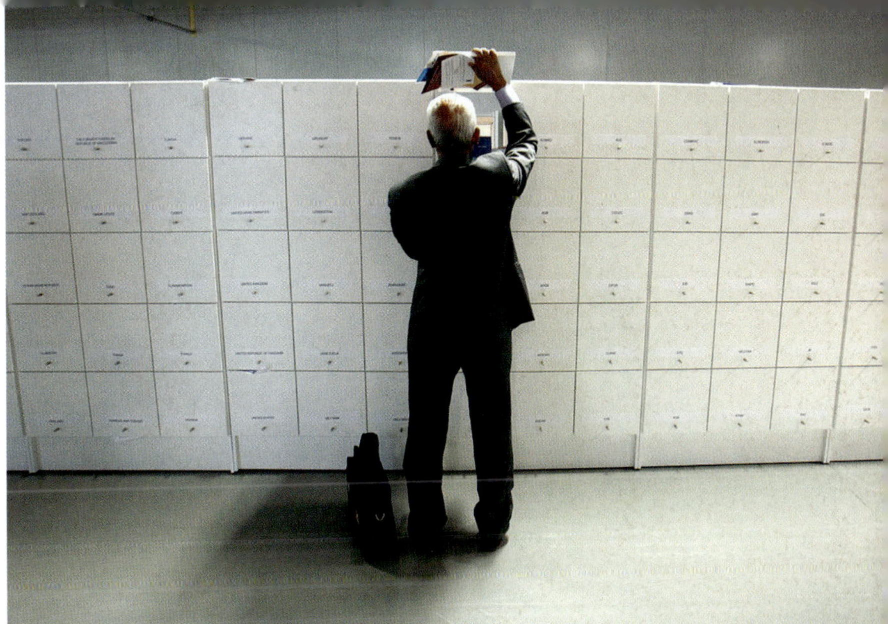

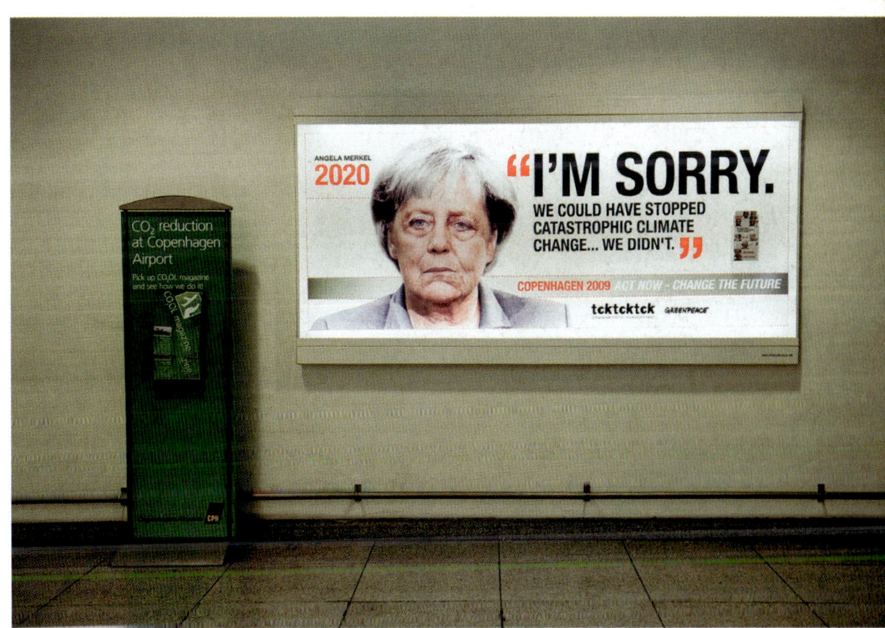

337 [TOP] 338 [ABOVE] Copenhagen, Denmark

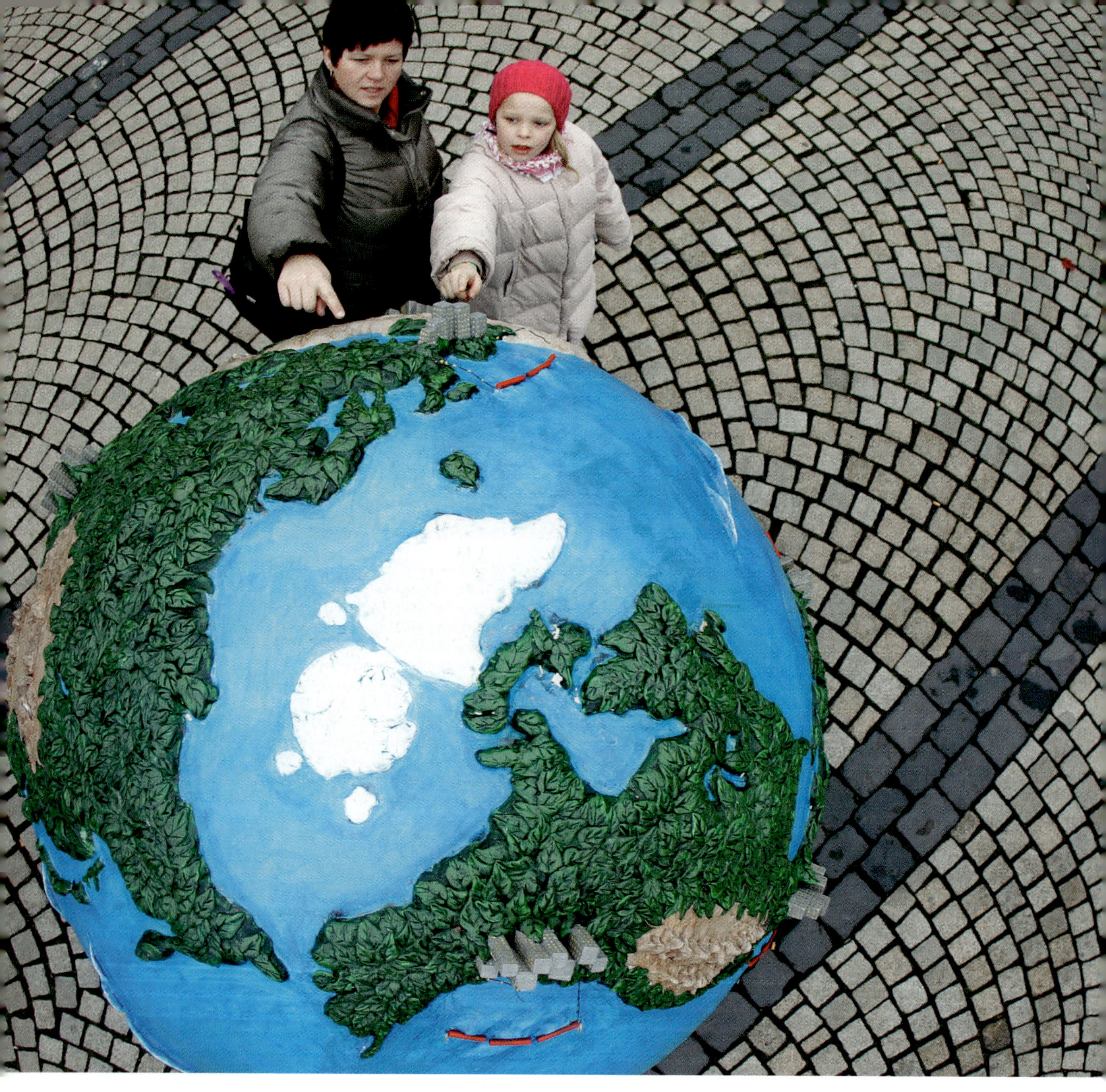

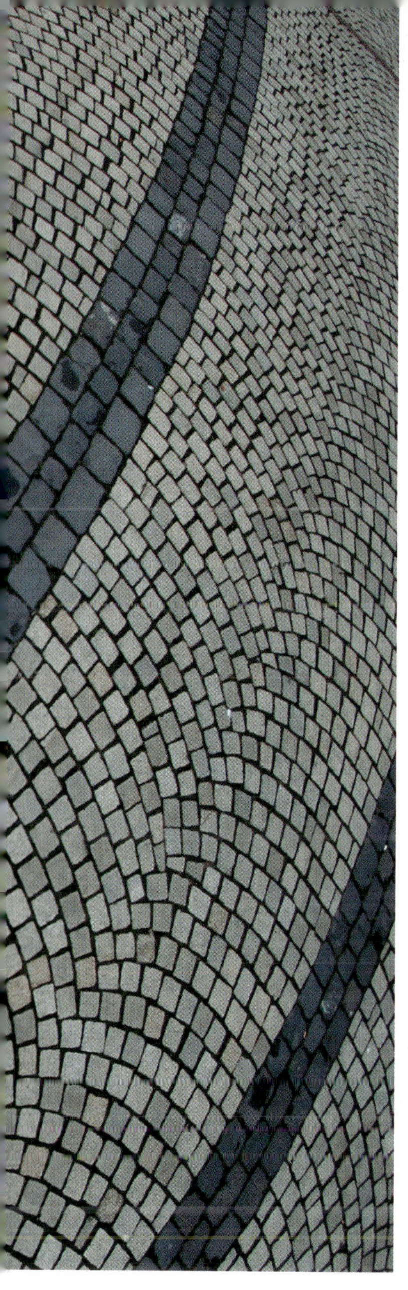

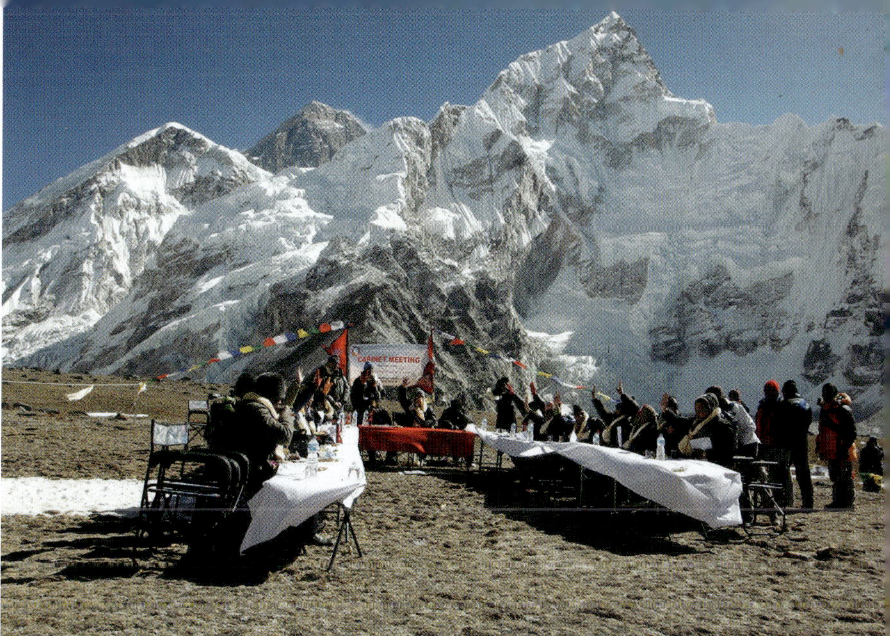

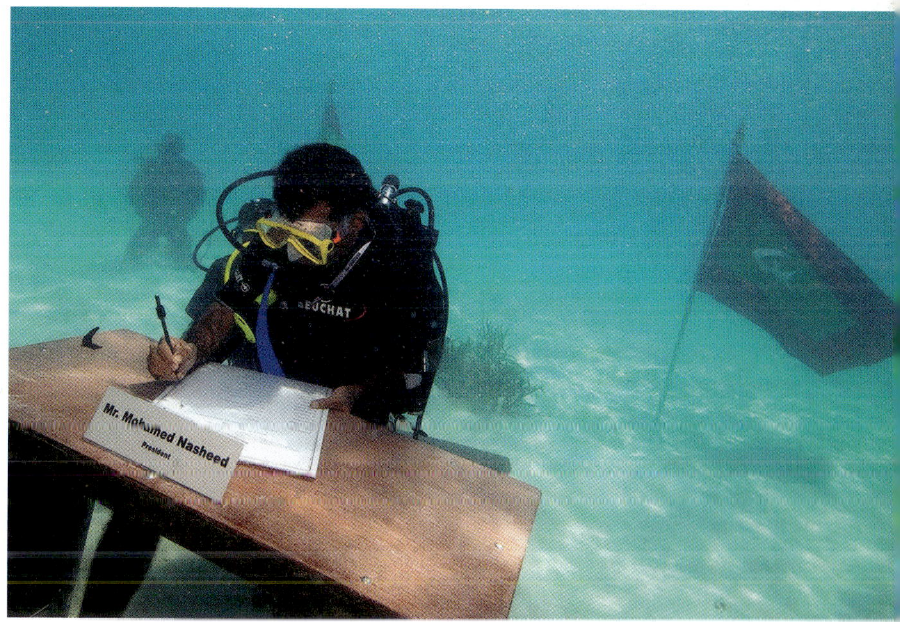

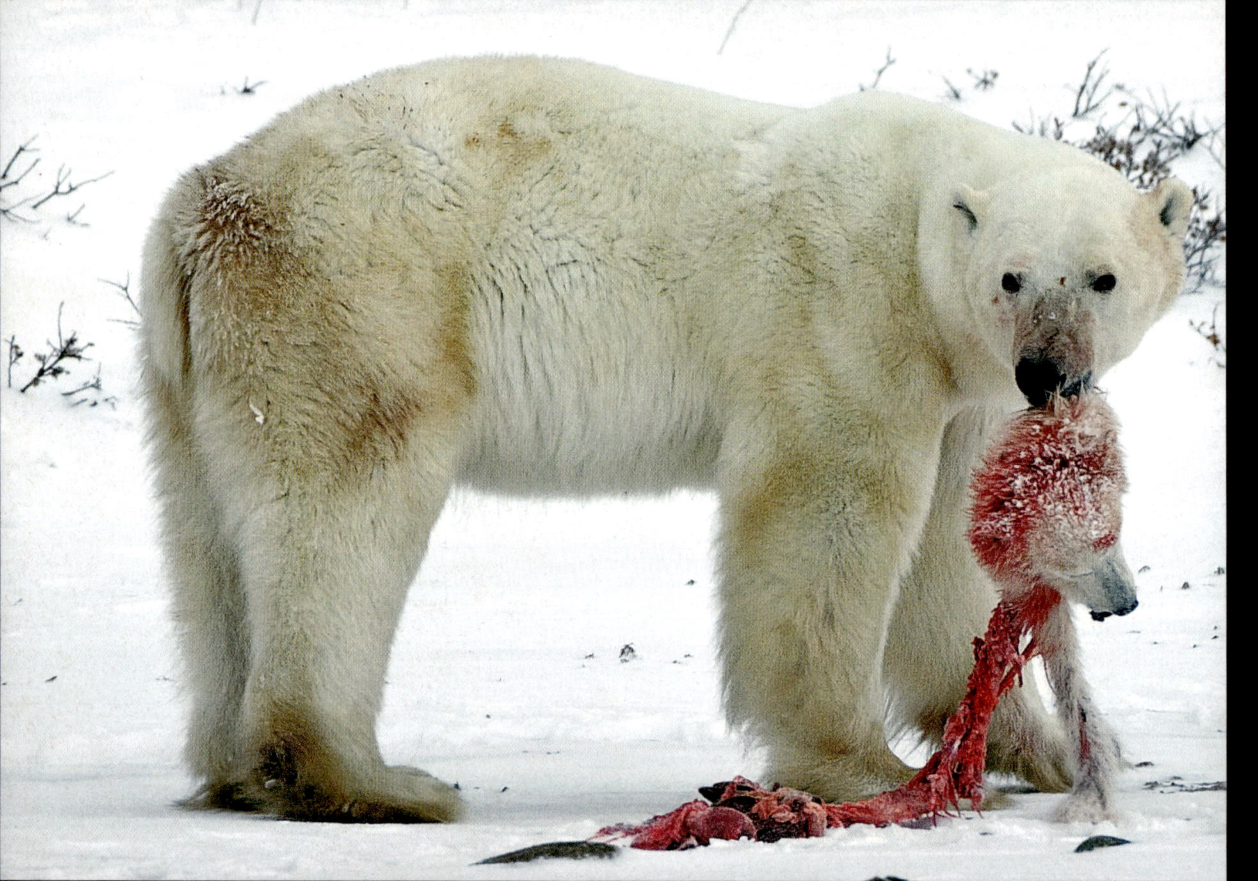

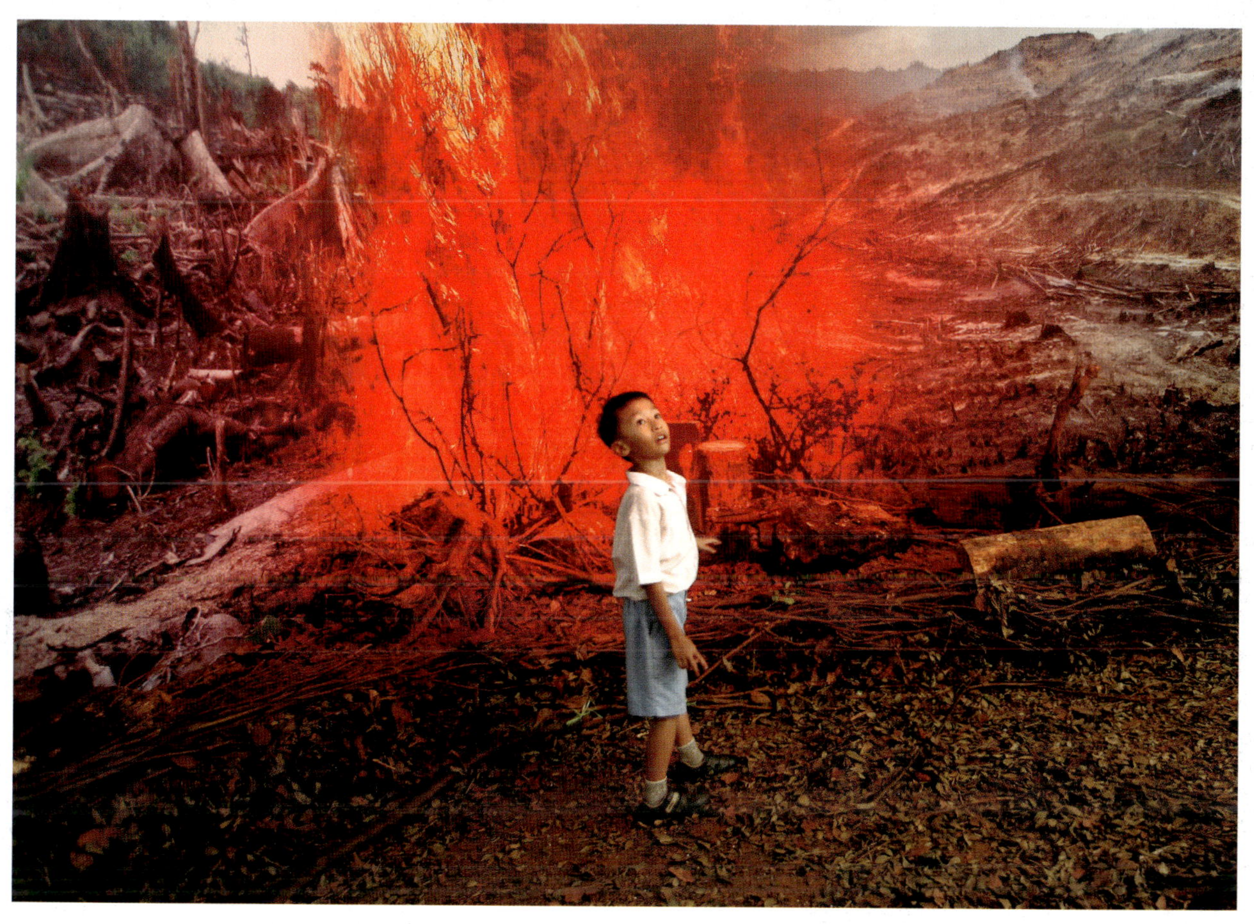

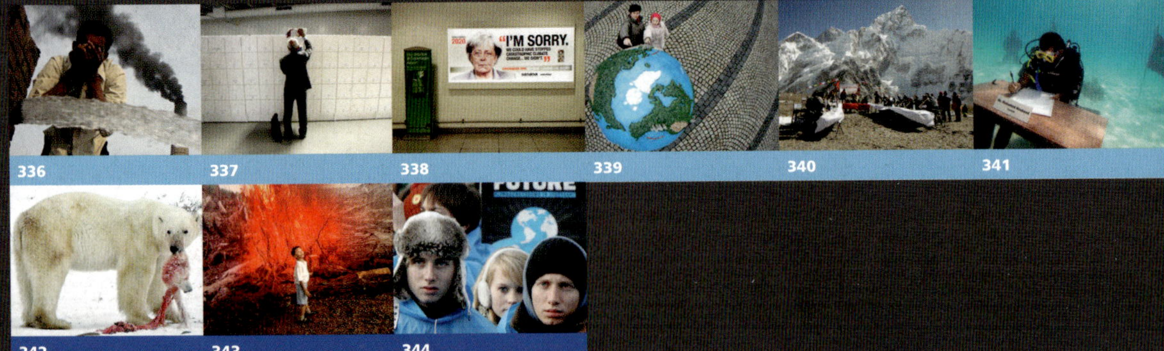

336 A labourer drinks water as smoke rises from the chimney of a brick factory at Togga village on the outskirts of the northern Indian city of Chandigarh. 6 December 2009. Chandigarh, India. Ajay Verma.

337 Somalia's Environment Minister Burci Hamza checks his mailbox at the 2009 U.N. Climate Change Conference in Copenhagen. 9 December 2009. Copenhagen, Denmark. Bob Strong.

338 A billboard depicting German Chancellor Angela Merkel is seen at Copenhagen International Airport. The poster was part of a Greenpeace campaign calling on world leaders to secure a 'fair, ambitious and binding deal' at the 2009 U.N. Climate Change Conference. 3 December 2009. Copenhagen, Denmark. Christian Aslund.

339 People look at a globe displayed in downtown Copenhagen, host city for the 2009 U.N. Climate Change Conference. 6 December 2009. Copenhagen, Denmark. Pawel Kopczynski.

340 Wearing oxygen masks, Nepal's cabinet meet at the Gorakshep base camp region of Mount Everest, 5,242 metres (17,200 feet) above sea level. The meeting was staged to send a message on the impact of global warming on the Himalayas, days before climate talks were scheduled to start in Copenhagen. Shrinking glaciers in the Himalayas could cause 10 major Asian rivers to go dry in the next five decades, experts say. 4 December 2009. Gorakshep, Nepal. Gopal Chitrakar.

341 Maldives President Mohamed Nasheed signs a declaration during the world's first underwater cabinet meeting. Clad in black diving suits and masks, Nasheed, 11 ministers, the vice president and cabinet secretary dived 3.8 metres (12 feet, 8 inches) to gather at tables on the sea bed. The event was a symbolic cry for help to avert rising sea levels that threaten the tropical archipelago's existence. If U.N. predictions are correct, most of the low-lying Maldives will be submerged by 2100. 17 October 2009. Maldives.

342 A male polar bear carries the head of a cub it killed and cannibalized in northern Manitoba, about 300 km (185 miles) north of the Canadian town of Churchill. Cannibalism is a known phenomenon among polar bears, but its incidence may be increased by the stresses caused by reduced habitat and hunting grounds as global warming melts the bears' Arctic terrain, according to a U.S.-led global scientific study. 20 November 2009. Northern Manitoba, Canada. Iain D. Williams.

343 A boy stands in front of a poster portraying a forest fire during the Green Festival in Jakarta to promote awareness of global warming. 6 December 2009. Jakarta, Indonesia. Supri.

344 Demonstrators meet before joining a larger march to the 2009 U.N. Climate Change Conference in Copenhagen. 12 December 2009. Copenhagen, Denmark. Bob Strong.

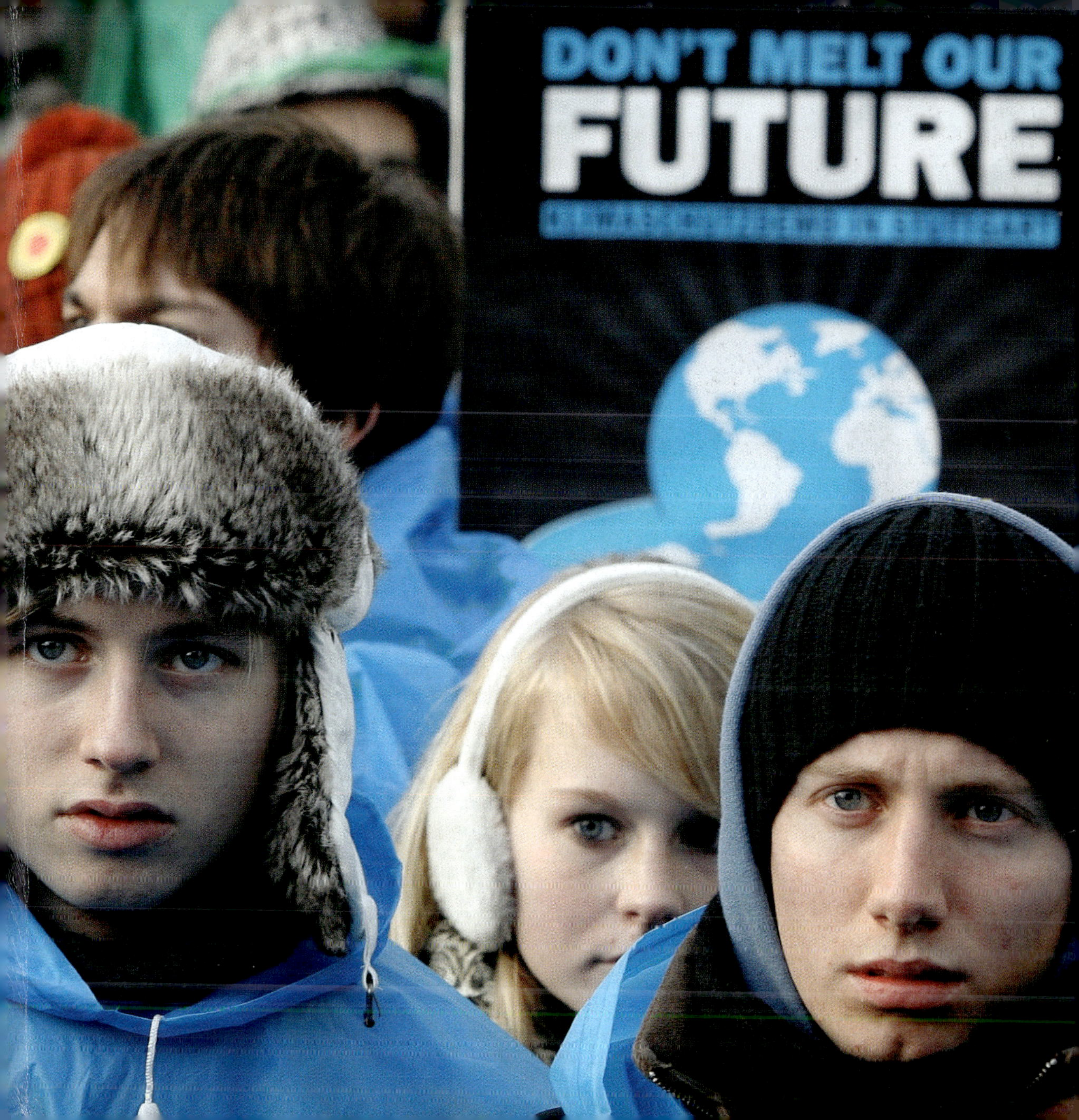

DON'T MELT OUR
FUTURE

Acknowledgments

Our World Now Picture Editor Ayperi Karabuda Ecer is Vice-President, Pictures at Reuters, with global responsibility for images. She was Editor-in-Chief of Magnum Photos Paris for 12 years and previously Bureau Chief for Sipa Press in New York. Ayperi was chair of the World Press Photo jury in 2010 and has shared her expertise at the Joop Swart Masterclass on four occasions.

At Reuters, she has helped shape the vision of news photography with her team by editing books, multimedia and exhibitions. These have included previous best-selling Reuters books, notably *The State of the World* (Thames & Hudson 2006), published in ten languages. Ayperi has produced an international programme of touring exhibitions, showcasing Reuters photographers' work in 50 cities from Shanghai to London. Ayperi led production of the award-winning multimedia essay *Bearing Witness*, reflecting on five years of war in Iraq, and initiated *Times of Crisis*, charting the global impact of the credit crunch.

With the support of
Head of Visual Projects Jassim Ahmad
Pictures Projects Manager Shannon Ghannam

With thanks to Paul Barker, Lynne Bundy, Hamish Crooks, Jeremy Gaunt, Ginny Liggitt, May Naji, Simon Newman, Dennis Owen, Corinne Perkins, Alexia Singh, Kate Slotover, Jane Steinbeck, Akio Suga, Thomas Szlukovenyi, Laurence Tan, Amanda Vinnicombe, Thomas White, Alison Williams.

Contributing Photographers

The country that follows each name represents the photographer's nationality

Adrees Latif, Pakistan/United States
Ahmad Masood, Afghanistan
Ahmed Jadallah, Palestinian Territories
Ajay Verma, India
Alejandro Bringas, Mexico
Alessandro Bianchi, Italy
Alessia Pierdomenico, Italy
Alex Almeida, Brazil
Alissa Everett, United States
Aly Song, China
Amir Cohen, Israel
Amit Dave, India
Amr Abdallah Dalsh, Egypt
Andres Stapff, Uruguay
Andrew Biraj, Bangladesh
Andrew Winning, Britain
Antony Njuguna, Kenya
Arko Datta, India
Arnd Wiegmann, Germany
Babu, India
Baz Ratner, Germany
Bazuki Muhammad, Malaysia
Beawiharta, Indonesia
Benoit Tessier, France
Bob Strong, United States
Bobby Yip, Japan
Bogdan Cristel, Romania
Bor Slana, Slovenia
Brian Snyder, United States
Carlos Barria, Argentina
Carlos Garcia Rawlins, Venezuela
Cathal McNaughton, Ireland
Charles Platiau, France
Chris Helgren, Canada
Claudia Daut, Germany
Crack Palinggi, Indonesia
Damir Sagolj, Bosnia
Daniel Aguilar, Mexico
Daniel LeClair, United States

Daniel Munoz, Colombia
Dario Bianchi, Switzerland
Darren Staples, Britain
Darren Whiteside, Canada
David Gray, Australia
David Mercado, Bolivia
Denis Sinyakov, Russia
Denise Balibouse, Switzerland
Dylan Martinez, Britain
Edgard Garrido Carrera, Chile
Eduard Korniyenko, Russia
Eduardo Munoz, Colombia
Eloy Alonso, Spain
Enrique De La Osa, Cuba
Eric Gaillard, France
Eric Thayer, United States
Erik de Castro, Philippines
Fabrizio Bensch, Germany
Fadi Arouri, Palestinian Territories
Farid Allouache, France
Fayaz Aziz, Pakistan
Feisal Omar, Somalia
Finbarr O'Reilly, Canada
Francois Lenoir, Belgium
Gary Hershorn, Canada
Gil Cohen Magen, Israel
Gleb Garanich, Ukraine
Gonzalo Fuentes, Mexico
Gopal Chitrakar, Nepalese
Gordon Jack, Britain
Herwig Prammer, Austria
Iain D Williams, Australia
Igor Pavicevic, Serbia
Ismail Zaydah, Palestinian Territories
Ivan Alvarado, Colombia
Jason Reed, Australia
Jean-Paul Pelissier, France
Jerry Lampen, Netherlands
Jessica Rinaldi, United States
Jianan Yu, China
Jim Young, Canada
Jo Yong-Hak, South Korea
Johannes Eisele, Germany
John Kolesidis, Greece

Jonathan Ernst, United States
Jorge Dan, Mexico
Jorge Silva, Mexico
Joshua Lott, United States
Juan Medina, Argentina
Kahtan al-Mesiary, Iraq
Kazbek Basaev, Russia
Kevin Coombs, Britain
Kevin Lamarque, United States
Kham, Vietnam
Kieran Doherty, Britain
Konstantin Chernichkin, Ukraine
Larry Downing, United States
Laszlo Balogh, Hungary
Lucas Jackson, United States
Lucy Nicholson, Britain
Luke MacGregor, Britain
Manuel Silvestri, Italy
Mario Anzuoni, Italy
Mark Blinch, Canada
Marko Djurica, Serbia
Max Rossi, Italy
Max Whittaker, United States
Maxi Jonas, Argentina
Michael Buholzer, Switzerland
Michael Dalder, Germany
Michaela Rehle, Germany
Mick Tsikas, Australia
Miguel Vidal, Spain
Mike Segar, United States
Mohammed Salem, Palestinian Territories
Mohsin Raza, Pakistan
Morteza Nikoubazl, Iran
Mukesh Gupta, India
Nicky Loh, Singapore
Nikola Solic, Croatia
Nir Elias, Israel
Ognen Teofilovski, Macedonia
Omar Sobhani, Afghanistan
Osman Orsal, Turkey
Pascal Rossignol, France
Paulo Santos, Brazil
Paulo Whitaker, Brazil

Pawel Kopczynski, Poland
Petr Josek, Czech Republic
Phil McCarten, United States
Philimon Bulawayo, Zimbabwe
Philip Brown, Britain
Philippe Wojazer, France
Punit Paranjpe, India
Rafael Marchante, Spain
Reinhard Krause, Germany
Remo Casilli, Italy
Ricardo Moraes, Brazil
Robert Galbraith, United States
Rogan Ward, South Africa
Romeo Ranoco, Philippines
Ronen Zvulun, Israel
Santiago Pandolfi, Argentina
Sergio Moraes, Brazil
Shamil Zhumatov, Kazakhstan
Shannon Stapleton, United States
Sigit Pamungkas, Indonesia
Singye Wangchuk, Bhutan
Siphiwe Sibeko, South Africa
Stefan Wermuth, Switzerland
Stephen Hird, Britain
Stoyan Nenov, Bulgaria
Suhaib Salem, Palestinian Territories
Sukree Sukplang, Thailand
Supri, Indonesia
Susana Vera, Spain
Thomas White, Britain
Tim Wimborne, Australia
Toby Melville, Britain
Tomas Bravo, Mexico
Tony Gentile, Italy
Toru Hanai, Japan
Vasily Fedosenko, Belarus
Vincent Kessler, France
Vivek Prakash, Australian
Vladimir Sindeyev, Russia
Yannis Behrakis, Greece
Yiorgos Karahalis, Greece
Yuri Gripas, Russia
Yuriko Nakao, Japan
Zainal Abd Halim, Malaysia